Jack Chan.

Essential Business Mathematics

Essential Business Mathematics

Seventh Edition

Llewellyn R. Snyder
Formerly, City College of San Francisco

William F. Jackson
Humboldt State University

McGraw-Hill Book Company

New York   St. Louis   San Francisco   Auckland   Bogotá   Düsseldorf
Johannesburg   London   Madrid   Mexico   Montreal   New Delhi   Panama   Paris   São Paulo
Singapore   Sydney   Tokyo   Toronto

ESSENTIAL BUSINESS MATHEMATICS

Copyright © 1979, 1972, 1967, 1963, 1958 by McGraw-Hill, Inc. All rights reserved.
Copyright 1953, 1947 by McGraw-Hill, Inc. All rights reserved.
Copyright renewed 1975 by Marie N. Snyder. Printed in the United States of America.
No part of this publication may be reproduced, stored in a retrieval system, or
transmitted, in any form or by any means, electronic, mechanical, photocopying,
recording, or otherwise, without the prior written permission of the publisher.

1 2 3 4 5 6 7 8 9 0 FGFG 7 8 3 2 1 0 9

This book was set in Zenith by York Graphic Services, Inc. The editors were Charles E. Stewart
and Frances A. Neal; the designer was Albert M. Cetta; the production supervisor
was Leroy A. Young. The cover photograph was taken by Rosmarie Hausherr.
Fairfield Graphics was printer and binder.

Library of Congress Cataloging in Publication Data

Snyder, Llewellyn R
    Essential business mathematics.

    Includes bibliographical references and index.
    1. Business mathematics. I. Jackson,
William F., joint author. II. Title.
HF5691.S62 1979   513'.93   78-11241
ISBN 0-07-059567-4

Contents

Preface

The purpose of this text is to increase the student's knowledge and skill in those essential quantitative areas which serve as the everyday, "bread and butter" computations for the financial problems of a business, civic, or personal nature. The text retains the basic philosophy of the late Professor Llewellyn R. Snyder and continues to be based in arithmetic, including the development of the arithmetical logic as well as the detailed "how-to," step-by-step arithmetical procedures. Formulas using symbolic terms are liberally employed, but their development, detailed explanation, examples, and accompanying exercises have been so designed that a prior knowledge of algebra is not required. Preparation of students for those courses in business requiring more sophisticated mathematical analysis is not within the scope of this book.

The Seventh Edition is an extensive revision and includes major re-writing with changes in emphasis of substantive material and style. A number of new problems have been added and other problems changed.

The metric system has been taken from the appendixes, expanded to two units, and placed in Chapter 3. The logic and coherence of the metric system are illustrated by presenting parallel problems in the metric and customary systems.

The chapter on the important area of Percentage, the common standard of measurement in the financial world, has been completely rewritten to introduce the concept of calculation models. In displaying, or "mapping" the elements of percentage problems in a calculation model format, the mental reasoning becomes more organized, and the path to the solution of these troublesome problems made more comprehensible.

The chapter in the previous editions on Simple Discount and the problems concerned with interest paid in advance have been eliminated since passage of the Truth in Lending Law has substantially decreased their relevance. Some of the alternative procedures of calculating simple interest have also been eliminated. The chapter on compound interest and annuities has been moved up to follow the chapter on simple interest. The material on consumer credit plans and the Truth in Lending Cost Disclosure (Regulation Z) is now presented in a separate chapter immediately following the chapters on simple and compound interest.

Business Graphs have been moved from the appendixes and included with the discussion of financial balance sheets and income statements. The material on the statistical concepts of central tendency, which has been rewritten and expanded, is also included with the chapter on balance sheets, income statements, and business graphs.

Appendix 1 contains a teaching description of binary, octal, and hexa-decimal number systems used with computers and computer programing. In deference to the wide use of pocket calculators, the examples and optional exercises in the better-known shortcuts in multiplication of whole numbers and fractions has been dropped from the Sixth Edition.

Appendix 2 retains the material on explanation of roots and powers and useful tables, figures and formulas used in the *customary system of weights and measures*. Appendix 2 also contains the description of the Roman System of notation.

For ease in reference and making assignments, style changes include a *renumbering system of the problems, tables, and figures*. The problems, tables, and figures are now double-numbered by chapter. *Objectives* at the beginning of each chapter provide a quick insight into the purpose and content of the chapter. Reference is made throughout the text to the use of *electronic pocket calculators;* their wide distribution among students sub-stantially increases motivation and accuracy, as well as freeing precious time from laborious calculations to spend on comprehension of the arithmetical logic. Although the calculators can be a most valuable "assist" to students, their use cannot and should not be substituted for the understanding of arithmetical concepts and the mental development of a "sense of figures." *Numerous problems* are included with each chapter in the text and its accompanying workbook to enable the instructor to vary assignments. Answers to the odd-numbered problems are provided at the end of the text and the workbook.

Previous editions of the text have advised the omission of the back-ground material contained in Part One for those students who have a satisfactory command of the basic arithmetical functions. This is still true of Chapters 1 and 2 which deal directly with the basic arithmetical functions of addition, subtraction, multiplication, and division of whole numbers and fractions. Chapters 3 and 4, however, which have been substantially rewrit-ten, contain the material on Fundamentals of Problem Solving, the Metric System, and Percentage. The author feels that these chapters can materially help any student. The remaining chapters and exercises in the text present the applications of arithmetic to typical business problems and procedures. The chapters and exercises are so structured and designed as to acquaint the student with the terms and description of many areas of the business world, and to develop within the student an appreciation of the numerical elements fundamental to the business decision process.

The separately published *Workbook for Essential Business Mathematics* is optional. Assignments in the workbook parallel the text exercises, but include worked-out solutions of a sample of the different types of problems and thus serve as a partial study-guide. Since the text contains tables and illustrations necessary to solve many problems in the workbook, the work-book cannot be used without the text.

A manual with worked-out solutions for many of the problems, in-cluding all the word problems, is available to the teacher. The manual includes not only the answers and worked-out solutions, but also such additional information as suggested teaching methods, an arithmetic ability test, and an appendix containing two alternate examinations for each chapter.

I want to express my sincere gratitude and appreciation to the many teachers who have communicated their observations and criticisms of the

Sixth Edition. Only by such comments can a revision be made more effective. I have used or adapted many of their ideas in the Seventh Edition, and I take sole responsibility for those accepted or rejected. I would like also to thank the reviewers who read the manuscript and offered many valuable suggestions. In particular I am grateful to Professors Joan W. Artz, Dutchess Community College, State University of New York; Robert H. Hale, Erie Community College; Craig S. Kuhns, City College of San Francisco; David N. McKelvey, Lakeland Community College; Kenneth Schoen, Worcester State College; and Etta F. Walker, Houston Community College.

To my colleagues and students who have "lived through" the trials and tribulations of this project with me, I feel a deep sense of gratitude. I especially want to thank Carolyn Falkenberg for assistance with the workbook and teacher's manual; Stew Fuller and George Jackson for substantial help with problem solutions; David Dillon, Erling Matsen, Jack Feigal, Herman and Harry Bistrin, Myron Abrahamson, Darrel Norberry, Walter Pieper, and many others active in business for assistance in updating the text to conform to modern business practice; Georgina Torgerson, Cheryl Edwards, Diane Eklund, and Kathy Brown for their invaluable assistance in typing; my sister Lois and her husband Lee for the use of their spare room to enable me to concentrate on the writing of the manuscript; and finally and most importantly my wife Peggy and our children for the help without which the task would simply not have been possible.

William F. Jackson

Part One

Essentials of Business Arithmetic

Chapter 1

Computing with Whole Numbers and Pure or Mixed Decimals

Objectives To Be Achieved in This Chapter

1 *Review the decimal system of notation and numeration.*

2 *Work with arithmetical approximation and rounding off.*

3 *Review the basic arithmetic functions of addition, subtraction, multiplication and division of whole numbers and decimal fractions.*

4 *Develop a sense of figures through use of convenient and simplified rules for performing the basic functions.*

Unit 1.1

Decimal System;
Notation and Numeration;
Approximation;
Rounding Off

The Base 10 (Decimal) Number System[1]

The base 10 number system, commonly known as the *decimal system,* probably originated in India and is now used worldwide. The number system was transmitted to Europe by the Arabs, and from Europe to America. The digits 0, 1, 2, 3, 4, 5, 6, 7, 8, and 9 are called Arabic or Hindu-Arabic numerals. The money system used in the United States is a decimal system. The metric system of weights and measures is also a decimal system.

The decimal system is a number system based on units of 10 and the various powers of 10. A *power* of a number is the product obtained when a number is multiplied by itself a specified number of times. Thus, the power of 4×4 is 16; the power of $4 \times 4 \times 4$ is 64. The frequency by which a number is to be multiplied by itself is expressed mathematically by placing a small figure to the upper right of the number to be multiplied. Thus 4×4 is written 4^2, and $4 \times 4 \times 4$ is written 4^3. The number to be multiplied is called the *base;* the small figure to the upper right indicating the frequency of multiplication is called an *exponent.* Base numbers with exponents are read as follows:

Number	*Read as*
4^2	"Four squared," or "4 to the second power"
4^3	"Four cubed," or "4 to the third power"
4^{25}	"Four to the 25th power"

Any base number, other than zero, with an exponent of 1 is equal to itself; any base number, other than zero, with an exponent of zero is another name for the number 1. Thus:

$$4^1 = 4$$
$$4^0 = 1$$

DETERMINING THE VALUE OF A DECIMAL NUMBER   The value of a decimal number is determined by each character (is it a 5 or an 8?) and the digit position it occupies in relation to the radix (decimal) point. Some of the values of the digit positions in a base 10 number system are presented in the following chart:

---

[1]Other systems of notation and numeration are presented in the appendices. The base 2 (binary), base 8 (octal), and base 16 (hexadecimal) number systems used with computers or by computer programmers are presented in Appendix One. The Roman system is presented in Appendix Two.

1,000,000,000 billions	100,000,000 hundred millions	10,000,000 ten millions	1,000,000 millions	100,000 hundred thousands	10,000 ten thousands	1000 thousands	100 hundreds	10 tens	1 units	Radix (decimal) point	$\frac{1}{10}$ tenths	$\frac{1}{100}$ hundredths	$\frac{1}{1000}$ thousandths	$\frac{1}{10,000}$ ten thousandths
10^9	10^8	10^7	10^6	10^5	10^4	10^3	10^2	10^1	10^0		10^{-1}	10^{-2}	10^{-3}	10^{-4}

The value of 6 in the first digit position to the left of the decimal point is determined by $6 \times 10^0 = 6$ $(6 \times 1 = 6)$. Proceeding to successive digital positions to the left of the decimal point, the value of each digital position increases by successive higher *positive* powers of 10. Thus the value of 6 in the second digit position to the left of the decimal point is determined by $6 \times 10^1 = 60$ $(6 \times 10 = 60)$. Proceeding to the right of the decimal point, each successive digital position is determined by successive *negative* powers of 10. Thus the value of 6 in the first digit position to the right of the decimal point is the product of:

$$6 \times 10^{-1} = 0.6 \qquad \left(6 \times 10^{-1} = 6 \times \frac{1}{10} = \frac{6}{10} = 0.6\right)$$

The numbers to the left of the decimal point (units, tens, hundreds, etc.) are termed *whole numbers* or *integers*. The numbers to the right of the decimal point are fractions with denominators of 10, or powers of 10, and are termed *decimal fractions*.

Example 1   **Determine the value of the decimal number 5467.23.**

Starting from the decimal point and proceeding to the left:

7×10^0	(7×1)	$= \quad 7$
6×10^1	(6×10)	$= \quad 60$
4×10^2	(4×100)	$= \quad 400$
5×10^3	(5×1000)	$= 5000$

Starting from the decimal point and proceeding to the right:

$$3 \times 10^{-1} \quad \left(2 \times \frac{1}{10}\right) = \quad .2$$

$$3 \times 10^{-2} \quad \left(3 \times \frac{1}{100}\right) = \quad .03$$

Sum   5467.23

Notation and Numeration

Notation refers to the writing of numbers. Table 1.1 summarizes common practice in the writing of numbers for different purposes. *Numeration* refers to the reading of numbers. In arithmetic, the word, "and," as used in the reading of numbers in the decimal system, should be used to indicate the separating point between the whole numbers to the left of the decimal point and the decimal fractions to the right of the decimal point. The word "and" is also used to indicate the separations between the decimal fractions and any common fractional endings.

TABLE 1.1 SUMMARY OF NOTATION OF DECIMAL NUMBERS

Description of purpose	Procedure	Example
Quantities or values other than those quantities used in the metric system	Starting from the decimal point, use commas to separate characters to the left of the decimal point in groups of three. (If there are only four digits to the left of the decimal point, no comma is needed.)	$1,234,567.89 20,540,000 shares $1480.00
	Characters to the right of the decimal point are not separated.	0.0246 cu in
Quantities or values used in the metric system	Starting from the decimal point, use a space (instead of the comma) to separate characters in groups of three to the left *and right* of the decimal point.	1 234.567 89 kg
Numbers that do not represent quantities or values (page numbers, code section numbers, dates, etc.)	Numbers are written together with no separations to the left or right of the decimal point.	1776 (year) 1234.5678 (code section) 5468 (page number)
Very large or very small numbers used in scientific notation	Numbers are written with no separation to the right of the decimal followed by a space and a positive or negative power of 10.*	$1.123456\ 10^3$ $= 1.123456 \times 1000$ $= 1123.456$ $2.98765\ 10^{-3}$ $= 2.98765 \div 1000$ $= 0.00298765$

*Some models of electronic pocket calculators on the market automatically switch over to scientific notation when a number is beyond their fixed decimal display.

Example 2   **Give the numerations of the following:**

(a) 5467.23   **(b)** 2,562,468   **(c)** $0.025\frac{2}{7}$

(d) $25.00\frac{2}{7}$ **(e)** 0.4718   **(f)** $312.89

Solution:
(a) Five thousand, four hundred sixty-seven, *and* twenty-three hundredths
(b) Two million, five hundred sixty-two thousand, four hundred sixty-eight
(c) Twenty-five thousandths *and* two-sevenths of one-thousandth
(d) Twenty-five *and* two-sevenths of one-hundredth
(e) Four thousand, seven hundred eighteen ten-thousandths
(f) Three hundred twelve *and* eighty-nine hundredths dollars

In the example above, note the following points:

1 The fractional term .00$\frac{2}{7}$ is two-sevenths of one-hundredth, not two-sevenths of one-thousandth.
2 The hyphen (-) is used in writing a compound number. Thus 23 is written twenty-three; 62 is written sixty-two.
3 The hyphen is also used in writing common fractions. Thus $\frac{2}{7}$ is written two-sevenths, $\frac{2}{3}$ is written two-thirds.

Exceptions to the above numerations exist in the reading of a year in a given date. The year 1776 is commonly read "seventeen seventy-six" instead of one thousand, seven hundred seventy-six. To avoid errors and to shorten the time in dictating numbers, it is common practice to dictate a number such as 312.89 as "three one two point eight nine" instead of three hundred twelve and eighty-nine hundredths.

Arithmetic Approximation

The uses of arithmetic do not end necessarily with the exact solution of a specific problem. We are often called upon to think in terms of comparative costs, general market trends, relative values, approximate weights or distances, etc. The development of *figure sense*, the ability to recognize and work with significant figures, is of great importance. If you understand quickly the significance of a number, you can communicate the number without putting your listener to sleep.
    Visualization of the relationships existing between quantities and qualities is a major part of everyone's daily life. Such a concept is dependent upon the ability to make rough estimates. It is therefore desirable that you develop skill in approximation, so that this proficiency may be carried over from your study of arithmetic and utilized in solving problems that will confront you in the future.
    Essential to approximation is the ability to recognize the figures in a given number that are significant not only to you but to others with whom you may be conversing. Thus if the number of shares sold on the New York Stock Exchange during a given day is 9,576,300, the significant figure sufficiently accurate for general information is "between nine million and ten

million shares." If it is required that the answer be to two significant figures, then we would say "nine million, six hundred thousand shares." To three significant figures, the answer would be "nine million, five hundred eighty thousand shares."

If an automobile is priced at $5018.95, the significant figure for most practical purposes is $5000; if a sweater is priced at $19.95, the significant figure for practical purposes may be $20; if the length of a fence is 469.364 ft, the significant figures for most purposes will be 475 ft, or even less accurately, 450 or 500 ft.

Constant practice in estimating will develop a skill that will avoid many serious errors. Particularly is this true in the proper location of decimal points. Approximating will aid greatly in eliminating errors in which answers are 10 or 100 times too large or too small.

The following are merely suggestions that may prove helpful to you; they are not to be construed as rules. Any method that achieves satisfactory results is acceptable. You may prefer to estimate in an entirely different manner. Obviously, those methods that are easiest, quickest, and most accurate for you are the ones that you should use.

In estimating, it is often helpful to reverse the process that is followed in the actual computation. Thus:

1 Approximate addition from left to right, reversing the direction of the original addition.
2 Approximate subtraction from left to right.
3 Approximate multiplication by rounding off the numbers of the factors and then multiplying from left to right. If one factor is rounded up, it is generally desirable to round down the other factor. For an even more accurate approximation, it is sometimes desirable to reverse the rounding off of the factors and then determine the average. A knowledge of the aliquot-parts method of multiplying (see Unit 3.1) may also be very helpful in adept approximation.
4 Approximate division by determining whether the quotient will be in thousands, hundreds, tens, units, tenths, hundredths, etc. To obtain a fairly accurate estimate, a knowledge of the aliquot-parts method of dividing (see Unit 3.1) will often be desirable. It may be advantageous to set the division problem in a fractional form. Thus 33,108 divided by 55 might be set as $\frac{33,108}{55}$. It would be apparent that the quotient should be in hundreds.

A convenient method of approximating a given sum of a series of numbers is to add the most significant digit on the left and retain the sum; count the number of items, divide by two, and add this quotient to the previous sum. The resulting approximate sum should be close to the true sum. This method, which is often used by auditors to check quickly the reasonableness of a given sum without using an adding machine, is a quick method of verifying your dinner check. Thus:

Example 3 **Problem**   **Approximation procedure**

+	2.25	*Step 1:*	2 + 8 + 6 = 16
+	8.50	*Step 2:*	4 items ÷ 2 = 2

Sum   18

+ 6.40   The approximation is close enough,
+ 0.60   and you may accept the given sum.

Sum   17.75

Rounding Off Numbers

The rounding off of a given number is simply the determination of its significant figures, as illustrated in the preceding paragraph. Whether a given quantity or value should be rounded off to thousands, to hundreds, to units, to tenths, to hundredths, etc., depends upon the purpose that the numerical value serves.

BUSINESS RULES FOR ROUNDING OFF To round off numbers, the general rules used in business are:

1 Drop all figures beyond the desired unit of accuracy if they are to the right of the decimal point; change them to zeros if they are to the left of the decimal point.
2 If the portion to be dropped off begins with the digit 5 or more, add 1 to the last figure retained.
3 If the portion to be dropped off begins with a digit less than 5, discard it and retain the last figure as is.

Example 4 **(a) Rounded off to thousands**   **(b) Rounded off to tenths**

565,743 to	566,000	0.356 to 0.4
27,499 to	27,000	27.04 to 27.0
5500 to	6000	3.051 to 3.1
1695.62 to	2000	0.049 to 0.0

(c) Rounded off to tens   **(d) Rounded off to hundredths**

27.26 to	30	0.4739 to 0.47
434.95 to	430	5.626 to 5.63
8.47 to	10	854.3 to 854.30
2056.75 to	2060	9.994 to 9.99

COMPUTER'S RULE FOR ROUNDING OFF The preceding rules and examples of rounding off, though normally used in business computations, are not valid in all instances. Where a considerable number of computations are made, the rounding up when the terminal digit is exactly 5 may result in cumulative errors in rounding off. To reduce the possibility of such error, statisticians, actuaries, scientists, etc., commonly use the *computer's rule:*

If a number is to be rounded off by one place and the terminal digit is exactly 5,

1 The 5 is dropped if the preceding digit is even.
2 The preceding digit is raised by 1 if the preceding digit is odd.

Thus the five-digit numbers 21.065 and 50.835 would be rounded off as four-digit numbers to 21.06 and 50.84, respectively. Note that when the computer's rule is used and the ending digit to be rounded off is exactly 5, the retained digit will always be an *even* number.

Exercise 1.1

1 Determine the value, expressed as a decimal number, of each set of characters in the base 10 system:

	Position from the decimal point (from left to right respectively)	
Character	Left	Right
(a) 8	6	
(b) 4, 3	5, 2	
(c) 6, 4	1	1
(d) 2, 5, 1	4	2, 3
(e) 9, 7, 3	6	1, 4
(f) 6, 7, 8, 4	5, 3, 1	4

Write the mathematically correct verbal form of the following:

2 726   **3** $506.12   **4** $0.46\frac{1}{4}$ **5** $48.03\frac{2}{7}$

6 $56\frac{5}{8}$ **7** 943   **8** 708.5   **9** 12.785

Write the following nonmetric values as Arabic numbers:

10 Eight hundred seven thousandths
11 Thirty-eight and five-sixths of one-hundredth
12 Eight thousand, five hundred seven, and six and one-third hundredths
13 Three million and two-tenths
14 Seventy-seven and seventy-seven thousandths
15 One thousand, three hundred and forty-two thousandths
16 Two hundred thousand, forty-four and two hundredths
17 Nineteen and two hundred sixty-nine ten-thousandths

Approximate the following, allowing only a few seconds for each answer:

18 614 + 18 + 797 + 1 + 1402 + 81
19 875 + 943 + 338 + 89 + 217
20 525 − 278 + 345 − 400 − 15   **21** 84 + 660 + 196 + 64 − 755
22 408 × 28   **23** 4680 ÷ 40

Round off the following numbers as indicated:

To hundredths		To tenths	
24	41.394	**28**	18.927
25	0.22495	**29**	0.30357
26	83.407	**30**	837.13
27	7.0926	**31**	76.56

To thousands		To hundreds	
32	9,214,902	**36**	22.844
33	12,598.7	**37**	8,678,149
34	500.019	**38**	91,627.7
35	3,400,591	**39**	417.01

To tens		To units	
40	807.3	**44**	318.564
41	306,755	**45**	3.1892
42	4.4844	**46**	2.098
43	481,514	**47**	5721.3

Unit 1.2   *Addition of Whole Numbers*
                                                         and Decimals

---

$$\left.\begin{array}{r} 26 \\ 2 \\ +40 \end{array}\right\} \text{Addends}$$

$\underline{}$
68   Sum or amount or total

Addition is the process of combining two or more numbers and expressing the result as a single quantity.

Addends are the numbers to be added.

The *sum* or *amount* or *total* is the result of the process of adding.

The sign representing addition is a plus sign (+). In reading, this sign is usually called "plus" or "and." Thus 8 + 5 is 8 plus 5, or 8 and 5.

Adding Whole Numbers

In the addition of whole numbers (integers), the digit positions of the number are added separately, starting with the least significant digit or units. From the sum of each series of digit positions, retain or write the number representing the units, and *carry over*, or redistribute the remaining tens, hundreds, etc., to the next significant digit position. Therefore, units are added to units, tens to tens, etc. Continue until the last digit position is reached, and write the entire sum of the last column of digits.

Example 1   **Problem**   **Procedure**

4638	Addend	*Step 1:* $8 + 3 = 11$	Retain 1 and carry over 1
+ 563	Addend		to ten's position.
5201	Sum		

Step 2: $1 + 3 + 6 = 10$ Retain 0 and carry over 1 to hundred's position.

Step 3: $1 + 6 + 5 = 12$ Retain 2 and carry over 1 to thousand's position.

Step 4: $1 + 4 = 5$ Write the 5.

Adding Decimals

The addition of decimals requires that the following rule be observed: *Place decimals of the same power in the same vertical column.* Thus, in the addends and in the sum, the decimal points must be placed directly above or below one another.

It is apparent that tenths are added to tenths, hundredths to hundredths, thousandths to thousandths, etc.

Example 2   **Find the sum of 2.35 and 354.4.**

```
    2.35
+ 354.4
  356.75
```

Example 3   **Find the sum of 8567.0138 and 28.97631.**

```
8567.0138
+ 28.97631
8595.99011
```

Example 4   **Find the sum of 0.067, 1.11, 54, 0.5678, and 324.6.**

```
    0.067
    1.11
  54.
    0.5678
+ 324.6
  380.3448
```

Two Methods of Adding Long Columns

In adding long columns it is sometimes helpful to divide the columns into two or more parts, obtaining a subtotal for each part, and then adding these subtotals to obtain the sum total:

Another method of increasing accuracy is to total each digit column separately and then obtain the sum total. This is helpful in doing a reverse-order check, as it records subtotals by columns:

```
  4,276
  3,849
  7,827
  4,834
+ 4,229    25,015 (subtotal)
  ─────
  2,275
  4,832
  7,439
  1,001
+ 8,157  + 23,704 (subtotal)
           ──────
           48,719 Sum total
```

```
  4,276
  3,849
  7,827
  4,834
  4,229
  2,275
  4,832
  7,439
  1,001
+ 8,157
  ─────
     59 ⎫
     36 ⎪ Subtotals of each column
     4 3 ⎬
  + 44 ⎭
  ──────
  48,719 Sum total
```

Checking Addition

Two methods of checking addition are in common use: (1) reverse-order check and (2) casting-out-nines check.

The reverse-order check is accomplished by adding again in the reverse direction. Thus if a column of figures has been added from bottom to top, reverse the operation and add from top to bottom. If the sums agree, it may be assumed that the answer is correct.

The casting-out-nines check is accomplished by eliminating nines or multiples of nine from the addends and the sum. The total of the remainders of the addends when nines have been eliminated will be equal to the remainder of the sum.

Several methods or techniques may be used in the casting-out-nines proof. The "adding plus canceling" method is preferred by most people and is illustrated as follows:

Numbers	Remainder after canceling nines
30	3̸
43	7̸
7̸1̸2̸	0
3̸4̸6	6̸
7̸1̸2̸	1
2,5̸1̸6̸	5
4̸6̸,6̸2̸2	2̸
Sum 50,3̸4̸1 (5 + 1) = 6, checking number	6 = checking number

Note that in the "numbers" column above, each line was inspected, and the combinations of numbers whose sum equals nine or a multiple thereof were crossed out or canceled. The sum of the remaining numbers on each line was placed in the column on the right. (There should be no number greater than eight in the "remainder" column.) The column of numbers setting forth the remainders is then inspected, and all combinations of nine or multiples thereof are also canceled. The sum of the remainders, or the checking number (6) is then found to equal the checking number (6) from the sum of the numbers in the left-hand column.

Example 5 **Add 376, 842, 936, and 742, proving by the casting-out-nines check.**

By canceling plus addition:

	Cancel and add:		Remainders
376	3̸ 7 6̸		= 7
842	8 4 2	8 + 4 + 2 = 14 and 1 + 4 =	5̸
936	9̸ 3̸ 6̸		= 0
+742	7 4 2̸		= +4̸

$\cdot$ Sum = 2896

Total of remainders in addends (cancel 5 + 4) $\qquad$ = 7

Sum = 2896, cancel 2896̸ and 2 + 8 + 6 = 16 and 1 + 6 = 7

The checking number is 7.[1]

The checking numbers obtained for both the sum and the total of remainders in the addends must be the same. If they are different, the work is incorrect, there being an error in the sum, in the check, or in both.

All methods of proving addition give only reasonable assurance of accuracy. Identical or coinciding mistakes will invalidate the reverse-order check. Shifting of decimals, reversing of numbers such as 74 for 47 (difference of 27 or three 9s), or any error totaling 9s in the sum will result in an error that will not be indicated when the casting-out-nines check is used.

For most problems in addition, the reverse-order check is satisfactory. However, when long columns of addends that are quite large must be totaled, the casting-out-nines check may be preferable.

---

[1]When the casting-out-nines checking procedure is used in actual practice, the crossouts are not to be made on the original presentation of the problem, nor is a rewrite of the problem on scratch paper necessary. By inspection, mentally cancel out the nines of each addend and the sum, noting the remainder of each addend and the checking number in the sum on a sheet of scratch paper. Proceed to cancel out the nines in the remainder column on your scratch paper to obtain the checking number of the addends.

Exercise 1.2

Add the following after rewriting to align whole numbers and decimals in the proper vertical columns:

1	212	2	3.05633	3	4766.99
	19,864		8500.38		1.6997
	776		446		688.01
	8,274,555		75.893		90.03
	789,401		258.08		3521
	71,007		19.19		42.3
	84,824		0.9066		856.51
	19,001		144.6		0.185
	3849		3578		5.98
	224,436		0.403		903.055
	924		970.00		6666.33
	17		544.3		3.0031

Add and check each problem by the reverse-order check:

4	814.72	5	904.02	6	987.051	7	244.8127
	889.17		244.99		4298.763		16.401
	236.89		617.93		627.367		999.969
	687.14		936.71		29.76		1284.07
	691.76		737.36		114.95		8177.8024
	355.27		763.33		5432.57		6.113
	179.49		763.76		0.0083		735.42
	927.96		94.38		92.83		669.454
	477.77		893.49		183.92		7547.804

Add and check each problem by the casting-out-nines check:

8	1.273	9	32.47	10	656.63	11	243.79
	6.948		68.97		871.79		18.924
	177.907		0.0041		0.3138		362.623
	2.41		2.501		15.9721		1848.912
	5.877		63.496		216.039		65.297
	1.206		5.9782		62.938		499.424
	1.260		105.6321		176.83		16.05
	18.354		72.6976		78.37		8.888
	12.887		81.7749		99.43		614.175

Solve the following:

12 A deposit slip made by Dan Sousa had the following entries: currency, $662.00; coin, $19.27; and checks for $91.75, $216.49, $100.00, $46.00, $200.14, $19.21, and $76.05. Find the total deposit.

13 The Houk Wholesale Company showed the following asset entries on its balance sheet: cash, $10,330; accounts receivable, $3020; notes receivable, $2780; inventory, $28,460; and equipment, $4900. Find the total assets.

14   Mr. Kuhns, who worked for Berston Realty, earned the following monthly commissions during a calendar year: $904.28, $1087.25, $981.37, $422.50, $750.75, $2545.80, $3100.40, $955.16, $1605.26, $1052.55, $920.30, and $238.49. Find his total commissions for the calendar year.

15   William Funke worked in a foundry and made the following castings in pounds: 834, 743.8, 890.75, 311.24, 843.9, and 408.03. Find the total of his castings in pounds.

16   A small business building for rent has the following square footage available: a basement containing a garage of 4862 sq ft, a storeroom of 3400 sq ft, a heater room of 378 sq ft, and a receiving dock of 1160 sq ft. The first and second floors each have the same square footage as does the basement. On the third floor there are 4284 sq ft of floor space. Find the total floor space of the building in square feet.

17   In addition to wages, an employer was required to pay the following per $100 of wages: $8.50 workmen's compensation insurance; $5.85 federal old-age, disability, and survivors insurance; $3.20 state unemployment insurance; $0.007 federal unemployment insurance; $2.60 medical care; and 94 cents for life insurance. Find the total of these added costs to the employer per $100 of wages.

Unit 1.3   *Subtraction of Whole Numbers and Decimals*

---

16   Minuend
− 9   Subtrahend
7   Remainder or difference

Subtraction is the process of finding the *difference* between numbers. The sign representing subtraction is the minus sign (−). In reading, this sign is usually read as "less" or "minus." Thus 7 − 3 is 7 less 3, or 7 minus 3.

The *minuend* is the number from which the subtraction is made.
The *subtrahend* is the number subtracted.
The *remainder* is the difference between the minuend and subtrahend.

The minuend is equal to the sum of the subtrahend and the remainder. The subtrahend is equal to the difference between the minuend and the remainder.

Subtraction of Whole Numbers

In subtraction, the units, tens, hundreds, etc., of the subtrahend are subtracted from the units, tens, hundreds, etc., of the minuend. Sometimes the digit value of a portion of the subtrahend is larger than the corresponding digit value in the minuend. In such instances, the number of units of the next higher denomination in the minuend (tens, hundreds, thousands, etc.) is "borrowed" and added to the next lower denomination (at the immediate right).

Thus in subtracting 28 from 73, 8 units cannot be taken from 3 units. One 10-unit portion is taken from, or "borrowed" from the tens column, leaving 6 tens instead of the original 7. The 10 "borrowed" units is then added to the 3 to get 13 units. Eight can then be subtracted from 13 and the difference of 5 obtained and written in the units position of the total difference. The 2 tens in this subtrahend is then subtracted from the remaining 6 tens in the minuend, and the difference of 4 written in the tens position of the total difference. The total remainder or difference is then 45. Thus:

Procedure

$$
\begin{array}{cc}
& 6 \\
7\ 3 & \cancel{7}^{1}3 \\
-2\ 8 & -2\ 8 \\
\hline
4\ 5 & 4\ 5
\end{array}
$$

Step 1: Borrow 10 units from tens column and add to the 3 units.

Step 2: Subtract 8 from 13 in the units column and write 5 as the difference.

Step 3: Subtract 2 from 6 in the tens column and write 4 as the difference.

Example 1

Minuend	8	25	154	639	23,310
−Subtrahend	−5	−7	−89	−231	−4,808
Remainder or difference	3	18	65	408	18,502

Decimals in Subtraction

When there are decimals in subtraction, the rule that must be observed is the same rule used for the addition of decimals: *Place decimals of the same power in the same vertical column.* Thus in minuend, subtrahend, and remainder, decimal points must be placed directly above or below one another.

Since only like numbers may be subtracted, tenths are subtracted from tenths, hundredths from hundredths, thousandths from thousandths, etc.

Example 2   **Subtract 47.062 from 1549.23.**

$$
\begin{array}{l}
1549.230 \ \text{(annex 0)} \\
\underline{-47.062} \\
\end{array}
$$
Remainder   1502.168

Example 3   **Subtract 356.1 from 4823.15.**

$$
\begin{array}{l}
4823.15 \\
\underline{-356.1} \\
\end{array}
$$
Remainder   4467.05

Example 4   **From 129.67 take 73.6438.**

$$129.6700 \text{ (annex 00)}$$
$$-73.6438$$
Remainder 56.0262

Example 5   **From 78.97825 subtract 9.387.**

$$78.97825$$
$$-9.387$$
Remainder 69.59125

Note that the annexation of zeros to digits to the right of the decimal point, as in Examples 2 and 4, does not change the value of the decimal.

Checking Subtraction

In checking subtraction, the most desirable method is to add the remainder to the subtrahend. The result should equal the minuend.

Example 6   Minuend   458,914
Subtrahend   − 290,478
Remainder   168,436
            + 290,478   Add subtrahend to remainder
            458,914   Sum equals minuend (check)

Since verifying the accuracy of subtraction is so easily accomplished, it is advisable to use this check frequently. The avoidance of errors will more than compensate for the time taken in checking.

Exercise 1.3

Find the differences in the following:

1 95	2 72	3 51	4 95	5 94	6 63
29	51	39	66	76	25

7 56	8 88	9 68	10 81	11 919	12 406
17	69	48	37	173	309

Subtract the following, aligning decimal points when necessary:

13 87.246	14 406.810	15 200.84	16 612.8
19.15	253.918	29.05	320.806

17 3.0074	**18** 87.31	**19** 737.6581	**20** 200.4
0.479061	9.02488	402.78	89.9973

21 486.273	**22** 172.34	**23** 5603.9	**24** 7692.74
35.106	75.984	489.127	7.6927

25 $36.942 - 36.101 =$ **26** $5.717 - 3.0675 =$

27 $975.53 - 72.4446 =$ **28** $2.003 - 0.0086705 =$

29 $1607 - 589.083011 =$ **30** $9.754 - 6.42177 =$

Subtract and check each problem by adding remainder to subtrahend:

31 123,456.78	**32** 84,197.609	**33** 3871.9489
98,382.89	399.897	89.6539

34 51,493.620	**35** 543,216.78	**36** 98,855.256
4,860.596	23.30	18,194.1

37 4787.8995	**38** 2247.7675	**39** 493,620.
9.7078	98.7759	46,938.70

40 4648.248	**41** 7897.6578	**42** 434.9715
.369	79.79	11.7924

43 497,248.6	**44** 18,997.7	**45** 1765.4329
787.79	9,897.879	1234.5615

46 110.010206
4.002487

Solve the following:

47 Mr. Frame's checkbook showed a balance of $719.24. He then wrote checks for $2.19, $104.77, and $400.00. Find his new balance.

48 The owner of an apartment house received cash rentals totaling $8733.36. During the same period the cash expenses were as follows: management, $627.50; taxes, $1438.83; utilities, $1071.44; repairs, $724.46; insurance, $199.80; interest, $1707.48; and miscellaneous, $79.37. Find his net cash flow from rentals.

49 An article sold for a total of $170.04 including selling price plus sales tax of $6.52. If the cost of the article was $109.88, what must have been the markup (difference between cost and selling price)?

50 The outside diameter of some copper tubing was 1.875 in. If the wall thickness was 0.193 in, what was the inside diameter?

51 An airplane is flying at an altitude of 7912 ft above sea level. The pilot plans to fly over Mt. Whitney, whose peak is 14,495 ft above sea level. If it is required that the airplane clear the peak by not less than 2550 ft, how much higher in feet must the airplane climb?

52 A welding shop during a 5-day workweek completed 650, 822, 409, 303, and 510 welds per day. Of those completed, inspection disclosed that 12, 19, 4, 42, and 14 welds were defective. What was the total number of acceptable welds?

Unit 1.4   *Multiplication of Whole Numbers and Decimals*

```
306    Multiplicand
×24    Multiplier
1224 ⎫
612  ⎬  Partial products
7344   Product
```

Multiplication is the process of taking one number as many times as there are units in another number.

It is a form of abbreviated addition. Thus, 5 × 3 means 3 added five times, or 5 added three times. Similarly, 5 + 5 + 5 = 15, or 5 multiplied by 3 = 15, and 3 + 3 + 3 + 3 + 3 = 15, or 3 multiplied by 5 = 15.

Three signs are in common use to indicate multiplication. Thus 5 multiplied by 3 may be noted as 5 × 3, 5 · 3, or (5)(3). One but not both of the sets of parentheses may be omitted, as in 5(3) or (5)3. Notice that the dot · is not placed on the writing line, and should not be confused with the decimal point. Usually these signs are read as "times" or "multiplied by."

The *multiplicand* is the number multiplied.

The *multiplier* is the number multiplied by (the number of times the multiplicand "is taken").

The *product* is the result of multiplication.

The *factors* in multiplication are the multiplicand and the multiplier. They are the numbers which when multiplied together result in the product.

Example 1 **Multiply 24 by 6, or 6 times 24, or 24 × 6.**

```
Factor   24  Multiplicand
Factor   ×6  Multiplier
        144  Product
```

Partial products are the result of multiplication of the multiplicand by the single digits composing the multiplier.

Example 2 **Multiply 24 by 56.**

```
  24
×56
 144   Partial product
120    Partial product
1344   Product
```

When Multiplicand or Multiplier Ends in Zeros

Multiplication may be simplified when either or both factors end in zeros. In such instances it is desirable to omit the ending zeros from the process of multiplication, the required product then being determined by annexing the number of zeros omitted.

Example 3   **Multiply 7200 by 23 (one factor ending in zeros).**

```
72  00   Factor
 23      Factor
216
144
165,600    Product (00 annexed)
```

Example 4   **Multiply 6400 by 850 (both factors ending in zeros).**

```
64  00   Factor
85   0   Factor
320
512
5,440,000   Product (000 annexed)
```

It is not necessary to write the ending zeros opposite the factors; merely count the ending zeros in both factors and annex that number to the product.

DECIMALS IN MULTIPLICATION   Because one of the factors in multiplication must always be an abstract number (a number without application to things), only after the digits comprising the product have been determined is it necessary to locate the position of the decimal point. Therefore it is immaterial whether the decimal points in the multiplicand and multiplier are in any particular position with respect to one another.

Thus the rule to observe when there are decimals in multiplication is: *A product will have as many decimal places as there are decimal places in the two factors together.*

If there are not as many decimals in the product as in both the multiplier and multiplicand together, then prefix as many zeros to the product as are necessary.

Example 5   **Find the product of 12.0765 and 2.31.**

```
12.0765
 ×2.31
120765
362295
241530
27896715
```

TABLE 1.2 MULTIPLICATION TABLE

	Products you must know								Products you should know							Products worth your effort to know								
	2	3	4	5	6	7	8	9	10	11	12	13	14	15	16	17	18	19	20	21	22	23	24	25
2	**4**	6	8	10	12	14	16	18	20	22	24	26	28	30	32	34	36	38	40	42	44	46	48	50
3	6	**9**	12	15	18	21	24	27	30	33	36	39	42	45	48	51	54	57	60	63	66	69	72	75
4	8	12	**16**	20	24	28	32	36	40	44	48	52	56	60	64	68	72	76	80	84	88	92	96	100
5	10	15	20	**25**	30	35	40	45	50	55	60	65	70	75	80	85	90	95	100	105	110	115	120	125
6	12	18	24	30	**36**	42	48	54	60	66	72	78	84	90	96	102	108	114	120	126	132	138	144	150
7	14	21	28	35	42	**49**	56	63	70	77	84	91	98	105	112	119	126	133	140	147	154	161	168	175
8	16	24	32	40	48	56	**64**	72	80	88	96	104	112	120	128	136	144	152	160	168	176	184	192	200
9	18	27	36	45	54	63	72	**81**	90	99	108	117	126	135	144	153	162	171	180	189	198	207	216	225
10	20	30	40	50	60	70	80	90	**100**	110	120	130	140	150	160	170	180	190	200	210	220	230	240	250
11	22	33	44	55	66	77	88	99	110	**121**	132	143	154	165	176	187	198	209	220	231	242	253	264	275
12	24	36	48	60	72	84	96	108	120	132	**144**	156	168	180	192	204	216	228	240	252	264	276	288	300
13	26	39	52	65	78	91	104	117	130	143	156	**169**	182	195	208	221	234	247	260	273	286	299	312	325
14	28	42	56	70	84	98	112	126	140	154	168	182	**196**	210	224	238	252	266	280	294	308	322	336	350
15	30	45	60	75	90	105	120	135	150	165	180	195	210	**225**	240	255	270	285	300	315	330	345	360	375
16	32	48	64	80	96	112	128	144	160	176	192	208	224	240	**256**	272	288	304	320	336	352	368	384	400
17	34	51	68	85	102	119	136	153	170	187	204	221	238	255	272	**289**	306	323	340	357	374	391	408	425
18	36	54	72	90	108	126	144	162	180	198	216	234	252	270	288	306	**324**	342	360	378	396	414	432	450
19	38	57	76	95	114	133	152	171	190	209	228	247	266	285	304	323	342	**361**	380	399	418	437	456	475
20	40	60	80	100	120	140	160	180	200	220	240	260	280	300	320	340	360	380	**400**	420	440	460	480	500
21	42	63	84	105	126	147	168	189	210	231	252	273	294	315	336	357	378	399	420	**441**	462	483	504	525
22	44	66	88	110	132	154	176	198	220	242	264	286	308	330	352	374	396	418	440	462	**484**	506	528	550
23	46	69	92	115	138	161	184	207	230	253	276	299	322	345	368	391	414	437	460	483	506	**529**	552	575
24	48	72	96	120	144	168	192	216	240	264	288	312	336	360	384	408	432	456	480	504	528	552	**576**	600
25	50	75	100	125	150	175	200	225	250	275	300	325	350	375	400	425	450	475	500	525	550	575	600	**625**

Note: The bold-faced number in each column is the square of the number at the head of the column.

Since there are six decimal places in the two factors, there should be six decimal places in the product. The correct answer would be

Product = 27.896715

Example 6   **Multiply 92.007 by 0.000032.**

$$
\begin{array}{r}
92.007 \\
\times 0.000032 \\
\hline
184014 \\
276021 \\
\hline
2944224
\end{array}
$$

Since the sum of the number of decimal places in the multiplicand and multiplier is nine, there should be nine decimal places in the product. As there are only seven digits in the product, two zeros are prefixed:

Product = 0.002944224

USEFUL SHORT METHODS OF MULTIPLYING   There are many shortcuts in multiplication, but with the ever-growing use of electronic pocket calculators, there is little necessity to learn them and not enough repeated use to retain them. However, there are a few practical shortcuts that everyone should know and use. One may not always have the opportunity or desire to use a calculator to perform small arithmetical tasks. To be aware of such shortcuts substantially increases your ability to work with arithmetical areas such as percentage and the metric system, and thus develop your "figure sense" for general problem solving.

SHORTCUTS BASED ON 10 AND POWERS OF 10
1 **To multiply by 10, 100, 1000, etc., move the decimal point in the multiplicand to the right as many places as there are zeros in the multiplier.**

Example 7 $42 \times 100 = 4200$ $27.6543 \times 1000 = 27,654.3$

This rule is reversed for multiplication by decimals such as 0.1, 0.01, 0.001 (equivalent to division by 10 or powers of 10). The decimal point in the multiplicand is moved to the *left* as many places as there are decimal places (excluding zeros to the right) in the multiplier.

Example 8 $8.6 \times 0.1 = 0.86$ $5385.402 \times 0.001 = 5.385402$

This shortcut is essential to utilize fully the potential of the coherent, decimally based metric system of weights and measures (Chapter 3). This shortcut also assists in checking the proper position of the decimal point in the multiplication of any decimal number.

2 **To multiply by equal parts of 100 (or 10 or any power of 10):**
   (a) To multiply by 50: multiply by 100 and divide by 2.
   (b) To multiply by 25: multiply by 100 and divide by 4.

Example 9   **(a)**   **(b)**

$742 \times 50 = (742 \times 100) \div 2 =$ $624 \times 25 = (624 \times 100) \div 4 =$
$74,200 \div 2 = 37,100$ $62,400 \div 4 = 15,600$

   Note: This procedure may be used whenever the multiplier is an equal part of 1, 10, 100, 1000, etc. See Unit 3.1 for an explanation of equal or aliquot parts, their multiples, and their use in multiplication and division.

3 **To multiply by a number slightly more or less than 10, 100, 1000, etc.:**
   (a) To multiply by 11: multiply by 10 and add multiplicand.
   (b) To multiply by 101: multiply by 100 and add multiplicand.
   (c) To multiply by 99: multiply by 100 and subtract multiplicand.
   (d) To multiply by 98: multiply by 100 and subtract two times the multiplicand.

Example 10   **(a)**   **(b)**

$437 \times 11 = (437 \times 10) + 437 =$ $38 \times 101 = (38 \times 100) + 38 =$
$4370 + 437 = 4807$ $3800 + 38 = 3838$

(c)   **(d)**

$52 \times 99 = (52 \times 100) - 52 =$ $27 \times 98 = (27 \times 100) - (2 \times 27) =$
$5200 - 52 = 5148$ $2700 - 54 = 2646$

   Note: Variations in this procedure may be used for numbers such as 102, 110, 89, 1011, 199, etc.

CHECKING THE PRODUCT OF MULTIPLICATION There are a number of commonly accepted ways of checking the result of multiplication. Among the most frequently used checks are the following:

1 **Transposing the factors and multiplying again.** If the products are the same, it may be assumed that the multiplication is correct.

Example 11   Check:

```
   285            36
  ×36          ×285
  ────          ────
  1710           180
   855           288
  ─────           72
 10260          ────
                10260
```

   Since pocket calculators have a visual display and do not have a printed tape, this method is useful in reentering the factors and checking on your original input of the factors.

2 **Division of the product by either of the factors** (preferably by the multiplier). The quotient thus obtained should equal the remaining factor.

Example 12

Check: Or check:

```
     95          95            42
    ×42      42)3990       95)3990
    190         378           380
    380         210           190
   3990         210           190
```

This shortcut provides a logical model for problem solving when one of the factors of a known product is unknown. This procedure is extensively used to solve problems in percentage (Chapter 4).

3 **Casting out nines.** This check is recommended only when the multiplier and multiplicand are large figures. If both factors exceed three digits, this check is sometimes the most desirable means of checking. The casting-out-nines check may be accomplished as follows:

(a) Use the canceling-plus-adding method to cast out nines from the multiplicand and the multiplier.
(b) Multiply one remainder by the other and again cast out nines.
(c) Cast out nines from the product.

The final remainder found in (b) should equal the remainder in the product (c).

Example 13

```
    7819  Remainder =   7
    ×281  Remainder = ×2
    7819                14  Remainder = 5
   62552
   15638
 2197139  Remainder in the product    = 5
```

Note: A zero remainder in either factor would immediately indicate that the remainder in the product must also be zero.

Exercise 1.4

Multiply the following:

1	7540	2	2400	3	58,300	4	6700	5	9720
	250		30		9,000		960		7290

Find the products of the following:

6	8.24	7	2.47	8	0.818	9	0.902	10	47.306
	7.7		0.581		3.5		0.403		0.20047

By inspection, determine the products of the following:

11	8.6 × 10	**12**	0.68 × 0.1	**13**	32.1 × 0.01
14	340.5 × 100	**15**	8.5241 × 1000	**16**	7290.9 × 0.0001

Multiply by the equal-parts method (see Table 3.1):

17	2400 × 25	**18**	20.7 × 50	**19**	526 × 250

Multiply the following and then check (a) by dividing the products by the multipliers, (b) by interchanging factors and multiplying, and (c) by casting-out-nines:

20	492,710	**21**	24.003	**22**	0.702	**23**	18.4
	44		4.6		32.2		82.7

Solve the following:

24 A kiln processes 57,600 board feet of lumber per 3-day period. What would be the total production of lumber over a 24-day period?

25 A flooded store basement was cleared of water by the use of three pumps after 4.25 hr of pumping. If one pump cleared 2448 gal of water per hr and the other two pumps each cleared 1956 gal of water per hr, how many gallons of water were pumped out of the basement?

26 An auditorium contains 18 rows with 52 seats per row, 18 rows with 46 seats per row, and 9 rows with 41 seats per row. Find the total number of seats in the auditorium.

27 On a map, 1 in represents 63 nautical miles. If each nautical mile represents approximately 1.15 common miles, approximately how far apart in common miles are two islands if they are 7.2 in apart on the map?

28 If the wage rate is $5.00 per hr during a standard workweek of 40 hr and 1.5 times the regular rate for work in excess of 40 hr per standard workweek, how much gross pay should a worker receive for a week during which he worked 46 hr?

29 If the charge for borrowing money was 0.094 times the sum of money borrowed for each year, find the charge for borrowing $4400 for 3 years.

Unit 1.5   *Division of Whole Numbers and Decimals*

```
           14  Quotient                        11  Partial quotient
Divisor  6)84  Dividend          Divisor  8)93  Dividend
           6                                 8
         ──                                ──
          24                                13
          24                                 8
         ──                                ──
           0  Remainder                      5  Remainder
```

The complete quotient is 14 since there is no remainder (a zero remainder).

The complete quotient is 11 with a remainder of 5.

Division is the process of finding how many times one number is contained within another number. It may be considered as a process of finding how many times one number is contained within another number or as a process of partitioning or separating a quantity into a number of equal parts.

Division is a short method of subtraction. Thus 9 may be subtracted three times from 27, or 27 may be divided three times by 9.

A sign frequently used indicating division is the division sign ($\div$), and in reading, this is usually called "divided by." Thus $9 \div 3$ is read "9 divided by 3." Division may also be indicated by a horizontal bar, the dividend being written above the bar, and the divisor being written below the bar. Among other symbols used to indicate division are $\overline{)\quad}$ or $)\quad$. Thus the following have the same meaning: $9 \div 3$ or $\frac{9}{3}$ or $3\overline{)9}$ or $3\underline{)9}$.

The *dividend* is the number divided.

The *divisor* is the number divided by.

The *quotient* is the result of division.

The *remainder*, if any, is the amount by which the dividend exceeds the product of the divisor and the partial quotient.

Division may also be thought of as the process of finding the unknown factor in a multiplication in which one of the factors and the product are known. For example, in dividing 324 by 6, the divisor 6 is the known factor; the dividend 324 is the known product; and the quotient, which is 54, is the unknown factor. Thus the divisor is a given factor; the dividend is the given product; and the quotient is therefore the required factor.

SHORT DIVISION   If the divisor is a single digit, do the operation mentally.

Example 1   **Divide 1981 by 7.**

Divisor $7\overline{)1981}$ Dividend
283 Quotient

Think as follows: "7 into 19 is 2, and 5 over. Write 2 and carry 5 to precede 8, making 58. 7 into 58 is 8, and 2 over. Write 8 and carry 2 to precede 1, making 21. 7 into 21 is 3. Write 3. The quotient is 283."

LONG DIVISION   If 748 is multiplied by 362, the product will be 270,776. Therefore if 270,776 is divided by 362, the quotient will be 748. In solving long-division problems, adept estimation is helpful. The following examples illustrate incorrect and correct estimating.

Example 2   **(a) Incorrect**   **(b) Incorrect**

6 8
$362\overline{)270776}$ $\qquad362\overline{)270776}$
2172 $\qquad2896$
$\overline{535}$

The number 6 is not large enough since the remainder of 535 is greater than the divisor.

The number 8 is too large since the product of $8 \times 362 = 2896$, which is larger than the dividend 2707.

(c)   Correct

$$
\begin{array}{r}
748 \\
362\overline{)\,270776} \\
2534 \\
\hline
1737 \\
1448 \\
\hline
2896 \\
2896 \\
\hline
\end{array}
$$

748   Quotient
Dividend

The procedure in solving Example 2c is as follows:
362 goes into 2707 seven times. Place 7 above the ending digit of 2707. Multiply 362 by 7 and place the product 2534 with its right digit below the right digit of 2707. Subtract and obtain 173. Annex 7 from the dividend to obtain the number 1737. Continue this process to obtain the final answer or quotient of 748.

REMAINDER If the divisor is not contained a whole number of times in the dividend, part of the dividend will remain after the divisor has been taken from the dividend the largest possible whole number of times. The remaining part of the dividend is called the *remainder*. The proper fraction "remainder over divisor" is part of the total quotient. Thus:

Example 3   **Divide 136 by 25.**

$$
\begin{array}{r}
5 \\
25\overline{)\,136} \\
125 \\
\hline
11 \\
\end{array}
$$

11   Remainder of dividend

Total quotient $= 5\dfrac{11}{25}$ $\left(\text{which means } 5 + \dfrac{11}{25}\right)$

The whole number 5 in the above calculation is commonly called the "quotient," but it is more properly called a *partial quotient* or the *integral quotient*. It is often desirable to continue the division process with the use of decimal fractions. The decimal is determined by placing a decimal point after the units digit (last whole digit) of the dividend and the partial quotient. Then zeros are annexed to the dividend and dividing is continued until the number of decimal places in the quotient produces sufficient accuracy in the value of the quotient. Thus:

Example 4   **Divide 136 by 25.**

$$
\begin{array}{r}
5.44 \\
25\overline{)136.00} \\
125 \\
\overline{110} \\
100 \\
\overline{100} \\
100 \\
\overline{0}
\end{array}
$$

Total quotient = 5.44

The total quotient could be expressed to the nearest tenth as 5.4, or five and four tenths; to the nearest hundredth (as above) as 5.44, or five and forty-four hundredths; or, similarly, to the nearest thousandth as 5.440, or five and four hundred forty thousandths.

WHEN THE DIVISOR ENDS IN ZEROS   If the divisor ends in zeros, canceling may be employed to simplify the process of division. Consider the following:

600 ÷ 200 = 3	1440 ÷ 500 = 2.88	3280 ÷ 1600 = 2.05
60 ÷ 20 = 3	144 ÷ 50 = 2.88	328 ÷ 160 = 2.05
6 ÷ 2 = 3	14.4 ÷ 5 = 2.88	32.8 ÷ 16 = 2.05

It is evident that canceling (rejection) of 10, 100, 1000, etc., from both dividend and divisor does not affect the quotient. Moving the decimal point in both divisor and dividend to the left one, two, three places, etc., is equivalent to dividing by 10, 100, 1000, etc.

The following rule may be applied to all problems in division: *The quotient will remain the same if both dividend and divisor are divided by the same number.*

Example 5   **(a)   Without canceling:**   **(b)   With canceling:**

5,472,000 ÷ 300   5,472,0̸0̸0̸ ÷ 3̸0̸0̸

$$
\begin{array}{r}
18240 \\
300\overline{)5472000} \\
300 \\
\overline{2472} \\
2400 \\
\overline{720} \\
600 \\
\overline{1200} \\
1200
\end{array}
\qquad
\begin{array}{r}
18240 \\
3̸0̸0̸\overline{)5472000̸0̸} \\
3 \\
\overline{24} \\
24 \\
\overline{7} \\
6 \\
\overline{12} \\
12
\end{array}
$$

DECIMALS IN THE DIVISOR   When decimals occur in the divisor, they may be eliminated by increasing both dividend and divisor proportionately.

Consider the following:

Original problem   *Restated problem*

	Multiply both factors by	

$$12 \div .6 = 20 \quad 10^1 \quad (10) \quad 120 \div 6 = 20$$
$$250 \div .05 = 5000 \quad 10^2 \quad (100) \quad 25{,}000 \div 5 = 5000$$
$$36 \div .004 = 9000 \quad 10^3 \quad (1000) \quad 36{,}000 \div 4 = 9000$$

It is evident that multiplication of both dividend and divisor by the same number does not affect the quotient.

The following rule is applicable not only to division problems that contain decimals in dividend or divisor, or both, but to all problems in division: *The quotient will remain the same if both dividend and divisor are multiplied by the same number.*

If the divisor contains decimals, it is recommended that they be eliminated by: (1) moving the decimal point to the right to make the divisor a whole number, (2) moving the decimal point in the dividend the same number of places to the right, annexing as many zeros as may be necessary, and (3) placing the decimal point of the quotient directly above the decimal point in this new dividend.

Note that each digit in the quotient must be placed directly over the right-hand digit of its product.

Example 6   **Divide 259.2386 by 0.542, giving answer in tenths.**

Change the divisor to whole numbers and move the decimal point in the dividend an equal number of places (three) to the right.

```
            478.3
542) 259238.6
     2168
      4243
      3794
       4498
       4336
        1626
        1626
```

This quotient is in tenths. If the answer is desired in hundredths, another zero is annexed to the dividend (259238.60). The quotient is then expressed in hundredths (478.30).

Example 7   **Divide 29.10489 by 3.81, giving answer to nearest thousandths.**

Change the divisor to whole numbers and move the decimal point in the dividend an equal number of places (two) to the right.

$$
\begin{array}{r}
7.639 \\
381\overline{)2910.489} \\
\underline{2667} \\
2434 \\
\underline{2286} \\
1488 \\
\underline{1143} \\
3459 \\
\underline{3429} \\
30 \quad \text{Remainder}
\end{array}
$$

The quotient is to the nearest thousandths, for the remainder is less than half of 381; the corrent answer is therefore 7.639. If the remainder were greater than one-half of 381, it would be proper to add one-thousandth to the quotient, giving an answer of 7.640.

If the answer is desired to the nearest hundredths, the remainder would be 345.9, more than half of 381, and the final digit or hundredth would be correctly increased from 3 to 4 so that the quotient would be 7.64.

SHORTCUTS IN DIVISION   Unlike multiplication, the number of shortcuts that may be used advantageously for division is very limited. However, the following practical shortcuts based on 10 and the powers of 10 should be understood and used.

SHORTCUTS BASED ON 10 AND POWERS OF 10:
1   **To divide by 10, 100, 1000, etc., move the decimal point in the dividend to the left as many places as there are zeros in the divisor.**

Example 8 $31.74 \div 10 = 3.174$ $8.467 \div 1000 = 0.008467$

This rule is reversed for division by decimals such as 0.1, 0.01, 0.001, etc. (equivalent to multiplication by 10 or the power of 10), the decimal point in the dividend being moved to the *right* as many places as there are decimal places (excluding zeros to the right) in the divisor.

Example 9 $50.3 \div 0.01 = 5030$ $2467.53 \div 0.10 = 24{,}675.3$

2   **To divide by equal parts of 100 (or 10 or any power of 10):** As with multiplication, a knowledge of numbers contained without remainder in 10 or powers of 10 will often prove useful. Thus to divide by 2.5, divide by 10 and then multiply by 4; to divide by 50, divide by 100 and then multiply by 2; etc.

Example 10   **(a)**   **(b)**

$624 \div 2.5 = (624 \div 10) \times 4$ $74.2 \div 50 = (74.2 \div 100) \times 2$
$= 62.4 \times 4 = 249.6$ $= 0.742 \times 2 = 1.484$

The procedure that is illustrated in Example 10a and b is known as the *aliquot-parts* method of division. For a complete explanation of aliquot parts and their use in division (and multiplication), see Unit 3.1.

SIMPLE AVERAGE   The quotient of the sum of a group of items divided by the number of items is a *simple average*. This is what is commonly known as "average" and may be more specifically designated by the terms "arithmetic mean" or "arithmetic average" to distinguish it from certain other types of averages used in statistics, business, and science.

Example 11 **Find the average sales (arithmetic mean) per clerk of five clerks whose individual sales were $367.85, $298.24, $315.37, $408.40, and $282.69.**

$$
\begin{array}{r}
\$ \quad 367.85 \\
298.24 \\
315.37 \\
408.40 \\
+282.69 \\
\hline
\end{array}
$$

Sum = $ 1672.55   Average = $1672.55 ÷ 5 = $334.51

CHECKING DIVISION BY MULTIPLYING FACTORS   Since the dividend equals the product of the divisor (given factor) and the quotient (required factor), checking accuracy in division may be determined by multiplying one factor by the other (preferably using the divisor as the multiplier) and then adding the remainder, if any. This number should equal the dividend.

Example 12 **Checking accuracy (see Example 6)**

$$
\begin{array}{r}
478.3 \\
\times 0.542 \\
\hline
9566 \\
19132 \\
23915 \\
\hline
259.2386 \\
\end{array}
$$

478.3   Factor (previous quotient)
×0.542   Factor (previous divisor)
259.2386   Product (previous dividend)

Example 13 **Checking accuracy (see Example 7)**

$$
\begin{array}{r}
7.639 \\
\times 3.81 \\
\hline
7639 \\
61112 \\
22917 \\
\hline
29.10459 \\
+30 \\
\hline
29.10489 \\
\end{array}
$$

7.639   Factor (previous quotient)
×3.81   Factor (previous divisor)
29.10459   Product
+30   Remainder
29.10489   Product + remainder (previous dividend)

If the product plus the remainder fails to equal the dividend, the division, the check, or both are incorrect.

CHECKING DIVISION BY CASTING OUT NINES The casting-out-nines check is recommended only when the divisor and the quotient are large figures. If both exceed three figures, this check is sometimes desirable. The casting-out-nines check may be accomplished as follows:

1 Use the canceling-plus-adding method to cast out nines from the quotient and the divisor.
2 Multiply any remainder from the quotient by any remainder from the divisor and again cast out nines.
3 Cast out nines from the remainder (of the division problem) and add this remainder to the product of (2).
4 Cast out nines from the sum totaled in (3).
5 Cast out nines in the dividend.

The remainder in (4) should equal the remainder in the dividend (5).

Example 14 **Divide 1,053,843 by 201 and check the accuracy of the quotient.**

```
        5243                    Check:
  201) 1053843   Quotient    5243, remainder =    5
        1005     Divisor      201, remainder = ×3
         488                                 15; 1 + 5 = remainder = 6
         402                   Dividend  1,053,843; 3 + 3 = remainder = 6
         864
         804
         603
         603
```

Since the final remainders are both 6, it may be assumed that the quotient of 5243 is correct.

Example 15 **Divide 7489.3 by 642 to tenths and check the accuracy of the quotient and remainder.**

Solution.

```
                                  Check:
       11.6       Quotient       11.6   remainder =     8
  642) 7489.3     × Divisor       642   remainder = ×  3
       642                                              24
      1069                                remainder         6
       642     + Remainder in
       427 3     division problem  42.1  remainder =      + 7
       385 2                                              13
       42.1
                                         remainder          4
             = Dividend          7489.3  remainder =        4
```

Since the final remainders are both 4, it may be assumed that the quotient of 11.6 with a remainder of 42.1 is correct.

Exercise 1.5

Divide, finding quotients to hundredths and showing remainders, if any, as fractions:

1 $76.23 \div 0.014$ 2 $800\overline{)48{,}364}$ 3 $\dfrac{120{,}000}{9{,}000}$

4 $0.384627 \div 0.003$ 5 $0.5082\overline{)48.2408}$ 6 $94.7\overline{)194{,}270.8}$

By inspection, determine the quotients of the following:

7 $84.7 \div 100$ 8 $0.8750 \div 0.01$ 9 $8.143 \div 10$
10 $5.064 \div 1000$ 11 $67.011 \div 0.001$ 12 $2964.12 \div 10$

Divide by the equal-parts method (see Table 3.1):

13 $3485 \div 25$ 14 $9108 \div 250$ 15 $47.2 \div 50$

Divide, finding quotient to decimal point only and then check (a) by multiplication of quotient by divisor and (b) by casting out nines:

16 $19.47\overline{)42{,}049.8}$

17 $17\overline{)81{,}003}$

18 $0.4062\overline{)36.1604}$

19 $0.0426\overline{)18.3921}$

Solve the following:

20 A manufacturing company pays its employees the following wages per month: manager, $1625; assistant manager, $1145; accountant, $1050; each of two bookkeepers, $655; each of 14 salespeople, $800; each of nine salespeople, $710; each of three stock clerks, $485; an elevator operator, $510; and a janitor, $510. Find the average monthly wage of the employees.

21 A factory completed a purchase order for 800 radios at a total price of $28,000. Another order at the same price per radio was received with a total of $22,750. How many radios were requested in the second purchase order?

22 One wheel makes 83 revolutions while a second wheel makes 61 revolutions. How many revolutions will the first wheel make while the second wheel makes 5063 revolutions?

23 A house cost five times more than the lot on which it was built. The total cost of the house and lot was $52,500. Find the cost of the house.

24 If the basic telephone charge is 6.4 cents for each of the first three message units and 3.4 cents for each additional message unit, how many

message units were charged for a telephone call with a total cost of 43 cents?

25 One cu ft equals 1728 cu in and 231 cu in equals 1 gal. In a tank containing 2050 gal, find the number of cubic feet (to nearest tenths).

Unit 1.6   *Common Factors and Divisibility of Numbers*

One of the most serious of the arithmetical deficiencies of many students is lack of knowledge and understanding of factors and multiples. Skill in recognizing factors common to both numerator and denominator is very helpful in solving problems in which canceling can be employed and also in reducing fractions to lower terms. The solution of certain problems in proportion and, more important, of many problems in adding or subtracting and even in multiplying or dividing fractions often depends upon the selection of a common denominator, the finding of which may require a knowledge of factors.

An exact divisor of a number is a factor of that number. Numbers multiplied together that produce a certain number are factors of that number.

A *prime number* is a natural number larger than 1 that has no factors other than itself and 1. Thus, 2, 3, 5, 7, 11, 13, 17, 19, 23, etc., are prime numbers. Each is divisible without remainder only by 1 and itself.

A *composite number* is a number that is the product of two or more factors other than 1 and itself. Thus 4, 6, 8, 9, 10, 12, 14, 15, 16, 18, etc., are composite numbers, since $2 \times 2 = 4$, $3 \times 2 = 6$, $2 \times 2 \times 2 = 8$, $3 \times 3 = 9$, $2 \times 5 = 10$, $2 \times 2 \times 3 = 12$, etc.

The number 1 is classified by itself, since it does not fit the definition of either a prime or composite number.

Rules of Divisibility

DIVISIBILITY BY PRIME NUMBERS In finding the factors of a number, there are several rules of divisibility that will enable you to determine readily whether a number is divisible without remainder by the smaller prime numbers 2, 3, 5, or 11.

A *number is divisible by 2 without remainder* if the ending digit is divisible by 2 without remainder. Thus, 386 is divisible by 2 without remainder, but 385 and 387 are not divisible by 2 into quotients expressed in whole numbers without remainder, since neither 5 nor 7 is divisible by 2 without remainder.

A *number is divisible by 3 without remainder* if the sum of its digits is divisible by 3 without remainder. Thus, 387 is divisible by 3 without remainder, since the sum of its digits $(3 + 8 + 7)$ totals 18, a number divisible by 3 without remainder. Since the digits in 385 total 16 and in 386 total 17, and since neither 16 nor 17 is divisible by 3 without remainder, the numbers 385 and 386 cannot be divided by 3 into quotients expressed in whole numbers without remainder.

A number is divisible by 5 without remainder if the ending digit is 5 or 0. Thus, 745 and 1180 are each divisible by 5 without remainder. But 746 or 1179 cannot be divided by 5 into quotients expressed in whole numbers without remainder, since their ending digits are neither 5 nor 0.

A number is divisible by 11 without remainder if the difference between the sum of every other digit and the sum of the remaining digits is 0 or is divisible by 11 without remainder. Thus, 22 is divisible by 11 without remainder, since the difference between 2 and 2 is 0, and $0 \div 11 = 0$. And 32,758 is divisible by 11 without remainder, since $3 + 7 + 8 = 18, 2 + 5 = 7$, and the difference between 18 and 7 is 11, a number divisible by 11 without remainder.

Other prime numbers, such as 7, 13, 17, 19, etc., which may also be factors of any given number, may best be determined by trial and error. Thus, 91 is divisible by 7 and 13, but not by 17 or 19, into quotients expressed in whole numbers without remainder.

TABLE 1.3   PRIME NUMBERS TO 1000

	59	139	233	337	439	557	653	769	883
2	61	149	239	347	443	563	659	773	887
3	67	151	241	349	449	569	661	787	907
5	71	157	251	353	457	571	673	797	911
7	73	163	257	359	461	577	677	809	919
11	79	167	263	367	463	587	683	811	929
13	83	173	269	373	467	593	691	821	937
17	89	179	271	379	479	599	701	823	941
19	97	181	277	383	487	601	709	827	947
23	101	191	281	389	491	607	719	829	953
29	103	193	283	397	499	613	727	839	967
31	107	197	293	401	503	617	733	853	971
37	109	199	307	409	509	619	739	857	977
41	113	211	311	419	521	631	743	859	983
43	127	223	313	421	523	641	751	863	991
47	131	227	317	431	541	643	757	877	997
53	137	229	331	433	547	647	761	881	

DIVISIBILITY BY COMPOSITE NUMBERS   In addition to the preceding rules of divisibility by prime numbers, there are also several helpful rules that aid in determining divisibility without remainder by the composite numbers 4, 8, 6, 9, and 10.

A number is divisible by 4 without remainder if the last two digits are divisible by 4 without remainder. Thus 132; 9720; 8516; and 992 are all divisible by 4 without remainder.

A number is divisible by 8 without remainder if the last three digits are divisible by 8 without remainder. Thus 7104; 52,480; 1328; and 69,064 are all divisible by 8 without remainder.

A number is divisible by 6 without remainder if it is an even number and if the sum of the digits is divisible by 3 without remainder. Thus 5718; 3414; 8190; and 7416 are all divisible by 6 without remainder.

A number is divisible by 9 without remainder if the sum of the digits is divisible by 9 without remainder. Thus 7110; 522; 9153; and 62,874 are all divisible by 9 without remainder.

A number is divisible by 10 without remainder if the ending digit is 0. Thus 40; 110; 550; and 3170 are all divisible by 10 without remainder. (If the ending digits are 00, as in 500; 1200; and 17,900; the number is also divisible by 100; if the ending digits are 000, as in 6000; 27,000; and 14,000; the number is divisible by 1000 as well as by 10 and 100, etc.)

Note that there are no exceptions to the preceding rules. Commit these rules of divisibility to memory. Their usefulness will become very apparent to you in the work that follows.

Common Factors or Common Divisors

The terms "common factor" and "common divisor" mean the same thing and are used synonymously. If two or more numbers are divisible by the same number (have the same number as a factor), this number is a common divisor (common factor).

Example 1   5 is a common divisor of 5, 25, and 40.
7 is a common factor of 14, 21, and 49.
9 is a common divisor of 18, 63, and 90.
3, 6, and 9 are common factors of 18, 36, 54, 72, and 144.
2, 6, and 15 are common divisors of 30, 60, 150, and 240.
4, 8, and 3 are common factors of 24, 48, 144, and 168.

THE GREATEST COMMON DIVISOR   The term "greatest common divisor" (g.c.d.) is synonymous in general use with the term "highest common factor" (h.c.f.).

The greatest common divisor is the largest whole number that can be divided into each of two or more numbers without remainder. The g.c.d. of two or more numbers is the product of all the prime factors common to all the numbers.

Example 2   2 is the greatest common divisor of 4, 8, and 10.
6 is the highest common factor of 12, 18, and 30.
10 is the greatest common divisor of 10, 30, and 70.

One of the most important uses of the g.c.d. is in changing a fraction to its lowest terms in a single operation. If the g.c.d. is not known, it is possible to change a fraction to its lowest terms by dividing both numerator and denominator by their common factors. These common factors may not be readily apparent, and the reduction will then be accomplished only after considerable effort by trial and error.

FINDING THE G.C.D.   The following procedure, known as the Euclidean algorithm, is recommended as the most desirable method to use in changing fractions to lowest terms if the common divisors of the numerator and denominator are not apparent. This procedure definitely determines the largest possible number that may be divided into the two terms of the fraction. If this method is used, you can be certain that you have found the g.c.d., and that the quotients of the numerator and denominator of the fraction after being divided by the g.c.d. will be the fraction expressed in the lowest possible terms.

The procedure is as follows:

1 Divide the larger number by the smaller.
2 Divide the divisor (the smaller number) by the remainder and continue this operation until there is no remainder (a 0 remainder).

The last divisor will be the g.c.d. (or h.c.f.).

Example 3   **Find the g.c.d. of 108 and 744.**

$$
\begin{array}{r} 6 \\ 108\overline{)744} \\ 648 \\ \hline 96 \end{array}
\qquad
\begin{array}{r} 1 \\ 96\overline{)108} \\ 96 \\ \hline 12 \end{array}
\qquad
\begin{array}{r} 8 \\ 12\overline{)96} \\ 96 \\ \hline 0 \end{array}
$$

The g.c.d. is 12.

$\frac{108}{744}$ could be expressed in its lowest terms by dividing its numerator and denominator by $12 = \frac{9}{62}$.

Example 4   **Find the h.c.f. of 9230 and 639.**

$$
\begin{array}{r} 14 \\ 639\overline{)9230} \\ 639 \\ \hline 2840 \\ 2556 \\ \hline 284 \end{array}
\qquad
\begin{array}{r} 2 \\ 284\overline{)639} \\ 568 \\ \hline 71 \end{array}
\qquad
\begin{array}{r} 4 \\ 71\overline{)284} \\ 284 \\ \hline 0 \end{array}
$$

The h.c.f. is 71.

$\frac{9230}{639}$ could be changed to its lowest terms by dividing its numerator and denominator by $71 = \frac{130}{9} = 14\frac{4}{9}$.

Example 5   **Find the g.c.d. or h.c.f. of 313 and 701.**

$$
\begin{array}{r}
2 \\
313\overline{)701} \\
626 \\
\hline
75
\end{array}
\quad
\begin{array}{r}
4 \\
75\overline{)313} \\
300 \\
\hline
13
\end{array}
\quad
\begin{array}{r}
5 \\
13\overline{)75} \\
65 \\
\hline
10
\end{array}
\quad
\begin{array}{r}
1 \\
10\overline{)13} \\
10 \\
\hline
3
\end{array}
\quad
\begin{array}{r}
3 \\
3\overline{)10} \\
9 \\
\hline
1
\end{array}
\quad
\begin{array}{r}
3 \\
1\overline{)3} \\
3 \\
\hline
0
\end{array}
$$

The g.c.d. or h.c.f. is 1.

$\frac{313}{701}$ is already expressed in its lowest terms, since the numerator and denominator divided by $1 = \frac{313}{701}$.

It is usually not necessary to complete all of the divisions as illustrated in Example 5, for as soon as it can be determined that the remainder and divisor are relatively prime (having the number 1 only as a common divisor), there is no need for further division. Thus in Example 5, most people would determine after the second division that the remainder 13 and divisor 75 are relatively prime, and certainly after the third division everyone should recognize that 10 and 13 are relatively prime.

Exercise 1.6

Find which of the prime numbers 2, 3, 5, 7, and 11 are factors in each of the following numbers:

1	3520	**2**	80,025	**3**	562,940	**4**	862,950
5	9,487,695	**6**	2550	**7**	821,467	**8**	1,530,914
9	42,386	**10**	72,184				

Find which of the composite numbers 4, 6, 8, 9, and 10 are factors in each of the following numbers:

11	75,292	**12**	679,128	**13**	29,160	**14**	562,959
15	53,838	**16**	12,036	**17**	17,246	**18**	363,999
19	7104	**20**	825,760				

Find which of the numbers 2, 3, 4, 5, 6, 7, 8, 9, 10, and 11 are factors in each of the following numbers:

21	224,921	**22**	807,680	**23**	642,841	**24**	247,960
25	30,632	**26**	492,768	**27**	343,600	**28**	102,564
29	98,406	**30**	854,727				

Find the g.c.d. and then use it as a divisor of the numerator and denominator of each of the following fractions to express them in lowest terms:

31 $\dfrac{28}{174}$	**32** $\dfrac{265}{1113}$	**33** $\dfrac{335}{469}$	**34** $\dfrac{334}{501}$	**35** $\dfrac{178}{4539}$
36 $\dfrac{468}{3125}$	**37** $\dfrac{387}{4902}$	**38** $\dfrac{5266}{6837}$	**39** $\dfrac{91}{117}$	**40** $\dfrac{2195}{2964}$

Unit 1.7   *Multiples and Canceling*

Multiples and Common Multiples

A *multiple* of a number is the product of which the number is one of the factors. Thus:

4, 8, 12, 16, etc., are multiples of 4 because each is the product of the factor 4 and some other factor.

6, 12, 18, 24, etc., are multiples of 6 because each is the product of the factor 6 and some other factor.

A *common multiple* of two or more numbers is a number which is a multiple of each of the numbers. It is a number into which each of the numbers will divide without a remainder. Thus:

Common multiples of 4 and 6 are 12, 24, 36, 48, etc.
Common multiples of 5 and 7 are 35, 70, 105, 140, etc.
Common multiples of 3, 4, and 5 are 60, 120, 180, 240, etc.
Common multiples of 2, 4, and 9 are 36, 72, 108, 144, etc.

A common multiple is used frequently in the addition or subtraction of fractions. The common denominator used to express two or more fractions in like terms is a common multiple of the denominators of the fractions.
The *least common multiple* (l.c.m.) of two or more numbers is the smallest number into which each number can be divided without remainder.
Adding or subtracting fractions may be greatly simplified if a "lowest common denominator" can be determined. A *lowest common denominator* (l.c.d.) is the least common multiple of the denominators of two or more fractions. Thus:

4 is the l.c.m. of 2 and 4
12 is the l.c.m. of 2, 3, 4, 6, and 12
35 is the l.c.m. of 5, 7, and 35

Two or more numbers are relatively prime to one another when they have no common factor other than 1. Their product is then the l.c.m. (or l.c.d.). Thus:

6 is the l.c.m. of 2 and 3
35 is the l.c.m. of 5 and 7
36 is the l.c.m. of 4 and 9

But 24 is not the l.c.m. of 4 and 6, because 2 is a common factor of 4 and 6, and therefore 4 and 6 are not prime to one another.

When three or more numbers are each prime to the other numbers, their product is the l.c.m. Thus 84 is the l.c.m. of 3, 4, and 7; 360 is the l.c.m. of 8, 9, and 5.

When the l.c.m. is not apparent by inspection, it may be found by determining the product of the prime factors of the numbers, each taken as many times as it occurs most frequently in any of the numbers.

A METHOD OF FINDING THE L.C.M. (OR L.C.D.)   Though there are a number of methods that may be used to find a l.c.m. (or a l.c.d.), the following is recommended:

1   Write the numbers (or denominators) in a horizontal row and then divide by a prime factor common to any two or more of the numbers.
2   Continue this process of division until there are no two quotients divisible by any prime number.

The product of the prime numbers and the final quotients will equal the l.c.m.

Example 1   **Find the l.c.m. of 36, 12, 32, and 48.**

2)36	12	32	48
2)18	6	16	24
2) 9	3	8	12
2) 9	3	4	6
3) 9	3	2	3
3	1	2	1

l.c.m. $= 2 \times 2 \times 2 \times 2 \times 3 \times 3 \times 2 = 288$

Example 2   **Find the l.c.d. of $\frac{1}{7}$, $\frac{5}{12}$, $\frac{3}{8}$, $\frac{1}{9}$, $\frac{5}{6}$, and $\frac{3}{14}$.**

2)7	12	8	9	6	14
2)7	6	4	9	3	7
3)7	3	2	9	3	7
7)7	1	2	3	1	7
1	1	2	3	1	1

l.c.d. $= 2 \times 2 \times 3 \times 7 \times 2 \times 3 = 504$

SHORTENING THE PROCESS OF FINDING THE L.C.M.   The process of solving for the l.c.m. may be shortened in two ways:

1   **Canceling:**
    (a)   Rejecting those given numbers which are factors of other numbers under consideration.
    (b)   Rejecting obtained quotients which are factors of other obtained quotients.
2   **Dividing by composite numbers:**
    (a)   Dividing by a composite number if it is divisible into all of the retained given numbers or obtained quotients.
    (b)   Dividing by a composite number if the numbers not so divided are prime to the composite number.

Example 3   **Same as Example 1.**

4)36	~~12~~	32	48	(Reject 12, as 12 is a factor of 48.)
3) 9		8	12	
3		8	~~4~~	(Reject 4, as 4 is a factor of 8.)

l.c.m. $= 4 \times 3 \times 3 \times 8 = 288$

Example 4   **Same as Example 2.**

2)~~7~~	12	8	9	~~6~~	14	(Reject 7 and 6, as each is a
2)	6	4	9		7	factor of 14 and 12, respectively.)
	~~3~~	2	9		7	(Reject 3, as 3 is a factor of 9.)

l.c.d. $= 2 \times 2 \times 2 \times 9 \times 7 = 504$

Example 5   **Find the l.c.m. of 48, 20, 32, 30, 15, and 40.**

2)48	~~20~~	32	30	~~15~~	40
4)24		16	15		20
2) 6		4	15		~~5~~
~~3~~		2	15		

l.c.m. $= 2 \times 4 \times 2 \times 2 \times 15 = 480$

Example 6   **Find the l.c.d. of fractions which have denominators of 14, 64, 56, 16, 42, and 80.**

2)~~14~~	64	56	~~16~~	42	80
4)	32	28		21	40
2)	8	~~7~~		21	10
	4			21	5

l.c.d. $= 2 \times 4 \times 2 \times 4 \times 21 \times 5 = 6720$

Take note that if improperly used, the methods used in Examples 3, 4, 5, and 6 to shorten the process of finding the l.c.m. or l.c.d. may result in a higher than necessary common multiple or common denominator.

Canceling

Reducing a fraction to its lowest terms may simplify computations materially. However, to cancel without forethought may increase rather than decrease the difficulty of the required computation. Thus, reducing $8 \div 1000$ or $\frac{8}{1000}$ to $1 \div 125$ or $\frac{1}{125}$ is not likely to simplify computation. Certainly $8 \div 900$ or $\frac{8}{900}$ is an easier computation than $2 \div 225$ or $\frac{2}{225}$. Almost everyone, no matter how experienced, tends to cancel merely because it may be done without first considering whether or not it will simplify the required calculation. Although not always true, generally such divisors or denominators as 10, 100, 1000 should not be reduced to other than lower powers of 10 (all of which are usually mechanical computations). Assuming that the divisor or denominator cannot be reduced to 10 or powers of 10, canceling will not usually be helpful unless the divisor or denominator can be reduced to figures that can be used as short divisors (e.g., 56 reduced to 7 or 8; 45 reduced to 5 or 9 or 3 or 15, etc.).

Either prime or composite numbers may be canceled. A common procedure in division is to place the factors of the dividend (numerator) above a horizontal line and the factors of the divisor (denominator) below, equal factors then being eliminated from the dividend (numerator) and the divisor (denominator).

As is illustrated in the following examples, canceling does not change the quotient.

Example 7 **Divide 144(12 × 6 × 2) by 48(6 × 2 × 4).**

$144 \div 48 = 3$

Canceling: $\dfrac{\overset{3}{\cancel{12}} \times \cancel{6} \times \cancel{2}}{\cancel{6} \times \cancel{2} \times \cancel{4}} = \dfrac{3}{1} = 3$

Example 8 **Divide 960(8 × 6 × 5 × 4) by 480(4 × 10 × 6 × 2).**

$960 \div 480 = 2$

Canceling: $\dfrac{\overset{\cancel{2}}{\cancel{8}} \times \cancel{6} \times \overset{2}{\cancel{5}} \times \cancel{4}}{\cancel{4} \times \underset{\cancel{2}}{\cancel{10}} \times \cancel{6} \times \cancel{2}} = \dfrac{2}{1} = 2$

Canceling may also be profitably employed in the multiplication and division of fractions. You will recall that a fraction is merely another form by which division is indicated and that the bar or line between the upper portion (numerator) and the lower portion (denominator) of a fraction has the same significance as the usual division sign. Thus the following have the same meaning:

$\dfrac{4}{5}$ and $4 \div 5$ $\dfrac{3}{7}$ and $3 \div 7$ $\dfrac{11}{8}$ and $11 \div 8$

When multiplying by one or a series of fractions, it is desirable to employ canceling whenever possible. Suppose it is required that 360 be multiplied by $\frac{3}{4}$, that their product be multiplied by $\frac{5}{6}$, and that this second product be multiplied by $\frac{2}{3}$. Each multiplication (and canceling) could be performed separately as follows:

$$\overset{90}{\cancel{360}} \times \frac{3}{\cancel{4}} = 270$$

$$\overset{45}{\cancel{270}} \times \frac{5}{\cancel{6}} = 225$$

$$\overset{45}{\cancel{225}} \times \frac{2}{\cancel{3}} = 90$$

Preferably, more factors could be canceled if all the multiplications were performed jointly as follows:

$$\overset{90}{\cancel{360}} \times \frac{\cancel{3}}{\cancel{4}} \times \frac{\cancel{5}}{\underset{\cancel{2}}{\cancel{6}}} \times \frac{\cancel{2}}{\cancel{3}} = 90$$

Perhaps even more desirable as a form for canceling would be the placing of all the numerators above, and all the denominators below, a single horizontal bar or line.

$$\frac{\overset{90}{\cancel{360}} \times \cancel{3} \times \cancel{5} \times \cancel{2}}{\cancel{4} \times \underset{\cancel{2}}{\cancel{6}} \times \cancel{5}} = 90$$

It will be apparent to you that the immediately preceding illustration (originally a problem in multiplication or division by fractions) is solved in exactly the same manner as might be used for the problem of dividing $360 \times 3 \times 5 \times 2$ by $4 \times 6 \times 5$. Note also that the sequence in which the factors are multiplied or canceled may be changed without affecting the result. Thus:

$$\frac{5 \times 3 \times \overset{\overset{\overset{3}{\cancel{15}}}{\cancel{90}}}{\cancel{360}} \times 2}{\cancel{5} \times \cancel{6} \times \cancel{4}} = 90$$

Before factors are canceled, the given quantities (or values) in both dividend and divisor must be expressed in similar values. Thus if the given quantities are in both dollars and cents, express all such terms in either dollars or cents; if the given quantities are in both inches and feet, express all such terms in either inches or feet.

ORDER OF OPERATIONS INDICATED BY SIGNS OR SYMBOLS Take special note that canceling cannot be performed when any one of the numbers in the numerator or denominator is separated from any of the others by addition or subtraction signs. Thus canceling cannot be performed in the examples that follow until the operations indicated in the numerators and denominators have been completed.

When the numerator or denominator or both contain signs other than multiplication, complete the operations indicated in the numerator and denominator in the following order:

1 Clear quantities within signs of aggregation such as parentheses ( ), brackets [ ], and braces { }; that is, perform the operations indicated.
2 Raise to powers indicated (see Unit 1.1 for explanation of powers).
3 Do all the multiplication (in any order desired).
4 Do all division in the order in which it occurs.
5 Do all addition and subtraction (in any order desired).

Example 9 **Perform the operations indicated in the following:**

(a) $\dfrac{24}{17 - (2 \times 4)} = \dfrac{24}{17 - 8} = \dfrac{\overset{8}{\cancel{24}}}{\underset{3}{\cancel{9}}} = \dfrac{8}{3} = 2\dfrac{2}{3}$

(b) $\dfrac{32 - (8 \div 4)}{6} = \dfrac{32 - 2}{6} = \dfrac{\overset{5}{\cancel{30}}}{\cancel{6}} = \dfrac{5}{1} = 5$

(c) $\dfrac{[(5 \times 6) - 9] \times [(90 : 5) \div 3]}{(4 \times 12) - [48 \div (4 \times 2)]} = \dfrac{(30 - 9) \times (18 \div 3)}{48 - (48 \div 8)}$

$$= \dfrac{21 \times 6}{48 - 6} = \dfrac{\overset{3}{\cancel{21}} \times \cancel{6}}{\underset{2}{\cancel{42}}} = \dfrac{3}{1} = 3$$

Exercise 1.7

Find the l.c.m. of the following groups of numbers:

1	3	23	42			

2	18	27	9	

3	5	18	9	10	3

4	32	56	42	80	

5 780   420   660   390

6 21   17   5   9   2   74   63

Find the l.c.d.'s of the following fractions:

7 $\dfrac{5}{18} \quad \dfrac{11}{42} \quad \dfrac{12}{19}$

8 $\dfrac{25}{15} \quad \dfrac{115}{6} \quad \dfrac{14}{25} \quad \dfrac{5}{3} \quad \dfrac{7}{30}$

9 $\dfrac{11 \quad 29 \quad 17 \quad 3 \quad 8}{24 \quad 16 \quad 30 \quad 20 \quad 5}$

10 $\dfrac{41 \quad 23 \quad 5 \quad 11}{252 \quad 48 \quad 98 \quad 63}$

11 $\dfrac{2 \quad 8 \quad 4 \quad 30}{9 \quad 27 \quad 72 \quad 108}$

12 $\dfrac{7 \quad 8 \quad 11 \quad 4 \quad 1}{6 \quad 11 \quad 4 \quad 18 \quad 30}$

Use canceling in solving the following:

13 $\dfrac{4 \times 20 \times 9 \times 12}{2 \times 7 \times 16 \times 14}$

14 $7 \times 2 \times 8 \times 25 \div 24 \times 5 \times 4 \times 14$

15 $\dfrac{209 \times 63 \times 640 \times 42 \times 78}{65 \times 56 \times 352 \times 14}$

16 $\dfrac{240 \times 195 \times 120 \times 74 \times 30}{33 \times 125 \times 4 \times 8 \times 10}$

Problems 17 through 22 should be set up in the same manner as Examples 7 and 8.

17 If a cord of wood requires a space equivalent to 8 by 4 by 4 ft, how many cords of wood are contained in a stack of wood that is 64 ft long, 15 ft wide, and 27 ft high?

18 A warehouse is 60 ft long, 42 ft wide, and 18 ft 9 in high. How many boxes 15 by 24 by 45 in will it contain?

19 A farmer sold 350 bu of wheat at $2.50 per bu, taking his pay in flour at 12.5 cents per lb. How many 100-lb sacks of flour did he receive? (*Note:* Express the price factors in the same kind of terms, e.g., in dollars or in cents.)

20 Laura Costa raised 1500 lb of apples valued at 45 cents per lb and traded them for gasoline at 60 cents per gal. How many gallons of gasoline would she receive?

21 A farmer's truck bed was $7\frac{1}{2}$ ft wide, 16 ft long, and he could stack hay bales 8 ft 4 in high. How many bales of hay 40 by 18 by 24 in could be put on the truck?

22 A loading pallet is 4 ft wide, 6 ft long, and concrete blocks can be stacked 3 ft high. How many concrete blocks 6 × 8 × 12 in will the pallet hold?

Chapter 2

Computing with Common or Complex Fractions and Complex Decimals

Objectives To Be Achieved in This Chapter

1   *Review the use, types, and fundamental principles of fractions.*
2   *Review the basic functions of addition, subtraction, multiplication, and division of fractions.*
3   *Learn procedures for simplifying fractions and finding the lowest common denominator.*
4   *Convert common fractions to decimal numbers and decimal numbers to fractions.*

Unit 2.1
Use and Fundamental Principles of Fractions: Addition of Fractions

Numerals such as $\frac{3}{4}, \frac{1}{3}, \frac{5}{8}, \frac{9}{7}$, and $\frac{6}{8}$ are fractions. The numbers represented by fractions are termed *fractional numbers*. Fractions are also known as *rational numbers,* to connote comparisons of a pair of numbers by division, as in a ratio. The number below the line or bar (———) is called a *denominator* and represents the whole unit or total set of which the number above the line or bar called the *numerator* is one or a number of equal parts. The numerator and the denominator together are the *terms of the fraction*.

The placing of a line or bar (———) between the numerator and the denominator has the same meaning as the sign indicating division ($\div$) or the words "divided by." Thus:

$\frac{3}{4}$ is the same as $3 \div 4$, or 3 divided by 4, whereby the numerator 3 is the dividend and the denominator 4 is the divisor.

If the division operation indicated by the bar is completed, the fractions would then be expressed as a *decimal fraction*. Thus:

Common fraction		Decimal fraction
$\frac{3}{4}$	$= 3 \div 4 =$	0.75
$\frac{3}{8}$	$= 3 \div 8 =$	0.375
$\frac{4}{5}$	$= 4 \div 5 =$	0.8

Kinds of Fractions

Fractions other than decimal fractions are known as *common* fractions. There are several types of common fractions, each distinguished by its own name.

A *proper fraction* is one in which the numerator is less than the denominator. Thus:

$\frac{2}{3}, \frac{6}{7}, \frac{21}{22}, \frac{1}{9}, \frac{7}{12}$ are proper fractions

An *improper fraction* is one in which the numerator is equal to or more than the denominator. Thus:

$\frac{5}{3}, \frac{8}{7}, \frac{21}{8}, \frac{6}{6}, \frac{11}{9}$ are improper fractions

A *complex fraction* is a fraction in which the numerator or denominator or both are fractional. Thus:

$$\frac{\frac{3}{4}}{10},\ \frac{\frac{4}{5}}{\frac{7}{2}},\ \frac{\frac{1}{2}}{\frac{8}{9}},\ \frac{\frac{1}{2}\times\frac{2}{7}}{\frac{2}{3}-\frac{1}{4}}\ \text{are complex fractions}$$

A *mixed number* is the sum of a whole number and a fraction. Thus:

$7\frac{1}{4}$ is a mixed number equivalent to $7+\frac{1}{4}$

$23\frac{2}{3}$ is a mixed number equivalent to $23+\frac{2}{3}$

A mixed number may also be expressed as an improper fraction; e.g., $2\frac{1}{4}$, equivalent to $2+\frac{1}{4}$, may be expressed as $\frac{9}{4}$. The mixed number $1\frac{2}{3}=\frac{5}{3}$; the mixed number $3\frac{3}{5}=\frac{18}{5}$, etc.

Use of Fractions

Fractions have many applications. The following illustrate some of the more common and practical uses:

Example 1 **To compare one or more equal parts of one unit to the total number of parts of that unit.**

David was to practice his music lessons 14 hr each week. He practiced 3 hr the first day. The fraction $\frac{3}{14}$ indicates the number of hours David practiced the first day compared to the total number of hours he was to practice during the week.

Example 2 **To indicate the division function between two numbers or sets of numbers.**

The total cost to transport 125.450 thousand board feet of redwood logs from the woods to the mill was $4390.75. The cost per 1000 board feet is $\dfrac{\$4390.75}{125.450}$ or $35 per 1000 board feet. The fraction $\dfrac{\$4390.75}{125.450}$ indicates that to find the cost per 1000 board feet you are to divide $4390.75 by 125.450.

Example 3 **To compare one number with another number by stating the quantity of the first number in terms of the second number as in a ratio.**

The Butte Company has current assets of $68,460 and current liabilities of $22,820 for a current ratio $\frac{3}{1}$ or 3 to 1. The fraction $\frac{3}{1}$ or ratio 3 to 1 states the comparison of current assets to current liabilities and results from performing the division operation indicated by the fraction $\frac{\$68,460}{\$22,820}$. In effect, current assets are being compared to current liabilities by stating that there exists $3 of current assets for every $1 of current liabilities.

Fundamental Principles of Fractions

In working with fractions, it is necessary to know and understand certain general principles that may be applied to all fractions. These principles are:

1   The value of the fraction is not changed by multiplying both numerator and denominator by the same number. Thus:

$$\frac{1}{2} = \frac{2}{4} \text{ or } \frac{3}{6} \text{ or } \frac{4}{8} \qquad \text{(Multipliers are 2, 3, and 4, respectively)}$$

$$\frac{2}{3} = \frac{4}{6} \text{ or } \frac{10}{15} \text{ or } \frac{14}{21} \qquad \text{(Multipliers are 2, 5, and 7, respectively)}$$

2   The value of the fraction is not changed by dividing both numerator and denominator by the same number. Thus:

$$\frac{32}{40} = \frac{16}{20} \text{ or } \frac{8}{10} \text{ or } \frac{4}{5} \quad \text{(Divisors are 2, 4, and 8, respectively)}$$

$$\frac{75}{150} = \frac{25}{50} \text{ or } \frac{5}{10} \text{ or } \frac{1}{2} \quad \text{(Divisors are 3, 15, and 75, respectively)}$$

3   An improper fraction may be expressed either as a whole number or as a mixed number, if the numerator is divided by the denominator. Thus:

$$\frac{24}{6} = 24 \div 6 = 4 \qquad \frac{23}{6} = 23 \div 6 = 3\frac{5}{6}$$

$$\frac{35}{7} = 35 \div 7 = 5 \qquad \frac{36}{7} = 36 \div 7 = 5\frac{1}{7}$$

4   A whole number may be stated as a fraction. Thus:

$$1 = \frac{1}{1} \text{ or } \frac{2}{2} \text{ or } \frac{3}{3}, \text{ etc.}$$

$$3 = \frac{3}{1} \text{ or } \frac{6}{2} \text{ or } \frac{9}{3}, \text{ etc.}$$

$$7 = \frac{7}{1} \text{ or } \frac{14}{2} \text{ or } \frac{21}{3}, \text{ etc.}$$

In performing this operation the numerator is determined by the product of the integer and the given denominator. Thus:

Express 8 in sevenths: $8 = \dfrac{8 \times 7}{7} = \dfrac{56}{7}$

Change 5 to ninths: $5 = \dfrac{5 \times 9}{9} = \dfrac{45}{9}$

General Rule for Operation in Fractions

Solution of many problems in fractions is dependent on a knowledge of the following general rule (which may be developed from the fundamental principles): *Fractions with a common denominator have the same relationship to each other as do their numerators.* Thus:

$\dfrac{3}{6}$ is to $\dfrac{4}{6}$ as 3 is to 4 $\dfrac{6}{2}$ is to $\dfrac{1}{2}$ as 6 is to 1

From this general rule, the following two very important applications can be made:

1   To apportion numbers, money, objects, or things having a fractional relationship, change the fractions to fractions with a common denominator and use the numerators as whole numbers in determining the proper apportionment.

   Thus, if a sum of money is divided so that John has $\frac{1}{4}$, Mary $\frac{1}{3}$, and James the remainder, the problem of determining what fractional part of the whole sum belongs to James may be solved as follows:

   A common denominator of 3 and 4 is 12. Therefore John has $\frac{1}{4}$, or $\frac{3}{12}$; and Mary has $\frac{1}{3}$, or $\frac{4}{12}$. But John and Mary together have $\frac{7}{12}$ of the whole. Since the unit 1, or the whole sum of money, is equivalent to $\frac{12}{12}$, then the remainder is $\frac{12}{12}$ less $\frac{7}{12}$, or $\frac{5}{12}$. James's share is the remainder, or $\frac{5}{12}$.

   Restated, it may be said that if the money is divided into 12 equal portions, then John has 3 portions, Mary has 4 portions, and James has the remainder of 5 portions, since

$$12 - (3 + 4) = 5$$

2   To add, subtract, divide, or multiply two or more fractions, change them to fractions having common denominators and then add, subtract, divide, or multiply the numerators. However, changing fractions to fractions expressed in common denominators is not necessary before dividing or multiplying by fractions and is not often a desirable method to use in multiplication.

   Note: In multiplying, the denominator is squared, cubed, etc., if a common denominator is found. Example: $\frac{4}{12} \times \frac{3}{12} \times \frac{1}{12} = \frac{12}{1728} = \frac{1}{144}$. Thus:

To add: $\dfrac{1}{3} + \dfrac{1}{4} = \dfrac{4}{12} + \dfrac{3}{12} = \dfrac{7}{12}$

To subtract: $\dfrac{1}{3} - \dfrac{1}{4} = \dfrac{4}{12} - \dfrac{3}{12} = \dfrac{1}{12}$

To divide: $\frac{1}{3} \div \frac{1}{4} = \frac{4}{12} \div \frac{3}{12} = \frac{4}{3} = 1\frac{1}{3}$

To multiply: $\frac{1}{3} \times \frac{1}{4} = \frac{4}{12} \times \frac{3}{12} = \frac{12}{144} = \frac{1}{12}$

Fractions or Whole Numbers of Equivalent Value

Fractions or any numbers may be expressed, changed, or reduced to denominations or forms of equivalent value. The term "reduce," when used in arithmetic, does not necessarily mean "to make smaller or lower," though it is generally used in this sense.

To express in higher terms:

$\frac{1}{2}$ may be changed to $\frac{2}{4}, \frac{3}{6}, \frac{4}{8}, \frac{5}{10}$, etc.

$\frac{2}{3}$ may be expressed as $\frac{4}{6}, \frac{6}{9}, \frac{8}{12}, \frac{10}{15}$, etc.

4 may be reduced to $\frac{8}{2}, \frac{12}{3}, \frac{16}{4}, \frac{20}{5}$, etc.

To reduce to lower terms:

$\frac{9}{18}$ may be changed to $\frac{8}{16}, \frac{7}{14}, \frac{6}{12}, \frac{5}{10}$, etc.

$\frac{18}{27}$ may be reduced to $\frac{16}{24}, \frac{14}{21}, \frac{12}{18}, \frac{10}{15}$, etc.

$\frac{36}{9}$ may be expressed as $\frac{32}{8}, \frac{28}{7}, \frac{24}{6}, \frac{20}{5}$, etc.

To change an improper fraction to a whole or mixed number: Divide the numerator by the denominator. Thus:

$\frac{18}{6} = 18 \div 6 = 3$

$\frac{22}{5} = 22 \div 5 = 4\frac{2}{5}$

To express a mixed number as an improper fraction: Multiply the whole number by the denominator of the fraction, add the numerator of the fraction to this product, and then place this sum over the given denominator of the fraction. Thus:

$$5\frac{1}{4} = \frac{(5 \times 4) + 1}{4} = \frac{20 + 1}{4} = \frac{21}{4}$$

$$17\frac{2}{3} = \frac{(17 \times 3) + 2}{3} = \frac{51 + 2}{3} = \frac{53}{3}$$

To change a fraction to a fraction in which the denominator is a multiple: Multiply the given numerator by the quotient of the required denominator divided by the given denominator, and then place this product (required numerator) over the required denominator. Thus:

$\frac{4}{7}$ expressed in 21sts: $\frac{(21 \div 7) \times 4}{21} = \frac{3 \times 4}{21} = \frac{12}{21}$

$\frac{7}{8}$ expressed as 40ths: $\frac{(40 \div 8) \times 7}{40} = \frac{5 \times 7}{40} = \frac{35}{40}$

To reduce a fraction to lower terms: Divide both terms by a common factor. Note that both numerator and denominator must be divisible by the number used as a factor. Thus:

$\frac{12}{30}$ can be reduced by dividing both terms by $2 = \frac{6}{15}$

$\frac{12}{30}$ can be reduced by dividing both terms by $3 = \frac{4}{10}$

$\frac{12}{30}$ can be reduced by dividing both terms by $6 = \frac{2}{5}$

To reduce a fraction to its lowest terms: Divide both terms by a common factor, divide the result by a common factor, and continue this process until the terms are prime to each other. Thus:

$\frac{20}{40}$, both terms divided by $2 = \frac{10}{20}$

$\frac{10}{20}$, both terms divided by $2 = \frac{5}{10}$

$\frac{5}{10}$, both terms divided by $5 = \frac{1}{2}$

To reduce a fraction to its lowest terms by use of only one divisor: Divide both terms by their greatest common divisor (highest common factor). Thus:

$\frac{12}{30}$, both terms divided by $6 = \frac{2}{5}$

$\frac{20}{40}$, both terms divided by $20 = \frac{1}{2}$

From the immediately preceding examples, it is obvious that the use of the greatest common divisor saves time and effort in expressing a fraction in its lowest terms.

If you do not have a thorough knowledge of the rules of divisibility for both prime and composite numbers (Unit 1.6), review them now, for their use will be of greatest assistance in completing the exercises that follow.

If it is required to change fractions to their lowest terms and you are not sure that both factors are prime to each other (that the fraction cannot be expressed in lower terms), find the g.c.d. by the division method (Unit 1.6). Use of this method will determine definitely the lowest terms in which any fraction can be expressed.

Addition of Fractions

Proper fractions, improper fractions, and mixed numbers after changing to improper fractions may be added by using the following order of procedure:

1   Change all addends to fractions with a common denominator (unless they are already so expressed).
2   Add the numerators of the addends to determine the numerator of the required sum.

The denominator of the required sum will be the common denominator of the addends.

The obtained sum will be a proper or improper fraction which should be reduced to lowest terms if it is not already thus expressed.

Example 4   **(a)   Add $\frac{2}{5}$, $\frac{4}{5}$, and $\frac{1}{5}$.**

$$\frac{2}{5}$$
$$\frac{4}{5}$$
$$\frac{1}{5}$$
$$\frac{7}{5} = 1\frac{2}{5}$$

(b)   Add $\frac{2}{3}$, $\frac{1}{2}$, and $\frac{5}{6}$.

$$\frac{2}{3} = \frac{4}{6}$$
$$\frac{1}{2} = \frac{3}{6}$$
$$\frac{5}{6} = \frac{5}{6}$$
$$\frac{12}{6} = 2$$

(c)   Add $4\frac{1}{4}$, $\frac{13}{6}$, $3\frac{1}{3}$, and $\frac{9}{2}$.

$$4\frac{1}{4} = \frac{17}{4} = \frac{51}{12}$$
$$\frac{13}{6} = \frac{26}{12}$$
$$3\frac{1}{3} = \frac{10}{3} = \frac{40}{12}$$
$$\frac{9}{2} = \frac{54}{12}$$
$$\frac{171}{12} = 14\frac{3}{12} = 14\frac{1}{4}$$

ADDITION OF MIXED NUMBERS   Mixed numbers need not be changed to improper fractions before they are added, for the addition of mixed numbers may be accomplished in two steps:

1   Find the sum of the fractional parts of the addends.
2   Add this sum to the whole digits of the addends.

If the sum of the fractional parts is an improper fraction, it may be changed to a mixed number before it is added to the whole numbers of the addends (see Example 2, below). In any event, the sum should be reduced to lowest terms if it is not already thus shown.

Example 5   **(a)   Add $1\frac{1}{3}$, $5\frac{1}{8}$, $3\frac{2}{5}$, and $9\frac{1}{10}$.**   **(b)   Add $\frac{3}{2}$, $\frac{6}{5}$, $\frac{9}{4}$, and $\frac{17}{10}$.**

$$1\frac{1}{3} = 1\frac{40}{120}$$

$$5\frac{1}{8} = 5\frac{15}{120}$$

$$3\frac{2}{5} = 3\frac{48}{120}$$

$$9\frac{1}{10} = 9\frac{12}{120}$$

$$18\frac{115}{120} = 18\frac{23}{24}$$

$$\frac{3}{2} = 1\frac{1}{2} = 1\frac{10}{20}$$

$$\frac{6}{5} = 1\frac{1}{5} = 1\frac{4}{20}$$

$$\frac{9}{4} = 2\frac{1}{4} = 2\frac{5}{20}$$

$$\frac{17}{10} = 1\frac{7}{10} = 1\frac{14}{20}$$

$$5\frac{33}{20} = 6\frac{13}{20}$$

Note: $\frac{33}{20} = 1\frac{13}{20}$, which, added to the whole digit total of 5, equals $6\frac{13}{20}$.

When the given addends are mixed numbers or improper fractions that are the equivalent of large whole or mixed numbers, addition as mixed numbers rather than as improper fractions is recommended except when the given improper fractions have the same denominator.

Exercise 2.1

Change to common denominators in adding each of the following, and then express each obtained sum in lowest terms as a proper fraction or mixed number:

1   $\frac{3}{11} + \frac{2}{8}$ 2 $\frac{4}{7} + \frac{1}{11}$ 3 $\frac{2}{3} + \frac{7}{9}$ 4 $\frac{5}{8} + \frac{5}{6}$

5   $2\frac{3}{4} + \frac{1}{5}$ 6 $2\frac{2}{3} + \frac{3}{4}$ 7 $6\frac{3}{7} + 8\frac{2}{3}$ 8 $5\frac{4}{9} + 2\frac{3}{4}$

9   $\frac{1}{4} + \frac{1}{5}$ 10 $\frac{1}{5} + \frac{1}{6}$ 11 $\frac{5}{7} + \frac{3}{8}$ 12 $\frac{2}{9} + \frac{1}{2}$

13   $4\frac{1}{15} + \frac{5}{8}$ 14 $7\frac{2}{3} + \frac{3}{4}$ 15 $8\frac{1}{2} + 9\frac{4}{5}$ 16 $6\frac{2}{3} + 4\frac{4}{5}$

17 $\dfrac{1}{6}$ 18 $\dfrac{1}{9}$ 19 $\dfrac{2}{9}$ 20 $\dfrac{7}{20}$

$\dfrac{1}{8}$ $\dfrac{1}{7}$ $\dfrac{3}{8}$ $\dfrac{5}{8}$

21 $6\dfrac{1}{4}$ 22 $2\dfrac{5}{6}$ 23 $17\dfrac{8}{9}$ 24 $18\dfrac{7}{23}$

$\dfrac{9}{4}$ $\dfrac{7}{2}$ $25\dfrac{4}{15}$ $6\dfrac{5}{10}$

Add and express sums as mixed numbers reduced to lowest terms:

25 $\dfrac{3}{8}$ 26 $\dfrac{5}{6}$ 27 $\dfrac{7}{12}$ 28 $\dfrac{2}{3}$

$\dfrac{4}{11}$ $\dfrac{2}{3}$ $\dfrac{2}{7}$ $\dfrac{5}{6}$

$\dfrac{1}{3}$ $\dfrac{1}{2}$ $\dfrac{1}{16}$ $\dfrac{1}{4}$

$\dfrac{6}{9}$ $\dfrac{1}{5}$ $\dfrac{3}{4}$ $\dfrac{1}{13}$

29 $\dfrac{3}{4}$ 30 $\dfrac{7}{18}$ 31 $1\dfrac{7}{8}$ 32 $\dfrac{1}{14}$

$\dfrac{3}{5}$ $\dfrac{4}{11}$ $\dfrac{5}{12}$ $2\dfrac{2}{3}$

$\dfrac{5}{8}$ $\dfrac{2}{18}$ $2\dfrac{3}{8}$ $\dfrac{9}{21}$

$\dfrac{3}{7}$ $\dfrac{5}{32}$ $\dfrac{1}{4}$ $1\dfrac{1}{4}$

$\dfrac{1}{6}$ $\dfrac{5}{6}$ $\dfrac{15}{16}$ $\dfrac{7}{28}$

Add and express sums as mixed numbers reduced to lowest terms:

33 $2\dfrac{1}{4}$ 34 $5\dfrac{1}{4}$ 35 $71\dfrac{3}{5}$

$5\dfrac{3}{8}$ $2\dfrac{1}{3}$ $16\dfrac{2}{3}$

$4\dfrac{2}{7}$ $1\dfrac{1}{5}$ $3\dfrac{1}{3}$

$\dfrac{1}{8}$ $3\dfrac{1}{7}$ $83\dfrac{1}{3}$

$2\dfrac{4}{5}$ $8\dfrac{3}{5}$ $19\dfrac{8}{15}$

36 $\dfrac{56}{11}$ **37** $\dfrac{15}{4}$ **38** $7\dfrac{2}{36}$

$11\dfrac{3}{4}$ $\dfrac{132}{3}$ $9\dfrac{3}{8}$

$239\dfrac{1}{2}$ $\dfrac{83}{7}$ $11\dfrac{2}{3}$

$14\dfrac{2}{5}$ $\dfrac{98}{9}$ $3\dfrac{8}{10}$

$\dfrac{85}{3}$ $\dfrac{115}{6}$ $19\dfrac{1}{24}$

Solve the following:

39 Find the total weight in ounces of a can and contents if the can weighs $1\frac{6}{8}$ oz and the contents weigh $32\frac{14}{16}$ oz.

40 Two pieces of wood are glued together. Find the thickness in inches if one piece of wood is $2\frac{11}{15}$ in thick, the second piece of wood is $2\frac{3}{4}$ in thick, and the joining glue is $\frac{4}{90}$ in thick.

41 Three pieces of pipe are joined together. If the joiners each add a net of 1 in to the length, find the total length of the joined pipe in inches if the three pieces of pipe are $11\frac{3}{4}$ in, $23\frac{4}{5}$ in, and $15\frac{2}{3}$ in, respectively.

42 Find the perimeter (distance around) in feet of a trapezoid (a four-sided plane figure) if one side is $7\frac{2}{3}$ ft, the second side is $6\frac{14}{12}$ ft, the third side is $\frac{9}{6}$ ft, and the fourth side is $16\frac{3}{9}$ ft.

43 Find the outside diameter in inches of a piece of tubing if its walls are $\frac{11}{16}$ in thick and the inside diameter is $4\frac{13}{24}$ in.

44 Find the outside dimensions in inches of a box made of $\frac{7}{12}$-in plywood if the inside dimensions are $18\frac{4}{9}$ by $13\frac{1}{4}$ by $9\frac{3}{5}$ in.

45 Find the total gallons of gasoline purchased on an automobile trip if the driver bought $14\frac{9}{10}$ gal, $18\frac{1}{4}$ gal, $9\frac{3}{8}$ gal, and $11\frac{7}{8}$ gal.

46 Find the total drapery yardage purchased in making three drapery sets if one set required $58\frac{1}{6}$ yd, the second set required $21\frac{5}{9}$ yd, and the third set required $65\frac{7}{12}$ yd.

47 Three workers require (a) 36 hr, (b) 44 hr, and (c) 56 hr, respectively, to singly complete a job. Expressing the answers in the same common denominator reduced to lowest terms, find what part of the job would be completed by each of the workers (a), (b), and (c) in 16 hr.

48 The length of a machine part consisted of four pieces measuring $14\frac{9}{16}$ in, $8\frac{17}{64}$ in, $19\frac{5}{8}$ in, and $3\frac{25}{32}$ in. Find the length of the machine part in inches.

49 A carton of groceries contained items weighing as follows: $4\frac{1}{4}$ lb, $2\frac{7}{8}$ lb, $3\frac{7}{32}$ lb, and $6\frac{5}{128}$ lb. If the carton weighed $3\frac{15}{64}$ lb, find the total weight in pounds of the carton and its contents.

50 A $3\frac{1}{4}$-ft-wide walk was placed 9 ft inside the boundaries of a 90-ft square backyard. Find in feet (a) the exterior perimeter (distance around) and (b) the interior perimeter of the walk.

Unit 2.2

Subtraction of Fractions and
Rounding Off Fractions

Proper fractions, improper fractions, and mixed numbers after changing to improper fractions may be subtracted by using the following order of procedure:

1 Unless already in terms of the same denominator, express both minuend and subtrahend as fractions with a common denominator (preferably the l.c.d.).

2 Subtract the numerator of the subtrahend from the numerator of the minuend to determine the numerator of the remainder.

3 The common denominator is the denominator of the remainder.

If the obtained remainder is not a fraction in lowest terms, reduce it to lowest terms as a proper fraction, whole number, or mixed number.

Example 1   **(a)   Subtract $\frac{1}{4}$ from $\frac{3}{4}$.**

$$\frac{3}{4}$$
$$-\frac{1}{4}$$
$$\frac{2}{4} = \frac{1}{2}$$

(b)   Subtract $\frac{2}{3}$ from $\frac{7}{8}$.

$$\frac{7}{8} = \frac{21}{24}$$
$$-\frac{2}{3} = \frac{16}{24}$$
$$\frac{5}{24}$$

(c)   Subtract $\frac{4}{5}$ from 8.

$$8 = \frac{40}{5}$$
$$-\frac{4}{5}$$
$$\frac{36}{5} = 7\frac{1}{5}$$

(d)   Subtract $\frac{3}{4}$ from $\frac{14}{5}$.

$$\frac{14}{5} = \frac{56}{20}$$
$$-\frac{3}{4} = \frac{15}{20}$$
$$\frac{41}{20} = 2\frac{1}{20}$$

(e)   Subtract $2\frac{1}{6}$ from $\frac{37}{5}$.

$$\frac{37}{5} = \frac{222}{30}$$
$$-2\frac{1}{6} = \frac{13}{6} = \frac{65}{30}$$
$$\frac{157}{30} = 5\frac{7}{30}$$

(f)   Subtract $1\frac{3}{4}$ from $5\frac{1}{3}$.

$$5\frac{1}{3} = \frac{16}{3} = \frac{64}{12}$$
$$-1\frac{3}{4} = \frac{7}{4} = \frac{21}{12}$$
$$\frac{43}{12} = 3\frac{7}{12}$$

Subtraction of Mixed Numbers

Mixed numbers may be subtracted without changing them to improper fractions. The procedure is as follows:

1 From the fractional part of the minuend subtract the fractional part of the subtrahend.
2 Add the fractional remainder to the difference between the whole numbers of the minuend and the subtrahend.

Example 2   **(a) Subtract 6 from $15\frac{3}{4}$.**

$$15\frac{3}{4}$$
$$-6$$
$$\overline{\quad 9\frac{3}{4}\quad}$$

(b) Subtract $8\frac{7}{15}$ from $53\frac{11}{12}$.

$$53\frac{11}{12} = 53\frac{55}{60}$$
$$-8\frac{7}{15} = 8\frac{28}{60}$$
$$\overline{45\frac{27}{60} = 45\frac{9}{20}}$$

When there is no fractional ending in the minuend and the subtrahend contains a fractional ending, subtract 1 from the minuend and express the minuend as an equivalent mixed number with a fractional ending having the same denominator as the fractional ending in the subtrahend.

Example 3   **(a) From 18 take $12\frac{3}{8}$.**

$$18 = 17\frac{8}{8}$$
$$-12\frac{3}{8}$$
$$\overline{\quad 5\frac{5}{8}\quad}$$

(b) Take $64\frac{11}{15}$ from 145.

$$145 = 144\frac{15}{15}$$
$$-64\frac{11}{15}$$
$$\overline{\quad 80\frac{4}{15}\quad}$$

When a fractional ending in the minuend is of lesser value than a fractional ending in the subtrahend, subtract 1 from the minuend and add the fractional value of 1 to the fractional ending of the minuend. Then the minuend will be expressed as a mixed number with a fractional ending that is an improper fraction. Thus:

$$6\frac{1}{3} = 5\frac{4}{3}, \ 9\frac{3}{8} = 8\frac{11}{8}, \ 26\frac{7}{10} = 25\frac{17}{10}, \text{ etc.}$$

Example 4   **(a) Take $8\frac{5}{9}$ from $24\frac{2}{9}$.**

$$24\frac{2}{9} = 23\frac{11}{9}$$
$$-8\frac{5}{9} = 8\frac{5}{9}$$
$$\overline{15\frac{6}{9} = 15\frac{2}{3}}$$

(b) Subtract $41\frac{3}{4}$ from $80\frac{1}{6}$.

$$80\frac{1}{6} = 79\frac{7}{6} = 79\frac{14}{12}$$
$$-41\frac{3}{4} = 41\frac{3}{4} = 41\frac{9}{12}$$
$$\overline{38\frac{5}{12}}$$

When subtraction of mixed numbers or improper fractions is necessary and the minuend or subtrahend is a large number, usually it is quicker and easier to subtract by the mixed-number method (changing improper fractions to mixed numbers before performing the required subtraction).

Rounding off Fractions[1]

In computing, a portion beyond the desired unit of accuracy will frequently be expressed as a fraction. Thus, it may be necessary to round off such numbers as $7\frac{2}{3}$ ft, $19\frac{7}{16}$ lb, $43.06\frac{5}{11}$ percent, $\$2.37\frac{1}{2}$. The rules to be followed in most types of business transactions (expressed as the fractional equivalents of the rules for rounding off decimals, Unit 1.1) are as follows:

1   If the portion to be dropped off is the fractional equivalent of $\frac{1}{2}$, or more, add 1 to the preceding digit.
2   If the portion to be dropped off is less than the fractional equivalent of $\frac{1}{2}$, discard it, leaving the preceding digit as is.

Example 5   **Fractions rounded off.**

Given	Round off to	Given	Round off to
$62\frac{1}{2}$	63	$\$3.06\frac{1}{3}$	$\$3.06$
$25\frac{7}{16}$	25	$\$57.83\frac{5}{9}$	$\$57.84$
$452\frac{7}{13}$	453	$15\frac{3}{8}\%$	15%
$\frac{9}{20}$	0	$46.12\frac{5}{8}\%$	46.13%

In business the most common exceptions to the rules for rounding off fractions or decimal equivalents occur in transactions involving weights and measures or between consumer and retailer. In such cases, the general practice is to raise by one unit any digit followed by a fraction, no matter how small that fraction may be. Thus, the purchaser of terra-cotta pipe priced in yard lengths will be required to purchase 14 yd of pipe even though only 13 yd and a very small fraction over is desired; a purchaser of $2415\frac{1}{4}$ board feet of lumber will be charged for 2416 board feet; the retail purchaser of canned milk will usually pay 9 cents per can if the price is 3 cans for 25 cents (an average of $8\frac{1}{3}$ cents per can).

---

[1]The rule for rounding off given here is the one generally used for business transactions. A modification is made in what is known as the computer's rule: If the portion to be dropped is exactly $\frac{1}{2}$, round up if the preceding digit is odd; discard if the preceding digit is even (see Unit 1.1).

Exercise 2.2

Change to common denominators in subtracting each of the following, and then express each obtained remainder in lowest terms:

1 $\dfrac{12}{15} - \dfrac{8}{12}$ **2** $1\dfrac{7}{8} - \dfrac{2}{3}$ **3** $\dfrac{9}{4} - \dfrac{2}{7}$ **4** $\dfrac{5}{2} - \dfrac{5}{7}$

5 $\dfrac{5}{7} - \dfrac{9}{14}$ **6** $\dfrac{3}{4} - \dfrac{2}{3}$ **7** $\dfrac{8}{15} - \dfrac{7}{16}$ **8** $\dfrac{9}{5} - \dfrac{3}{4}$

9 $\begin{array}{c}\dfrac{2}{3}\\[4pt]\dfrac{1}{4}\\ \hline\end{array}$ **10** $\begin{array}{c}\dfrac{2}{3}\\[4pt]\dfrac{1}{2}\\ \hline\end{array}$ **11** $\begin{array}{c}\dfrac{5}{8}\\[4pt]\dfrac{1}{3}\\ \hline\end{array}$ **12** $\begin{array}{c}\dfrac{18}{6}\\[4pt]\dfrac{6}{7}\\ \hline\end{array}$

Round off the fractions or common fractional endings of the following:

13 $\dfrac{5}{11}$ **14** $\dfrac{4}{5}$ **15** $4\dfrac{7}{13}$ **16** $4\dfrac{7}{15}$

17 $23.2\dfrac{5}{9}$ **18** $0.4\dfrac{3}{7}$ **19** $\$2.28\dfrac{6}{13}$ **20** $\$4.72\dfrac{3}{4}$

Perform the indicated subtraction *first* and then round off the remainder to nearest whole units:

21 $36\dfrac{3}{7} - 14$ **22** $38 - 26\dfrac{2}{5}$ **23** $17\dfrac{4}{5} - 6\dfrac{1}{3}$ **24** $72\dfrac{1}{8} - 20\dfrac{15}{21}$

Change all improper fractions to whole or mixed numbers before performing subtraction. Express answers as whole or mixed numbers reduced to lowest terms.

25 $\begin{array}{c}36\dfrac{18}{23}\\[4pt]17\\ \hline\end{array}$ **26** $\begin{array}{c}42\dfrac{3}{7}\\[4pt]19\\ \hline\end{array}$ **27** $\begin{array}{c}86\dfrac{4}{9}\\[4pt]38\\ \hline\end{array}$ **28** $\begin{array}{c}45\dfrac{2}{3}\\[4pt]27\\ \hline\end{array}$

29 $\begin{array}{c}89\\[4pt]43\dfrac{2}{9}\\ \hline\end{array}$ **30** $\begin{array}{c}47\dfrac{1}{7}\\[4pt]40\dfrac{3}{7}\\ \hline\end{array}$ **31** $\begin{array}{c}53\\[4pt]28\dfrac{2}{3}\\ \hline\end{array}$ **32** $\begin{array}{c}62\\[4pt]47\dfrac{3}{11}\\ \hline\end{array}$

33 $\begin{array}{c}18\dfrac{2}{3}\\[4pt]6\dfrac{4}{9}\\ \hline\end{array}$ **34** $\begin{array}{c}56\dfrac{5}{8}\\[4pt]19\dfrac{4}{9}\\ \hline\end{array}$ **35** $\begin{array}{c}60\dfrac{2}{3}\\[4pt]18\dfrac{3}{5}\\ \hline\end{array}$ **36** $\begin{array}{c}74\dfrac{16}{21}\\[4pt]42\dfrac{9}{11}\\ \hline\end{array}$

37 $\begin{array}{c}19\dfrac{9}{12}\\[4pt]16\dfrac{5}{8}\\ \hline\end{array}$ **38** $\begin{array}{c}27\dfrac{2}{5}\\[4pt]13\dfrac{5}{6}\\ \hline\end{array}$ **39** $\begin{array}{c}42\dfrac{8}{9}\\[4pt]25\dfrac{14}{15}\\ \hline\end{array}$ **40** $\begin{array}{c}69\dfrac{2}{7}\\[4pt]20\dfrac{5}{8}\\ \hline\end{array}$

41 $\dfrac{195}{5}$ 42 $\dfrac{184}{7}$ 43 $\dfrac{625}{5}$ 44 $\dfrac{173}{11}$

$\dfrac{253}{11}$ $\dfrac{216}{20}$ $\dfrac{419}{6}$ $\dfrac{195}{17}$

45 $324\dfrac{5}{13}$ 46 $291\dfrac{2}{5}$ 47 $48\dfrac{7}{9}$ 48 $88\dfrac{6}{11}$

$\dfrac{283}{3}$ $\dfrac{784}{9}$ $14\dfrac{525}{25}$ $14\dfrac{2}{3}$

Solve the following:

49 A container was $\frac{5}{8}$ full of oil. Enough oil was added to fill the container to $\frac{15}{16}$ full. How much of a full container of oil was added?

50 A $8\frac{5}{12}$-ft post was set $3\frac{1}{2}$ ft in the ground. What was the exact length in feet of the post above ground level?

51 The opening price of a stock was $63\frac{5}{8}$. If the closing price was $59\frac{1}{4}$, find the net reduction in price.

52 If one worker can complete a job in $8\frac{7}{12}$ hr and a second worker can complete the same job in $6\frac{9}{10}$ hr, how much more time in hours does the first worker require?

53 If the outside diameter of a pipe is $4\frac{8}{15}$ in and the walls are $\frac{7}{16}$ in thick, find the inside diameter in inches of the pipe.

54 A piece of lumber $15\frac{3}{8}$ ft long was cut into three pieces. The length of the first piece was $3\frac{15}{32}$ ft and the length of the second piece was $8\frac{7}{12}$ ft. If the cutting waste was $\frac{1}{72}$ ft, find the exact length of the third piece in feet.

55 From a $68\frac{5}{8}$-ft length of rope two pieces each $12\frac{3}{4}$ ft long were cut off. Then three pieces each $10\frac{7}{36}$ ft long were cut off. Find the length of the remaining piece of rope in feet.

56 A job was partially completed as follows: $\frac{1}{6}$ the first day, $\frac{5}{16}$ the second day, and $\frac{4}{15}$ the third day. What portion of the job remained to be completed?

57 If the perimeter (distance around) of a triangle is $61\frac{9}{32}$ in, one side is $21\frac{5}{8}$ in, and the second side is $17\frac{13}{16}$ in, find the length in inches of the third side.

58 In a partnership, one man owned $\frac{5}{14}$ of the capital, the second man owned $\frac{3}{8}$, and a woman owned the remainder. Find the fractional part owned by the woman.

59 A man left $\frac{2}{7}$ of his estate to his widow, $\frac{1}{6}$ each to his two daughters, $\frac{1}{10}$ to his son, and the remainder to charitable organizations. What fractional part of the estate did the charitable organizations receive?

60 A couple built a home on a $160\frac{1}{2}$-ft-wide lot. If the house was set back $6\frac{1}{4}$ ft from the lot line on one side and the home was $60\frac{3}{4}$ ft wide, find the distance that the home was situated from the lot line on the second side.

Unit 2.3   *Multiplication of Fractions and Mixed Numbers*

In multiplying fractions there is no need for the denominators to be common, as is usual in adding or subtracting fractions.

A procedure in multiplying proper or improper fractions (mixed numbers may be expressed as improper fractions) is as follows:

1 Multiply the numerators to determine the numerator of the product.
2 Multiply the denominators to determine the denominator of the product.

When the numerators and denominators have common factors, canceling before multiplication may be employed to simplify the required operations. The product will be either a proper or improper fraction. Normally it is desirable to reduce the obtained product to lowest terms as a proper fraction, whole number, or mixed number.

Example 1   **Multiply $\frac{7}{9}$ by 24 (or multiply 24 by $\frac{7}{9}$).**

(a) Without canceling before multiplication   **(b) With canceling**

$$\frac{7}{9} \times 24 = \frac{168}{9} = 18\frac{6}{9} = 18\frac{2}{3} \qquad \frac{7}{\overset{}{\underset{3}{9}}} \times \overset{8}{24} = \frac{56}{3} = 18\frac{2}{3}$$

Example 2   **Multiply $\frac{5}{18}$ by $\frac{23}{3}$.**

$$\frac{5}{18} \times \frac{23}{3} = \frac{115}{54} = 2\frac{7}{54}$$ (In this problem there is no opportunity for canceling.)

Find the product of $\frac{28}{15}$ multiplied by $2\frac{5}{8}$.

The mixed number $2\frac{5}{8} = \frac{21}{8}$

Example 3   **(a) Without canceling before multiplication**   **(b) With canceling**

$$\frac{28}{15} \times \frac{21}{8} = \frac{588}{120} = 4\frac{108}{120} = 4\frac{9}{10} \qquad \frac{\overset{7}{28}}{\underset{5}{15}} \times \frac{\overset{7}{21}}{\underset{2}{8}} = \frac{49}{10} = 4\frac{9}{10}$$

Example 4   **Find the product of $\frac{3}{2} \times \frac{4}{9} \times \frac{9}{5} \times 8 \times \frac{25}{24}$, canceling when possible.**

(a) This form may be used:

$$\frac{\cancel{3}}{\cancel{2}} \times \frac{\overset{2}{\cancel{4}}}{\cancel{9}} \times \frac{\cancel{9}}{\cancel{5}} \times \cancel{8} \times \frac{\overset{5}{\cancel{25}}}{\underset{\cancel{3}}{24}} = 10$$

(b) This form may be preferable:

$$\frac{\cancel{3} \times \overset{2}{\cancel{4}} \times \cancel{9} \times \cancel{8} \times \overset{5}{\cancel{25}}}{\cancel{2} \times \cancel{9} \times \cancel{3} \times \cancel{24}} = 10$$

Partial-Product Method of Multiplying Mixed Numbers

Mixed numbers need not be changed to improper fractions before multiplication. When the number values of the mixed numbers or improper fractions
(after expressing as mixed numbers) are large, the partial-product method of
multiplying is usually quicker and easier.

Use the following steps in determining the partial products and the
product:

Step 1: Find the partial product of the fractional parts of both factors.
Step 2: Find the partial product of the fractional part of the multiplier and
the integers of the multiplicand.
Step 3: Find the partial product of the integers of the multiplier and the
fractional part of the multiplicand.
Step 4: Find the partial products of the integers in both factors.
Step 5: Total the partial products to determine the required product.

Note in the following examples that the fractional endings of the
partial products of the fractional parts (steps 1, 2, and 3) are placed directly
under the fractional part of the multiplier and that digits representing units,
tens, hundreds, etc., in the partial products are placed directly under units,
tens, hundreds, etc., of the multiplier.

Example 5   **(a) Multiply 24 by $15\frac{3}{8}$.**   **(b) Find the product of $35\frac{2}{3}$ and 28.**

$$24$$
$$\times 15\frac{3}{8}$$

Step 2 $9 \quad \left(24 \times \frac{3}{8} = 9\right)$

Step 4 $\begin{cases} 120 \\ 24 \end{cases}$

Step 5 369

$$35\frac{2}{3}$$
$$\times 28$$

Step 3 $18\frac{2}{3} \left(\frac{2}{3} \times 28 = \frac{56}{3} = 18\frac{2}{3}\right)$

Step 4 $\begin{cases} 280 \\ 70 \end{cases}$

Step 5 $998\frac{2}{3}$

(c) Multiply $32\frac{3}{5} \times 25\frac{3}{4}$.   **(d) Find the product of $32\frac{3}{4}$ and $25\frac{3}{5}$.**

$$32\frac{3}{5}$$
$$\times 25\frac{3}{4}$$

Step 1 $\frac{9}{20} \left(\frac{3}{5} \times \frac{3}{4} = \frac{9}{20}\right)$

Step 2 $24 \quad \left(32 \times \frac{3}{4} = 24\right)$

Step 3 $15 \quad \left(\frac{3}{5} \times 25 = 15\right)$

Step 4 $\begin{cases} 160 \quad (32 \times 5) \\ 640 \quad (32 \times 20) \end{cases}$

Step 5 $839\frac{9}{20}$

$$32\frac{3}{4}$$
$$\times 25\frac{3}{5}$$

Step 1 $\frac{9}{20} \left(\frac{3}{4} \times \frac{3}{5} = \frac{9}{20}\right)$

Step 2 $19\frac{4}{20} \left(32 \times \frac{3}{5} = \frac{96}{5} = 19\frac{1}{5} = 19\frac{4}{20}\right)$

Step 3 $18\frac{15}{20} \left(\frac{3}{4} \times 25 = \frac{75}{4} = 18\frac{3}{4} = 18\frac{15}{20}\right)$

Step 4 $\begin{cases} 160 \quad (32 \times 5) \\ 640 \quad (32 \times 20) \end{cases}$

Step 5 $837\frac{28}{20} = 838\frac{8}{20} = 838\frac{2}{5}$

Note that in Example 5*d*, the fractional endings in the partial products were changed to a common denominator before they were added to obtain the final product. The l.c.d. can be determined as soon as the first partial product is obtained. Thus:

Fractional endings in partial products (Example 5*d*)

$$+\frac{9}{20} \qquad \frac{9}{20}$$

$$+\frac{1}{5} \qquad \frac{4}{20}$$

$$+\frac{3}{4} \qquad \frac{15}{20}$$

Sum $\qquad \frac{28}{20}$

Exercise 2.3

Multiply, reducing answers to lowest terms as proper fractions or whole or mixed numbers:

1 $\frac{2}{3} \times \frac{3}{6}$ **2** $\frac{1}{6} \times \frac{4}{7}$ **3** $\frac{3}{4} \times \frac{2}{3}$

4 $\frac{4}{5} \times \frac{5}{6}$ **5** $\frac{4}{9} \times \frac{3}{5}$ **6** $\frac{9}{13} \times \frac{11}{12}$

7 $\frac{5}{8} \times \frac{4}{17}$ **8** $\frac{3}{7} \times \frac{6}{9}$ **9** $\frac{13}{19} \times \frac{7}{11}$

10 $\frac{6}{18} \times \frac{16}{19}$ **11** $\frac{9}{11} \times \frac{5}{2}$ **12** $\frac{7}{3} \times \frac{9}{5}$

13 $\frac{15}{7} \times \frac{14}{5}$ **14** $\frac{11}{17} \times \frac{7}{8}$ **15** $\frac{7}{8} \times \frac{3}{4}$

Multiply, reducing answers to lowest terms as proper fractions or whole or mixed numbers:

16 $18 \times \frac{6}{9}$ **17** $\frac{5}{12} \times 8$ **18** $54 \times \frac{9}{4}$ **19** $\frac{13}{6} \times 88$

20 $4 \times 6\frac{1}{2}$ **21** $46 \times 7\frac{2}{3}$ **22** $9\frac{7}{8} \times 6$ **23** $6\frac{7}{13} \times 25$

24 $\frac{3}{5} \times 8\frac{1}{3}$ **25** $\frac{4}{10} \times 12\frac{1}{3}$ **26** $16\frac{2}{3} \times \frac{5}{8}$ **27** $23\frac{4}{5} \times \frac{2}{3}$

28 $\frac{9}{6} \times 8\frac{1}{2}$ **29** $24\frac{1}{9} \times \frac{7}{4}$ **30** $28\frac{9}{14} \times 84\frac{2}{7}$ **31** $16\frac{1}{3} \times 400\frac{1}{4}$

Multiply by the partial-product method and reduce products to lowest terms. Do not change factors to improper fractions or to mixed decimals in completing this exercise:

32	$14\frac{1}{4}$	33	32	34	$73\frac{5}{9}$	35	$84\frac{3}{5}$
	$\underline{62}$		$\underline{52\frac{1}{2}}$		$\underline{33}$		$\underline{24}$

36	46	37	35	38	51	39	63
	$\underline{19\frac{7}{8}}$		$\underline{84\frac{4}{7}}$		$\underline{47\frac{5}{6}}$		$\underline{31\frac{4}{11}}$

40	$32\frac{5}{9}$	41	$63\frac{2}{11}$	42	$22\frac{3}{15}$	43	$51\frac{1}{6}$
	$\underline{18\frac{3}{4}}$		$\underline{44\frac{5}{7}}$		$\underline{40\frac{9}{14}}$		$\underline{96\frac{11}{17}}$

44	$126\frac{2}{3}$	45	$204\frac{5}{7}$	46	$32\frac{5}{6}$	47	$18\frac{5}{6}$
	$\underline{93\frac{11}{12}}$		$\underline{143\frac{4}{9}}$		$\underline{24\frac{7}{8}}$		$\underline{42}$

Solve the following:

48 If ice weighs $\frac{9}{10}$ as much as water and water weighs $62\frac{1}{2}$ lb per cu ft, find the weight in pounds of a block of ice 60 cu ft in size.

49 If an automobile owner used $318\frac{3}{4}$ gal of gasoline during the year and averaged $16\frac{2}{3}$ miles per gal, find the total mileage.

50 A piece of brass weighing $8\frac{1}{2}$ lb contained $\frac{2}{3}$ copper and the remainder zinc. Find the weight in pounds of (a) the copper and (b) the zinc.

51 Find the cubic feet in a box $4\frac{2}{3} \times 7\frac{1}{12} \times 4\frac{7}{8}$ ft.

52 If a common mile is approximately $\frac{7}{8}$ of a nautical mile, how many nautical miles (to eighths) are there in a course measuring 73 common miles?

53 A tank holding 375 lb of seawater contains $\frac{7}{200}$ of dissolved solids. Find the weight in pounds (to eighths) of the dissolved solids.

54 Find the total dollar amount of 300 shares of stock purchased at $38\frac{1}{2}$ per share plus 28 shares of stock purchased at $38\frac{5}{8}$ per share.

55 An automobile averages $18\frac{8}{10}$ miles per gal of gasoline. How far could the automobile travel on a tank of gasoline that holds $26\frac{3}{4}$ gal?

56 The premium rate for a 3-year casualty policy is $2\frac{7}{10}$ times the annual rate. Find the 3-year rate (to fractional cents) per $100 on policies for which the basic annual rate is (a) 14 cents per $100 and (b) 37 cents per $100.

57 Not considering the resistance of air, a falling body increases its speed of fall at the end of each second by 32 ft. Velocity at the end of a given number of seconds of fall may be found by multiplying 32 by the given number of seconds. Find the velocity in feet per second after $6\frac{3}{8}$ sec of fall if it is assumed that there is no resistance of air.

58 Celsius temperature can be found by subtracting 32 from the Fahrenheit temperature and multiplying by $\frac{5}{9}$. Find the degrees of Celsius temperature if the Fahrenheit temperature is 131 deg.

59 Kevin purchased $8\frac{5}{10}$ gal of gasoline at $59\frac{3}{5}$ cents per gal. Find the total cost of the purchase.

60 The Pooler family had salary after deductions of $34,800. The income was spent as follows: Food $\frac{1}{8}$; mortgage payment, property taxes, and home maintenance $\frac{3}{16}$; clothing $\frac{1}{10}$; vacation and recreation $\frac{1}{4}$; miscellaneous $\frac{1}{6}$; and the balance was placed in the savings account. Find the amount placed in savings.

Unit 2.4   *Division of Fractions*

Division by (or of) fractions may be accomplished in several ways. Three of the methods of solution generally used are the following:

1 Multiplication of the dividend by the reciprocal of the divisor (frequently called "inverting the divisor").

2 Expressing both dividend and divisor as fractions with a common denominator before dividing.

3 Changing both dividend and divisor to whole numbers before dividing.

RECIPROCALS The quotient obtained by dividing 1 by a number is the *reciprocal* of that number. When the product of two numbers is 1, the numbers are reciprocal to each other. Consider the following:

$$\frac{5}{8} \times \frac{8}{5} = 1 \qquad \frac{2}{3} \times \frac{3}{2} = 1 \qquad \frac{6}{1} \times \frac{1}{6} = 1 \qquad \left(\text{or } 6 \times \frac{1}{6} = 1\right)$$

You will recall that in division with whole numbers and decimals the product of the divisor and the complete quotient equals the dividend. This is also true of fractions. Therefore:

$$1 \div \frac{5}{8} = \frac{8}{5} \qquad 1 \div \frac{2}{3} = \frac{3}{2} \qquad 1 \div \frac{6}{1} = \frac{1}{6}$$

$$1 \div \frac{8}{5} = \frac{5}{8} \qquad 1 \div \frac{3}{2} = \frac{2}{3} \qquad 1 \div \frac{1}{6} = \frac{6}{1} \text{ or } 6$$

Note that the reciprocal of a fraction (that is, 1 divided by the fraction) is the fraction "inverted." Thus the reciprocal of $\frac{3}{4}$ is $\frac{4}{3}$, of $\frac{9}{2}$ is $\frac{2}{9}$, of 5 (meaning $\frac{5}{1}$) is $\frac{1}{5}$, of $\frac{17}{3}$ is $\frac{3}{17}$, etc.

DIVISION BY MULTIPLICATION OF DIVIDEND BY RECIPROCAL OF DIVISOR You may reason that if $1 \div \frac{3}{4} = \frac{4}{3}$, then $12 \div \frac{3}{4}$ should produce a quotient 12 times as large. Thus:

$$12 \div \frac{3}{4} = 12 \times \frac{4}{3} = 16$$

Similarly, if $1 \div \frac{5}{2} = \frac{2}{5}$, then $15 \div \frac{5}{2}$ should produce a quotient 15 times as large:

$$15 \div \frac{5}{2} = 15 \times \frac{2}{5} = 6$$

If the preceding explanation seems unclear to you, consider the following:

$$\frac{1}{4} \div \frac{1}{2} \text{ may be written as } \frac{\frac{1}{4}}{\frac{1}{2}}$$

If the denominator $\frac{1}{2}$ can be changed to 1, this new denominator can be eliminated. Since $\frac{1}{2} \times 2 = 1$, then:

$$\frac{\frac{1}{4}}{\frac{1}{2}} = \frac{\frac{1}{4} \times 2}{\frac{1}{2} \times 2} = \frac{\frac{1}{4} \times 2}{1} = \frac{1}{4} \times 2 = \frac{2}{4} \text{ or } \frac{1}{2}$$

Thus, a general rule for division of fractions may be stated: *To divide by a fraction, multiply by its reciprocal.*

Since the reciprocal of a fraction (or whole number) may be formed by interchanging the terms (inverting the terms), a similar rule for division of fractions may be stated: *To divide by a fraction, invert the terms of the fraction and proceed as in the multiplication of fractions.*

Note that in the following Examples 1a and 1b, whole numbers are expressed as fractions with a denominator of 1.

Example 1   **Proper or improper fractions: Divide (a) $\frac{5}{7}$ by 2, (b) 6 by $\frac{4}{5}$, (c) $\frac{3}{4}$ by $\frac{2}{3}$, and (d) $\frac{49}{6}$ by $\frac{35}{27}$.**

(a) $\dfrac{5}{7} \div 2 = \dfrac{5}{7} \div \dfrac{2}{1} = \dfrac{5}{7} \times \dfrac{1}{2} = \dfrac{5}{14}$

(b) $6 \div \dfrac{4}{5} = \dfrac{6}{1} \div \dfrac{4}{5} = \dfrac{\overset{3}{\cancel{6}}}{1} \times \dfrac{5}{\underset{2}{\cancel{4}}} = \dfrac{15}{2} = 7\dfrac{1}{2}$

(c) $\dfrac{3}{4} \div \dfrac{2}{3} = \dfrac{3}{4} \times \dfrac{3}{2} = \dfrac{9}{8} = 1\dfrac{1}{8}$

(d) $\dfrac{49}{6} \div \dfrac{35}{27} = \dfrac{\overset{7}{\cancel{49}}}{\underset{2}{\cancel{6}}} \times \dfrac{\overset{9}{\cancel{27}}}{\underset{5}{\cancel{35}}} = \dfrac{63}{10} = 6\dfrac{3}{10}$

If a dividend or divisor (or both) are mixed numbers, express them as improper fractions before division.

Example 2   **Mixed numbers: Divide (a) $6\frac{1}{4}$ by $3\frac{2}{7}$ and (b) $8\frac{1}{6}$ by $1\frac{5}{9}$.**

(a) $6\dfrac{1}{4} \div 3\dfrac{2}{7} = \dfrac{25}{4} \div \dfrac{23}{7} = \dfrac{25}{4} \times \dfrac{7}{23} = \dfrac{175}{92} = 1\dfrac{83}{92}$

(b) $8\dfrac{1}{6} \div 1\dfrac{5}{9} = \dfrac{49}{6} \div \dfrac{14}{9} = \dfrac{\overset{7}{\cancel{49}}}{\underset{2}{\cancel{6}}} \times \dfrac{\overset{3}{\cancel{9}}}{\underset{2}{\cancel{14}}} = \dfrac{21}{4} = 5\dfrac{1}{4}$

EXPRESSING BOTH DIVIDEND AND DIVISOR AS FRACTIONS WITH A COMMON DENOMINATOR BEFORE DIVIDING   The general rule, *fractions having a common denominator are to each other as are their numerators,* may be applied to division as well as to other operations in fractions. Thus fractions may be divided by changing them to fractions with a common denominator, discarding the common denominator, and then performing the division indicated by the numerators. Preferably, the common denominator used will be the l.c.d.

Example 3   **Divide 23 by $\frac{2}{3}$ (a) by multiplying by the reciprocal of the divisor and (b) by changing both dividend and divisor to fractions with a common denominator discarding the common denominator, and then dividing by the numerators.**

(a) $23 \div \dfrac{2}{3} = 23 \times \dfrac{3}{2} = \dfrac{69}{2} = 34\dfrac{1}{2}$

(b) $23 \div \dfrac{2}{3} = \dfrac{69}{\cancel{3}} \div \dfrac{2}{\cancel{3}} = 34\dfrac{1}{2}$ or $\dfrac{23}{\dfrac{2}{3}} = \dfrac{\dfrac{69}{\cancel{3}}}{\dfrac{2}{\cancel{3}}} = 34\dfrac{1}{2}$

Example 4   **Divide $32\frac{1}{2}$ by $5\frac{2}{3}$ (a) by multiplying by the reciprocal of the divisor and (b) by changing both dividend and divisor to fractions with a common denominator, discarding the common denominator, and then dividing by the numerators.**

(a) $32\dfrac{1}{2} \div 5\dfrac{2}{3} = \dfrac{65}{2} \div \dfrac{17}{3} = \dfrac{65}{2} \times \dfrac{3}{17} = \dfrac{195}{34} = 5\dfrac{25}{34}$

(b) The l.c.d. is 6.

$32\dfrac{1}{2} \div 5\dfrac{2}{3} = \dfrac{65}{2} \div \dfrac{17}{3} = \dfrac{195}{\cancel{6}} \div \dfrac{34}{\cancel{6}} = 5\dfrac{25}{34}$

or $\dfrac{32\dfrac{1}{2}}{5\dfrac{2}{3}} = \dfrac{\dfrac{65}{2}}{\dfrac{17}{3}} = \dfrac{\dfrac{195}{\cancel{6}}}{\dfrac{34}{\cancel{6}}} = 5\dfrac{25}{34}$

CHANGING BOTH DIVIDEND AND DIVISOR TO WHOLE NUMBERS BE-FORE DIVIDING   It is a fact that the product of a fraction and any multiple of that fraction's denominator will be a whole number. As examples:

$$\frac{3}{4} \times 4 = 3 \quad \frac{3}{4} \times 8 = 6 \quad \frac{3}{4} \times 12 = 9 \quad \frac{3}{4} \times 16 = 12 \text{ etc.}$$

$$\frac{7}{5} \times 5 = 7 \quad \frac{7}{5} \times 10 = 14 \quad \frac{7}{5} \times 15 = 21 \quad \frac{7}{5} \times 20 = 28 \text{ etc.}$$

A rule of division (see Unit 1.5) applying to fractions as well as to whole numbers is: *The quotient will remain the same if both dividend and divisor are multiplied by the same number.*

Thus both dividend and divisor will always be expressed as whole numbers when they are multiplied by a common multiple of their denominators, and the quotient of the dividend and divisor will remain the same. Preferably, the common multiple used will be the l.c.m.

Example 5   **Divide 12 by $\frac{4}{5}$ (a) by multiplying by the reciprocal of the divisor and (b) by multiplying both dividend and divisor by a common multiple of their denominators and then performing the indicated division.**

(a) $12 \div \frac{4}{5} = \overset{3}{\cancel{12}} \times \frac{5}{\cancel{4}} = 15$

(b)   The l.c.m. is 5.

$$12 \div \frac{4}{5} = (12 \times 5) \div \frac{4}{\cancel{5}} \times \cancel{5} = 60 \div 4 = 15$$

or $\dfrac{12}{\frac{4}{5}} = \dfrac{12 \times 5}{\frac{4}{\cancel{5}} \times \cancel{5}} = \dfrac{60}{4} = 15$

Example 6   **Divide $16\frac{3}{5}$ by $7\frac{1}{3}$ by (a) changing both dividend and divisor to fractions with a common denominator, discarding the common denominator, and then dividing by the numerators and (b) by multiplying both numerator and denominator (dividend and divisor) by a common multiple of their denominators and then performing the indicated division.**

The l.c.d. or l.c.m. is 15.

(a) $\dfrac{16\frac{3}{5}}{7\frac{1}{3}} = \dfrac{\frac{83}{5}}{\frac{22}{3}} = \dfrac{\frac{249}{\cancel{15}}}{\frac{110}{\cancel{15}}} = 2\frac{29}{110}$

(b) $\dfrac{16\frac{3}{5}}{7\frac{1}{3}} = \dfrac{\frac{83}{5}}{\frac{22}{3}} = \dfrac{\frac{83}{\cancel{5}} \times \overset{3}{\cancel{15}}}{\frac{22}{\cancel{3}} \times \cancel{15}} = \dfrac{249}{110} = 2\frac{29}{110}$

From Example 6 it will be apparent that the methods of dividing fractions by first expressing both dividend and divisor as fractions with a common denominator *or* by first expressing both dividend and divisor as whole numbers are much the same and require almost identical computations.

No single method of performing division in fractions will always be most desirable. It is recommended that you become thoroughly familiar with the use of the reciprocal (inverted divisor), the common denominator, and the common multiple in the division of fractions. Sometimes one method will be distinctly preferable, and only experience will enable you to select the best solution.

Common fractions may also be divided after they have been expressed as decimal fractions.

Exercise 2.4

Divide by the use of the reciprocal. Express quotients in lowest terms as proper fractions or whole or mixed numbers.

1 $36 \div \frac{3}{6}$	**2** $30 \div \frac{3}{4}$	**3** $24 \div \frac{8}{3}$	**4** $42 \div \frac{7}{5}$
5 $\frac{4}{7} \div 22$	**6** $\frac{3}{8} \div 14$	**7** $\frac{11}{3} \div 36$	**8** $\frac{16}{5} \div 24$
9 $\frac{4}{5} \div \frac{8}{9}$	**10** $\frac{3}{8} \div \frac{3}{5}$	**11** $\frac{9}{11} \div \frac{13}{5}$	**12** $\frac{7}{9} \div \frac{8}{3}$
13 $\frac{17}{9} \div \frac{5}{8}$	**14** $\frac{14}{13} \div \frac{8}{11}$	**15** $\frac{19}{5} \div \frac{12}{4}$	**16** $\frac{13}{5} \div \frac{9}{7}$
17 $\frac{7}{9} \div 4\frac{1}{4}$	**18** $\frac{3}{8} \div 4\frac{2}{5}$	**19** $8\frac{1}{4} \div \frac{11}{3}$	**20** $7\frac{2}{7} \div \frac{15}{4}$
21 $3\frac{1}{2} \div 5\frac{2}{3}$	**22** $4\frac{2}{3} \div 1\frac{1}{4}$	**23** $18\frac{5}{7} \div 5\frac{1}{4}$	**24** $7\frac{8}{9} \div 2\frac{1}{3}$

Divide after changing both dividend and divisor to fractions with a common denominator. Express quotients in lowest terms as proper fractions or whole or mixed numbers.

25 $\dfrac{24}{\frac{1}{6}}$	**26** $\dfrac{15}{\frac{3}{4}}$	**27** $\dfrac{\frac{5}{9}}{16}$	**28** $\dfrac{12}{\frac{7}{16}}$
29 $\dfrac{\frac{4}{15}}{\frac{8}{45}}$	**30** $\dfrac{\frac{3}{8}}{\frac{5}{12}}$	**31** $\dfrac{\frac{9}{2}}{\frac{7}{8}}$	**32** $\dfrac{\frac{7}{3}}{\frac{11}{12}}$
33 $\dfrac{2\frac{5}{6}}{\frac{3}{5}}$	**34** $\dfrac{\frac{3}{4}}{5\frac{1}{3}}$	**35** $\dfrac{17\frac{4}{5}}{20\frac{1}{2}}$	**36** $\dfrac{2\frac{1}{4}}{2\frac{1}{7}}$

Divide after changing both dividend and divisor to whole numbers. Express quotients in lowest terms as proper fractions or whole or mixed numbers.

37 $\dfrac{\dfrac{12}{1}}{\dfrac{1}{6}}$ 38 $\dfrac{\dfrac{25}{5}}{\dfrac{5}{3}}$ 39 $\dfrac{\dfrac{2}{3}}{18}$ 40 $\dfrac{\dfrac{2}{7}}{16}$

41 $\dfrac{\dfrac{7}{11}}{\dfrac{17}{3}}$ 42 $\dfrac{\dfrac{5}{8}}{\dfrac{9}{2}}$ 43 $\dfrac{\dfrac{22}{5}}{\dfrac{5}{6}}$ 44 $\dfrac{\dfrac{17}{4}}{\dfrac{3}{7}}$

45 $\dfrac{\dfrac{19}{4}}{3\dfrac{1}{3}}$ 46 $\dfrac{7\dfrac{5}{8}}{\dfrac{16}{7}}$ 47 $\dfrac{8\dfrac{5}{9}}{15\dfrac{1}{4}}$ 48 $\dfrac{5\dfrac{1}{4}}{3\dfrac{1}{3}}$

Solve the following:

49 If a flywheel makes four revolutions each $\frac{7}{8}$ sec, how many revolutions will it make in 160 sec?

50 A certain liquid expands on freezing by $\frac{1}{3}$ of its volume. If after freezing there is 516 gal of the liquid, how many gallons of liquid were there before freezing?

51 If each piece of a required tubing is to be $3\frac{3}{8}$ in long, (a) how many pieces can be cut from a 48-in length of tubing and (b) what is the length of the remaining piece of tubing?

52 If a flywheel makes 35,003 revolutions in $35\frac{1}{2}$ min, find the number of revolutions the flywheel makes per minute.

53 If real property is assessed at $\frac{11}{30}$ of its probable sales value, what is the probable sales value of property assessed at $15,400?

54 A ship traveled $66\frac{7}{12}$ nautical miles in $4\frac{1}{2}$ hr. Find its exact average speed in knots (1 knot = 1 nautical mile per hour).

55 On a map, each inch represents $96\frac{1}{2}$ land miles. How many inches on the map would be required to represent $844\frac{3}{8}$ land miles?

56 If 1 cu ft of water weighs $62\frac{1}{4}$ lb, how many cubic feet (exactly) is occupied by a column of water weighing $7770\frac{5}{6}$ lb?

57 A board 244 in in length is divided into nine equal lengths. If each of the required saw cuts wastes $\frac{1}{8}$ in, find the length in inches of each equal length.

58 How many stairway steps that are $38\frac{1}{4}$ in in length including cutting waste can be cut from a 16-ft board?

59 If a merchant's cost is $\frac{1}{5}$ less than the selling price, find the selling price of an article that cost $360.

60 If a piece of jewelry is priced at $117 including an excise tax of $\frac{1}{12}$ of the basic sales price, find the cost to the purchaser if the excise tax is removed but $\frac{1}{25}$ sales tax is added to the reduced price.

Unit 2.5   *Simplifying Complex and Compound-Complex Fractions*

A *complex fraction* is a fraction which has a fraction or mixed number as numerator or denominator or both. Thus the following are complex fractions:

$$\frac{\frac{7}{5}}{\frac{5}{6}} \qquad \frac{\frac{2}{3}}{4} \qquad \frac{\frac{3}{5}}{\frac{7}{4}} \qquad \frac{\frac{8}{3}}{2\frac{1}{2}}$$

As you know, the bar or line between the numerator and denominator of a fraction is merely another means of indicating division. Thus the divisions indicated in the preceding complex fractions are really no more complex than equivalent problems in the division of fractions. Thus:

$$\frac{7}{\frac{5}{6}} = 7 \div \frac{5}{6} \qquad \frac{\frac{2}{3}}{4} = \frac{2}{3} \div 4 \qquad \frac{\frac{3}{5}}{\frac{7}{4}} = \frac{3}{5} \div \frac{7}{4} \qquad \frac{\frac{8}{3}}{2\frac{1}{2}} = \frac{8}{3} \div 2\frac{1}{2}$$

SIMPLIFYING COMPLEX FRACTIONS The fractions in the numerator or denominator of a complex fraction may be changed to whole numbers and the complex fraction thus simplified into its equivalent in the form of a proper or improper fraction. This simplification is accomplished by performing the division operation indicated, namely, dividing the numerator by the denominator.

As with any division involving fractions, there is a choice of methods:

1   Use of the reciprocal of the denominator (divisor)
2   Use of a common denominator (preferably the l.c.d.)
3   Use of a common multiple of the denominators (preferably the l.c.m.)

Example 1   **Simplifying by the use of the reciprocal.**

(a) $\dfrac{7}{\frac{5}{6}} = 7 \div \frac{5}{6} = 7 \times \frac{6}{5} = \frac{42}{5} = 8\frac{2}{5}$

(b) $\dfrac{\frac{2}{3}}{4} = \frac{2}{3} \div 4 = \frac{2}{3} \times \frac{1}{4} = \frac{2}{12} = \frac{1}{6}$

(c) $\dfrac{\frac{3}{5}}{\frac{7}{4}} = \frac{3}{5} \div \frac{7}{4} = \frac{3}{5} \times \frac{4}{7} = \frac{12}{35}$

(d) $\dfrac{\dfrac{8}{3}}{2\dfrac{1}{2}} = \dfrac{8}{3} \div 2\dfrac{1}{2} = \dfrac{8}{3} \div \dfrac{5}{2} = \dfrac{8}{3} \times \dfrac{2}{5} = \dfrac{16}{15} = 1\dfrac{1}{15}$

Example 2   **Simplifying by the use of a common denominator.**

(a) $\dfrac{\dfrac{7}{5}}{\dfrac{5}{6}} = \dfrac{\dfrac{42}{\cancel{6}}}{\dfrac{5}{\cancel{6}}} = \dfrac{42}{5} = 8\dfrac{2}{5}$

(b) $\dfrac{\dfrac{2}{3}}{4} = \dfrac{\dfrac{2}{\cancel{3}}}{\dfrac{12}{\cancel{3}}} = \dfrac{1}{6}$

(c) $\dfrac{\dfrac{3}{5}}{\dfrac{7}{4}} = \dfrac{\dfrac{12}{\cancel{20}}}{\dfrac{35}{\cancel{20}}} = \dfrac{12}{35}$

(d) $\dfrac{\dfrac{8}{3}}{2\dfrac{1}{2}} = \dfrac{\dfrac{8}{3}}{\dfrac{5}{2}} = \dfrac{\dfrac{16}{\cancel{6}}}{\dfrac{15}{\cancel{6}}} = \dfrac{16}{15} = 1\dfrac{1}{15}$

Example 3   **Simplifying by the use of a common multiple.**

(a) $\dfrac{\dfrac{7}{5}}{\dfrac{5}{6}} = \dfrac{7 \times 6}{\dfrac{5}{\cancel{6}} \times \cancel{6}} = \dfrac{42}{5} = 8\dfrac{2}{5}$

(b) $\dfrac{\dfrac{2}{3}}{4} = \dfrac{\dfrac{2}{\cancel{3}} \times \cancel{3}}{4 \times 3} = \dfrac{2}{12} = \dfrac{1}{6}$

(c) $\dfrac{\dfrac{3}{5}}{\dfrac{7}{4}} = \dfrac{\dfrac{3}{\cancel{5}} \times \cancel{20}^{\,4}}{\dfrac{7}{\cancel{4}} \times \cancel{20}_{\,5}} = \dfrac{12}{35}$

(d) $\dfrac{\dfrac{8}{3}}{2\dfrac{1}{2}} = \dfrac{\dfrac{8}{3}}{\dfrac{5}{2}} = \dfrac{\dfrac{8}{\cancel{3}} \times \cancel{6}^{\,2}}{\dfrac{5}{\cancel{2}} \times \cancel{6}_{\,3}} = \dfrac{16}{15} = 1\dfrac{1}{15}$

SIMPLIFYING COMPOUND-COMPLEX FRACTIONS   Frequently complex fractions are expressed in a more complicated form, as illustrated by the following:

(a) $\dfrac{147}{1 - \left(\dfrac{4}{9} \times \dfrac{9}{200}\right)}$

(b) $\dfrac{\dfrac{2}{3} + \dfrac{3}{4}}{\dfrac{1}{6} \times 1\dfrac{2}{3}}$

(c) $\dfrac{6\dfrac{2}{5}}{\dfrac{1}{6} \times \dfrac{2}{25}}$

(d) $\dfrac{24\dfrac{9}{25}}{1 + \left(\dfrac{1}{4} \times \dfrac{3}{50}\right)}$

The preceding types of complex fractions are also known as *compound* or *compound-complex* fractions. When expressed in this manner, a usual procedure in simplifying is to clear the numerator and denominator (perform the operations indicated in the numerator and denominator) and then solve by any of the methods used to divide fractions.

In Example 4 that follows, once the compound-complex fractions have been changed to complex fractions, the final steps in simplifying may be as illustrated in Examples 1, 2, or 3. However, many rules and definitions lend themselves to expression in equation forms known as *formulas*. Frequently, formulas are so written that required divisions are in fractional form and substitution of quantities in the formulas results in complex or compound-complex fractions. When such fractions occur, it is generally not desirable either to rewrite the problems and simplify by the use of the reciprocal or to simplify by the use of a common denominator. Thus, as illustrated in Examples 3 and 4, it is usual practice to solve by using a common multiple to change both numerator and denominator to whole numbers before division.

Example 4 **Simplifying compound-complex fractions.**

(a) $\dfrac{147}{1 - \left(\dfrac{\cancel{4}}{\cancel{9}} \times \dfrac{\cancel{9}}{\cancel{200}}\right)} = \dfrac{147}{1 - \dfrac{1}{50}} = \dfrac{147}{\dfrac{49}{50}} = \dfrac{147 \times 50}{\dfrac{49}{\cancel{50}} \times \cancel{50}} = \dfrac{7{,}350}{49} = 150$

(b) $\dfrac{\dfrac{2}{3} + \dfrac{3}{4}}{\dfrac{1}{6} \times 1\dfrac{2}{3}} = \dfrac{\dfrac{17}{12}}{\dfrac{5}{18}} = \dfrac{\dfrac{17}{\cancel{12}} \times \cancel{36}^{\,3}}{\dfrac{5}{\cancel{18}} \times \cancel{36}} = \dfrac{51}{10} = 5\dfrac{1}{10}$

(c) $\dfrac{6\dfrac{2}{5}}{\dfrac{1}{\cancel{6}}_{3} \times \dfrac{\cancel{2}}{25}} = \dfrac{\dfrac{32}{5}}{\dfrac{1}{75}} = \dfrac{\dfrac{32}{\cancel{5}} \times \cancel{75}^{\,15}}{\dfrac{1}{\cancel{75}} \times \cancel{75}} = \dfrac{480}{1} = 480$

(d) $\dfrac{24\dfrac{9}{25}}{1 + \left(\dfrac{1}{4} \times \dfrac{3}{50}\right)} = \dfrac{\dfrac{609}{25}}{1 + \dfrac{3}{200}} = \dfrac{\dfrac{609}{25}}{\dfrac{203}{200}} = \dfrac{\dfrac{609}{\cancel{25}} \times \cancel{200}^{\,8}}{\dfrac{203}{\cancel{200}} \times \cancel{200}} = \dfrac{4872}{203} = 24$

Exercise 2.5

Simplify the following complex fractions by any method desired:

1 $\dfrac{50}{2\dfrac{3}{5}}$ 2 $\dfrac{12\dfrac{5}{9}}{300}$ 3 $\dfrac{3\dfrac{2}{9}}{100}$

4 $\dfrac{120}{\dfrac{4}{5}}$ 5 $\dfrac{9\dfrac{1}{3}}{8\dfrac{5}{6}}$ 6 $\dfrac{\dfrac{44}{7}}{\dfrac{3}{8}}$

Simplify the following compound-complex fractions by changing numerators and denominators to whole numbers or mixed decimals before performing the required division:

7 $\dfrac{146\frac{1}{4}}{\dfrac{15}{60} \times \dfrac{5}{20}}$ **8** $\dfrac{68\frac{2}{5}}{\dfrac{19}{40} \times \dfrac{9}{200}}$

9 $\dfrac{5225\frac{3}{5}}{1 - \left(\dfrac{4}{15} \times \dfrac{7}{100}\right)}$ **10** $\dfrac{7113\frac{3}{5}}{1 - \left(\dfrac{1}{5} \times \dfrac{3}{50}\right)}$

11 $\dfrac{1520\frac{5}{8}}{1 + \left(\dfrac{11}{60} \times \dfrac{3}{40}\right)}$ **12** $\dfrac{87\frac{2}{3}}{\dfrac{18}{60} \times \dfrac{2\frac{1}{6}}{24}}$

Solve the following. If you can, first establish each computation in a complex-fraction form rather than as a series of separate computations:

13 Fahrenheit temperature can be determined if Celsius temperature is known, by dividing the degrees Celsius by $\frac{5}{9}$ and then adding 32 to the obtained quotient. Find the Fahrenheit temperature (to nearest 0.1 F) if the degrees Celsius is 62.

14 A container and its contents of water weighs $2279\frac{11}{16}$ lb. Find the number of gallons of water if the container weighs $621\frac{7}{8}$ lb, and if 1 cu ft of water weighs $62\frac{1}{2}$ lb and contains $7\frac{1}{2}$ gal.

15 A strip of metal $198\frac{1}{8}$ in long is to be cut into six equal pieces. Allowing $\frac{1}{8}$ in waste for each required cut, exactly how long will each piece be?

16 If the assessed valuation of a piece of property is $\frac{5}{24}$ of its actual value and if assessed valuation can be determined by dividing the tax by the tax rate, find the actual sales value of a piece of property on which the tax is $220.50 and the tax rate is 10.5 cents.

17 During the month of November, a retail salesman earned $675.30 based on a salary of $450 per month and $\frac{4}{80}$ commission on all sales. Find his sales for the month of November.

18 The maturity value of a discounted note may be found by dividing the discount by the following: the fractional part that the number of days of discount is of 360 multiplied by the rate of discount. If the discount is $3\frac{3}{4}$, the number of days of discount 90, and the rate of discount $\frac{2}{50}$, find the maturity value of the discounted note.

Unit 2.6   Decimal Fractions: Pure, Mixed, Complex; Repeating Decimals

---

Reading and writing of decimals have already been discussed (see Unit 1.1). Placement of the decimal point in addition, subtraction, multiplication, and division was treated in connection with the fundamental processes. Restated briefly:

In adding decimals place the decimal points in the addends and sum in the same vertical column.

In subtracting decimals place the decimal points in minuend, subtrahend, and remainder in the same vertical column.

In multiplying decimals place the decimal point in the product (after multiplication) so that the product will contain the same number of decimal places as the factors combined.

In dividing decimals clear the divisor of decimals (by multiplying divisor and dividend by 10, 100, 1000, or some other power of 10), thus placing the decimal point in the quotient directly above the relocated decimal point in the dividend *before* beginning the process of division.

A decimal fraction is a fraction with a denominator of 10 or some power of 10 which is not expressed by numbers but is shown by the placing of a decimal point.

The digits to the right of the decimal point are really fractions with a numerator of the number indicated by those digits and a denominator of 1 with as many zeros annexed as there are decimal places in the given decimal. Thus:

$$12.4 = 12\frac{4}{10} \qquad 6.25 = 6\frac{25}{100} \qquad 0.007 = \frac{7}{1000}$$

Classification of Decimal Fractions

Just as fractions are classified as proper fractions, improper fractions or mixed numbers, and complex fractions, so may decimal fractions be classified as pure decimals, mixed decimals, and complex decimals.

Pure decimals	Mixed decimals	Complex decimals
0.5	3.1	$0.0\frac{2}{3}$
0.12	25.07	$0.675\frac{1}{7}$
0.375	1.402	$4.3\frac{1}{6}$
0.06	860.3125	$18.91\frac{5}{9}$

Note that there is no separate classification of decimals similar to improper fractions. The decimal equivalent of an improper fraction will be a mixed decimal or a complex decimal.

EXPRESSING DECIMALS AS COMMON FRACTIONS Since a decimal is a fraction with a denominator of 10 or some power of 10, to change from a decimal-fraction form to a common-fraction form, proceed as follows:

1 Write the figures in the given decimal as a numerator.
2 Write 1 in the denominator and annex as many zeros as there are decimal places in the given decimal (decimal fraction).

The obtained fraction will then be expressed in tenths, hundredths, thousandths, etc. If it is complex, simplify it (see Unit 2.5). If it can be reduced to lower terms, reduce it.

Decimals

(a) $0.4 = \dfrac{4}{10} = \dfrac{2}{5}$

(b) $0.056 = \dfrac{56}{1,000} = \dfrac{7}{125}$

Mixed decimals

(a) $9.25 = 9\dfrac{25}{100} = 9\dfrac{1}{4}$

or $9.25 = \dfrac{925}{100} = 9\dfrac{1}{4}$

(b) $14.625 = 14 + \dfrac{625}{1,000} = 14\dfrac{5}{8}$

or $14.625 = \dfrac{14,625}{1,000} = 14\dfrac{5}{8}$

Complex decimals[1]

(a) $0.3\dfrac{1}{3} = \dfrac{3\frac{1}{3}}{10} = \dfrac{10}{30} = \dfrac{1}{3}$

(b) $8.28\dfrac{4}{7} = 8 + \dfrac{28\frac{4}{7}}{100} = 8\dfrac{200}{700} = 8\dfrac{2}{7}$

or $8.28\dfrac{4}{7} = \dfrac{828\frac{4}{7}}{100} = \dfrac{5800}{700} = 8\dfrac{2}{7}$

Note that a mixed decimal or a complex decimal containing a whole integer may be changed to a mixed number in two ways:

1 By directly changing only the decimal-fraction ending of the mixed decimal (or complex decimal) to its common-fraction equivalent and then adding this equivalent to the whole integers.
2 By first changing the entire mixed decimal (or complex decimal) to an improper fraction and then reducing.

It is obvious that the first method is the more desirable.

EXPRESSING COMMON FRACTIONS AS DECIMALS   To change from a common-fraction form to a decimal-fraction form, proceed as follows:

1 Write the numerator of the common fraction as a dividend, annexing as many zeros as decimal places are desired in the decimal fraction.
2 Divide this obtained dividend by the denominator of the common fraction.

---

[1]After a complex decimal is changed to a fraction, it will be first in a complex-fraction form. This complex fraction may be simplified by any of the methods illustrated in Unit 2.5, but the changing of both numerator and denominator to whole numbers by multiplying by a common multiple is usually the easiest and most desirable method.

If it is desired to express the decimal fractions in tenths, annex one zero to the dividend; to express in hundredths, annex two zeros; to express in thousandths, annex three zeros; etc.

Tenths

(a) $\dfrac{2}{5} = 5\overline{)2.0}^{\,0.4}$

(b) $\dfrac{8}{3} = 3\overline{)8.0}^{\,2.6\frac{2}{3}}$

(c) $5\dfrac{3}{7} = 5 + 7\overline{)3.0}^{\,0.4\frac{2}{7}} = 5.4\dfrac{2}{7}$ or $5\dfrac{3}{7} = \dfrac{38}{7} = 7\overline{)38.0}^{\,5.4\frac{2}{7}}$

Hundredths

(a) $\dfrac{3}{4} = 4\overline{)3.00}^{\,0.75}$

(b) $\dfrac{11}{6} = 6\overline{)11.00}^{\,1.83\frac{1}{3}}$

(c) $3\dfrac{5}{8} = 3 + 8\overline{)5.00}^{\,0.62\frac{1}{2}} = 3.62\dfrac{1}{2}$ or $3\dfrac{5}{8} = \dfrac{29}{8} = 8\overline{)29.00}^{\,3.62\frac{1}{2}}$

Thousandths

(a) $\dfrac{7}{20} = 20\overline{)7.000}^{\,0.350}$

(b) $\dfrac{32}{9} = 9\overline{)32.000}^{\,3.555\frac{5}{9}}$

(c) $12\dfrac{5}{6} = 12 + 6\overline{)5.000}^{\,0.833\frac{1}{3}} = 12.833\dfrac{1}{3}$ or $12\dfrac{5}{6} = \dfrac{77}{6} = 6\overline{)77.000}^{\,12.833\frac{1}{3}}$

Note that mixed numbers may be changed to decimals in two ways:

1 By changing only the fractional ending of the mixed number to its decimal equivalent and then adding this equivalent to the whole integers in the mixed number.
2 By first expressing the mixed number as an improper fraction and then changing this improper fraction to its decimal equivalent.

The first method is preferable.

Repeating or Circulating Decimals

Some common fractions and mixed numbers when expressed as decimals do not terminate but continue repeating. Decimals that will not terminate are called *repeating decimals*. They are also commonly known as *circulating decimals, periodic decimals,* or *repetends*.

The fraction $\frac{1}{3}$ expressed decimally is 0.333 etc. And $\frac{1}{6}$ is expressed decimally as 0.1666 etc. Such fractions cannot be expressed as exact or finite decimals. Some common fractions (and mixed numbers) may be expressed exactly as finite decimals. Thus $\frac{1}{2}$ is exactly 0.5; $\frac{3}{8}$ is exactly 0.375; and $\frac{3}{40}$ is exactly 0.075. Such fractions do terminate when expressed as decimals.

Any common fraction in lowest terms cannot be changed to a finite decimal if its denominator has in it any prime factors other than 2 or 5. Thus the fractions $\frac{1}{7}, \frac{5}{12}, \frac{2}{3}, \frac{11}{15}$, etc., will not terminate if expressed as decimals. But any common fraction in lowest terms will be expressed as a finite decimal if its denominator has in it only the prime factors 2 or 5, or 2 and 5. Thus the fractions $\frac{1}{8}, \frac{9}{10}, \frac{4}{25}, \frac{3}{4}$, etc., will terminate if carried sufficient places as decimals.

If the denominator of a fraction contains neither a 2 nor a 5 as a factor, it will be a *pure* circulate. For example, $\frac{5}{9}$ is expressed decimally as 0.555 etc., and $\frac{1}{7}$ as 0.142857 142857 142857 etc.

If the denominator contains only 2s and/or 5s as factors, there will be as many places in the decimal as there are 2s *or* 5s in the denominator. Thus, $\frac{1}{10}$, containing a 2 and a 5 (2 × 5), is expressed decimally as 0.1; $\frac{3}{8}$, containing three 2s (2 × 2 × 2); is expressed decimally as 0.375; and $\frac{1}{20}$, containing two 2s and a 5 (2 × 2 × 5), is expressed decimally as 0.05.

If the denominator contains 2s or 5s and some other factor or factors, the decimal will be a *mixed circulate*; that is, it will be part finite and part circulating. Thus, $\frac{1}{6}$, containing one 2 (2 × 3), may be expressed as $0.1\frac{2}{3}$; $\frac{1}{15}$, containing one 5 (5 × 3), may be expressed as $0.0\frac{2}{3}$; and $\frac{1}{36}$, containing two 2s (2 × 2 × 3 × 3), may be expressed as $0.02\frac{7}{9}$.

INDICATING A REPEATING DECIMAL   Rather than indicating that a decimal is repeating by such expressions as 0.333 etc. or 0.333 . . . , it is understood that the decimal is repeating if a dot (˙) or short bar (‾) is placed above the figure or figures that constitute the circulating portion of the decimal.

Example 1 $\frac{1}{9} = 0.\dot{1}$ $\frac{2}{7} = 0.\dot{2}8571\dot{4}$ $\frac{11}{6} = 1.8\dot{3}$

$\frac{7}{30} = 0.2\dot{3}$ $\frac{1}{11} = 0.\dot{0}\dot{9}$ $\frac{17}{110} = 0.1\dot{5}\dot{4}$

CHANGING THE FORM OF A REPEATING DECIMAL   Repeating decimals may be expressed as common fractions, mixed numbers, or complex decimals as follows

1   Use the circulate as the numerator of a fraction.
2   For the denominator, write as many 9s as there are decimal places in the circulate.

Example 2 $0.\dot{3} = \frac{3}{9} = \frac{1}{3}$ $1.\dot{2}\dot{5} = 1\frac{25}{99}$ $0.2\dot{6} = 0.2\frac{6}{9} = 0.2\frac{2}{3}$

$$7.6\dot{1}2\dot{3} = 7.6\frac{123}{999} = 7.6\frac{41}{333}$$

It will be observed that in so changing its form, a pure circulate will be expressed as a proper fraction or mixed number, and a mixed circulate will be expressed as a complex decimal fraction. A mixed circulate when expressed as an equivalent complex decimal fraction may then be changed to a proper fraction or mixed number.

CHANGING MIXED CIRCULATES DIRECTLY TO PROPER FRACTIONS OR MIXED NUMBERS   A mixed circulate may be directly changed to a proper fraction or mixed number by the following procedure:

1   From the decimals (including the repeating portion), subtract the finite decimals and use this remainder as the numerator of a fraction.
2   For the denominator, write as many 9s as there are places in the repeating portion (the circulate) and annex as many zeros as there are finite decimal places.

Example 3 $0.1\dot{6} = \frac{(16-1)}{90} = \frac{15}{90} = \frac{1}{6}$ $0.43\dot{5}1\dot{8} = \frac{(43{,}518 - 43)}{99{,}900} = \frac{43{,}475}{99{,}900} = \frac{47}{108}$

$4.8\dot{3} = 4 + \frac{(83-8)}{90} = 4\frac{75}{90} = 4\frac{5}{6}$ $5.15\dot{4} = 5 + \frac{(154-1)}{990} = 5\frac{153}{990} = 5\frac{17}{110}$

Exercise 2.6

Change to common-fraction equivalents expressed in lowest terms. If equivalents are improper fractions, express as mixed numbers.

1 0.84	2 $0.1\frac{1}{3}$	3 $0.00\frac{2}{3}$	4 $2.000\frac{1}{4}$
5 $9.74\frac{1}{6}$	6 60.9824	7 $4.102\frac{1}{4}$	8 $45.2\frac{8}{9}$
7 $0.00\frac{4}{11}$	10 $21.30\frac{2}{7}$	11 $3.1\frac{5}{9}$	12 $4.96\frac{1}{2}$

Change to decimal-fraction equivalents. Work to nearest ten-thousandths.

13 $\frac{3}{8}$	14 $\frac{5}{7}$	15 $\frac{18}{26}$	16 $\frac{13}{41}$
17 $\frac{103}{64}$	18 $\frac{17}{7}$	19 $\frac{188}{125}$	20 $\frac{27}{19}$
21 $1\frac{4}{15}$	22 $3\frac{18}{79}$	23 $6\frac{11}{13}$	24 $14\frac{10}{31}$

Change the following fractions to circulating decimals. Indicate the repeating portion by placement of dot or dots.

25 $\dfrac{3}{9}$ **26** $\dfrac{5}{6}$ **27** $\dfrac{3}{7}$ **28** $\dfrac{4}{15}$

29 $\dfrac{13}{75}$ **30** $\dfrac{7}{18}$ **31** $\dfrac{449}{150}$ **32** $\dfrac{37}{18}$

Change only the repeating portion of the following to common fractions of fractional endings expressed in lowest terms

33 $0.\dot{4}$ **34** $10.2\dot{5}\dot{0}$ **35** $0.7\dot{1}$ **36** $0.1\dot{5}$

37 $0.11\dot{3}\dot{6}$ **38** $0.\dot{3}8461\dot{5}$ **39** $13.8\dot{7}$ **40** $8.1\dot{8}$

Change the following mixed circulates to common fractions or mixed numbers expressed in lowest terms:

41 $6.4\dot{6}$ **42** $3.5\dot{1}$ **43** $1.07\dot{2}$ **44** $0.4\dot{7}\dot{2}$

45 $0.034\dot{5}$ **46** $0.201\dot{8}$ **47** $6.01\dot{3}$ **48** $27.\dot{2}\dot{4}$

Chapter 3

Fundamentals of Problem Solving and the Metric System of Weights and Measurements

Objectives To Be Achieved in This Chapter

1 *Learn basic techniques and procedures for approaching and solving problems by arithmetic more easily and more quickly.*
2 *Work with aliquot parts, the laws of proportion, simple equations, and formulas in problem solving to achieve a sense of figures.*
3 *Learn the metric system of weights and measures.*
4 *Develop understanding of the logic and coherence of the metric system by solving parallel problems in both the metric and the customary systems.*

Some students may possess an innate ability to solve problems in arithmetic easily. Such persons are often considered to have a "sense of figures." However, just as in athletics or other fields of endeavor, both those persons who have an abundance of such ability and those persons who may not be so fortunate can increase their effectiveness by learning and practicing certain basic fundamentals, techniques, or procedures.

Solving word problems has long been the nemesis of students. Just the term "word problem" has been enough to strike fear in the hearts and minds of some students. Word problems quickly "turn them off" or close their minds to the attempt at a solution.

If there be a single rule or principle that can be stated to apply to all word problems, it might be:

Be aware of what information is given and what information is required.

Merely reading the problem, even several times, may not accomplish this awareness. Many students—even scholars who make their living solving the word problems of numerous disciplines—must take paper and pencil (or chalk and chalkboard) and prepare an outline, map, or diagram, of what is known and what is required.[1]

Once the knowledge of what information is given and what is required begins to "sink in," your awareness of the arithmetical processes learned here and elsewhere should lead you through the problem to its solution. The following suggested summary of procedural steps, together with the explanation and examples of the material that follows in this chapter, should increase your sense of figures and enable you to solve problems in arithmetic more easily and in less time.

SUGGESTED PLAN FOR SOLVING WORD PROBLEMS:
Step 1   Read the problem carefully.
Step 2   Prepare outlines, maps, diagrams, pictures—anything that helps you in being aware of what information is given, just what is required, and any relationships you can see among the given information.
Step 3   Proceed to a solution.
Step 4   Attempt to estimate a "ballpark" or reasonable answer, and compare it with your solution.
Step 5   Check your solution with the original statement to prove its correctness.

Unit 3.1   *Aliquot Parts and Their Use in Problem Solving*

Can you divide 12 by $3\frac{1}{3}$ in your head in 3 sec or less? If not, a knowledge of aliquot parts can help.

---

[1]Computers are "taught" to solve problems by having a model (a procedural outline) for the solution designed for them, and then the variable information is fed to them to be placed in the model. An attempt at solving word problems by use of calculation models is presented in the important area of Percentage, Chapter 4.

An aliquot part is a number contained in another number a whole number of times without remainder. Thus $3\frac{1}{3}$ is an aliquot part of the base number 10, because 10 can be divided 3 times by $3\frac{1}{3}$ without remainder; $12\frac{1}{2}$ is an aliquot part of the base number 100, because 100 can be divided 8 times by $12\frac{1}{2}$ without remainder. Stated another way, $3\frac{1}{3}$ is $\frac{1}{3}$ of 10; $12\frac{1}{2}$ is $\frac{1}{8}$ of 100; and $166\frac{2}{3}$ is $\frac{1}{6}$ of 1000. The fractions $\frac{1}{3}$, $\frac{1}{8}$, and $\frac{1}{6}$ are the fractional equivalents or *aliquot fractions* of the aliquot parts $3\frac{1}{3}$, $12\frac{1}{2}$, and $166\frac{2}{3}$, respectively.

Knowledge of aliquot parts and their aliquot fractions is useful in multiplication and division, as it enables many calculations to be performed in "your head," or without use of a pocket calculator and with a minimum of pencil-and-paper work.

TO MULTIPLY BY THE ALIQUOT-PARTS METHOD:
Step 1   Find the product of the multiplicand and the basic number 1; 10; 100; 1000; or 10,000 (move the decimal point to the *right* as many places as there are zeros in the basic number).
Step 2   Multiply this product by the aliquot fraction.

TO *DIVIDE* BY THE ALIQUOT-PARTS METHOD:
Step 1   Find the quotient of the dividend and the basic number 1; 10; 100; 1000; or 10,000 (move the decimal point to the left as many places as there are zeros in the basic number).
Step 2   Divide this quotient by the aliquot fraction.

Example 1   **Multiply 67.44 by $12\frac{1}{2}$**

Since $12\frac{1}{2}$ is an aliquot part ($\frac{1}{8}$) of 100:

Step 1   Multiply multiplicand by 100 (move decimal point two places to the right)

$67.44 \times 100 = 6744$

Step 2   Multiply by $\frac{1}{8}$ (same as dividing by 8)

$6744 \div 8 = 843$ (use short division)

Example 2   **Divide 12 by $3\frac{1}{3}$**

Since $3\frac{1}{3}$ is an aliquot part ($\frac{1}{3}$) of 10:

Step 1   Divide dividend by 10 (move decimal point one place to the left)

$12 \div 10 = 1.2$

Step 2   Divide by $\frac{1}{3}$ (same as multiplying by 3)

$1.2 \times 3 = 3.6$

Example 3   **Multiply 921.72 by $166\frac{2}{3}$**

Since $166\frac{2}{3}$ is an aliquot part ($\frac{1}{6}$) of 1000:

Step 1   Multiply multiplicand by 1000 (move decimal point three places to the right)

921.72 × 1000 = 921,720

Step 2   Multiply by $\frac{1}{6}$ (same as dividing by 6)

921,720 ÷ 6 = 153,620 (use short division)

If this shortcut is to be of practical value, it is necessary to memorize the more common aliquot parts listed in Table 3.1. In this table, it is suggested that you memorize first the aliquot parts and their fractional equivalents of the basic number 100. Knowledge of the aliquot parts of 100 can then be extended readily to the adjoining columns listing the aliquot parts of the basic numbers 1; 10; 1000; and 10,000. Note that the numerator of an aliquot fraction is 1. The aliquot-parts shortcut in multiplication and division can be extended to *multiples* of an aliquot part ($\frac{3}{8}$ is a multiple of $\frac{1}{8}$). The fractional equivalent of a multiple of an aliquot part always has a numerator other than 1. The rules for multiplication and division by a multiple of an aliquot part are the same as for the aliquot part. However, since the numerator of the aliquot fraction is greater than 1, the procedure does not lend itself so readily to mental calculations and is not illustrated here. An extended table of the aliquot parts, and their multiples of the basic number 100 is included in Chapter 4, Percentage, as Table 4.1.

TABLE 3.1   COMMON ALIQUOT PARTS OF 1; 10; 100; 1000; AND 10,000

Aliquot fractions	The basic numbers				
	1	10	100	1000	10,000
$\frac{1}{2}$	0.50	5	50	500	5000
$\frac{1}{3}$	$0.33\frac{1}{3}$	$3\frac{1}{3}$	$33\frac{1}{3}$	$333\frac{1}{3}$	$3333\frac{1}{3}$
$\frac{1}{4}$	0.25	$2\frac{1}{2}$	25	250	2500
$\frac{1}{5}$	0.20	2	20	200	2000
$\frac{1}{6}$	$0.16\frac{2}{3}$	$1\frac{2}{3}$	$16\frac{2}{3}$	$166\frac{2}{3}$	$1666\frac{2}{3}$
$\frac{1}{8}$	$0.12\frac{1}{2}$	$1\frac{1}{4}$	$12\frac{1}{2}$	125	1250
$\frac{1}{10}$	0.10	1	10	100	1000
$\frac{1}{12}$	$0.08\frac{1}{3}$	$\frac{5}{6}$	$8\frac{1}{3}$	$83\frac{1}{3}$	$833\frac{1}{3}$
$\frac{1}{16}$	$0.06\frac{1}{4}$	$\frac{5}{8}$	$6\frac{1}{4}$	$62\frac{1}{2}$	625

Exercise 3.1
Solve by the aliquot-parts method (refer to Table 3.1).

1   $45 \times 3\frac{1}{3}$

2   $\$180 \times 16\frac{2}{3}$

3   $81 \times 33\frac{1}{3}$

4   $10.7 \times 12\frac{1}{2}$

5   $0.96 \times 83\frac{1}{3}$

6   $6\frac{1}{4} \times 21.12$

7   $0.0786 \times 16\frac{2}{3}$

8   125×2.200

9 625 × 4.16

10 $144 \times \frac{5}{6}$

11 $440 \times 2\frac{1}{2}$

12 $0.36 \times 83\frac{1}{3}$

13 $128 \times \frac{5}{8}$

14 2500 × 16.5204

15 $96 \div 16\frac{2}{3}$

16 $681 \div 3\frac{1}{3}$

17 7560 ÷ 250

18 $6241 \div 166\frac{2}{3}$

19 $4250 \div 12\frac{1}{2}$

20 623 ÷ 125

21 $240 \div \frac{5}{6}$

22 $12 \div 8\frac{1}{3}$

23 423 ÷ 25

24 $462 \div 1\frac{1}{4}$

25 $1001 \div \frac{5}{8}$

26 $16 \div 6\frac{1}{4}$

27 $144 \div 83\frac{1}{3}$

28 320 ÷ 625

Solve the following:

29 Cynthia Moore sold 320 shares of stock of the Hair Co. for $125 per share. Find the total amount of the sale.

30 Jack Zumbrunnen's property was valued at $49,920 and was assessed for property taxes at 25 percent of its value. If the tax rate was 8\frac{1}{3}$ per $100 of assessed valuation (0.08\frac{1}{3}$ per $1), find the total property tax.

31 Cheryl Harper worked 32 hr at the rate of $6.25 per hr. Find her gross pay.

32 A salesman sold 7290 pounds of fertilizer at 16$\frac{2}{3}$ cents per lb. The salesman also received a commission of $12.50 for each $100 of fertilizer sold. Find (a) the amount of sale and (b) the amount of his commission.

33 Joe Williams paid $300 for 625 lb of pig feed. Find the price per pound.

34 Alice Warren was attending an auction where the auctioneer was inviting bids for a truck and trailer load of hay (25 tons). The bidding had reached a total amount of $1700, and Alice felt that if she upped the bid by $50 she would be the winner. Alice could obtain the same quality of hay locally for $85 per ton. The auctioneer was ready to close the bids—should Alice bid $1750?

Unit 3.2   Finding a Required Quantity When the Quantity of a Fractional Part of the Whole Quantity Is Known

---

Methods of Determining Required Quantities

If $\frac{2}{3}$ of a cake costs 90 cents, how much does the whole cake cost? How much does $\frac{5}{8}$ of the cake cost? When the quantity of a fractional part of the whole quantity is known, solution of many problems requires finding of the whole quantity. In other similar problems, the requirement is to find the quantity of a different fractional part of the same whole quantity.

Example 1   **Finding whole quantity. If $\frac{3}{8}$ of a cake costs 90 cents, find the cost of the whole cake.**

Solution using the fractional-unit procedure:

Step 1   Divide the known quantity by the numerator of its related fractional equivalent. The quotient will then equal the quantity of one part:

$0.90 ÷ 3 = $0.30 (cost of one part)

Step 2   Multiply this obtained quantity of one part by the denominator of the fractional unit which represents the entire number of parts:

$0.30 × 8 = $2.40 (cost of all parts or the whole cake)

Solution using the procedure of proving the product of two factors in the multiplication process by dividing the known product by one of the factors:

Step 1   If $\frac{3}{8}$ times the cost of the whole cake is $0.90, then the problem could be viewed as:

$$? = \text{factor (cost of whole cake)}$$
$$\times \frac{3}{8} = \text{factor}$$
$$\overline{\$0.90} = \text{product}$$

Step 2   Divide the product by the one known factor. The quotient will be the other factor (unknown in the problem):

$$\$0.90 ÷ \frac{3}{8} = \$0.90 \times \frac{8}{3} = \$2.40$$

Note that the calculations in both procedures find the required whole quantity by multiplying the known quantity by the reciprocal (see Unit 2.4) of the related fractional equivalent. Thus (the reciprocal of the related fractional equivalent of $\frac{3}{8}$ is $\frac{8}{3}$):

$$\$0.90 \times \frac{8}{3} = \$2.40$$

Although both procedures are basically the same, each procedure follows a somewhat different mental approach and may thus contribute to a better understanding.

Example 2   **Finding whole quantity. New partner Cox is willing to pay $8000 for a $\frac{2}{3}$ interest in the existing partnership of Albright and Buchanan. What is the existing partnership worth?**

Fractional-unit procedure:

Step 1 $8000 ÷ 2 = $4000 (value of one part)
Step 2 $4000 × 3 = $12000 (value of entire partnership)

Proving the product, or reciprocal procedure:

$\qquad$?   Factor (value of entire partnership)

$\underline{\times \frac{2}{3}}$ Factor

8000 Product

$$\$8000 \div \frac{2}{3} = \$8000 \times \frac{3}{2} = \$12{,}000$$

Example 3   **Finding fractional quantity. If $\frac{5}{12}$ yd of silk costs $1.20, find the cost of $\frac{7}{12}$ yd.**

Fractional-unit procedure:

Step 1 $1.20 ÷ 5 = $0.24 (cost of one part)
Step 2 $0.24 × 7 = $1.68 (cost of seven parts)

Proving the product, or reciprocal procedure

Step 1 $\qquad$?   factor [cost of whole quantity (1 yd)]

$\underline{\times \frac{5}{12}}$ factor

1.20 Product

$$\$1.20 \div \frac{5}{12} = \overset{0.24}{\cancel{1.20}} \times \frac{12}{\underset{1}{\cancel{5}}} = \$2.88 \text{ [cost of whole quantity (1 yd)]}$$

Step 2 $\overset{0.24}{\cancel{\$2.88}} \times \frac{7}{\underset{1}{\cancel{12}}} = \$1.68 \left(\text{cost of } \frac{7}{12} \text{ yd} \right)$

Example 4   **Finding fractional quantity. John earned $14.40 or $\frac{3}{5}$ as much as Mary. Henry earned $\frac{11}{8}$ times as much as Mary. Find Mary's earnings and Henry's earnings.**

Fractional-unit procedure:

Step 1 $14.40 ÷ 3 = $4.80 (one part of Mary's earnings)
Step 2 $4.80 × 5 = $24.00 (Mary's entire earnings)

Step 3 $\overset{3.00}{\cancel{\$24.00}} \times \frac{11}{\underset{1}{\cancel{8}}} = \$33.00$ (Henry's earnings)

Proving the product, or reciprocal procedure:

Step 1   ?   factor (Mary's entire earnings)

$$\times \frac{3}{5} \quad \text{factor}$$

$$\overline{\$14.40} \quad \text{Product}$$

$$\$14.40 \div \frac{3}{5} = \$\cancel{14.40}^{4.80} \times \frac{5}{\cancel{3}_1} = \$24.00 \text{ (Mary's entire earnings)}$$

Step 2 $\$\cancel{24.00}^{3.00} \times \frac{11}{\cancel{8}_1} = \$33.00$ (Henry's earnings)

Exercise 3.2

Find the whole quantity of each of the following by the fractional-unit method:

1   $\frac{1}{6}$ of a quantity = 40

2   $\frac{3}{4}$ of a quantity = 270

3   $\frac{7}{8}$ of a quantity = $27\frac{5}{8}$

4   $\frac{5}{11}$ of a quantity = $43.20

5   $\frac{9}{4}$ of a quantity = $18\frac{1}{3}$

6   $2\frac{3}{8}$ times a quantity = 360

Find the whole quantity of each of the following by the reciprocal method:

7   $\frac{3}{8}$ of a quantity = 16

8   $\frac{5}{7}$ of a quantity = 385

9   $\frac{4}{9}$ of a quantity = $22\frac{1}{2}$

10   $\frac{8}{13}$ of a quantity = $38.64

11   $\frac{9}{7}$ of a quantity = $30\frac{1}{3}$

12   $3\frac{1}{3}$ times a quantity = $15\frac{2}{3}$

Given the equations on the left, find the following whole quantities or fractional parts of the whole quantities:

		(a)	(b)	(c)
13	$\frac{7}{8}$ of a quantity = 28	1	$\frac{9}{8}$	$\frac{1}{4}$
14	$\frac{8}{5}$ of a quantity = 120	$\frac{7}{12}$	$2\frac{3}{4}$	$\frac{4}{15}$
15	$\frac{7}{30}$ of a quantity = 259	$\frac{5}{6}$	1	$8\frac{1}{5}$
16	$\frac{1}{6}$ of a quantity = $66.00	$\frac{1}{4}$	$3\frac{1}{2}$	$\frac{3}{8}$

17   $\frac{7}{6}$ of a quantity = $17.50 $\frac{5}{3}$ $\frac{1}{6}$ $3\frac{1}{2}$

18   $3\frac{1}{3}$ times a quantity = $24\frac{1}{4}$ $\frac{1}{12}$ 1 $4\frac{3}{8}$

Solve the following:

19   A man drove $39\frac{6}{10}$ miles, which was $\frac{3}{15}$ of the distance to his destination. Find the total distance in miles that he planned to drive.

20   If $\frac{1}{33}$ of a worker's monthly paycheck was $30.60, find her total earnings for the month.

21   If $\frac{5}{16}$ of an item weighed $7\frac{7}{10}$ lb, find the total weight in pounds of the item.

22   If $\frac{11}{24}$ in on a blueprint represented 154 ft, find the distance in feet represented by 1 in on the blueprint.

23   If a house requires $\frac{7}{9}$ of the width of a lot and the house is 68.6 ft wide, find the width in feet of the lot.

24   A can of dried parsley weighed 27.62 g. If the dried weight was $\frac{3}{28}$ of the fresh weight of the parsley, find in grams the fresh weight of the parsley before drying.

25   If $\frac{2}{15}$ of the total cost of a diamond ring was $107.50 in taxes, find the price of the ring before taxes.

26   If $\frac{7}{48}$ of the total cost of an automobile was tax and delivery charge in the amount of $436.80, find the cost of the auto excluding the tax and delivery charge.

27   An estate was divided among three people. The first person received $\frac{2}{11}$ of the estate and $6336 less than the second person, who received $\frac{2}{9}$ of the estate. Find (a) the value of the estate and (b) the amount received by the third person.

28   Three workers on a piece-rate basis completed a work order. If the first worker completed $\frac{4}{11}$ of the job and 45 pieces less than the second worker, who completed $\frac{3}{7}$ of the job, (a) how many pieces did the three workers together produce and (b) how many pieces were completed by the third worker?

29   If $\frac{8}{11}$ of the commission earned by a salesman in November was $560 and if his December earnings were $1\frac{5}{8}$ times his commissions for November, find his commission earnings for December.

30   If $\frac{16}{47}$ of the drapery material required for a pair of drapes is 360 in, find the required length in inches of the lining if it must be $\frac{14}{18}$ of the length of the drapery material.

Unit 3.3   *Simple Equations and Use of Formulas*

The solution to many problems is often found through the determination of the quantity or value of an unknown part of an equation.

An *equation* expresses the equality of two quantities or values. Thus the following are equations:

$$8 = 6 + 2 \qquad 12 = 4 \times 3$$
$$6 = 8 - 2 \qquad 4 = 12 \div 3$$

The two parts (left and right of the = sign) are known as the *sides* or *members* of the equation.

In arithmetical computations, usually the problem (and the equation) is satisfied if the value of some one unknown is found. This unknown may be named, as "retail," "cost," "area," "length," etc., or it may be indicated by a symbol or abbreviation such as R, C, A, I, etc. This symbol may or may not be mnemonic (when letter or letters indicate the meaning of the unknown, as R, C, A, or I), and frequently such letters as x, y, a, b, c, d, etc., are used to symbolize the unknown quantity or value without in themselves implying what the unknown represents. The symbols x, y, or z are commonly used to represent such an unknown.

Formulas

Formulas are merely a concise method of describing the procedure to reach a certain objective. Frequently, formulas will contain signs of aggregation, such as parentheses ( ), brackets [ ], and braces { }, which are used to simplify and make plain the order of operations to be performed. When a formula contains such a sign of aggregation, all quantities within the sign are to be treated as a single quantity, and the operations indicated should be performed first.

After substituting known quantities in a formula, solve by applying the following order of procedure:

1 Clear quantities within signs of aggregation (perform the operations indicated).
2 Raise to powers indicated (see Unit 1.1 for explanation of powers).
3 Do all multiplication (in any order desired).
4 Do all division in the order in which it occurs.
5 Do all addition and subtraction (in any order desired).

Note that multiplication should be performed before division. Thus, $24 \div 3 \times 2 = 24 \div 6 = 4$ (not $8 \times 2 = 16$).

And division should be performed in the order in which it occurs. Thus $48 \div 4 \div 2 = 12 \div 2 = 6$ (not $48 \div 2 = 24$).

However, factors may be rejected (canceled) from dividend and divisor before the indicated operations are performed:

$$\overset{4}{\cancel{\underset{\cancel{8}}{24}}} \div \cancel{3} \times \cancel{2} = 4 \qquad \text{or} \qquad \overset{4}{\cancel{\underset{\cancel{12}}{24}}} \div \cancel{3} \times \cancel{2} = 4$$

The dividend is 24.
The divisor is 3×2.

6   6
~~12~~   ~~24~~
$\cancel{48} \div \cancel{4} \div \cancel{2} = 6$ or $\cancel{48} \div \cancel{4} \div \cancel{2} = 6$

The dividend is 48.
The divisors are 4 and 2.

Ordinarily, problems are so stated that there will be no uncertainty as to their meanings. Thus the preceding might have been written:

$$24 \div (3 \times 2) \text{ or } \frac{24}{3 \times 2} \qquad (48 \div 4) \div 2 \text{ or } \frac{48 \div 4}{2} \text{ or } \frac{\frac{48}{4}}{2}$$

Observe that the following formulas are expressed in two forms, each form having the same meaning:

$$V = \frac{1}{3} \times b \times h \qquad \text{or} \qquad V = \frac{1}{3}bh \text{ or } \frac{bh}{3}$$

$$S = B \times (1 + r) \qquad \text{or} \qquad S = B(1 + r)$$

$$2s = 2 \times (1 + i)^n \qquad \text{or} \qquad 2s = 2(1 + i)^n$$

$$B = P \div r \qquad \text{or} \qquad B = \frac{P}{r}$$

$$P = I \div n \times i \qquad \text{or} \qquad P = \frac{I}{ni}$$

Generally, formulas are written as in the right-hand grouping. As you will observe, the multiplication sign ($\times$) need not be used between an abstract number and symbol, between symbols, or between a symbol or abstract number and a sign of aggregation. Also, as is indicated, the division process is ordinarily shown in the fractional form rather than by the division sign ($\div$).

Since both parts of an equation are equalities, the unknown may be placed in either side of the equation, but it is customary to place the unknown in the left side and then substitute all known quantities before proceeding with the solution.

Solving Simple Equations

The following axioms (established truths) are used in solving simple equations:

1 The same number may be added to both members of an equation without destroying the equality. Thus:

If $8 = 6 + 2$ If $A = 9 - 2$
then $8 + 4 = 6 + 2 + 4$ then $A + 3 = 9 - 2 + 3$

2   The same number may be subtracted from both members of an equation
without destroying the equality. Thus:

If $6 = 8 - 2$ If $B = 12 \times 5$
then $6 - 3 = 8 - 2 - 3$ then $B - 7 = 12 \times 5 - 7$

3   Both members of an equation may be multiplied by the same number
without destroying the equality. Thus:

If $12 = 4 \times 3$ If $C = 6 + 4$
then $2 \times 12 = 2(4 \times 3)$ then $5C = 5(6 + 4)$

4   Both members of an equation may be divided by the same number
without destroying the equality. Thus:

If $4 = 12 \div 3$ If $D = 15 \times 5$

then $4 \div 2 = (12 \div 3) \div 2$ then $\dfrac{D}{3} = \dfrac{15 \times 5}{3}$

There are several mechanical methods that may be used to solve simple
equations. Two of these follow:

1   *Transposition.* A term may be transposed from one member of an equation to another if the sign is changed to its opposite (from $+$ to $-$; from
$-$ to $+$; from $\times$ to $\div$; from $\div$ to $\times$). Thus:

If $8 = 6 + 2$ If $c = a + b$
then $8 - 2 = 6$ then $c - b = a$
and $8 - 6 = 2$ and $c - a = b$

If $12 = 4 \times 3$ If $x = yz$
then $12 \div 3 = 4$ then $x \div z = y$
and $12 \div 4 = 3$ and $x \div y = z$

2   *Canceling.* A term (with the same sign of operation) appearing in both
members of an equation may be canceled. Thus:

If $8 + \cancel{4} = 6 + 2 + \cancel{4}$ If $X + \cancel{3} = 7 + \cancel{3}$
then $8 = 6 + 2$ then $X = 7$

If $6 - \cancel{3} = 8 - 2 - \cancel{3}$ If $Y - \cancel{6} = 9 - \cancel{6}$
then $6 = 8 - 2$ then $Y = 9$

If $\cancel{2} \times 12 = \cancel{2}(4 \times 3)$ If $\cancel{7}A = \cancel{7} \times 5$
then $12 = 4 \times 3$ then $A = 5,$

If $4 \div \cancel{2} = (12 \div 3) \div \cancel{2}$ If $B \div \cancel{9} = 2 \div \cancel{9}$
then $4 = 12 \div 3$ then $B = 2$

Finding One Unit (Whole or 100 Percent) of the Unknown

If in solving, the unknown is expressed as a multiple or fractional part of the whole quantity, the quantity of value of *one* unit (the whole quantity) of the unknown may be found by applying Axiom 3 (multiplying by the reciprocal), Axiom 4 (dividing by the multiple or fractional part), or by transposition. As you know, $4A$ means 4 times A, $6Y$ means 6 times Y, $\frac{2}{3}B$ means $\frac{2}{3}$ times B, etc.

Example 1   **Find the quantities of C in the following equations by applying Axiom 3, Axiom 4, and transposition: (a) $4C = 35$, (b) $\frac{3}{4}C = 26$.**

By Axiom 3 (multiplying by reciprocal)

(a) $4C = 35$

$$\frac{1}{4} \times 4C = \frac{1}{4} \times 35$$

$$C = 8\frac{3}{4}$$

(b) $\frac{3}{4}C = 26$

$$\frac{3}{4}C \times \frac{4}{3} = 26 \times \frac{4}{3}$$

$$C = \frac{104}{3} = 34\frac{2}{3}$$

By Axiom 4 (dividing by multiple or fractional part)

(a) $4C = 35$

$$\frac{4C}{4} = \frac{35}{4}$$

$$C = 8\frac{3}{4}$$

(b) $\frac{3}{4}C = 26$

$$\frac{3}{4}C \div \frac{3}{4} = 26 \div \frac{3}{4}$$

$$\frac{3}{4}C \times \frac{4}{3} = 26 \times \frac{4}{3}$$

$$C = \frac{104}{3} = 34\frac{2}{3}$$

By transposition (changing signs)

(a) $4C = 35$

$$C = \frac{35}{4}$$

$$C = 8\frac{3}{4}$$

(b) $\frac{3}{4}C = 26$

$$C = 26 \div \frac{3}{4}$$

$$C = 26 \times \frac{4}{3}$$

$$C = \frac{104}{3} = 34\frac{2}{3}$$

As is illustrated by these examples, the method of solution is optional. It is possible that you may prefer to solve by the mechanical rule for transposition.

Exercise 3.3

Find the value of b in each of the following equations:

1 $5b = 12 \times 18$

2 $2b - 1 = 19$

3 $5 + 6b + 4 = 22 - 8 + 3$

4 $18b - 14 = 19 + 7b$

5 $10(3b - 4) = 5(b + 16)$

6 $\dfrac{12b}{3} = \dfrac{6(b + 2)}{2}$

7 $\dfrac{18(b - 2)}{9} = \dfrac{12 \times 5}{4}$

8 $\dfrac{4b + 2}{7} = \dfrac{8 \times 7}{4}$

Find the numerical value of each of the following if $a = 9$, $b = 4$, $c = 5$, $y = 2$, and $z = 10$:

9 $a + c$

10 $3b + 2y$

11 $z - 2b$

12 $6az + bc + ay$

13 $az + bcy$

14 $\dfrac{y}{z} + \dfrac{b}{a}$

15 $\dfrac{5c}{2y} + \dfrac{\dfrac{ac}{y}}{a}$

16 $\dfrac{4\left(\dfrac{ab}{y} - b + az\right)}{by + y}$

Select the appropriate formula from the following listing and then solve the numbered problems:

$A = lw$	Area of a rectangle = length $\times$ width
$d = rt$	Distance = rate $\times$ time
$N = L(1 - d)$	Net price = list price $\times$ (1 − discount rate)
$I = Prt$	Interest in dollars = principal $\times$ rate $\times$ time in years
$l = \dfrac{A}{w}$	Length of a rectangle = area $\div$ width
$V = \dfrac{1}{3}Bh$	Volume of a regular pyramid = one-third area of base $\times$ height
$P = a + b + c$	Perimeter of a triangle = sum of lengths of three sides (a, b, c, respectively)
$w = \dfrac{A}{l}$	Width of a rectangle = area $\div$ length
$A = \dfrac{1}{2}bh$	Area of a triangle = half base $\times$ height
$M = R - C$	Markup in dollars = retail price − cost

17 A rectangular garden plot is 36 ft long and 14 ft wide. Find the area in square feet.

18   A concrete monument is shaped in the form of a regular pyramid. If the base has an area of 75 sq ft and the height is 18 ft, find the number of cubic feet of concrete that compose the monument.

19   A boat has a triangular sail with a base of 8 yd and a height of $9\frac{1}{4}$ yd. Find the area of the sail in square yards.

20   Find the width of a desk top in inches if the surface area of the desk top is 836 sq in and its length is 38 in.

21   What will be the simple interest charge for the use of $2700 for 4 years if the rate of interest is 5 percent (equivalent to 0.05 or $\frac{5}{100}$)?

22   A train averaged $45\frac{1}{2}$ mph for $2\frac{2}{3}$ hr. How many miles did the train travel?

23   A radio with a retail price of $312 cost $204.50. Find the markup in dollars.

24   A CB radio is listed in a catalog at $500 less a discount of 20 percent. Find the net price.

Unit 3.4   *Ratio and Proportion*

Ratio

A *ratio* is a method of comparing one quantity with another quantity.

Example 1   On the Gant farm, there are 150 sheep and 50 hogs. The number of sheep compared to the number of hogs is $\frac{150}{50}$, or $\frac{3}{1}$ or *in the ratio of 3 to 1.*

Example 2   The Quinn Company has total sales of $4,542,748 and total assets of $908,550. If sales are compared to assets, the comparison can be expressed $\dfrac{\$4,542,748}{\$\ 908,550}$, or $\frac{5}{1}$ or in the ratio of 5 to 1. This ratio communicates the comparison of sales to assets by stating that the Quinn Company has $5 of sales for every $1 of assets.

The ratios in the examples above of 3 to 1 and 5 to 1 express and communicate the comparison of the actual quantities in a more convenient and simple manner than using the actual quantities. Note that a ratio does not tell how many or how much, but merely gives a comparison. Such comparisons are all that is needed in the analysis of many relationships in business.

Also note that a ratio is considered a fraction. Therefore, problems involving ratios may be solved by application of the same principles that are used for fractions (see Unit 2.1).

A ratio is expressed in its lowest terms, usually with the denominator dividing the numerator so that one term of the ratio will always be 1. If the numerator has a fractional ending, both terms of the fraction may be multiplied by a common factor to eliminate the fractional ending in the numerator.

Example 3   The Pomeroy Public School has 195 boys and 130 girls. The ratio of boys to girls could be stated:

$$\frac{195}{130} = \frac{1\frac{1}{2}}{1} \qquad \text{or} \qquad 1\frac{1}{2} \text{ to } 1$$

To eliminate the fractional ending, multiply both terms of the ratio by 2:

$$1\frac{1}{2} \times \frac{2}{1} = 3 \qquad 1 \times 2 = 2$$

Therefore the ratio $1\frac{1}{2}$ to 1 can be restated as 3 to 2.

Proportion

A *proportion*[1] is a statement that two ratios—or two fractions—are equal. By using this statement and observing the rules concerned with proportion, many practical, everyday problems can be solved by arithmetic.

Consider the following problem in converting a fraction to an equivalent fraction with a different denominator.

$$\frac{5}{8} = \frac{x}{32}$$

The procedure presented in Chapter 2 to make this conversion was:

Step 1 $32 \div 8 = 4$ Divide the required denominator (32) by the given denominator (8) and obtain the quotient (4).

Step 2 $4 \times 5 = 20$ Multiply the obtained quotient (4) by the given numerator (5) and obtain the required numerator (20).

Therefore: $\dfrac{5}{8} = \dfrac{20}{32}$

This equality of fractions ($\frac{5}{8} = \frac{20}{32}$) can be stated as terms in a proportion as 5 is to 8 as 20 is to 32. This means that 5 has the same ratio to 8 as 20 has to 32. It also means that the ratio of 5 to 8 equals the ratio of 20 to 32. A proportion is symbolically expressed as $5:8::20:32$, or $5:8 = 20:32$.

The numbers forming the proportion are called the *terms* of the proportion. They are numbered consecutively from left to right thus:

(1) (2)   (3) (4)
$5 : 8 :: 20 : 32$

---

[1] Proportion has played an important role in arithmetic as is attested by this excerpt from a book first published in 1892: "Proportion forms one of the most useful sections in arithmetic. In our grandfathers' arithmetics, it was called the 'Rule of Three.'" I.C.S. Reference Library, *Arithmetic, Elements of Algebra; Logarithms, Geometry and Trigonometry*, sec. 2., p. 59, International Textbook Company, Scranton, 1905.

The first term is the numerator of the first fraction; the second term, the denominator of the first fraction; the third term, the numerator of the second fraction; and the fourth term, the denominator of the second fraction. The first and fourth terms are identified as the *extremes,* and the second and third terms as the *means.* Thus, in the preceding proportion:

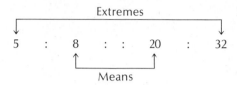

Extremes

5 : 8 : : 20 : 32

Means

CALCULATION RULES IN PROPORTION The principles governing statements of proportion, and thus the rules for solving problems by proportion, are:

Rule 1 *The product of the means equals the product of the extremes.*
In the preceding proportion:
$$8 \times 20 = 160 \qquad 5 \times 32 = 160$$

Rule 2 *The product of the extremes, divided by either mean, gives the other mean:*
$$5 \times 32 = 160 \div 8 = 20$$
or
$$5 \times 32 = 160 \div 20 = 8$$

Rule 3 *The product of the means, divided by either extreme, gives the other extreme:*
$$8 \times 20 = 160 \div 5 = 32$$
$$8 \times 20 = 160 \div 32 = 5$$

In problems in proportion, three of the four terms will always be given, and the remaining term can be derived.

Example 4 **Find the missing terms by the rules of proportionality.**

(a) $\dfrac{5}{15} = \dfrac{12}{x}$

(b) $\dfrac{24}{x} = \dfrac{15}{40}$

(c) $\dfrac{x}{85} = \dfrac{10}{17}$

(d) $\dfrac{16}{64} = \dfrac{x}{4}$

Solutions:

(a) 5:15::12:x
$$15 \times 12 = 180$$
$$\frac{180}{5} = 36 \quad Answer \text{ (Rule 3)}$$

(b) 24:x::15:40
$$24 \times 40 = 960$$
$$\frac{960}{15} = 64 \quad Answer \text{ (Rule 2)}$$

(c) $x:85::10:17$
    $85 \times 10 = 850$

$\dfrac{850}{17} = 50$ *Answer* (Rule 3)

(d) $16:64::x:4$
    $16 \times 4 = 64$

$\dfrac{64}{64} = 1$ *Answer* (Rule 2)

SOLVING WORD PROBLEMS BY PROPORTION   The keys to solving word problems by proportions are:

Step 1   Determine the type of relationship that exists (or does not exist) between two ratios:

Direct proportion exists when two ratios are related to each other and vary *directly, at the same rate,* with one another; i.e., as the first becomes greater, the second becomes greater; or as the first becomes smaller, the second becomes smaller; all at the same rate.

Inverse proportion exists when two ratios are related to each other and vary *inversely, at the same rate,* with each other; i.e., as the first becomes greater, the second becomes smaller; or as the first becomes smaller, the second becomes greater; all at the same rate.

It may be that *no relation* exists logically between two ratios, or they may not vary at the same rate. If so, then an attempt to solve by proportion will obtain an erroneous answer.

Step 2   Write the correct statement of the proportion. A "failsafe" method is to write the statements in fraction form first, paying attention to the following relationships:

Direct proportion:
(a) Like items are placed over like items (gallons over gallons, distance over distance, time over time, etc.).
(b) One set of related factors is placed as numerators of both fractions.
(c) The second set of related factors is placed as denominators of both fractions.
Note: "Related" factors are the cause and effect of each statement. Consider the statement: If 4 people can earn $820 in one week, what can 12 people earn at the same rate? The 4 people earning $820 is one set of related factors, and the amount of money 12 people can earn is the other set of related factors.
Inverse proportion:
(a) Like items are placed over like items.
(b) One set of related factors is set as the numerator of the first fraction and the denominator of the second fraction.
(c) The second set of related factors is set as the denominator of the first fraction and the numerator of the second fraction.

Example 5   **Direct proportion.**

A pump produces 4800 gal of water in 120 min. How long will it take to pump 5700 gal of water? (*Note:* As the time *increases,* the number of gallons also increases.)

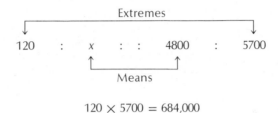

Then:

Extremes

120   :   *x*   : :   4800   :   5700

Means

$120 \times 5700 = 684{,}000$

$$\frac{684{,}000}{4800} = 142.50 \text{ min} \quad Answer \text{ (Rule 2)}$$

Therefore: $\dfrac{120}{142.5} = \dfrac{4800}{5700}$

Example 6   Direct proportion.

An investment of $3000 yields $240. At the same rate of return, what will be the yield of an investment of $2100? (*Note:* As the size of the investment *decreases*, and if the rate of return remains the same, the amount of the yield will also *decrease*.)

$$\frac{240}{x} = \frac{3000}{2100}$$

Then: $240 : x :: 3000 : 2100$
$240 \times 2100 = 504{,}000$

$$\frac{504{,}000}{3000} = \$168 \text{ yield} \quad Answer \text{ (Rule 2)}$$

Therefore:

$$\frac{240}{168} = \frac{3000}{2100}$$

Example 7   Inverse proportion.

If 60 people can weed a field of beets in 8 days, how many will be required to weed the field in 5 days? (*Note:* As the number of days *decreases*, the number of people should *increase*.)

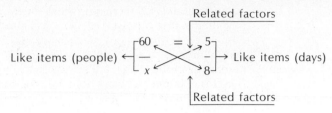

Then:

Extremes

60   :   x   : :   5   :   8

Means

$$8 \times 60 = 480$$

$$\frac{480}{5} = 96 \text{ people} \quad Answer \text{ (Rule 2)}$$

Therefore:

$$\frac{60}{96} = \frac{5}{8}$$

Example 8   **Inverse proportion.**

An airplane travels from one city to another in 160 min at the rate of 270 mph. How long will it take to make the return trip if headwinds slow the plane to 240 mph? (*Note:* As the mph *decreases,* the total number of minutes should *increase.*)

$$\frac{160}{x} = \frac{240}{270}$$

Then:

$$160:x::240:270$$
$$160 \times 270 = 43,200$$

$$\frac{43,200}{240} = 180 \text{ min} \quad Answer \text{ (Rule 2)}$$

Therefore:

$$\frac{160}{180} = \frac{240}{270}$$

The greatest chance for error in solving problems by proportion is in determining whether the proportion is direct or inverse, and in writing the correct fraction or statement. When in doubt, the student can check by first writing the proportion in fraction form as described above *as if* the proportion were *direct.*

Step 1   *In direct or inverse proportion,* if the numerator of the first fraction is smaller than its denominator, then the numerator of the second fraction should also be smaller than its denominator. If the numerator of the first fraction is larger than its denominator, then the numerator of the second fraction should also be larger than its denominator.

Step 2 Reread the problem and reason if the required term (unknown term) is in this relationship. If so, then the proportion is, in fact, direct. If not, then invert one fraction as the proportion is inverse.

Example 9   **Same as Example 7.**

Write the statement as if it were in direct proportion:

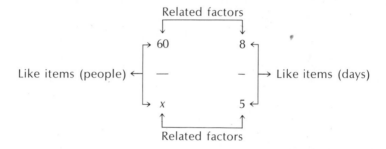

However, when rereading the problem, you would reason that it should take *more than 60 people* to weed the field in three less days! Therefore, the number of people represented by x should be larger than 60, and thus the denominator of the first fraction is larger than its numerator. Therefore, the denominator of the second fraction should also be larger than its numerator. Since our initial expression of the proportion does not show this relationship, we should invert one of the fractions (it makes no difference which one). Then:

$$\frac{60}{x} = \frac{5}{8}$$

$$60:x::5:8$$

$$8 \times 60 = 480$$

$$\frac{480}{5} = 96 \text{ people}   \textit{Answer}$$

Example 10 **When not to use proportion:**

A girl grew 50 in in the first 10 years of life. How tall would she be at 30 years of age?

These quantities are not logically related and do not vary at the same rate. The growing period of a human being is normally completed in 18–20 years. Solving by proportion would result in an erroneous answer.

Example 11 **When not to use proportion:**

If one young boy could weed the garden in 2 hr, how long would it take him and two of his pals to weed the garden?

Again, there is probably no logical relationship here due to the nature of young boys. The rate of work could speed up if all three wanted to go swimming, or they could "play around" and take all day!

Allocating Quantities in a Ratio

Partnership profits, estates, departmental overhead costs, bulk purchases, etc., are often (1) allocated by a ratio containing two or more terms; or (2) expressed in fractions with different denominators and whose sum is more or less than a whole number.

ALLOCATION WITH A RATIO OF TWO OR MORE TERMS. Add the terms to determine the whole. Use this sum as the denominator of a series of fractions of which the ratio terms are the numerators. Then allocate in accordance with the fractions the sum of which constitutes a whole number.

Example 12 **Agliolo, Barlow, Connett, and Daly, attorneys at law, share profits in the ratio of 5:4:3:2. If the profits for the past year were $96,180, find the share for each partner.**

(a) The sum of the terms and the denominator is $5 + 4 + 3 + 2 = 14$.
(b) Allocation is then:

Agliolo $\dfrac{5}{14} \times \$96{,}180 = \$34{,}350$

Barlow $\dfrac{4}{14} \times \$96{,}180 = 27{,}480$

Connett $\dfrac{3}{14} \times \$96{,}180 = 20{,}610$

Daly $\dfrac{2}{14} \times \$96{,}180 = 13{,}740$

Total $\dfrac{14}{14}$ $= \$96{,}180$

Note: If you are using a calculator which is capable of locking in a constant factor, a convenient calculation procedure is to divide the quantity to be allocated by the denominator, lock in the quotient, and then multiply by each numerator. Thus:

$\$96{,}180 \div 14 = \$6870$

Then:

$$\$6870 \times 5 = \$34{,}350$$
$$\times 4 = \quad 27{,}480$$
$$\times 3 = \quad 20{,}610$$
$$\times 2 = \quad \underline{13{,}740}$$
$$\$96{,}180$$

Example 13 **Guynup Enterprises purchased an apartment complex that was advertised as follows:**

Land	$ 50,500
Building	94,750
Carpets and draperies	15,640
Appliances	21,967
Total	$182,857

By negotiation, Guynup Enterprises purchased the entire complex for $160,000. For income tax purposes, Guynup Enterprises wanted to allocate the $160,000 purchase price to the various components in the same ratio as the components were advertised. Find the cost allocation to each component.

The sum of the terms and the denominator is $182,857.
Allocation is then (160,000 ÷ 182,857 = 0.875):

Land	0.875 × $50,500 =	$ 44,188
Building	0.875 × $94,750 =	82,906
Carpets and draperies	0.875 × $15,640 =	13,685
Appliances	0.875 × $21,967 =	19,221
Total		= $160,000

ALLOCATION WITH A RATIO EXPRESSED IN FRACTIONS WHOSE SUM IS MORE OR LESS THAN A WHOLE NUMBER. For a general rule for operations of fractions see Unit 2.1: *fractions having a common denominator are in the same ratio to each other as are their numerators.* From this rule, reduce the fractions to fractions having a common denominator; then after discarding the common denominator, proceed as Example 12 above.

Example 14 **Zebo, Zobel, and Ziegler, real estate brokers, are to divide a sales commission of $6325 in a ratio of $\frac{2}{3}$ to $\frac{3}{4}$ to $\frac{1}{2}$, respectively. Find the share of each broker.**

Convert given fractions to equivalent fractions with a common denominator.

$$\frac{2}{3} = \frac{8}{12}$$

$$\frac{3}{4} = \frac{9}{12}$$

$$\frac{1}{2} = \frac{6}{12}$$

Discarding the denominator of 12, we now have a ratio of 8:9:6. Allocation of the $6400 as in Example 12 above:

The sum of the terms and the denominator is $8 + 9 + 6 = 23$.

Allocation is then ($6325 \div 23 = 275):

Zebo	$275 \times 8 =$	$2200
Zobel	$\times 9 =$	2475
Ziegler	$\times 6 =$	1650
Total	$=$	$6325

Exercise 3.4

Express the ratios of the following in fractional form reduced to lowest terms:

1 84 to 12

2 65 to 195

3 168 to 42

4 $22\frac{1}{2}$ to 9

5 $5\frac{1}{9}$ to $31\frac{17}{18}$

6 $\frac{1}{4}$ to $\frac{5}{7}$

7 $\frac{14}{8}$ to $\frac{15}{5}$

8 1.74 to 0.29

9 $5.2\frac{1}{3}$ to 8.6

10 $\frac{7}{8}$ to $\frac{16}{4}$

Restate the following statements of proportion in fractional form:

11 $3:8::24:64$

12 $2:3::32:48$

13 $4:1::16:4$

14 $18:3::8466:1411$

15 $60:40::7\frac{1}{2}:5$

16 $15:16::75:80$

Restate the following in statements of proportion and find the missing quantity:

17 $\dfrac{2400}{300} = \dfrac{600}{x}$

18 $\dfrac{3500}{700} = \dfrac{x}{100}$

19 $\dfrac{45.6}{x} = \dfrac{229.5}{76.5}$

20 $\dfrac{x}{3\frac{3}{4}} = \dfrac{24}{36}$

21 $\dfrac{\frac{6}{4}}{\frac{6}{12}} = \dfrac{168}{x}$

22 $\dfrac{0.19}{x} = \dfrac{15.2}{8.8}$

23 $\dfrac{\frac{9}{8}}{\frac{3}{8}} = \dfrac{x}{8\frac{1}{2}}$

24 $\dfrac{x}{2\frac{1}{4}} = \dfrac{12\frac{1}{2}}{6\frac{1}{4}}$

25 If $300 is received as the profit on an investment of $3600, what return might be expected on an investment of $4800?

26 Brown invests $4400 and Black $5200 in a partnership. If profits are to be shared in the ratio that each partner's investment bears to the total amount invested, what return should Black receive if Brown's share of the profits is $900?

27 Ms. Johnson invested $39,600 in an apartment house earning a profit of $4250 yearly. She invests $26,400 in another apartment house, expecting to earn a profit $\frac{1}{3}$ larger in ratio to the amount invested. How much yearly profit does Ms. Johnson expect on the $26,400 apartment house?

28 In a partnership, A invested $7500; B, $6000; and C, $4500. If their profits totaled $10,500, how much did each partner receive if the profits were to be divided in the ratio that each partner's investment bore to the total investment?

29 The framework of a building requires the labor of 21 workers for 15 days. If it is desired to complete the job in 6 days less time, how many workers will be needed?

30 Two flywheels are joined by a belt. The circumference of the larger is 133 ft, and it makes 48 rpm. Find how many revolutions per minute the smaller flywheel makes if its circumference is 84 ft.

31 Rosie Wakeman started to San Francisco with a full tank (14 gal) of gasoline. She traveled 62 miles and stopped to fill the tank. It took 3.4 gal. How far will her car go on a tankful of gasoline?

32 If Judy can do a job in 4 days and George can do the same job in 7 days, how long will it take Judy to do a job that takes George 63 days?

33 Bill's pump can fill a pond in 20 hr pumping at the rate of 4 gal per min. How long will it take Bill Jr.'s pump to fill the same pond pumping at the rate of 12 gal per min?

34 A gain of $32,580 is to be divided between X, Y, and Z in the ratio 5:3:1, respectively. How much should each receive?

35 An estate of $116,000 is left to four heirs, W, X, Y, and Z. It is to be divided in the ratio of $\frac{3}{5}, \frac{2}{3}, \frac{1}{2}, \frac{1}{6}$, respectively. What inheritance should each receive?

36 Joe Edwards listed a piece of property for sale and originally advertised it as follows:

Orchard	$ 40,000
Land with residence	10,000
Residence	70,000
Barn	5,000
Total	$125,000

Because of rapid inflation, Joe eventually sold the property for $160,000. Allocate the selling price to the components in the same ratio as originally advertised.

Unit 3.5   The Metric System of Measurement

The United States constitution gave Congress the power to "fix the standard of weights and measures." The United States retained from England a system using such terms as inches, ounces, and gallons, which is now known as the *customary system* of weights and measures. An Act of Congress in 1866 made use of the metric system legal in the United States, but left implementation to the various states and did *not make it compulsory.* Although the fields of medicine and engineering have made extensive use of the metric system, the metric system has not been adopted in the United States for everyday use.[1]

At the present time, a renewed effort is being made in the United States for the wider adoption of the metric system. Education programs on metrics in schools have increased; television cartoons present numerous educational metric "spots"; bumper stickers urging "Go Metric" have appeared; and conversion tables, rulers, thermometers, slide rules, and programmed pocket electronic calculators abound to assist in the conversion of our customary units to metric units.

What Is the Metric System?

The metric system is a *decimal system* of weights and measures which is so designed, labeled, and interrelated as to promote more precise measurements, logical use, and ease of understanding than the customary system. This text will concern itself only with measures of length, mass (weight), area, and capacity and will not attempt to describe the other measures established by the International System of Units of major interest to the sciences.[2]

---

[1] Many consumer products in the United States today state the contents of packages in both customary units and metric units, but retain the customary unit package size:

   A 12-oz can of a soft drink is also labeled 355 milliliters (ml).
   A 2-lb can of coffee is also labeled 907 grams (g).

Some consumer products are even identified exclusively by their metric designations:

   A certain brand of cigarettes contains "11 milligrams (mg) tar and 0.7 milligram (mg) nicotine."
   One can ask for and purchase a 35-millimeter (mm) camera, a 750-milliliter bottle of wine, or a liter of wine with a meal at a restaurant.

[2] The International System of Units (SI) is the metric system of measurements established in 1960 in Paris under the Treaty of the Meter. In this system, there are seven base units:

Measure	SI Base Units	Symbol
Length	meter	m
Mass and weight	kilogram	kg
Time	second	s
Temperature	kelvin	K
Electric current	ampere	A
Amount of substance	mole	mol
Luminous intensity	candela	cd

All other units are obtained from these seven by derivation or combination. Note that the *liter* (dry and liquid measure of capacity, pronounced lē´tēr) is not a base SI unit. In 1964, the General Conference on Weights and Measures adopted the name *litre* (or liter) as a special name for a cubic decimeter (0.001 of a cubic meter or 1000 cubic centimeters).

TABLE 3.2 METRIC PREFIXES AND CORRESPONDING VALUES FOR ALL UNITS

Prefix	Value	Decimal number	Name in the United States
tera	10^{12}	1 000 000 000 000	trillion
giga	10^{9}	1 000 000 000	billion
mega	10^{6}	1 000 000	million
kilo	10^{3}	1 000	thousand
hecto	10^{2}	100	hundred
deka	10^{1}	10	ten
no prefix (Base Unit)	10^{0}	1	one
deci	10^{-1}	0.1	tenth
centi	10^{-2}	0.01	hundredth
milli	10^{-3}	0.001	thousandth
micro	10^{-6}	0.000 001	millionth
nano	10^{-9}	0.000 000 001	billionth
pica	10^{-12}	0.000 000 000 001	trillionth

Table 3.2 presents the prefixes and values for all metric units. Notice that the format is similar to the chart of the powers of 10 introducing the decimal system in Chapter 1. The values to the positive powers of ten are assigned prefixes which are Greek in origin (deka, hecto, kilo, etc.). The values to the negative powers of ten are assigned prefixes which are Latin in origin (deci, centi, milli, etc.).

Converting Within the Metric System

To convert a prefix with a larger power of 10 to a prefix with a smaller power of 10, *multiply* by the value of the intervening powers of 10 (move the decimal point the proper number of places to the *right*). If kilometers (10^3) are to be changed to meters (10^0), the power *decreases* by 10^3, or 1000. To change 1.5 kilometers to meters, *multiply* by 1000 (1.5 × 1000 = 1500 meters). To convert a prefix with a smaller power of 10 to a larger power of 10, *divide* by the value of the intervening powers of 10 (move the decimal point to the *left*). If centimeters (10^{-2}) are to be changed to decimeters (10^{-1}), the power *increases* by 10^1, or 10. To change 800 centimeters to decimeters, *divide* by 10 (800 ÷ 10 = 80 decimeters). Remember, if the power *decreases,* the resulting units are of a *lower value* and *more numerous;* therefore you must *multiply.* If the power *increases,* the resulting units are of a *higher value* and are *less numerous;* therefore you must *divide.*

When converting a square or cubic metric unit to another square or cubic metric unit, multiply or divide by the square or cube of the intervening powers of 10 of the unit being squared or cubed. One hectare [square hectometer (10^2)] is 10,000 ($10^2 \times 10^2$, or 100 × 100) times greater than one square meter (10^0). To convert hectares to square meters, you would multiply by 10,000. One cubic centimeter (10^{-2}) is 1,000,000 ($10^2 \times 10^2 \times 10^2$, or 100 × 100 × 100) times smaller than one cubic meter (10^0). To convert cubic centimeters to cubic meters, you would divide by 1,000,000.

Example 1   **(a)**   Convert 200 dekameters to hectometers
(b)   Convert 2.5 dekameters to meters
(c)   Convert 1.75 kilometers to meters
(d)   Convert 300 decimeters to meters
(e)   Convert 25 square dekameters to square meters
(f)   Convert 2800 cubic centimeters to cubic meters

Solutions:

(a)   deka (10^1) to hecto (10^2); power *increases* by 1 (10); *divide:*

   200 dekameters ÷ 10 = 20 hectometers

(b)   deka (10^1) to no prefix (10^0); power *decreases* by 1 (10); *multiply:*

   2.5 dekameters × 10 = 25 meters

(c)   kilo (10^3) to no prefix (10^0); power *decreases* by 3 (1000); *multiply:*

   1.75 kilometers × 1000 = 1750 meters

(d)   deci (10^{-1}) to no prefix (10^0); power *increases* by 1 (10); *divide:*

   300 decimeters ÷ 10 = 30 meters

(e)   square deka (10^1) to square meters (10^0); power *decreases* by 1 (10); *multiply* by *square of 10,* or 100:

   25 square dekameters × 100 = 2500 square meters

(f)   cubic centi (10^{-2}) to cubic meters (10^0); power *increases* by 2 (100); *divide* by cube of 100, or 1,000,000:

   2800 cubic centimeters ÷ 1,000,000 = 0.0028 cubic meter

Conversions of Selected Metric Units to Customary Units

Because the United States is in a state of conversion and probably will be for many years, conversion tables to the customary system and vice versa are essential. In everyday use, not all the metric units or derivations are used, much as all the customary units are not used. Table 3.3 presents the metric terms that will be used most frequently and the conversion factors to translate metric units to customary units and customary units to metric units. Table 3.3 shows the conversion factors from known customary units to metric units in reciprocal fractional form without calculating the decimal fraction. In this manner, just one set of factors need be learned. *Multiply* by this factor to convert *metric to customary; divide* by the same factor to convert *customary to metric.* (See Table 3.3, pages 112–113.)

Example 2   **Convert the following metric units to the indicated customary units (to one decimal place):**

(a)   85 kilometers per hour to miles per hour
(b)   16 liters of gasoline to gallons (US)
(c)   12 kilograms of potatoes to pounds

(d) 75 grams of salt to ounces (avdp)
(e) 750 milliliters of wine to quarts

Solutions:

(a)   85 km × 0.6214 = 52.8 miles per hour
(b)   16 liters × 0.2642 = 4.2 gal (US)
(c)   12 kg × 2.2046 = 26.5 pounds
(d)   75 g × 0.0353 = 2.7 oz
(e)   750 ml = 0.75 liter (750 ÷ 1000)
      0.75 liter × 1.0567 = 0.8 quart (US)

Example 3   **Convert the following customary units to the indicated metric units (to one decimal place)**

(a)   25 miles per hour to kilometers per hour
(b)   10 pounds of potatoes to kilograms
(c) $\frac{1}{2}$ gallon (US) of milk to liters
(d)   8-oz glass of water to milliliters
(e)   46-oz can of orange juice to liters

Solutions:

(a) $25 \text{ mph} \times \dfrac{1}{0.6214} = 25 \div 0.6214 = 40.2 \text{ km per hr}$

(b) $10 \text{ lb} \times \dfrac{1}{2.2046} = 10 \div 2.2046 = 4.5 \text{ kg}$

(c) $0.5 \text{ gal} \times \dfrac{1}{0.2642} = 0.5 \div 0.2642 = 1.9 \text{ liters}$

(d) $8 \text{ oz} \times \dfrac{1}{0.0338} = 8 \div 0.0338 = 236.7 \text{ ml}$

(e) $46 \text{ oz} \times \dfrac{1}{0.0338} = 46 \div 0.0338 = 1361 \text{ ml}$

$$= 1.4 \text{ liters } (1361 \div 1000)$$

Note: If a conversion factor is not given for a particular metric to a customary unit, it is often easier to adapt the metric unit to another metric unit for which the conversion factor is given rather than adapt the customary unit [See Example 2(e) and Example 3(e) above].

Exercise 3.5

Change units within the metric system (to two decimal places):

1   1.875 kilometers to meters
2   120 decimeters to meters
3   6.47 kilograms to grams
4   1620 grams to kilograms
5   750 milliliters to liters
6   5.46 liters to milliliters

TABLE 3.3   SELECTED METRIC UNITS AND APPROXIMATE CONVERSION FACTORS TO RELATED CUSTOMARY UNITS AND VICE VERSA*

Metric unit	×	Conversion factor	=	Customary unit	×	Conversion factor†	=	Metric unit and symbol
Length								
millimeter	×	0.0394		0.0394 in	×	$\frac{1}{0.0394}$		1 mm
centimeter	×	0.3937		0.3937 in	×	$\frac{1}{0.3937}$		1 cm
meter	×	39.37		39.37 in	×	$\frac{1}{39.37}$		1 m
meter	×	3.2808		3.2808 ft	×	$\frac{1}{3.2808}$		1 m
meter	×	1.0936		1.0936 yd	×	$\frac{1}{1.0936}$		1 m
kilometer	×	0.6214		0.6214 mile	×	$\frac{1}{0.6214}$		1 km
Area								
square centimeter	×	0.155		0.155 sq in	×	$\frac{1}{0.155}$		1 cm²
square meter	×	10.7639		10.7639 sq ft	×	$\frac{1}{10.7639}$		1 m²
hectare (square hectometer)	×	2.47		2.47 acres	×	$\frac{1}{2.47}$		1 ha
Mass, volume, or capacity (solid)								
cubic centimeter	×	0.061		0.061 cu in	×	$\frac{1}{0.061}$		1 cm³
cubic meter	×	35.3147		35.3147 cu ft	×	$\frac{1}{35.3147}$		1 m³
cubic meter	×	1.308		1.308 cu yd	×	$\frac{1}{1.308}$		1 m³
cubic meter	×	0.0008		0.0008 acre ft	×	$\frac{1}{0.0008}$		1 m³
cubic meter	×	423.776		423.776 board ft	×	$\frac{1}{423.776}$		1 m³

* It is interesting to note that in 1893, T. C. Mendenhall, then Superintendent of Weights and Measures, issued an order, with the approval of the Secretary of the Treasury, establishing the French meter and kilogram as the official standard for the American yard and pound, respectively. Therefore, the American yard is *not legally* 36 inches; it is $\frac{1}{1.0936}$ or 0.9144+ of a meter. The American pound is *not legally* 16 ounces; it is $\frac{1}{2.20462}$ or 0.4535+ of a kilogram. Frank Donavon, *Prepare Now for a Metric Future*, pp. 34–35, Popular Library, New York, 1970,

† To convert from known customary units to metric, multiply the customary unit by the *reciprocal* of the conversion factor used to convert from metric to customary.

To convert pounds to kilograms:

$$5 \text{ lb} \times \frac{1}{2.2046} = 5 \div 2.2046 = 2.3 \text{ kg}$$

To convert gallons (Imp) to liters:

$$10 \text{ gal (Imp)} \times \frac{1}{0.22} = 10 \div 0.22 = 45.5 \text{ liters}$$

TABLE 3.3   SELECTED METRIC UNITS AND APPROXIMATE CONVERSION FACTORS TO RELATED CUSTOMARY UNITS AND VICE VERSA* (Continued)

Metric unit	×	Conversion factor	=	Customary unit	×	Conversion factor†	=	Metric unit and symbol
Mass, volume, or capacity (liquid and dry)								
milliliter	×	0.0338		0.0338 fl oz	×	$\frac{1}{0.0338}$		1 ml
milliliter	×	0.0002		0.0002 liquid pt	×	$\frac{1}{0.0002}$		1 ml
liter	×	1.0567		1.0567 qt	×	$\frac{1}{1.0567}$		1 liter
liter	×	0.2642		0.2642 gal (US)	×	$\frac{1}{0.2642}$		1 liter
liter	×	0.22		0.22 gal (Imp)	×	$\frac{1}{0.22}$		1 liter
liter	×	0.2838		0.2838 stricken bu	×	$\frac{1}{0.2838}$		1 liter
Weight (avoirdupois)								
gram	×	0.0353		0.0353 oz	×	$\frac{1}{0.0353}$		1 g
kilogram	×	2.2046		2.2046 lb	×	$\frac{1}{2.2046}$		1 kg
kilogram	×	0.0011		0.0011 short ton	×	$\frac{1}{0.0011}$		1 kg
kilogram	×	0.00098		0.00098 long ton	×	$\frac{1}{0.00098}$		1 kg
metric ton	×	1.1023		1.1023 short tons	×	$\frac{1}{1.1023}$		1 t

7   6.78 hectares to square meters

8   14,500 sq meters to hectares

9   1.285 cubic meters to cubic centimeters

10   168,572 cubic centimeters to cubic meters

Change metric units to customary units (to two decimal places):

11   90 km to miles

12   1500 m to yards

13   1125 g to pounds

14   25 liters to gallons (US)

15   550 ml to ounces

16   5 kg to pounds

17   10 m^3 to cubic feet

18   145 m^3 to board feet

19   28 ha to acres

20   2680 cm^2 to square feet

Change customary units to metric units (to two decimal places):

21   28 short tons to metric tons

22   15 gal (Imp) to liters

23   180 lb to kilograms

24   34 in to centimeters

25   5 ft 2 in to centimeters

26   12 oz (fl) to milliliters

27   1200 sq ft to square meters

28   160 acres to hectares

29   1000 board feet to cubic meters

30   300 miles to kilometers

Miscellaneous problems in conversion:

31   A man is 6 ft 4 in tall and weighs 205 lb. State his height and weight in centimeters and kilograms, respectively (to one decimal place).

32   A woman is 163 cm tall and weighs 52 kg. State her height to the nearest inch and her weight to the nearest pound.

33   A French liner 300 m long is docked beside a New York pier 330 yd long. Does the liner extend past the dock or vice versa? Express the answer in meters and in feet (to the nearest tenth).

34   Marsha Pooler owns a parcel of land in Trinity County 2 ha in area. Erica Pooler owns a parcel of land in Humboldt County of 5 acres. Who has the larger parcel and by how much? Express the difference in hectares and in acres.

35   George consumed 1500 ml of water on a warm day and his friend Barbara consumed 48 oz of water. Who consumed more and by how much? Express the difference in milliliters and ounces (fl).

36   Stephen traveled from Blue Lake to Arcata, a distance of 12 miles, at an average speed of 50 mph. Leonard traveled the same distance at an average speed of 70 km per hr. Who got to Arcata first and by how much time? Express the difference to the nearest minute.

Unit 3.6 *Solving Problems in Metric Units*

One of the logical features built in to the metric system is the coherent relationships[1] of one metric measure to another. For example, 1 liter of water at its greatest density is 0.001 m^3, will fill a 1-kg container, and weighs 1 kg. One thousand liters will fill a container 1 m^3 in size. There are 10 cm in 1 dm, 10 dm in 1 m, and 1000 m in 1 km. This is contrasted with the knowledge in the customary system that there are 4 qt in 1 gal, 1 gal fills a container of 231 cu in, and water weighs approximately $8\frac{1}{3}$ lb per gal, 0.036 lb per cu in, or $62\frac{1}{2}$ lb per cu ft. Also, there are 12 in in 1 ft, 3 ft in 1 yd, and 1760 yd in 1 mile.

The meter is the common base unit, and all other measures are defined and/or derived from this one base unit. Since all of the metric units are interrelated by the decimal system, conversions are logical and the arithmetic is simple.

Table 3.4 presents some of the interrelationships of the metric units most common in everyday use.

Example 1   **Tank A, a rectangular tank filled with water, is 3 m long, 2 m wide, and 1 m deep. Tank B, another rectangular tank filled with water, is 9 ft long, 7 ft wide, and 3 ft deep. In parallel columns, find:**

For tank A	For tank B
(a) Volume in cubic meters	**(a)** Volume in cubic feet
(b) Capacity of tank in liters	**(b)** Capacity of tank in gallons (US)

---

[1] A system of units is coherent if the product or quotient of any two unit quantities in the system is the unit of the resultant quantity.

TABLE 3.4 DEFINITION, DERIVATION, AND INTERRELATIONSHIPS OF METRIC UNITS IN EVERYDAY USE

Metric unit	Definition or derivation	Approximate customary equivalent
Length		
meter (m)	A precise distance measured in terms of the wavelength of light in a vacuum*	3+ ft or 1+ yd
millimeter (mm)	0.001 of a meter	$\frac{1}{32}$+ in
centimeter (cm)	0.01 of a meter	$\frac{3}{8}$+ in
Area		
hectare (ha)	10,000 square meters	$2\frac{1}{2}$− acres
Volume or capacity (solids)		
cubic meter (m³)	One meter cubed; contains 1000 liters; if filled with water at its greatest density would weigh 1000 kilograms	35+ cu ft or $1\frac{1}{3}$− cu yd or 424 board ft
cubic centimeter (cm³)	0.000 000 001 cubic meter; contains 1 milliliter; 1 cm³ of water at its greatest density weighs 1 gram	$\frac{6}{100}$ cu in
Volume or capacity (dry and liquid)		
liter	0.001 of a cubic meter; 1000 cubic centimeters; fills a 1-kilogram container; 1 liter of water at its greatest density weighs 1 kilogram	$\frac{1}{4}$+ gal (US) or $\frac{1}{4}$− gal (Imp) or $\frac{1}{4}$+ stricken bushel
milliliter (ml)	One cubic centimeter; if filled with water at its greatest density would weigh 1 gram	$\frac{3}{100}$+ fl oz
Weight		
kilogram (kg)	A prototype cylinder of platinum-iridium alloy containing 1000 grams; the cylinder has a volume of approximately 0.001 m³ or 1000 cubic centimeters; 1 liter of water (1000 cm³) at its greatest density weighs 1 kg	2+ lb
gram (g)	0.001 of kilogram and approximately one cubic centimeter in volume; 1 milliliter of water at its greatest density weighs 1 gram	$\frac{3}{100}$+ fl oz
metric ton (mt)	1000 kilograms of weight or 1 cubic meter of water at its greatest density	1+ short ton

* The precise definition of the meter is "1 650 763.73 wavelengths in vacuum of the orange-red line of the spectrum of the krypton-86 atom."

For tank A	**For tank B**
(c) Weight of water in kilograms	**(c)** Weight of water in pounds
(d) Weight of water in metric tons	**(d)** Weight of water in short tons
	Note:
	1 cu ft = 1728 cu in
	231 cu in = 1 gal
	1 gal = 8.33 lb of water
	2000 lb = 1 short ton

Solutions:

For tank A	**For tank B**

<table>
<tr><td>(a) $3 \times 2 \times 1 = 6 \text{ m}^3$</td><td>(a) $9 \times 7 \times 3 = 189$ cu ft</td></tr>
<tr><td>(b) $6 \text{ m}^3 \times 1000 = 6000$ liters</td><td>(b) $189 \times 1728 = 326{,}592$ cu in
$326{,}592 \div 231 = 1413.82$ gal</td></tr>
<tr><td>(c) 6000 liters $\times 1 = 6000$ kg</td><td>(c) $1413.82 \times 8.33 = 11{,}777.1$ lb</td></tr>
<tr><td>(d) 6000 kg $\div 1000 = 6$ t</td><td>(d) $11{,}777.1 \div 2000 = 5.89$ short tons</td></tr>
</table>

Example 2   **Garage A is 6 m long and 4 m wide. A concrete floor is poured 1 dm thick. Garage B is 20 ft long and 10 ft wide. A concrete floor is poured 4 in thick. In parallel columns, find:**

For garage A	**For garage B**
(a) Volume of concrete in cubic meters	**(a)** Volume of concrete in cubic feet
(b) Weight of concrete in metric tons if concrete weighs $2\frac{1}{2}$ times same volume of water	**(b)** Weight of concrete in short tons if concrete weighs $2\frac{1}{2}$ times same volume of water
(c) Total cost of concrete if price is \$4 per cubic decimeter	**(c)** Total cost of concrete if price is \$31 per cu yd

Note:
27 cu ft $= 1$ cu yd

1 cu ft of water $= 62\frac{1}{2}$ lb

2000 lb $= 1$ short ton

Solutions:

(a) $6 \times 3 \times 0.1 = 1.8 \text{ m}^3$

(a) $20 \text{ ft} \times 10 \text{ ft} \times \frac{1}{3} \text{ ft} = 66\frac{2}{3}$ cu ft

(b) $1.8 \times 1000 \times 2\frac{1}{2} = 4500$ kg

(b) $66\frac{2}{3} \times 62\frac{1}{2} \times 2\frac{1}{2} = 10{,}416\frac{2}{3}$ lb

4500 kg $\div 1000 = 4.5$ t

$10{,}416\frac{2}{3} \div 2000 = 5.21$ short tons

(c) $1.8 \text{ m}^3 \times 10 = 18 \text{ dm}^3$

(c) $66\frac{2}{3} \div 27 = 2.47$ cu yd

$18 \times \$4 = \$72$

$2.47 \times \$31 = \$76.57$

Note that in the two examples above, the arithmetic was shorter and less complex in the metric system than in the customary system. Whereas the calculations might be performed "in one's head" under the metric system, pencil and paper and/or an electronic calculator are needed for the calculations under the customary system. Moreover, the noncoherent relationships between cubic inches and cubic feet, gallons and cubic feet, weight and gallons and cubic feet, etc., are not readily known or recalled by most of us. We therefore must refer to tables and/or recalculate them. The longer the calculations and the looking up of factors, the longer the time and the greater the possibility of error.

Conclusions on Metric System

"Going metric," or converting to the metric system in the United States, will be costly and frustrating for many citizens. Signs, maps, gauges, tools, etc., will all have to be changed. More importantly, citizens will have to rethink distances, sizes, and quantities, and be able to visualize the metric items in order to make intelligent decisions. It is understandable why a great number of citizens in the United States are uncomfortable and oppose the change.

However, when more and more consumer products are marketed in metric sizes and consumers can purchase a 2-liter container of milk, a "kilo" (kilogram) of instant potatoes, and read 90 km in their cars and know that such speed is the legal speed limit, it should not take long for them to be comfortable with the metric system. Even though the sacrifice is great, the rewards will be greater.

Exercise 3.6

(When necessary, consult Appendix Two for customary system of weights and measurements.)

1 The legal weight limit of a truck is 10 metric tons. How many cubic meters of lumber can it haul if the particular type of lumber weighs 0.8 of the same volume of water?

2 The legal weight limit of a truck is 14 short tons. How many board feet of lumber can it haul if the particular type of lumber weighs 0.8 of the same volume of water? (Answer to the nearest board foot.)

3 Catherine just bought a new water bed 6 ft wide, 7 ft long, and 9 in thick (answer to two decimal places):

   (a) Find the number of gallons it will hold.
   (b) Find the total weight of the water in pounds.
   (c) Find the pounds per square inch that the floor must bear.

4 Margery just bought a new water bed 183 cm wide, 213 cm long, and 23 cm thick (answer to two decimal places):

   (a) Find the number of liters it will hold.
   (b) Find the total weight of water in kilograms.
   (c) Find grams per square centimeter that the floor must bear.

5 Bob Hines is paneling a room 316 cm by 387 cm. The walls are 244 cm high.

   (a) How many square meters of paneling is required?
   (b) Assuming no waste factor and a cost of $3.23 per m² find the cost of the paneling.

6 Lee Pooler is paneling a room with dimensions of 10 ft $4\frac{1}{2}$ in by 12 ft $8\frac{1}{4}$ in. The walls are 8 ft high.
   (a) How many square feet of paneling is required?
   (b) Assuming no waste factor and a cost of 30 cents per ft², find the cost of the paneling (to nearest cent).

7 Lester desires to seed a lawn which measures 35 ft 5 in by 26 ft 4 in. If 1 lb of seed covers 75 sq ft and costs $5, find the cost to seed the lawn.

8 Ms. Steinhauser wants to seed her lawn, which measures 805 cm by 1080 cm. One kilogram of seed covers 15 m² and costs $11.00. Find the cost to seed the lawn.

9 The A & E Company was asked to detail the price of a certain mix of concrete which sells for $40 per m³. This concrete mix weighs $2\frac{1}{2}$ times the same volume of water. State the equivalent price for the following quantities (answer to the nearest cent):
   (a) Metric ton   (b) Kilogram
   (c) Cubic yard   (d) Short tons
   (e) Per 100 lb

10 The No-Harm-Done Company was asked to detail the price of a fertilizer which sells for $20 per 55-gal (US) drum. The fertilizer weighs the same as water. State the equivalent price for the following quantities (answer to the nearest cent):
   (a) Per short ton   (b) Per 100 lb
   (c) Per gallon   (d) Per metric ton
   (e) Per kilogram   (f) Per liter

11 Marc Pooler's pecan pie recipe includes the following ingredients for one pie:

Ingredients	Customary units	Metric units
Eggs	3	3
Sugar	$\frac{2}{3}$ cup	166 ml
Melted butter	$\frac{1}{3}$ cup	83 ml
Salt	$\frac{1}{2}$ teaspoon	2.5 ml
Corn syrup	$\frac{3}{4}$ cup	188 ml
Pecan halves	1 cup	250 ml

He wishes to make five pies and therefore must increase the ingredients proportionately.

In parallel columns, show your calculations for increasing the recipe under the customary system and under the metric system.

Chapter 4

Percentage

Objectives To Be Achieved in This Chapter

1 *Restate common fractions and decimal fractions into percent and vice versa.*
2 *Become familiar with the terms used in percentage and be able to recognize and identify such terms in word problems in percentage.*
3 *Solve word problems in percentage by use of calculation models and/or by use of formulas.*
4 *Adapt percentage problem-solving techniques to problems in accounting and retailing involving percentage.*

Unit 4.1

Percent: Rules for Equivalencies of Percent, Common Fractions, and Decimal Fractions; Aliquot Parts of 1.00 and 100 Percent

Percentage is the common standard of measurement in the financial world. Taxes, interest, expenses, return on investment, etc.,—all are expressed in percent as well as in dollars.

"Corporate income taxes are *46 percent* of net income over $50,000."
"Home mortgage interest rates are lowered to *9½ percent."*
"Investment in this property can return as much as *15 percent!"*

These are examples of the communication of financial information in terms of percent. The advertisement that announces sales of up to *50 percent off,* the news that employees were given a *7½ percent wage raise,* that the cost of living is up another *2½ percent,* that a forest fire is *40 percent* contained, or that there is an *80 percent* chance of rain tomorrow are other examples of the wide use of percents in communicating many types of information to the general public.

WHAT IS PERCENT? Percent is the number of hundredths of a certain number included in a particular other number. Percents facilitate comparisons of several numbers to a common base by reducing the various number quantities to hundredths of the common base. Thus costs, expenses, profits, etc., are compared to each other by each being stated in hundredths of the base number, net sales. Similarly, percents are used to indicate increases and decreases and differences and likenesses and for many other purposes in which comparison, ratio, or proportion are of use. Percents are not spoken of as 8 hundredths, 10 hundredths, or 14 hundredths of the base number so and so. Common usage is to annex the percent sign (%) to the number of hundredths, and state the relationship as 8%, 10%, or 14% (read 8 percent, 10 percent, etc.). The base number used in the comparison should be mentioned, or be easily identified from the context of the statements.

General Rules for Restating Percents as Common Fractions, Decimal Fractions, and Vice Versa

To effect the arithmetical computations in percent, the percents are restated in terms of decimal fractions, and sometimes in common fractions. Conversely, simplicity of communication is accomplished by restating decimal fractions and common fractions as percents.[1]

---

[1]Many electronic calculators (including the smaller hand-sized models) on the market today are programmed so that the operator can perform calculations in percentage directly by using a percent key. This key eliminates the necessity of restating the percent numbers in decimal fractions and "keying in" the decimal points. However, not all electronic calculators are programmed in this manner, and some of those that are, are not programmed in a manner that will enable them to handle all the necessary calculations in percentage. It is then incumbent upon the student to be able to convert percents to decimal fractions so that all the arithmetical functions in percentage can be performed without regard to the type of calculator available.

CHANGING PERCENT (%) TO A COMMON FRACTION   *Rule:* Write a common fraction, the numerator of which is the number in percent (omit the word "percent" or the % sign) and the denominator of which is 100.

Example 1   **Express 8 percent, 12 percent, and 20 percent as common fractions.**

$$8\% = \frac{8}{100} \qquad 12\% = \frac{12}{100} \qquad 20\% = \frac{20}{100}$$

Example 2   **Express $\frac{5}{6}$ percent and $7\frac{1}{4}$ percent as common fractions.**

$$\frac{5}{6}\% = \frac{\frac{5}{6}}{100} = \frac{5}{600} = \frac{1}{120}$$

$$7\frac{1}{4}\% = \frac{7\frac{1}{4}}{100} = \frac{\frac{29}{4}}{100} = \frac{29}{400}$$

Note: To simplify $\frac{\frac{5}{6}}{100}$ and $\frac{7\frac{1}{4}}{100}$ see the rules presented in Unit 2.5.

CHANGING PERCENT TO A DECIMAL FRACTION   *Rule:* Divide the number in percent by 100 (move the decimal point two places to the left) and eliminate the percent sign.

Example 3   **Express 8 percent, 12 percent, and 20 percent as decimal fractions.**

$$8\% = 0.08 \qquad 12\% = 0.12 \qquad 20\% = 0.20$$

Example 4   **Express $\frac{5}{6}$ percent and $7\frac{1}{4}$ percent as decimal fractions.**

Perform the division indicated by the fraction, divide the quotient by 100, and eliminate the percent sign.

$$\frac{5}{6}\% = 0.00833 \qquad \left(6\overline{)5}^{\,0.833} = 0.00833 \right)$$

$$7\frac{1}{4}\% = 0.0725 \qquad \left(\frac{29}{4} = 7.25 = 0.0725 \right)$$

CHANGING COMMON FRACTIONS TO PERCENT   *Rule:* Perform the division indicated by the common fractions, multiply the quotient by 100 (move the decimal point two places to the right), and annex the percent sign.

Example 5   **Express $\frac{9}{100}$ as a percent.**

$$\frac{9}{100} = 100\overline{)9}^{\;0.09} = 9\%$$

Example 6   **Express $\frac{2}{3}$, $\frac{3}{8}$, and $3\frac{1}{8}$ as percents.**

$$\frac{2}{3} = 3\overline{)2}^{\;0.666} = 66.67\% \text{ (to two decimal places)}$$

$$\frac{3}{8} = 8\overline{)3}^{\;0.375} = 37.5\%$$

$$3\frac{1}{8} = \frac{25}{8} = 8\overline{)25}^{\;3.125} = 312.5\%$$

Note: To change a mixed number to a percent, first change the mixed number to an improper fraction and then proceed with above rule.

CHANGING DECIMAL FRACTIONS TO PERCENTS *Rule:* Multiply by 100 and annex the percent sign or word.

Example 7   **Express 0.15, 0.04928, and 3.25 as percents.**

$0.15 \quad\;= 15\%$
$0.04928 = 4.93\% \text{ (to two decimal places)}$
$3.25 \quad\;= 325\%$

Aliquot Parts of 1.00 or 100 Percent and Their Multiples

In many computations involving percents, the use of aliquot parts or their multiples will greatly shorten the time required for solution. Since percent is equivalent to hundredths, it is the aliquot parts of 1.00 or 100 and their multiples that will be of particular value. (See Unit 3.1 for additional explanation of the use of aliquot parts in multiplication and division.) Table 4.1 presents the aliquot parts of 1.00 (100 percent) and their multiples that are most likely to prove useful in rapid calculations. In the table, the first vertical column (at the left) indicates the denominators of the fractional equivalents of 1.00 and 100 percent; the first horizontal row (at the top) indicates the numerators of the fractional equivalents of 1.00 and 100 percent. The aliquot parts and multiples of aliquot parts are shown in the squares at which the two, columns and rows, meet. Thus $\frac{1}{2}$ is 0.50 or 50 percent of 1.00 or 100 percent; $\frac{1}{8}$ is 0.125 or $12\frac{1}{2}$ percent; or $\frac{3}{4}$ is 0.75 or 75 percent. Reading the table the other way, 0.50 or 50 percent is $\frac{1}{2}$; 0.125 or $12\frac{1}{2}$ percent is $\frac{1}{8}$; or 0.75 or 75 percent is $\frac{3}{4}$.

TABLE 4.1 CERTAIN ALIQUOT PARTS OF 1.00 OR 100 PERCENT AND THEIR MULTIPLES (The basic number is 1.00 or 100 percent)

1.00 or 100%	1	2	3	4	5	6	7	8	9	10	11	12	13	14	15
2	0.50 50%														
3	0.33⅓ 33⅓%	0.66⅔ 66⅔%													
4	0.25 25%	0.50 50%	0.75 75%												
5	0.20 20%	0.40 40%	0.60 60%	0.80 80%											
6	0.16⅔ 16⅔%	0.33⅓ 33⅓%	0.50 50%	0.66⅔ 66⅔%	0.83⅓ 83⅓%										
7	0.14²⁄₇ 14²⁄₇%	0.28⁴⁄₇ 28⁴⁄₇%	0.42⁶⁄₇ 42⁶⁄₇%	0.57¹⁄₇ 57¹⁄₇%	0.71³⁄₇ 71³⁄₇%	0.85⁵⁄₇ 85⁵⁄₇%									
8	0.12½ 12½%	0.25 25%	0.37½ 37½%	0.50 50%	0.62½ 62½%	0.75 75%	0.87½ 87½%								
9	0.11⅑ 11⅑%	0.22²⁄₉ 22²⁄₉%	0.33⅓ 33⅓%	0.44⁴⁄₉ 44⁴⁄₉%	0.55⁵⁄₉ 55⁵⁄₉%	0.66⅔ 66⅔%	0.77⁷⁄₉ 77⁷⁄₉%	0.88⁸⁄₉ 88⁸⁄₉%							
10	0.10 10%	0.20 20%	0.30 30%	0.40 40%	0.50 50%	0.60 60%	0.70 70%	0.80 80%	0.90 90%						
11	0.09¹⁄₁₁ 9¹⁄₁₁%	0.18²⁄₁₁ 18²⁄₁₁%	0.27³⁄₁₁ 27³⁄₁₁%	0.36⁴⁄₁₁ 36⁴⁄₁₁%	0.45⁵⁄₁₁ 45⁵⁄₁₁%	0.54⁶⁄₁₁ 54⁶⁄₁₁%	0.63⁷⁄₁₁ 63⁷⁄₁₁%	0.72⁸⁄₁₁ 72⁸⁄₁₁%	0.81⁹⁄₁₁ 81⁹⁄₁₁%	0.90¹⁰⁄₁₁ 90¹⁰⁄₁₁%					
12	0.08⅓ 8⅓%	0.16⅔ 16⅔%	0.25 25%	0.33⅓ 33⅓%	0.41⅔ 41⅔%	0.50 50%	0.58⅓ 58⅓%	0.66⅔ 66⅔%	0.75 75%	0.83⅓ 83⅓%	0.91⅔ 91⅔%				
13	0.07⁹⁄₁₃ 7⁹⁄₁₃%	0.15⁵⁄₁₃ 15⁵⁄₁₃%	0.23¹⁄₁₃ 23¹⁄₁₃%	0.30¹⁰⁄₁₃ 30¹⁰⁄₁₃%	0.38⁶⁄₁₃ 38⁶⁄₁₃%	0.46²⁄₁₃ 46²⁄₁₃%	0.53¹¹⁄₁₃ 53¹¹⁄₁₃%	0.61⁷⁄₁₃ 61⁷⁄₁₃%	0.69³⁄₁₃ 69³⁄₁₃%	0.76¹²⁄₁₃ 76¹²⁄₁₃%	0.84⁸⁄₁₃ 84⁸⁄₁₃%	0.92⁴⁄₁₃ 92⁴⁄₁₃%			
14	0.07¹⁄₇ 7¹⁄₇%	0.14²⁄₇ 14²⁄₇%	0.21³⁄₇ 21³⁄₇%	0.28⁴⁄₇ 28⁴⁄₇%	0.35⁵⁄₇ 35⁵⁄₇%	0.42⁶⁄₇ 42⁶⁄₇%	0.50 50%	0.57¹⁄₇ 57¹⁄₇%	0.64²⁄₇ 64²⁄₇%	0.71³⁄₇ 71³⁄₇%	0.78⁴⁄₇ 78⁴⁄₇%	0.85⁵⁄₇ 85⁵⁄₇%	0.92⁶⁄₇ 92⁶⁄₇%		
15	0.06⅔ 6⅔%	0.13⅓ 13⅓%	0.20 20%	0.26⅔ 26⅔%	0.33⅓ 33⅓%	0.40 40%	0.46⅔ 46⅔%	0.53⅓ 53⅓%	0.60 60%	0.66⅔ 66⅔%	0.73⅓ 73⅓%	0.80 80%	0.86⅔ 86⅔%	0.93⅓ 93⅓%	
16	0.06¼ 6¼%	0.12½ 12½%	0.18¾ 18¾%	0.25 25%	0.31¼ 31¼%	0.37½ 37½%	0.43¾ 43¾%	0.50 50%	0.56¼ 56¼%	0.62½ 62½%	0.68¾ 68¾%	0.75 75%	0.81¼ 81¼%	0.87½ 87½%	0.93¾ 93¾%

Exercise 4.1

Find the missing terms in the following equivalents. Express decimals in hundredths, showing all fractional remainders in lowest terms.

	Fraction	= Decimal	= Percent			Fraction	= Decimal	= Percent
1	$\frac{1}{8}$	____	____%	2		____	0.33	____%
3	____	____	36%	4	$\frac{4}{7}$	____	____%
5	____	0.7	____%	6		____		4%
7	$\frac{9}{8}$	____	____%	8		____	$0.28\frac{4}{7}$	____%
9	____	____	$\frac{1}{6}$%	10	$8\frac{1}{4}$		____	____%
11	____	$1.87\frac{1}{2}$	____%	12		____		$318\frac{3}{4}$%

Solve the following:

13 Is $\frac{11}{16}$ greater or less than 75 percent, and by how much, expressed as a common fraction?

14 Is $\frac{8}{35}$ greater or less than 21 percent, and by how much, expressed as a decimal fraction?

15 Is 55 percent greater or less than $\frac{7}{12}$ and by how much, expressed in percent (to tenths)?

16 From the sum of 86.25 percent, $0.69\frac{1}{3}$, and $\frac{5}{12}$ subtract the sum of 30.75 percent, $0.47\frac{1}{5}$, and $\frac{3}{8}$. Express the difference in percent.

Refer to Table 4.1 of aliquot parts of 1.00 or 100 percent and their multiples and complete the following blanks:

	Fraction	Percent			Fraction	Percent
17	$\frac{2}{3}$	____	18	$\frac{5}{6}$	____
19	$\frac{1}{8}$	____	20	$\frac{5}{8}$	____
21	$\frac{5}{12}$	____	22	$\frac{4}{9}$	____
23	$\frac{3}{16}$	____	24	$\frac{7}{16}$	____
25	$\frac{2}{7}$	____	26	$\frac{7}{12}$	____

Unit 4.2

Definitions of Terms, Formulas, and Calculation Models Used in Percentage

---

The key to solving problems in percentage is a clear understanding of the definitions and interrelationships of but five terms. The terms are defined below, and their interrelationships are presented by means of formulas and calculation models in the paragraphs that follow.

Definition of Terms

1 *Base* is the number which represents the whole and to which the percent or rate relates. The base number is always represented by 100 percent or 1.00 and serves as the most fundamental term in percentage.

2   *Percent or rate per 100* represents the proportion to the base number of 100. Percent means the number of hundredths a particular number is of a certain base number. Thus, 5 percent means a proportion *or rate* of 5 for every 100; 12 percent means 12 for every 100. Percent is symbolized by annexing the sign "%" or the word "percent" to the number (i.e., 5% and 12% or 5 percent and 12 percent). 5 percent would be expressed as a common fraction as $\frac{5}{100}$ and as a decimal fraction as 0.05. The words "percent" and "rate" are often used interchangeably. This is accurate if "rate" refers to the rate or proportion to 100. Thus, in the context of problems in percentage, interest, discounts, etc., the word "rate" is commonly employed as a synonym for percent. However, the word "rate" can refer to other concepts, i.e., the single *rate* of a hotel room, *rate* of weight gain or loss, mortality *rate* per 1000 persons, etc.

3   *Percentage* is the quantity obtained by multiplying the base by the percent; the name given to the quantity that represents *the percent of a given number.* Thus:

100	(Base)		150	(Base)
×0.05	(Percent)		×0.12	(Percent)
5	(Percentage)		18	(Percentage)

The word "percentage" is dropped when stating that 5 (the percentage of) is 5 percent (5%) of 100; 18 is 12 percent of 150. "Percentage" is also used as a generic term to describe the field of mathematics that concerns itself with percents.

4   *Amount* is obtained by adding the percentage to the base. Thus:

100	(Base)		150	(Base)
+ 5	(Percentage)		+ 18	(Percentage)
105	(Amount)		168	(Amount)

5   *Difference* is obtained by subtracting the percentage from the base. Thus:

100	(Base)		150	(Base)
− 5	(Percentage)		− 18	(Percentage)
95	(Difference)		132	(Difference)

Symbols, Formulas, and Calculation Models Used in Percentage

Brevity and mathematical preciseness is achieved by representing the various terms used in percentages by letters (symbols) and expressing certain inter-relationships by formulas and/or calculation models. These symbols are used in the formulas and calculation models that follow:

B = base $B\%$ = percent B is of the base (always 100 percent or 1.00)

r = percent or rate per 100
P = percentage

$A = amount$ $A\% =$ percent A is of the base (found by
                                                      dividing A by B and always more
                                                      than 100 percent)

$D = difference$ $D\% =$ percent D is of the base (found
                                                      by dividing D by B and always less
                                                      than 100 percent)

These basic formulas are obtained from the definitions of the terms used in percentage:

Definition	*Formula*
1 Percentage is equal to the base multiplied by the percent or rate per hundred.	To find percentage (P): $P = B \times r;\; P = Br$
2 Amount is equal to the base plus the percentage.	To find amount (A): $A = B + P$
3 Difference is equal to the base less the percentage.	To find difference (D): $D = B - P$

Numerous auxiliary formulas can be derived from the basic formulas. The auxiliary formulas are useful when one or more of the apparent essential terms are unknown, and it becomes necessary to derive the unknown terms from what information is available.

For those students comfortable with symbolic terms, simple equations, and factoring (usually such knowledge and skills are acquired in the study of elementary algebra) derivation of these auxiliary formulas offers no difficulty. However, all students should find the partial list of formulas and examples below a handy reference.

From the basic formulas given above:

$$P = Br \qquad A = B + P \qquad D = B - P$$

the following auxiliary formulas may be derived:

$$B = \frac{P}{r} \qquad B = A - P \qquad B = D + P$$

$$r = \frac{P}{B} \qquad P = A - B \qquad P = B - D$$

By substitution of Br for P, the following may be derived:

If $A = B + P$ If $D = B - P$
then $A = B + Br$ then $D = B - Br$
          $= B(1 + r)$ $= B(1 - r)$

and $B = \dfrac{A}{1 + r}$ and $B = \dfrac{D}{1 - r}$

SUMMARIZING OF FORMULAS AND EXAMPLES[1] The preceding formulas for percentage may be capitulated as follows:

To find base (always 100 percent of itself):

		Given	Solution
1	$B = A - P$	$A = 235; P = 25$	$B = 235 - 25$ $= 210$
2	$B = D + P$	$D = 385; P = 45$	$B = 385 + 45$ $= 430$
3	$B = \dfrac{P}{r}$	$P = 4.80; r = 4\%$	$B = \dfrac{4.80}{0.04}$ $= 120$
4	$B = \dfrac{A}{100\% + r}$	$A = 459; r = 2\%$	$B = \dfrac{459}{1 + 0.02} = \dfrac{459}{1.02} = 450$
5	$B = \dfrac{D}{100\% - r}$	$D = 342; r = 5\%$	$B = \dfrac{342}{1 - 0.05} = \dfrac{342}{0.95} = 360$

To find percentage:

		Given	Solution
6	$P = Br$	$B = 300; r = 6\%$	$P = 300 \times 0.06 = 18$
7	$P = A - B$	$A = 420; B = 390$	$P = 420 - 390 = 30$
8	$P = B - D$	$B = 320; D = 280$	$P = 320 - 280 = 40$

To find rate (the percent of the base that is the percentage):

		Given	Solution
9	$r = \dfrac{P}{B}$	$P = 7.50; B = 150$	$r = \dfrac{7.50}{150} = 0.05 = 5\%$
10	$r = A\% - 100\%$	$A\% = 115\%$	$r = 115\% - 100\% = 15\%$
11	$r = 100\% - D\%$	$D\% = 76\%$	$r = 100\% - 76\% = 24\%$

To find amount (expressed in percents as the base of 100 percent plus the rate in percent):

		Given	Solution
12	$A = B + P$	$B = 325; P = 30$	$A = 325 + 30$ $= 355$
13	$A\% = 100\% + r$	$r = 20\%$	$A\% = 100\% + 20\% = 120\%$
14	$A = B \times A\%$	$B = 400; A\% = 108\%$	$A = 400 \times 1.08$ $= 432$
15	$A\% = \dfrac{A}{B}$	$A = 321; B = 300$	$A\% = \dfrac{321}{300} = 1.07 = 107\%$

[1]If the solution of the complex or compound-complex fractions in the examples is not clear to you, review Unit 2.5.

To find difference (expressed in percents as the base of 100 percent less the rate in percent):

		Given		Solution	
16	$D = B - P$	$B = 45;$	$P = 5$	$D = 45 - 5$	$= 40$
17	$D\% = 100\% - r$	$r = 8\%$		$D\% = 100\% - 8\% = 92\%$	
18	$D = B \times D\%$	$B = 250;$	$D = 96\%$	$D = 250 \times 0.96 = 240$	
19	$D\% = \dfrac{D}{B}$	$D = 120;$	$B = 200$	$D\% = \dfrac{120}{200} = 0.60 = 60\%$	

The formula to be selected in any given problem depends on what terms are identifiable and given in the problem. A particular formula is selected when the term on the left of the equals sign is unknown, and all the terms on the right of the equals sign are known.

Solving Problems in Percentage—Use of Calculation Models

In solving problems in percentage, the following procedural steps are essential:

1 *Identify* the quantities given with their related percentage terms. (Is a given number the base, percent, percentage, amount, or difference?)
2 *Relate* the quantities to each other, whether known or unknown, in the format of a calculation model or formula.
3 *Complete* the solution.

Calculation models provide a format in which the problem terms can be entered as they are identified. Once identified and properly labeled, the model visually displays and relates what is known and the arithmetical procedures to calculate what is unknown. By "mapping" or "displaying" the elements of a problem in the model format, the mental reasoning becomes more organized, and the path to the solution is made more comprehensible.

The basic models used for solving problems in percentage include a model for finding the *percentage,* the *amount,* and the *difference.*

USING THE PERCENTAGE MODEL The percentage model is used when just the percentage is to be found and the base and percent are given; or whenever the percentage is one of the given terms and either the base or the percent is to be found.

PERCENTAGE MODEL

Number	%*	Description†
————	1.00	Base/B%
× ————	× ————	Percent/r
════	════	Percentage/r

*Expressed in decimal fractions.
†Base/B%; Percent/r; and Percentage/r represent the description of the quantities entered in the number and % columns, respectively.

Example 1   **Find the percentage if the base is 240 and the rate is 5%.**

Solution:

Step 1   Identify the terms and place the given information in the model format.

PERCENTAGE MODEL

Number	%	Description
240 (step 1)	1.00	Base/B%
×.05 (step 1)	×.05 (step 1)	Percent/r
		Percentage/r

Step 2   Perform the arithmetical procedure indicated by the model and write in the answer.

PERCENTAGE MODEL

Number	%	Description
240 (step 1)	1.00	Base/B%
×.05 (step 1)	×.05 (step 1)	Percent/r
12 (step 2 answer)	0.05 (step 2)	Percentage/r

Alternate solution procedure by use of formula:

$$P = Br \qquad P = 240 \times 05 = 12$$

Example 2   **Find the base if the percentage is 7.68 and the rate is 8 percent.**

Solution:

Step 1   Identify the terms and place the given information in the model format.

PERCENTAGE MODEL

Number	%	Description
	1.00	Base/B%
×.08 (step 1)	×.08 (step 1)	Percent/r
7.68 (step 1)	0.08 (step 1)	Percentage/r

Step 2   The model shows that when the unknown base number (multiplicand) is multiplied by 8 percent (multiplier), the percentage (product) of 7.68 results. From your knowledge of the multiplication
process, when the product is divided by either one of the other two
factors, the remaining factor is obtained.[1] Thus, the unknown base
number is obtained by dividing 7.68 by .08.

7.68 ÷ .08 = 96

Write in the number 96 as the answer for the unknown base number.
A brief inspection of the completed model then indicates the
correctness of your answer.

PERCENTAGE MODEL

Number	%	Description
(step 2		
96 answer)	1.00	Base/B%
×.08 (step 1)	×.08 (step 1)	Percent/r
7.68 (step 1)	0.08 (step 1)	Percentage/r

Alternate solution procedure by use of formula:

$$B = \frac{P}{r} \qquad B = \frac{7.68}{.08} = 96$$

Example 3   **Find the percent if the base is 755 and the percentage is 453. Or, what
percent is 453 (the percentage) of 755 (the base)?**

Solution:

Step 1   Identify the terms and place the given information in the model:

PERCENTAGE MODEL

Number	%	Description
755 (step 1)	1.0	Base/B%
×	×	Percent/r
453 (step 1)		Percentage/r

[1] For an example of this quality, see *Division of the Product by Either of the Factors,* page 25, and/or
division of whole numbers and decimals, Unit 1.5.

Step 2   The model shows that when the base number 755 (multiplicand) is multiplied by the unknown percent (multiplier), the percentage of 453 (product) results. Again from your knowledge of the factors in the multiplication process, the unknown factor can be found by dividing the product by the other factor. Thus, the unknown percent can be obtained by dividing 453 (product) by 755 (one of the factors):

$$453 \div 755 = .60$$

Write in the number .60 as the answer for the unknown percent. A brief inspection of the completed model then indicates the correctness of your answer.

PERCENTAGE MODEL

Number		%		Description
755	(step 1)	1.0		Base/B%
×0.60	(step 2 answer)	×0.60	(step 2)	Percent/r
453	(step 1)	0.60	(step 2)	Percentage/r

Alternate solution procedure by use of formula:

$$r = \frac{P}{B} \qquad R = \frac{453}{755} = .60$$

In the exercise that follows, draw the percentage calculation model and proceed to enter the given information and reason through to the solution. When the model is completed, check the arithmetical calculations and prove your answer.

Exercise 4.2

Find the missing quantities in each of the following:

	Base	Percent	Percentage
1	820	12%	——
2	4100	110%	——
3	——	15%	375
4	——	12%	.0192
5	15,000	——	900
6	1400	——	112
7	30	7%	——
8	56	125%	——
9	440	——	39.60
10	54	——	10.80
11	——	$7\frac{1}{2}$%	16.50
12	——	3%	2.85

Unit 4.3

The Amount
and Difference Models
Used in Percentage

The amount and difference models include provisions to calculate the percentage as well as the amount or difference. The amount and difference models are similar to each other in basic design. In the *amount model,* the percentage and percent are added to the base and 1.00 to obtain the *amount* and *A%,* respectively. In the *difference model,* the percentage and percent are subtracted from the base and 1.00 to obtain the *difference* and *D%,* respectively.

Using the Amount Model

The amount model is used whenever the amount is to be found or whenever the amount is one of the given terms.

AMOUNT MODEL

Number	%*	Description†
_____	1.00	Base/*B*%
+ _____	+ _____	Percentage/*r*
======	======	Amount/*A*%

* Expressed in decimal fractions.
† Base/*B*%; Percentage/*r*; and Amount/*A*% represent the description of the quantities in the number and % columns, respectively.

Example 1   **Find the amount if the base number is 1500 and the percent is 2%.**

Solution:

Step 1   Enter the given information and perform the arithmetical calculations that are indicated.

AMOUNT MODEL

Number	%	Description
1500 (step 1a)	1.00	Base/*B*%
+ 30 (step 1b)	+0.02 (step 1a)	Percentage/*r*
======	1.02 (step 1a)	Amount/*A*%

(a) The base number (1500) and the percent, or rate (.02) are given and entered on the appropriate lines and columns. The .02 can then be added to the base of 1.00 and the A% obtained of 1.02.

(b) Since the base number and the percent are given, the percentage can be calculated with the formula (1500 × .02 = 30). This is a side calculation in this model and is an example of the inclusion in the amount model of the calculations illustrated in the percentage model. The percentage (30) is then placed in the number column on the Percentage/r line.

Step 2 Complete the arithmetical procedures indicated and write in the answer.

Step 3 Further observation of the partially completed model after step 1a, discloses that the A% (the percent that the amount is of the base) was calculated as 1.02. The amount could then have been directly determined by multiplying the base number by the A%:

$$A = B \times A\%$$
$$A = 1500 \times 1.02 = 1530$$

Step 4 Observation of the completed model then indicates the correctness of your answer.

$$1500 + 30 = 1530$$

AMOUNT MODEL

Number	%	Description
1500 (step 1a)	1.00	Base/B%
+ 30 (step 1b)	+0.02 (step 1a)	Percentage/r
1530 (step 2 or step 3 answer)	1.02 (step 1a)	Amount/A%

Alternate solution procedure by use of formula:

$$A = B(1 + r)$$
$$A = 1500(1.02) = 1530$$

Example 2 **Find the base if the amount is $1944 and the percent is .08.**

Solution:

Step 1 Enter the given information and perform the arithmetical calculations that are indicated.

AMOUNT MODEL

Number	%	Description
_____	1.00	Base/B%
+ _____	+0.08 (step 1)	Percentage/r
1944 (step 1)	1.08 (step 1a)	Amount/A%

(a) After the amount (1944) and the percent or rate (.08) are entered, the A% (1.08) can be obtained by performing the arithmetical operation in the % column.

(b) Since the amount (1944) is given and the A% has been calculated (1.08), the unknown base can now be computed. The amount is the product of the base multiplied by the A% ($B \times A\% = A$, see Example 1, step 3 above). Therefore, since the product and one of the factors are known, the other factor can be obtained:

$$A \div A\% = B$$
$$1944 \div 1.08 = 1800 \qquad \text{(base and answer)}$$

Note: Whenever you have a known quantity *and* its equivalent percent, the other percentage terms can always be found.

Step 2 Write in the answer and complete the model. The percentage of 144 is obtained by subtracting the base from the amount (1944 − 1800 = 144), or by multiplying the base times the percent (1800 × .08 = 144).

AMOUNT MODEL

Number		%	Description
1800	(step 1b answer)	1.00	Base/B%
+ 144	(step 2)	+ .08 (given)	Percentage/r
1944	(given)	1.08 (step 1)	Amount/A%

Alternate solution procedure by use of formula:

$$B = \frac{A}{A\%}$$

$$B = \frac{A}{100\% + r} \qquad \text{(substituting } 100\% + r \text{ for } A\%)$$

$$B = \frac{1944}{1.08} = 1800$$

Example 3   **Find the percentage and the percent if the base number is 1400 and the amount is 1526.**

AMOUNT MODEL

Number	%	Description
1400 (step 1)	1.00	Base/B%
(step 1 + 126 1st answer)	+	Percentage/r
1526 (step 1)		Amount/A%

Solution:

Step 1   Enter the given information in the model and perform the arithmetical operations.

Step 2   Observation of the partially completed model indicates that the base number and the percentage are now known. By definition, percentage is the product of the base times the percent ($P = Br$). Therefore, the unknown factor can be found by dividing the product by the other factor:

$$126 \div 1400 = .09 \text{ (second answer)}$$

AMOUNT MODEL

Number	%	Description
1400 (step 1)	1.00	Base/B%
(step 1 + 126 1st answer)	(step 2 + .09 2d answer)	Percentage/r
1526 (step 1)	1.09	Amount/A%

Alternate solution procedure by use of formula:

$$P = A - B \qquad r - \frac{P}{B}$$

$$P = 1526 - 1400 = 126 \qquad \text{(first answer)}$$

$$r = \frac{126}{1400} = .09 \qquad \text{(second answer)}$$

Using the Difference Model

The difference model is used whenever the difference is to be found, or whenever the difference is one of the given terms.

DIFFERENCE MODEL

Number	%*	Description†
	1.00	Base/B%
−	−	Percentage/r
		Difference/D%

*Expressed in decimal fractions.

†Base/B%; Percentage/r; and Difference/D% represent the description of the quantities in the number and % columns, respectively.

Example 4   **Find the difference if the base is 900 and the percent is $8\frac{1}{4}$.**

DIFFERENCE MODEL

Number	%	Description
900.00 (step 1)	1.00	Base/B%
− 74.25 (step 1b)	− .0825 (step 1)	Percentage/r
	.9175 (step 1a)	Difference/D%

Solution:

Step 1   Enter the given information in the model and perform the indicated arithmetical operations.

    (a)   The D% can be obtained by subtracting the percent (.0825) from the base (1.00).

    (b)   The percentage can be obtained by multiplying the base (900) by the percent (.0825).

Step 2   The difference can now be obtained by subtracting the percentage from the base.

$$900 - 74.25 = 825.75$$

Step 3   Further observation of the partially completed model shows that the D% (the *percent* the difference is of the base, as determined in solution step 1a), can be used to find the difference directly by multiplying the base number by the D%.

$$D = B \times D\%$$
$$D = 900 \times .9175 = 825.75$$

DIFFERENCE MODEL

Number	%	Description
900.00 (step 1)	1.00	Base/B%
− 74.25 (step 1b)	− .0825 (step 1)	Percentage/r
825.75 (step 2 or step 3 answer)	.9175 (step 1a)	Difference/D%

Alternate solution procedure by formula:

$$D = B(1 - r)$$
$$D = 900(.9175) = 825.75 \quad \text{(answer)}$$

Example 5   **Find the base and the percentage if the difference is 528 and the percent is 12.**

DIFFERENCE MODEL

Number	%	Description
_____	1.00	Base/B%
−	− .12 (step 1)	Percentage/r
528 (step 1)	.88 (step 1)	Difference/D%

Solution:

Step 1   Enter the given information in the model and perform the arithmetical calculations.

Step 2   Observation of the partially completed model discloses that both the difference (528) and the D% (.88) are now known. The difference is the product of the base multiplied by the D% (B × D% = D. See Example 4, step 3 above). Therefore, since the product and one of the factors are known, the other factor is found:

$$B = D \div D\%$$
$$B = 528 \div .88 = 600 \text{ base and first answer}$$

Place the first answer in the model and complete the model.

Step 3   Perform the remaining arithmetical calculations indicated by the model format. The percentage and second answer of 72 is then obtained.

DIFFERENCE MODEL

Number	%	Description
(step 2)		
600 1st answer)	1.00	Base/B%
(step 3		
− 72 2d answer)	− .12 (step 1)	Percentage/r
528 (step 1)	.88 (step 1)	Difference/D%

Alternate solution procedure by formula:

$$B = \frac{D}{1 - r} \qquad B = \frac{528}{.88} = 600 \qquad \text{(first answer)}$$

$$P = D - B \qquad P = 600 - 528 = 72 \qquad \text{(second answer)}$$

Example 6 **Find the percentage and the percent if the base number is 1300 and the difference is 988.**

Solution:

Step 1 Enter the given information in the difference model and perform the arithmetical operations.

DIFFERENCE MODEL

Number	%	Description
1300 (step 1)	1.00	Base/B%
(step 1	(step 2	
− 312 1st answer)	− .24 2d answer)	Percentage/r
988 (step 1)	.76 (step 2)	Difference/D%

Step 2 Observation of the partially completed model indicates that the base number (1300) and the percentage (312) are now known. By definition, percentage is the product of the base times the percent ($P = Br$). Therefore the unknown factor (percent) can be found by dividing the product by the other factor:

$$312 \div 1300 = .24$$

Alternate solution procedure by formula:

$$P = B - D \qquad P = 1300 - 982 = 312 \qquad \text{(first answer)}$$

$$r = \frac{P}{B} \qquad r = \frac{312}{1300} = .24 \qquad \text{(second answer)}$$

Exercise 4.3

Draw the calculation model, enter the given quantities, and proceed to the solution.

Find the missing quantities in each of the following:

	Base	Percentage	Percent, r	Amount
1	2000	——	2%	——
2	1400	——	6%	——
3	——	15.30	——	86.20
4	——	660	——	61.60
5	——	.48	12%	——
6	——	3162	25.5%	——
7	——	——	5%	315
8	——	——	15%	1725
9	800	——	——	840
10	1975	——	——	2291
11	7.50	.4125	——	——
12	6600	44	——	——

Find the missing quantities in each of the following:

	Base	Percentage	Percent, r	Difference
13	2200	——	12%	1936
14	55	——	24%	41.80
15	19,750	4345	——	——
16	4200	3570	——	——
17	——	——	8%	138
18	——	——	3%	383.15
19	69	——	——	54.51
20	220	——	——	198
21	——	21.25	5%	——
22	——	286.90	38%	——
23	——	112	——	1288
24	——	5096	——	67,704

Find the missing quantities in each of the following:

	Base	Percentage	Percent, r	Amount	A%
25	800	40	5%	——	——
26	1500	225	15%	——	——
27	——	17.25	——	342.65	——
28	——	900	——	15,900	——
29	125,000	——	28%	——	——
30	1370	——	2%	——	——
31	93.50	——	——	——	106
32	150	——	——	——	195
33	7	——	——	140	——
34	500	——	——	560	——

	Base	Percentage	Percent, r	Amount	A%
35	——	——	——	22,950	127.5
36	——	——	——	99.11	106
37	——	——	15%	460	——
38	——	——	3%	2575	——
39	——	60	5%	——	——
40	——	48	12%	——	——

Find the missing quantities in each of the following:

	Base	Percentage	Percent, r	Difference	D%
41	320	12.80	4%	——	——
42	180	10.80	6%	——	——
43	——	54	——	546	——
44	——	162.50	——	1087.50	——
45	15,000	——	21%	——	——
46	1460	——	12%	——	——
47	2000	——	——	——	86
48	350	——	——	——	98
49	1400	——	——	1064	——
50	1975	——	——	1659	——
51	——	——	——	861.60	96
52	——	——	——	32.39	82
53	——	——	19%	4050	——
54	——	——	9%	1456	——
55	——	26.55	36%	——	——
56	——	315	7%	——	——

Unit 4.4 *Solving Word Problems in Percentage*

In actual practice, the base, the percentage, the amount, or the difference are not ordinarily identified and labeled as they have been in Units 4.2 and 4.3. However, once these terms are identified with the quantities given in a problem and placed in the calculation models, the interrelationships among the terms can be visualized and the steps in the solution made clear.

Identification of Quantities Given in Word Problems

The identification of the quantities given in a word problem with their respective percentage terms requires careful analysis of the definition of the terms given in Unit 4.2. The following nine word-problem examples follow the sequence used in the introduction of the calculation models in Units 4.2 and 4.3. Keys to proper identification of the terms are given with each

example. It is recommended that you carefully follow the sequential procedural steps and observe the model at the end of each step.

Example 1 **If raw wool decreases 15 percent in weight during the cleaning process, find
the decrease in weight of 250 kilograms (kg) of raw wool when it is put
through the cleaning process.**

Solution:

Step 1 The ". . . *decrease in weight* of 250 kg of raw wool" requested in the
problem is the quantity that represents the percent of a given
number and therefore matches the definition of *percentage*. The
percentage model is then drawn and the terms entered in the model
as they are identified:

PERCENTAGE MODEL

Number	%	Description
250 (step 3)	1.00	Base/B%
×.15 (step 2)	×.15 (step 2)	Percent/r
37.50 (step 4 answer)	.15	Percentage/r

Step 2 15% is identified as the *percent or rate* and is entered in the model.
Step 3 250 kg of raw wool is identified as the *base number* as this is the
quantity to which the 15% relates.
Step 4 Since all the given terms are now identified and entered, the model
format indicates the remaining arithmetical steps. The decrease in
weight of 37.50 kg is determined (250 × .15) and the model completed.

Example 2 **A retailer purchases merchandise and then adds 60 percent of the purchase
price in order to determine the sales price. If the retailer adds $15 to the
purchase price of an item of merchandise, find the purchase price of the
item.**

Solution:

Step 1 This problem gives an unknown number (the purchase price) and
then states that a given percent of that number represents a certain
figure ($15). The $15 then represents a percent of a given number
and matches the definition of percentage. The percentage model is
drawn and the given terms identified and entered.

PERCENTAGE MODEL

Number	%	Description
(step 4 25 answer)	1.00	Base/B%
×.60 (step 2)	×.60 (step 2)	Percent/r
$15 (step 3)	.60	Percentage/r

Step 2   60 percent is identified as the *percent or rate* and is entered in the model.

Step 3 $15 is identified as the *percentage* as this is the quantity that is 60% of a certain number.

Step 4   *The base number* is not given and its calculation is the requirement of the problem. The model format at this point, however, indicates the *percentage* and the *percent,* and therefore the *base* can be calculated by dividing the product by one known factor:

Base   × percent = percentage
(Factor)   (Factor)   (Product)

or

$B = P \div r$
$B = 15 \div .60 = 25$ (answer)

Example 3   **If 264 lugs of peaches are spoiled on a truck loaded with 2200 lugs of peaches, find the percent of the entire load that was spoiled.**

Solution:

Step 1   The phrase ". . . find the percent of the entire load that was spoiled . . ." implies finding the rate or percent that is used in multiplying the entire load of peaches in order to obtain the given number of spoiled lugs of peaches. The number of lugs of spoiled peaches then represents the percent of a number and matches the definition of percentage. The *percentage* model is drawn and the given information identified and entered.

PERCENTAGE MODEL

Number	%	Description
2200 (step 3)	1.00	Base/B%
×.12 (step 4)	×.12 (step 4 answer)	Percent/r
264 (step 2)	.12	Percentage/r

Step 2 The 264 lugs of spoiled peaches is identified as the *percentage* as this is the quantity that represents a percent of the total load of peaches.

Step 3 The 2200 lugs of peaches is identified as the *base number* as this number represents the whole to which the 264 lugs of spoiled peaches is to relate.

Step 4 The *percent or rate* is not given. The model format at this point, however, indicates the *base* and the *percentage* and therefore the percent can be obtained by dividing the product by one known factor:

Base   × percent = percentage
(Factor)   (Factor)   (Product)

or

$r = P \div B$
$r = 264 \div 2200 = 12\%$ (answer)

Example 4 **An item of merchandise is sold at 75% above cost. If the item cost $42, find the selling price.**

Solution:

Step 1 This problem gives a number which is to be increased by a given percent of itself. The "percent of itself," or the percent of a given number, matches the definition of *percentage*. If the *percentage* is then added to the *base* number, it matches the definition of *amount*. The amount model is drawn and the given terms identified and entered.

AMOUNT MODEL

Number		%		Description
42.00 (step 3)		1.00		Base/B%
+31.50 (step 4)		+ .75 (step 2)		Percentage/r
73.50	(step 5 answer)	1.75 (step 2)		Amount/A%

Step 2 The *percent or rate* is identified and placed in the model. The rate can then be added to the *B%* and the *A%* obtained.

Step 3 The cost of $42 is identified as the *base number* as this is the number to which the 75 percent relates.

Step 4 The *percentage* can then be calculated as now the *base number* and the *percent* are identified:

$P = Br$
$P = 42 \times .75 = \$31.50$

Step 5　After the percentage of $31.50 is entered in the model, the indicated arithmetical calculation is performed and the *amount* (sales price) is obtained.

　　　　Note: The *amount* could have been more directly calculated by multiplying the *base number* by the *A%* that was calculated in step 2:

Base × A% = Amount
42　× 1.75 = $73.50　　(answer)

Example 5　**A valve sells for $18.90, and this price is 26 percent above the cost price. Find the cost price.**

Solution:

Step 1　This problem requires finding an unknown quantity that when increased by a percent of itself will be equal to a given number. The given number then represents the sum of a base number and its percentage and matches the definition of amount. The amount model is then drawn and the given terms identified and entered.

AMOUNT MODEL

Number		%		Description
15.00	(step 5 answer)	1.00		Base/B%
+ 3.90	(step 5)	+ .26	(step 2)	Percentage/r
18.90	(step 4)	1.26	(step 2)	Amount/A%

Step 2　The percent or *r* is identified and is entered in the model. The *A%* can then be calculated.

Step 3　The base number is not given, but this is the quantity (the cost) to which the rate or 26 percent relates.

Step 4　The selling price of $18.90 represents the unknown base number plus the percentage, and is therefore identified and entered as the *amount*.

Step 5　Since the amount and the *A%* are known and displayed in the model, the unknown base number can be computed by dividing the product by one of the factors:

B　　× A%　　= A
(Factor)　(Factor)　(Product)

or

B = A ÷ A%
18.90 ÷ 1.26 = 15　　(answer)

When the base number is entered, the arithmetical procedures are completed and the percentage of $3.90 obtained.

Example 6 **A solution consisting of 18 kiloliters (kl) of a concentrate was diluted with water to produce a usable solution of 450 kl. How much water was added and what percent of the concentrate is represented by the quantity of water added?**

Solution:

Step 1 This problem gives a beginning and ending quantity and requests a rate or percent of increase on the beginning quantity. Since the base number and the amount are given, the amount model is selected and the terms entered as identified:

AMOUNT MODEL

Number	%	Description
18 (step 2)	1.00	Base/B%
(step 4 +432 1st answer)	(step 5 +24.00 2d answer)	Percentage/r
450 (step 3)	25.00	Amount/A%

Step 2 18 kl of concentrate is identified as the *base* as this is the number to which the water added is to relate, or of which the water added is the percentage.

Step 3 450 kl is identified as the *amount* as this is the quantity which results when the percentage is added to the base.

Step 4 The model format then indicates the calculation of the *percentage* and it is calculated and entered:

$$P = A - B$$
$$P - 450 - 18 = 432 \text{ kl} \qquad \text{(first answer)}$$

Step 5 Since the base number and percentage are now known, the percent or rate can be calculated:

$$r = P \div B$$
$$r = 432 \div 18 = 24 \quad (2400\%) \qquad \text{(second answer)}$$

Example 7 **Stu Fuller earns a gross monthly salary of $2400. If deductions for all purposes total 14 percent of gross earnings, how much money does Mr. Fuller "take home" each month?**

Solution:

Step 1 This problem gives a number which is to be reduced by a certain percent of itself. The problem therefore requires the calculation of the *percentage* and the *difference*. The difference model is drawn and the given terms identified and entered.

DIFFERENCE MODEL

Number		%		Description
2400 (step 2)		1.00		Base/B%
− 336 (step 4)		− .14 (step 3)		Percentage/r
2064	(step 5 answer)	.86		Difference/D%

Step 2   The $2400 gross earnings is identified and entered as the *base* number as this is the number to which the 14 percent relates.

Step 3   The 14 percent is identified as the *rate*.

Step 4   Since the base number and the percent or rate are now known, the *percentage* can be calculated:

$$P = B \times r$$
$$P = 2400 \times .14 = 336$$

Step 5   The model format then indicates the calculation of the *difference*, and the "take home" pay and final answer is obtained.

$$D = B - P$$
$$D = 2400 - 336 = \$2064 \quad \text{(answer)}$$

Example 8   **The Urban Enterprises reports a profit after income taxes of $60,000. If the tax rate is 40% of profit before income taxes, find the income taxes and the profit before income taxes.**

Solution:

Step 1   The $60,000 profit after taxes is the profit remaining after deducting a given percent from a base number. This matches the definition of *difference* and the difference model is drawn and the given terms identified and entered.

DIFFERENCE MODEL

Number		%		Description
100,000 (step 4 2d answer)		1.00		Base/B%
− 40,000 (step 5 1st answer)		− .40		Percentage/r
60,000 (step 2)		.60 (step 3)		Difference/D%

Step 2 The $60,000 is identified as the *difference* since this number represents the quantity remaining after 40 percent of the base number (profit before taxes) is deducted from the base number.

Step 3 The *percent (r)* is then identified and entered in the model and the subtraction performed to obtain the *D%*.

Step 4 The *base* number, the number to which the 40 percent relates, is not given. However, the difference and the *D%* are now known, and since $B \times D\% = D$, the base number can be obtained by dividing the product by one of the factors:

$$B = D \div D\%$$
$$B = 60,000 \div 60 = \$100,000 \qquad \text{(second answer)}$$

Step 5 The model format then indicates the calculation of the *percentage* and the final answer.

$$P = B - D$$
$$P = 100,000 - 60,000 = 40,000 \qquad \text{(first answer)}$$

Example 9 **The perpetual inventory records of the Anokhi Dress Shop indicated that $30,000 of merchandise should be on hand. An actual inventory of the merchandise disclosed that only $29,100 was on hand. Find the "shrinkage" of merchandise and the percent of shrinkage of the perpetual inventory.**

Solution:

Step 1 The $29,100 actual inventory represents the *difference* remaining after the "shrinkage" is subtracted from the perpetual inventory. The difference model is drawn and the given information identified and entered.

DIFFERENCE MODEL

Number		%		Description
30,000 (step 2)		1.00		Base/B%
− 900	(step 4 1st answer)	− .03	(step 5 2d answer)	Percentage/r
29,100 (step 3)		.97		Difference

Step 2 The $30,000 is identified as the *base* as this is the number to which the percent of shrinkage is to relate.

Step 3 The $29,100 is identified as the *difference* as this is the quantity of merchandise remaining after the "shrinkage" is subtracted from the perpetual inventory.

Step 4 The model format then indicates the calculation of the *percentage*.

$$P = B - D$$
$$P = 30,000 - 29,100 = 900 \qquad \text{(first answer)}$$

Step 5   Since the base and percentage are now known, the percent (factor) can be calculated by dividing the product by the other factor.

$r = P \div B$
$r = 900 \div 30,000 = 3\%$ (second answer)

Exercise 4.4

Identify the known and unknown terms, enter them in the appropriate calculation model, observe and study the semicompleted model, and proceed to the solution.

1   The present enrollment of the Blue Lake Elementary School is 92 percent of the enrollment for the previous year. Find the present enrollment if the enrollment for the previous year was 500 students.

2   Fat lambs will suffer a 6 percent weight loss while being shipped to market. Find the weight loss of a truckload of fat lambs that started their trip weighing 4000 kg.

3   Mr. Rocha lost $96, which was 20 percent of the sales price, on the sale of a case of rare wine. Find the sales price of the case of rare wine.

4   A fuel tank lost 176 liters of gasoline by evaporation. This loss represented 8 percent of the original contents. Find the number of liters of gasoline in the tank before evaporation.

5   A steer weighing 540 pounds was fed for 60 days and gained 180 pounds. Find the percent of gain of the steer's starting weight.

6   Genevieve Varnes had gross weekly earnings of $450. Her employer deducted $63 for federal income taxes. Find the percent of her gross earnings that were deducted for federal income taxes.

7   Daniel Leonard purchased a pair of calk logging boots for $80, and sold them one year later for 15 percent more than cost. Find the sales price of the boots.

8   A quantity of water representing 400 percent of the concentrate was used to dilute 200 liters of a fertilizer concentrate. Find the number of liters of usable fertilizer that was obtained.

9   A building lot is sold for $8500, which was 25 percent more than its cost. What was the cost of the lot?

10   Product Y decreases 16 percent in weight in the manufacturing process. If 3780 pounds of Product Y was manufactured, how many pounds of raw material were started in the manufacturing process?

11   A used car costing $1200 is sold for $1440. What percent of the cost price is represented by the profit?

12   David Matthew deposited $250 in the savings bank from the sale of his pig at the County Fair. One year later, and with no additional deposits or withdrawals, his savings account had grown to $270. What percent of growth on his original deposit did David earn?

13   Randy Smith weighed 130 kg when he commenced his diet. In the next six months, he reduced his weight by 22 percent. How many kilograms did Randy weigh at the end of the six-month period?

14 An engine tune-up decreased the gasoline consumption by 8 percent. If an automobile consumed 35 gallons of fuel in traveling from Eureka to Los Angeles before the tune-up, how many gallons would be consumed on the same trip after the tune-up?

15 An automobile now priced at $3612 has just been reduced by 14 percent of its original price. Find the original price.

16 The Arcata High School's current enrollment of 3000 students represents a 6 percent reduction of last year's enrollment. Find last year's enrollment.

17 A used car costing $1200 is sold for $1000. What percent of the cost price is represented by the loss?

18 The average stay of patients in a hospital was reduced from 4.5 days to 2.7 days. By what percent of the original number of days was the length of time reduced?

Unit 4.5

Adaptation of Percentage Calculation Models to Common Accounting Schedules and Statements

---

Up to this point, three calculation models were illustrated for finding the various terms used in problems in percentage; the *percentage model,* the *amount model,* and the *difference model.* The models were designed to present the precise sequence of the formulas to find the percentage, amount, and difference. The problem data was then identified and arranged to match that sequence. As soon as the numbers were identified with the percentage terms and visualized in the calculation models, the relationships of the numbers and their respective percentage terms should have turned on the light and illuminated the procedure to the solution.

One must learn to walk before trying to run. However, when the student is sufficiently knowledgeable in identifying and relating percentage terms from the use of the models and/or the formulas, it should no longer be necessary to rearrange the problem data into the format of the calculation models. It is sufficient merely to identify the quantities in any given format with their corresponding percentage term. Once so identified, the knowledge gained from the calculation models should be sufficient to proceed to the solution.

Procedure for Adapting Percentage Models to an Accounting Schedule

1 Using the particular accounting schedule as the basic format, add a column in which to write the labels of the related percentage term. (In due time and after solving several problems in percentage, the student can identify and relate the quantities in the accounting format to their

respective percentage terms without the need of actually labeling the quantities as the base, percentage, and amount or difference.)

2   From the problem data, enter the numbers opposite their accounting description. If a number is not given for a particular accounting term, leave that number line blank.

3   Identify the accounting description (with or without numbers) and write in the appropriate percentage term (base, percentage, amount, or difference).

4   Complete the more obvious blanks, observe and study the partially completed form, and then proceed to the solution.

Example 1   **The Buckhorn Tire Shop earns a margin of 35 percent on sales (sales − cost of goods sold = margin). If the margin for the current year is $21,000, find the sales and the cost of goods sold.**

Solution:

Step 1   An appropriate accounting schedule is drawn and the given information entered and identified:

Accounting terms	Number	%	Percentage terms
Sales	_____	1.00 (step 1a)	Base (step 1a)
Less cost of goods sold	− _____	− _____	Percentage/r (step 1c)
Margin	21,000 (step 1b)	.35 (step 1b)	Difference/D% (step 1b)

(a)   The most important percentage identification to be made is the number or accounting term which represents the *base*. In this problem, sales can be identified as the *base* since sales is the term to which the 35 percent relates (". . . 35 percent *on sales*").

(b)   The $21,000 and 35 percent are then entered opposite their respective accounting terms. The margin and the 35 percent are then identified as the *difference* and D%. These quantities can be so identified since they represent that which remains when a quantity (the cost of goods sold) is subtracted from the base number (sales).

(c)   Since the base, difference and D% are now identified, the *cost of goods sold* can be identified as the *percentage* and *percent*. The arithmetical calculation can be performed in the % column and the percent (r) obtained.

Step 2   The model now indicates that $21,000 is 35 percent of the base and therefore the *base number* (and *sales*) can be calculated and entered.

Base = Difference ÷ D%
Base = $21,000 ÷ .35 = $60,000

Step 3   After the base number (sales) of $60,000 is entered, the remaining arithmetical procedure indicated in the model is completed and the final answer obtained.

Accounting terms	Number	%	Percentage terms
Sales	60,000 (step 2)	1.00 (step 1a)	Base (step 1a)
Less cost of goods sold	−39,000 (step 3)	− .65 (step 1c)	Percentage/r (step 1c)
Margin	21,000 (step 1b)	.35 (step 1b)	Difference/D% (step 1b)

Example 2   **A used car is purchased for $1000 and is marked up to sell for a profit margin of 25 percent of sales. Find the sales price and the proposed profit margin.**

Solution:

Step 1   The appropriate accounting schedule is drawn and the given data entered and identified.

Accounting terms	Number	%	Percentage terms
Sales	1333 (step 2)	1.00 (step 1a)	Base (step 1a)
Less cost of goods sold	1000 (step 1b)	− .75 (step 1c)	Percentage/r (step 1c)
Margin	333 (step 3)	.25 (step 1b)	Difference/D% (step 1b)

(a)   Sales is identified as the *base* since this is the term to which the profit margin is to relate (". . . to sell for a margin of 25 percent *of sales*").

(b)   The cost of $1000 is entered opposite its accounting term (cost of goods sold), and .25 is entered opposite the margin line in the % column. The margin term and the .25 are then identified as the *difference* and *D%*. These quantities can be so identified because they represent that which remains after a quantity is subtracted from the base.

(c)   The $1000 is then identified as the *percentage* since it is the number which is subtracted from the base to obtain the difference. The *percent* (*r*) can then be calculated by performing the indicated arithmetical procedure in the % column.

$$1.00 - ?   = .25$$
$$1.00 - .75 = .25$$

Step 2   The model now indicates that $1000 is 75 percent of base (and sales) and therefore the *base* can be calculated and entered:

Base = Percentage ÷ r
Base = 1000 ÷ .75 = $1333

Step 3   After the base number (sales) is entered, the arithmetical procedure indicated in the number column is completed and the final answer obtained.

$1333 − 1000 = $333

Example 3   **The employees of the Mad River Angus Farm receive a bonus of 24 percent of the profit after the bonus is subtracted from the profit before bonus. If the profit before bonus was $186,000, find the bonus received by the employees.**

Solution:

Step 1   An appropriate accounting schedule is drawn and the given data entered and identified:

Accounting terms	Number	%	Percentage terms
Profit before bonus	$186,000 (step 1c)	1.24 (step 1c)	Amount/A% (step 1d)
Less bonus	− 36,000 (step 3)	− .24 (step 1b)	Percentage/r (step 1b)
Profit after bonus	$150,000 (step 2)	1.00 (step 1a)	Base (step 1a)

(a)   Profit after bonus is identified as the *base* since this is the term to which the bonus percent relates (". . . a bonus of 24 percent *of the profit after the bonus is subtracted . . .*").

(b)   The 24 percent is entered on the bonus line in the % column and the bonus line identified as the *percentage/r.* These identifications can be made since the bonus is derived by multiplying the base number by the percent. This procedure matches the definition of percentage:

$P = B \times r$

(c)   The 186,000 is entered opposite its accounting term profit before bonus. The arithmetic procedure indicated in the % column is performed.

? − .24 = 1.00
1.24 − .24 = 1.00

(d) The profit before bonus line is then identified as the *amount* and *A%* because the profit before bonus is obtained by adding the percentage (bonus) to the base number (profit after bonus).

Step 2 The model now indicates the amount and the *A%* and the *base* can be calculated and entered:

Base = Amount ÷ A%
Base = 186,000 ÷ 1.24 = 150,000

Step 3 After the base number (profit after bonus) is entered, the arithmetical procedure indicated in the number column is completed and the percentage (bonus) obtained.

$186,000 − ? = $150,000
186,000 − 36,000 = 150,000

Note that once the base number and the percent become known after step 1c, the percentage (bonus) could have been calculated:

$P = B \times r$
$P = 150,000 \times .24 = 36,000$

Example 4 **The Baird Bulb Farms sold some excess fertilizer for $481.60 which resulted in a loss of $78.40 on the original purchase price. Find the percent of loss on the original purchase price.**

Solution:

Step 1 The accounting schedule is drawn with the given information entered and identified as follows:

Accounting terms	Number	%	Percentage terms
Sales	$481.60 (step 1b)	.86	Difference/D% (step 1b)
Less purchase price	−560.00 (step 1b)	−1.00 (step 1a)	Base (step 1a)
Profit (loss)*	(78.40) (step 1b)	(−.14) (step 2)	Percentage/r (step 1b)

* Parentheses denote loss.

(a) The purchase price can be identified as the *base* since this is the term to which the percent of loss is to relate ("Find the percent of loss *on the original purchase price*").

(b) The $481.60 and (78.40) are entered opposite their respective accounting terms. The arithmetical procedure indicated in the number column is performed and the quantity $560.00 obtained for the base number. The loss of $78.40 can be identified as the *percentage* since this quantity is derived by multiplying the base number by percent. The sales price of $481.60 can be identified as the *difference* since this is the quantity that remains when the percentage (loss of $78.40) is subtracted from the base number (purchase price of $560).

Step 2   The partially completed model now indicates that the percentage and the base number are known. The *percent* can then be calculated:

$$r = P \div B$$
$$r = 78.40 \div 560 = .14$$

Step 3   Although not required in the problem, the arithmetical procedure in the % column is performed and .86 obtained on the sales line for the D%. Due to the accounting format selected, a negative number appeared and the illustrated solution may appear cumbersome. However, negative numbers do appear in accounting schedules and statements, and business students must be able to cope with them. If the accounting schedule had been rearranged so as to eliminate the negative number, the same solution would have been calculated as follows:

Accounting terms	Number	%	Percentage terms
Purchase price	$560.00 (step 1b)	1.00 (step 1d)	Base (step 1a)
Less loss on purchase price	− 78.40 (step 1b)	− .14 (step 2)	Percentage/r (step 1b)
Sales price	481.60 (step 1b)	.86 (step 3)	Difference/D% (step 1b and step 3)

Example 5   **The profit and loss statement of the Stephen Enterprises indicated that the profit margin on sales was 40 percent of sales, and percent of profit before income taxes was 15 percent of sales. If the profit before income taxes was $36,750, find the sales, the cost of sales, margin on sales and the operating expenses.**

Solution:

Step 1   The accounting statement is drawn and the given terms identified and entered:

Accounting terms	Number	%	Percentage terms
Sales	$245,000 (step 2)	1.00 (step 1a)	Base (step 1a)
Less cost of goods sold	147,000 (step 3)	.60 (step 1c)	Percentage/r (step 1b)
Margin on sales	98,000 (step 3)	.40 (step 1b)	Difference/D% (step 1b)
Less operating expenses	61,250 (step 3)	.25 (step 1c)	Percentage/r (step 1b)
Profit before income taxes	36,750 (step 1a)	.15 (step 1b)	Difference/D% (step 1b)

(a) Sales is identified as the *base* since this is the term to which the percent figures relate (". . . margin on sales was 40 percent *of sales* . . . profit before income taxes was 15 percent *of sales*").

(b) The given percents and the number for profit before income taxes are entered opposite their respective accounting terms. The profit before income taxes and the margin on sales are identified as the *difference/D%* since they represent quantities remaining after certain numbers are subtracted from the base. The operating expenses and cost of goods sold are identified as *percentage/r* since these quantities are obtained by multiplying the base by a percent of the base.

(c) The arithmetical procedure is completed in the % column and *.60* is obtained for *r* opposite cost of goods sold, and *.25* is obtained for *r* opposite operating expenses.

Step 2 Observation of the partially completed model at this stage indicates that the *difference* and *D%* are known (profit before income taxes). The base number (sales) can then be calculated:

$$B = D \div D\%$$
$$B = \$36,750 \div .15 = \$245,000$$

Step 3 Once the base is known, the remaining quantities can be calculated:

$$\text{Cost of goods sold} = Br = 245,000 \times .60 = 147,000$$
$$\text{Margin on sales} = B - P = 245,000 - 147,000 = 98,000$$

or

$$B \times D\% = 245,000 \times .40 = 98,000$$
$$\text{Operating expenses} = Br = 245,000 \times .25 = 61,250$$

Exercise 4.5

Draw the appropriate accounting schedule, enter the given quantities opposite their respective accounting terms, identify the accounting term with its appropriate percentage term, observe the semicompleted model, and then proceed to the solution.

1   Elmer's Market budgets for a 25 percent profit margin on sales. If the sales were budgeted at $275,000, find budgeted profit margin on sales.

2   The Whitely Tire Company sells fuel for a profit margin of 20 percent on sales. If a sale amounted to $288.20, find the profit margin.

3   The sales tax rate in a certain state is 6 percent of the sales price. Find the sales price if the sales taxes paid were $1.74.

4   Mike Strahan has 14 percent deducted from his total earnings for federal income tax. If the deduction was $115.36, find his total earnings.

5   A dealer in used cars purchased two cars, each at a cost of $1500. He sold one at a gain of 25 percent of the sales price and the other at a loss of 25 percent of the sales price. Find the total gain or loss on the two cars. (*Hint:* Draw a calculation model for each car.)

6   A wholesaler purchased two items of machinery, each at a cost of $2250. He sold one item at a loss of $\frac{3}{8}$ of the cost price, and the other at a profit of $\frac{2}{3}$ of the sales price. Find the total profit or loss. (*Hint:* Convert the common fractions to percent and proceed with the calculation models.)

7   A wholesaler sold a violin that cost him $65 for a price which was 350 percent of his cost. Find the selling price and his profit margin.

8   If merchandise costs $1234.50, find the markup and the selling price if the markup is 80 percent of the cost.

9   A redwood furniture manufacturer produces tables at a cost of $90 each. His operating expenses are 30 percent of sales. If he wants to make a profit of 25 percent of sales, find the necessary sales price of the table.

10   The cash operating expenses of a commercial rental were 40 percent of total rents. If the only other cash outflow was the mortgage payment of $500 per month, for how much would the landlord have to rent the property to obtain a net cash inflow before taxes of $220 per month?

11   Total sales of a store were $92,340, but return sales and allowances (total sales — return sales and allowances = net sales) were 8 percent of net sales. Find the net sales.

12   A salesman received $96.25 for selling a vacuum cleaner for $275. What rate of commission on the sales price did the salesman receive?

13   LaFenetre Dress Shop earns a profit which represents a 22 percent return on the owners' investment. If the profit earned was $19,800, what was the amount of the owners' investment?

14   A taxpayer pays income taxes at the rate of 35 percent of his taxable income (taxable income × tax rate = income taxes). If the taxpayer wanted to reduce his income taxes by $4200, by how much would he have to reduce his taxable income?

15   In the processing of coffee beans, it is discovered that coffee beans lose 12 percent in the roasting process. How many grams of coffee beans must be roasted to yield 1 kg of roasted coffee beans?

16   One hundred grams of apples will yield 75 ml of apple cider. How many grams of apples must be run through the cider press to yield 1 kl of cider?

Part Two

Essentials of Business Mathematics

Chapter 5

Simple Interest

Objectives To Be Achieved in This Chapter

1 *To calculate time used in interest problems.*
2 *To develop and use the more common formulas in calculating simple interest.*
3 *To develop and illustrate interest factor tables used by bankers and others who work frequently with simple interest.*
4 *To find simple-interest rates, time, principal and amount through adaptations of the simple-interest formula.*

Unit 5.1   *Types of Interest;*
                                              Calculation of Time

Interest is rent paid for the use of money.[1] As investors, people rent their savings for use by banks, credit unions, large corporations, and other financial institutions. As borrowers, people and business firms rent money from these same banks, credit unions, etc., to purchase homes, cars, and furniture and acquire commercial loans. People and business firms also acquire goods and services on credit (use now—pay later). The money paid for the use of this money and credit is called *interest*. The calculation of interest is similar to the calculation of percentage—with the added factor of *time*.

Types of Interest

There are two basic methods in general use today for calculating interest: (1) simple interest and (2) compound interest. *Simple interest* is interest on the amount invested or borrowed at a given rate and for a given time. *Compound interest* involves not only the interest on the amount invested or borrowed, but also includes interest on interest as it is earned over time. Compound interest measures the *time* value of money more accurately than does simple interest and is used extensively in many areas of business such as repayment schedules of loans, pension plans, valuation of bonds, criteria for choice among alternative investments, and many others. Calculation in and applications of compound interest are presented in Chapter 6. Simple interest, however, is in wide use among businesses and individuals for certain types of loans and credit.

Calculation of Time in Interest Calculations

Time is the number of years, months, and/or days for which interest may be earned or charged on a sum of money invested or borrowed. *Time is a factor in every interest calculation*. In the modern business world the passage of time is determined by the *Gregorian calendar* and is based on the true solar year of 365 days, 5 hr, 48 min, and 46 sec, or almost $365\frac{1}{4}$ days, the time the earth takes for a complete revolution around the sun. Because of this fractional part of a day, an extra day is added to the years *divisible by 4 without remainder*. The extra day is added to the month of February. Thus every fourth year has 366 days instead of 365 and is called a leap year. Adding 1 day every 4 years is a little too much, and adds approximately 3 extra days every 450 years. A correction is made by considering only century years

---

[1] In previous editions of this text, bank discount was presented in a separate chapter. *Bank discount* was defined as interest calculated on the amount due at maturity for an exact number of days at a given rate (the so called interest taken-out-in-advance type of note). Many problems were presented to students to distinguish this type of loan and to compare its interest rates and amount with loans which stated and calculated interest on the amount actually borrowed. Regulation Z of the Federal Truth and Lending Law required the Annual Percentage Rate (the actual rate on the amount borrowed) to be calculated and clearly stated on each loan. This requirement changed the method by which banks negotiate and write such loans. The previous material on bank discount has either been eliminated or included with other chapters where appropriate.

divisible by 400 without remainder as a leap year. Thus the years 1800 and 1900, although divisible by 4 without remainder, were not leap years because they were not divisible by 400 without remainder. The year 2000, however, will be a leap year. Even this correction leaves a variation from the true solar year of 1 day in approximately 20,000 years. However, for practical purposes, the Gregorian calendar is sufficiently accurate.

Because some methods of interest calculation call for the exact number of days between two dates and because all the months do not have the same number of days, it is necessary that the student know the number of days in each month. Also, because dates are often written with the number of the month instead of its name (8/5/77 instead of August 5, 1977),[1] and because numbering the month facilitates the determination of the exact number of days when starting and ending dates fall in different months, it is also necessary to know the month number.

Table 5.1 presents the month numbers and number of days in each month. To calculate time in interest calculations, all students should commit the information in Table 5.1 to memory and be able to recall it instantly.

If the time in dated years is stated, it must be determined whether any are leap years. Unless otherwise stated, February is to be considered as having 28 days. The old rhyme

Thirty days hath September,
April, June, and November;
All the rest have thirty-one,
Excepting February alone,
Which hath but twenty-eight, in fine,
Till leap year gives it twenty-nine.

[1] Dates written within military organizations and in some countries have the day of the month first, the month second, and the year third. Thus August 5, 1977 is written as 5 August 1977. When converting this order to number of the months, confusion may arise unless you are aware of the source of the date. Thus does 5/8/77 mean May 8, 1977 *or* 5 August 1977?

TABLE 5.1   MONTHS AND NUMBERS OF DAYS IN EACH MONTH IN THE GREGORIAN CALENDAR

Calendar quarters	Month number	Month name	Abbreviation	Number of days
First	1	January	Jan.	31
	2	February	Feb.	28 (or 29 in leap years)*
	3	March	Mar.	31
Second	4	April	Apr.	30
	5	May	May	31
	6	June	June	30
Third	7	July	July	31
	8	August	Aug.	31
	9	September	Sept.	30
Fourth	10	October	Oct.	31
	11	November	Nov.	30
	12	December	Dec.	31

* Leap years are years divisible by 4 without remainder, and those century years which can also be divided by 400 without remainder.

was intended to facilitate the memorization of the number of days in each month.[1]

Methods of Computing Time

Since several methods are used to calculate time, it is necessary that you understand the different ways by which time is determined in actual business practice. Two measurements of time in common use are (1) 30-day-month time and (2) exact time.

THIRTY-DAY-MONTH TIME   The year is considered as 360 days, divided into 12 months of 30 days each. Each month, quarter, half-year, or year is considered as having the same number of days as a corresponding period, thus simplifying the comparison of one period with another.

Thirty-day-month time is used most frequently for long-term loans in which periodic payments are made on both principal and interest. Typical examples of periodic-payment plans include certain forms of personal borrowing, real estate loans, and obligations arising out of the purchase of such items as home furnishings, clothing, jewelry, or automobiles. In such instances, interest charges for each month are computed upon the assumption that each month contains 30 days and is $\frac{1}{12}$ year (regardless of whether the month actually is 28, 29, 30, or 31 days). Thirty-day-month time is sometimes called "bond time" because it is always used in computing interest accruing to the seller of corporate bonds.

USUAL METHOD OF COMPUTING 30-DAY-MONTH TIME   In calculating short periods of time, particularly those of less than 1 year, the usual method of computation is recommended.

1   *When the stipulated date of the earlier month* (date of origin) *is less than the stipulated date of the later month* (due date), determine the time in whole months (each considered as 30 days) from the date of the earlier month to the same date in the later month. To this number add the difference between the stipulated dates of the earlier month and the later month.

Example 1   **Find the time from May 17 to August 26.**

5/17 to 8/17 = 3 months =   90 days
Plus 26 − 17   = + 9 days
                Time =   99 days

[1] Counting the months on your doubled-up fist is another way of determining the number of days in each month. On the fist of either hand, count January on the top of the first knuckle (forefinger), February is between the first and second knuckle, March on top of the second knuckle, April between the second and third knuckle, etc., until you arrive at July on top of the fourth knuckle (little finger). Continue with August on the top of the fourth knuckle, September in between the fourth and third knuckles, October on top of the third knuckle, etc., through December. The months falling on top the knuckles have 31 days; the months falling in between the knuckles have 30 days, except February, which has 28 in regular years and 29 in leap years.

2 *When the stipulated date of the earlier month* (date of origin) *is greater than the stipulated date of the later month* (due date), determine the time in whole months (each considered as 30 days) from the date of the earlier month to the same date in the later month. From this number subtract the difference between the stipulated dates of the earlier month and the later month.

Example 2   **Find the time from May 17 to August 6.**

5/17 to 8/17 = 3 months =   90 days
Less 17 − 6   = −11 days
                Time =   79 days

In counting, notice that the first day is not counted, but that the last day is included in the total. Also notice that in the preceding examples both May and July, although actually having 31 days, are considered as 30-day months. This is also true of the other 31-day months; and February, whether it has 28 or 29 days, is also considered as a 30-day month *if* 30-day-month time is used.

COMPOUND-TIME METHOD OF COMPUTING 30-DAY-MONTH TIME   In calculating long periods of time, particularly those in excess of 1 year, the compound-time method of computation is recommended.

In computing the elapsed time period at 30-day-month time by the compound-time method, change the date of origin if 31 (days) to 30 unless both date of origin and maturity (due) date are 31 (see Example 4 following).

Example 3   **Find the number of days at 30-day-month time from November 16, 1975 to May 9, 1980.**

Year	Month	Day
	16	
79	4̸	39
19̸8̸0̸	5̸	9̸
−1975	−11	−16
4 years	5 months	23 days
(1440 days) +	(150 days) +	(23 days) = 1613 days

Since 16 days cannot be subtracted from 9 days, 1 month or 30 days is borrowed from the month column, making 4 the number of months and 39 the number of days. Since 11 months cannot be subtracted from 4 months, 1 year or 12 months is borrowed from the year column, making 1979 the number of years and 16 the number of months.

At this point, the problem is merely that of subtraction and conversion of the remainders in years, months, and days to their equivalent total of days.

Example 4   **Find the number of days at 30-day-month time from October 31, 1895 to June 8, 1899.**

Year	Month	Day
	17	
98	5̶	38
189̶9̶	6̶	8̶
−1895	−10	−3̶1̶ 30[1]
3 years	7 months	8 days
(1080 days) +	(210 days) +	(8 days) = 1298 days

[1] *Note:* 31 days is changed to 30 days in 30-day-month time.

EXACT TIME   Exact time is the actual number of days. It is the time basis used for most interest calculations, and in general may be said to be used for most loans except real estate loans and installment loans.

Since loans other than security loans, government obligations, real estate loans, and installment loans rarely extend over time periods in excess of a few months, it is usually not necessary to calculate exact time (with the exception of security loans and government obligations) for periods in excess of 120 to 180 days.

When exact time is used, as with 30-day-month time, the first day is excluded and the last day included in the total. Merely subtracting the first day from the last day accomplishes this result. The following examples emphasize the need of knowing the number of days in each month and whether February has 28 or 29 days.

Example 5   **Find the exact time from June 4 to September 2.**

	Exact days
Remaining days in June (30 − 4)	26
July	31
August	31
September	2
Exact time total	90 days

Example 6   **Find the exact time from January 15, 1976 to April 15, 1976.**

	Exact days
Remaining days in January (31 − 15)	16
February (1976 was a leap year)[1]	29
March	31
April	15
Exact time total	91 days

[1] 1976 ÷ 4 = 494

THE DATE OF ORIGIN AND THE DUE DATE OF A LOAN   The *date* (or date of origin) of a loan is the date on which the loan is incurred.

The *due date* (or maturity date) of a loan is the date on which the loan is due and payable.

The time of a loan is frequently expressed in either of two ways: (1) a specified number of days, (2) a specified number of months or years.

WHEN TIME OF A NOTE IS EXPRESSED IN DAYS   The time period of most loans is expressed as a stipulated number of days from the date of the loan. Thus the due date of a 30-day loan is exactly 30 days after date; the due date of a 72-day loan is exactly 72 days after date; etc.

Example 7   **Find the due date of a 30-day loan dated June 25.**

Total days	30
Less days remaining in June (30 − 25)	− 5
Remaining days	25

Since the number of remaining days is less than the number of days in the following month (July), the due date is July 25.

Example 8   **Find the due date of a 90-day loan dated August 17.**

Total days	90
Less remaining days in August (31 − 17)	−14
Remainder	76
Days in September	− 30
Remainder	46
Days in October	− 31
Remainder	15
Due date	November 15

CALCULATING TIME AND DUE DATES FROM TABLES   Lending agencies and other businesses having frequent need to calculate elapsed days, save time and ensure greater accuracy by utilizing one or more of the several types of calendar-day tables that are available. Table 5.2 is an example of such a table used to determine the exact number of days. The table is also used to determine the due date of a loan.

FINDING EXACT NUMBER OF DAYS   For determining the exact number of days between two given dates, Table 5.2 is used as follows:

1   In the left-hand column find the day of the month corresponding to the date of maturity, and read horizontally to locate the day of the year underneath the month of maturity.
2   In the left-hand column find the day of the month corresponding to the date of origin, and read horizontally to locate the day of the year underneath the month of origin.
3   Subtract the figure obtained in (2) from the figure obtained in (1).

TABLE 5.2 NUMBER OF THE DAYS IN A CALENDAR YEAR
If a leap year, add 1 day to the terminal date if the time period includes February 29

Day of month	J	F	M	A	M	J	J	A	S	O	N	D
1	1	32	60	91	121	152	182	213	244	274	305	335
2	2	33	61	92	122	153	183	214	245	275	306	336
3	3	34	62	93	123	154	184	215	246	276	307	337
4	4	35	63	94	124	155	185	216	247	277	308	338
5	5	36	64	95	125	156	186	217	248	278	309	339
6	6	37	65	96	126	157	187	218	249	279	310	340
7	7	38	66	97	127	158	188	219	250	280	311	341
8	8	39	67	98	128	159	189	220	251	281	312	342
9	9	40	68	99	129	160	190	221	252	282	313	343
10	10	41	69	100	130	161	191	222	253	283	314	344
11	11	42	70	101	131	162	192	223	254	284	315	345
12	12	43	71	102	132	163	193	224	255	285	316	346
13	13	44	72	103	133	164	194	225	256	286	317	347
14	14	45	73	104	134	165	195	226	257	287	318	348
15	15	46	74	105	135	166	196	227	258	288	319	349
16	16	47	75	106	136	167	197	228	259	289	320	350
17	17	48	76	107	137	168	198	229	260	290	321	351
18	18	49	77	108	138	169	199	230	261	291	322	352
19	19	50	78	109	139	170	200	231	262	292	323	353
20	20	51	79	110	140	171	201	232	263	293	324	354
21	21	52	80	111	141	172	202	233	264	294	325	355
22	22	53	81	112	142	173	203	234	265	295	326	356
23	23	54	82	113	143	174	204	235	266	296	327	357
24	24	55	83	114	144	175	205	236	267	297	328	358
25	25	56	84	115	145	176	206	237	268	298	329	359
26	26	57	85	116	146	177	207	238	269	299	330	360
27	27	58	86	117	147	178	208	239	270	300	331	361
28	28	59	87	118	148	179	209	240	271	301	332	362
29	29		88	119	149	180	210	241	272	302	333	363
30	30		89	120	150	181	211	242	273	303	334	364
31	31		90		151		212	243		304		365

Note: If the time period extends from one year into the following year, add 365 days to the number of the maturity date found in step (1).

Example 9   **Find the exact time from June 5 to August 27.**

Date	Day number
August 27	239
June 5	−156
Exact number of days	83 days

Example 10 **Find the exact time from January 24, 1976 to April 29, 1976.**

Date	Day number
April 29, 1976	119
Add 1 day for leap year	+ 1
	120
January 24, 1976	− 24
Exact number of days	96 days

Example 11 **Find the exact time from September 21 to May 7 of the following year.**

Date	Day number
May 7	127
Add 365 for extending into the next year	+365
	492
September 21	−264
Exact number of days	228 days

FINDING DUE DATE To determine the due date of a loan for an exact number of days, Table 5.2 is used as follows:

1 In the left-hand column find the day of the month corresponding to the date of origin and read horizontally to locate the day of the year underneath the month of origin.
2 Add the number of exact days of the loan to the number of the day of origin. The sum is the number of the day of maturity.
3 Locate the number of the day of maturity in the table. The due date is the month listed at the top of the column of the day of maturity, and the day listed in the left-hand column opposite the day of maturity.

Note: If the sum of the day of origin and the term of the note found in (2) exceeds 365, the maturity date then falls in the next year. Subtract 365 from the sum and proceed with (3). If the term of the loan includes the date of February 29 of a leap year, subtract 1 day from the number of the maturity day before finding the maturity date in (3).

Example 12 **Find the maturity date of a 90-day loan dated August 8.**

Date	Day number
August 8	220
Add terms of loan	+ 90
Day number of maturity date	310
Maturity date is	November 6

Example 13 **Find the maturity date of a 180-day loan dated November 14.**

	Date	Day number
November 14		318
Add term of loan		+180
Subtotal (exceeds 365 days)		498
Less		−365
Day number of maturity date		133
Maturity date is		May 13

Example 14 **Find the maturity date of a 60-day loan dated February 5, 1976.**

	Date	Day number
February 5, 1976		36
Add term of loan		+60
Subtotal		96
Less 1 day for leap year		− 1
Day number of maturity date		95
Maturity date is		April 5

WHEN TIME OF A NOTE IS EXPRESSED IN MONTHS (OR YEARS)   If the time period of a loan is expressed as a specified number of months (or years), the due date of the loan is found by 30-day-month time. Thus the due date of a 1-month loan dated January 25 would be February 25; the due date of a 3-month loan dated June 7 would be September 7; etc.

If there is not the required number of days in the maturity month, the maturity date is the *last day* of the maturity month. Thus a 1-month loan dated January 31 is due on February 28 (or February 29 in a leap year). And a 4-month loan dated May 31 will fall due on September 30.

Likewise, a 1-year loan falls due on the same day (date) of the following year; a 2-year loan falls due on the same day (date) of the second year following; etc.

Take special note that, *even though the maturity date is established by 30-day-month time, the number of days at interest may be computed by either 30-day-month time or exact time,* the latter being the more frequently used for short-term business and commercial bank transactions.

WHEN THE DUE DATE IS A NONBUSINESS DAY   If the due date of a loan falls on a nonbusiness day, such as a Sunday or legal holiday, the due date is considered to be the first business day following, and the additional day or days are added to the period for which interest is charged. Thus if a 90-day loan falls due on December 25, the note is considered as due December 26 (if a business day) and interest is charged for 91 days. Similarly, if the due date falls on a Sunday, interest is considered as due the first business day following, and the additional day or days are added to the interest period. In many states, Saturdays as well as Sundays are nonbusiness days.

Example 15 **Find the due date on a 2-month loan dated November 1.**

Two months after November 1 is January 1.
But January 1 is a legal holiday.
        Therefore the due date is January 2 (if a business day), and interest is charged for 61 days if 30-day-month time is used or for 62 days if exact time is used.

Example 16 **Find the due date on a 90-day loan dated April 5.**

Date	Day number
Total days	90
Less days remaining in April (30 − 5)	− 25
Remainder	65
Days in May	− 31
Remainder	34
Days in June	− 30
Remainder	4
Maturity date	July 5

        Ordinarily, the maturity date would be July 4. But July 4 is a holiday, and the due date would be July 5 (if a business day), and interest would be charged for 91 days.

Exercise 5.1

In computing time in the following exercise, assume January 1, July 4, and December 25 due dates to be the only nonbusiness days.

Find 30-day-month time by the usual method:

	Date of origin	Maturity (due) date
1	June 3, 1977	December 26, 1977
2	September 4, 1977	February 12, 1978
3	August 22, 1977	March 25, 1978
4	September 18, 1977	December 12, 1977
5	May 14, 1978	October 10, 1978
6	November 30, 1978	March 31, 1979

Find the 30-day-month time by the compound-time method in (a) years, months, and days and (b) total number of days:

	Date of origin	Maturity date
7	April 15, 1977	June 30, 1980
8	January 14, 1972	September 20, 1974
9	May 10, 1978	January 4, 1981
10	October 4, 1976	March 16, 1980
11	November 16, 1975	October 5, 1978
12	September 15, 1977	April 10, 1979

Find the exact time by the manual method (do not use Table 5.2):

	Date of origin	Maturity date
13	January 15, 1977	April 15, 1977
14	September 15, 1976	April 15, 1977
15	June 15, 1976	April 15, 1977
16	October 10, 1978	January 22, 1979
17	January 22, 1976	June 3, 1976
18	November 16, 1977	March 14, 1978

Find the exact time by use of Table 5.2:

	Date of origin	Date of maturity
19	May 16, 1977	November 16, 1977
20	February 3, 1952	September 3, 1952
21	July 18, 1978	December 14, 1978
22	February 12, 1976	February 4, 1977
23	December 14, 1978	March 8, 1979
24	November 22, 1979	April 10, 1980

Find the due dates:

	Date of origin	Time		Date of origin	Time
25	July 8	3 months	26	February 25	6 months
27	May 19	2 months	28	October 6	9 months
29	4/15	5 months	30	3/18	4 months

Find the due dates by the manual method (do not use Table 5.2):

	Date of origin	Time		Date of origin	Time
31	November 4	90 days	32	April 10	60 days
33	December 12	30 days	34	October 16	180 days
35	February 14, 1976	45 days	36	January 15, 1977	120 days

Find the due dates by use of Table 5.2:

	Date of origin	Time		Date of origin	Time
37	April 16	60 days	38	August 17	90 days
39	February 4, 1980	120 days	40	January 12, 1980	180 days
41	December 6, 1979	45 days	42	November 16, 1979	150 days

Unit 5.2   *Fraction and Cancellation Method and Dollar-Day Method of Computing Simple Interest; Maturity Value*

Calculations in simple interest are the same as finding the *percentage*, and then multiplying the *percentage* by a time factor expressed either in years, or a fraction of a year, or both. Most simple interest calculations are for periods of time less than one year, but there are numerous instances when simple interest calculations are needed for time periods in excess of one year.

Terms and Symbols Used in Simple Interest

Term and symbol	Definition
Principal (*P*)	The amount invested or borrowed. Principal is the same as the *base number* that was used in problems in percentage. Principal is also known as the *present value* in simple interest.
Rate (*r*)	The amount of money charged for every $100 of principal. It is expressed as a percent (%), means the same, and is used in calculations the same as the percent or rate in percentage problems.
Time (*t*)	The length of time that interest is being earned or charged on the principal at the specified rate. Time may be expressed in years, months, or days, but is used in the simple interest formula in terms of years or a fraction thereof.
Interest (*I*)	The amount of money charged for the use of the principal for a specified time at a given rate.
Exact (accurate) interest	The interest amount that is found when time is computed in exact days and a 365 day year is used in the interest formula. At the present time this method is the most common for individual loans.
Ordinary interest at exact time	The interest amount that is found when time is computed in exact days but a 360-day year is used in the interest formula.
Ordinary interest at 30-day-month time	The interest amount that is found when time is computed by 30 day-month time and a 360-day year is used in the interest formula.
Maturity value (*S*)	The sum of the principal and the interest at the given rate and for the specified time. The maturity value is similar to *amount* in percentage. Maturity value is also known as *future value*.

Formulas for Calculating Simple Interest

Simple interest is the product of the *principal* × *rate* × *time*. Expressed as a formula with the symbols given above, it is

$$I = Prt$$

As a consequence of the different methods of computing time (*t* in the above formula) three different amounts can be computed for simple interest on the same principal and interest rate.

Example 1   **Find the simple interest on $1000 at 9 percent from April 30 to June 30 by:**
(a) Exact interest
(b) Ordinary interest at exact time
(c) Ordinary interest at 30-day-month time

(a) Exact interest (exact time is 61 days)

$$\$1000 \times 9\% \times \frac{61}{365} = \$15.04$$

(b) Ordinary interest at exact time:

$$\$1000 \times 9\% \times \frac{61}{360} = \$15.25$$

(c) Ordinary interest at 30-day-month time (30-day-month time is 60 days)

$$\$1000 \times 9\% \times \frac{60}{360} = \$15.00$$

A theoretically possible but never used hybrid is with time computed by 30-day-month time and with a 365-day year used in the interest formula.

Ordinary interest with 30-day-month time or exact time as the numerator, and 360 as the denominator for *t*, is used primarily for commercial-type loans and mortgage payments.

Whether 30-day-month or exact time is used depends primarily upon custom, although in general, *ordinary interest at 30-day-month time* is used only for periodic-repayment plans such as monthly payments on real estate mortgages, installment purchases, and certain types of personal borrowing and in computing accrued interest on corporate bonds. *Ordinary interest at exact time* is commonly used for most commercial, industrial, and personal notes.

As is readily apparent, the lender gains 5 days additional interest yearly by the use of ordinary interest at exact time (365 days for the numerator and 360 days for the denominator). The gaining of the 5 days interest (6 days in leap years) has been the subject of controversy between borrowers and lenders. As you can observe from the example above, ordinary interest at exact time results in the most interest. When millions of dollars are loaned by this method, the lenders stand to gain considerably.

Exact (or accurate) interest, although not customary in most business transactions and personal loans, is sometimes used when the borrower is in an advantageous position. Interest payments on government obligations (rediscounting of notes for member banks by Federal Reserve banks) are calculated on the basis of the 365-day year. The interest payment is $\frac{5}{365}$, or $\frac{1}{73}$, less than when interest is computed as ordinary interest at exact time. Take special note that exact interest, frequently called accurate interest, is not the same as ordinary interest at exact time.

Exact interest is calculated by taking the exact time (actual number of days) and using the 365-day year as the denominator for *t*.

Many different methods or procedures exist for solving the simple-interest formula. A great many persons involved with making simple-interest calculations use prepared simple-interest tables and/or pocket calculators programmed for the computation of simple interest. Such tables and pro-grammed pocket calculators most definitely shorten the time and increase the accuracy of the calculations. However, the author feels that the business student should be able to find simple interest without depending on such aids or should use calculators only to perform some of the multiplication and division operations within the formula. Knowledge of the formula and the procedures will also enable students to perform *reverse operations* (see Unit 5.4) in simple interest, and thus provide a much deeper understanding of simple interest than merely being able to find the interest from a table or to follow the step-by-step procedures of a calculator instruction manual.

FRACTIONS AND CANCELLATION METHOD The most straightforward method is to view the calculation as a problem in finding the product of three fractions. The fraction factors are

Principal	Although a whole number, it would be expressed as a fraction. Thus the principal of $5400 is written $\frac{\$5400}{1}$.
Rate	The rate is usually given as a percent. Express the percent in fraction form. Thus a 9 percent interest rate is written $\frac{9}{100}$.
Time	Time is usually given or computed as an exact number of days or the 30-day-month time is given or computed. The number of days is then placed as the numerator of a fraction with either 360 or 365 as the denominator, depending on whether *ordinary* or *exact* interest, respectively, is to be found.

The product of the three factors can then be computed. Cancellation techniques are used, when they are obvious, to simplify the arithmetical operations.

Example 2   **Ordinary interest at 30-day-month time.**

Find the ordinary interest, using 30-day-month time, on $800 at 9 percent from April 25 to June 15.

$$P = 800$$

$$r = 9\% = \frac{9}{100}$$

$$t = 50 \text{ days } (60 \text{ days} - 10 \text{ days})$$

$$I = \frac{\overset{\overset{0.2}{\cancel{20}}}{\cancel{800}}}{1} \times \frac{\overset{1}{\cancel{9}}}{\cancel{100}} \times \frac{50}{\underset{\underset{1}{40}}{\cancel{360}}} = \$10.00$$

Example 3   **Ordinary interest at exact time.**

Find the ordinary interest at exact time on $800 at 9 percent from April 25 to July 24.

$P = \$800$

$r = 9\% = \dfrac{9}{100}$

$t = 90$ days

$$I = \frac{\overset{20}{\cancel{800}}}{1} \times \frac{\overset{1}{\cancel{9}}}{\underset{1}{\cancel{100}}} \times \frac{\overset{0.9}{\cancel{90}}}{\underset{1}{\underset{\cancel{40}}{\cancel{360}}}} = \$18.00$$

Example 4   **Exact interest.**

Find the exact interest on $800 at 9 percent from April 25 to August 23.

$P = 800$

$r = 9\% = \dfrac{9}{100}$

$t = 120$ days

$$I = \frac{\overset{8}{\cancel{800}}}{1} \times \frac{9}{\underset{1}{\cancel{100}}} \times \frac{120}{365} = \frac{8640}{365} = \$23.67$$

You will observe from Examples 2, 3, and 4 above that more opportunities for cancellation are possible with ordinary interest than with exact interest. The denominator 365 in the exact interest formula has but two factors, 5 and 73, both prime numbers; the denominator 360 has the following pairs of factors:

360	
2	180
3	120
4	90
5	72
6	60
8	45
9	40
10	36
12	30
15	24
18	20

To increase your speed and accuracy in use of cancellation in the ordinary simple-interest formula, thoroughly memorize all of the above factors of 360, most of which you probably already know.

RELATIONSHIP OF ACCURATE INTEREST OR EXACT INTEREST AND ORDINARY INTEREST AT EXACT TIME   If the base for the time calculation is 365 days, the interest charge is $\frac{5}{365}$, or $\frac{1}{73}$, less than if 360 days is used as the base for the time calculation. Restated, if the base for the time calculation is 360 days, the interest charge is $\frac{5}{360}$, or $\frac{1}{72}$, more than if 365 days is used as the base for the time calculation.

Two rules for conversion follow:[1]

1   To find accurate interest or exact interest, if ordinary interest at exact time is known, deduct $\frac{1}{73}$. Thus, in Example 3 of ordinary interest at exact time, where the interest charge was determined as $18.00, subtraction of $\frac{1}{73} \times$ $18.00, or 25 cents, would give accurate interest of $17.75.
2   To find ordinary interest at exact time, if accurate (or exact) interest is known, add $\frac{1}{72}$ of the accurate interest to the accurate interest. Thus in Example 4 of accurate interest, where the interest charge was determined as $23.67, addition of $\frac{1}{72} \times$ $23.67, or 33 cents, would give ordinary interest at exact time of $24.00.

Note: These rules for conversion are applicable to ordinary interest at 30-day-month time only when the number of days at interest is the same as in accurate interest.

DOLLAR-DAY PRODUCT METHOD OF COMPUTING ORDINARY AND EXACT INTEREST   The dollar-day product method of computing ordinary and exact interest is preferred by banks and other financial institutions as it lends itself to the preparation of convenient factor tables and facilitates the use of calculating machines. Bank employees, with the aid of these factor tables and calculating machines, can make their numerous computations in simple interest much faster and with a minimum of error. Unless calculating machines are available, the dollar-day product method is not the most desirable method of solving the simple-interest formula. This is especially true of the calculation for exact interest. However, most persons, including students, who must make numerous calculations in simple interest, do have calculating machines available.

FORMULA AND FACTORS FOR ORDINARY INTEREST BY THE DOLLAR-DAY PRODUCT METHOD   The basic formula for simple ordinary interest is restated in such a manner as to facilitate the use of fewer calculations for a specific principal and a specific interest rate. Thus:

1   To find simple ordinary interest

$$I = Pr\frac{t}{360}$$

---

[1]Some pocket calculators are programmed in this manner. The basic program in simple interest is performed in ordinary or exact interest. To convert from one to the other, you merely press one or two keys to multiply by $\frac{1}{73}$ and subtract, or multiply by $\frac{1}{72}$ and add.

2 Since *t* is the number of 360ths taken, the formula can be written

$$I = Prt\frac{1}{360}$$

3 Statement (2) is equivalent to

$$I = Pt\frac{1}{360}r$$

4 If the rate of interest (*r*) is 1 percent substituting its equivalent, $\frac{1}{100}$, in statement (3) gives the following:

$$I = Pt\left(\frac{1}{360} \times \frac{1}{100}\right) = Pt\frac{1}{36,000} = \frac{Pt}{36,000} = \text{ordinary interest at 1\%}$$

5 Ordinary interest at 1 percent is then multiplied by 36 to obtain ordinary interest at 36 percent. Thus

$$\frac{Pt}{36,000} \times \frac{36}{1} = \frac{Pt}{1000} = \text{ordinary interest at 36\%}$$

6 Multiply the interest at 36 percent by the fraction that the required rate in number of percent bears to 36 percent to find the interest at any required rate.

Example 5 **Find the ordinary interest on $1600 for 48 days at 9 percent by the dollar-day product method.**

$$\frac{Pt}{1000} \times \frac{\text{required rate in number of percent}}{36}$$

$$\frac{\cancel{1600}^{\,\overset{.4}{\cancel{1.6}}} \times 48}{\cancel{1000}_{1}} \times \frac{\cancel{9}^{1}}{\cancel{36}_{\substack{4 \\ 1}}} = \$19.20$$

The formula can be made easier by converting the fractions that the required rate in number of percent bears to 36 percent to a fraction whose numerator is 1. Then divide the interest at 36 percent by the denominator. Thus:

$\dfrac{\text{Required rate}}{36\%}$	=	$\dfrac{\text{Reduced}}{\text{fraction}}$	=	$\dfrac{\text{Same as}}{\text{dividing by}}$
$\dfrac{5}{36}$	=	$\dfrac{1}{7.2}$	=	7.2
$\dfrac{6}{36}$	=	$\dfrac{1}{6}$	=	6
$\dfrac{7\frac{1}{2}}{36}$	=	$\dfrac{1}{4.8}$	=	4.8

$$\frac{8}{36} \quad = \quad \frac{1}{4.5} \quad = \quad 4.5$$

$$\frac{9}{36} \quad = \quad \frac{1}{4} \quad = \quad 4$$

$$\frac{10}{36} \quad = \quad \frac{1}{3.6} \quad = \quad 3.6$$

$$\frac{12}{36} \quad = \quad \frac{1}{3} \quad = \quad 3$$

Example 6   **Find the ordinary interest on $727 for 90 days at 8 percent.**

$$\frac{Pt}{1000} \times \frac{1}{4.5}$$

$$\frac{0.727}{\cancel{727} \times \cancel{90}^{20}}{\cancel{1000}} \times \frac{1}{\cancel{4.5}} = \$14.54$$

The formula can be further simplified to an expression which then forms the basis for the various factor tables mentioned at the beginning of this section. Thus we develop factors for $7\frac{1}{2}$, 8, 9, and 10 percent, which are used in some factor tables:

Interest rate	Product formula		Formula restated	Division factor
$7\frac{1}{2}$%	$\frac{Pt}{1000} \times \frac{1}{4.8}$	$=$	$\frac{Pt}{4800}$	4800
8%	$\frac{Pt}{1000} \times \frac{1}{4.5}$	$=$	$\frac{Pt}{4500}$	4500
9%	$\frac{Pt}{1000} \times \frac{1}{4}$	$=$	$\frac{Pt}{4000}$	4000
10%	$\frac{Pt}{1000} \times \frac{1}{3.6}$	$=$	$\frac{Pt}{3600}$	3600

Factor tables are then prepared which instruct the user to multiply the principal times the number of days and then divide by the factor opposite the appropriate interest rate. An example of a portion of such a table is illustrated in Table 5.3.

Example 7   **Find the ordinary interest on $4600 at $8\frac{1}{4}$% for 93 days (use Table 5.3).**

$$\frac{Pt}{\text{Divisor for } 8\frac{1}{4}\%} = \frac{\$4600 \times 93}{4363.64} = \frac{\$427,800}{4363.64} = \$98.04$$

Example 8   **Find the ordinary interest on $1800 at $9\frac{5}{8}$ percent for 105 days (use Table 5.3).**

$$\frac{\$1800 \times 105}{3740.26} = \frac{\$189,000}{3740.26} = \$50.53$$

Another type of factor table carries the formula one step further and develops factors for the different number of days for a specified interest rate. Thus to develop factors for 30, 31, and 120 days at 9 percent ($\frac{9}{36} = \frac{1}{4}$):

Days	Dollar-day product formula		Formula restated		Formula restated		Factor
30	$\dfrac{Pt}{1000} \times \dfrac{1}{4}$	$=$	$\dfrac{P(30)}{4000}$	$=$	$P\left(\dfrac{30}{4000}\right)$	$=$	$P(0.007\ 500\ 0)$
31	$\dfrac{Pt}{1000} \times \dfrac{1}{4}$	$=$	$\dfrac{P(31)}{4000}$	$=$	$P\left(\dfrac{31}{4000}\right)$	$=$	$P(0.007\ 750\ 0)$
120	$\dfrac{Pt}{1000} \times \dfrac{1}{4}$	$=$	$\dfrac{P(120)}{4000}$	$=$	$P\left(\dfrac{120}{4000}\right)$	$=$	$P(0.030\ 000\ 0)$

Factor tables are then prepared which instruct the user to multiply the principal times the factor found opposite the appropriate interest rate and under the column for the proper number of days. An example of a portion of such a table is presented in Table 5.5.

Example 9   **Find the ordinary interest on $1250.75 for 90 days at 9$\frac{3}{4}$ percent (use Table 5.5).**

P = $1250.75
Multiplier for 9$\frac{3}{4}$ percent for 90 days × 243750
(Point off nine decimal places in answer.) $30.49

FORMULA AND FACTORS FOR EXACT INTEREST BY THE DOLLAR-DAY PRODUCT METHOD The same arithmetical procedures used to develop the dollar-day product formula and factor tables for ordinary interest are used to develop a similar formula and factor tables for exact interest. Instead of finding interest at 36 percent for a 360-day year, the exact interest formula finds interest at 36$\frac{1}{2}$ percent for a 365-day year before converting to any specified rate other than 36$\frac{1}{2}$ percent.

The following arithmetical procedures illustrate the development of the simple-interest formula to find *exact* interest by the dollar-day method:

1 To find simple exact interest,

$$I = Pr\frac{t}{365}$$

2 Since t is the number of 365ths taken, the formula is restated

$$I = Prt\frac{1}{365}$$

3 Statement (2) is equivalent to

$$I = Pt\frac{1}{365}r$$

4   If the rate (r) is 1 percent, substituting its fractional equivalent $(\frac{1}{100})$ in statement (3) gives

$$I = Pt\left(\frac{1}{365} \times \frac{1}{100}\right) = Pt\left(\frac{1}{36500}\right) = \frac{Pt}{36500} = \begin{array}{l}\text{exact}\\\text{interest}\\\text{at 1\%}\end{array}$$

5   Exact interest at 1 percent is then multiplied by 36.5 to obtain exact interest at $36\frac{1}{2}$ percent.

$$\frac{Pt}{36500} \times \frac{36.5}{1} = \frac{Pt}{1000}$$

6   Multiply the interest at $36\frac{1}{2}$ percent by the fraction that the required rate in number of percent bears to $36\frac{1}{2}$ percent to find the interest at any required rate.

Example 10   **Find the exact interest on $1600 for 28 days at 9 percent by the dollar-day product method.**

$$\frac{Pt}{1000} \times \frac{\text{required rate in number of percent}}{0.365}$$

$$\frac{\$1600 \times 28}{1000} \times \frac{0.09}{0.365} = \frac{\$4032}{365} = \$11.05$$

Example 11   **Find the exact interest on $1500 for 45 days at $8\frac{3}{4}$ percent by the dollar-day product method.**

$$\frac{\$1500 \times 45}{1000} \times \frac{0.0875}{0.365} = \frac{\$5906.25}{365} = \$16.18$$

The formula procedures to develop factor tables for exact interest parallel those illustrated for ordinary interest and will not be presented again. Examples of a portion of the factor tables for exact interest are presented in Tables 5.4 and 5.6.

Example 12   **Find the exact interest on $1400 for 31 days at $10\frac{1}{2}$ percent (use Table 5.4).**

$$\frac{Pt}{\text{Divisor for } 10\frac{1}{2}\%} = \frac{\$1400 \times 31}{3476.19} = \$12.48$$

Example 13   **Find the exact interest on $687.45 for 90 days at $9\frac{3}{4}$ percent (use Tabe 5.6).**

$$\begin{array}{lr}P & \$687.45\\\text{Multiplier for 90 days at } 9\frac{3}{4}\% & \times 240{,}411\\\text{(Point off nine decimal places in answer.)} & \$16.53\end{array}$$

WHEN TO DROP DECIMALS Although commercial practice varies in computing interest, the preferred and accurate rule to follow is: *Do* not *drop or raise decimal parts of 1 cent until the final result is determined.* With the cent, the smallest coin used in the United States, business practice is as follows: *If the result is a fractional part of 1 cent amounting to $\frac{1}{2}$ cent ($0.005) or more, raise the amount 1 cent and drop the fraction of a cent; if the result is a fractional part of 1 cent amounting to less than $\frac{1}{2}$ cent, drop the fraction of a cent.* Thus $10.915 is raised to $10.92, and $10.9149 is considered as $10.91.

Remember, do not drop or raise decimal parts of 1 cent until all computations have been made.

Maturity Value or Amount

By definition, maturity value is the sum (or amount) of the principal plus any interest accumulated at the time at which the obligation is due and payable. If *S* is used to symbolize maturity value, then

$$S = P + I$$

Since *I* is usually unknown, most problems in finding maturity value require that the interest be determined and then added to the given principal. Thus:

$$I = Prt$$
$$S = P + I$$

Example 14 **Find the maturity value of a note for $540 at 8 percent ordinary simple interest for 135 days.**

$$I = \$540.00 \times \frac{8}{100} \times \frac{135}{360} = \$16.20$$

$$S = \$540.00 + \$16.20 = \$556.20$$

Example 15 **Find the amount due at maturity of $292 at 10 percent exact interest for 216 days (use Table 5.4).**

$$I = \frac{\$292 \times 216}{3650} = \$17.28$$

$$S = \$292 + \$17.28 = \$309.28$$

Exercise 5.2

Find ordinary simple interest (360-day year). Use the fraction and cancellation method.

1 $5000 for 40 days at 9%   2 $6200 for 60 days at 12%

3 $7200 for 168 days at $8\frac{1}{2}$%   4 $165.50 for 45 days at 8%

TABLE 5.3   SIMPLE INTEREST DIVISORS—360-DAY BASIS[1]
(PORTION OF TABLE)

		Interest rate			
6%	7%	8%	9%	10%	%
6000.	5142.86	4500.	4000.	3600.	
5938.14	5097.35	4465.12	3972.41	3577.64	$\frac{1}{16}$
5877.55	5052.63	4430.77	3945.21	3555.56	$\frac{1}{8}$
5818.18	5008.70	4396.95	3918.37	3533.74	$\frac{3}{16}$
5760.	4965.52	4363.64	3891.89	3512.20	$\frac{1}{4}$
5702.97	4923.08	4330.83	3865.77	3490.91	$\frac{5}{16}$
5647.06	4881.36	4298.51	3840.	3469.88	$\frac{3}{8}$
5592.23	4840.34	4266.67	3814.57	3449.10	$\frac{7}{16}$
5538.46	4800.	4235.29	3789.47	3428.57	$\frac{1}{2}$
5485.71	4760.33	4204.38	3764.71	3408.28	$\frac{9}{16}$
5433.96	4721.31	4173.91	3740.26	3388.24	$\frac{5}{8}$
5383.18	4682.93	4143.88	3716.13	3368.42	$\frac{11}{16}$
5333.33	4645.16	4114.29	3692.31	3348.84	$\frac{3}{4}$
5284.40	4608.	4085.11	3668.79	3329.48	$\frac{13}{16}$
5236.36	4571.43	4056.34	3645.57	3310.34	$\frac{7}{8}$
5189.19	4535.43	4027.97	3622.64	3291.43	$\frac{15}{16}$

[1] Multiply the principal times the number of days and then divide by the divisor corresponding to interest rate.

TABLE 5.4   SIMPLE INTEREST DIVISORS—365-DAY BASIS[1]
(PORTION OF TABLE)

		Interest rate			
6%	7%	8%	9%	10%	%
6083.33	5214.29	4562.50	4055.56	3650.	
6020.62	5168.14	4527.13	4027.59	3627.33	$\frac{1}{16}$
5959.18	5122.81	4492.31	4000.	3604.94	$\frac{1}{8}$
5898.99	5078.26	4458.02	3972.79	3582.82	$\frac{3}{16}$
5840.	5034.48	4424.24	3945.95	3560.98	$\frac{1}{4}$
5782.18	4991.45	4390.98	3919.46	3539.39	$\frac{5}{16}$
5725.49	4949.15	4358.21	3893.33	3518.07	$\frac{3}{8}$
5669.90	4907.56	4325.93	3867.55	3497.01	$\frac{7}{16}$
5615.38	4866.67	4294.12	3842.11	3476.19	$\frac{1}{2}$
5561.90	4826.45	4262.77	3817.	3455.62	$\frac{9}{16}$
5509.43	4786.89	4231.88	3792.21	3435.29	$\frac{5}{8}$
5457.94	4747.97	4201.44	3767.74	3415.20	$\frac{11}{16}$
5407.41	4709.68	4171.43	3743.59	3395.35	$\frac{3}{4}$
5357.80	4672.	4141.84	3719.75	3375.72	$\frac{13}{16}$
5309.09	4634.92	4112.68	3696.20	3356.32	$\frac{7}{8}$
5261.26	4598.43	4083.92	3672.96	3337.14	$\frac{15}{16}$

[1] Multiply the principal times the number of days and then divide by the divisor corresponding to interest rate.

TABLE 5.5 INTEREST MULTIPLIERS—360-DAY BASIS[1] (PORTION OF TABLE)

	Number of days						
%	28	29	30	31	60	90	120
9	70000	72500	75000	77500	150000	225000	300000
$9\frac{1}{4}$	71944	74514	77083	79653	154167	231250	308333
$9\frac{1}{2}$	73889	76528	79167	81806	158333	237500	316667
$9\frac{3}{4}$	75833	78542	81250	83958	162500	243750	325000
10	77778	80556	83333	86111	166667	250000	333333
$10\frac{1}{4}$	79722	82569	85417	88264	170833	256250	341663
$10\frac{1}{2}$	81667	84583	87500	90417	175000	262500	350000
$10\frac{3}{4}$	83611	86597	89583	92569	179167	268750	358333

[1] Multiply principal by above factor and point off seven decimal places plus the number of decimal places in the principal.

TABLE 5.6 INTEREST MULTIPLIERS—365-DAY BASIS[1] (PORTION OF TABLE)

	Number of days						
%	28	29	30	31	60	90	120
9	69041	71507	73973	76438	147945	221918	295890
$9\frac{1}{4}$	70959	73493	76027	78562	152055	228082	304110
$9\frac{1}{2}$	72877	75479	78082	80685	156164	234247	312329
$9\frac{3}{4}$	74795	77466	80137	82808	160274	240411	320548
10	76712	79452	82192	84932	164384	246575	328767
$10\frac{1}{4}$	78630	81438	84247	87055	168493	252740	336986
$10\frac{1}{2}$	80548	83425	86301	89178	172603	258904	345205
$10\frac{3}{4}$	82466	85411	88356	91301	176712	265068	353425

[1] Multiply principal by above factor and point off seven decimal places plus the number of decimal places in the principal.

5 $825.00 for 216 days at 5%

6 $1500 for 180 days at 12%

7 $1440 for 200 days at 7%

8 $3000 for 221 days at 6%

9 $1750 for 72 days at 10%

10 $1800 for 200 days at 11%

Find exact simple interest (365-day year). Use the fraction and cancellation method.

11 $10,000 for 73 days at 10%

12 $730 for 200 days at 9%

13 $1095 for 60 days at 7%

14 $1500 for 95 days at 10%

15 $6100 for 180 days at $9\frac{1}{2}$%

16 $9000 for 146 days at $8\frac{1}{4}$%

17 $2500 for 300 days at 12%

18 $1825 for 100 days at $9\frac{5}{8}$%

19 $2190 for 55 days at 8%

20 $3650 for 80 days at $10\frac{1}{2}$%

Find ordinary simple interest (360-day year). Use dollar-day product method and Tables 5.3 and 5.5 when possible.

21    $400 for 78 days at 6%   22 $900 for 90 days at 8%

23    $650 for 72 days at 10%   24 $1500 for 96 days at $7\frac{1}{2}$%

25    $2000 for 120 days at 12%   26 $1650 for 144 days at 5%

27    $2500 for 96 days at $9\frac{5}{8}$%   28 $2450 for 84 days at $8\frac{7}{8}$%

29    $5000 for 108 days at 14%   30 $3600 for 75 days at 11%

Find ordinary exact interest (365-day year). Use dollar-day product method and Tables 5.4 and 5.6 when possible:

31    $7300 for 45 days at 11%   32 $500 for 73 days at 12%

33    $1000 for 31 days at $9\frac{3}{4}$%   34 $2500 for 28 days at $10\frac{1}{2}$%

35    $5000 for 70 days at $8\frac{1}{2}$%   36 $100 for 120 days at $9\frac{1}{2}$%

37    $2840.25 for 150 days at $10\frac{7}{8}$%   38 $315.40 for 400 days at $8\frac{3}{4}$%

39    $3750.75 for 28 days at 9%   40 $4820.16 for 29 days at $10\frac{3}{4}$%

Find the maturity value (amount) of the following interest obligations. You may compute the interest by any method.

41   A note dated August 20 for $5000 is due in 3 months at 9 percent ordinary interest. Find the maturity value (a) at 30-day-month time and (b) at exact time.

42   Stephen Joseph borrowed $450 on February 2 at 8 percent ordinary interest at exact time. He sold his pigs at the county fair, and repaid the loan August 8. What was the amount of the loan repayment?

43   Marsha Byers borrowed $500 September 15 to start college. She obtained summer employment and paid off the loan July 8 of the following year. Find the total principal and interest paid if exact interest was charged at $10\frac{1}{2}$ percent.

44   Mr. Griffith borrowed $10,000 on April 15 at 9 percent exact interest for 90 days. When the note was due, he paid $3000 plus interest on the $10,000 and renewed the note for $7000 for another 90 days at 10 percent. He paid the last note in full September 28. Find the total principal and interest paid on both notes.

45   Lester Pedrazinni obtained a personal loan of $3400 on January 15, 1976. He was able to collect his back salary and paid off the loan May 18, 1976. Sue Rockletz at the bank calculated the total amount due at $9\frac{3}{4}$ percent exact interest. Find that total amount.

46   Ms. Sonia Brown, a renowned building contractor, arranged with her bank for construction loans at 12 percent ordinary interest at exact time. On one building, she borrowed $3200 on July 25, $6400 on August 22, and $6400 on October 17. If she made payment in full including interest on November 22, find the total payment.

Unit 5.3
The 60-Day, 6 Percent Method of Computing Ordinary Interest

The 60 day, 6 percent method of solving the *ordinary* simple-interest formula is perhaps the best known and the most widely used. Although its popularity has been dimmed by the easy availability of the pocket calculator, numerous interest tables, higher "normal" interest rates, and the growing adoption of exact interest for more types of interest computations, there is still much practical use for this method. It is a method which can be performed mentally, with a minimum of pencil and paper work, and practically no need of a calculator.

Development of the 60-Day, 6 Percent Procedure

The basic principle of the procedure is based on the 6 and 60 pair of factors of the denominator 360 used for time in the ordinary interest formula.[1] Observe the interest calculation to find the ordinary interest on $100 for 60 days at 6 percent:

$$100 \times \frac{\overset{1}{\cancel{6}}}{100} \times \frac{\overset{1}{\cancel{60}}}{\underset{\underset{1}{\cancel{60}}}{360}} \qquad \text{or} \qquad \begin{array}{r} \$100 \text{ Principal} \\ \times 0.06 \text{ Rate} \\ \hline 6.00 \end{array}$$

$$= 100 \times \frac{1}{100} = \$1.00 \qquad \qquad \begin{array}{r} \times \frac{1}{6} \text{ Time} \left(\frac{60}{360} = \frac{1}{6} \right) \\ \hline \$1.00 \end{array}$$

Note that in multiplying the principal by the rate ($\frac{6}{100}$) and the time ($\frac{60}{360}$ or $\frac{1}{6}$), you are actually multiplying by $\frac{1}{100}$. This is the same as dividing by 100, and to divide by 100, you simply move the decimal point two places to the left.

To find ordinary interest for any number of days at 6 percent you "construct" the desired number of days from the base of 60 days. Thus the interest for 30 days would be one-half the interest for 60 days, the interest for 200 days would be one-third the interest for 600 days (60 days × 10), or the interest for 12 days would be one-fifth the interest for 60 days or twice the interest for 6 days (60 days ÷ 10).

FINDING COMBINATIONS OF DAYS To become adept in the use of the 60-day, 6 percent method requires the selection of easy-to-use combinations of factors and multiples of 6, 60, 600, and 6000 days. The following are some examples.

Example 1   10 days $= \frac{1}{6}$ of 60 days   1 day $= \frac{1}{6}$ of 6 days

15 days $= \frac{1}{4}$ of 60 days   2 days $= \frac{1}{3}$ of 6 days

---

[1]Certain other combinations of rates and number of days which are factors of 360 could lend themselves to the same procedures as the 60-day, 6 percent method. Thus the following could be used if desired: 90 day, 4 percent; 30-day, 12 percent; 120-day, 3 percent, etc.

$20 \text{ days} = \frac{1}{3} \text{ of } 60 \text{ days}$ $3 \text{ days} = \frac{1}{2} \text{ of } 6 \text{ days}$

$45 \text{ days} = \frac{1}{4} \text{ less than } 60 \text{ days}$ $4 \text{ days} = \frac{1}{3} \text{ less than } 6 \text{ days}$

$50 \text{ days} = \frac{1}{6} \text{ less than } 60 \text{ days}$ $5 \text{ days} = \frac{1}{6} \text{ less than } 6 \text{ days}$

$150 \text{ days} = 2 \times 60 \text{ days plus } 30 \text{ days} \left(\text{or } \frac{1}{4} \text{ of } 600 \text{ days} \right)$

$90 \text{ days} = 60 \text{ days plus } 30 \text{ days}$
$54 \text{ days} = 60 \text{ days minus } 6 \text{ days (or } 6 \text{ days} \times 9)$
$183 \text{ days} = 60 \text{ days} \times 3 \text{ plus } 3 \text{ days}$
$118 \text{ days} = 60 \text{ days} \times 2 \text{ minus } 2 \text{ days}$

Example 2   **Find the ordinary interest on $832 for 60 days at 6 percent.**

$\$8.32 =$ interest for 60 days (point off two places)

Example 3   **Find the ordinary interest on $560 for 96 days at 6 percent.**

$\$5.60 =$ interest for 60 days (point off two places)
$2.80 =$ interest for 30 days (half of 60 days)
$\underline{+0.56} =$ interest for 6 days (point off three places)
$\$8.96 =$ interest for 96 days

Example 4   **Find the ordinary interest on $960 for 673 days at 6 percent.**

$\$\ 96.00 =$ interest for 600 days (point off one place)
$9.60 =$ interest for 60 days (point off two places)
$1.92 =$ interest for 12 days (point off three places, multiply by 2, or

find $\frac{1}{5}$ of 60 days)

$+0.16 =$ interest for   1 day $\left(\frac{1}{6} \text{ of } 6 \text{ days} \right)$

$\overline{\$107.68 =}$ interest for 673 days

It is possible to select various combinations of days into which the time may be divided. In using the 60-day, 6 percent method, attempt to select that combination of days which seems easiest to use. Thus if interest at 6 percent is to be found on $240 for 88 days, the following are among many possible combinations of days that might be used:

(a)	**(b)**	**(c)**
$2.40 for 60 days	$2.40 for 60 days	$2.40 for 60 days
0.80 for 20 days	+1.20 for 30 days	0.60 for 15 days
0.24 for 6 days	3.60 for 90 days	0.24 for 6 days
+0.08 for 2 days	−0.08 for −2 days	0.24 for 6 days
$3.52 for 88 days	$3.52 for 88 days	+0.04 for 1 day
		$3.52 for 88 days

TRANSPOSING Transposition of the principal and the days will often simplify the use of the 60-day, 6 percent method; e.g., $1 for 360 days will result in the same interest as $360 for 1 day, or $10 for 39 days will result in the same interest as $39 for 10 days, etc.

Example 5   **Find the ordinary interest on $600 for 127 days at 6 percent.**

(a)
$ 6.00 for   60 days
6.00 for   60 days
0.60 for   6 days
+ 0.10 for   1 day
$12.70 for 127 days

(b)
By transposition:

$600.00 for 127 days = $127.00 for 600 days

$12.70 for 600 days

Since the principal in many interest problems often lends itself to transposition, always consider whether such a change is advisable before proceeding with the solution.

USING THE 60-DAY, 6 PERCENT METHOD FOR RATES OTHER THAN 6 PERCENT When the ordinary interest at 6 percent for the desired number of days has been found, it can then be converted to the desired rate. Thus if the ordinary interest at 6 percent for $600 for 127 days is $12.70 (see Example 5), the interest at 12 percent would be twice $12.70, or $25.40, and the interest at 9 percent would be $1\frac{1}{2}$ times as great, or $19.05 ($12.70 + $6.35). A number of interest rates lend themselves to such conversion (see Table 5.7).

Example 6   **Find the ordinary interest on $240 for 60 days at 7 percent.**

$2.40 = interest for 60 days at 6%

+0.40 = $\frac{1}{6}$ interest at 6% = full interest at 1%

$2.80 = interest for 60 days at 7%

Example 7   **Find the ordinary interest on $320 for 93 days at $7\frac{1}{2}$ percent.**

$3.20 = interest for 60 days at 6%

1.60 = interest for 30 days at 6% $\left(\frac{1}{2} \text{ of } 60\right)$

0.16 = interest for 3 days at 6% $\left(\frac{1}{10} \text{ of 30 days}\right)$

$4.96 = interest for 93 days at 6%

+1.24 = $\frac{1}{4}$ of interest at 6% $\left(1\frac{1}{2}\%\right)$

$6.20 = interest for 93 days at $7\frac{1}{2}\%$

TABLE 5.7 CONVERSION TO RATES OTHER THAN 6 PERCENT IN THE 60-DAY, 6 PERCENT METHOD

Rate required, %	For the same number of days and the same principal, the interest will be:	Because
1	$\dfrac{1}{6}$ of the interest at 6%	1 is $\dfrac{1}{6}$ of 6
$1\dfrac{1}{2}$	$\dfrac{1}{4}$ of the interest at 6%	$1\dfrac{1}{2}$ is $\dfrac{1}{4}$ of 6
2	$\dfrac{1}{3}$ of the interest at 6%	2 is $\dfrac{1}{3}$ of 6
3	$\dfrac{1}{2}$ of the interest at 6%	3 is $\dfrac{1}{2}$ of 6
4	6% interest *minus* $\dfrac{1}{3}$ of interest at 6%	$4 = 6 - \dfrac{1}{3}$ of 6
$4\dfrac{1}{2}$	6% interest *minus* $\dfrac{1}{4}$ of interest at 6%	$4\dfrac{1}{2} = 6 - \dfrac{1}{4}$ of 6
5	6% interest *minus* $\dfrac{1}{6}$ of interest at 6%	$5 = 6 - \dfrac{1}{6}$ of 6
7	6% interest *plus* $\dfrac{1}{6}$ of interest at 6%	$7 = 6 + \dfrac{1}{6}$ of 6
$7\dfrac{1}{2}$	6% interest *plus* $\dfrac{1}{4}$ of interest at 6%	$7\dfrac{1}{2} = 6 + \dfrac{1}{4}$ of 6
8	6% interest *plus* $\dfrac{1}{3}$ of interest at 6%	$8 = 6 + \dfrac{1}{3}$ of 6
9	6% interest *plus* $\dfrac{1}{2}$ of interest at 6%	$9 = 6 + \dfrac{1}{2}$ of 6
12	Twice the interest at 6%	$12 = 6 \times 2$

COMPUTING INTEREST AT RATES NOT EASILY CONVERTED FROM INTEREST AT 6 PERCENT A number of interest rates may not be converted readily from 6 percent, and sometimes the interest at 6 percent does not lend itself to easy conversion. In any instance, the interest at the required rate may be found by use of the following formula:

$$\text{Required interest} = \frac{\text{interest at 6\% } \times \text{ required rate in number of percent}}{6}$$

Example 8   **Find the ordinary interest on $920 for 72 days at 3.5 percent.**

$\$9.20 =$ interest for 60 days at 6%

$+ \ 1.84 =$ interest for 12 days at 6% $\left(\dfrac{1}{5} \text{ of 60 days, or } 2 \times 6 \text{ days}\right)$

$\overline{\$11.04} =$ interest for 72 days at 6%

$\quad 1.84$

$\dfrac{\$11.04 \times 3.5}{\underset{1}{\cancel{6}}} = \$6.44 =$ interest for 72 days at 3.5%

Example 9   **If the ordinary interest at 6 percent is *exactly* \$7.523, find the ordinary interest at 7 percent.**

$$\frac{\$7.523 \times 7}{6} = \frac{\$52.661}{6} = \$8.776\frac{5}{6} = \$8.78$$

As Example 9 indicates, decimal places in the computation should be retained (not rounded off) until the required interest in dollars and cents has been determined.

Exercise 5.3

Find the ordinary interest at 6 percent by use of the 60-day, 6 percent method:

1	\$156.48 for 60 days	2	\$92.40 for 30 days
3	\$240.00 for 78 days	4	\$86.00 for 9 days
5	\$840.20 for 5 days	6	\$410.00 for 150 days
7	\$204.30 for 54 days	8	\$320.50 for 178 days
9	\$1069.00 for 183 days	10	\$43.75 for 75 days
11	\$600.00 for 126 days	12	\$1536.00 for 4 days
13	\$4880.00 for 3 days	14	\$837.38 for 77 days
15	\$95.66 for 45 days	16	\$720.00 for 88 days
17	\$48.60 for 666 days	18	\$5802.40 for 45 days
19	\$17.04 for 6000 days	20	\$2135.08 for 20 days
21	\$140.00 for 60 days	22	\$400.00 for 30 days
23	\$85.00 for 120 days	24	\$245.00 for 9 days
25	\$50.00 for 72 days	26	\$164.00 for 88 days
27	\$560.00 for 61 days	28	\$22.00 for 33 days
29	\$660.00 for 73 days	30	\$300.00 for 125 days
31	\$240.00 for 857 days	32	\$73.50 for 2 months 2 days
33	\$82.17 for 29 days	34	\$180.00 for 121 days
35	\$36.50 for 1 month 27 days	36	\$145.35 for 8 days
37	\$621.00 for 3 months 10 days	38	\$345.20 for 2 months 27 days
39	\$51.25 for 6000 days	40	\$942.15 for 6 months 3 days

Find the ordinary interest by use of the 60-day, 6 percent method (use Table 5.7 when appropriate):

41	\$986.00 for 99 days at $7\frac{1}{2}$%	42	\$600.00 for 84 days at 12%
43	\$564.00 for 117 days at 9%	44	\$504.00 for 62 days at 10%
45	\$180.00 for 149 days at $10\frac{1}{2}$%	46	\$84.12 for 110 days at 7%
47	\$568.70 for 66 days at 8%	48	\$96.84 for 76 days at 9%
49	\$325.40 for 60 days at 5%	50	\$673.27 for 80 days at $4\frac{1}{2}$%

51   \$840.00 at 10%, February 16, to March 15
52   \$3600.00 at 9%, March 30 to April 29

53 $440.80 at 8%, April 12 to June 17

54 $96.40 at $7\frac{1}{2}$%, March 29 to May 15

55 $302.10 at 12%, May 31 to August 31

56 $495.00 at 15%, June 18 to December 5

57 $4850.00 at 7%, January 3 to July 31

58 $260.00 at $7\frac{1}{2}$%, August 15 to September 23

59 $318.45 at 9%, December 15 to April 16

60 $7011.90 at $10\frac{1}{2}$%, November 27 to January 26

Solve the following by the use of the 60-day, 6 percent method:

61 In order to extend the due date from April 17 to July 1 on a net invoice of $2856.80, the Harvey Hardware Store agreed to pay 10 percent ordinary interest at 30-day-month time. Find (a) interest and (b) maturity value.

62 Mr. Everett Linville made a construction loan of $9300 from his bank at $7\frac{1}{2}$ percent ordinary interest at exact time. If the date of the loan was October 26 and payment in full was made on December 29, find (a) interest and (b) maturity value.

63 A business firm was able to borrow at 9 percent ordinary interest at exact time. If $45,600 was borrowed from December 22 of 1978 to May 10 of 1979, find (a) interest and (b) maturity value.

64 The sum of $720 is invested at 7 percent ordinary interest at 30-day-month time from July 16 to October 10. Find (a) interest and (b) maturity value.

65 Ms. Charlotte Doan borrowed $644.40 at 8 percent ordinary interest at 30-day-month time from May 31 to October 31. Find (a) interest and (b) maturity value.

66 Ms. Lorraine Watkins made a construction loan from her bank at $10\frac{1}{2}$ percent ordinary interest at exact time. If she borrowed $4800 from February 7 to June 3, how much did she pay (a) in interest and (b) at maturity?

67 A business firm was able to borrow at $8\frac{1}{2}$ percent ordinary interest computed at exact time. If $10,000.00 was borrowed from December 28, 1971, to May 22, 1973, find (a) interest and (b) amount due at maturity.

68 The Alpine Co. borrowed $5250 from May 12 to July 18. At 12 percent ordinary interest, find (a) interest and (b) amount due at maturity.

69 Mio Takada owes $8640.41 balance on his 9 percent mortgage on his house as of May 12. His monthly payments are $260 and are due the 12th of each month. At 30-day-month time, find (a) the amount of the June payment allocable to interest, and (b) the amount of the payment used to reduce the principal. (Ordinary interest is charged on the mortgage at 30-day-month time.)

70 Maxine Plank owes $6280.15 on her 10 percent mortgage as of August 21. Payments of $168.40 are due the 21st of each month. At 30-day-month time, find (a) the portion of the September 21 payment allocable to interest, and (b) the balance of the mortgage after the September 21 payment is made. (Ordinary interest at 30-day-month time is charged on the mortgage.)

Unit 5.4   *Reverse Operations in Simple Interest*

From the basic formulas to find ordinary or exact interest and maturity value, auxiliary formulas can be derived to find the value of a missing quantity or factor, as long as the other factors in the formula are known. From the basic formulas to find interest and maturity value

$I = Prt$
$S = P + I$

the following auxiliary formulas can be derived.

TO FIND THE INTEREST RATE r   From the basic formula to find interest, restate the formula so that the rate (r) stands alone on one side of the equation (see Unit 3.3 for rules governing equations).

(a) $I = Prt$
(b)   Divide both sides of the equation by Pt:

$$\frac{I}{1} \div \frac{Pt}{1} = \frac{I}{1} \times \frac{1}{Pt} = \frac{I}{Pt} \qquad \frac{Prt}{1} \div \frac{Pt}{1} = \frac{Prt}{1} \times \frac{1}{Pt} = r$$

Therefore

$$r = \frac{I}{Pt} \quad \text{or} \quad r = I \div Pt$$

Example 1   **Find the interest rate if the ordinary simple interest on $450 for 60 days is $3.75.**

$$r = \frac{I}{Pt}$$

$$r = \frac{3.75}{450 \times \dfrac{60}{360}} = \frac{3.75}{75} = 0.05 = 5\%$$

Example 2   **Find the interest rate if the exact simple interest on $4260 for 90 days is $94.54.**

$$r = \frac{1}{Pt}$$

$$r = \frac{94.54}{4260 \times \dfrac{90}{365}} = \frac{94.54}{1050.41} = 0.09 = 9\%$$

TO FIND THE TIME t   Again from the basic formula to find interest, restate the formula so that t stands alone on one side of the equation:

(a) $I = Prt$
(b) Divide both sides of the equation by Pr:

$$\frac{I}{Pr} = t \quad \text{or} \quad t = I \div Pr$$

Example 3   **Find the time if the ordinary simple interest on $6000 at 10 percent is $200.**

$$t = \frac{I}{Pr}$$

$$= \frac{200}{6000 \times 0.10} = \frac{200}{600} = \frac{1}{3} \text{ year (360-day year)}$$

$$360 \text{ days} \times \frac{1}{3} = 120 \text{ days}$$

Example 4   **Find the time if the exact simple interest on $2500 at 9 percent is $55.48.**

$$t = \frac{I}{Pr}$$

$$= \frac{55.48}{2500 \times 0.09} = \frac{55.48}{225} = 0.2466 \text{ of 1 year (365 days)}$$

$$365 \text{ days} \times 0.2466 = 90 \text{ days}$$

Since the time period in most simple-interest problems is less than 1 year, it is desirable to find the time directly in days rather than in a fraction of a year and then convert to days.

Formula to find number of days directly in ordinary simple interest is

(a) $t = \dfrac{\text{days}}{360}$

Substituting in formula to find time $t = \dfrac{I}{Pr}$ yields

(b) $\dfrac{\text{Days}}{360} = \dfrac{I}{Pr}$

Multiply both sides of (b) by 360:

(c) $\dfrac{\text{Days}}{360} \times \dfrac{360}{1} = \text{days} \qquad \dfrac{I}{Pr} \times \dfrac{360}{1} = \dfrac{I \times 360}{Pr}$

Therefore

$$\text{Days} = \frac{I \times 360}{Pr} \qquad \text{For ordinary interest}$$

$$\text{Days} = \frac{I \times 365}{Pr} \qquad \text{For exact interest}$$

Example 5   **Same as Example 3.**

$$\text{Days} = \frac{200 \times 360}{6000 \times 0.10} = \frac{72{,}000}{600} = 120 \text{ days}$$

Same as Example 4.

$$\text{Days} = \frac{55.48 \times 365}{2500 \times 0.09} = \frac{20{,}250.20}{225} = 90 \text{ days}$$

TO FIND MATURITY VALUE S   Combine the two basic formulas to find interest and maturity value into one formula:

(a) $I = Prt$
(b) $S = P + I$

Substitute the value of I in (b):

(c) $S = P + Prt$

Factor (c):

$$S = P(1 + rt)$$

Example 6   **Find the maturity value of the principal \$425 at ordinary simple interest at 8 percent for 135 days.**

$$S = P(1 + rt)$$

$$= \$425\left[1 + \left(\frac{135}{360} \times \frac{8}{100}\right)\right]$$

$$= \$425\,(1 + 0.03)$$
$$= \$425\,(1.03) = \$437.75$$

Example 7   **Find the maturity value of the principal \$2500 at exact simple interest at 9 percent for 90 days.**

$$S = P(1 + rt)$$

$$= \$2500\left[1 + \left(\frac{90}{365} \times \frac{9}{100}\right)\right]$$

$$= \$2500\,(1 + 0.022\,19)$$
$$= \$2500\,(1.022\,19) = \$2555.48$$

TO FIND PRINCIPAL P   Using the same formula for finding maturity value, isolate P on one side of the equation:

(a) $S = P(1 + rt)$

Divide both sides of the equation by $(1 + rt)$:

(b) $\dfrac{S}{1 + rt} = P$ or $P = S \div (1 + rt)$

Example 8 **Find the principal if the maturity value is \$1575 and ordinary interest at 8 percent for 75 days has been earned.**

$$P = \dfrac{S}{(1 + rt)}$$

$$= \dfrac{\$525}{1 + \left(\dfrac{8}{100} \times \dfrac{75}{360}\right)}$$

$$= \dfrac{\$1525}{1.016\ 67} = \$1500$$

Example 9 **Find the principal if the maturity value is \$1286.99 and exact interest at 9 percent for 120 days has been earned.**

$$P = \dfrac{S}{1 + rt}$$

$$= \dfrac{\$1286.99}{1 + \left(\dfrac{9}{100} \times \dfrac{120}{365}\right)}$$

$$= \dfrac{\$1286.99}{1.029\ 59} = \$1250$$

The principal can also be found if the maturity value (*S*) is unknown:

From the basic formula

$$I = Prt$$

Divide both sides of the equation by *rt*:

$$\dfrac{I}{rt} = P \qquad \text{or} \qquad P = I \div rt$$

Example 10 **The ordinary interest on a loan for 180 days at 12 percent is \$48. Find the principal of the note.**

$$P = \dfrac{I}{rt}$$

$$= \dfrac{\$48}{\left(\dfrac{12}{100} \times \dfrac{180}{360}\right)}$$

$$= \dfrac{\$48}{0.06} = \$800$$

Example 11 **The exact interest on a loan for 200 days at 11 percent is $60.27. Find the principal of the note.**

$$P = \frac{I}{rt}$$

$$= \frac{\$60.27}{\left(\dfrac{11}{100} \times \dfrac{200}{365}\right)}$$

$$= \frac{\$60.27}{0.060\ 27} = \$1000$$

SUMMARY OF AUXILIARY FORMULAS The preceding formulas in simple interest are summarized for easy reference as follows:

Basic formulas
    To find interest $I = Prt$
    To find maturity value $S = P + I$
Auxiliary formulas

    To find rate $r = \dfrac{I}{Pt}$

    To find time (fraction of a year) $t = \dfrac{I}{Pr}$

    To find time (number of days) $\text{Days} = \dfrac{I \times 360\ (\text{or } 365)}{Pr}$

    To find maturity value $S = P(1 + rt)$

    To find principal (if S is known) $P = \dfrac{S}{1 + rt}$

    To find principal (if S is not known) $P = \dfrac{I}{rt}$

Note: If working with ordinary interest, use 360 as the denominator for t in the above formulas; if working with exact interest, use 365 as the denominator for t.

Exercise 5.4

Find the time in days:

	Principal	Maturity value	Ordinary interest	Rate, %
1	$400.00		$ 8.00	6
2	522.00		10.44	8
3	326.42	$338.66		$7\frac{1}{2}$
4		270.83	20.83	10

Solve the following:

5   Ms. Andrews paid $56.00 ordinary interest at exact time due on her 12 percent note for $1400.00. Find the time in days for which interest was paid.

6   A student borrowed $500 at $7\frac{1}{2}$ percent exact interest in order to pay his tuition charges. At a later date he was unable to make any payment on the principal, but he did pay $18.49, the interest due at that time. How many days had lapsed before he made the interest payment?

7   A borrower of $1875 at 9 percent ordinary interest cleared his debt and interest due with a payment of $2015.63. How many days did he have the use of the lender's money?

Find the percent rate of ordinary interest charged on the following notes:

	Principal	Maturity value	Ordinary interest	Time, days
8	$500.00		$ 8.75	90
9	312.50		15.23	270
10	425.50	$456.32		745
11		187.05	2.30	64

Solve the following:

12   A borrower of $400 made an interest payment of $21.94 due at the end of 282 days. Find the percent rate of ordinary interest at exact time paid by the borrower.

13   550 days after Ms. Perez borrowed $500.00, she paid her note in full and exact interest due in an amount totaling $575.34. Find the percent rate of exact interest that was charged Ms. Perez.

14   Mr. Stenberg paid both principal and exact interest in an amount of $761.10 on an obligation which he had incurred 639 days preceding the date of payment. If interest due was $103.60, find the percent rate of ordinary interest paid by Mr. Stenberg.

Find (a) the principal and then (b) the maturity value in the following:

	Ordinary interest	Time, days	Rate, %
15	$ 18.75	180	6
16	333.33	800	$7\frac{1}{2}$
17	120.17	247	8
18	24.27	56	12

19   After 133 days, Ms. Wattle made an exact interest payment of $24.60 due on her 9 percent note. How much was the principal?

20   On the due date, the ordinary interest owed at 30-day-month time on a 7 percent note was $298.40 after 1 year, 2 months, and 3 days. Find the maturity value.

21   Mr. Kinkade received $231 ordinary interest at exact time due after

630 days on a loan that he had made to a friend. If the interest rate was $16\frac{1}{2}$ percent, how much did he lend his friend?

Find (a) the principal and then (b) the interest on the following notes at ordinary interest:

	Maturity value	Time, days	Rate, %
22	$ 794.43	111	6
23	367.83	180	$7\frac{1}{2}$
24	1335.67	1272	$9\frac{1}{2}$
25	6242.69	25	8

Solve the following:

26 A bank made a 240-day loan at 7 percent ordinary interest at exact time, receiving at maturity an amount of $3180.00. How much was the principal?

27 One year and 9 months after Ms. McMillan borrowed some money at $10\frac{1}{2}$ percent ordinary interest at 30-day-month time, she paid off her note in full, including the interest, with a check for $2959.38. How much did she borrow?

28 Ms. O'Neill borrowed some money at 15 percent exact interest in order to pay cash for some furniture. She cleared the note in full, including the interest, 105 days later, with a payment of $521.58. How much did she borrow?

Chapter 6

Compound Interest, Annuities, Sinking Funds, Amortization

Objectives To Be Achieved in This Chapter

1   To work with compound interest and annuity formulas and tables.

2   To find unknown rates and time periods by adaptation of the compound interest and annuity formulas and use of the tables.

3   To apply compound interest and annuity concepts to problems in sinking funds, amortization of loans, and capital-budgeting decisions.

The interest earned on savings accounts; determination of the monthly payment of home mortgage loans, automobile loans, and personal loans; comparison of alternative investments—all use compound interest in their calculations.

Unit 6.1   *Compound Interest;*
Finding the Compound Interest

Whereas *simple interest* was defined as interest (money rent) on a principal sum for a specified time and at an expressed rate per year, *compound interest* is not only interest on the principal sum for a specified time and at an expressed rate per year, but as the interest is earned, it becomes part of the principal and also earns interest. The interest may be added to the principal and start earning interest in intervals of 1 year, $\frac{1}{2}$ year, $\frac{1}{4}$ year (every 3 months), 1 month, 1 day, or even continuously. Compound interest is illustrated and compared to simple interest as follows:

Example 1   **Find the amount due at the end of 4 years if $500 is invested at 5 percent, at**

(a) Simple interest
(b) Compound interest with interest credited annually

(a) Simple interest:

Interest→	$25.00	$25.00	$25.00	$25.00	
$500	year 1	year 2	year 3	year 4	= $600

Principal   Amount or
or present value   future value

Interest for each year:

$I = Prt$
$= \$500 \times .05 \times 1 = \$25.00$

(b) Compound interest:

Interest→	$25.00	$26.25	$27.56	$28.94	
$500	year 1	year 2	year 3	year 4	= $607.75

Principal   Amount or
or present value   future value

Interest for each year:

$$l_1 = \text{interest for year 1}$$
$$l_2 = \text{interest for year 2, etc.}$$

Year 1:	$l_1 = Prt$	$= \$500 \times .05 \times 1 = \$25.00$
Year 2:	$l_2 = (P + l_1)rt$	$= \$525.00 \times .05 \times 1 = \$26.25$
Year 3:	$l_3 = (P + l_1 + l_2)rt$	$= \$551.25 \times .05 \times 1 = \$27.56$
Year 4:	$l_4 = (P + l_1 + l_2 + l_3)rt$	$= \$578.81 \times .05 \times 1 = \$28.94$

The difference between the amounts for simple and compound interest ($607.75 − $600.00 = $7.75) is due to calculating "interest on interest" in the amount determined by the compound interest method. Thus:

Year			Interest on interest
1		=	$0.00
2	$25.00 × .05 × 1	=	1.25
3	($25.00 + $26.25) × .05 × 1	=	2.56
4	($25.00 + $26.25 + $27.56) × .05 × 1	=	3.94

Note: Interest is added to the principal at the end of each year. Therefore, no interest on interest is earned for year 1; interest on the interest added at the end of year 1 is earned in year 2; etc.

Terms and Symbols Used in Compound Interest

Term and symbol	Definition
Principal (P) or present value	The initial sum that was invested or borrowed. The symbol PV is sometimes used, especially on pocket calculator keys.
Amount (S) or future value	The principal plus the interest due at a future date. The symbol FV is also used with pocket calculators.
Nominal rate (j)	The given *annual* rate per $100 of principal which is to be converted some number of times during a year.
Conversion periods per year (m)	The number of times per year the nominal rate (j) is converted, or "compounded."
Interest rate per conversion period (i)	The rate of interest for each conversion period during the year. Found by dividing the nominal rate (j) by the conversion periods per year (m).
Interest periods (n)	The number of conversion periods during the entire term. Found by multiplying the number of years times the conversion periods per year (m).
Effective rate	The amount of interest earned in 1 year.

Example 2   **Find the interest rate per conversion period (i) of the following nominal rates:**

(a)   8%, $m = 1$ (b)   6%, $m = 12$
(c)   10%, $m = 4$ (d)   5%, $m = 365$

$$i = \frac{j}{m}$$

(a) $i = \dfrac{8}{1} = 8\%$ (b) $i = \dfrac{6}{12} = \dfrac{1}{2}\%$

(c) $i = \dfrac{10}{4} = 2\dfrac{1}{2}\%$ (d) $i = \dfrac{5}{365} = .0137\%$

Example 3   **Find the number of conversion periods (n) for the terms of the following obligations:**

(a)   25 years, $m = 12$ (b)   10 years, $m = 4$
(c)   15 years, $m = 1$ (d)   20 years, $m = 365$

Solution: $n =$ years (m)

(a) $n = 25(12) = 300$ (b) $n = 10(4) = 40$
(c) $n = 15(1) = 15$ (d) $n = 20(365) = 7300$

Formula to Find the Maturity Value by Compound Interest

To calculate the maturity value at compound interest in the manner illustrated in Example 1b would be an unnecessarily laborious process, and therefore formulas and tables have been developed to perform calculations in compound interest.[1] The formula to find maturity value at compound interest is developed as follows:

$P =$ the original principal
$i =$ the interest rate per period
$S =$ maturity value

1   The interest due at the end of one period equals Pi.
2   The maturity value at the end of one period and also the principal at the beginning of the next period is $P + Pi = S$.
3   By factoring, the expression $(P + Pi)$ becomes $P(1 + i)$.
4   The interest for the second period is $P(1 + i)i$.

[1] Programs for computers and pocket calculators have long been developed to make calculations in compound interest. In fact, without such computers and their speed and capacity, many savings banks and other financial institutions would not be offering many of the savings plans they have today.

5 The maturity value at the end of the second period *and also* the principal at the beginning of the third period is then

$$P(1 + i) + [P(1 + i)]i$$

6 By factoring, the expression in (5) becomes $P(1 + i)(1 + i) = P(1 + i)^2$.

7 The maturity value at the end of the third period would be found by multiplying the maturity value at the end of the second period by $(1 + i)$:

$$P(1 + i)^2(1 + i) = P(1 + i)^3$$

8 It follows that the maturity value S for *n periods* on the principal P, at the rate i, is then

$$S = P(1 + i)^n$$

The total compound interest is obtained by the same formula used in simple interest:

$$I = S - P$$

A *characteristic of exponents* can be observed from the development of the above formula to find the maturity value at compound interest.

Since an *exponent* is a number that tells how many times another number, called the *base,* is used as a factor in a product, $(1 + i)^3$ means that the quantity $(1 + i)$ is multiplied by itself three times. The numerical value of $(1 + i)^2$, when multiplied by $(1 + i)^1$, would give $(1 + i)^3$. Therefore, when the base numbers are *multiplied* by each other, you express the multiplication by *adding* their exponents. Thus:

$$(1 + i)^{100} \times (1 + i)^{20} = (1 + i)^{120}$$
$$(1 + i)^{50} \times (1 + i)^{50} = (1 + i)^{100}$$

Stating this characteristic another way, you can find the numerical value of a base number with a given exponent by *multiplying the numerical values of any addends* of the exponent of that base number. Thus:

$$(1 + i)^{120} = (1 + i)^{100} \times (1 + i)^{20} \quad \text{or} \quad (1 + i)^{60} \times (1 + i)^{60} \quad \text{etc.}$$
$$(1 + i)^{100} = (1 + i)^{50} \times (1 + i)^{50} \quad \text{or} \quad (1 + i)^{75} \times (1 + i)^{25} \quad \text{etc.}$$

This feature of exponents may be used to determine a factor which is not given in the factor table. An example is included later in this unit.

Example 4 Find **(a) the maturity value of $500 at the end of 4 years at the nominal rate of 5 percent, converted annually, and (b) the total compound interest.**

(a) $P = \$500$

$$i = \frac{j}{m} = \frac{5\%}{1} = 5\%$$

$$n = \text{years } (m) = 4(1) = 4$$

$$S = \$500 \, [(1.05)^1 \, (1.05)^1 \, (1.05)^1 \, (1.05)^1]$$

$$= \$500 \, (1.05)^4 = \$500 \, (1.215 \, 5062) = \$607.75$$

(b) $\; I = S - P$

$$I = \$607.75 - \$600.00 = \$7.75$$

COMPOUND INTEREST ACCUMULATION FACTOR TABLE If $P = \$1$, it is customary to replace S by s and state the formula $s = (1 + i)^n$. The factor $(1 + i)^n$ is calculated for various values of i and successive periods of n and tables are prepared.

Table 6.1 presents a sample of such interest factor tables. Table 6.1 is presented for illustrative purposes and to use in solving the problems that are presented in the text to find the compound amount. Tables that contain many more interest rates and n periods can be purchased and are available in libraries.[1] To use Table 6.1 proceed as follows:

1 Locate the proper column corresponding to i, the interest rate per period. Note that i is not the annual nominal rate, and care must be taken not to confuse the two rates.
2 Find under n the number of periods during which interest is to be accumulated.
3 The number found at the point of intersection of n and i is the factor to be used.

Example 5 **Find the factor in Table 6.1 for the compound amount of $1 for 5 years at the following nominal rates (j) and conversion periods (m):**

(a)   8%, $m = 2$
(b)   6%, $m = 12$
(c) 12%, $m = 4$

Solution:

(a) $i = \dfrac{8\%}{2} = 4\%$; $n = 5(2) = 10$; factor is 1.480 2443

(b) $i = \dfrac{6\%}{12} = \dfrac{1}{2}\%$; $n = 5(12) = 60$; factor is 1.348 8502

(c) $i = \dfrac{12\%}{4} = 3\%$; $n = 5(4) = 20$; factor is 1.806 1112

---

[1] Figure 6.1 illustrates the type of interest tables that are available. Computers and some pocket calculators are programmed to solve the compound-interest formulas directly without the need of prepared tables.

TABLE 6.1   AMOUNT OF $1 AT COMPOUND INTEREST $s = (1 + i)^n$

Formulas:

To find amount	$S = P(1 + i)^n$
To find interest	$I = S - P$
	$= P[(1 + i)^n - 1]$
To find time or rate	$(1 + i)^n = \dfrac{S}{P}$
To find present value	$P = \dfrac{S}{(1 + i)^n}$ { Also see Table 6.2, which is preferable when available.

n	$\frac{1}{2}$%	1%	2%	3%	4%	5%	6%
1	1.005 0000	1.010 0000	1.020 0000	1.030 0000	1.040 0000	1.050 0000	1.060 0000
2	1.010 0250	1.020 1000	1.040 4000	1.060 9000	1.081 6000	1.102 5000	1.123 6000
3	1.015 0751	1.030 3010	1.061 2080	1.092 7270	1.124 8640	1.157 6250	1.191 0160
4	1.020 1505	1.040 6040	1.082 4322	1.125 5088	1.169 8586	1.215 5062	1.262 4770
5	1.025 2513	1.051 0100	1.104 0808	1.159 2741	1.216 6529	1.276 2816	1.338 2256
6	1.030 3775	1.061 5202	1.126 1624	1.194 0523	1.265 3190	1.340 0956	1.418 5191
7	1.035 5294	1.072 1354	1.148 6857	1.229 8739	1.315 9318	1.407 1004	1.503 6303
8	1.040 7070	1.082 8567	1.171 6594	1.266 7701	1.368 5690	1.477 4554	1.593 8481
9	1.045 9106	1.093 6853	1.195 0926	1.304 7732	1.423 3118	1.551 3282	1.689 4790
10	1.051 1401	1.104 6221	1.218 9944	1.343 9164	1.480 2443	1.628 8946	1.790 8477
11	1.056 3958	1.115 6684	1.243 3743	1.384 2339	1.539 4541	1.710 3394	1.898 2986
12	1.061 6778	1.126 8250	1.268 2418	1.425 7609	1.601 0322	1.795 8563	2.012 1965
13	1.066 9862	1.138 0933	1.293 6066	1.468 5337	1.665 0735	1.885 6491	2.132 9283
14	1.072 3211	1.149 4742	1.319 4788	1.512 5897	1.731 6764	1.979 9316	2.260 9040
15	1.007 6827	1.160 9690	1.345 8683	1.557 9674	1.800 9435	2.078 9282	2.396 5582
16	1.083 0712	1.172 5786	1.372 7857	1.604 7064	1.872 9812	2.182 8746	2.540 3517
17	1.088 4865	1.184 3044	1.400 2414	1.652 8476	1.947 9005	2.292 0183	2.692 7728
18	1.093 9289	1.196 1475	1.428 2462	1.702 4331	2.025 8165	2.406 6192	2.854 3392
19	1.099 3986	1.208 1090	1.456 8112	1.753 5061	2.106 8492	2.526 9502	3.025 5995
20	1.104 8956	1.220 1900	1.485 9474	1.806 1112	2.191 1231	2.653 2977	3.207 1355
21	1.110 4201	1.232 3919	1.515 6663	1.860 2946	2.278 7681	2.785 9626	3.399 5636
22	1.115 9722	1.224 7159	1.545 9797	1.916 1034	2.369 9188	2.925 2607	3.603 5374
23	1.121 5520	1.257 1630	1.576 8993	1.973 5865	2.464 7155	3.071 5238	3.819 7497
24	1.127 1598	1.269 7346	1.608 4372	2.032 7941	2.563 3042	3.225 0999	4.048 9346
25	1.132 7956	1.282 4320	1.640 6060	2.093 7779	2.665 8363	3.386 3549	4.291 8707
26	1.138 4596	1.295 2563	1.673 4181	2.156 5913	2.772 4698	3.555 6727	4.549 3830
27	1.144 1519	1.308 2089	1.706 8865	2.221 2890	2.883 3686	3.773 4563	4.822 3459
28	1.149 8726	1.321 2910	1.741 0242	2.287 9277	2.998 7033	3.920 1291	5.111 6867
29	1.155 6220	1.334 5039	1.775 8447	2.356 5655	3.118 6514	4.116 1356	5.418 3879
30	1.161 4001	1.347 8489	1.811 3616	2.427 2625	3.243 3975	4.321 9424	5.743 4912
40	1.220 7942	1.488 8637	2.208 0397	3.262 0378	4.801 0206	7.039 9887	10.285 7179
50	1.283 2258	1.644 6318	2.691 5880	4.383 9060	7.106 6834	11.467 3998	18.420 1543
60	1.348 8502	1.816 6967	3.281 0308	5.891 6031	10.519 6274	18.679 1859	32.987 6908
70	1.417 8305	2.006 7634	3.999 5582	7.917 8219	15.571 6184	30.426 4255	59.075 9302
80	1.490 3386	2.216 7152	4.875 4392	10.640 8906	23.049 7991	49.561 4411	105.795 9935
90	1.566 5547	2.448 6327	5.943 1331	14.300 4671	34.119 3333	80.730 3650	189.464 5112
100	1.646 6685	2.704 8138	7.244 6461	19.218 6320	50.504 9482	131.501 2578	339.302 0835

Example 6 **Find (a) the maturity value of $500 if it can earn 5 percent per year compounded annually for 4 years and (b) the total compound interest (same as Example 1b).**

(a) $P = \$500$

$$i = \frac{5\%}{1} = 5\%$$

$$n = 4(1) = 4$$

From $S = P(1 + i)^n$

$$S = \$500(1.05)^4$$
$$= \$500(1.215\ 5062) \qquad \text{(Table 6.1)}$$
$$= \$607.75$$

(b) $I = S - P$
$$= \$607.75 - \$500.00 = \$107.75$$

Example 7 **Find the compound amount of $600 invested at 8 percent compounded quarterly for 7 years.**

$P = \$600$

$$i = \frac{8\%}{4} = 2\%$$

$$n = 7(4) = 28$$

From $S = P(1 + i)^n$

$$S = \$600(1.02)^{28}$$
$$= \$600(1.741\ 0242) \qquad \text{(Table 6.1)}$$
$$= \$1044.61$$

Remember that rates in compound interest are stated as *nominal rates* and time is stated in terms of years. Before you can find the proper compound-interest factor, you must convert the given nominal rate j to i by $\dfrac{j}{m}$ and convert the given time (years) to n by years (m).

FINDING THE EFFECTIVE RATE OF INTEREST PER YEAR   It becomes necessary to compare investment plans, savings accounts, and loans of various types when different *nominal rates* of interest are compounded more than once per year. A comparison can be made by calculating the total interest to be earned or charged over the entire life of the investment or loan. However, since any two interest rates, whether nominal or effective rates, are equivalent if their compound amounts at the end of one year are equivalent, a more convenient comparison is to compare the effective annual rates.

To calculate the effective annual rate:

1 Find the amount of $1 at the nominal rate and for the number of periods contained in 1 year.
2 Subtract the principal of $1 from the amount to obtain the interest earned in 1 year.

Example 8   **Find the effective annual rates of the following:**

(a)   6%, $m = 12$
(b)   8%, $m = 4$
(c)   12%, $m = 2$

Solutions:

(a) $i = \dfrac{6\%}{12} = \dfrac{1}{2}\%$ $n = 1(12) = 12$

$(1.005)^{12} = 1.061\ 6778$ (Table 6.1)
$1.0617 - 1 = .0617 = 6.17\%$ (Effective annual rate)

(b) $i = \dfrac{8\%}{4} = 2\%$ $n = 1(4) = 4$

$(1.02)^4 = 1.082\ 4322$ (Table 6.1)
$1.082\ 4322 - 1 = .0824 = 8.24\%$ (Effective annual rate)

(c) $i = \dfrac{12\%}{2} = 6\%$ $n = 1(2) = 2$

$(1.06)^2 = 1.1236$ (Table 6.1)
$1.1236 - 1 = .1236 = 12.36\%$ (Effective annual rate)

Rates and Conversion Periods, Not Found in Sample Tables

Since the coming of the computer, and the more recent wide availability of programmed pocket calculators, investment plans and loan contracts can be and are created with a much wider range of interest rates and conversion periods than was customary when just interest factor tables were available. For example, savings banks advertise interest on savings accounts *compounded daily*. Savings banks customarily use 30-day-month time in crediting interest to customer savings accounts and have developed tables to find the compound amount based on a 360-day year. Table 6.2 calculates some selected entries from the table for the nominal rates of 5.25 and 6 percent. To find the compound interest directly in one mathematical operation, subtract 1 from the factor listed for the compound amount, and multiply by *P*. Thus:

1 From $I = S - P$
2 Substitute the formula $P + P(1 + i)$ for S:

$I = P + P(1 + i) - P$

3 Factoring the equation in (2):

$I = P[(1 + i) - 1]$

TABLE 6.2 AMOUNT OF $1 AT COMPOUND INTEREST COMPOUNDED DAILY, 360-DAY YEAR

	Nominal rate	
n	$5\frac{1}{4}\%$	6%
1	1.000 1458	1.001 1667
30	1.004 3843	1.003 0121
60	1.008 7877	1.010 0493
90	1.013 2105	1.015 1118
360	1.053 8985	1.061 8312
720	1.110 7021	1.127 4856
1080	1.170 5673	1.197 1994
1440	1.233 6591	1.271 2237
1800	1.300 1516	1.349 8251
3600	1.690 3941	1.822 0277

Example 9 Jack Fiegal invested $1000 in the Buckhorn Savings and Loan on April 1. At 5.25 percent compounded daily, find (a) the interest credited to Mr. Fiegal's account for the second quarter ending June 30 and (b) the maturity value of the investment at the end of 2 years.

(a) $P = \$1000$

$$i = \frac{5\frac{1}{4}\%}{360}$$

$n = 90$ (30-day-month time)

$I = P[(1 + i)^n - 1]$

$$I = \$1000\left[\left(1 + \frac{5\frac{1}{4}\%}{360}\right)^{90} - 1\right]$$

$$= \$1000\,[(1.013\ 2105) - 1]\ \text{(Table 6.2)}$$

$$= \$13.21$$

(b) $S = P\left(1 + \dfrac{5\frac{1}{4}\%}{360}\right)^{720}$

$$= \$1000\,(1.110\ 7021)\ \text{(Table 6.2)}$$

$$= \$1110.70$$

INTEREST RATES NOT REPRESENTED IN THE TABLE When an *interest rate* is not represented in the interest tables that are available for solving a problem, the use of logarithms or programmed calculators is necessary. This will be the case with the many rates of interest that are compounded daily and compounded continuously. Solving problems by logarithms is not within the scope of this text, and all problems involving compound interest included in the text can be solved by use of the tables illustrated. A comparison of the same nominal rate of interest compounded quarterly, daily, and continuously shows that a limit is reached when the compounding periods are increased and the difference is not as great as it might appear.

Example 10 **Find the effective rate of 6 percent compounded**

    (a) Monthly
    (b) Daily
    (c) Continuously

Solution:

    (a) $\left(1 + \dfrac{6}{12}\right)^{12} - 1 = (1.005)^{12} - 1 = .061\,6778$ (Table 6.1)

    (b) $\left(1 + \dfrac{.06}{365}\right)^{365} - 1$ $= .061\,8315$ (By logarithms)[1]

    (c) $(e^{.06} - 1)$ $= .061\,8365$ (By logarithms)[1]

CONVERSION PERIODS NOT REPRESENTED IN THE TABLE Conversion periods can be found by following the characteristic of exponents explained on page 201 if an interest table with sufficient addends for the desired number of periods is available. The problem could also be solved by use of logarithms or programmed calculators.

Example 11 **Find the compound amount if $2000 is invested at 6 percent, compounded monthly for 10 years.**

    $P = \$2000$

    $i = \dfrac{6\%}{12} = \dfrac{1}{2}\%$

    $n = 10(12) = 120$
    $S = \$2000(1.005)^{120}$

Solution:

Since $(1.005)^{120}$ is not listed in Table 6.1, the numerical value can be determined:

$$^1\left[365\,\log_e\left(1 + \frac{.06}{365}\right)\right] - 1 = [365\,\log_e(1.000\,164\,384)] - 1$$

$$= e^{.0599952} - 1$$

$$= 1.061\,8315 - 1 = .061\,8315+$$

$$(e^{.06} - 1) = .06e^z = 1.061\,8365 = .061\,8365+$$

$(1.005)^{120} = (1.005)^{100} (1.005)^{20}$
$(1.005)^{120} = (1.646\ 6685)\ (1.104\ 8956) = 1.819\ 3968$
$S = \$2000(1.819\ 3968)$
$\quad = \$3638.79$

Exercise 6.1

Find the interest rate per period (i) from the following nominal rates:

1	5%, $m = 4$	**2**	6%, $m = 4$
3	12%, $m = 2$	**4**	10%, $m = 2$
5	9%, $m = 12$	**6**	12%, $m = 12$
7	8%, $m = 360$	**8**	7%, $m = 365$

Find the number of conversion periods:

9 20 years, $m = 1$ **10** 25 years, 5 months, $m = 12$

11 $10\frac{3}{4}$ years, $m = 4$ **12** $5\frac{1}{2}$ years, $m = 2$

13 January 15, 1976 to   **14** January 15, 1976 to
February 20, 1986, $m = 360$ March 12, 1981, $m = 365$

Find the compound amounts (use Tables 6.1 or 6.2):

	Principal	Nominal rate	Term	Conversion periods per year
15	1200	8%	5 years	4
16	6000	12%	5 years	12
17	1500	6%	20 years	2
18	2500	$5\frac{1}{4}\%$	10 years	360
19	1800	$5\frac{1}{4}\%$	4 years	360

Find the compound interest (use Tables 6.1 or 6.2):

20	10,000	6%	5 years	12
21	10,000	6%	5 years	360
22	4000	12%	20 years	4
23	1250	8%	50 years	2
24	6000	10%	40 years	2

Solve the following:

25 On Julio's sixth birthday, his father placed $1000 in a savings account that earns 8 percent compounded quarterly. What would be in the account on Julio's twenty-first birthday?

26 Martha Rhea invested $2500 in a term savings account that earned

3,372.13   3,500   Alice by 127.87

6 percent, $m = 12$. Her daughter Alice invested the same amount at 8 percent simple interest. At the end of 5 years, find (a) who has the greater amount and (b) by how much.

27 The Blue Lake Savings Bank advertises interest paid on savings accounts at 8 percent compounded quarterly. The Fieldbrook Savings and Loan advertises interest paid on savings accounts at 6 percent compounded daily. Both banks use 30-day-month time in calculating interest. In which bank would your savings account earn more?

1.0824
vs
1.0618

28 The St. Martins Hospital sold 10 acres of land no longer needed for its purposes for net proceeds of $100,000. It could deposit the money in a savings bank earning $5\frac{1}{4}$ percent compounded daily or in another savings bank earning 6 percent compounded monthly. Both banks use 30-day-month time. Which bank should be selected in order to maximize the interest earned?

29 Judy Holding received an inheritance of $50,000. If she invests it at 8 percent, $m = 4$ for 5 years, and 6 percent, $m = 360$ for 5 more years, what will be the amount of the inheritance at the end of 10 years?

100,288.45

30 The Acme Co. placed $10,000 in a fund on July 1, 1970. If the fund earns interest at 12 percent, $m = 4$, what will be in the fund on March 31, 1977?

Unit 6.2

Reverse Operations in Compound Interest

If you deposited $1000 in a savings account at 6 percent, compounded monthly, how long would it take to double? How much would you have to deposit in a savings account at 8 percent, compounded quarterly, to be able to withdraw $5000 five years from now? These and other questions can be answered by restating the basic compound amount formula and finding any of these factors in the compound-interest table.

To Find Present Value at Compound Interest

From the equation to find the amount at compound interest, restate the formula to isolate the principal or present value. Thus:

$$S = P(1 + i)^n$$

or

$$P(1 + i)^n = S$$

Divide both sides of equation by $(1 + i)^n$:

$$P = \frac{S}{(1 + i)^n}$$

Example 1   **Find the principal which will amount to $5000 in 5 years at 8 percent, *m* = 4.**

P = principal = unknown
S = amount = $5000

$$i = \frac{j}{4} = \frac{8\%}{4} = 2\%$$

$n = 5 \text{ years} \times m = 5(4) = 20$

$$P = \frac{S}{(1 + i)^n} = \frac{\$5000}{(1.02)^{20}}$$

$$P = \frac{\$5000}{1.4859474} \text{ (from Table 6.3)}$$

$$= \$3364.86$$

The expression $\dfrac{S}{(1 + i)^n}$ can be factored to form the basis of a table to find the present value by a multiplication operation rather than the division operation illustrated in Example 1. Thus:

$$\frac{S}{(1 + i)^n} = S\frac{1}{(1 + i)^n}$$

The expression $\dfrac{1}{(1 + i)^n}$, the reciprocal of $(1 + i)^n$, is calculated for different values of i and successive periods for n and presented in tables. Selected values for $\dfrac{1}{(1 + i)^n}$, identified in the table as v^n, are presented in Table 6.3.

Example 2   **Same problem as Example 1.**

$$P = S\frac{1}{(1 + i)^n} \text{ or } P = Sv^n$$

$$P = \$5000\left(\frac{1}{(1.02)^{20}}\right)$$

$$= \$5000(.672\ 9713)$$
$$= \$3364.86$$

Example 3   **Gerald Fielding desires to discharge a debt of $15,000, not due until 10 years hence. However, his creditor will charge him a "penalty amount" for an early payoff. Therefore, Mr. Fielding chooses to invest a sum of money now that will pay off the $15,000 when due. Find the investment needed if it can earn 12 percent compounded quarterly.**

The sum of money needed to invest represents the *present value* of $15,000 due 10 years hence at 12 percent.

$m = 4$

P = present value needed = unknown

TABLE 6.3   PRESENT VALUE OF $1 AT COMPOUND INTEREST[1] $v^n = \dfrac{1}{(1+i)^n}$

Formula:

To find present value $P = S\left[\dfrac{1}{(1+i)^n}\right] = Sv^n$

n	$\frac{1}{2}$%	1%	2%	3%	4%	5%	6%
1	0.995 0249	0.990 0990	0.980 3922	0.970 8738	0.961 5385	0.952 3810	0.943 3962
2	0.990 0745	0.980 2960	0.961 1688	0.942 5959	0.924 5562	0.907 0295	0.889 9964
3	0.985 1488	0.970 5902	0.942 3223	0.915 1417	0.888 9964	0.863 8376	0.839 6193
4	0.980 2475	0.960 9803	0.923 8454	0.888 4870	0.854 8042	0.822 7025	0.792 0937
5	0.975 3707	0.951 4657	0.905 7308	0.862 6088	0.821 9271	0.783 5262	0.747 2582
6	0.970 5181	0.942 0452	0.887 9714	0.837 4843	0.790 3145	0.746 2154	0.704 9605
7	0.965 6896	0.932 7180	0.870 5602	0.813 0915	0.759 9178	0.710 6813	0.665 0571
8	0.960 8852	0.923 4832	0.853 4904	0.789 4092	0.730 6902	0.676 8394	0.627 4124
9	0.956 1047	0.914 3398	0.836 7553	0.766 4167	0.702 5867	0.644 6089	0.591 8985
10	0.951 3479	0.905 2870	0.820 3483	0.744 0939	0.675 5642	0.613 9132	0.558 3948
11	0.946 6149	0.896 3237	0.804 2630	0.722 4213	0.649 5809	0.584 6793	0.526 7875
12	0.941 9053	0.887 4492	0.788 4932	0.701 3799	0.624 5970	0.556 8374	0.496 9694
13	0.937 2192	0.878 6626	0.773 0325	0.680 9513	0.600 5741	0.530 3214	0.468 8390
14	0.932 5565	0.869 9630	0.757 8750	0.661 1178	0.577 4751	0.505 0680	0.442 3010
15	0.927 9169	0.861 3495	0.743 0147	0.641 8619	0.555 2645	0.481 0171	0.417 2651
16	0.923 3004	0.852 8213	0.728 4458	0.623 1669	0.533 9082	0.458 1115	0.393 6463
17	0.918 7068	0.844 3775	0.714 1626	0.605 0164	0.513 3732	0.436 2967	0.371 3644
18	0.914 1362	0.836 0173	0.700 1594	0.587 3946	0.493 6281	0.415 5206	0.350 3438
19	0.909 5882	0.827 7399	0.686 4308	0.570 2860	0.474 6424	0.395 7340	0.330 5130
20	0.905 0629	0.819 5445	0.672 9713	0.553 6758	0.456 3870	0.376 8895	0.311 8047
21	0.900 5601	0.811 4302	0.659 7758	0.537 5493	0.438 8336	0.358 9424	0.294 1554
22	0.896 0797	0.803 3962	0.646 8390	0.521 8925	0.421 9554	0.341 8499	0.277 5051
23	0.891 6216	0.795 4418	0.634 1559	0.506 6917	0.405 7263	0.325 5713	0.261 7973
24	0.887 1857	0.787 5661	0.621 7215	0.491 9337	0.390 1215	0.310 0679	0.246 9786
25	0.882 7718	0.779 7684	0.609 5309	0.477 6056	0.375 1168	0.295 3028	0.232 9986
26	0.878 3799	0.772 0480	0.597 5793	0.463 6947	0.360 6892	0.219 8100	0.281 2407
27	0.874 0099	0.764 4039	0.585 8620	0.450 1891	0.346 8166	0.207 3680	0.267 8483
28	0.869 6616	0.756 8356	0.574 3746	0.437 0768	0.333.4775	0.195 6301	0.255 0936
29	0.865 3349	0.749 3422	0.563 1123	0.424 3464	0.320 6514	0.184 5567	0.242 9463
30	0.861 0297	0.741 9229	0.552 0709	0.411 9868	0.308 3187	0.174 1101	0.231 3774
40	0.819 1389	0.671 6531	0.452 8908	0.306 5568	0.208 2890	0.142 0457	0.097 2222
50	0.779 2861	0.608 0388	0.371 5279	0.228 1071	0.140 7126	0.087 2037	0.054 2884
60	0.741 3722	0.550 4496	0.304 7823	0.169 7331	0.095 0604	0.053 5355	0.030 3143
70	0.705 3029	0.498 3149	0.250 0276	0.126 2974	0.064 2194	0.032 8662	0.016 9274
80	0.670 9885	0.451 1179	0.205 1097	0.093 9771	0.043 3843	0.020 1770	0.009 4522
90	0.638 3435	0.408 3912	0.168 2614	0.069 9278	0.029 3089	0.012 3869	0.005 2780
100	0.607 2868	0.369 7112	0.138 0330	0.052 0328	0.019 8000	0.007 6045	0.002 9472

[1] Note that each factor in this table is reciprocal to the accumulation factor in Table 6.1.

S = amount = \$15,000

$i = \dfrac{12\%}{4} = 3\%$

$n = 10(4) = 40$

$$P = S\left(\frac{1}{(1 + i)^n}\right)$$

$$P = \$15{,}000\left(\frac{1}{(1.03)^{40}}\right)$$

$$= \$15{,}000(.306\ 5568) = \$4598.35$$

TO FIND THE NUMBER OF COMPOUND-INTEREST PERIODS   The basic compound-interest formula to find the amount is restated to isolate $(1 + i)^n$. By reference to Table 6.1, the value for n can be determined. Thus:

1   $S = P(1 + i)^n$
2   Divide both sides of equation by P:

$$\frac{S}{P} = (1 + i)^n$$

Example 4   **If $1000 is deposited in a credit union, how long would it take to accumulate a fund of $1485.95 if it can earn 8 percent, $m = 4$?**

1   $P = \$1000.00$

  $S = \$1485.95$

  $i = \dfrac{8\%}{4} = 2\%$

  $n = $ years $(4) = $ not given

2   $\dfrac{S}{P} = (1 + i)^n$

  $\dfrac{1485.95}{1000.00} = (1.02)^n$

  $1.48595 = (1.02)^n$

3   Refer to Table 6.1
   (a)   Select the 2% column.
   (b)   Scan down the 2% column until you reach the value 1.48595 opposite 20 periods in the n column.

4   $n = $ years (m); therefore years $= \dfrac{n}{m}$

  Years $= \dfrac{20}{4} = 5$ years

TO FIND THE PERIODIC RATE OF INTEREST i AND THE NOMINAL RATE j
Similarly, the same procedure used to find an unknown value for n can be used to find an unknown value for i. Once i is found, it can then be converted to j.

Example 5   **Four years after borrowing $1500, Mr. Hobbs repaid the loan with interest, the amount required being $2407.06. What rate of interest, compounded quarterly, did Mr. Hobbs pay?**

1   $P = \$1500$
$S = \$2407.06$
$n = 4(4) = 16$

$i = \dfrac{j}{4} = \text{not given}$

2   $\dfrac{S}{P} = (1 + i)^n$

$\dfrac{2407.06}{1500.00} = (1 + i)^{16}$

$1.604\ 7064 = (1 + i)^{16}$

3   Refer to Table 6.1.
   (a)   Select the horizontal line where $n = 16$.
   (b)   Scan across the values in the various percent columns until you reach the value 1.604704 in the 3% column.

4   $i = \dfrac{j}{m}$; therefore $j = (i)(m)$

$j = 3\% \times 4 = 12\%$

WHEN THE VALUES FOR n AND i ARE NOT PRECISELY REPRESENTED IN THE TABLE[1] If the value represented by the quotient in step 2 in the procedures above is not exactly represented in Table 6.1, you may:

(a)   State your answer approximately by converting to their annual equivalents the periods (n) or the periodic interest rate (i) that bracket (are above and below) the values for n and i indicated by the quotient in step 2.
(b)   Interpolate in the tables to obtain a more precise rate.

The approximate time or rate may be all that is necessary in most on-the-spot business decisions. They can be found relatively simply by use of the compound-interest tables.

Example 6   **Ms. Dirksen deposits $800 in a savings account at 6 percent interest compounded semiannually. Approximately how long will it take to double?**

1   $(1 + i)^n = \dfrac{S}{P}$

---

[1]Unknown values for n and i can also be determined by the use of logarithms and determined quite easily by use of a programmed pocket calculator.

$$P = \$800$$
$$S = \$1600$$
$$j = 6 \text{ percent}$$
$$m = 2$$

$$i = \frac{j}{m} = \frac{6}{2} = 3 \text{ percent}$$

$$n = \text{years} \times m = \text{unknown}$$

2 $(1.03)^n = \dfrac{1600}{800} = 2.0$

3 Refer to Table 6.1. (Note that in the 3 percent column, the values given for 23 periods and 24 periods bracket the value 2.0.)

4 Since n lies between $11\frac{1}{2}$ years $\left[\dfrac{23(n)}{2(m)}\right]$ and 12 years $\left[\dfrac{24(n)}{2(m)}\right]$, an *approxi-*

mate answer suitable in many cases would be "between $11\frac{1}{2}$ and 12

years."

Example 7 **Ms. Patenaude borrows $1500 and repays the loan 10 years later. The amount paid, including interest, was $2500. By use of Table 6.1, find the *approximate* rate of interest converted annually paid by Ms. Patenaude.**

1 $(1 + i)^n = \dfrac{S}{P}$

$$P = \$1500$$
$$S = \$2500$$
$$j = \text{unknown}$$
$$m = 1$$
$$i = \text{unknown}$$
$$n = \text{years} \times m = 10 \times 1 = 10$$

2 $(1 + i)^{10} = \dfrac{2500}{1500} = 1.66667$

3 Refer to Table 6.1. (Note that in the $n = 10$ line the values given in the 5 percent and 6 percent columns bracket the value 1.66667.)

4 Since i lies between 5 percent and 6 percent (and since $m = 1$, 5 and 6 percent also represents the effective annual rate), an approximate answer suitable in many cases would be "between 5 and 6 percent."[1]

Interpolation in the compound interest tables develops a more precise rate, which may be significant for some business decisions. Interpolation to obtain a more precise value for n, however, may not be significant. When the time falls within a conversion period, the interpolation procedure assumes a simple interest calculation for the fractional portion of one period.

[1] In a book of interest tables, the gradations in i for the more common rates of interest are as small as $\frac{1}{32}$ percent. With such tables, a much closer approximation could be made.

Interpolation in tables is performed as follows:

1 Locate the values that bracket (are above and below) the calculated value.
2 Obtain the *total difference* between the values that bracket the calculated value.
3 Obtain the *partial difference* between the lower value and the calculated value.
4 The actual rate is then:
   (a) The rate indicated by the lower value used in (3), plus
   (b) The same proportion of the total rate difference as the partial difference bears to the total difference found in (3) and (2) respectively.

Example 8 **Ms. Patenaude borrows $1500 and repays the loan 10 years later. The amount paid including interest, was $2500. By interpolation, find rate of interest, converted annually, paid by Ms. Patenaude (same problem data as Example 7).**

From the solution to Example 7, the calculated value of 1.6666667 was bracketed by the 5 and 6 percent columns (see Table 6.1).

| Total rate difference 1% | ⌈5% Actual rate ⌊6% | 1.6288946⌉ 1.6666667⌋ 1.7908477 | Partial difference .0377721 | Total difference .1619531 |

$$\text{Actual rate} = .05 + \left(\frac{.0377721}{.1619531} \times .01\right)$$

$$= .05 + .0023326$$

$$= .0523326 = 5.23\%[1]$$

Example 9 **Mr. Dirksen deposits $800 in a savings account at 6 percent interest compounded semiannually. By interpolation, find the time it will take to double (same problem data as Example 6).**

From the solution to Example 6, the calculated value 2.0 falls between 23 and 24 periods.

| 1 period $\left(\frac{1}{2} \text{ year}\right)$ | ⌈23 periods Actual time ⌊24 periods | 1.9735865⌉ 2.0 2.0327941 | .0264135 .0592076 |

$$\text{Actual time} = 23 \text{ periods} + \frac{.0264135}{.0592076} \times 1 = 23.446 \text{ periods}$$

[1]This rate and time may vary from the true rate and time depending upon the number of decimal places used in the factor tables. However, with the seven-place Table 6.1, the above values should not vary by more than .01 percent (.0001).

$$\text{Years} = \frac{n}{m}$$

$$= \frac{23.446}{2} = 11.723 \text{ years or approximately } 11\frac{264}{365} \text{ years}[1]$$

Exercise 6.2

Find the present value by use of Table 6.1:

1 $2000 due in 10 years at 6%, $m = 2$.
2 $5500 due in 40 years at 5%, $m = 1$.
3 $10,000 due in 25 years at 8%, $m = 4$.
4 $25,000 due in 5 years at 12%, $m = 12$.

Find the present value by use of Table 6.3.

5 $1500 due in 20 years at 8%, $m = 2$.
6 $1000 due in 5 years at 6%, $m = 12$.
7 $1600 due in 15 years at 12%, $m = 4$.
8 $6000 due in 10 years at 5%, $m = 1$.

Find the *approximate value* for the nominal rate:

	Present value	Amount	Years	Conversion periods per year
9	$1000	$2000	13	2
10	$3000	$4000	5	12
11	$1950	$5000	20	1
12	$1750	$2750	10	1

Find the approximate time:

	Present value	Amount	Nominal rate	Conversion periods per year
13	$800	$1400	8%	4
14	$1200	$2500	10%	2
15	$5000	$21,000	6%	1
16	$15,000	$55,000	5%	1

Find a more precise nominal rate by interpolation [to 5 decimal places (.00000)]:

[1]This rate and time may vary from the true rate and time depending upon the number of decimal places used in the factor tables. However with the seven-place Table 6.1, the above values should not vary by more than .01 percent (.0001).

	Present value	Amount	Years	Conversion periods per year
17	$1600	$2400	5	12
18	$1400	$2500	10	2
19	$1250	$21,500	60	1
20	$20,000	$37,500	15	2

Find a more precise time by interpolation:

	Present value	Amount	Nominal rate	Conversion periods per year
21	$ 500	$1000	12%	12
22	$ 750	$2200	8%	4
23	$1680	$7000	6%	1
24	$4400	$9000	5%	1

Solve the following:

25 How long does it take $1200 to amount to $2277.96 at 6%, $m = 1$?

26 $2650 will amount to $7946.56 in approximately how many years at 8%, $m = 2$?

27 After 15 years, a loan of $1000 was repaid by an amount of $10,519.62. Find the nominal rate, converted quarterly, that was charged on the loan.

28 Essex Savings and Loan credits interest at 8 percent, compounded quarterly. On the date of their daughter's birth, Thomas and Ellen deposited a sum of money that would amount to $10,000 on their daughter's twentieth birthday. How much money should they deposit?

29 Peggy and Bill want to have a vacation fund of $4000 in 5 years. They have $2750 to invest. At what rate, compounded quarterly, must they invest the $2750 in order to reach the $4000?

30 The Hair Company is scheduled to receive $50,000 in 4 years when the final installment becomes due on the sale of a patent. If the Board of Directors wanted to sell the final installment to an investor who was charging 10%, $m = 2$, how much would the Hair Company receive?

Unit 6.3   *Annuities: Finding Amount;*
                                                                    Tables

---

Annuities are perhaps the most widely used application of compound interest. Pension and retirement plans, determination of monthly payments to retire short- and long-term loans, capital-budgeting decisions, and a great many other areas concerned with the time-value of money—all are based on the concepts of compound interest and annuities.

An *annuity* is a series of payments, usually equal, made at regular intervals of time. Although the word "annuity" indicates an annual or yearly payment, its meaning has been broadened to include payments at regular intervals which may be more or less than one year. Annuities may be of several types:

Type	Description
Annuities certain	The number of payments and time periods are fixed and certain. A series of equal payments each month for 10 years is an annuity certain.
Contingent annuity	The starting date, number of payments, or ending date depend on the happening of an unknown event. A pension which pays a certain payment for the life of an individual is a contingent annuity. Pure contingent annuities will not be taken up in this text.
Ordinary annuity	The periodic payment comes at the *end* of each regular period.
Annuity due	The periodic payment comes at the *beginning* of each regular period.
Simple annuity	The payment and the number of times interest is compounded each year are the same. An annuity of 12 equal payments, when the interest rate is 6 percent, compounded 12 times a year is a simple annuity.
General annuity	The payment interval and the number of times interest is compounded per year *do not coincide*. An annuity of one annual payment when interest is compounded quarterly is a general annuity. General annuities will not be taken up in this text.
Perpetuities	The payments continue forever. The payment of a scholarship to a university forever is an example of a perpetuity. The present value of a perpetuity is equal to $A = \dfrac{I}{i}$.

Terms and Symbols Used with Annuities

Term and symbol	Definition
Rent (R)	The periodic payment made at regular intervals throughout the annuity.
Rent period	The unit of time for which one payment is made. Since this text will be concerned with simple annuities only, the rent period will be the same as m, the number of times interest is compounded each year.
Term of annuity	The time from the beginning of the first rent period to the end of the last rent period.
Nominal interest rate (j)	The annual rate of interest per $100 which is converted one or more times each year.

Conversion periods per year (*m*)	The number of periods the nominal rate is converted each year or the number of payments per year of a simple annuity.
Rate per period (*i*)	The rate of interest per payment or conversion period. Found by $\dfrac{j}{m}$.
Number of payments (*n*)	The total number of annuity payments in the term of the annuity.
Amount (*S*)	The accumulated value of all the rent payments at the end of the annuity term.
Present value (*P*)	The value of all the rent paymens at the beginning of the annuity term.

TO FIND THE AMOUNT OF AN ORDINARY ANNUITY AND AN ANNUITY DUE

An *ordinary annuity* and a visual presentation of what value make up the *amount* are illustrated by Example 1 and the following map.

Example 1   **Find the amount of $500 invested at the end of each year for 4 years at 5 percent interest compounded annually.**

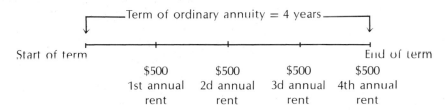

To find the amount of an ordinary annuity, find the value of each periodic rent payment at the maturity date. Thus:

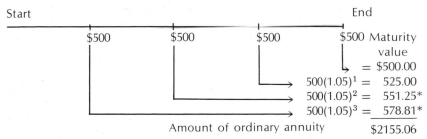

* Values for $(1 + i)^n$ obtained from Table 6.1. Although the procedure illustrated above will find the amount of an ordinary annuity, a formula and table have been developed to simplify the calculation.

1   Notice that what was done in the preceding calculation to find the amount of an ordinary annuity can be expressed as:

$$S = 500 + 500(1.05)^1 + 500(1.05)^2 + 500(1.05)^3$$

2 Factoring the expression in (1),

$$S = 500[1 + (1.05)^1 + (1.05)^2 + (1.05)^3]$$

3 Notice that within the brackets [ ] in (2) a *geometric progression* is present, whereby there is a sequence of terms each of which, after the first, is obtained by multiplying the preceding term by a common ratio.

$$1 = \text{first term}$$
$$(1.05)^1 = \text{common ratio as is seen by}$$

$$1 \times (1.05)^1 = (1.05)^1 = \text{second term}$$
$$(1.05)^1 \times (1.05)^1 = (1.05)^2 = \text{third term}$$
$$(1.05)^2 \times (1.05)^1 = (1.05)^3 = \text{fourth term}$$
$$(1.05)^3 = \text{last term in this example}$$

4 From the formula to find the sum of a geometric progression:

$$\left(\begin{array}{c}\text{Sum of a} \\ \text{geometric progression}\end{array}\right) = \frac{\text{common ratio} \times \text{last term} - \text{first term}}{\text{common ratio} - 1}$$

a formula is constructed so that the calculations to find the amount of an ordinary annuity are greatly simplified. Thus:

$$\text{Sum of items inside the brackets in (2)} = \frac{(1.05)^1(1.05)^3 - 1}{(1.05)^1 - 1}$$

$$= \frac{(1.05)^4 - 1}{0.05}$$

5 The amount of the ordinary annuity in Example 1 is then found:

$$\left.\begin{array}{l}S = 500\dfrac{(1.05)^4 - 1}{0.05} \\[3mm] = 500\dfrac{1.2155062 - 1}{0.05}\end{array}\right\} \quad (1.05)^4 = 1.2155062 \text{ (Table 6.1)}$$

$$= 500(4.310125) = \$2155.06$$

6 In symbolic terms, the formula to find the sum of an ordinary annuity S is presented as:

$$S = R\frac{(1 + i)^n - 1}{i}$$

where R = periodic rent payments
$\qquad n$ = number of rents in the term, determined by (years in term) $\times$ (number of rents per year)
$\qquad i$ = interest rate per compounding periods per year determined by $\dfrac{j}{m}$

Table 6.4 presents the values of the amount of ordinary annuities of $1 per period for selected term lengths n and for various periodic interest rates i. It is customary to express the formula $\dfrac{(1 + i)^n - 1}{i}$ in its abbreviated symbolic form as $s_{\overline{n}|i}$. The symbol $s_{\overline{n}|i}$ is read "s sub n at rate i" and means the amount of an ordinary annuity of $1 per period payable for n periods at the periodic rate i.

Example 2   **Same as Example 1.**

S = amount of ordinary annuity
R = periodic annual rent = $500
n = number of periods in term = $4(1) = 4$

i = interest rate per period = $\dfrac{5\%}{1} = 5\%$

Hence,

$S = 500(s_{\overline{4}|0.05})$
$ = 500(4.3101250)$ (Table 6.4)
$ = \$2155.06$

An *annuity due* and a visual presentation of what values make up the *amount* are illustrated by Example 3 and an adaptation of the map used for an ordinary annuity.

Example 3   **Find the amount of $500 invested at the *beginning of each year* for 4 years at 5 percent interest compounded annually (use Table 6.1).**

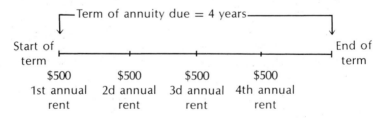

To find the amount of an annuity due, find the value of all periodic payments at the maturity date. Thus (using Table 6.1):

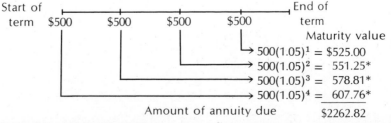

*Values of $(1 + i)^n$ obtained from Table 6.1.

Note that the amount of an annuity due is larger than that of an ordinary annuity with the same periodic rent and interest rate (see Example 2). In checking the "maps," the reasons for the difference become apparent, as indicated by the following comparison.

	Ordinary annuity	Annuity due
First payment	Earns interest for 3 years	Earns interest for 4 years
Last payment	Earns no interest	Earns interest for 1 year

The formula to find the amount of an ordinary annuity, together with Table 6.4, can be adapted to find the amount of an annuity due.

1   An annuity due of 4 rent periods is the same as an ordinary annuity of 5 rent periods less 1 payment, as illustrated by the following:

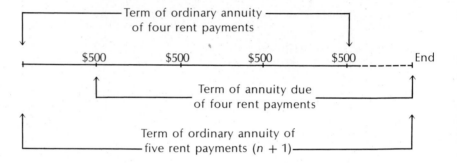

2   Since the last rent payment in an ordinary annuity earns no interest, we can assume a rent payment at the end of the dotted line above for inclusion in the ordinary annuity formula, and then subtract the face value of that payment from the answer to obtain the amount of an annuity due. (See Example 4.)

Example 4   Same as Example 3.

(a)   The amount of an ordinary annuity of $n + 1$ rent payments $(4 + 1) = 5$.

$$S = \$500(s_{\overline{5}|0.05})$$
$$= 500(5.5256312) \quad \text{(Table 6.4)}$$
$$= \$2762.82$$

(b)   Subtract the face value of the last payment
$2762.82 - \$500 = \$2262.82$.

TABLE 6.4 AMOUNT OF $1 PER PERIOD AT COMPOUND INTEREST $s_{\overline{n}|i} = \dfrac{(1 + i)^n - 1}{i}$

Formulas:

To find amount of an ordinary annuity $S = R\dfrac{(1 + i)^n - 1}{i} = Rs_{\overline{n}|i}$

To find amount of an annuity due $S = R\dfrac{(1 + i)^{n+1} - 1}{i} - R = R(s_{\overline{n+1}|i} - 1)$

n	$\frac{1}{2}\%$	1%	2%	3%	4%	5%	6%
1	1.000 0000	1.000 0000	1.000 0000	1.000 0000	1.000 0000	1.000 0000	1.000 0000
2	2.005 0000	2.010 0000	2.020 0000	2.030 0000	2.040 0000	2.050 0000	2.060 0000
3	3.015 0250	3.030 1000	3.060 4000	3.090 9000	3.121 6000	3.152 5000	3.183 6000
4	4.030 1001	4.060 4010	4.121 6080	4.183 6270	4.246 4640	4.310 1250	4.374 6160
5	5.050 2506	5.101 0050	5.204 0402	5.309 1358	5.416 3226	5.525.6312	5.637 0930
6	6.075 5019	6.152 0151	6.308 1210	6.468 4099	6.632 9755	6.801 9128	6.975 3185
7	7.105 8794	7.213 5352	7.434 2834	7.662 4622	7.898 2945	8.142 0084	8.393 8376
8	8.141 4088	8.285 6706	8.582 9691	8.892 3360	9.214 2263	9.549 1089	9.897 4679
9	9.182 1158	9.368 5273	9.754 6284	10.159 1061	10.582 7953	11.026 5643	11.491 3160
10	10.228 0264	10.462 2125	10.949 7210	11.463 8793	12.006 1071	12.577 8925	13.180 7949
11	11.279 1665	11.566 8347	12.168 7154	12.807 7957	13.486 3514	14.206 7872	14.971 6426
12	12.335 5624	12.682 5030	13.412 0897	14.192 0296	15.025 8055	15.917 1265	16.869 9412
13	13.397 2402	13.809 3280	14.680 3315	15.617 7904	16.626 8377	17.712 9828	18.882 1377
14	14.464 2264	14.947 4213	15.973 9382	17.086 3242	18.291 9112	19.558 6320	21.015 0659
15	15.536 5475	16.096 8955	17.293 4169	18.598 9139	20.023 5876	21.578 5636	23.275 9699
16	16.614 2303	17.257 8645	18.639 2853	20.156 8813	21.824 5311	23.657 4918	25.672 5281
17	17.697 3014	18.430 4431	20.012 0710	21.761 5877	23.697 5124	25.840 3664	28.212 8798
18	18.785 7879	19.614 7476	21.412 3124	23.414 4354	25 645 4129	28.132 3047	30.905 6526
19	19.879 7168	20.810 8950	22.840 5586	25.116 8684	27.671 2294	30.539 0039	33.759 9917
20	20.979 1154	22.019 0040	24.297 3698	26.870 3745	29.778 0786	33.065 9541	36.785 5912
21	22.084 0110	22.239 1940	25.783 3172	28.676 4857	31.969 2017	35.719 2518	39.992 7267
22	23.194 4311	24.471 5860	27.298 9835	30.536 7803	34.247 9698	38.505 2144	43.392 2903
23	24.310 4032	25.716 3018	28.844 9632	32.452 8837	36.617 8886	41.430 4751	46.995 8277
24	25.431 9552	26.973 4648	30.421 8625	34.426 4702	39.082 6041	44.501 9989	50.815 5774
25	26.559 1150	28.243 1995	32.030 2997	36.459 2643	41.645 9083	47.727 0988	54.864 5120
26	27.691 9106	29.525 6315	33.670 9057	38.553 0423	44.311 7446	51.113 4538	59.156 3827
27	28.830 3702	30.820 8878	35.344 3238	40.709 6335	47.084 2144	54.669 1264	63.705 7657
28	29.974 5220	32.129 0967	37.015 2103	42.930 9225	49.967 5830	58.402 5828	68.528 1116
29	31.124 3946	33.450 3877	38.792 2345	45 218 8502	52.966 2863	62.322 7119	73.639 7983
30	32.280 0166	34.784 8915	40.568 0792	47.575 4157	56.084 9378	66.438 8475	79.058 1862
40	44.158 8473	48.886 3734	60.401 9832	75.401 2597	95.025 5157	120.799 7742	154.761 9656
50	56.645 1630	64.463 1822	84.579 4015	112.796 8673	152 667 0837	209.347 9957	290.335 9046
60	69.770 0305	81.669 6699	114.051 5394	163.053 4368	237.990 6852	353.583 7179	533.128 1809
70	83.566 1055	100.676 3368	149.977 9111	230.594 0637	364.290 4588	588.528 5107	967.932 1696
80	98.067 7136	121.671 5217	193.771 9578	321.363 0185	551.244 9768	971.228 8213	1746.599 8914
90	113.310 9358	144.863 2675	247.156 6563	443.348 9037	827.983 3335	1594.607 3010	3141.075 1872
100	129.333 6984	170.481 3829	312.232 3059	607.287 7327	1237.623 7046	2610.025 1569	5638.368 0586

(c) The subtraction of the face value of the last payment could have been accomplished by subtracting 1 from the value of $s_{\overline{5}|0.05}$ from Table 6.4 before multiplying by the periodic rent of $500. Thus:

$$s_{\overline{5}|0.05} = 5.5256312 \quad \text{(Table 6.4)}$$

$$(-) 1.$$
$$\overline{4.5256312} \times \$500 = \$2262.82$$

3 In symbolic terms, the formula for finding the amount of an annuity due is then:

$$S = R(s_{\overline{n+1}|i}) - 1$$

Substituting the data of Example 4,

$$S = \$500(s_{\overline{5}|0.05}) - 1$$
$$= \$500(5.525\ 6312 - 1) \quad \text{(Table 6.4)}$$
$$= \$500(4.525\ 6312)$$
$$= \$2262.82$$

Exercise 6.3

Find the amount of the following ordinary annuities:

	Rent	Nominal rate	Payments per year and m	Total number of payments
1	$ 100	6%	12	90
2	$1000	8%	4	60
3	$1500	5%	1	24
4	$1800	12%	4	30
5	$ 250	8%	2	12
6	$4500	10%	2	6

Find the amount of the following annuities due:

7	$ 600	8%	4	20
8	$ 750	6%	1	18
9	$1640	12%	4	24
10	$1100	10%	2	12
11	$ 400	16%	4	15
12	$ 250	12%	12	12

Note: In the problems that follow, draw a map of the term of the annuity and when the payments are made. In this manner, you can visualize the distinction between an ordinary annuity and an annuity due and choose the proper formula.

Solve the following:

13 On his son's sixth birthday, and every birthday thereafter, Bob Hines deposited $150 in a savings account that earned 6 percent compounded annually. What was in the account *just after* Mr. Hines made the payment on his son's twenty-first birthday?

14 On her daughter's fourth birthday, and every birthday thereafter, Mary Wright deposited $300 in a savings account which earned 6 percent compounded annually. What was in the account *just before* Ms. Wright made the payment for her nineteenth birthday?

15 Art McCune wanted to save enough money to make a downpayment on a new fishing boat. If he deposited $4000 into a fund at the end of every 3 months, how much would be in the fund at the end of 60 months if the fund earned 8%, $m = 4$?

16 To provide for replacement of equipment, a trucking firm deposited $2000 at the beginning of each month for 24 months. How much was in the fund *just after the 24th payment was made* if the account could earn 12%, $m = 12$?

17 Find the amount of $250 deposited at the end of each month just after the sixth payment was made. The account earns 6%, $m = 12$. Assume that Table 6.4 was not available and you had to use Table 6.1.

18 Find the amount of $600 deposited at the beginning of each quarter, one quarter after the tenth payment was made. The account earns 12%, $m = 4$. Assume that Table 6.4 was not available and you had to use Table 6.1.

19 On July 1, 1978, Jill Mannix opened a savings account with $750. If Ms. Mannix deposited $750 in the account on January 1 and July 1 of each year thereafter, how much would be in the account just after the payment was made January 1, 1986? The account earns 8%, $m = 2$.

20 On December 1, 1979, Greg Ennes deposited $100 in a savings account that earns 6%, $m = 12$. If Mr. Ennes deposited a like amount on the first of every month, how much would be in the fund just before Mr. Ennes made his payment on May 1, 1982?

Unit 6.4   *Annuities: Finding Present Value; Tables*

The present value of an *ordinary annuity* finds the value of all the rent payments at the beginning of the annuity term. Example 1 and the following map illustrate the determination of the present value of an ordinary annuity.

Example 1   **Find the present value of $300 received at the end of each 3 months for the next $1\frac{1}{2}$ years at 8 percent interest compounded quarterly (use Table 6.3).**

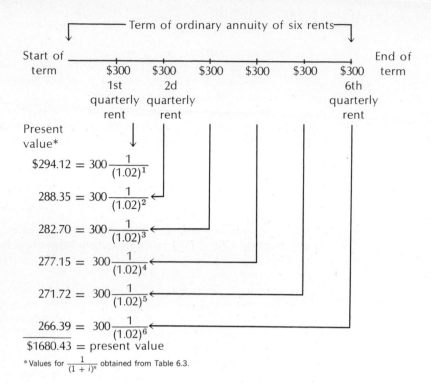

$294.12 = 300\dfrac{1}{(1.02)^1}$

$288.35 = 300\dfrac{1}{(1.02)^2}$

$282.70 = 300\dfrac{1}{(1.02)^3}$

$277.15 = 300\dfrac{1}{(1.02)^4}$

$271.72 = 300\dfrac{1}{(1.02)^5}$

$266.39 = 300\dfrac{1}{(1.02)^6}$

$\overline{\$1680.43} = $ present value

* Values for $\dfrac{1}{(1+i)^n}$ obtained from Table 6.3.

As was the case in developing a formula to find the amount of an ordinary annuity, a formula is developed for finding the present value of an ordinary annuity.

$A = $ present value of ordinary annuity

$R = $ periodic rent payments $= \$300$

$n = $ number of rents in the term $= $ years $(m) = 1\dfrac{1}{2}(4) = 6$

$i = $ interest rate per compounding periods per year $= \dfrac{j}{m} = \dfrac{8}{4} = 2\%$

1 $A = 300\dfrac{1}{(1.02)^1} + 300\dfrac{1}{(1.02)^2} + \cdots + 300\dfrac{1}{(1.02)^6}$

2 By applying a formula to find the sum of a geometric progression:

3 $A = 300\dfrac{1 - \dfrac{1}{(1.02)^6}}{0.02}$

4 $A = 300\dfrac{1 - 0.8879714}{0.02}$ $\left(\text{Table 6.3 for } \dfrac{1}{(1.02)^6}\right)$

5 $A = 300(5.60143)$

6 $A = \$1680.43$

7 In symbolic terms and with the symbols as defined above:

$$A = R\frac{1 - \dfrac{1}{(1 + i)^n}}{i}$$

Table 6.5 presents the present values of ordinary annuities of $1 per period for selected term lengths n and for various periodic interest rates i. It is customary to express the formula

$$\frac{1 - \dfrac{1}{(1 + i)^n}}{i}$$

in its abbreviated symbolic form as $a_{\overline{n}|i}$. The symbol $a_{\overline{n}|i}$ is read "a sub n at rate i" and means the present value of $1 per period for n periods at the periodic rate i.

Example 2   **Same as Example 1 (use Table 6.5).**

$$\begin{aligned}
A &= Ra_{\overline{n}|i} \\
&= \$300(a_{\overline{6}|0.02}) \\
&= 300(5.6014309) \quad \text{(Table 6.5)} \\
&= \$1680.43
\end{aligned}$$

The present value of an *annuity due* is illustrated by Example 3 and visualized on the following map.

Example 3   **Find the present value of $300 received at the beginning of each 3 months for the next $1\frac{1}{2}$ years at 8 percent compounded quarterly.**

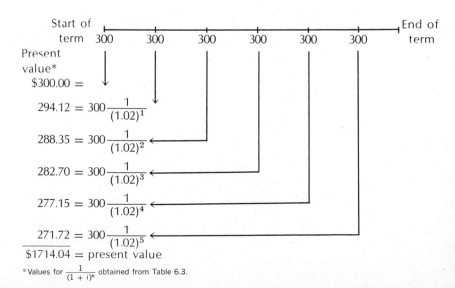

Start of term   300   300   300   300   300   300   End of term

Present value*

$$\$300.00 =$$

$$294.12 = 300\frac{1}{(1.02)^1}$$

$$288.35 = 300\frac{1}{(1.02)^2}$$

$$282.70 = 300\frac{1}{(1.02)^3}$$

$$277.15 = 300\frac{1}{(1.02)^4}$$

$$271.72 = 300\frac{1}{(1.02)^5}$$

$$\overline{\$1714.04} = \text{present value}$$

* Values for $\dfrac{1}{(1 + i)^n}$ obtained from Table 6.3.

As was the case in adapting the formula and Table 6.4 to find the amount of an ordinary annuity for use with an annuity due, the formula and table can be similarly adapted from the formula and Table 6.5 used to find the present value of an ordinary annuity.

TABLE 6.5   PRESENT VALUE OF $1 PER PERIOD AT COMPOUND INTEREST $a_{\overline{n}|i} = \dfrac{1 - \dfrac{1}{(1 + i)^n}}{i}$

Formulas:

To find present value of an ordinary annuity $A = R(a_{\overline{n}|i})$

To find present value of an annuity due $A = R(1 + a_{\overline{n-1}|i})$

n	½%	1%	2%	3%	4%	5%	6%
1	0.995 0249	0.990 0990	0.980 3922	0.970 8738	0.961 5385	0.952 3810	0.943 3962
2	1.985 0994	1.970 3951	1.941 5609	1.913 4697	1.886 0947	1.859 4104	1.833 3927
3	2.970 2481	2.940 9852	2.883 8833	2.828 6114	2.775 0910	2.723 2480	2.673 0120
4	3.950 4957	3.901 9656	3.807 7287	3.717 0984	3.629 8952	3.545 9505	3.465 1056
5	4.925 8663	4.853 4312	4.713 4595	4.579 7072	4.451 8223	4.329 4767	4.212 3638
6	5.896 3844	5.795 4765	5.601 4309	5.417 1914	5.242 1369	5.075 6921	4.917 3243
7	6.862 0740	6.728 1945	6.471 9911	6.230 2830	6.002 0547	5.786 3734	5.582 3814
8	7.822 9592	7.651 6778	7.325 4814	7.019 6922	6.732 7449	6.463 2128	6.209 7938
9	8.779 0639	8.566 0176	8.162 2367	7.786 1089	7.435 3316	7.107 8217	6.801 6923
10	9.730 4119	9.471 3045	8.982 5850	8.530 2028	8.110 8958	7.721 7349	7.360 0870
11	10.677 0267	10.367 6282	9.786 8480	9.252 6241	8.760 4767	8.306 4142	7.886 8746
12	11.618 9321	11.255 0775	10.575 3412	9.954 0040	9.385 0738	8.863 2516	8.383 8439
13	12.556 1513	12.133 7401	11.348 3737	10.634 9553	9.985 6478	9.393 5730	8.852 6830
14	13.488 7078	13.003 7030	12.106 2488	11.296 0731	10.563 1229	9.898 6409	9.294 9839
15	14.416 6246	13.865 0525	12.849 2635	11.937 9351	11.118 3874	10.379 6580	9.712 2490
16	15.339 9250	14.717 8738	13.577 7093	12.561 1020	11.652 2956	10.837 7696	10.105 8953
17	16.258 6319	15.562 2513	14.291 8719	13.166 1185	12.165 6688	11.274 0662	10.477 2597
18	17.172 7680	16.398 2686	14.992 0313	13.753 5131	12.659 2970	11.689 5869	10.827 6035
19	18.082 3562	17.226 0085	15.678 4620	14.323 7991	13.133 9394	12.085 3209	11.158 1165
20	18.987 4192	18.045 5530	16.351 4333	14.877 4749	13.590 3263	12.462 2103	11.469 9212
21	19.887 9792	18.856 9831	17.011 2092	15.415 0241	14.029 1600	12.821 1527	11.764 0766
22	20.784 0590	19.660 3793	17.658 0482	15.936 9166	14.451 1153	13.163 0026	12.041 5817
23	21.675 6806	20.455 8211	18.292 2041	16.443 6084	14.856 8417	13.488 5739	12.303 3790
24	22.562 8662	21.243 3873	18.913 9256	16.935 5421	15.246 9631	13.798 6418	12.550 3575
25	23.445 6380	22.023 1557	19.523 4565	17.413 1477	15.622 0799	14.093 9446	12.783 3562
26	24.324 0179	22.795 2037	20.121 0358	17.876 8424	15.982 7692	14.375 1853	13.003 1662
27	25.198 0278	23.559 6076	20.706 8978	18.327 0315	16.329 5858	14.643 0336	13.210 5341
28	26.067 6894	24.316 4432	21.281 2724	18.764 1082	16.663 0632	14.898 1273	13.406 1643
29	26.933 0242	25.065 7853	21.844 3847	19.188 4546	16.983 7146	15.141 0736	13.590 7210
30	27.794 0540	25.807 7082	22.396 4556	19.600 4414	17.292 0333	15.372 4510	13.764 8312
40	36.172 2279	32.934 6861	27.355 4792	23.114 7720	19.792 7739	17.159 0864	15.046 2969
50	44.142 7864	39.196 1175	31.423 6059	25.729 7640	21.482 1846	18.255 9255	15.761 8606
60	51.725 5608	44.955 0384	34.760 8867	27.675 5637	22.623 4900	18.929 2895	16.161 4277
70	58.939 4176	50.168 5144	37.493 6193	29.123 4214	23.394 5150	19.342 6766	16.384 5439
80	65.802 3054	54.888 2061	39.744 5136	30.200 7634	23.915 3918	19.596 4605	16.509 1308
90	72.331 2996	59.160 8815	41.586 9292	31.002 4071	24.267 2776	19.752 2617	16.578 6994
100	78.542 6448	63.028 8788	43.098 3516	31.598 9053	24.504 9990	19.847 9102	16.617 5462

1 An annuity due of 6 rent payments is the same as an ordinary annuity of 5 rent payments plus 1 payment, as illustrated by the following:

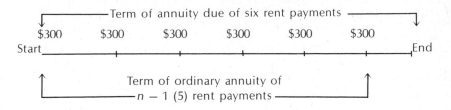

2 Since the present value of the first rent payment is equal to its face, we can omit it from the ordinary annuity formula, and then add the face value of the first payment back to the answer to obtain the present value of an annuity due.

Example 4 **Same as Example 3.**

   (a) The present value of an ordinary annuity of $n - 1$ rent payments $= 6 - 1 = 5$.

$$A = \$300(a_{\overline{5}|0.02})$$
$$= 300(4.7134595) \quad \text{(Table 6.5)}$$
$$= \$1414.04$$

   (b) Add the face value of the first payment:

$$A = \$1414.04 + \$300 = \$1714.04$$

   (c) The addition of the face value of the first payment could have been accomplished by adding 1 to the value of $a_{\overline{5}|0.02}$ in Table 6.5 before multiplying by the periodic rent of $300. Thus:

$$a_{\overline{5}|0.02} = 4.7134595$$
$$\underline{+\ 1.}$$
$$5.7134595 \times 300 = \$1714.04$$

3 In symbolic terms, the formula to find the present value of an annuity due is then

$$A = R(a_{\overline{n-1}|i} + 1)$$

Substituting the data of Example 4,

A = present value
R = \$300
$$n = \text{years}(m) = 1\frac{1}{2}(4) = 6$$

$$i = \frac{j}{m} = \frac{8}{4} = 2\%$$

$$\begin{aligned}
A &= \$300(a_{\overline{5}|0.02} + 1) \\
&= 300(4.7134595 + 1) \qquad \text{(Table 6.5)} \\
&= 300(5.7134595) \\
&= \$1714.04
\end{aligned}$$

Exercise 6.4

Find the present value of the following ordinary annuities:

	Rent	Nominal rate	Payments per year and m	Total number of payments
1	$ 600	8%	4	6
2	$ 1000	12%	12	24
3	$ 300	16%	4	20
4	$ 1250	6%	1	60
5	$10,000	6%	1	25
6	$ 450	10%	2	50

Find the present value of the following annuities due:

7	$1600	10%	2	20
8	$ 200	12%	12	30
9	$ 150	16%	4	18
10	$ 75	20%	4	24
11	$1300	6%	1	25
12	$4000	8%	2	15

Note: In the problems that follow, draw a map of the term of the annuity and indicate the payments thereon. In this manner there is less chance of confusing an ordinary annuity with an annuity due or vice versa.

Solve the following:

13 The installment price on a television set is nothing down and 24 monthly payments of $26.44, the first payment due one month from date of sale. If the contract was written for 24%, $m = 12$, what was the cash price of the TV set?

14 The estimated net return from a piece of mining property is $75,000 at the end of each year for the next 10 years. If money is worth 6%, $m = 1$, what is the present value of the property?

15 Ms. Thompson has her boat for sale. She receives one offer for $1000 down and a note which calls for monthly payments of $125 per month for 24 months. The second offer is for $1000 down and $102.50 per month for 30 months. Find the present value of each offer. The payment is due at the end of the month for both offers. Money is worth 12%, $m = 12$.

16 Mr. Hunt receives the following offers for 10 acres of land:

(a) $5000 down and a note which calls for 20 quarterly payments of $350.00, due at the end of the quarter.

(b) $5000 down and a note which calls for 16 payments of $422.00, due at the beginning of the quarter.

Find the present value of both offers if money is worth 12%, $m = 4$.

17 Find the present value of an annuity of $300 per year if the first payment is due today and then yearly for 10 consecutive payments. Money is worth 6%, $m = 1$.

18 Find the present value of a 15-year lease on a store building at $3000 per annum, payable in advance each year. Money is worth 6%, $m = 1$.

19 On March 1, 1978, Don Jackman signed a contract to pay $1000 every 3 months until December 1, 1983. If Mr. Jackman wanted to pay it off on March 1, 1978, find the payoff price if money is worth 12%, $m = 4$.

20 By inheritance, Ms. Hoffman received a bequest of $2000 on April 1 and October 1 of each year. The bequest started March 1, 1978, and was to run until October 1, 1988. If money is worth 8%, $m = 2$, find the present value of the bequest on March 1, 1978.

Unit 6.5

Reverse Operations in Annuity Formulas

What will be the monthly payment to pay off that new car loan for $4000 in 30 months at 12 percent interest?

This and other questions can be answered by finding the unknown values for R, n, and i from the various annuity tables.

To Find the Periodic Rent R

Example 1 **Larry Johnson desires to save enough money to have an emergency fund of $3000 at the end of 5 years. How much would Mr. Johnson have to deposit at the end of each month in a savings bank that pays 6 percent interest compounded monthly to reach his goal?**

The $3000 that Mr. Johnson wants to save represents the maturity value or the *amount S* of a series of monthly payments spread over the next 5 years. A map should be drawn and the known information inserted where appropriate. From the map, the correct formula to use is selected. Thus:

```
          ┌─ 60 payments of $R, made at end of each period ─┐
          ↓                                                 ↓
Start ├─┼─┼─┼─┼─┼──────────────────────────────┼─┼─┤ End
     $R $R $R $R, etc.,                          $R $R $R
```

$$i = \frac{j}{m} = \frac{6\%}{12} = .5\% \qquad \$3000 = \text{desired funds } (S)$$

The map indicates an ordinary annuity for which the amount (S) is given. Therefore, the formula to find the *amount* (S) of an ordinary annuity is selected.

1 $S = Rs_{\overline{n}|i}$

2 $\dfrac{S}{s_{\overline{n}|i}} = R$ [Divide (1) by $s_{\overline{n}|i}$]

Equation (2) could be solved by using Table 6.4 to find the value of $s_{\overline{n}|i}$ and then performing the long-division operation. However, Equation (2) can be factored and restated as:

3 $R = S\dfrac{1}{s_{\overline{n}|i}}$

Table 6.6 has the calculated values of $\dfrac{1}{s_{\overline{n}|i}}$ for selected terms n at various rates i, and use of Table 6.6 involves the relatively easier manual multiplication operation in place of the manual division operation. If calculating machines are available, the choice of Table 6.4 or Table 6.6 is indifferent.

4   Thus, to solve Example 1:

   (a)   Use of Table 6.4

$R = $ not known
$S = \$3000$
$n = 60$

$R = \dfrac{S}{s_{\overline{n}|i}}$ or $R = \dfrac{3000}{s_{\overline{60}|1/2}}$

$= \dfrac{3000}{69.770\ 0305} = \$43.00$

   (b)   Use of Table 6.6

$R = S\dfrac{1}{s_{\overline{n}|i}}$ or $R = 3000\dfrac{1}{s_{\overline{60}|1/2}}$

$R = 3000(0.0143328) = \$43.00$

Example 2   **Ellen Lindstrand purchased a new automobile for $5000 with terms of $1000 down and the balance of $4000 payable in equal monthly installments payable at the end of each month for the next $2\frac{1}{2}$ years. Interest is charged on the contract at 12 percent compounded monthly. Find the equal monthly payment.**

A map drawn for the transaction and the known information inserted would appear as follows:

TABLE 6.6   ANNUITY WHICH AT COMPOUND INTEREST AMOUNTS TO $1

$$\frac{1}{s_{\overline{n}|i}} = \frac{i}{(1+i)^n - 1} \qquad \left[\frac{1}{a_{\overline{n}|i}} = \frac{1}{s_{\overline{n}|i}} + i\right]^1$$

Formula:

To find rent in a sinking fund $R = S\dfrac{1}{s_{\overline{n}|i}}$

n	½%	1%	2%	3%	4%	5%	6%
1	1.000 0000	1.000 0000	1.000 0000	1.000 0000	1.000 0000	1.000 0000	1.000 0000
2	0.498 7531	0.497 5124	0.495 0495	0.492 6108	0.490 1961	0.487 8049	0.485 4369
3	0.331 6722	0.330 0221	0.326 7547	0.323 5304	0.320 3485	0.317 2086	0.314 1098
4	0.248 1328	0.246 2811	0.242 6238	0.239 0271	0.235 4901	0.232 0118	0.228 5915
5	0.198 0100	0.196 0398	0.192 1584	0.188 3546	0.184 6271	0.180 9748	0.177 3964
6	0.164 5955	0.162 5484	0.158 5258	0.154 5975	0.150 7619	0.147 0175	0.143 3626
7	0.140 7285	0.138 6283	0.134 5120	0.130 5064	0.126 6096	0.122 8198	0.119 1350
8	0.122 8289	0.120 6903	0.116 5098	0.112 4564	0.108 5278	0.104 7218	0.101 0359
9	0.108 9074	0.106 7404	0.102 5154	0.098 4339	0.094 4930	0.090 6901	0.087 0222
10	0.097 7706	0.095 5821	0.091 3265	0.087 2305	0.083 2909	0.079 5046	0.075 8680
11	0.088 6590	0.086 4541	0.082 1779	0.078 0775	0.074 1490	0.070 3889	0.066 7929
12	0.081 0664	0.078 8488	0.074 5596	0.070 4621	0.066 5522	0.062 8254	0.059 2770
13	0.074 6422	0.072 4148	0.068 1184	0.064 0295	0.060 1437	0.056 4558	0.052 9601
14	0.069 1361	0.066 9012	0.062 6020	0.058 5263	0.054 6690	0.051 0240	0.047 5849
15	0.064 3644	0.062 1238	0.057 8255	0.053 7666	0.049 9411	0.046 3423	0.042 9628
16	0.060 1894	0.057 9446	0.053 6501	0.049 6109	0.045 8200	0.042 2699	0.038 9521
17	0.056 5058	0.054 2581	0.049 9698	0.045 9525	0.042 1985	0.038 6991	0.035 4448
18	0.053 2317	0.050 9021	0.046 7021	0.042 7087	0.038 9933	0.035 5462	0.032 3565
19	0.050 3025	0.048 0518	0.043 7818	0.039 8139	0.036 1386	0.032 7450	0.029 6209
20	0.047 6665	0.045 4153	0.041 1567	0.037 2157	0.033 5818	0.030 2426	0.027 1846
21	0.045 2816	0.043 0308	0.038 7848	0.034 8718	0.031 2801	0.027 9961	0.025 0046
22	0.043 1138	0.040 8637	0.036 6314	0.032 7474	0.029 1988	0.025 9705	0.023 0456
23	0.041 1347	0.038 8858	0.034 6681	0.030 8139	0.027 3091	0.024 1368	0.021 2785
24	0.039 3206	0.037 0734	0.032 8711	0.029 0474	0.025 5868	0.022 4709	0.019 6790
25	0.037 6519	0.035 4068	0.031 2204	0.027 4279	0.024 0120	0.020 9525	0.018 2267
26	0.036 1116	0.033 8689	0.029 6992	0.025 9383	0.022 5674	0.019 5643	0.016 9044
27	0.034 6857	0.032 4455	0.028 2931	0.024 5642	0.021 2385	0.018 2919	0.015 6972
28	0.033 3617	0.031 1244	0.026 9897	0.023 2932	0.020 0130	0.017 1225	0.014 5926
29	0.032 1291	0.029 8950	0.025 7784	0.022 1147	0.018 8799	0.016 0455	0.013 5796
30	0.030 9789	0.028 7481	0.024 6499	0.021 0193	0.017 8301	0.015 0514	0.012 6489
40	0.022 6455	0.020 4556	0.016 5558	0.013 2624	0.010 5235	0.008 2782	0.006 4615
50	0.017 6538	0.015 5127	0.011 8232	0.008 8655	0.006 5502	0.004 7767	0.003 4443
60	0.014 3328	0.012 2445	0.008 7680	0.006 1330	0.004 2019	0.002 8282	0.001 8757
70	0.011 9666	0.009 9328	0.006 6677	0.004 3366	0.002 7451	0.001 6992	0.001 0331
80	0.010 1970	0.008 2189	0.005 1607	0.003 1118	0.001 8141	0.001 0296	0.000 5725
90	0.008 8253	0.006 9031	0.004 0460	0.002 2556	0.001 2078	0.000 6271	0.000 3184
100	0.007 7319	0.005 8657	0.003 2027	0.001 6467	0.000 8080	0.000 3831	0.000 1774

[1] Note that through slight modification in the formula presented, Tables 6.6 and 6.7 may be used interchangeably. This is due to the fact that the rent of the present value of an annuity of $1 is equal to the rent of the amount of an annuity of $1 plus the interest rate per period.

┌ 30 payments of R made at end of each period ┐

Start ├─┼─┼─┼─┼─┼─────────────────────┼─┼─┤ End

　　　↑　R　R　R　R, etc.,　　　　　　　　R　R　R

　　　│　$4000 = $ present value of loan (A)　　$i = \dfrac{j}{m} = \dfrac{12\%}{12} = 1\%$

The map indicates an ordinary annuity for which the present value (A) is given. Therefore, the formula to find the present value (A) of an ordinary annuity is selected.

1　$A = Ra_{\overline{n}|i}$

2　$\dfrac{A}{a_{\overline{n}|i}} = R$　　[Divide (1) by $a_{\overline{n}|i}$]

　　　Equation (2) could be solved by use of Table 6.5 to find the value of $a_{\overline{n}|i}$ and the long-division operation performed. However, Equation (2) can also be factored and restated as

3　$R = A\dfrac{1}{a_{\overline{n}|i}}$

　　　Table 6.7 has the calculated values of $\dfrac{1}{a_{\overline{n}|i}}$ for selected terms n at various rates i.

　　　Note the relationship between $\dfrac{1}{s_{\overline{n}|i}}$ (Table 6.6) and $\dfrac{1}{a_{\overline{n}|i}}$ (Table 6.7). The difference between the two tables is merely the addition or subtraction of i for each of the values given. Thus:

$$\frac{1}{s_{\overline{n}|i}} + i = \frac{i}{a_{\overline{n}|i}}$$

and　$\dfrac{i}{a_{\overline{n}|i}} - i = \dfrac{1}{s_{\overline{n}|i}}$

Hence, Tables 6.6 and 6.7 could be used interchangeably by adding or subtracting i, respectively.

4　Use of Table 6.5

$R = \dfrac{A}{a_{\overline{n}|i}}$

$R = $ unknown
$A = \$4000$
$n = 30$
$i = 1\%$

$R = \dfrac{\$4000}{a_{\overline{30}|1}}$

$R = \dfrac{4000}{25.8077082} = \$154.99$

TABLE 6.7   ANNUITY THAT $1 WILL PURCHASE OR ANNUITY WHOSE PRESENT VALUE IS $1

$$\frac{1}{a_{\overline{n}|i}} = \frac{i}{1 - (1 + i)^n} \qquad \left[\frac{1}{s_{\overline{n}|i}} = \frac{1}{a_{\overline{n}|i}} - i\right]$$

Formula:

To find rent in amortization $R = A\dfrac{1}{a_{\overline{n}|i}}$

n	$\frac{1}{2}$%	1%	2%	3%	4%	5%	6%
1	1.005 0000	1.010 0000	1.020 0000	1.030 0000	1.040 0000	1.050 0000	1.060 0000
2	0.503 7531	0.507 5124	0.515 0495	0.522 6108	0.530 1961	0.537 8049	0.545 4369
3	0.336 6722	0.340 0221	0.346 7547	0.353 5304	0.360 3485	0.367 2086	0.374 1098
4	0.253 1328	0.256 2811	0.262 6238	0.269 0271	0.275 4901	0.282 0118	0.288 5915
5	0.203 0100	0.206 0398	0.212 1584	0.218 3646	0.224 6271	0.230 9740	0.237 3964
6	0.169 5955	0.172 5484	0.178 5258	0.184 5975	0.190 7619	0.197 0175	0.203 3626
7	0.145 7285	0.148 6283	0.154 5120	0.160 5064	0.166 6096	0.172 8198	0.179 1350
8	0.127 8289	0.130 6903	0.136 5098	0.142 4564	0.148 5278	0.154 7218	0.161 0359
9	0.113 9074	0.116 7404	0.122 5154	0.128 4339	0.134 4930	0.140 6901	0.147 0222
10	0.102 7706	0.105 5821	0.111 3265	0.117 2305	0.123 2909	0.129 5046	0.135 8680
11	0.093 6590	0.096 4541	0.102 1779	0.108 0775	0.114 1490	0.120 3889	0.126 7929
12	0.086 0664	0.088 8488	0.094 5596	0.100 4621	0.106 5522	0.112 8254	0.119 2770
13	0.079 6422	0.082 4148	0.088 1184	0.094 0295	0.100 1437	0.106 4558	0.112 9601
14	0.074 1361	0.076 9012	0.082 6020	0.088 5263	0.094 6690	0.101 0240	0.107 5849
15	0.069 3644	0.072 1238	0.077 8255	0.083 7666	0.089 9411	0.096 3423	0.102 9628
16	0.065 1894	0.067 9446	0.073 6501	0.079 6109	0.085 8200	0.092 2699	0.098 9521
17	0.061 5058	0.064 2581	0.069 9698	0.075 9525	0.082 1985	0.088 6991	0.095 4448
18	0.058 2317	0.060 9821	0.066 7021	0.072 7087	0.078 9933	0.085 5462	0.092 3565
19	0.055 3025	0.058 0518	0.063 7818	0.069 8139	0.076 1386	0.082 7450	0.089 6209
20	0.052 6665	0.055 4153	0.061 1567	0.067 2157	0.073 5818	0.080 2426	0.087 1846
21	0.050 2816	0.053 0308	0.058 7848	0.064 8718	0.071 2801	0.077 9961	0.085 0046
22	0.048 1138	0.050 8637	0.056 6314	0.062 7474	0.069 1988	0.075 9705	0.083 0456
23	0.046 1347	0.048 8858	0.054 6681	0.060 8139	0.067 3091	0.074 1368	0.081 2785
24	0.044 3206	0.047 0735	0.052 8711	0.059 0474	0.065 5868	0.072 4709	0.079 6790
25	0.042 6519	0.045 4068	0.051 2204	0.057 4279	0.064 0120	0.070 9525	0.078 2267
26	0.041 1116	0.043 8689	0.049 6992	0.055 9383	0.062 5674	0.069 5643	0.076 9044
27	0.039 6857	0.042 4455	0.048 2931	0.054 5642	0.061 2385	0.068 2919	0.075 6972
28	0.038 3617	0.041 1244	0.046 9897	0.053 2932	0.060 0130	0.067 1225	0.074 5926
29	0.037 1291	0.039 8950	0.045 7784	0.052 1147	0.058 8799	0.066 0455	0.073 5796
30	0.035 9789	0.038 7481	0.044 6499	0.051 0193	0.057 8301	0.065 0514	0.072 6489
40	0.027 6455	0.030 4556	0.036 5558	0.043 2624	0.050 5235	0.058 2782	0.066 4615
50	0.022 6538	0.025 5127	0.031 8232	0.038 8655	0.046 5502	0.054 7767	0.063 4443
60	0.019 3328	0.022 2445	0.028 7680	0.036 1330	0.044 2019	0.052 8282	0.061 8757
70	0.016 9666	0.019 9328	0.026 6677	0.034 3366	0.042 7451	0.051 6992	0.061 0331
80	0.015 1970	0.018 2189	0.025 1607	0.033 1118	0.041 8141	0.051 0296	0.060 5725
90	0.013 8253	0.016 9031	0.024 0460	0.032 2557	0.041 2078	0.050 6271	0.060 3184
100	0.012 7319	0.015 8657	0.023 2027	0.031 6467	0.040 8080	0.050 3831	0.060 1774

5   Use of Table 6.7

$$R = A \frac{1}{a_{\overline{n}|i}}$$

$$R = 4000 \frac{1}{a_{\overline{30}|1}}$$

$$R = 4000(0.0387481) = \$154.99$$

Caution: To find R in the case of an annuity due, *Tables 6.4 and 6.5 must be used* and the division operation performed, and *Tables 6.6 and 6.7, respectively, cannot be used.* Tables 6.6 and 6.7 represent the reciprocal values of $s_{\overline{n}|i}$ and $a_{\overline{n}|i}$, and

$$\frac{1}{s_{\overline{n}|i}} \quad \text{and} \quad \frac{1}{a_{\overline{n}|i}}$$

are *not the same* as the respective reciprocal values of $s_{\overline{n+1}|i} - 1$ and $a_{\overline{n+1}|i} + 1$.

Example 3   **Joe Costa signed a 2-year lease for a building for a total of $30,000 due at the start of the lease. Mr. Costa desires to make 8 quarterly payments at the beginning of each quarter. Find the amount of each payment if money is worth 12%, $m = 4$.**

A map drawn for the above problem would indicate an *annuity due* for which the present value was given. Therefore, to find the unknown payments (R), the annuity due formula is selected.

1 $R = \dfrac{A}{a_{\overline{n}|i} + 1}$

$R =$ unknown
$A = \$30,000$
$n = 2(4) = 8$

$$i = \frac{j}{m} = \frac{12\%}{4} = 3\%$$

2 $R = \dfrac{\$30,000}{a_{\overline{7}|0.03} + 1}$

3 $R = \dfrac{\$30,000}{6.2302830 + 1}$ (Table 6.5)

4 $R = \dfrac{\$30,000}{7.2302830} = \$4149.22$

To Find the Number of Periods, n

Example 4   **Ben Simpson can save $15 at the end of each month toward the accumulation of a special fund of $381.48. If Mr. Simpson can invest his money in a savings bank which pays 6 percent compounded monthly, how long must Mr. Simpson wait to accumulate the $381.48?**

All the items are known except the number of periods n, and the $381.48 would appear on the map at the end of the line and thus represent the amount of an ordinary annuity, or S.

1   $S = Rs_{\overline{n}|i}$
     $S = \$381.48$
     $R = \$15$
     $n = $ unknown

$$i = \frac{j}{m} = \frac{6\%}{12} = \frac{1}{2}\%$$

2   $\$381.48 = 15(s_{\overline{n}|1/2})$

3   $\dfrac{\$381.48}{15} = s_{\overline{n}|1/2}$ [Divide (2) by 15]

4   $25.432 = s_{\overline{n}|1/2}$

5   Refer to Table 6.4 and select the $\dfrac{1}{2}$ percent column and scan the values for

     n until the value of 25.432 is found opposite 24. Hence,

6   $n = 24$

7   Since $n = $ years(m), the number of years $= \dfrac{n}{m} = \dfrac{24}{12} = 2$ years

To find the number of periods n when the *present value of an ordinary annuity A* is known, use the formula to find the present value of an ordinary annuity, $A = Ra_{\overline{n}|i}$, and proceed as with Example 4.

Example 5   **Joan Kerker owes a debt of $18,929.29 which she can pay off at the rate of $1000 every 6 months. How long will it take Ms. Kerker to pay off the debt if the debt calls for interest at 10 percent compounded semiannually?**

The $18,929.29 would appear on the map at the *start* of the line and thus represent the *present value* or A.

1   $A = Ra_{\overline{n}|i}$
     $A = \$18,929.29$
     $R = \$1000$
     $n = $ unknown

$$i = \frac{j}{m} = \frac{10}{2} = 5\%$$

2 $\$18{,}929.29 = \$1000(a_{\overline{n}|0.05})$

3 $\dfrac{\$18{,}929.29}{1000} = a_{\overline{n}|0.05}$ [Divide (2) by $1000]

4 $18.92929 = a_{\overline{n}|0.05}$

5 Refer to Table 6.5 and scan down the 5 percent column. The value 18.92929 is found opposite line 60. Hence,

6 $n = 60$

7 Years $= \dfrac{n}{m} = \dfrac{60}{2} = 30$ years

WHEN THE PRECISE VALUE FOR $a_{\overline{n}|i}$ OR $s_{\overline{n}|i}$ IS NOT REPRESENTED IN THE TABLES When precise numbers are not present in the tables for the values calculated in step (4) of the above examples, the answer for n is stated as a certain number of full payments, and a smaller final payment.

Example 6 **Van Baldwin owes $860 and wants to pay off the loan at $50 per month. How many months will be necessary if interest is charged at 12%, $m = 12$?**

The $860 would appear on the map as the present value, and the present value formula is selected.

1 $A = R(a_{\overline{n}|i})$
  $A = \$860$
  $R = 50$

  $i = \dfrac{j}{m} = \dfrac{12\%}{12} = 1\%$

  $n = $ unknown

2 $860 = 50(a_{\overline{n}|0.01}$

3 $\dfrac{860}{50} = a_{\overline{n}|0.01}$

4 $17.20 = a_{\overline{n}|0.01}$

5 Refer to Table 6.5 and scan down the 1% column. The value 17.20 is bracketed by the values for $n = 18$ (16.3982686) and $n = 19$ (17.2260085). Therefore, 18 months at $50 per month is necessary and a smaller payment at the end of 19 months. The amount of the smaller payment is calculated in accordance with the Merchant's Rule described in Unit 7.3.

$860(1.01)^{18} = $ $1028.69
$-50(s_{\overline{18}|0.01}) = $ $\underline{\quad 990.54}$
Balance after 18th payment $= \$\ \underline{\underline{\quad 38.15}}$

Simple interest at 12 percent would then be added to the $38.15 for the number of days the amount remains unpaid during the 19th month.

To Find the Interest Rate

The nominal rate (j) is also the *effective annual interest rate* in those annuities where the number of payments per year equals the number of interest conversions per year (simple annuities). As the effective annual interest rate, it becomes the *annual percentage rate* (APR), which is required to be stated for many types of consumer obligations by Regulation Z of the Federal Truth in Lending Law.[1] The nominal and effective interest rates for simple annuities are also used extensively in comparing and making decisions on alternative investments.

Example 7   **Russell Connett can invest $75 at the end of each month for the next 24 months. At what annual rate of interest, compounded monthly, must Mr. Connett invest his monthly amount in order to have a fund of $2023.01 at the end of the 24-month period?**

The $2023.01 would appear on the map at the *end* of the line and thus represents the *amount S* of an ordinary annuity where all the terms, except i, are known.

1   $S = Rs_{\overline{n}|i}$
    $S = \$2023.01$
    $R = \$75$
    $n = 24$
    $i = $ unknown

2   $\$2023.01 = \$75(s_{\overline{24}|i})$

3   $\dfrac{2023.01}{75} = s_{\overline{24}|i}$

4   $26.97346 = s_{\overline{24}|i}$

5   Refer to Table 6.4 and scan across line 24. The value 26.97346 appears in the 1 percent column. Hence,

6   $i = 1\%$

7   $j = im = 1\% \times 12 = 12\%$

Example 8   **Ann Raymond purchased a used houseboat. The amount to be financed was $3186.51. Ms. Raymond signed a conditional sales contract for 24 monthly payments of $150, the first payment due 1 month after the date of the contract. Find the effective annual interest rate.**

The $3186.51 would appear on the map at the start of the line and thus would represent the present value A of an ordinary annuity.

[1] Regulation Z and the annual percentage rate will be presented more fully in Chapter 7.

1 $A = Ra_{\overline{n}|i}$
$A = \$3186.51$
$R = \$150$
$n = 24$
$i = $ unknown

2 $\$3186.51 = \$150(a_{\overline{n}|i})$

3 $\dfrac{3186.51}{150} = a_{\overline{24}|i}$

4 $21.2434 = a_{\overline{24}|i}$

5   Refer to Table 6.5 and scan across line 24. The value of 21.2434 appears in the 1 percent column. Hence,

6 $i = 1\%$

7 $j = mi = 12 \times 1\% = 12\% = $ APR   (Effective annual interest rate)

WHEN THE PRECISE VALUE FOR $s_{\overline{n}|i}$ AND $a_{\overline{n}|i}$ IS NOT REPRESENTED IN THE TABLES   If the precise value is not represented in the annuity tables, state the rate *approximately* or interpolate in the tables for a more precise rate.

More complete interest tables, which are available in most libraries or can be purchased, contain more interest rates and consecutive interest periods. The compound interest and annuity tables presented in the text, although adequate for the illustrative purposes intended, could be used only with a limited variety of actual problems. Sample pages from a book of published compound-interest and annuity tables are reproduced in Figure 6.1 and are used to solve the following example.

Example 9   **Clara Jackson purchased a new automobile and signed a conditional sales contract to finance the unpaid balance of \$4497.22. The contract calls for 48 payments of \$123.99, with the first payment to start 1 month from the date of the contract.**

Using Figure 6.1 find (a) the approximate interest rate and (b) a more precise interest rate by interpolation.

The \$4497.22 represents the present value of a series of 48 equal payments. The formula to find the present value of an ordinary annuity is selected.

Approximate interest rate:

1 $A = R(a_{\overline{n}|i})$
$A = \$4497.22$
$R = \$123.99$
$n = 48$
$i = $ unknown

2 $\$4497.22 = \$123.99(a_{\overline{48}|i})$

3 $\dfrac{4497.22}{123.99} = a_{\overline{48}|i}$

4 $36.270\ 828\ 29 = a_{\overline{48}|i}$

P E R I O D S	AMOUNT OF 1 *How $1 left at compound interest will grow.*	AMOUNT OF 1 PER PERIOD *How $1 deposited periodically will grow.*	SINKING FUND *Periodic deposit that will grow to $1 at future date.*
1	1.011 875 0000	1.000 000 0000	1.000 000 0000
2	1.023 891 0156	2.011 875 0000	.497 048 7729
3	1.036 049 7214	3.035 766 0156	.329 406 1515
4	1.048 352 8119	4.071 815 7371	.245 590 6811
5	1.060 802 0015	5.120 168 5489	.195 306 0706
6	1.073 399 0253	6.180 970 5505	.161 786 8896
7	1.086 145 6387	7.254 369 5757	.137 847 9535
8	1.099 043 6182	8.340 515 2145	.119 896 6700
9	1.112 094 7611	9.439 558 8326	.105 937 1542
10	1.125 300 8864	10.551 653 5938	.094 771 8754
11	1.138 663 8345	11.676 954 4802	.085 638 7684
12	1.152 185 4675	12.815 618 3146	.078 029 7895
13	1.165 867 6699	13.967 803 7821	.071 593 2165
14	1.179 712 3485	15.133 671 4520	.066 077 8188
15	1.193 721 4326	16.313 383 8005	.061 299 3608
16	1.207 896 8746	17.507 105 2332	.057 119 6658
17	1.222 240 6500	18.715 002 1078	.053 433 0691
18	1.236 754 7577	19.937 242 7578	.050 157 3870
19	1.251 441 2205	21.173 997 5156	.047 227 7377
20	1.266 302 0850	22.425 438 7361	.044 592 2156
21	1.281 339 4223	23.691 740 8211	.042 208 8021
22	1.296 555 3279	24.973 080 2433	.040 043 1180
23	1.311 951 9224	26.269 635 5712	.038 066 7633
24	1.327 531 3515	27.581 587 4936	.036 256 0712
25	1.343 295 7863	28.909 118 8451	.034 591 1615
26	1.359 247 4237	30.252 414 6314	.033 055 2127
27	1.375 388 4869	31.611 662 0551	.031 633 8951
28	1.391 721 2252	32.987 050 5421	.030 314 9261
29	1.408 247 9147	34.378 771 7672	.029 087 7175
30	1.424 970 8587	35.787 019 6820	.027 943 0925
31	1.441 892 3877	37.211 990 5407	.026 873 0585
32	1.459 014 8598	38.653 882 9284	.025 870 6220
33	1.476 340 6612	40.112 897 7881	.024 929 6375
34	1.493 872 2066	41.589 238 4494	.024 044 6817
35	1.511 611 9390	43.083 110 6560	.023 210 9517
36	1.529 562 3308	44.594 722 5950	.022 424 1781
37	1.547 725 8835	46.124 284 9258	.021 680 5529
38	1.566 105 1284	47.672 010 8093	.020 976 6692
39	1.584 702 6268	49.238 115 9377	.020 309 4692
40	1.603 520 9705	50.822 818 5644	.019 676 2011
41	1.622 562 7820	52.426 339 5349	.019 074 3815
42	1.641 830 7150	54.048 902 3169	.018 501 7634
43	1.661 327 4548	55.690 733 0319	.017 956 3088
44	1.681 055 7183	57.352 060 4866	.017 436 1652
45	1.701 018 2549	59.033 116 2049	.016 939 6445
46	1.721 217 8467	60.734 134 4598	.016 465 2054
47	1.741 657 3086	62.455 352 3066	.016 011 4380
48	1.762 339 4892	64.197 009 6152	.015 577 0496
49	1.783 267 2706	65.959 349 1044	.015 160 8531
50	1.804 443 5695	67.742 616 3750	.014 761 7564
51	1.825 871 3368	69.547 059 9444	.014 378 7530
52	1.847 553 5590	71.372 931 2813	.014 010 9140
53	1.869 493 2575	73.220 484 8402	.013 657 3802
54	1.891 693 4899	75.089 978 0977	.013 317 3564
55	1.914 157 3501	76.981 671 5876	.012 990 1050
56	1.936 887 9686	78.895 828 9377	.012 674 9413
57	1.959 888 5133	80.832 716 9064	.012 371 2284
58	1.983 162 1894	82.792 605 4196	.012 078 3734
59	2.006 712 2404	84.775 767 6090	.011 795 8236
60	2.030 541 9482	86.782 479 8494	.011 523 0632
n	$s=(1+i)^n$	$s_{\overline{n}}=\dfrac{(1+i)^n-1}{i}$	$\dfrac{1}{s_{\overline{n}}}=\dfrac{i}{(1+i)^n-1}$

.011875
per period

ANNUALLY
If compounded
annually
nominal annual rate is

$1\frac{3}{16}\%$

SEMIANNUALLY
If compounded
semiannually
nominal annual rate is

$2\frac{3}{8}\%$

QUARTERLY
If compounded
quarterly
nominal annual rate is

$4\frac{3}{4}\%$

MONTHLY
If compounded
monthly
nominal annual rate is

$14\frac{1}{4}\%$

$i = .011875$
$j_{(2)} = .02375$
$j_{(4)} = .0475$
$j_{(12)} = .1425$

438

FIGURE 6.1 *Source: These interest tables appear in* Financial Compound Interest and Annuity Tables, *5th ed., and are reproduced with permission of the Financial Publishing Company, 82 Brookline Avenue, Boston, Mass. 02215.*

PRESENT WORTH OF 1 *What $1 due in the future is worth today.*	PRESENT WORTH OF 1 PER PERIOD *What $1 payable periodically is worth today.*	PARTIAL PAYMENT *Annuity worth $1 today.* *Periodic payment necessary to pay off a loan of $1.*	P E R I O D S	RATE **1³⁄₁₆%**
.988 264 3607	.988 264 3607	1.011 875 0000	1	
.976 666 4467	1.964 930 8074	.508 923 7729	2	
.965 204 6415	2.930 135 4489	.341 281 1515	3	.011875
.953 877 3480	3.884 012 7970	.257 465 6811	4	*per period*
.942 682 9876	4.826 695 7845	.207 181 0706	5	
.931 620 0001	5.758 315 7846	.173 661 8896	6	
.920 686 8438	6.679 002 6284	.149 722 9535	7	
.909 881 9951	7.588 884 6235	.131 771 6700	8	
.899 203 9482	8.488 088 5717	.117 812 1542	9	
.888 651 2150	9.376 739 7867	.106 646 8754	10	
.878 222 3249	10.254 962 1116	.097 513 7684	11	
.867 915 8245	11.122 877 9361	.089 904 7895	12	
.857 730 2775	11.980 608 2136	.083 468 2165	13	
.847 664 2643	12.828 272 4779	.077 952 8188	14	
.837 716 3823	13.665 988 8602	.073 174 3608	15	
.827 885 2450	14.493 874 1052	.068 994 6658	16	
.818 169 4824	15.312 043 5876	.065 308 0691	17	
.808 567 7405	16.120 611 3281	.062 032 3870	18	
.799 078 6811	16.919 690 0092	.059 102 7377	19	
.789 700 9820	17.709 390 9912	.056 467 2156	20	ANNUALLY If compounded *annually* nominal annual rate is
.780 433 3361	18.489 824 3273	.054 083 8021	21	
.771 274 4520	19.261 098 7793	.051 918 1180	22	
.762 223 0532	20.023 321 8326	.049 941 7633	23	
.753 277 8784	20.776 599 7110	.048 131 0712	24	
.744 437 6810	21.521 037 3920	.046 466 1615	25	**1³⁄₁₆%**
.735 701 2289	22.256 738 6208	.044 930 2127	26	
.727 067 3046	22.983 805 9255	.043 508 8951	27	
.718 534 7050	23.702 340 6305	.042 189 9261	28	
.710 102 2409	24.412 442 8714	.040 962 7175	29	
.701 768 7371	25.114 211 6085	.039 818 0925	30	SEMIANNUALLY If compounded *semiannually* nominal annual rate is
.693 533 0324	25.807 744 6409	.038 748 0585	31	
.685 393 9789	26.493 138 6198	.037 745 6222	32	
.677 350 4424	27.170 489 0622	.036 804 6375	33	
.669 401 3019	27.839 890 3641	.035 919 6817	34	
.661 545 4497	28.501 435 8138	.035 085 9517	35	**2³⁄₈%**
.653 781 7909	29.155 217 6048	.034 299 1781	36	
.646 109 2437	29.801 326 8485	.033 555 5529	37	
.638 526 7387	30.439 853 5871	.032 851 6692	38	
.631 033 2192	31.070 886 8063	.032 184 4692	39	
.623 627 6409	31.694 514 4472	.031 551 2011	40	QUARTERLY If compounded *quarterly* nominal annual rate is
.616 308 9719	32.310 823 4191	.030 949 3815	41	
.609 076 1921	32.919 899 6112	.030 376 7634	42	
.601 928 2936	33.521 827 9049	.029 831 3088	43	
.594 864 2803	34.116 692 1852	.029 311 1652	44	
.587 883 1677	34.704 575 3529	.028 814 6445	45	**4³⁄₄%**
.580 983 9829	35.285 559 3357	.028 340 2054	46	
.574 165 7644	35.859 725 1002	.027 886 4380	47	
.567 427 5621	36.427 152 6623	.027 452 0496	48	
.560 768 4369	36.987 921 0993	.027 035 8531	49	
.554 187 4608	37.542 108 5601	.026 636 7564	50	MONTHLY If compounded *monthly* nominal annual rate is
.547 683 7167	38.089 792 2768	.026 253 7530	51	
.541 256 2982	38.631 048 5750	.025 885 9140	52	
.534 904 3095	39.165 952 8845	.025 532 3802	53	
.528 626 8655	39.694 579 7500	.025 192 3564	54	
.522 423 0913	40.217 002 8412	.024 865 1050	55	**14¼%**
.516 292 1223	40.733 294 9635	.024 549 9413	56	
.510 233 1042	41.243 528 0677	.024 246 2284	57	
.504 245 1925	41.747 773 2603	.023 953 3734	58	i = .011875
.498 327 5528	42.246 100 8131	.023 670 8236	59	$j_{(2)}$ = .02375
.492 479 3604	42.738 580 1735	.023 398 0632	60	$j_{(4)}$ = .0475 $j_{(12)}$ = .1425
$v^n = \dfrac{1}{(1+i)^n}$	$a_{\overline{n}|} = \dfrac{1-v^n}{i}$	$\dfrac{1}{a_{\overline{n}|}} = \dfrac{i}{1-v^n}$	**n**	

439

FIGURE 6.1 (Continued.)

242

RATE 1 7/32%	P E R I O D S	AMOUNT OF 1 *How $1 left at compound interest will grow.*	AMOUNT OF 1 PER PERIOD *How $1 deposited periodically will grow.*	SINKING FUND *Periodic deposit that will grow to $1 at future date.*
.0121875 *per period*	1	1.012 187 5000	1.000 000 0000	1.000 000 0000
	2	1.024 523 5352	2.012 187 5000	.496 971 5794
	3	1.037 009 9157	3.036 711 0352	.329 303 6408
	4	1.049 648 4741	4.073 720 9509	.245 475 8222
	5	1.062 441 0649	5.123 369 4250	.195 184 0512
	6	1.075 389 5653	6.185 810 4899	.161 660 3033
	7	1.088 495 8757	7.261 200 0552	.137 718 2824
	8	1.101 761 9192	8.349 695 9309	.119 764 8403
	9	1.115 189 6425	9.451 457 8500	.105 803 7835
	10	1.128 781 0163	10.566 647 4926	.094 637 3957
	11	1.142 538 0350	11.695 428 5089	.085 503 4939
	12	1.156 462 7173	12.837 966 5438	.077 893 9559
	13	1.170 557 1066	13.994 429 2611	.071 457 0049
	14	1.184 823 2714	15.164 986 3677	.065 941 3715
	15	1.199 263 3050	16.349 809 6391	.061 162 7916
	16	1.213 879 3265	17.549 072 9440	.056 983 0670
	17	1.228 673 4808	18.762 952 2706	.053 296 5168
	18	1.243 647 9388	19.991 625 7514	.050 020 9444
	19	1.258 804 8981	21.235 273 6902	.047 091 4580
	20	1.274 146 5828	22.494 078 5883	.044 456 1441
ANNUALLY If compounded *annually* nominal annual rate is 1 7/32%	21	1.289 675 2413	23.768 225 1711	.042 072 9774
	22	1.305 393 1613	25.057 900 4154	.039 907 5734
	23	1.321 302 6405	26.363 293 5767	.037 931 5277
	24	1.337 406 0164	27.684 596 2171	.036 121 1698
	25	1.353 705 6522	29.022 002 2335	.034 456 6165
	26	1.370 203 9399	30.375 707 8858	.032 921 0435
	27	1.386 903 3004	31.745 911 8256	.031 500 1190
	28	1.403 806 1843	33.132 815 1260	.030 181 5586
	29	1.420 915 0722	34.536 621 3103	.028 954 7721
	30	1.438 232 4747	35.957 536 3826	.027 010 5816
SEMIANNUALLY If compounded *semiannually* nominal annual rate is 2 7/16%	31	1.455 760 9529	37.395 768 8572	.026 740 9932
	32	1.473 503 0193	38.851 529 7902	.025 739 0122
	33	1.491 461 3374	40.325 032 8095	.024 798 4919
	34	1.509 638 5224	41.816 494 1469	.023 914 0086
	35	1.528 037 2419	43.326 132 6693	.023 080 7584
	36	1.546 660 1958	44.854 169 9112	.022 294 4712
	37	1.565 510 1169	46.400 830 1070	.021 551 3386
	38	1.584 589 7715	47.966 340 2239	.020 847 9529
	39	1.603 901 9593	49.550 929 9954	.020 181 2559
	40	1.623 449 5144	51.154 831 9547	.019 548 4955
QUARTERLY If compounded *quarterly* nominal annual rate is 4 7/8%	41	1.643 235 3054	52.778 281 4691	.018 947 1876
	42	1.663 262 2357	54.421 516 7745	.018 375 0851
	43	1.683 533 2442	56.084 779 0102	.017 830 1496
	44	1.704 051 3056	57.768 312 2544	.017 310 5282
	45	1.724 819 4309	59.472 363 5600	.016 814 5327
	46	1.745 840 6677	61.197 182 9909	.016 340 6214
	47	1.767 118 1008	62.943 023 6586	.015 887 3842
	48	1.788 654 8527	64.710 141 7595	.015 453 5282
	49	1.810 454 0837	66.498 796 6121	.015 037 8661
	50	1.832 518 9929	68.309 250 6959	.014 639 3057
MONTHLY If compounded *monthly* nominal annual rate is 14 5/8%	51	1.854 852 8181	70.141 769 6887	.014 256 8402
	52	1.877 458 8368	71.996 622 5068	.013 889 5404
	53	1.900 340 3664	73.874 081 3436	.013 536 5473
	54	1.923 500 7646	75.774 421 7100	.013 197 0654
	55	1.946 943 4302	77.697 922 4746	.012 870 3570
i = .0121875 $j_{(2)}$ = .024375 $j_{(4)}$ = .04875 $j_{(12)}$ = .14625	56	1.970 671 8032	79.644 865 9047	.012 555 7371
	57	1.994 689 3658	81.615 537 7079	.012 252 5689
	58	2.018 999 6425	83.610 227 0737	.011 960 2593
	59	2.043 606 2006	85.629 226 7162	.011 678 2556
	60	2.068 512 6512	87.672 832 9168	.011 406 0418
	n	$s = (1+i)^n$	$s_{\overline{n}\|} = \dfrac{(1+i)^n - 1}{i}$	$\dfrac{1}{s_{\overline{n}\|}} = \dfrac{i}{(1+i)^n - 1}$

445-1

FIGURE 6.1 (*Continued.*)

PRESENT WORTH OF 1 — What $1 due in the future is worth today.	PRESENT WORTH OF 1 PER PERIOD — What $1 payable periodically is worth today.	PARTIAL PAYMENT — Annuity worth $1 today. Periodic payment necessary to pay off a loan of $1.	P E R I O D S	RATE — $1\,\frac{7}{32}\%$
.987 959 2467	.987 959 2467	1.012 187 5000	1	
.976 063 4731	1.964 022 7198	.509 159 0794	2	.0121875
.964 310 9336	2.928 333 6534	.341 491 1408	3	
.952 699 9035	3.881 033 5569	.257 663 3222	4	
.941 228 6790	4.822 262 2359	.207 371 5512	5	*per period*
.929 895 5767	5.752 157 8126	.173 847 8033	6	
.918 698 9334	6.670 856 7460	.149 905 7824	7	
.907 637 1062	7.578 493 8522	.131 952 3403	8	
.896 708 4717	8.475 202 3238	.117 991 2835	9	
.885 911 4262	9.361 113 7500	.106 824 8957	10	
.875 244 3852	10.236 358 1352	.097 690 9939	11	
.864 705 7835	11.101 063 9187	.090 081 4559	12	
.854 294 0745	11.955 357 9932	.083 644 5049	13	
.844 007 7302	12.799 365 7234	.078 128 8715	14	
.833 845 2414	13.633 210 9648	.073 350 2916	15	
.823 805 1165	14.457 016 0813	.069 170 5670	16	
.813 885 8823	15.270 901 9636	.065 484 0168	17	
.804 086 0832	16.074 988 0468	.062 208 4444	18	
.794 404 2810	16.869 392 3278	.059 278 9580	19	
.784 839 0550	17.654 231 3828	.056 643 6441	20	ANNUALLY — If compounded *annually* nominal annual rate is
.775 389 0016	18.429 620 3844	.054 260 4774	21	
.766 052 7339	19.195 673 1183	.052 095 0734	22	
.756 828 8819	19.952 502 0001	.050 119 0277	23	
.747 716 0920	20.700 218 0921	.048 308 6698	24	$1\,\frac{7}{32}\%$
.738 713 0270	21.438 931 1191	.046 644 1165	25	
.729 818 3657	22.168 749 4848	.045 108 5435	26	
.721 030 8027	22.889 780 2875	.043 687 6190	27	
.712 349 0487	23.602 129 3362	.042 369 0586	28	
.703 771 8295	24.305 901 1658	.041 142 2721	29	
.695 297 8865	25.001 199 0523	.039 998 0816	30	SEMIANNUALLY — If compounded *semiannually* nominal annual rate is
.686 925 9762	25.688 125 0285	.038 928 4932	31	
.678 654 8700	26.366 779 8985	.037 926 5122	32	
.670 483 3541	27.037 263 2526	.036 985 9919	33	
.662 410 2294	27.699 673 4821	.036 101 5086	34	$2\,\frac{7}{16}\%$
.654 434 3113	28.354 107 7933	.035 268 2584	35	
.646 554 4292	29.000 662 2225	.034 481 9712	36	
.638 769 4268	29.639 431 6493	.033 738 8386	37	
.631 078 1617	30.270 509 8110	.033 035 4529	38	
.623 479 5052	30.893 989 3162	.032 368 7559	39	
.615 972 3423	31.509 961 6585	.031 735 9955	40	QUARTERLY — If compounded *quarterly* nominal annual rate is
.608 555 5713	32.118 517 2297	.031 134 6876	41	
.601 228 1037	32.719 745 3335	.030 562 5851	42	
.593 988 8645	33.313 734 1979	.030 017 6496	43	
.586 836 7911	33.900 570 9890	.029 498 0282	44	$4\,\frac{7}{8}\%$
.579 770 8340	34.480 341 8230	.029 002 0327	45	
.572 789 9564	35.053 131 7795	.028 528 1214	46	
.565 893 1339	35.619 024 9133	.028 074 8842	47	
.559 079 3542	36.178 104 2676	.027 641 0282	48	
.552 347 6176	36.730 451 8852	.027 225 3661	49	
.545 696 9362	37.276 148 8215	.026 826 8057	50	MONTHLY — If compounded *monthly* nominal annual rate is
.539 126 3340	37.815 275 1555	.026 444 3402	51	
.532 634 8468	38.347 910 0024	.026 077 0404	52	
.526 221 5220	38.874 131 5244	.025 724 0473	53	
.519 885 4185	39.394 016 9429	.025 384 5654	54	$14\,\frac{5}{8}\%$
.513 625 6064	39.907 642 5493	.025 057 8570	55	
.507 441 1672	40.415 083 7165	.024 743 2371	56	
.501 331 1933	40.916 414 9098	.024 440 0689	57	
.495 294 7881	41.411 709 6979	.024 147 7593	58	$i = .0121875$
.489 331 0657	41.901 040 7636	.023 865 7556	59	$j_{(2)} = .024375$
.483 439 1510	42.384 479 9146	.023 593 5418	60	$j_{(4)} = .04875$ $j_{(12)} = 14625$
$v^n = \dfrac{1}{(1+i)^n}$	$a_{\overline{n}\rceil} = \dfrac{1-v^n}{i}$	$\dfrac{1}{a_{\overline{n}\rceil}} = \dfrac{i}{1-v^n}$	n	

445-2

FIGURE 6.1 (*Continued.*)

Refer to Figure 6.1 (the nominal rate if compounded monthly shows $14\frac{1}{4}$ percent in the lower right-hand corner). For line 48 and in the column headed Present worth of $1 per period, the value 36.427 152 66 (to 8 decimal places) is shown. Figure 6.1 (for the nominal rate of $14\frac{5}{8}$ percent compounded monthly) line 48 and in the column for the present value of an ordinary annuity shows the value 36.178 104 27 (to 8 decimal places).

5 The value in (4) for $a_{\overline{48}|}i$ of 36.270 828 29 is thus bracketed by the *periodic rates* of $14\frac{1}{4}$ and $14\frac{5}{8}$ percent. The approximate rate could then be stated "between $14\frac{1}{4}$ and $14\frac{5}{8}$ percent."

By interpolation:

$$\frac{1}{32}\% \leftarrow \begin{bmatrix} 1\frac{6}{32}\% & 36.427\,152\,66 \\[2em] i & 36.270\,828\,29 \\[2em] 1\frac{7}{32}\% & 36.178\,104\,27 \end{bmatrix} \begin{array}{l} \rightarrow 0.156\,324\,37 \\[1em] \rightarrow 0.249\,048\,39 \end{array}$$

$$i = 1\frac{6}{32}\% + \frac{0.156\,324\,37}{0.249\,048\,39}\left(\frac{1}{32}\%\right)$$

$$= 0.011\,875 + 0.000\,1962$$

$$= 0.012\,0712$$

$$12i = 14.49\%$$

Exercise 6.5

Find the following missing factors:

	A	S	R	n	j	m
1	$5000	$ xxx	———	20	6%	12
2	xxxxx	4000	———	24	8%	4
3	xxxxx	6000	$222.24	—	12%	12
4	4500	xxxx	426.01	—	8%	2
5	5200	xxxx	229.85	60	—	4
6	xxxx	2500	11.94	50	—	2

State the unknown number of periods approximately:

	A	S	R	n	j	m
7	$1500	$xxxx	$107.31	—	5%	1
8	——	1600	22.85	—	6%	1

Interpolate in the tables to find the unknown interest rate:

	A	S	R	n	j	m
9	$850	$xxxx	$75.00	18	——	1
10	——	1600	36.81	25	——	1

Solve the following by the use of Table 6.6 or 6.7. (*Hint:* Draw a map of the transaction before you decide which formula to use.)

11   On the day of their daughter's birth, Thomas and Ellen decided to accumulate a fund of $21,000 by the time their daughter reached her 21st birthday. If a fund paid 6%, $m = 1$, how much would Tom and Ellen have to invest on each birthday, including the 21st birthday, to reach the $21,000?

12   When Evelyn Ladd retired, she had accumulated $25,000 in a special fund. She desires to withdraw this fund over the next 90 months, the first payment to be received one month from the date of retirement. If the fund is earning 6%, $m = 12$, what will be the monthly payment?

13   Dave Dillon desires a fund of $19,500 at the end of 10 years. If he makes $1500 deposits at the end of each year, what approximate interest rate would his fund have to earn?

14   Carlotta Green purchased some land for $25,000 and is to make 10 annual payments of $3277.04, the first due one year from the signing of the contract. Find the approximate rate of interest.

15   Carolyn Falkenberg borrowed $6500, which she is paying off at the rate of $1000 per year for 8 years including interest. Find, by interpolation, the annual effective rate of interest to the nearest .01 percent.

16   Bill Wilbur is paying off a loan of $5000 with annual payments of $495 for 15 years. Find, by interpolation, the annual effective rate of interest to the nearest .01 percent.

17   Mr. and Mrs. Aucker agree to pay off a loan of $2275 bearing interest at 6 percent compounded monthly in 24 equal monthly payments. Find the size of each payment.

18   Ms. Chabot purchased an Arabian stallion for $5000. She agreed to pay the $5000 in equal quarterly payments over the next 4 years, with the first payment due on delivery of the stallion. If the debt bears interest at 8 percent compounded quarterly, find the amount of the quarterly payment.

19   Dave and Eileen Zebo owe $2500 and can pay $100 at the end of each month until the loan is paid. If the loan bears interest at 12 percent compounded monthly, *approximately* how long will it take to pay off the loan?

20 Ron Huang purchased a boat for $1101.16. Ron can pay $50 at the end of each month. If the contract calls for 12 percent compounded monthly, how long will it take Ron to pay for the boat?

21 Mr. and Mrs. Stewart desire to accumulate $6500 at the end of 8 years. How much money must be put aside in equal installments at the end of each year if it will earn 5 percent interest compounded annually?

22 Mr. Buttimer plans to accumulate $10,000 in 20 years by depositing an equal amount at the end of a 6-month period in a building and loan association that pays 6 percent interest compounded semiannually. How much money must Mr. Buttimer deposit at the end of each 6-month period?

Unit 6.6   *Other Applications of Compound Interest and Annuity Formulas to Business Decisions*

In addition to the applications to business of compound-interest and annuity formulas illustrated in the previous examples and exercises, the areas listed below involve decisions, the solution to which include calculations in compound-interest and annuity formulas. The following list is not intended to be exhaustive:

Capital budgeting
Sinking funds
Loan amortization schedules
Actuarial method of computing unearned interest
Valuation of bonds
Yield rates on bonds
Amortization of bond premium and discount
Valuation of certain assets, especially intangible assets
Depreciation and amortization of certain assets
Calculation of life insurance premiums, retirement plan deposits, etc.

All the above applications of compound-interest and annuity formulas are presented in depth in the various courses in business. A few are presented here to illustrate how such formulas are adapted for use in business decisions and problems.

APPLICATIONS IN CAPITAL BUDGETING Capital budgeting involves the decision in choosing among alternative investments. Whereas operating budgets are concerned with sales forecasts, production programs, and operating expenses, capital budgeting is concerned with the acquisition of long-lived assets, decisions to replace or repair, or whether investment in a particular business venture should be made.

Example 1   The Zebo Industries Inc. has a policy of not acquiring any asset unless the net return of the asset yields 15 percent per annum. Two investments have been proposed and are under consideration. Each plan has been estimated to return the following after all operating expenses have been deducted:

Plan A: $4000 each quarter for 5 years, costing $59,510
Plan B: $3000 each quarter for 6 years, costing $45,750

The yield rate, or effective annual rate, is computed for each plan and the answer becomes a problem in finding i and j in an ordinary annuity.

Plan A:

1 $A = Ra_{\overline{n}|i}$

2 $\dfrac{A}{R} = a_{\overline{n}|i}$

    A = present value, or cost = $59,510
    R = periodic rent, or amount of quarterly return = $4000
    n = number of periods, or quarterly periods in life of asset
      = $4 \times 5 = 20$

3 $\dfrac{\$59,510}{\$4000} = a_{\overline{20}|i}$

4 $14.8775 = a_{\overline{20}|i}$
5 $i = 3\%$ (Refer to Table 6.5)
6   Yield rate = $4i = 4 \times 3\% = 12\%$

Plan B:

1 $\dfrac{A}{R} = a_{\overline{n}|i}$

2 $\dfrac{\$45,750}{\$3000} = a_{\overline{24}|i}$

3 $15.25 = a_{\overline{24}|i}$
4 $i = 4\%$ (Refer to Table 6.5)
5   Yield rate = $4i = 4 \times 4\% = 16\%$

Hence Plan B qualifies on the basis of the annual yield rate and Plan A does not.

APPLICATIONS TO SINKING FUNDS AND AMORTIZATION   A *sinking fund* is money accumulated by means of equal periodic deposits at compound interest for the purpose of meeting an obligation (principal) at maturity. Among the many examples of sinking funds to be found in business are the accumulations of moneys through periodic savings in order to meet bond obligations or real estate mortgages at maturity or periodic savings to provide replacement of capital loss through depreciation or obsolescence.

    Amortization is a method of payment in which borrowings with current interest (amounts) are repaid in equal periodic installments. Examples of amortization are such periodic payments as those made on installment purchases, personal borrowing, and the monthly payments to both principal and interest on real estate loans.

Although there is some disagreement among authorities as to the scope of the meaning of the term "sinking fund," it is rather generally agreed that if the obligation is interest bearing (that is, if the principal earns interest until maturity), the problem is one of amortization rather than of a sinking fund.

Note the following differences which distinguish a sinking fund from amortization:

In a sinking fund:

1 The principal equals the maturity value or amount; that is, the debt does not earn interest.
2 Installments (rent) are sufficient to accumulate a fund equal to the principal due at maturity.
3 The debt or principal remains constant to maturity.
4 Finally, the mathematical problem is that of determining what rent must be provided to accumulate the sum of the principal at maturity.

In amortization:

1 The principal earns interest to maturity.
2 Installments are sufficient to pay interest on the outstanding debt (decreasing principal) and a partial payment of the principal.
3 The amount (principal + interest) is reduced with each payment, the final payment at maturity retiring the debt obligation.
4 Finally, the mathematical problem is that of determining what rent must be provided to retire by maturity the present value of an amount (interest-bearing obligation).

From the preceding it will be apparent that a series of payments into a sinking fund or amortization, if made at regular intervals and in identical amounts, constitutes an annuity in which the mathematical problem will be the determination of the required value of each periodic payment (rent).

Example 2 **The Taggart Corporation is required to make an annual deposit into a sinking fund in order to redeem $100,000 face value of bonds due at the end of 20 years. If the deposits in the sinking fund can earn 6 percent compounded annually for the next 20 years, how much money will the Taggart Corporation have to deposit into the sinking fund at the end of each year?**

The $100,000 represents the *amount* S of an ordinary annuity of $\$R$ for 20 annual periods. Hence:

1 $S = Rs_{\overline{n}|i}$

2 $R = \dfrac{S}{s_{\overline{n}|i}} = S\dfrac{1}{s_{\overline{n}|i}}$

R = unknown periodic payment
S = $100,000
n = 20 annual periods
i = 6 percent

3   $R = \$100,000\dfrac{1}{s_{\overline{20}|0.06}}$

4   $R = \$100,000(0.027\ 1846)$ (Table 6.6)

5   $R = \$2718.46$

Example 3   **On December 31, 1978 Ruth Dunaway purchased a building lot from Agnes Fielding and signed a mortgage note for $5016.85. The note includes 12 percent interest, and $100 per month payments until paid. The first payment was due January 31, 1979, and Ms. Dunaway made all the payments in 1979.**

Construct an amortization schedule of the note for 1979 and find

(a) total interest paid in 1979, and (b) balance of the note as of December 31, 1979.

The amortization schedule appears as Table 6.8.

Reading from the schedule:

(a)   Total interest paid in 1979, $568.01
(b)   Balance of note, December 31, 1979, $4384.86

Example 4   **Same problem data as Example 3. Without constructing an amortization schedule, find**

(a) balance of principal, December 31, 1979; (b) amount of interest paid, year 1979; and (c) number of months to pay off the note.

(a)   The "Merchants Rule," described in Unit 7.3, is used to answer (a) and (b).
        Balance of loan January 1, 1979 brought forward to December 31, 1979:
        $$\$5016.85(1.01)^{12} = \$5016.85(1.126\ 825) = \$5653.11$$
     Less amount of payments to December 31, 1979:
        $$\$100(s_{\overline{12}|1}) = \$100(12.6825030) = \underline{1268.25}$$
        Balance of loan, December 31, 1979 = $\overline{\$4384.86}$

(b)   Total amount paid in 1979:

12 payments at $100	$1200.00
Less reduction of principal:	
Balance, January 1, 1979 $5016.85	
Balance, December 31, 1979 [from (a) above] 4384.86	
Reduction in principal	631.99
Remainder represents interest paid in 1979:	$ 568.01

(c)   To find *n* in total term of note:

1   $A = Ra_{\overline{n}|i}$
    $A = \$5016.85$
    $R = \$100$

$$i = \frac{j}{m} = \frac{12\%}{12} = 1\%$$

$n = $ unknown

2 $\$5016.85 = \$100(a_{\overline{n}|0.01})$

3 $\dfrac{5016.85}{100} = a_{\overline{n}|0.01}$

4 $50.1685 = a_{\overline{n}|0.01}$

Refer to Table 6.5. Scan the values in the 1% column until you find 50.1685 opposite 70 periods.

5 $n = 70$ periods *or* $\dfrac{70}{12} = 5$ years and 10 months

TABLE 6.8 AMORTIZATION SCHEDULE PREPARED FOR DUNAWAY NOTE. RATE OF INTEREST, 12 PERCENT

Payment		Applied to		
Number	Amount	Interest	Principal	Unpaid balance
Start				$5016.85
1	$ 100	$ 50.17	$ 49.83	4967.02
2	100	49.67	50.33	4916.69
3	100	49.17	50.83	4865.86
4	100	48.66	51.34	4814.52
5	100	48.14	51.86	4762.66
6	100	47.63	52.37	4710.29
7	100	47.10	52.90	4657.39
8	100	46.57	53.43	4603.96
9	100	46.04	53.96	4550.00
10	100	45.50	54.50	4495.50
11	100	44.96	55.04	4440.46
12	100	44.40	55.60	4384.86
Annual totals	$1200	$568.01	$631.99	

The periodic portion of any payment is computed from

$I = Pi$, where, in the example above:

$I = $ interest for period (1 month)

$P = $ principal, or previous unpaid balance

$i = $ interest rate per period $\dfrac{j}{m} = \dfrac{12\%}{12} = 1\%$

The interest portion of the seventh payment is calculated as follows:

$I = Pi$

$I = \$4710.29 \times .01 = \$47.10$

Prepared amortization schedules are available for loans of any amount, interest rate, term, or payment. With the help of their computers, most financial institutions furnish their cusomters with annual statements similar to the above.

ACTUARIAL METHOD OF COMPUTING THE UNEARNED FINANCE CHARGE

When an interest add-on type of contract or note is paid prior to the end of the term, finding the amount of the unearned finance charge is another application of the compound-interest and annuity formula.

Example 5   Jerry Simone is repaying a loan with 18 monthly payments of $33.35 each. The total finance charge was $100.32, and the effective annual percentage rate was 24 percent. With 12 payments remaining, Mr. Simone desires to pay the loan in full. Find (a) the amount to pay off the loan assuming the unearned finance charge is calculated by the actuarial method, and (b) the amount of the unearned finance charge.

(a)   The amount necessary to pay the loan in full with 12 payments remaining is merely the present value of an ordinary annuity of 12 payments.

1    $A = R(a_{\overline{n}|i})$

$A =$ unknown

$R = \$33.35$

$n = 12$

$$i = \frac{24\%}{12} = 2\%$$

2    $A = \$33.35(a_{\overline{12}|0.02})$

$A = 33.35(10.5753412)$

$A = \$352.69$

(b)   Face value of remaining payments ($33.35 × 12) $400.20

Amount necessary to pay in full, (a) above   352.69

Unearned finance charge $ 47.51

Exercise 6.6

1   The Dutra Trucking Company is considering the purchase of a new truck and has received the following proposals for a truck which meets the minimum specifications for size, weight, accessory equipment, etc.

Proposal A:
    Cost $17,248; life, 6 years; and an average net return (excess of revenues over all operating expenses) of $1250 each 3 months for 6 years.
Proposal B:
    Cost, $19,996; life, 7 years; and an average net return of $1200 each 3 months for 7 years.
Which proposal should be accepted?

2   Phyllis Henry inherited some money and is considering investment in one of three apartment buildings for student housing. She has established a minimum yield rate of 10 percent for acceptance of any investment. Which, if any, of the three alternative apartment buildings should she accept?

	Cost	Net return	Frequency	Life, years
(a)	$40,000	$1672.56	Quarterly	20
(b)	35,000	2024.05	Semiannually	15
(c)	50,000	1582.33	Quarterly	25

3   To provide for the redemption in 25 years at maturity of a $140,000 bond issue, the Ranier Corporation plans to establish a sinking fund in which equal semiannual payments will earn 6 percent interest compounded semiannually. How much money must be placed in the sinking fund at the end of each 6-month period?

4   The Parton Company plans to accumulate $150,000 in 15 years by depositing an equal amount at the end of each 3-month period in a building and loan association that pays 8 percent compounded quarterly. Find the amount of the quarterly payments the Parton Company must make.

5   Carol Bella borrows $4500 at 6 percent interest compounded annually, agreeing to amortize the loan in equal installments at the end of each year for the next 10 years. Find the size of the annual payments.

6   Cliff Elliott borrowed $29,754.95 which he is paying off at the rate of $2000 at the end of each 6 months for 10 years at 6 percent interest compounded semiannually. Find (a) the unpaid balance just after he makes the fourteenth payment, and (b) how much of the fifteenth payment is interest.

7   Larry Eitzen borrowed $2124.34 and signed an add-on-interest type of note that calls for 24 monthly payments of $100 each due at the end of each month. The effective annual interest rate for the note is 12 percent. Find (a) the finance charge unearned if Mr. Eitzen pays off the note with six payments remaining and (b) the amount necessary to pay the note in full under the assumption that the creditor rebates unearned finance charges by the actuarial method.

8   Deborah Rowe borrowed $173.86 from the local credit union and is repaying the loan in six monthly installments of $30 payable at the end of each month. The effective annual interest rate is 12 percent. Construct an amortization schedule for all six payments similar to the one illustrated in Table 6.8.

Chapter 7

Consumer Credit Plans: The Truth-in-Lending Cost Disclosure

Objectives To Be Achieved in This Chapter

1 *Learn to understand the various types of consumer credit and loan plans.*
2 *Calculate the annual percentage rate (APR) by use of tables and by use of the annuity formula.*
3 *Find the balance on loans on which partial payments have been made, or periodic payments have been missed.*
4 *Calculate approximate interest rates on installment loans without the use of tables.*
5 *Determine the unearned finance charge for early payoff of loans.*
6 *Make decisions on the choice of credit plans.*

Consumer credit plans have become so numerous, varied, and widely used that the government of the United States deemed it necessary in the public interest to enact what is known as the Federal Truth in Lending Act. Pursuant to this law, the Board of Governors of the Federal Reserve System have issued Regulation Z requiring suppliers of consumer credit to disclose certain essential information covering the cost of consumer credit.[1]

The purpose of Regulation Z is to let borrowers and customers know the cost of the credit privilege so that they can compare the cost with those of other credit sources and avoid the uninformed use of credit. Regulation Z does not fix maximum, minimum, or any charges for credit. The various states have enacted laws establishing maximum rates of interest for the various types of credit, and some states have laws of credit disclosure similar to Regulation Z.

Unit 7.1 *Consumer Credit Plans*

Main Points in Regulation Z

The types of credit covered under Regulation Z include all real estate transactions and open-end and installment credit extended to consumers in amounts less than $25,000 for personal, family, household, or agriculture purposes. The types of credit *not covered* under Regulation Z involve business and commercial credit (except agriculture credit); credit extended to federal, state, and local governments; transactions in securities and commodities accounts with a broker dealer registered with the Securities and Exchange Commission; transactions under certain public utility tariffs; and consumer credit over $25,000 not involving real estate transactions.

THE FINANCE CHARGE The items comprising the total finance charge must be clearly disclosed. The finance charge is the total of all costs which the customer *must pay,* directly or indirectly, for obtaining credit. Some of the more common items included in the finance charge are: interest; loan fees; finder's fee or similar charge; service, transaction, or other carrying charge; points; appraisal fee (except in real estate transactions); premium for credit life or other insurance, should this be made a condition for giving credit; and investigation or credit report fee (except in real estate transactions). Costs such as taxes, registration fees, etc., and those which would be paid if credit were not employed, are excluded from the finance charge.

---

[1] The effective date of Regulation Z was July 1, 1969. All suppliers of credit should be familiar with the full text of the Regulation. The treatment in this book is illustrative of regular transactions only, and should not be relied upon as a full treatment of all the provisions in the Regulation. The full text of Regulation Z may be obtained from most banks or financial institutions or by writing to the Federal Reserve Bank serving your area or to the Board of Governors of the Federal Reserve System, Washington, DC 20551.

Example 1   **Laura Ingvardsen purchased a new automobile on credit, the price of which included the following charges: invoice price, $5200; sales taxes, $312; registration fees, $125; appraisal fee on old auto trade-in, $25; premium for insurance to continue payments if buyer dies or is disabled, $160 (optional); fire, theft, and casualty insurance premium, $360 (required); interest on deferred balance, $1151; and credit investigation fee, $10. What items are *excluded* and what items are *included* in the finance charge?**

Item	Excluded from finance charge	Included in finance charge
Invoice price	$5200	
Sales tax	312	
Registration fees	125	
Appraisal fee on old auto	25	
Optional disability insurance	160	
Required fire, theft, and casualty insurance		$ 360
Interest on deferred balance		1151
Credit investigation fee		10
	$5822	$1521

THE ANNUAL PERCENTAGE RATE   The annual percentage rate (APR) must in most cases be disclosed, and disclosed in such a manner that it will not escape the attention of the customer or borrower. The APR is the effective or true annual interest rate, calculated on an actuarial (compound interest) basis, that the total finance charge bears to the amount financed. The APR must be accurate within $\frac{1}{4}$ of 1 percent (.25 percent or 0.0025). The APR is readily ascertained on open-end credit accounts, but tables are usually employed to determine the APR on installment contracts and notes. Use of the tables is illustrated in the examples and exercises that follow, and the mathematical calculation of the APR on installment contracts and notes was presented in Unit 6.5.

Consumer Credit Plans

Goods sold by stores are purchased either by paying cash or through the medium of credit. When purchased for cash, payment is made at the time of sale and the transaction is closed. If credit is desired, the buyer may defer payment by one of several credit plans.

REGULAR CHARGE ACCOUNT   If the buyer plans to pay the entire amount of the purchase by the end of the following month, a regular charge account—or 30-day account—is opened. There is usually no direct charge for this credit service, although the initial price of the goods may be slightly higher than if the store sold for cash only, because of the additional costs of record keeping, monthly customer statements, and losses from uncollectible accounts. If the buyer fails to pay the balance when due, most stores will add a delinquent charge for late payment. The charge is usually a stated monthly percentage of the delinquent balance.

Example 2   Ms. Joann Varnes has a 30-day charge account with Hoops Bootery, which charges 2 percent per month on delinquent accounts. The balance on her July 31st statement was $44.20. Ms. Varnes did not make any charges or payments in August, and the statement she received August 31st indicated a *delinquent charge* of $0.88, calculated as follows:

Delinquent balance	$44.20
Monthly rate for delinquent accounts	×0.02
	$ 0.88

Note: A monthly rate of 2 percent is equivalent to an annual rate of 24 percent.

$i = 2\%$ = rate per period (1 month in this example)
$12i = 24\%$ = annual percentage rate[1]

CONSUMER OPEN-END CREDIT   The customer or buyer may arrange to make purchases from time to time and have the privilege of paying the balance in full or in installments. The credit arrangements can be made directly with the store, with banks, or with other credit-granting institutions. This type of credit typically covers most revolving charge accounts and credit cards. The number of installments is not fixed; however, the amount of the minimum installment is usually a certain percentage of the ending balance rounded to even multiples of $5.00 or $10.00. If the balance is paid in full, no direct interest charge is made. If payments are made in installments, a direct interest charge, or finance charge, is computed on the previous balance.

Example 3   Mrs. Gabriel Vallee has a revolving charge account with Meyer Bistrins, a department store offering their customers open-end credit under their "B-10" plan. On September 7, 1977, Mrs. Vallee received her statement for the month of August (Figure 7.1). The finance charge of $8.73 is computed as follows:

Previous balance	$581.81
Finance charge rate per month	× 0.015
Finance charge	$ 8.73

Calculation of APR in Figure 7.1.

Finance charge per billing cycle (1 month)	$ 8.73
Previous balance, or principal	$581.81

From $r = \dfrac{I}{Pt}$ (page 190)

---

[1] The APR rate indicated here does not have to be disclosed to the customer under the requirements of Regulation Z. A charge for late payment, delinquency, default, reinstatement, or other such charge is *not a finance charge if imposed for actual unanticipated late payment, delinquency, default, or other such occurrence* [Sec. 226.4(b) Regulation Z].

meyer Bistrins inc

CORPORATE OFFICE

535 FIFTH STREET   EUREKA, CALIFORNIA 95501   707-443-6787

MRS. GABRIEL VALLEE   593894   ACCT. NO.
BOX 367   ←
BLUE LAKE, CA   95525

PAGE   1   CLOSING DATE   7-20-77

$ _____

PLEASE DETACH AND RETURN WITH YOUR REMITTANCE   AMOUNT ENCLOSED

BISTRINS

Transactions during the last nine days of the month will appear on your next statement.

DATE	CLASS	DESCRIPTION	PURCHASES		PAYMENTS
6-25-77	104	ALTERATIONS	4.00		
6-25-77	324	MEN PROM. OUTERWEAR	16.99		
6-25-77	324	MEN PROM. OUTERWEAR	12.99		
6-25-77	355	MEN LS TOPS	25.00		
6-25-77	329	Y.M. SUIT/SPT. COAT	90.00		
6-25-77	777	SALES TAX	8.94	157.92	
6-25-77		CASH RECEIVED			150.00-
7-20-77	461	LDS MISSEY DRESS	12.00		
7-20-77	777	SALES TAX	.72	12.72	

FINANCE CHARGE is computed by a periodic rate of 1½% per month (or a minimum charge of 50 cents for balances of $33.00 and less) which is an ANNUAL PERCENTAGE RATE of 18% applied to the previous balance without deducting current payments and/or credits appearing on this statement.

PREVIOUS BALANCE	FINANCE CHARGE	PURCHASES	PAYMENTS	NEW BALANCE
581.81	8.73	170.64	150.00	611.18

MINIMUM PAYMENT	
PAST DUE	
CURRENT	65.00
MINIMUM NOW DUE	65.00

FIGURE 7.1 *Open-end revolving charge account. Source: Printed with permission of Meyer Bistrins, Inc.*

$$r = \frac{\$8.73}{\$581.81 \times \frac{30}{360}} = 18\%$$

When Mrs. Vallee in Example 3 above opened her account at Meyer Bistrins, she was required, under Regulation Z, to sign a disclosure statement indicating that she had been informed of the finance charges and how they

would be computed. Figure 7.2 shows that portion of the disclosure statement concerned with the finance charge. Note the boldface and/or larger
type used whenever the *finance charge* and *annual percentage rate* are
mentioned. Regulation Z requires that information relating to the cost of
credit be displayed in a manner to attract the buyer's attention and not lost
"in the fine print."

$\boxed{B}$*istrins*   ALL PURPOSE CHARGE ACCOUNT
Terms of Agreement

Customer agrees as follows with respect to this account:

(1) To pay the cash sale price of all purchases made on the account and a **Finance Charge**, if applicable, as provided herein.

(2) If full payment of the closing balance (New Balance) of a billing period is received by Bistrins
before the close of the next billing period, no **Finance Charge** will be added in the billing period in
which payment is received. In each billing period (current period) in which full payment of the New
Balance of the previous billing period is not received, a **Finance Charge** may be imposed, computed
on the Previous Balance of the current period (New Balance of the previous period, without deducting payments and credits or adding purchases made in the current period.

The **Finance Charge** is computed by applying periodic rates of $1\frac{1}{2}\%$ per month to the first
$1,000.00 of the **Previous Balance** and **1%** to such balance in excess of **$1,000.00**, corresponding
to **Annual Percentage Rates** of **18%** and **12%** respectively.

If the New Balance of the previous period is not paid in full and special payment terms have
not been arranged, to pay at least $1/10$th of the New Balance shown on each monthly billing statement (but not less than $10.00, or the balance, if less) within 10 days of receipt of such statement.

FIGURE 7.2 *Portion of disclosure statement required by Regulation Z to be signed by customer
upon opening of an open-end credit account. Source: Printed with permission of Meyer Bistrins,
Inc.*

Exercise 7.1

1   Ron Brunson's purchase of a waterbed included the following charges:
    invoice price, $550; sales tax, $33; disability insurance, $40 (required);
    credit check, $25; delivery fee, $15; interest on deferred balance, $151. Find
    the total finance charge.

2   Mike Luzzi was working in the woods and finally received the following
    statement from the Chain Saw Shop for the month of July.

Previous balance	$840.00
Finance charge	10.50
Delinquency charge	5.00
	$855.50

Find the annual percentage rate (APR) charged by the Chain Saw Shop.

3   Milly Burgess maintains a revolving charge account at the A & B Body
    Shop, which charges a finance charge on the unpaid balance as follows:

$1\frac{1}{2}$ percent per month on first $1000 of previous balance

1 percent per month on amounts over $1000

The previous unpaid balance was $1280. Find (a) the monthly finance charge and (b) the annual percentage rate (APR) for the total finance charge.

4   Daniel Leonard has a credit card for use with miscellaneous purchases. The credit card indicates finance charge rates on the previous balance as follows:

2 percent per month on balances up to $100

$1\frac{1}{2}$ percent per month on balances from $101 to $250

1 percent per month on balances over $250

Find (a) the finance charge and (b) the APR if Daniel Leonard had a previous balance of $540.

5   Riley Baxter received his monthly statement from Umpires' Suppliers, Inc., on which was indicated a previous balance of $280 and a finance charge of $4.90. Find (a) the monthly rate for charging finance charges, and (b) the APR.

6   Stephen Joseph received his monthly statement from Larry's Pitching Aids, on which was indicated a previous balance of $460 and a finance charge of $5.75. Find (a) the monthly rate for charging finance charges, and (b) the APR.

7   Beryl Herres received her monthly statement from A&E Department Store on which was indicated a previous balance of $650. If the A&E Department Store charges finance charges on the previous balance equivalent to an APR of 12 percent, find the monthly service charge on Mrs. Herres's statement.

8   Tex Box received his monthly statement from Monty's Sporting Shop, on which was indicated an APR of 16 percent. If Mr. Box's previous balance was $100, compute the monthly finance charges.

Unit 7.2   *Periodic Payment Plans; Using Annual Percentage Rate Tables*

The APR on customer credit plans involving periodic payments must be calculated by the actuarial or compound-interest method. To assist the large numbers of people concerned with disclosing the APR for customers, tables have been prepared[1] from which the APR can be obtained.

---

[1] The Board of Governors of the Federal Reserve System publishes in Volume I rate tables for regular transactions (applicable to a week or month, or a multiple or a fraction of a week or month). Volume II contains factor tables for irregular transactions (all combinations of irregular advances and payments). These volumes can be obtained at nominal cost from any Federal Reserve Bank or the Board of Governors of the Federal Reserve System, Washington, DC 20551. Rate tables produced by other publishers can also be obtained from most banks and other financial institutions.

USING THE APR TABLES The tables in Figure 7.3 are used as follows:

1 Find the finance charge (FC) per $100 of amount financed:

FC = finance charge

B = amount financed

$\dfrac{B}{100}$ = amount financed in hundreds

ANNUAL PERCENTAGE RATE TABLE FOR MONTHLY PAYMENT PLANS
SEE INSTRUCTIONS FOR USE OF TABLES   FRB-103-M

NUMBER OF PAYMENTS	10.00%	10.25%	10.50%	10.75%	11.00%	11.25%	11.50%	11.75%	12.00%	12.25%	12.50%	12.75%	13.00%	13.25%	13.50%	13.75%
					(FINANCE CHARGE PER $100 OF AMOUNT FINANCED)											
1	0.83	0.85	0.87	0.90	0.92	0.94	0.96	0.98	1.00	1.02	1.04	1.06	1.08	1.10	1.12	1.15
2	1.25	1.28	1.31	1.35	1.38	1.41	1.44	1.47	1.50	1.53	1.57	1.60	1.63	1.66	1.69	1.72
3	1.67	1.71	1.76	1.80	1.84	1.88	1.92	1.96	2.01	2.05	2.09	2.13	2.17	2.22	2.26	2.30
4	2.09	2.14	2.20	2.25	2.30	2.35	2.41	2.46	2.51	2.57	2.62	2.67	2.72	2.78	2.83	2.88
5	2.51	2.58	2.64	2.70	2.77	2.83	2.89	2.96	3.02	3.08	3.15	3.21	3.27	3.34	3.40	3.46
6	2.94	3.01	3.08	3.16	3.23	3.31	3.38	3.45	3.53	3.60	3.68	3.75	3.83	3.90	3.97	4.05
7	3.36	3.45	3.53	3.62	3.70	3.78	3.87	3.95	4.04	4.12	4.21	4.29	4.38	4.47	4.55	4.64
8	3.79	3.88	3.98	4.07	4.17	4.26	4.36	4.46	4.55	4.65	4.74	4.84	4.94	5.03	5.13	5.22
9	4.21	4.32	4.43	4.53	4.64	4.75	4.85	4.96	5.07	5.17	5.28	5.39	5.49	5.60	5.71	5.82
10	4.64	4.76	4.88	4.99	5.11	5.23	5.35	5.46	5.58	5.70	5.82	5.94	6.05	6.17	6.29	6.41
11	5.07	5.20	5.33	5.45	5.58	5.71	5.84	5.97	6.10	6.23	6.36	6.49	6.62	6.75	6.88	7.01
12	5.50	5.64	5.78	5.92	6.06	6.20	6.34	6.48	6.62	6.76	6.90	7.04	7.18	7.32	7.46	7.60
13	5.93	6.08	6.23	6.38	6.53	6.68	6.84	6.99	7.14	7.29	7.44	7.59	7.75	7.90	8.05	8.20
14	6.36	6.52	6.69	6.85	7.01	7.17	7.34	7.50	7.66	7.82	7.99	8.15	8.31	8.48	8.64	8.81
15	6.80	6.97	7.14	7.32	7.49	7.66	7.84	8.01	8.19	8.36	8.53	8.71	8.88	9.06	9.23	9.41
16	7.23	7.41	7.60	7.78	7.97	8.15	8.34	8.53	8.71	8.90	9.08	9.27	9.46	9.64	9.83	10.02
17	7.67	7.86	8.06	8.25	8.45	8.65	8.84	9.04	9.24	9.44	9.63	9.83	10.03	10.23	10.43	10.63
18	8.10	8.31	8.52	8.73	8.93	9.14	9.35	9.56	9.77	9.98	10.19	10.40	10.61	10.82	11.03	11.24
19	8.54	8.76	8.98	9.20	9.42	9.64	9.86	10.08	10.30	10.52	10.74	10.96	11.18	11.41	11.63	11.85
20	8.98	9.21	9.44	9.67	9.90	10.13	10.37	10.60	10.83	11.06	11.30	11.53	11.76	12.00	12.23	12.46
21	9.42	9.66	9.90	10.15	10.39	10.63	10.88	11.12	11.36	11.61	11.85	12.10	12.34	12.59	12.84	13.08
22	9.86	10.12	10.37	10.62	10.88	11.13	11.39	11.64	11.90	12.16	12.41	12.67	12.93	13.19	13.44	13.70
23	10.30	10.57	10.84	11.10	11.37	11.63	11.90	12.17	12.44	12.71	12.97	13.24	13.51	13.78	14.05	14.32
24	10.75	11.02	11.30	11.58	11.86	12.14	12.42	12.70	12.98	13.26	13.54	13.82	14.10	14.38	14.66	14.95
25	11.19	11.48	11.77	12.06	12.35	12.64	12.93	13.22	13.52	13.81	14.10	14.40	14.69	14.98	15.28	15.57
26	11.64	11.94	12.24	12.54	12.85	13.15	13.45	13.75	14.06	14.36	14.67	14.97	15.28	15.59	15.89	16.20
27	12.09	12.40	12.71	13.03	13.34	13.66	13.97	14.29	14.60	14.92	15.24	15.56	15.87	16.19	16.51	16.83
28	12.53	12.86	13.18	13.51	13.84	14.16	14.49	14.82	15.15	15.48	15.81	16.14	16.47	16.80	17.13	17.46
29	12.98	13.32	13.66	14.00	14.33	14.67	15.01	15.35	15.70	16.04	16.38	16.72	17.07	17.41	17.75	18.10
30	13.43	13.78	14.13	14.48	14.83	15.19	15.54	15.89	16.24	16.60	16.95	17.31	17.66	18.02	18.38	18.74
31	13.89	14.25	14.61	14.97	15.33	15.70	16.06	16.43	16.79	17.16	17.53	17.90	18.27	18.63	19.00	19.38
32	14.34	14.71	15.09	15.46	15.84	16.21	16.59	16.97	17.35	17.73	18.11	18.49	18.87	19.25	19.63	20.02
33	14.79	15.18	15.57	15.95	16.34	16.73	17.12	17.51	17.90	18.29	18.69	19.08	19.47	19.87	20.26	20.66
34	15.25	15.65	16.05	16.44	16.85	17.25	17.65	18.05	18.46	18.86	19.27	19.67	20.08	20.49	20.90	21.31
35	15.70	16.11	16.53	16.94	17.35	17.77	18.18	18.60	19.01	19.43	19.85	20.27	20.69	21.11	21.53	21.95
36	16.16	16.58	17.01	17.43	17.86	18.29	18.71	19.14	19.57	20.00	20.43	20.87	21.30	21.73	22.17	22.60
37	16.62	17.06	17.49	17.93	18.37	18.81	19.25	19.69	20.13	20.58	21.02	21.46	21.91	22.36	22.81	23.25
38	17.08	17.53	17.98	18.43	18.88	19.33	19.78	20.24	20.69	21.15	21.61	22.07	22.52	22.99	23.45	23.91
39	17.54	18.00	18.46	18.93	19.39	19.86	20.32	20.79	21.26	21.73	22.20	22.67	23.14	23.61	24.09	24.56
40	18.00	18.48	18.95	19.43	19.90	20.38	20.86	21.34	21.82	22.30	22.79	23.27	23.76	24.25	24.73	25.22
41	18.47	18.95	19.44	19.93	20.42	20.91	21.40	21.89	22.39	22.88	23.38	23.88	24.38	24.88	25.38	25.88
42	18.93	19.43	19.93	20.43	20.93	21.44	21.94	22.45	22.96	23.47	23.98	24.49	25.00	25.51	26.03	26.55
43	19.40	19.91	20.42	20.94	21.45	21.97	22.49	23.01	23.53	24.05	24.57	25.10	25.62	26.15	26.68	27.21
44	19.86	20.39	20.91	21.44	21.97	22.50	23.03	23.57	24.10	24.64	25.17	25.71	26.25	26.79	27.33	27.88
45	20.33	20.87	21.41	21.95	22.49	23.03	23.58	24.12	24.67	25.22	25.77	26.32	26.88	27.43	27.99	28.55
46	20.80	21.35	21.90	22.46	23.01	23.57	24.13	24.69	25.25	25.81	26.37	26.94	27.51	28.08	28.65	29.22
47	21.27	21.83	22.40	22.97	23.53	24.10	24.68	25.25	25.82	26.40	26.98	27.56	28.14	28.72	29.31	29.89
48	21.74	22.32	22.90	23.48	24.06	24.64	25.23	25.81	26.40	26.99	27.58	28.18	28.77	29.37	29.97	30.57
49	22.21	22.80	23.39	23.99	24.58	25.18	25.78	26.38	26.98	27.59	28.19	28.80	29.41	30.02	30.63	31.24
50	22.69	23.29	23.89	24.50	25.11	25.72	26.33	26.95	27.56	28.18	28.80	29.42	30.04	30.67	31.29	31.92
51	23.16	23.78	24.40	25.02	25.64	26.26	26.89	27.52	28.15	28.78	29.41	30.05	30.68	31.32	31.96	32.60
52	23.64	24.27	24.90	25.53	26.17	26.81	27.45	28.09	28.73	29.38	30.02	30.67	31.32	31.98	32.63	33.29
53	24.11	24.76	25.40	26.05	26.70	27.35	28.00	28.66	29.32	29.98	30.64	31.30	31.97	32.63	33.30	33.97
54	24.59	25.25	25.91	26.57	27.23	27.90	28.56	29.23	29.91	30.58	31.25	31.93	32.61	33.29	33.98	34.66
55	25.07	25.74	26.41	27.09	27.77	28.44	29.13	29.81	30.50	31.18	31.87	32.56	33.26	33.95	34.65	35.35
56	25.55	26.23	26.92	27.61	28.30	28.99	29.69	30.39	31.09	31.79	32.49	33.20	33.91	34.62	35.33	36.04
57	26.03	26.73	27.43	28.13	28.84	29.54	30.25	30.97	31.68	32.39	33.11	33.83	34.56	35.28	36.01	36.74
58	26.51	27.23	27.94	28.66	29.37	30.10	30.82	31.55	32.27	33.00	33.74	34.47	35.21	35.95	36.69	37.43
59	27.00	27.72	28.45	29.18	29.91	30.65	31.39	32.13	32.87	33.61	34.36	35.11	35.86	36.62	37.37	38.13
60	27.48	28.22	28.96	29.71	30.45	31.20	31.96	32.71	33.47	34.23	34.99	35.75	36.52	37.29	38.06	38.83

FIGURE 7.3 Source: Truth in Lending, Regulation Z, Annual Percentage Rate Tables, vol. 1, Board of Governors of the Federal Reserve System, Washington, DC.

ANNUAL PERCENTAGE RATE TABLE FOR MONTHLY PAYMENT PLANS
SEE INSTRUCTIONS FOR USE OF TABLES   FRB-104-M

NUMBER OF PAYMENTS	ANNUAL PERCENTAGE RATE															
	14.00%	14.25%	14.50%	14.75%	15.00%	15.25%	15.50%	15.75%	16.00%	16.25%	16.50%	16.75%	17.00%	17.25%	17.50%	17.75%
	(FINANCE CHARGE PER $100 OF AMOUNT FINANCED)															
1	1.17	1.19	1.21	1.23	1.25	1.27	1.29	1.31	1.33	1.35	1.37	1.40	1.42	1.44	1.46	1.48
2	1.75	1.78	1.82	1.85	1.88	1.91	1.94	1.97	2.00	2.04	2.07	2.10	2.13	2.16	2.19	2.22
3	2.34	2.38	2.43	2.47	2.51	2.55	2.59	2.64	2.68	2.72	2.76	2.80	2.85	2.89	2.93	2.97
4	2.93	2.99	3.04	3.09	3.14	3.20	3.25	3.30	3.36	3.41	3.46	3.51	3.57	3.62	3.67	3.73
5	3.53	3.59	3.65	3.72	3.78	3.84	3.91	3.97	4.04	4.10	4.16	4.23	4.29	4.35	4.42	4.48
6	4.12	4.20	4.27	4.35	4.42	4.49	4.57	4.64	4.72	4.79	4.87	4.94	5.02	5.09	5.17	5.24
7	4.72	4.81	4.89	4.98	5.06	5.15	5.23	5.32	5.40	5.49	5.58	5.66	5.75	5.83	5.92	6.00
8	5.32	5.42	5.51	5.61	5.71	5.80	5.90	6.00	6.09	6.19	6.29	6.38	6.48	6.58	6.67	6.77
9	5.92	6.03	6.14	6.25	6.35	6.46	6.57	6.68	6.78	6.89	7.00	7.11	7.22	7.32	7.43	7.54
10	6.53	6.65	6.77	6.88	7.00	7.12	7.24	7.36	7.48	7.60	7.72	7.84	7.96	8.08	8.19	8.31
11	7.14	7.27	7.40	7.53	7.66	7.79	7.92	8.05	8.18	8.31	8.44	8.57	8.70	8.83	8.96	9.09
12	7.74	7.89	8.03	8.17	8.31	8.45	8.59	8.74	8.88	9.02	9.16	9.30	9.45	9.59	9.73	9.87
13	8.36	8.51	8.66	8.81	8.97	9.12	9.27	9.43	9.58	9.73	9.89	10.04	10.20	10.35	10.50	10.66
14	8.97	9.13	9.30	9.46	9.63	9.79	9.96	10.12	10.29	10.45	10.62	10.78	10.95	11.11	11.28	11.45
15	9.59	9.76	9.94	10.11	10.29	10.47	10.64	10.82	11.00	11.17	11.35	11.53	11.71	11.88	12.06	12.24
16	10.20	10.39	10.58	10.77	10.95	11.14	11.33	11.52	11.71	11.90	12.09	12.28	12.46	12.65	12.84	13.03
17	10.82	11.02	11.22	11.42	11.62	11.82	12.02	12.22	12.42	12.62	12.83	13.03	13.23	13.43	13.63	13.83
18	11.45	11.66	11.87	12.08	12.29	12.50	12.72	12.93	13.14	13.35	13.57	13.78	13.99	14.21	14.42	14.64
19	12.07	12.30	12.52	12.74	12.97	13.19	13.41	13.64	13.86	14.09	14.31	14.54	14.76	14.99	15.22	15.44
20	12.70	12.93	13.17	13.41	13.64	13.88	14.11	14.35	14.59	14.82	15.06	15.30	15.54	15.77	16.01	16.25
21	13.33	13.58	13.82	14.07	14.32	14.57	14.82	15.06	15.31	15.56	15.81	16.06	16.31	16.56	16.81	17.07
22	13.96	14.22	14.48	14.74	15.00	15.26	15.52	15.78	16.04	16.30	16.57	16.83	17.09	17.36	17.62	17.88
23	14.59	14.87	15.14	15.41	15.68	15.96	16.23	16.50	16.78	17.05	17.32	17.60	17.88	18.15	18.43	18.70
24	15.23	15.51	15.80	16.08	16.37	16.65	16.94	17.22	17.51	17.80	18.09	18.37	18.66	18.95	19.24	19.53
25	15.87	16.17	16.46	16.76	17.06	17.35	17.65	17.95	18.25	18.55	18.85	19.15	19.45	19.75	20.05	20.36
26	16.51	16.82	17.13	17.44	17.75	18.06	18.37	18.68	18.99	19.30	19.62	19.93	20.24	20.56	20.87	21.19
27	17.15	17.47	17.80	18.12	18.44	18.76	19.09	19.41	19.74	20.06	20.39	20.71	21.04	21.37	21.69	22.02
28	17.80	18.13	18.47	18.80	19.14	19.47	19.81	20.15	20.48	20.82	21.16	21.50	21.84	22.18	22.52	22.86
29	18.45	18.79	19.14	19.49	19.83	20.18	20.53	20.89	21.23	21.58	21.94	22.29	22.64	22.99	23.35	23.70
30	19.10	19.45	19.81	20.17	20.54	20.90	21.26	21.62	21.99	22.35	22.72	23.08	23.45	23.81	24.18	24.55
31	19.75	20.12	20.49	20.87	21.24	21.61	21.99	22.37	22.74	23.12	23.50	23.88	24.26	24.64	25.02	25.40
32	20.40	20.79	21.17	21.56	21.95	22.33	22.72	23.11	23.50	23.89	24.28	24.68	25.07	25.46	25.86	26.25
33	21.06	21.46	21.85	22.25	22.65	23.06	23.46	23.86	24.26	24.67	25.07	25.48	25.88	26.29	26.70	27.11
34	21.72	22.13	22.54	22.95	23.37	23.78	24.19	24.61	25.03	25.44	25.86	26.28	26.70	27.12	27.54	27.97
35	22.38	22.80	23.23	23.65	24.08	24.51	24.94	25.36	25.79	26.23	26.66	27.09	27.52	27.96	28.39	28.83
36	23.04	23.48	23.92	24.35	24.80	25.24	25.68	26.12	26.57	27.01	27.46	27.90	28.35	28.80	29.25	29.70
37	23.70	24.16	24.61	25.06	25.51	25.97	26.42	26.88	27.34	27.80	28.26	28.72	29.18	29.64	30.10	30.57
38	24.37	24.84	25.30	25.77	26.24	26.70	27.17	27.64	28.11	28.59	29.06	29.53	30.01	30.49	30.96	31.44
39	25.04	25.52	26.00	26.48	26.96	27.44	27.92	28.41	28.89	29.38	29.87	30.36	30.85	31.34	31.83	32.32
40	25.71	26.20	26.70	27.19	27.69	28.18	28.68	29.18	29.68	30.18	30.68	31.19	31.68	32.19	32.69	33.20
41	26.39	26.89	27.40	27.91	28.41	28.92	29.44	29.95	30.46	30.97	31.49	32.01	32.52	33.04	33.56	34.08
42	27.06	27.58	28.10	28.62	29.15	29.67	30.19	30.72	31.25	31.78	32.31	32.84	33.37	33.90	34.44	34.97
43	27.74	28.27	28.81	29.34	29.88	30.42	30.96	31.50	32.04	32.58	33.13	33.67	34.22	34.76	35.31	35.86
44	28.42	28.97	29.52	30.07	30.62	31.17	31.72	32.28	32.83	33.39	33.95	34.51	35.07	35.63	36.19	36.76
45	29.11	29.67	30.23	30.79	31.36	31.92	32.49	33.06	33.63	34.20	34.77	35.35	35.92	36.50	37.08	37.66
46	29.79	30.36	30.94	31.52	32.10	32.68	33.26	33.84	34.43	35.01	35.60	36.19	36.78	37.37	37.96	38.56
47	30.48	31.07	31.66	32.25	32.84	33.44	34.03	34.63	35.23	35.83	36.43	37.04	37.64	38.25	38.86	39.46
48	31.17	31.77	32.37	32.98	33.59	34.20	34.81	35.42	36.03	36.65	37.27	37.88	38.50	39.13	39.75	40.37
49	31.86	32.48	33.09	33.71	34.34	34.96	35.59	36.21	36.84	37.47	38.10	38.74	39.37	40.01	40.65	41.29
50	32.55	33.18	33.82	34.45	35.09	35.73	36.37	37.01	37.65	38.30	38.94	39.59	40.24	40.89	41.55	42.20
51	33.25	33.89	34.54	35.19	35.84	36.49	37.15	37.81	38.46	39.12	39.79	40.45	41.11	41.78	42.45	43.12
52	33.95	34.61	35.27	35.93	36.60	37.27	37.94	38.61	39.28	39.96	40.63	41.31	41.99	42.67	43.36	44.04
53	34.65	35.32	36.00	36.68	37.36	38.04	38.72	39.41	40.10	40.79	41.48	42.17	42.87	43.57	44.27	44.97
54	35.35	36.04	36.73	37.42	38.12	38.82	39.52	40.22	40.92	41.63	42.33	43.04	43.75	44.47	45.18	45.90
55	36.05	36.76	37.46	38.17	38.88	39.60	40.31	41.03	41.74	42.47	43.19	43.91	44.64	45.37	46.10	46.83
56	36.76	37.48	38.20	38.92	39.65	40.38	41.11	41.84	42.57	43.31	44.05	44.79	45.53	46.27	47.02	47.77
57	37.47	38.20	38.94	39.68	40.42	41.16	41.91	42.65	43.40	44.15	44.91	45.66	46.42	47.18	47.94	48.71
58	38.18	38.93	39.68	40.43	41.19	41.95	42.71	43.47	44.23	45.00	45.77	46.54	47.32	48.09	48.87	49.65
59	38.89	39.66	40.42	41.19	41.96	42.74	43.51	44.29	45.07	45.85	46.64	47.42	48.21	49.01	49.80	50.60
60	39.61	40.39	41.17	41.95	42.74	43.53	44.32	45.11	45.91	46.71	47.51	48.31	49.12	49.92	50.73	51.55

FIGURE 7.3 *(Continued)*

The finance charge per $100 of amount financed (symbolized FC/100) is then:

$$FC \div \frac{B}{100} = FC \times \frac{100}{B} = \frac{FC(100)}{B}$$

2   Locate the number of payments in the extreme left-hand column of the proper monthly or weekly payment schedule and read across on the selected payment line to the value that is *nearest* FC/100 found in step 1. The APR listed at the top of this column represents the APR within $\frac{1}{4}$ of 1 percent of the true effective rate.

ANNUAL PERCENTAGE RATE TABLE FOR MONTHLY PAYMENT PLANS
SEE INSTRUCTIONS FOR USE OF TABLES

FRB-106-M

NUMBER OF PAYMENTS	22.00%	22.25%	22.50%	22.75%	23.00%	23.25%	23.50%	23.75%	24.00%	24.25%	24.50%	24.75%	25.00%	25.25%	25.50%	25.75%
	(FINANCE CHARGE PER $100 OF AMOUNT FINANCED)															
1	1.83	1.85	1.87	1.90	1.92	1.94	1.96	1.98	2.00	2.02	2.04	2.06	2.08	2.10	2.12	2.15
2	2.76	2.79	2.82	2.85	2.88	2.92	2.95	2.98	3.01	3.04	3.07	3.10	3.14	3.17	3.20	3.23
3	3.69	3.73	3.77	3.82	3.86	3.90	3.94	3.98	4.03	4.07	4.11	4.15	4.20	4.24	4.28	4.32
4	4.62	4.68	4.73	4.78	4.84	4.89	4.94	5.00	5.05	5.10	5.16	5.21	5.26	5.32	5.37	5.42
5	5.57	5.63	5.69	5.76	5.82	5.89	5.95	6.02	6.08	6.14	6.21	6.27	6.34	6.40	6.46	6.53
6	6.51	6.59	6.66	6.74	6.81	6.89	6.96	7.04	7.12	7.19	7.27	7.34	7.42	7.49	7.57	7.64
7	7.47	7.55	7.64	7.73	7.81	7.90	7.99	8.07	8.16	8.24	8.33	8.42	8.51	8.59	8.68	8.77
8	8.42	8.52	8.62	8.72	8.82	8.91	9.01	9.11	9.21	9.31	9.40	9.50	9.60	9.70	9.80	9.90
9	9.39	9.50	9.61	9.72	9.83	9.94	10.04	10.15	10.26	10.37	10.48	10.59	10.70	10.81	10.92	11.03
10	10.36	10.48	10.60	10.72	10.84	10.96	11.08	11.21	11.33	11.45	11.57	11.69	11.81	11.93	12.06	12.18
11	11.33	11.47	11.60	11.73	11.86	12.00	12.13	12.26	12.40	12.53	12.66	12.80	12.93	13.06	13.20	13.33
12	12.31	12.46	12.60	12.75	12.89	13.04	13.18	13.33	13.47	13.62	13.76	13.91	14.05	14.20	14.34	14.49
13	13.30	13.46	13.61	13.77	13.93	14.08	14.24	14.40	14.55	14.71	14.87	15.03	15.18	15.34	15.50	15.66
14	14.29	14.46	14.63	14.80	14.97	15.13	15.30	15.47	15.64	15.81	15.98	16.15	16.32	16.49	16.66	16.83
15	15.29	15.47	15.65	15.83	16.01	16.19	16.37	16.56	16.74	16.92	17.10	17.28	17.47	17.65	17.83	18.02
16	16.29	16.48	16.68	16.87	17.06	17.26	17.45	17.65	17.84	18.03	18.23	18.42	18.62	18.81	19.01	19.21
17	17.30	17.50	17.71	17.92	18.12	18.33	18.53	18.74	18.95	19.16	19.36	19.57	19.78	19.99	20.20	20.40
18	18.31	18.53	18.75	18.97	19.19	19.41	19.62	19.84	20.06	20.28	20.50	20.72	20.95	21.17	21.39	21.61
19	19.33	19.56	19.79	20.02	20.26	20.49	20.72	20.95	21.19	21.42	21.65	21.89	22.12	22.35	22.59	22.82
20	20.35	20.60	20.84	21.09	21.33	21.58	21.82	22.07	22.31	22.56	22.81	23.05	23.30	23.55	23.79	24.04
21	21.38	21.64	21.90	22.16	22.41	22.67	22.93	23.19	23.45	23.71	23.97	24.23	24.49	24.75	25.01	25.27
22	22.42	22.69	22.96	23.23	23.50	23.77	24.04	24.32	24.59	24.86	25.13	25.41	25.68	25.96	26.23	26.50
23	23.46	23.74	24.03	24.31	24.60	24.88	25.17	25.45	25.74	26.02	26.31	26.60	26.88	27.17	27.46	27.75
24	24.51	24.80	25.10	25.40	25.70	25.99	26.29	26.59	26.89	27.19	27.49	27.79	28.09	28.39	28.69	29.00
25	25.56	25.87	26.18	26.49	26.80	27.11	27.43	27.74	28.05	28.36	28.68	28.99	29.31	29.62	29.94	30.25
26	26.62	26.94	27.26	27.59	27.91	28.24	28.56	28.89	29.22	29.55	29.87	30.20	30.53	30.86	31.19	31.52
27	27.68	28.02	28.35	28.69	29.03	29.37	29.71	30.05	30.39	30.73	31.07	31.42	31.76	32.10	32.45	32.79
28	28.75	29.10	29.45	29.80	30.15	30.51	30.86	31.22	31.57	31.93	32.28	32.64	33.00	33.35	33.71	34.07
29	29.82	30.19	30.55	30.92	31.28	31.65	32.02	32.39	32.76	33.13	33.50	33.87	34.24	34.61	34.98	35.36
30	30.90	31.28	31.66	32.04	32.42	32.80	33.18	33.57	33.95	34.33	34.72	35.10	35.49	35.88	36.26	36.65
31	31.98	32.38	32.77	33.17	33.56	33.96	34.35	34.75	35.15	35.55	35.95	36.35	36.75	37.15	37.55	37.95
32	33.07	33.48	33.89	34.30	34.71	35.12	35.53	35.94	36.35	36.77	37.18	37.60	38.01	38.43	38.84	39.26
33	34.17	34.59	35.01	35.44	35.86	36.29	36.71	37.14	37.57	37.99	38.42	38.85	39.28	39.71	40.14	40.58
34	35.27	35.71	36.14	36.58	37.02	37.46	37.90	38.34	38.78	39.23	39.67	40.11	40.56	41.01	41.45	41.90
35	36.37	36.83	37.28	37.73	38.18	38.64	39.09	39.55	40.01	40.47	40.92	41.38	41.84	42.31	42.77	43.23
36	37.49	37.95	38.42	38.89	39.35	39.82	40.29	40.77	41.24	41.71	42.19	42.66	43.14	43.61	44.09	44.57
37	38.60	39.08	39.56	40.05	40.53	41.02	41.50	41.99	42.48	42.96	43.45	43.94	44.43	44.93	45.42	45.91
38	39.72	40.22	40.72	41.21	41.71	42.21	42.71	43.22	43.72	44.22	44.73	45.23	45.74	46.25	46.75	47.26
39	40.85	41.36	41.87	42.39	42.90	43.42	43.93	44.45	44.97	45.49	46.01	46.53	47.05	47.57	48.10	48.62
40	41.98	42.51	43.04	43.56	44.09	44.62	45.16	45.69	46.22	46.76	47.29	47.83	48.37	48.91	49.45	49.99
41	43.12	43.66	44.20	44.75	45.29	45.84	46.39	46.94	47.48	48.04	48.59	49.14	49.69	50.25	50.80	51.36
42	44.26	44.82	45.38	45.94	46.50	47.06	47.62	48.19	48.75	49.32	49.89	50.46	51.03	51.60	52.17	52.74
43	45.41	45.98	46.56	47.13	47.71	48.29	48.87	49.45	50.03	50.61	51.19	51.78	52.36	52.95	53.54	54.13
44	46.56	47.15	47.74	48.33	48.93	49.52	50.11	50.71	51.31	51.91	52.51	53.11	53.71	54.31	54.92	55.52
45	47.72	48.33	48.93	49.54	50.15	50.76	51.37	51.98	52.59	53.21	53.82	54.44	55.06	55.68	56.30	56.92
46	48.89	49.51	50.13	50.75	51.37	52.00	52.63	53.26	53.89	54.52	55.15	55.78	56.42	57.05	57.69	58.33
47	50.06	50.69	51.33	51.97	52.61	53.25	53.89	54.54	55.18	55.83	56.48	57.13	57.78	58.44	59.09	59.75
48	51.23	51.88	52.54	53.19	53.85	54.51	55.16	55.83	56.49	57.15	57.82	58.49	59.15	59.82	60.50	61.17
49	52.41	53.08	53.75	54.42	55.09	55.77	56.44	57.12	57.80	58.48	59.16	59.85	60.53	61.22	61.91	62.60
50	53.59	54.28	54.96	55.65	56.34	57.03	57.73	58.42	59.12	59.81	60.51	61.21	61.92	62.62	63.33	64.03
51	54.78	55.48	56.19	56.89	57.60	58.30	59.01	59.73	60.44	61.15	61.87	62.59	63.31	64.03	64.75	65.47
52	55.98	56.69	57.41	58.13	58.86	59.58	60.31	61.04	61.77	62.50	.63.23	63.97	64.70	65.44	66.18	66.92
53	57.18	57.91	58.65	59.38	60.12	60.87	61.61	62.35	63.10	63.85	64.60	65.35	66.11	66.86	67.62	68.38
54	58.38	59.13	59.88	60.64	61.40	62.16	62.92	63.68	64.44	65.21	65.98	66.75	67.52	68.29	69.07	69.84
55	59.59	60.36	61.13	61.90	62.67	63.45	64.23	65.01	65.79	66.57	67.36	68.14	68.93	69.72	70.52	71.31
56	60.80	61.59	62.38	63.17	63.96	64.75	65.54	66.34	67.14	67.94	68.74	69.55	70.36	71.16	71.97	72.79
57	62.02	62.83	63.63	64.44	65.25	66.06	66.87	67.68	68.50	69.32	70.14	70.96	71.78	72.61	73.44	74.27
58	63.25	64.07	64.89	65.71	66.54	67.37	68.20	69.03	69.86	70.70	71.54	72.38	73.22	74.06	74.91	75.76
59	64.48	65.32	66.15	67.00	67.84	68.68	69.53	70.38	71.23	72.09	72.94	73.80	74.66	75.52	76.39	77.25
60	65.71	66.57	67.42	68.28	69.14	70.01	70.87	71.74	72.61	73.48	74.35	75.23	76.11	76.99	77.87	78.76

FIGURE 7.3 (Continued)

3   If you desire to obtain a more precise APR, you can interpolate in the APR tables.

Example 1   The amount to be financed in a 36-month payment contract is $260. The finance charge is $42.38. Find (a) the APR within $\frac{1}{4}$ of 1 percent and (b) a more precise rate by interpolation.

$$FC/100 = \frac{\$42.38(100)}{\$260} = \$16.30$$

ANNUAL PERCENTAGE RATE TABLE FOR MONTHLY PAYMENT PLANS
SEE INSTRUCTIONS FOR USE OF TABLES   FRB-316-M

NUMBER OF PAYMENTS	ANNUAL PERCENTAGE RATE														
	10.00%	10.25%	10.50%	10.75%	11.00%	11.25%	11.50%	11.75%	12.00%	12.25%	12.50%	12.75%	13.00%	13.25%	13.50%	13.75%

(FINANCE CHARGE PER $100 OF AMOUNT FINANCED)

301	173.31	178.64	184.00	189.40	194.83	200.29	205.78	211.30	216.85	222.43	228.04	233.67	239.33	245.01	250.72	256.45
302	174.02	179.37	184.75	190.17	195.62	201.11	206.62	212.17	217.74	223.34	228.97	234.63	240.31	246.01	251.74	257.50
303	174.73	180.10	185.50	190.95	196.42	201.93	207.46	213.03	218.63	224.25	229.91	235.58	241.29	247.02	252.77	258.55
304	175.43	180.83	186.26	191.72	197.22	202.75	208.31	213.90	219.52	225.16	230.84	236.54	242.27	248.02	253.80	259.60
305	176.14	181.56	187.01	192.49	198.01	203.57	209.15	214.76	220.41	226.08	231.77	237.50	243.25	249.03	254.82	260.65
306	176.85	182.29	187.76	193.27	198.81	204.39	209.99	215.63	221.30	226.99	232.71	238.46	244.23	250.03	255.85	261.70
307	177.55	183.02	188.51	194.05	199.61	205.21	210.84	216.50	222.19	227.90	233.65	239.42	245.21	251.04	256.88	262.75
308	178.26	183.75	189.27	194.82	200.41	206.03	211.68	217.37	223.08	228.82	234.58	240.38	246.20	252.04	257.91	263.80
309	178.97	184.48	190.02	195.60	201.21	206.85	212.53	218.23	223.97	229.73	235.52	241.34	247.18	253.05	258.94	264.86
310	179.68	185.21	190.78	196.38	202.01	207.68	213.38	219.10	224.86	230.65	236.46	242.30	248.17	254.06	259.97	265.91
311	180.39	185.95	191.53	197.16	202.81	208.50	214.22	219.97	225.75	231.56	237.40	243.26	249.15	255.07	261.01	266.97
312	181.10	186.68	192.29	197.94	203.62	209.33	215.07	220.85	226.65	232.48	238.34	244.23	250.14	256.08	262.04	268.02
313	181.82	187.41	193.05	198.72	204.42	210.15	215.92	221.72	227.54	233.40	239.28	245.19	251.13	257.09	263.07	269.08
314	182.53	188.15	193.81	199.50	205.22	210.98	216.77	222.59	228.44	234.32	240.22	246.16	252.11	258.10	264.11	270.14
315	183.24	188.89	194.56	200.28	206.03	211.81	217.62	223.46	229.33	235.24	241.17	247.12	253.10	259.11	265.14	271.19
316	183.96	189.62	195.32	201.06	206.83	212.63	218.47	224.34	230.23	236.16	242.11	248.09	254.09	260.12	266.18	272.25
317	184.67	190.36	196.08	201.84	207.64	213.46	219.32	225.21	231.13	237.08	243.05	249.05	255.08	261.13	267.21	273.31
318	185.39	191.10	196.84	202.63	208.44	214.29	220.17	226.09	232.03	238.00	244.00	250.02	256.07	262.15	268.25	274.37
319	186.10	191.83	197.60	203.41	209.25	215.12	221.03	226.96	232.93	238.92	244.94	250.99	257.06	263.16	269.29	275.43
320	186.82	192.57	198.37	204.19	210.06	215.95	221.88	227.84	233.83	239.84	245.89	251.96	258.06	264.18	270.32	276.49
321	187.53	193.31	199.13	204.98	210.86	216.78	222.73	228.71	234.73	240.77	246.83	252.93	259.05	265.19	271.36	277.55
322	188.25	194.05	199.89	205.76	211.67	217.61	223.59	229.59	235.63	241.69	247.78	253.90	260.04	266.21	272.40	278.62
323	188.97	194.79	200.65	206.55	212.48	218.45	224.44	230.47	236.53	242.61	248.73	254.87	261.04	267.23	273.44	279.68
324	189.69	195.53	201.42	207.34	213.29	219.28	225.30	231.35	237.43	243.54	249.68	255.84	262.03	268.24	274.48	280.74
325	190.41	196.28	202.18	208.13	214.10	220.11	226.15	232.23	238.33	244.46	250.62	256.81	263.02	269.26	275.52	281.81
326	191.13	197.02	202.95	208.91	214.91	220.95	227.01	233.11	239.23	245.39	251.57	257.78	264.02	270.28	276.57	282.87
327	191.85	197.76	203.71	209.70	215.72	221.78	227.87	233.99	240.14	246.32	252.52	258.76	265.02	271.30	277.61	283.94
328	192.57	198.51	204.48	210.49	216.54	222.62	228.73	234.87	241.04	247.25	253.47	259.73	266.01	272.32	278.65	285.01
329	193.29	199.25	205.25	211.28	217.35	223.45	229.59	235.75	241.95	248.17	254.43	260.71	267.01	273.34	279.70	286.07
330	194.01	199.99	206.01	212.07	218.16	224.29	230.45	236.64	242.85	249.10	255.38	261.68	268.01	274.36	280.74	287.14
331	194.73	200.74	206.78	212.86	218.98	225.13	231.31	237.52	243.76	250.03	256.33	262.66	269.01	275.39	281.79	288.21
332	195.46	201.49	207.55	213.65	219.79	225.96	232.17	238.40	244.67	250.96	257.28	263.63	270.01	276.41	282.83	289.28
333	196.18	202.23	208.32	214.45	220.61	226.80	233.03	239.29	245.58	251.89	258.24	264.61	271.01	277.43	283.88	290.35
334	196.90	202.98	209.09	215.24	221.42	227.64	233.89	240.17	246.48	252.82	259.19	265.59	272.01	278.46	284.93	291.42
335	197.63	203.73	209.86	216.03	222.24	228.48	234.75	241.06	247.39	253.76	260.15	266.57	273.01	279.48	285.97	292.49
336	198.35	204.47	210.63	216.83	223.06	229.32	235.62	241.94	248.30	254.69	261.10	267.54	274.01	280.50	287.02	293.56
337	199.08	205.22	211.40	217.62	223.87	230.16	236.48	242.83	249.21	255.62	262.06	268.52	275.02	281.53	288.07	294.63
338	199.81	205.97	212.18	218.42	224.69	231.00	237.34	243.72	250.12	256.56	263.02	269.50	276.02	282.56	289.12	295.70
339	200.53	206.72	212.95	219.21	225.51	231.84	238.21	244.61	251.03	257.49	263.97	270.49	277.02	283.58	290.17	296.78
340	201.26	207.47	213.72	220.01	226.33	232.69	239.08	245.50	251.95	258.42	264.93	271.47	278.03	284.61	291.22	297.85
341	201.99	208.22	214.50	220.81	227.15	233.53	239.94	246.38	252.86	259.36	265.89	272.45	279.03	285.64	292.27	298.93
342	202.72	208.98	215.27	221.60	227.97	234.37	240.81	247.27	253.77	260.30	266.85	273.43	280.04	286.67	293.32	300.00
343	203.45	209.73	216.05	222.40	228.79	235.22	241.68	248.16	254.68	261.23	267.81	274.41	281.04	287.70	294.37	301.08
344	204.18	210.48	216.82	223.20	229.61	236.06	242.54	249.06	255.60	262.17	268.77	275.40	282.05	288.73	295.43	302.15
345	204.91	211.23	217.60	224.00	230.44	236.91	243.41	249.95	256.51	263.11	269.73	276.38	283.06	289.76	296.48	303.23
346	205.64	211.99	218.38	224.80	231.26	237.75	244.28	250.84	257.43	264.05	270.69	277.37	284.06	290.79	297.54	304.30
347	206.37	212.74	219.15	225.60	232.08	238.60	245.15	251.73	258.34	264.99	271.65	278.35	285.07	291.82	298.59	305.38
348	207.10	213.50	219.93	226.40	232.91	239.45	246.02	252.63	259.26	265.93	272.62	279.34	286.08	292.85	299.64	306.46
349	207.83	214.25	220.71	227.20	233.73	240.29	246.89	253.52	260.18	266.87	273.58	280.32	287.09	293.88	300.70	307.54
350	208.57	215.01	221.49	228.00	234.56	241.14	247.76	254.41	261.10	267.81	274.56	281.31	288.10	294.92	301.76	308.62
351	209.30	215.76	222.27	228.81	235.38	241.99	248.63	255.31	262.01	268.75	275.51	282.30	289.11	295.95	302.81	309.70
352	210.03	216.52	223.05	229.61	236.21	242.84	249.51	256.20	262.93	269.69	276.47	283.29	290.12	296.99	303.87	310.78
353	210.77	217.28	223.83	230.41	237.03	243.69	250.38	257.10	263.85	270.63	277.44	284.27	291.13	298.02	304.93	311.86
354	211.50	218.04	224.61	231.22	237.86	244.54	251.25	258.00	264.77	271.57	278.41	285.26	292.15	299.06	305.99	312.94
355	212.24	218.80	225.39	232.02	238.69	245.39	252.13	258.89	265.69	272.52	279.37	286.25	293.16	300.09	307.05	314.02
356	212.98	219.55	226.17	232.83	239.52	246.24	253.00	259.79	266.61	273.46	280.34	287.24	294.17	301.13	308.11	315.11
357	213.71	220.31	226.95	233.63	240.35	247.10	253.88	260.69	267.54	274.41	281.31	288.23	295.19	302.16	309.17	316.19
358	214.45	221.07	227.74	234.44	241.18	247.95	254.75	261.59	268.45	275.35	282.27	289.23	296.20	303.20	310.23	317.27
359	215.19	221.84	228.52	235.25	242.01	248.80	255.63	262.49	269.38	276.30	283.24	290.22	297.22	304.24	311.29	318.36
360	215.93	222.60	229.31	236.05	242.84	249.65	256.50	263.39	270.30	277.24	284.21	291.21	298.23	305.28	312.35	319.44

FIGURE 7.3 (Continued)

(a) By following step 2, you determine that in the 36-month payment line (Figure 7.3), the $16.30 falls less than halfway between the columns headed 10.00 percent ($16.16) and 10.25 percent ($16.58). An acceptable APR would then be 10.00 percent.

(b) APR table, 36-month payment line (Figure 7.3). The more precise APR is the same fraction of the difference from 10.00 percent to 10.25 percent as 16.30 is of the difference from 16.16 to 16.58. Thus:

$$\left.\begin{array}{c} \text{10.00\%} \\ \\ 0.25\% \quad \leftarrow \quad \text{APR} \\ \\ \text{10.25\%} \end{array}\right[\quad \begin{array}{l} \$16.16 \\ \\ \$16.30 \\ \\ \$16.58 \end{array}\right] \quad \begin{array}{l} \\ \rightarrow \quad 0.14 \\ \\ \\ \rightarrow 0.42 \end{array}\right]$$

$$APR = 10.00\% + \frac{14}{42}(.25\%)$$

$$= 10.00\% + .08\% = 10.08\%$$

THE INSTALLMENT SALES CONTRACT   The buyer may desire to extend the period of payment over a specified number of weeks, months, or years. A conditional sales contract is usually signed whereby the seller retains title to the goods until the account is paid in full. Certain charges may be added to the original purchase price, and the downpayment, consisting of a stipulated sum or precentage of the total charges, is deducted. The balance remaining is the amount to be financed.

An interest, or finance, charge is then added to the amount to be financed. The total is then divided by the number of months or weeks of the desired contract term, and the periodic payment is obtained. Installment sales contracts typically cover such larger consumer items as household appliances, furniture, and automobiles.

Example 2   **A customer purchased a TV set for an invoice price of $500. A 6 percent sales tax and other miscellaneous charges were added in the amount of $45.17. A down payment of $60 was made, and the balance was to be financed. A finance charge of $77.63 was added to obtain a total amount to be paid in 24 equal payments. Find the value of each payment.**

Invoice price	$500.00
Sales taxes	30.00
Other charges	15.17
Subtotal	$545.17
Down payment	−60.00
Amount to be financed	$485.17
Add finance charge	77.63
Total	$562.80

Paid in 24 equal payments:

$562.80 ÷ 24 = $23.45

The finance charge is normally calculated by one of two methods:

1   A flat percentage per year is based on the initial amount to be financed. This type of calculation is known as the add-on interest type of contract. The finance charge and the annual percentage rate (APR) must be calculated and prominently displayed on the contract.
2   The finance charge is determined by reference to a preselected APR. The finance charge and the APR must also be prominently displayed on the

contract. (The calculation of the finance charge by this method is illus-trated later on in Example 5.)

Example 3 **Add-on type of contract. Henry Johnson purchased a new automobile from the Harvey M. Harper Company and signed the Federal Truth in Lending Disclosure Statement illustrated in Figure 7.4. Using the APR tables shown in Figure 7.3, (a) determine the APR within $\frac{1}{4}$ of 1 percent and (b) find by interpolation in the tables the APR disclosed in Figure 7.4.**

The FC/100 is

Finance charge	$1454.30
Amount to be financed	4497.22

$$FC/100 \qquad \frac{\$1454.30 \times 100}{\$4497.22} = \$32.34$$

(a) Refer to APR tables, Monthly Payment Plans:

Col.	(14.25%)	(14.50%)
Line 48	31.77	32.37

The FC/100 of $32.34 is nearest the factor 32.37; therefore an acceptable APR would be 14.5 percent.

(b) By interpolation:

$$
\begin{array}{c}
\quad\;14.25\% \quad\qquad \$31.77 \\
0.25\% \quad \leftarrow\; \text{APR} \qquad \$32.34 \quad\; \rightarrow 0.57 \qquad \rightarrow 0.60 \\
\quad\;14.50\% \qquad\quad \$32.37
\end{array}
$$

$$APR = 14.25\% + \frac{57}{60}(0.25\%)$$

$$= 14.25\% + .24\%$$

$$= 14.49\%[1]$$

PERSONAL BORROWING   Personal loan repayment plans are, in general, of three types: (1) *open-end credit,* whereby the borrower may pay in full or pay a minimum percentage of the unpaid balance together with a monthly interest charge; (2) *promissory notes,* whereby the borrower repays the principal borrowed plus interest in one lump sum on demand or at some designated future date; (3) *installment note,* whereby the borrower repays principal and interest in equal weekly, monthly, or other periodic payments.

Open-end credit accounts maintained with banks or other financial institutions are often used for personal cash borrowing. A credit card or a special arrangement attached to a regular commercial checking account is made available to the borrower, who either presents the credit card or writes a check to borrow cash. The interest charge is a specified percentage on the

[1] The rate computed for this same example by interpolation in the ten-decimal place tables of Figure 6.1 was 14.4849%. The rate calculated above to four decimal places is 14.4875%. The difference of .0026% (.000026) arises from calculating with an FC/100 of two decimal places in the APR tables. For practical purposes, the margin of error in the APR tables is insignificant.

HARVEY M. HARPER COMPANY
(NAME OF CREDITOR)

To: Credit sale applicant(s):
Date <u>September 10, 1977</u>

The following disclosures regarding the credit sale of <u>1977 Pinto 3D RBT</u> are given in compliance with the Federal Truth in Lending Act.

(DESCRIBE)

1. Cash price (including sales tax of $ <u>277.14</u>) . . . . $ <u>4,896.14</u> (1)
2. Down payment: Cash down payment . . . . $ <u>None</u>
   Trade-in (net). $ <u>857.87</u>
   Total down payment . . . . $ <u>857.87</u> (2)
3. Unpaid balance of cash price (1 minus 2) . . . . $ <u>4,038.27</u> (3)
4. Charges to be financed:
   a. Credit life . . . . $ <u>119.03</u>
   b. Credit disability insurance . . . . $ <u>255.92</u>
   c. Other insurance, see paragraph 16 . . . . $ <u>-0-</u>
   d. License fee . . . . $ <u>11.00</u>
   e. Registration fee . . . . $ <u>73.00</u>
   Total . . . . $ <u>458.95</u> (4)
5. Unpaid balance (3 + 4) . . . . $ <u>4,497.22</u> (5)
6. Pick-up payment . . . . $ <u>-0-</u> (6)
7. Amount financed (5 minus 6) . . . . $ <u>4,497.22</u> (7)
8. *Finance charge* (time-price differential) . . . . $ <u>1,454.30</u> (8)
9. *Annual percentage rate* . . . . $ <u>14.49%</u>(9)
10. Deferred payment price (1 + 4 + 8) . . . . $ <u>6,809.39</u> (10)
11. Total of payments (total of 6 + 7 + 8) . . . . $ <u>5,951.52</u> (11)

The total of payments is payable in <u>48</u> installments as follows: <u>48</u> equal successive monthly installments of $ <u>123.99</u> each on the <u>10th</u> day of each month, commencing <u>October 10,</u> 19 <u>77</u> plus * <u>   </u>

*(Here date and describe as "balloon payment" any payment, including a pickup payment, which is more than twice the amount of a regular installment. Any balloon payment shown above will not be refinanced.)

12. A late charge of **5%** is payable on any payment past due 10 days.
13. This credit sale will be secured by a "Security Agreement (Purchase Money) Motor Vehicle" covering:
    Year model <u>1977</u> Model <u>Ford</u> Body style <u>Pinto 3 DRBT</u> I.D. number <u>7R11Y 109788</u>
14. Upon full prepayment, any unearned, precomputed time-price differential, calculated by the "sum of the balances" method, less $25, will be refunded if $1 or more.
15. Credit life, or credit disability insurance:
    The creditor does not require <u>Accident, health or life</u> insurance in connection with this credit sale. The estimated cost of this insurance if obtained from <u>Harvey M. Harper Co.</u> is $ <u>374.95</u> for the term of the credit transaction. <u>September 10,</u> 19 <u>77</u> . I want this insurance <u>yes</u>

    Henry Johnson
(SIGNATURE OF PERSON TO BE INSURED)

16. Other insurance—terms as checked below:
    ☐ <u>Fire, theft & collision</u> insurance, if written in connection with this credit sale may be obtained by you through any person of your choice. The insurer must be acceptable to the creditor.
    ☐ This insurance is not obtainable from or through the creditor.
    ☐ This insurance is obtainable from or through the creditor. Based on current information the estimated cost for the term of <u> </u> months is $<u>   </u>.
    NOTE: Information on line numbers <u>15</u> is estimated. If any information in paragraphs 1, 2, 4, or 8 is an estimate, the finance charge, annual percentage rate, and total of payments are estimates, as are other calculations based on the estimated information.

    Creditor: Harvey M. Harper Company

        By *H. A. Hesse*

I have received a copy of this disclosure statement and have not yet signed any documents evidencing or securing the proposed credit sale.
Sept. 10, 19 *77*
        Henry Johnson
        (CREDIT SALE APPLICANT)

FIGURE 7.4 *Truth in lending disclosure statement. (This form has been adapted by the author for illustrative purposes only. It does not represent that of any particular bank or lending institution, nor does it purport to comply precisely with the requirements of the Federal Truth in Lending Act and the comparable laws of the various states.)*

previous unpaid balance and a minimum monthly payment is required. The calculation of the monthly interest charge and APR is the same as Example 3 in Unit 7.1. This method offers convenience in borrowing cash and is generally used in borrowing small sums for short periods of time.

   Promissory notes are usually loans with simple interest computed on the amount borrowed. Payments of both principal and interest are made at or before maturity, no intervening payments being required. Such loans are usually for short terms, up to six months, and are designed to match the borrower's repayment ability. The loans are ordinarily available to borrowers with good credit ratings or easily liquidated collateral. The actual note is sometimes made out to include the interest for the term of the note, but the interest is computed on the amount borrowed.

Example 4   **Anokhi Imports has immediate need of $5000 to pay for an incoming shipment. Their bank loans the $5000 and prepares a 60-day note which includes the following language:**

>   "Sixty days from date, we promise to pay the ABC Bank, or order, the sum of $5086.30."

A finance charge and annual percentage rate disclosure are also signed which show the following detail:

Amount borrowed	$5000.00
Finance charge, simple interest on $5000 for 60 days,	
365-day basis, at the annual percentage rate of $10\frac{1}{2}$ percent	86.30
Amount to be repaid	$5086.30

   Installment notes are written for any length of time and usually involve equal weekly or monthly payments. The finance charge is sometimes calculated as a certain sum depending on the size, length, and payment period of the loan. This finance charge is then "added on" to the amount borrowed and the sum divided by the number of payments. The APR would have to be calculated and prominently displayed on the note. The Henry Johnson automobile contract presented as Example 3 is a similar type of "interest add-on" type of contract. Since the passage of Regulation Z, loan companies specializing in small loans to the public determine the finance charge by reference to a specific rate in the APR tables.

Example 5   **Determining finance charge from APR tables. Walter Pieper needs $1200 cash and borrows from the Buckham Finance Company. He offers his automobile and some household appliances as collateral. The note is written for 20 monthly installments of $64.35, with an APR of $25\frac{1}{2}$ percent.**

   Calculation of finance charge:

Desired rate	$25\frac{1}{2}\%$
Amount to be financed	$1200

Number of monthly payments   24

Refer to the APR tables for monthly payment plans. In the 25.50 percent column, line 24, find the FC/100: $28.69

Finance charge:

If the FC/100 was determined by

$$FC/100 = \frac{FC(100)}{B \text{ (amount financed)}}$$

then to find the finance charge:

$$\frac{FC/100 \times B}{100} = FC \qquad \left(\text{Multiply both sides of equation by } \frac{B}{100}\right)$$

$$\frac{28.69 \times 1200}{100} = \$344.28$$

Monthly payment:

Amount borrowed	$1200.00
Add finance charge	344.28
Total	$1544.28

24 equal payments of $\dfrac{\$1544.28}{24}$ $64.35

To accommodate customers who prefer to repay a loan in payments of even dollars, finance companies have prepared tables with APR's precalculated to fulfill this need. Table 7.1 presents some selected APR's for typical small loans with 12, 24, and 36 monthly payment plans. If the customer desires life and disability insurance, the premium is deducted from the cash advance. Since the life and disability insurance are not compulsory for the granting of the loan, their deduction from the cash advance does not affect the APR.

TABLE 7.1 PAYMENT CHART FOR PERSONAL BORROWING (PORTION OF CHART)

12 monthly payments				24 monthly payments				36 monthly payments			
Pay-ment	Cash advance	Finance charge	APR	Pay-ment	Cash advance	Finance charge	APR	Pay-ment	Cash advance	Finance charge	APR
$10	$102.37	$17.63	30.40	$25	$453.19	$146.81	28.54	$ 84	$2220.67	$ 803.33	21.29
11	112.60	19.40	30.41	30	546.77	173.23	27.96	94	2510.29	873.71	20.55
12	122.84	21.16	30.41	35	640.64	199.36	27.50	100	2685.26	914.74	20.15
13	133.08	22.92	30.40	40	735.98	224.02	26.94	125	3420.78	1079.22	18.77
14	143.31	24.69	30.41	50	929.98	270.02	25.78	150	4134.75	1265.25	18.25

Example 6   **Ven Vagin needs money for a vacation and decides to borrow money on his 1973 ½-ton Ford pickup. His budget will allow 36 monthly payments of approximately $85 each. The loaning officer at the West End Finance Company refers to his chart and has all the figures necessary to write up the loan.**

From Table 7.1, 36 monthly payment section

Monthly payment	$ 84.00
Cash advance	$2220.67
Finance charge	$803.33
Annual percentage rate	21.29%

REAL ESTATE LOANS   The requirements under Regulation Z differ somewhat for *credit sales of real estate*, as compared with the consumer credit plans listed above. The main points of difference are the following:

1   *The total dollar amount of the finance charge* on a credit sale or first mortgage loan to finance the purchase of the customer's dwelling *does not have to be shown* on the disclosure statement.

2   The finance charge does not include such customary real estate "closing costs" as title insurance premiums, fees for preparing and notarizing deeds and other documents, deposits for future payments of taxes and insurance, appraisal fees, and credit reports (even though they are required for the loan, provided they are reasonable in amount and not for the purpose of circumvention or evasion of the purpose of Regulation 7)

3   In many instances, the customer has the right to cancel a credit arrangement within three business days if his residence is used as collateral for credit. It is important to note that the APR for the entire credit transaction may not be the effective rate of interest which the customer is paying on his mortgage note.

Example 7   **Robert and Sally Sheridan purchased a new home, and the summary of the transaction is as follows:**

List price	$ 65,000.
Normal closing costs to be paid by buyer (title insurance, drawing deeds, etc.)	2500.
Loan origination fee and buyers' points	1800.
Credit report	100.
Total	$ 69,400.

Met by	
Down payment	9400.
10¼ percent note secured by first trust deed in favor of bank and calling for 360 payments of $537.66	60,000.
	$ 69,400.

Find (*a*) total finance charges, (*b*) APR on entire transaction to nearest ¼ of 1 percent, and (*c*) more precise APR by interpolation.

(a) Total finance charge:

Loan origination fee		1800.
Interest on note		
Total payments (360 × $537.66)	$193,557.88	
Less amount borrowed	−60,000.00	133,557.88
Total finance charge		$135,357.88

(b) FC/100:

Finance charge			$135,357.88
Amount to be financed			
Total charges		$ 69,400.	
Less			
Loan origination fee classified as a finance charge	$1800.		
Down payment	9400.	11,200.	
Amount to be financed:			$ 58,200.00

$$FC/100 = \frac{\$135,357.88}{\$58,200 \div 100} = \$232.57$$

Refer to APR tables, 360 monthly payment line

$$
\begin{array}{lll}
10.50\% = \$229.31 \\
& 3.26 \\
\text{Calculated} \\
\text{amount} = \$232.57 \\
& 3.48 \\
10.75\% = \$236.05
\end{array}
$$

The calculated $232.57 is nearest the FC/100 for 10.50 percent, therefore $10\frac{1}{2}$ percent is an acceptable APR.

(c) By interpolation:

$$
\begin{array}{llll}
& 10.50\% & \$229.31 \\
& & & 3.26 \\
.25\% \leftarrow & \text{APR} & \$232.57 & \rightarrow 6.74 \\
& 10.75\% & \$236.05
\end{array}
$$

$$APR = 10.50\% + \frac{326}{674}(.25\%)$$

$$= 10.50\% + .12\%$$

$$= 10.62\%$$

Exercise 7.2

Calculate the FC/100 from the following:

	Amount to be financed	Monthly payments Number	Amount
1	$14,500	144	$162.37
2	$2000	24	$100.79
3	$1021.51	9	$125.00
4	$ 828.43	15	$ 65.00
5	$1552.63	18	$101.00
6	$1000.00	12	$ 94.41

Find the items indicated by the blank spaces. The APR is to be determined to $\frac{1}{4}$ of 1 percent by use of the APR tables, Figure 7.3.

	Amount to be financed	Finance charge	Monthly payments Number	Amount	APR
7	___	$ 37.20	12	$53.10	___
8	___	$346.68	30	$69.89	___
9	$1000	___	24	$52.42	___
10	$1500	___	36	$50.65	___
11	$1600	$443.20	___	$34.05	___

	Amount to be financed	Finance charge	Monthly payments Number	Amount	APR
12	$20,000	$49,168.00	___	$192.13	___
13	$15,000	$37,665.00	330	___	___
14	$2000	$ 836.00	48	___	___
15	$5600	___	30	___	15.75
16	$10,000	___	320	___	10.75

Find the APR by interpolation:

	Amount to be financed	Finance charge	Number of monthly payments	APR by interpolation
17	$2500	$ 333.75	24	___
18	$1500	$ 144.60	12	___
19	$2000	$ 707.00	30	___
20	$6000	$13,500.00	312	___

Solve the following:

21 Juan and Maria found a home they want to purchase. The price was finally settled at $52,500. Juan and Maria can pay $10,000 down. All closing costs, other than the loan origination fee, are $1200. The loan origination fee is $525. The banker will grant them a 30-year loan at 10 percent. Find (a) finance charge, (b) amount to be financed, (c) APR to nearest $\frac{1}{4}$ of 1 percent, and (d) the total amount paid for the house.

22 Chris Hake purchased a new motorbike for $3000 plus $180 sales tax and
    $60 license fee. Chris also voluntarily agreed to pay $130 for life and
    disability insurance. Chris paid $900 down, and the dealer put the
    balance on a 30-month contract. The dealer added an interest charge of
    $500. Find (a) the amount to be financed and (b) the APR to the nearest
    $\frac{1}{4}$ of 1 percent.

23 Ed Howell sold some used equipment for $3000. The buyer paid $500
    down, and Ed will accept the balance in 12 monthly payments with an
    APR of 16 percent. Find (a) the finance charge and (b) the monthly
    payment.

24 Sheila Kurwitz sold a parcel of land for $15,000 including normal closing
    costs. The buyer paid $2000 down, and Sheila will accept the balance in
    60 equal monthly payments at an annual percentage rate of $14\frac{1}{2}$ percent.
    Find (a) the finance charge and (b) the monthly payment.

25 Jack Young needed at least $900. He dropped in to the West End Finance
    Company and informed them of his needs and that he could afford to
    repay the loan at $50 per month for at least 2 years. Using Table 7.1, find
    (a) cash advance received, (b) total finance charge, and (c) the APR.

Unit 7.3

Unearned Finance Charges;
Partial Payments; and
Approximate Effective
Annual Interest Rates

Unearned Finance Charges

An early payoff of an installment note or contract in which the finance charge
is included in the equal periodic payment will cause an abatement of a
portion of the finance charge. *Regulation Z requires disclosure* of the
method used by the creditor to compute the amount of this abatement. Two
methods in general use and acceptable under Regulation Z are (1) the *"sum
of the balances,"* or what has been known as the *Rule of 78,* and (2) the
actuarial or compound-interest method.

SUM OF BALANCES OR RULE OF 78 This method is an adaptation of the
"sum-of-the-years'-digits" method of determining proportions. In accounting, the sum-of-the-years' depreciation method assigns larger portions of the
cost to the earlier years in the depreciable asset's life. So it should be with
the earning of a finance charge. The greater portion of the finance charge is
earned in the early periods of the loan when the outstanding balance—the
amount "at interest"—is the greater.

   *The unearned finance charge is the same proportion of the total finance
charge as the sum of the number of remaining payments bears to the sum of
the number of total payments.* There is no difference in the answer if the sum

of the loan balances after each payment is used, or is merely just the sum of the number of the payments.

Example 1 **Donna Sorensen took out a loan of $1080 for 12 months at an APR of 13 percent. The total finance charge was $83.76, and the monthly payments were $96.98. Total amount of payments was $1163.76. The loan was paid off with four payments remaining. By use of the Rule of 78, find (a) the unearned finance charge and (b) the amount necessary to pay off the loan.**

The sum of the number of payments, and the sum of the remaining number of payments when the note is paid in full are illustrated as follows:

Payments	Payments remaining
Date of note	12
Payment 1	11
2	10
3	9
4	8
5	7
6	6
7	5
8	4
9	3
10	2
11	1
12	0
Sum of payments	78
Sum of remaining number of payments when note is paid in full	10

Notice that the above is an arithmetical progression whereby each number differs from the preceding number by the same number or a *common difference*. Utilizing the formula to find the sum of an arithmetical progression, the totals can be obtained without the necessity of adding the column:

Sum of an arithmetic progression:

$$\text{Largest term in series} \times \frac{\text{number of items} + 1}{2}$$

Thus:

$$\text{Sum of total number of payments} = 12 \times \frac{12 + 1}{2} = 78$$

$$\begin{array}{l}\text{Sum of remaining payments} \\ \quad \text{when note is paid in full}\end{array} = 4 \times \frac{4 + 1}{2} = 10$$

(a) Unearned finance charge is then calculated by the law of proportions (see Unit 3.4):

$$\frac{\text{Unearned finance charge}}{\$83.76 \text{ (finance charge)}} = \frac{10}{78}$$

or

Unearned finance charge: $83.76 :: 10:78

Therefore:

$$\text{Unearned finance charge} = \frac{83.76(10)}{78} = \$10.74$$

(b) Amount of remaining payments 96.98(4) = $387.92
        Less abatement of unearned finance charge   −10.74
          Balance to pay off the loan $377.18

Using the sum of the remaining balances of the note does not change the amount of the unearned finance charge:

Sum of balances $\quad\quad = \$1163.70\dfrac{12 + 1}{2} = \$7564.05$

Sum of remaining balances
  when note is paid in full $= \$387.92 \times \dfrac{4 + 1}{2} = \$969.80$

$$\frac{\text{Unearned finance charge}}{83.76} = \frac{969.80}{7564.05}$$

$$\text{Unearned finance charge} = \frac{83.76(969.80)}{7564.05} = \$10.74$$

Tables are available to determine more quickly the amount of the unearned finance charge by use of the Rule of 78.

ACTUARIAL METHOD   The actuarial method is based in compound interest. The amount to pay off the loan with n number of payments remaining was found to be the present value of an ordinary annuity of n payments (see Unit 6.6). However, the APR tables can also be used to calculate the unearned finance charge by the actuarial method.

Example 2   **Buck Buchanan is repaying a loan with 18 monthly payments of $33.35 each. The total finance charge was $100.32, and the APR was 24 percent. With 12 payments remaining, Mr. Buchanan pays the loan in full. Find (a) the unearned finance charge and (b) the amount of the loan payoff.**

(a) Calculation of the unearned finance charge by use of the APR tables:

1 Let RP = dollar amount of remaining payments
  Let h = FC/100 in a contract or loan the number of installments of which are equal to the number of remaining payments, and the APR of which is equal to the APR of the contract or loan that is being paid off (find from APR tables).
2 Calculate the unearned finance charge from the formula:

$$\frac{RP \times h}{100 + h}$$

$RP = 33.35(12) = \$400.20$
h = FC/100 in a loan with 12 payments and an APR of 24% = \$13.47 (from APR table)

$$\frac{400.20 \times 13.47}{100 + 13.47} = \$47.51 \text{ (Unearned finance charge)}$$

(b)
Amount of remaining payments	\$400.20
Less abatement of finance charge	-47.51
Amount of payoff on loan	\$352.69[1]

Example 3 **Same problem data as Example 2. Find the unearned finance charge by the Rule of 78.**

1 Sum of number of total payments:

$$18 \times \frac{18 + 1}{2} = 171$$

Sum of number of remaining payments:

$$12 \times \frac{12 + 1}{2} = 78$$

Finance charge = \$100.32

2 Unearned finance charge (by law of proportion, Unit 3.4)

$$\frac{\text{Unearned finance charge}}{100.32} = \frac{78}{171}$$

$$\text{Unearned finance charge} = \frac{\$100.32 \times 78}{171} = \$45.76$$

Although the Rule of 78 abates less of the finance charge than does the actuarial method, the amounts are reasonably close. Most installment con-

---

[1] Refer to Unit 6.6, and note that in Example 5, the payoff calculated as the present value of an ordinary annuity of 12 payments was exactly the same amount, \$352.69.

tracts provide for a deduction of a specified amount from the unearned finance charge (usually $25) and will abate the balance if $1 or more.

Partial Payments and Missed Periodic Installments

In bankruptcy settlements of long-term loans and in the purchase of merchandise and other forms of property, it happens frequently that payments on account have been made or periodic installments on notes have been missed. The question immediately arises as to the amount of interest and principal that is due at any point in the life of the debt or at its maturity.

A *partial payment,* or payment on account, is the payment of any part of a note or similar obligation.

On non-interest-bearing obligations the computation is of course quite simple, for the partial payment need only be deducted from the sum due in order to obtain the remainder due.

On interest-bearing obligations, the two common methods of finding the amount due are (1) by the United States rule or (2) by the merchants' rule.

THE UNITED STATES RULE   The United States rule was first used as a method of settling government obligations. Its legality, established by the United States Supreme Court, has subsequently been affirmed by many of the states. Hence it is called the United States rule.

The following excerpt from a decision by the United States Supreme Court is the basis for solving partial-payment problems on interest-bearing obligations:

> *The rule for casting interest when partial payments have been made is to apply the payment, in the first place, to the discharge of the interest then due.*
>
> *If the payment exceeds the interest, the surplus goes toward discharging the principal, and the subsequent interest is to be computed on the balance of the principal remaining due.*
>
> *If the payment is less than the interest, the surplus of interest must not be taken to augment the principal, but the interest continues on the former principal until the period when the payments, taken together, exceed the interest due, and then the surplus is applied toward discharging the principal, and the interest is to be computed on the balance as aforesaid.*

It is evident that two fundamental principles must be applied in solving partial-payment problems by the United States rule: (1) accrued interest must be paid before the principal can be diminished and (2) interest must never draw interest (i.e., simple interest is involved).

Therefore the procedure to find the amount due *at any given time* is as follows:

1 Compute the interest on the face of the note following the date of the note to and including the date of the first payment.
2 From the first payment deduct the interest.
3 Apply the remainder of the first payment to reduce the face, obtaining a

new face; that is, the excess of the payment over the interest due is subtracted from the previous face to obtain a new face as of the date of the payment.

For any subsequent payments continue the above procedure. The amount due at any time is the sum of the last face plus accrued interest from the date of that face.

If any payment does not equal the interest due at the time the payment is made, no change is made in the face, interest continues on the face, and the payment is held until sufficient payments, taken together, exceed the interest due, at which time the excess is applied to determine a new face, as above.

THE MERCHANTS' RULE   Under the merchants' rule, the face of the note draws interest following its date to and including the date of settlement, and each payment draws interest following its date to and including the date of settlement. To determine the amount due at the date of settlement, the sum of the amounts (payment + interest) of the payments is deducted from the amount (face + interest) of the note or obligation.

Therefore the procedure to find the amount due at *any given settlement date* is as follows:

1   Find the amount (face + interest) of the note to the date of settlement.
2   Find the amount (face + interest) of each payment from the date of payment to the date of settlement.
3   From the amount of the note subtract the sum of the amounts of the payments. The remainder is the amount due on the settlement date.

TO COMPUTE TIME ON PARTIAL PAYMENTS   You will note that in the preceding explanation of the United States rule, the term "at any given time" was used, and that in the explanation of the merchants' rule, the term "at any given settlement date" was used. These terms, rather than "maturity date," were used on the assumption that the payee would accept final payment prior to any fixed date. Of course, if the final date of payment is the maturity date, the amounts due will be determined by the stipulated maturity date rather than any given time or any given settlement date.

However, since partial payments are commonly applied on obligations that may have no fixed or predetermined date of maturity, such as payments on merchandise, accounts payable, this terminology is desirable.

Because of banking regulations, most banks prefer to make out entirely new notes at the time of each payment. At times, this is impossible because of the unavailability of one or more of the makers or for other reasons, and in such instances banks will ordinarily apply the United States rule.

In obligations arising from merchandise transactions, sometimes the merchants' rule is used.

For both rules, a 360-day business year and either exact time or 30-day-month time may be used. Although both banks and business concerns generally use exact time, on some occasions 30-day-month time is used.

Example 4   **The United States rule, using exact time. On April 17 Ralph Johnson contracted the following obligation:**

$8500.00	SAN FRANCISCO, CALIF.	April 17, 1978

ON OR BEFORE ONE YEAR _____ AFTER DATE _____ I _____ PROMISE TO PAY TO

THE ORDER OF_____ American National Bank _____

Eighty-Five Hundred and $\overline{100}^{\text{no}}$ _____ DOLLARS

at American National Bank

VALUE RECEIVED — — — — — WITH INTEREST AT _____ 6% _____

NO. ___ 5736 ___   DUE ___ April 17, 1979 ___   *Ralph Johnson*

FIGURE 7.5

The following payments were endorsed on the back of the note:

7/13/78	$1200.00
9/22/78	$1500.00
12/26/78	$2000.00

Find the amount due at *maturity,* using the United States rule and exact time:

Face of note, 4/17/78		$8500.00
First payment, 7/13/78	$1200.00	
Interest, 4/17 to 7/13 (87 days on $8500)	−123.25	
Balance applied to face		−1076.75
Reduced face of note, 7/13/78		$7423.25
Second payment, 9/22/78	$1500.00	
Interest, 7/13 to 9/22 (71 days on $7423.25)	−87.84	
Balance applied to face		−1412.16
Reduced face of note, 9/22/78		$6011.09
Third payment, 12/26/78	$2000.00	
Interest, 9/22 to 12/26 (95 days on $6011.09)	−95.18	
Balance applied to face		−1904.82
Reduced face of note, 12/26/78		$4106.27
Interest, 12/26/78 to maturity 4/17/79 (112 days on $4106.27)		+76.65
Amount due at *maturity*		$4182.92

Example 5   **The merchants' rule, using 30-day-month time and simple interest. Compute the amount due at *maturity* on the $8500 note of Ralph Johnson, using the merchants' rule and 30-day-month time.**

Face of note, 4/17/78		$8500.00
Interest 4/17/78 to maturity 4/17/79		+510.00
Maturity value of note		$9010.00
First payment, 7/13/78	$1200.00	
Interest, 7/13/78 to 4/17/79 (274 days)	+54.80	
Amount of first payment		$1254.80
Second payment, 9/22/78	$1500.00	
Interest, 9/22/78 to 4/17/79 (205 days)	+51.25	
Amount of second payment		1551.25
Third payment, 12/26/78	$2000.00	
Interest, 12/26/78 to 4/17/79 (111 days)	+37.00	
Amount of third payment		2037.00
Sum of amounts of payments		−4843.05
Amount due at *maturity*		$4166.95

Example 6   **The merchants' rule, using compound interest. Larry Marx had sold a parcel of real estate and was collecting on a mortgage note. The note had a face amount of $25,000 and called for equal annual payments for 5 years at 6 percent interest. The payments came to $5934.91 per year. The debtor made the first three payments on schedule, but defaulted on the fourth and fifth payments. It is now six years after the date of the note, and Mr. Marx needs to know the amount due. Assuming the note contains provision to charge interest at the note rate for all delinquencies, find the amount due on the note.**

Amount of note due six years after starting date:

$\qquad$ $25,000(1.06)^6$ $\qquad\qquad\qquad\qquad$ = $35,462.98

Less value of payments made to end of sixth year:

First payment

$\qquad$ $5934.91(1.06)^5 = $7942.25

Second payment

$\qquad$ $5934.91(1.06)^4 = $ 7492.69

Third payment

$\qquad$ $5934.91(1.06)^3 = $ 7068.57 $\qquad\qquad\qquad$ 22,503.51

Amount due on note: $\qquad\qquad\qquad\qquad$ $12,959.47[1]

Example 7   **Same problem data as Example 6 except that debtor missed the third installment and desires to "catch up" by paying whatever amount is necessary with the fourth installment to bring the payments "back on schedule."**

[1]Values for $(I + i)^n$ obtained from Table 6.1.

Accumulate the missed payment for the number of periods missed at the note rate:

Third payment
$5934.91(1.06)	= $ 6,291.00
Fourth payment (face value)	= 5,934.91
Amount due at end of fourth year to remain "on schedule"	$12,225.91[1]

Approximate Effective Annual Interest Rates

FINDING APPROXIMATE EFFECTIVE INTEREST RATES FOR INSTALLMENT CONTRACTS WITHOUT USE OF FACTOR TABLES   There are many times when it is useful to know the approximate effective rate of ordinary interest on periodic-payment plans of the add-on interest type, but APR tables, compound-interest tables, or programmed pocket calculators are not immediately available. The following arithmetical procedure gives a useful approximation to the true effective rate. It should be observed that these approximations are not accurate within the $\frac{1}{4}$ of 1 percent tolerance of Regulation Z, and should not be used as a substitute procedure for determining the APR.

TO FIND THE APPROXIMATE EFFECTIVE ANNUAL RATE FOR INSTALLMENT CONTRACTS   The procedure is as follows:

1   Find the total finance charge.
2   Determine the average balance of the principal outstanding during the term of the loan or contract. [The average balance is best determined by finding the sum of the balances (use the arithmetic progression formula, page 275), and dividing by the total number of items.]
3   Divide the finance charge by the average balance. The product is the effective rate of interest for the entire term of the contract or loan, *as if* the loan or contract was *one* interest period.
4   Convert the interest rate found in step 3 to 1 year by multiplying by the fraction formed by the periods in 1 year divided by the number of periods in the loan.

Expressing the procedure in a formula:

Let FC = finance charge
    AP = average principal outstanding
     E = approximate effective annual interest rate
     m = periods in 1 year
     n = number of periods in loan or contract

---

[1]There are many routes one may take in solving problems in compound interest. The procedure illustrated for this example is probably the shortest. Perhaps you can work out other routes to arrive at the same answer.

Therefore:

$$E = \frac{FC}{AP} \times \frac{m}{n}$$

Example 8   **An electric refrigerator is advertised for $475 cash, or $25 down and $50.31 per month for 10 months on an "easy pay plan." Find (a) finance charge, (b) the approximate annual interest rate, and (c) the APR as determined from the APR tables.**

(a) Finance charge:

Total payments (50.31 × 10)		= $503.10
Less amount financed:		
Cash price	$475	
Less down payment	25	450.00
Finance charge		= $ 53.10

(b) Finance charge (FC)   = $ 53.10

$$\text{Average principal (AP)} = \frac{450 \times \dfrac{10 + 1}{2}}{10} = 247.50$$

Periods in 1 year (m)   =   12
Periods in loan (n)   =   10

From

$$E = \frac{FC}{AP} \times \frac{m}{n}$$

$$= \frac{53.10}{247.50} \times \frac{12}{10} \qquad\qquad = 25.75\%$$

(c) $FC/100 = \dfrac{53.10(100)}{450} = 11.80$

From (Figure 7.3) APR table (line 10)   = 25.00%

Example 9   **A pressure pump is priced at $310 cash or $40 down and $4.51 per week for 75 weeks. Find (a) the finance charge and (b) the approximate effective annual interest rate.**

(a) Finance charge:

Total payments $4.51 × 75 =		$338.25
Less amount financed:		
Cash price	$310.00	
Less down payment	40.00	270.00
Finance charge		$ 68.25

(b) FC   = $ 68.25

$$AP \quad \frac{270 \times \dfrac{75 + 1}{2}}{75} \quad = \ 136.80$$

m   =   52

n   =   75

From

$$E = \frac{FC}{AP} \times \frac{m}{n}$$

$$E = \frac{\$68.25}{\$136.80} \times \frac{52}{75} \qquad = 34.59\%[1]$$

RELATIONSHIP BETWEEN NOMINAL INTEREST RATE AND APPROXIMATE EFFECTIVE ANNUAL INTEREST RATE   To find the approximate effective rate for any given nominal rate and number of periods, the formulas presented above are factored to obtain

$$E = \frac{2nj}{n + 1}$$

where E = approximate effective annual interest rate
            n = number of periods in contract or loan
            j = nominal interest rate

Example 10   **Find the approximate effective annual interest rate equivalent to a 12 percent nominal rate for 26 equal weekly payments.**

$$E = \frac{2nj}{n + 1}$$

$$= \frac{2(26 \times .12)}{26 + 1} = 23.1\%$$

Conversely, the above formula can be rearranged to find the approximate nominal rate for a given number of periods that is equivalent to a given effective annual rate. The formula obtained is

$$j_a = \frac{r(n + 1)}{2n}$$

where

j_a = approximate nominal rate
 r = effective annual rate
 n = number of periods

---

[1]APR tables for weekly rates have not been reproduced in this text. However, for this example, the APR to the nearest $\frac{1}{4}$ of 1 percent is 32.25 percent. The disparity between the approximate effective annual rate and the APR increases as the number of periods increases.

Example 11 **Find the approximate nominal rate of interest for eight monthly payments that is equivalent to the annual effective rate of 25 percent.**

$$j_a = \frac{r(n+1)}{2n}$$

$$= \frac{0.25(8+1)}{2(8)} = 14.1\%$$

Exercise 7.3

Find (1) the unearned finance charge, and (2) the amount necessary to pay off each of the following contracts or notes assuming the unearned finance charge is rebated in full and calculated by (a) the Rule of 78 and (b) the actuarial method calculated from the APR tables.

	Finance charge	APR	Monthly payments Total number	Monthly payments Amount	Remaining number of payments
1	$ 62.10	11.50	24	$ 23.42	8
2	138.45	13.00	36	21.90	12
3	99.72	15.00	12	108.31	3
4	98.55	16.00	18	47.14	10
5	1376.17	12.00	48	137.26	12
6	908.24	24.00	30	119.45	20

Refer to Table 6.5 and calculate the amount necessary to pay off the contracts assuming the unearned finance charge is abated in full:
7 Same data as Problem 5 above.
8 Same data as Problem 6 above.

Solve the following:
9 A 9-month note for $6000 dated September 5, 1977 and bearing ordinary interest at 9 percent had the following payments endorsed on its back:

12/15/77 $1000
3/1/78 $3000

Compute the amount owed at maturity by the United States rule, using exact time.
10 Same data as Problem 9. Compute the amount owed at maturity by the merchants' rule, using exact time.
11 Herbert Urban was collecting on a $40,000 mortgage note which called for 30 equal annual payments of $2905.96 at 6 percent. The debtor made the first two payments and missed the third and fourth payments. At the end of 5 years, Mr. Urban demanded full payment of the note. Find the value of the note by the merchants' rule and use of compound interest.
12 Stella Hahn was encouraging one of her customers to "catch up" his delinquent payments. Her customer was discharging a debt of $1200

with 20 quarterly payments of $73.39 and 8 percent interest compounded four times a year. The sixth payment was due and her customer had missed the fourth and fifth payments. Find the amount due, including the sixth payment.

13   A 6-month note for $4500 dated May 20, 1978, and bearing ordinary interest at 7 percent had the following payments endorsed on its back:

6/19/78 $ 800
8/18/78 $1500

Compute the amount owed at maturity of this note by the United States rule, using exact time.

14   George Alvers was the maker of a note for $6500 dated June 22, 1978, and bearing ordinary interest at 9 percent. Payments were endorsed on the back of the note as follows:

7/7/78 $1165.00
10/12/78 $ 50.00
11/6/78 $3600.00
12/8/78 $1500.00

Use the United States rule and exact time to compute the amount George Alvers owed on this note as of February 16, 1979.

15   The following payments were made on a 12-month, 10 percent ordinary interest note for $2750, dated February 14, 1979:

4/19/79 $ 750.00
10/26/79 $1200.00

Compute the amount due at maturity by the merchants' rule, using exact time.

16   A 9 percent ordinary interest note for $6000, dated October 18, 1979, and due on or before 18 months after date, was given in payment of some merchandise. The following partial payments had been made:

5/16/80 $3000
9/16/80 $1000

Using the merchants' rule, find the amount of final settlement made on December 30, 1980, if computed by 30-day-month time.

Find the approximate effective rate of ordinary interest to nearest $\frac{1}{10}$ percent on the following installment purchases and personal loans paid in full by equal periodic payments:

17   A stereo power unit is advertised at $650 cash, or $50 down and $31.13 per month for 24 months.

18   A personal loan was obtained for $500 and is to be repaid in 20 monthly installments of $30.83.

19   Mr. Harvey borrowed $300 from the Auto Finance Company and repaid the loan in weekly payments of $10.50 for 32 weeks. Find the approximate percent rate of interest charged Mr. Harvey.

20   A lending institution charges 9 percent rate of nominal interest on the

original balance repaid in 15 months. Find the approximate effective rate of ordinary interest.

21   If the approximate effective rate of ordinary interest charged by a lending agency on loans repaid in nine equal monthly installments is 13.5 percent, find the nominal rate of interest charged (to nearest $\frac{1}{10}$ percent).

22   A color TV is advertised at $525 cash or $75.00 down and $22.50 per month for 24 months on the installment plan.

23   A washing machine is priced at $205 cash or nothing down and $4.50 per week for 52 weeks on the installment plan.

24   A used automobile is priced at $645 cash or one-third down and $13 per week for 39 weeks on the installment plan.

25   Find the approximate percent rate of interest charged on a loan of $320 if the amount of $350 is to be paid in eight equal monthly installments.

26   Same data as Problem 17. Find the APR from the APR tables.

27   Same data as Problem 18. Find the APR from the APR tables.

Unit 7.4
Decisions of Choice of Credit Plans

The purpose of Regulation Z is to disclose the important cost features of credit transactions so as to enable consumers to better evaluate the desirability of credit and the alternative credit plans available. With the aid of Regulation Z, customers are made aware of the total dollar cost of credit (except in real estate transactions), and through comparison of the APRs, the relative cost of one plan can be compared with alternative plans. It should be noted that there are other features of credit plans which may not be measured in such quantitative terms. The urgency of the need, convenience of obtaining credit, availability of terms to match repayment ability, and collateral needed are all factors to be taken into account. The consumer must weigh these characteristics along with the quantitative factors in making a decision on the desirability of using personal credit and making a choice among alternative plans.

Example 1   **David Mathew wants to borrow $300 and repay the loan in equal installments over the next 6 months. Credit source A will loan him the money and charge $1\frac{3}{4}$ percent per month on the remaining balance. Credit source B will also loan him $300 to be repaid in 6 monthly installments of $52.62. From which credit source should David Mathew borrow the $300?**

Compare the two credit sources by their APRs:

APR from source A:

$i = 1\frac{3}{4}\%$ per month on declining balance

$12i = 21.00\% = $ APR

APR from source B:

Finance charge:

Total amount of payments (6 × $52.62)		$315.72
Less amount borrowed		300.00
Finance charge		$ 15.72

$$FC/100 = \frac{FC(100)}{B} = \frac{\$15.72(100)}{300} = \$5.24$$

From the APR tables:

$$\text{APR to nearest } \frac{1}{4} \text{ of } 1\% = 17.75\%$$

Credit source B has the lower APR, and so, assuming indifference as to other factors concerning the loan, David Mathew should choose credit source B.

Example 2 **Sharon Buchanan purchased a new carpet and is financing $1200 for 30 months at $49.38 per month for an APR of 17 percent and a total finance charge of $281.40. After making six payments, she inherited some money and wants to know if she should pay off the installment loan. Her creditor refunds the unearned finance charge by the actuarial method, less $25. If Sharon placed her money in a savings bank, she could earn 8 percent, converted quarterly. What should she do? Show details.**

(a) Calculation of payoff:

RP = remaining payments = $49.38(24) = $1185.12
h = FC/100 in a 24-month loan with an APR
      of 17% (from APR table) $18.66

$$\frac{RP \times h}{150 + h} = \frac{1185.12 \times 18.66}{100 + 18.66} \qquad = \$186.37$$

Less withheld by creditor		25.00
Abatement of finance charge		161.37
Payoff amount		$1023.75

(b) Calculation of new APR:[1]

FC = finance charge $1185.12 − $1023.75 = $ 161.37

B = amount financed = $1023.75

$$\frac{FC}{100} = \frac{161.37(100)}{1023.75} = \quad 15.76$$

$$n = 24 \text{ months}$$

[1]An investor would view the transaction at this point as the opportunity to receive 24 future payments of $49.38 each for a present investment of $1023.75. This represents a return equal to the APR of 14.50 percent.

APR to nearest $\frac{1}{4}$ of 1 percent (from
APR tables)   = 14.50%

(c)   Effective annual rate of 8 percent, $m = 4$ (APR):

$$[(1.02)^4 - 1] = .082\ 4322 \text{ (Table 6.1)} = 8.24\%$$

Ms. Buchanan should pay off the installment loan as her effective annual earnings would be 14.50 percent compared to 8.24 percent in the savings account.

Exercise 7.4

Assume all credit plans are equal with respect to convenience and ability of debtor to qualify for the credit desired and to meet the respective payment terms indicated.

1   Alice Jones has an immediate need for cash and is considering borrowing $500 under one of the following two plans. Which one should she prefer? Why? (a) $45.78 per month for 12 months, (b) $89.00 per month for 6 months.

2   William Lambert is purchasing a new automobile and must finance $2400. (a) The automobile dealer will finance the sum under a plan calling for $113 per month for 24 months or (b) a financial institution will loan him the $2400 for 30 months at $94.13 per month. What plan should he prefer? Why?

3   Jerry Chapman is buying a color TV set. He needs to finance only $200 and may obtain this amount from (a) his open-end credit card plan which charges $1\frac{1}{2}$ percent per month on the unpaid balance, or (b) from a personal finance company which will loan him the $200 on a loan calling for 6 monthly payments of $35.85 each. Which plan should he prefer? Why?

4   Norma Smith has allowed her open-end revolving charge account with the Blue Lake Department store to reach a balance of $600, and although the store will continue to carry the account, the monthly service charge is $1\frac{1}{4}$ percent per month. A bank will loan her the $600, payable in 12 monthly installments of $53.31 each. Should Ms. Smith (a) continue paying on the revolving charge account or (b) borrow the money and pay it off? Why?

5   Mr. Osborn is purchasing a house. He has the opportunity to (a) assume an existing loan with a balance of $12,500, on which there remain 60 monthly payments of $284.42 including interest or (b) refinance the existing loan with a new loan which requires 10 percent interest on the declining balance. Which plan should Mr. Osborn choose? Why?

6   Ms. Jarboe is buying a piece of property and is able to borrow $15,000 from either of two alternative banks. (a) One will loan her the $15,000 for 25 years with interest on the unpaid balance at $10\frac{1}{4}$ percent. Payments on principal and interest are payable monthly. (b) A second bank will offer a loan at 10 percent on the unpaid balance which calls for 360 payments of $131.64, but will charge 5 "points" (5 percent of $15,000, or

$750.00) payable at the time the loan is made. Which plan should Ms. Jarboe choose? Why?

7   Clifford Sorensen purchased a truck and was financing $1500 for 24 months at $72.73 per month. After making four payments, his sister said she would be happy to pay off the balance of Clifford's loan and allow Clifford to pay her 24 additional installments at $64.99 per month. Clifford's creditor will abate the unearned finance charge by the actuarial method less $25. Assuming Clifford is indifferent as to the 4 months additional time, should he accept the offer? Show details.

8   Cathy Silvio has purchased a new waterbed for her home. She needs to finance $400 and credit source A will finance it for $36.29 per month for 12 months. Credit source B will finance it for a monthly payment calculated at 12 percent, $m = 12$. Which should she choose? Why?

9   Glenda Gant is financing $6000 for a parcel of real estate. Credit source A will finance it for 120 monthly payments of $78.46. Credit source B will also finance it for 120 months at a 12 percent annual effective rate of interest. Which one should she choose? Why? (Use the method for finding the approximate effective rate of interest from credit source A.)

10 Sidney Carver is buying a new dishwasher and must finance $300. Credit source A will finance it for 36 months at $9.54 per month. Credit source B will finance for 36 months at an APR of 14 percent. Which should he choose? (Use the approximate effective rate of interest for credit source A.)

Chapter 8

Payrolls, Wages, and Commission Accounts

Objectives To Be Achieved in This Chapter

1 Work with the payroll deductions imposed by the federal government and calculate the net pay of employees.
2 Calculate gross earnings from individual and group wage incentive plans and formulas.
3 Determine and analyze labor wage variances.
4 Calculate gross earnings from various commission arrangements and complete commission accounts.

Unit 8.1　　　　　　　　　　　　　　　　　　*Net Pay After Deductions*

After determining gross wages, further computations are usually necessary in determining the net pay due employees. With the exception of certain exempt services, deductions must be made by employers for federal old-age, disability, and survivors insurance (Federal Insurance Contributions Act), federal income tax withholding, and in some states, state and city income taxes, and disability fund taxes. Additionally, payroll deductions may be made for union dues, group life insurance premiums, savings plans, hospital and medical insurance premiums, etc.

OLD-AGE, DISABILITY, AND SURVIVORS INSURANCE TAX　Federal old-age, disability, and survivors insurance (FICA tax) is paid for by a tax on the workers' earnings and matching contributions by the employers—and by self-employed persons on the net earnings from their profession, trade, or business. The self-employed pay approximately $1\frac{1}{2}$ times as much as employees (or employers) would pay on the same earnings, but about $\frac{1}{4}$ less than the combined payments of employees and employers. The employees' contributions are deducted from their wages each pay day. The employers send the employees' contributions and their own matching contributions to the Internal Revenue Service not later than the month following the end of each calendar quarter. The self-employed make their contributions quarterly when they file their federal income tax estimates, and/or annually with their final income tax returns.

Table 8.1 shows the FICA tax rates that have been in effect since January 1, 1937 and the scheduled increases.[1]

An employee having more than one employer is taxed separately for the income received from each employer and thus may pay a tax in excess of the stipulated percentage. Any excess payment by the employee beyond maximum contributions required should be applied as a payment on the employee's federal income tax return, though the employers cannot claim any refund or credit for such excess contributions to the FICA.

Beginning with 1968, the percent contributions by the employee, employer, and the self-employed also include payments for hospital insurance benefits.[2]

Individuals with earnings from both employment and self-employment pay contributions on their wages earned as employees and on that part of their self-employment earnings that may be necessary to bring the total earnings up to the maximum for the current year.

Example 1　**Mark Gooden, an office worker, was paid $782.75 per month in January of 1977. Find the FICA deductions made from his January salary check.**

$782.75 \times 0.0585 = $45.79

[1]Rates and maximums quoted were in effect as of January 1, 1978, and may (probably will) be changed by future acts of Congress.

[2]FICA wage bracket tables are furnished without charge by the Internal Revenue Service, U.S. Treasury Department, for the rapid determination of the FICA tax to be withheld from employees.

TABLE 8.1   FICA TAX RATES EFFECTIVE THROUGH 1978

Calendar years	Maximum earnings	Employee, %	Employer, %	Self-Employed, %
1937–1950	$3,000	1	1	Not covered
1951–1953	3,600	$1\frac{1}{2}$	$1\frac{1}{2}$	$2\frac{1}{4}$
1954	3,600	2	2	3
1955–1956	4,200	2	2	3
1957–1958	4,200	$2\frac{1}{4}$	$2\frac{1}{4}$	$3\frac{3}{8}$
1959	4,800	$2\frac{1}{2}$	$2\frac{1}{2}$	$3\frac{3}{4}$
1960–1961	4,800	3	3	4.5
1962	4,800	$3\frac{1}{8}$	$3\frac{1}{8}$	4.7
1963–1965	4,800	$3\frac{5}{8}$	$3\frac{5}{8}$	5.4
1966	6,600	4.20	4.20	6.15
1967	6,600	4.40	4.40	6.40
1968	7,800	4.40	4.40	6.90
1969–1970	7,800	4.80	4.80	6.90
1971	7,800	5.20	5.20	7.50
1972	9,000	5.20	5.20	7.50
1973	10,800	5.85	5.85	8.00
1974	13,200	5.85	5.85	7.90
1975	14,100	5.85	5.85	7.90
1976	15,300	5.85	5.85	7.90
1977	16,500	5.85	5.85	7.90
1978	17,700	6.05	6.05	8.10

Example 2   **Sara Baker earned $38,000 as division manager of an insurance company in 1977. Find the total FICA deductions made from her yearly earnings.**

The deductions are limited to the first $16,500 of earnings. Therefore,

$16,500 \times 0.0585 = 965.25

Example 3   **John Sander, self-employed as an accountant in 1977, had net business income of $38,480, as well as $4,640 as an employee of a public warehouse firm. Find (a) his FICA tax as an employee, (b) his FICA self-employment tax, and (c) his total FICA tax for the year.**

Earnings as employee: $4640
Balance from self-employment: $11,860
Total FICA income: $16,500

(a) $ 4,640 × .0585 = $ 271.44   FICA tax as employee
(b) $\underline{11,860}$ × .079 = $\underline{936.94}$ Self-employment FICA tax
(c) $16,500 $1208.38   Total FICA tax

UNEMPLOYMENT FUND BENEFITS   In addition to federal old-age, disability, and survivors insurance (plus hospital insurance benefits beginning July 1, 1966), the Social Security Act of 1935 established unemployment benefit funds to be administered by the various state departments of unemployment. The result has been considerable variation among the states as to eligibility requirements, minimum and maximum benefits, and the period of time for which unemployment benefits are paid. At present in California, minimum weekly benefits are $30, maximum weekly benefits are $104, and payments are normally limited to 26 weeks.

The cost of unemployment fund benefits is paid entirely by the employers. In California at the present time, employers who are subject to the unemployment provisions of the state law pay the state government a maximum of 3.6 percent on each employee's wages up to $7000. The federal law assesses an unemployment tax of 3.4 percent on the first $4200 of employees' earnings, but allows a credit up to 2.7 percent for unemployment taxes paid the state governments. Both the federal and state governments have provisions in the law for a merit-rating reduction of the unemployment premiums for a record of steady employment.

Due to the relatively rapid changes in rates, earnings maximums, varying qualifications, etc., the latest provisions of the state and federal laws are best found by consulting your local state and federal agencies that administer these laws.

DISABILITY INSURANCE AND EMPLOYEE TAXES   In some states, weekly compensation is provided for disability as well as for certain hospital benefits. In general, the number of weekly periods during which such payments may be made are usually limited to the same number of weeks which unemployment fund benefits are paid. Thus in certain combinations, benefits or compensation may be made for 1 year or more.

Some states require employees to contribute to a disability insurance fund (employers do not contribute). Payments for disability are, in general, similar to those provided for unemployment (in California the minimum is the same, $30 per week, but the maximum is somewhat higher, $119 per week).

Disability deductions from employees' pay vary from 1 to $1\frac{1}{2}$ percent of earnings with varying maximums to which the percent is applied. Thus in California, a 1 percent disability insurance deduction from an employee's pay is limited to the first $11,400 of earnings. As with FICA taxes, the maximum base and the percent of withholding may be expected to increase in the future.

Example 4   **Employee disability insurance tax deductions. James Green, an office manager residing in California, earned $550 per week from his employer during the year 1977. Find (a) the disability insurance tax deductions made from his weekly pay and (b) the total disability insurance deductions made for the year 1977.[1]**

(a) $550 × .01 = $5.50
Deductions at this rate to continue until maximum wages of $11,400 are reached

(b) $11,400 × .01 = $114 (Maximum disability insurance deduction)

[1]If James Green had worked for more than one employer during 1977 and had earned the same salary, each employer would have deducted 1 percent of his weekly salary up to $11,400. Upon the timely filing of a refund claim to the state, Mr. Green could claim a refund for disability insurance premiums deducted in excess of $114 for the year. Just as with the FICA tax, employers in California cannot claim any refund or credit for excess contributions to the California Disability Insurance Fund.

FEDERAL INCOME TAX WITHHOLDING   The federal tax laws require that the employer withhold from his employees' pay certain stipulated amounts of percents of their earnings for income and FICA taxes. The employer then deposits such amounts with an authorized bank accompanied by Federal Tax Deposit Form 501. The time of the deposits depends upon the amount withheld. Unless the amounts withheld are less than $200 for any calendar quarter, the deposits must be made either once or four times each month. If the amounts withheld are less than $200 per quarter, employers pay the amount quarterly.

One month after the end of each calendar quarter, the employer must submit a report to the Internal Revenue Service (Form 941) which sets forth the total taxable wages earned by the employees for the quarter. In addition, the report shows the total income and FICA taxes withheld from the employees, the amount of the employer's share of the FICA tax, and the federal tax deposit receipts indicating that all withheld taxes and taxes owed by the employer have been timely paid. If any additional amount is shown to be due, the employer's check for the balance should accompany the quarterly report. On or before January 31 of each year, or at the termination of employment, the employer is required to furnish each employee with a statement (usually in quadruplicate) setting forth the employee's total earnings for the year, the amount of income taxes withheld, the amount of FICA earnings, the FICA taxes withheld and relevant state and/or city wage information (Form W-2). Also on or before January 31 of each year, the employer is required to submit copies to the federal government of all earnings statements furnished to each employee and to reconcile the total of all taxes withheld to the previously submitted quarterly reports. When the employee files a federal income tax return, one copy of the earnings statement (Form W-2) is attached to the income tax return.

The employer withholds income taxes from employees on the basis of a withholding certificate (Form W-4) filed by the employee with the employer. The certificate sets forth the employee's name, social security number, marital status, and the number of exemptions being claimed by the employee.

As taxpayers, employees are entitled to exemptions for themselves, their spouses, and for each person who qualifies as a dependent by meeting *all* of the following tests:

1   Received over one-half of support from taxpayer
2   Is within a certain specified area of relationship with the taxpayer or has lived in taxpayer's home for the entire year
3   Earned less than $750, or was a *child of the taxpayer* and was either a full-time student or under the age of 19
4   Does not file a joint return with his or her spouse and thereby receive a tax benefit
5   Must meet certain citizenship tests

In addition to the above exemptions, taxpayers are entitled to additional exemptions if they or their spouses are 65 years of age or older or are blind. The 1969 Tax Reform Act made it possible under certain circumstances for a taxpayer to claim additional withholding allowances (which have the same effect as claiming additional exemptions) based upon a larger than normal amount of personal deductions.[1]

Federal Income Tax Wage-Bracket Withholding Tables

Income tax withholding tables have been prepared by the Internal Revenue Service, U.S. Treasury Department, and are available without charge for the following time periods: weekly, biweekly, semimonthly, monthly, and daily or miscellaneous. For other payroll periods, the percentage method of withholding must be used by the employer. From May 1, 1966, separate tables or separate computations have been required for single persons and for married persons.[2]

HOW TO USE THE WAGE-BRACKET TABLE METHOD OF INCOME TAX WITHHOLDING Income tax withholding tables for single and married taxpayers for the weekly payroll period are shown in Figure 8.1. The payroll period and marital status of the employee determines the table to be used.

If the wages exceed the highest wage bracket in the applicable table in determining the amount to be deducted and withheld, the wages may, at the option of the employer, be rounded to the nearest dollar.

Income Tax Withholding—Percentage Method[3]

HOW TO USE THE PERCENTAGE METHOD OF INCOME TAX WITHHOLDING (This section may be disregarded by any employer using the wage-bracket tables.) Employers who prefer not to use the wage-bracket tables in computing the amount of income tax to be deducted and withheld from a payment of wages to an employee will make a percentage computation based upon the following percentage method withholding table and the appropriate rate table.

PERCENTAGE METHOD INCOME TAX WITHHOLDING TABLE

Payroll period	Amount of one withholding exemption
Weekly	$ 14.40
Biweekly	28.80
Semimonthly	31.30
Monthly	62.50
Quarterly	187.50
Semiannual	375.00
Annual	750.00
Daily or miscellaneous (per day of such period)	2.10

[1] Detailed instructions on the filing of the federal income tax returns are furnished annually to each taxpayer by the Internal Revenue Service. The taxpayer should read these instructions carefully, and if additional explanation on exemptions or any other phase of the income tax law is needed, the taxpayer may seek assistance from any office of the Internal Revenue Service.

[2] The wage-bracket tables and percentage method rate tables included here were effective as of January 1, 1978. Current tables may be obtained from your local office of the Internal Revenue Service.

[3] Based on information from the Internal Revenue Service, U.S. Treasury Department.

SINGLE Persons — WEEKLY Payroll Period

And the wages are—		And the number of withholding allowances claimed is—										
At least	But less than	0	1	2	3	4	5	6	7	8	9	10 or more
		The amount of income tax to be withheld shall be—										
$0	$33	$0	$0	$0	$0	$0	$0	$0	$0	$0	$0	$0
33	34	.10	0	0	0	0	0	0	0	0	0	0
34	35	.30	0	0	0	0	0	0	0	0	0	0
35	36	.40	0	0	0	0	0	0	0	0	0	0
36	37	.60	0	0	0	0	0	0	0	0	0	0
37	38	.80	0	0	0	0	0	0	0	0	0	0
38	39	.90	0	0	0	0	0	0	0	0	0	0
39	40	1.10	0	0	0	0	0	0	0	0	0	0
40	41	1.20	0	0	0	0	0	0	0	0	0	0
41	42	1.40	0	0	0	0	0	0	0	0	0	0
42	43	1.60	0	0	0	0	0	0	0	0	0	0
43	44	1.70	0	0	0	0	0	0	0	0	0	0
44	45	1.90	0	0	0	0	0	0	0	0	0	0
45	46	2.00	0	0	0	0	0	0	0	0	0	0
46	47	2.20	0	0	0	0	0	0	0	0	0	0
47	48	2.40	.10	0	0	0	0	0	0	0	0	0
48	49	2.50	.20	0	0	0	0	0	0	0	0	0
49	50	2.70	.40	0	0	0	0	0	0	0	0	0
50	51	2.80	.50	0	0	0	0	0	0	0	0	0
51	52	3.00	.70	0	0	0	0	0	0	0	0	0
52	53	3.20	.90	0	0	0	0	0	0	0	0	0
53	54	3.30	1.00	0	0	0	0	0	0	0	0	0
54	55	3.50	1.20	0	0	0	0	0	0	0	0	0
55	56	3.60	1.30	0	0	0	0	0	0	0	0	0
56	57	3.80	1.50	0	0	0	0	0	0	0	0	0
57	58	4.00	1.70	0	0	0	0	0	0	0	0	0
58	59	4.10	1.80	0	0	0	0	0	0	0	0	0
59	60	4.30	2.00	0	0	0	0	0	0	0	0	0
60	62	4.50	2.20	0	0	0	0	0	0	0	0	0
62	64	4.80	2.50	.20	0	0	0	0	0	0	0	0
64	66	5.20	2.90	.60	0	0	0	0	0	0	0	0
66	68	5.50	3.20	.90	0	0	0	0	0	0	0	0
68	70	5.80	3.50	1.20	0	0	0	0	0	0	0	0
70	72	6.10	3.80	1.50	0	0	0	0	0	0	0	0
72	74	6.40	4.10	1.80	0	0	0	0	0	0	0	0
74	76	6.80	4.50	2.20	0	0	0	0	0	0	0	0
76	78	7.10	4.80	2.50	.20	0	0	0	0	0	0	0
78	80	7.50	5.10	2.80	.50	0	0	0	0	0	0	0
80	82	7.80	5.40	3.10	.80	0	0	0	0	0	0	0
82	84	8.20	5.70	3.40	1.10	0	0	0	0	0	0	0
84	86	8.60	6.10	3.80	1.40	0	0	0	0	0	0	0
86	88	8.90	6.40	4.10	1.80	0	0	0	0	0	0	0
88	90	9.30	6.70	4.40	2.10	0	0	0	0	0	0	0
90	92	9.60	7.00	4.70	2.40	.10	0	0	0	0	0	0
92	94	10.00	7.40	5.00	2.70	.40	0	0	0	0	0	0
94	96	10.40	7.80	5.40	3.00	.70	0	0	0	0	0	0
96	98	10.70	8.10	5.70	3.40	1.10	0	0	0	0	0	0
98	100	11.10	8.50	6.00	3.70	1.40	0	0	0	0	0	0
100	105	11.70	9.10	6.60	4.20	1.90	0	0	0	0	0	0
105	110	12.60	10.00	7.40	5.00	2.70	.40	0	0	0	0	0
110	115	13.50	10.90	8.30	5.80	3.50	1.20	0	0	0	0	0
115	120	14.40	11.80	9.20	6.60	4.30	2.00	0	0	0	0	0
120	125	15.30	12.70	10.10	7.50	5.10	2.80	.50	0	0	0	0
125	130	16.20	13.60	11.00	8.40	5.90	3.60	1.30	0	0	0	0
130	135	17.10	14.50	11.90	9.30	6.70	4.40	2.10	0	0	0	0
135	140	18.00	15.40	12.80	10.20	7.60	5.20	2.90	.60	0	0	0
140	145	18.90	16.30	13.70	11.10	8.50	6.00	3.70	1.40	0	0	0
145	150	20.00	17.20	14.60	12.00	9.40	6.80	4.50	2.20	0	0	0
150	160	21.60	18.60	16.00	13.40	10.80	8.20	5.70	3.40	1.10	0	0
160	170	23.80	20.60	17.80	15.20	12.60	10.00	7.40	5.00	2.70	.40	0

(Continued on next page)

FIGURE 8.1 Source: Circular E (Supplement) Employer's Tax Guide, Department of the Treasury, Internal Revenue Service, May, 1977.

SINGLE Persons — WEEKLY Payroll Period

And the wages are—		And the number of withholding allowances claimed is—										
At least	But less than	0	1	2	3	4	5	6	7	8	9	10 or more
		The amount of income tax to be withheld shall be—										
$170	$180	$26.00	$22.80	$19.70	$17.00	$14.40	$11.80	$9.20	$6.60	$4.30	$2.00	$0
180	190	28.30	25.00	21.90	18.80	16.20	13.60	11.00	8.40	5.90	3.60	1.30
190	200	30.70	27.20	24.10	20.90	18.00	15.40	12.80	10.20	7.60	5.20	2.90
200	210	33.10	29.60	26.30	23.10	19.90	17.20	14.60	12.00	9.40	6.80	4.50
210	220	35.50	32.00	28.60	25.30	22.10	19.00	16.40	13.80	11.20	8.60	6.10
220	230	38.10	34.40	31.00	27.50	24.30	21.20	18.20	15.60	13.00	10.40	7.80
230	240	40.90	36.80	33.40	29.90	26.50	23.40	20.20	17.40	14.80	12.20	9.60
240	250	43.70	39.60	35.80	32.30	28.80	25.60	22.40	19.20	16.60	14.00	11.40
250	260	46.50	42.40	38.40	34.70	31.20	27.80	24.60	21.40	18.40	15.80	13.20
260	270	49.30	45.20	41.20	37.20	33.60	30.20	26.80	23.60	20.40	17.60	15.00
270	280	52.10	48.00	44.00	40.00	36.00	32.60	29.10	25.80	22.60	19.50	16.80
280	290	54.90	50.80	46.80	42.80	38.70	35.00	31.50	28.10	24.80	21.70	18.60
290	300	57.70	53.60	49.60	45.60	41.50	37.50	33.90	30.50	27.00	23.90	20.70
300	310	60.80	56.40	52.40	48.40	44.30	40.30	36.30	32.90	29.40	26.10	22.90
310	320	64.00	59.40	55.20	51.20	47.10	43.10	39.00	35.30	31.80	28.30	25.10
320	330	67.20	62.60	58.00	54.00	49.90	45.90	41.80	37.80	34.20	30.70	27.30
330	340	70.40	65.80	61.20	56.80	52.70	48.70	44.60	40.60	36.60	33.10	29.70
340	350	73.60	69.00	64.40	59.70	55.50	51.50	47.40	43.40	39.40	35.50	32.10
350	360	76.80	72.20	67.60	62.90	58.30	54.30	50.20	46.20	42.20	38.10	34.50
360	370	80.40	75.40	70.80	66.10	61.50	57.10	53.00	49.00	45.00	40.90	36.90
370	380	84.00	78.80	74.00	69.30	64.70	60.10	55.80	51.80	47.80	43.70	39.70
380	390	87.60	82.40	77.20	72.50	67.90	63.30	58.70	54.60	50.60	46.50	42.50
390	400	91.20	86.00	80.80	75.70	71.10	66.50	61.90	57.40	53.40	49.30	45.30
400	410	94.80	89.60	84.40	79.20	74.30	69.70	65.10	60.50	56.20	52.10	48.10
410	420	98.40	93.20	88.00	82.80	77.60	72.90	68.30	63.70	59.10	54.90	50.90
420	430	102.00	96.80	91.60	86.40	81.20	76.10	71.50	66.90	62.30	57.70	53.70
430	440	105.60	100.40	95.20	90.00	84.80	79.60	74.70	70.10	65.50	60.90	56.50
440	450	109.20	104.00	98.80	93.60	88.40	83.20	78.00	73.30	68.70	64.10	59.40
450	460	112.80	107.60	102.40	97.20	92.00	86.80	81.60	76.50	71.90	67.30	62.60
460	470	116.40	111.20	106.00	100.80	95.60	90.40	85.20	80.10	75.10	70.50	65.80
470	480	120.00	114.80	109.60	104.40	99.20	94.00	88.80	83.70	78.50	73.70	69.00
480	490	123.60	118.40	113.20	108.00	102.80	97.60	92.40	87.30	82.10	76.90	72.20
490	500	127.20	122.00	116.80	111.60	106.40	101.20	96.00	90.90	85.70	80.50	75.40
500	510	130.80	125.60	120.40	115.20	110.00	104.80	99.60	94.50	89.30	84.10	78.90
510	520	134.40	129.20	124.00	118.80	113.60	108.40	103.20	98.10	92.90	87.70	82.50
520	530	138.00	132.80	127.60	122.40	117.20	112.00	106.80	101.70	96.50	91.30	86.10
530	540	141.60	136.40	131.20	126.00	120.80	115.60	110.40	105.30	100.10	94.90	89.70
540	550	145.20	140.00	134.80	129.60	124.40	119.20	114.00	108.90	103.70	98.50	93.30
550	560	148.80	143.60	138.40	133.20	128.00	122.80	117.60	112.50	107.30	102.10	96.90
560	570	152.40	147.20	142.00	136.80	131.60	126.40	121.20	116.10	110.90	105.70	100.50
570	580	156.00	150.80	145.60	140.40	135.20	130.00	124.80	119.70	114.50	109.30	104.10
580	590	159.60	154.40	149.20	144.00	138.80	133.60	128.40	123.30	118.10	112.90	107.70
590	600	163.20	158.00	152.80	147.60	142.40	137.20	132.00	126.90	121.70	116.50	111.30
600	610	166.80	161.60	156.40	151.20	146.00	140.80	135.60	130.50	125.30	120.10	114.90
610	620	170.40	165.20	160.00	154.80	149.60	144.40	139.20	134.10	128.90	123.70	118.50
620	630	174.00	168.80	163.60	158.40	153.20	148.00	142.80	137.70	132.50	127.30	122.10
630	640	177.60	172.40	167.20	162.00	156.80	151.60	146.40	141.30	136.10	130.90	125.70
640	650	181.20	176.00	170.80	165.60	160.40	155.20	150.00	144.90	139.70	134.50	129.30
650	660	184.80	179.60	174.40	169.20	164.00	158.80	153.60	148.50	143.30	138.10	132.90
660	670	188.40	183.20	178.00	172.80	167.60	162.40	157.20	152.10	146.90	141.70	136.50
670	680	192.00	186.80	181.60	176.40	171.20	166.00	160.80	155.70	150.50	145.30	140.10
680	690	195.60	190.40	185.20	180.00	174.80	169.60	164.40	159.30	154.10	148.90	143.70
690	700	199.20	194.00	188.80	183.60	178.40	173.20	168.00	162.90	157.70	152.50	147.30
700	710	202.80	197.60	192.40	187.20	182.00	176.80	171.60	166.50	161.30	156.10	150.90
710	720	206.40	201.20	196.00	190.80	185.60	180.40	175.20	170.10	164.90	159.70	154.50
		36 percent of the excess over $720 plus—										
$720 and over		208.20	203.00	197.80	192.60	187.40	182.20	177.00	171.90	166.70	161.50	156.30

FIGURE 8.1 (Continued)

MARRIED Persons — WEEKLY Payroll Period

And the wages are—		And the number of withholding allowances claimed is—										
At least	But less than	0	1	2	3	4	5	6	7	8	9	10 or more
		The amount of income tax to be withheld shall be—										
$0	$60	$0	$0	$0	$0	$0	$0	$0	$0	$0	$0	$0
60	62	.10	0	0	0	0	0	0	0	0	0	0
62	64	.40	0	0	0	0	0	0	0	0	0	0
64	66	.70	0	0	0	0	0	0	0	0	0	0
66	68	1.00	0	0	0	0	0	0	0	0	0	0
68	70	1.30	0	0	0	0	0	0	0	0	0	0
70	72	1.60	0	0	0	0	0	0	0	0	0	0
72	74	1.90	0	0	0	0	0	0	0	0	0	0
74	76	2.20	0	0	0	0	0	0	0	0	0	0
76	78	2.50	.30	0	0	0	0	0	0	0	0	0
78	80	2.80	.60	0	0	0	0	0	0	0	0	0
80	82	3.10	.90	0	0	0	0	0	0	0	0	0
82	84	3.40	1.20	0	0	0	0	0	0	0	0	0
84	86	3.70	1.50	0	0	0	0	0	0	0	0	0
86	88	4.00	1.80	0	0	0	0	0	0	0	0	0
88	90	4.30	2.10	0	0	0	0	0	0	0	0	0
90	92	4.60	2.40	.20	0	0	0	0	0	0	0	0
92	94	4.90	2.70	.50	0	0	0	0	0	0	0	0
94	96	5.20	3.00	.80	0	0	0	0	0	0	0	0
96	98	5.50	3.30	1.10	0	0	0	0	0	0	0	0
98	100	5.80	3.60	1.40	0	0	0	0	0	0	0	0
100	105	6.30	4.10	2.00	0	0	0	0	0	0	0	0
105	110	7.10	4.90	2.70	.50	0	0	0	0	0	0	0
110	115	8.00	5.60	3.50	1.30	0	0	0	0	0	0	0
115	120	8.90	6.40	4.20	2.00	0	0	0	0	0	0	0
120	125	9.80	7.20	5.00	2.80	.60	0	0	0	0	0	0
125	130	10.70	8.10	5.70	3.50	1.40	0	0	0	0	0	0
130	135	11.60	9.00	6.50	4.30	2.10	0	0	0	0	0	0
135	140	12.50	9.90	7.30	5.00	2.90	.70	0	0	0	0	0
140	145	13.40	10.80	8.20	5.80	3.60	1.50	0	0	0	0	0
145	150	14.30	11.70	9.10	6.50	4.40	2.20	.10	0	0	0	0
150	160	15.70	13.10	10.50	7.90	5.50	3.00	1.20	0	0	0	0
160	170	17.50	14.90	12.30	9.70	7.10	4.80	2.70	.50	0	0	0
170	180	19.30	16.70	14.10	11.50	8.90	6.30	4.20	2.00	0	0	0
180	190	21.10	18.50	15.90	13.30	10.70	8.10	5.70	3.50	1.40	0	0
190	200	22.90	20.30	17.70	15.10	12.50	9.90	7.30	5.00	2.90	.70	0
200	210	24.70	22.10	19.50	16.90	14.30	11.70	9.10	6.50	4.40	2.20	0
210	220	26.50	23.90	21.30	18.70	16.10	13.50	10.90	8.30	5.90	3.70	1.50
220	230	28.40	25.70	23.10	20.50	17.90	15.30	12.70	10.10	7.50	5.20	3.00
230	240	30.60	27.50	24.90	22.30	19.70	17.10	14.50	11.90	9.30	6.70	4.50
240	250	32.80	29.60	26.70	24.10	21.50	18.90	16.30	13.70	11.10	8.50	6.00
250	260	35.00	31.80	28.60	25.90	23.30	20.70	18.10	15.50	12.90	10.30	7.70
260	270	37.20	34.00	30.80	27.70	25.10	22.50	19.90	17.30	14.70	12.10	9.50
270	280	39.40	36.20	33.00	29.80	26.90	24.30	21.70	19.10	16.50	13.90	11.30
280	290	41.80	38.40	35.20	32.00	28.90	26.10	23.50	20.90	18.30	15.70	13.10
290	300	44.30	40.70	37.40	34.20	31.10	27.90	25.30	22.70	20.10	17.50	14.90
300	310	46.80	43.20	39.60	36.40	33.30	30.10	27.10	24.50	21.90	19.30	16.70
310	320	49.30	45.70	42.10	38.60	35.50	32.30	29.10	26.30	23.70	21.10	18.50
320	330	51.80	48.20	44.60	41.00	37.70	34.50	31.30	28.20	25.50	22.90	20.30
330	340	54.30	50.70	47.10	43.50	39.90	36.70	33.50	30.40	27.30	24.70	22.10
340	350	56.80	53.20	49.60	46.00	42.40	38.90	35.70	32.60	29.40	26.50	23.90
350	360	59.30	55.70	52.10	48.50	44.90	41.30	37.90	34.80	31.60	28.40	25.70
360	370	62.10	58.20	54.60	51.00	47.40	43.80	40.10	37.00	33.80	30.60	27.50
370	380	64.90	60.80	57.10	53.50	49.90	46.30	42.60	39.20	36.00	32.80	29.60
380	390	67.70	63.60	59.60	56.00	52.40	48.80	45.10	41.50	38.20	35.00	31.80
390	400	70.50	66.40	62.40	58.50	54.90	51.30	47.60	44.00	40.40	37.20	34.00
400	410	73.30	69.20	65.20	61.20	57.40	53.80	50.10	46.50	42.90	39.40	36.20
410	420	76.10	72.00	68.00	64.00	59.90	56.30	52.60	49.00	45.40	41.80	38.40
420	430	78.90	74.80	70.80	66.80	62.70	58.80	55.10	51.50	47.90	44.30	40.70
430	440	81.80	77.60	73.60	69.60	65.50	61.50	57.60	54.00	50.40	46.80	43.20

(Continued on next page)

FIGURE 8.1 (Continued)

MARRIED Persons — WEEKLY Payroll Period

And the wages are—		And the number of withholding allowances claimed is—										
At least	But less than	0	1	2	3	4	5	6	7	8	9	10 or more
		The amount of income tax to be withheld shall be—										
$440	$450	$85.00	$80.40	$76.40	$72.40	$68.30	$64.30	$60.30	$56.50	$52.90	$49.30	$45.70
450	460	88.20	83.60	79.20	75.20	71.10	67.10	63.10	59.00	55.40	51.80	48.20
460	470	91.40	86.80	82.20	78.00	73.90	69.90	65.90	61.80	57.90	54.30	50.70
470	480	94.60	90.00	85.40	80.80	76.70	72.70	68.70	64.60	60.60	56.80	53.20
480	490	97.80	93.20	88.60	84.00	79.50	75.50	71.50	67.40	63.40	59.30	55.70
490	500	101.00	96.40	91.80	87.20	82.60	78.30	74.30	70.20	66.20	62.10	58.20
500	510	104.20	99.60	95.00	90.40	85.80	81.10	77.10	73.00	69.00	64.90	60.90
510	520	107.70	102.80	98.20	93.60	89.00	84.30	79.90	75.80	71.80	67.70	63.70
520	530	111.30	106.10	101.40	96.80	92.20	87.50	82.90	78.60	74.60	70.50	66.50
530	540	114.90	109.70	104.60	100.00	95.40	90.70	86.10	81.50	77.40	73.30	69.30
540	550	118.50	113.30	108.10	103.20	98.60	93.90	89.30	84.70	80.20	76.10	72.10
550	560	122.10	116.90	111.70	106.50	101.80	97.10	92.50	87.90	83.30	78.90	74.90
560	570	125.70	120.50	115.30	110.10	105.00	100.30	95.70	91.10	86.50	81.90	77.70
570	580	129.30	124.10	118.90	113.70	108.50	103.50	98.90	94.30	89.70	85.10	80.50
580	590	132.90	127.70	122.50	117.30	112.10	106.90	102.10	97.50	92.90	88.30	83.70
590	600	136.50	131.30	126.10	120.90	115.70	110.50	105.30	100.70	96.10	91.50	86.90
600	610	140.10	134.90	129.70	124.50	119.30	114.10	108.90	103.90	99.30	94.70	90.10
610	620	143.70	138.50	133.30	128.10	122.90	117.70	112.50	107.30	102.50	97.90	93.30
620	630	147.30	142.10	136.90	131.70	126.50	121.30	116.10	110.90	105.70	101.10	96.50
630	640	150.90	145.70	140.50	135.30	130.10	124.90	119.70	114.50	109.30	104.30	99.70
640	650	154.50	149.30	144.10	138.90	133.70	128.50	123.30	118.10	112.90	107.70	102.90
650	660	158.10	152.90	147.70	142.50	137.30	132.10	126.90	121.70	116.50	111.30	106.10
660	670	161.70	156.50	151.30	146.10	140.90	135.70	130.50	125.30	120.10	114.90	109.70
670	680	165.30	160.10	154.90	149.70	144.50	139.30	134.10	128.90	123.70	118.50	113.30
680	690	168.90	163.70	158.50	153.30	148.10	142.90	137.70	132.50	127.30	122.10	116.90
690	700	172.50	167.30	162.10	156.90	151.70	146.50	141.30	136.10	130.90	125.70	120.50
700	710	176.10	170.90	165.70	160.50	155.30	150.10	144.90	139.70	134.50	129.30	124.10
710	720	179.70	174.50	169.30	164.10	158.90	153.70	148.50	143.30	138.10	132.90	127.70
720	730	183.30	178.10	172.90	167.70	162.50	157.30	152.10	146.90	141.70	136.50	131.30
730	740	186.90	181.70	176.50	171.30	166.10	160.90	155.70	150.50	145.30	140.10	134.90
740	750	190.50	185.30	180.10	174.90	169.70	164.50	159.30	154.10	148.90	143.70	138.50
750	760	194.10	188.90	183.70	178.50	173.30	168.10	162.90	157.70	152.50	147.30	142.10
760	770	197.70	192.50	187.30	182.10	176.90	171.70	166.50	161.30	156.10	150.90	145.70
770	780	201.30	196.10	190.90	185.70	180.50	175.30	170.10	164.90	159.70	154.50	149.30
780	790	204.90	199.70	194.50	189.30	184.10	178.90	173.70	168.50	163.30	158.10	152.90
790	800	208.50	203.30	198.10	192.90	187.70	182.50	177.30	172.10	166.90	161.70	156.50
800	810	212.10	206.90	201.70	196.50	191.30	186.10	180.90	175.70	170.50	165.30	160.10
810	820	215.70	210.50	205.30	200.10	194.90	189.70	184.50	179.30	174.10	168.90	163.70
820	830	219.30	214.10	208.90	203.70	198.50	193.30	188.10	182.90	177.70	172.50	167.30
830	840	222.90	217.70	212.50	207.30	202.10	196.90	191.70	186.50	181.30	176.10	170.90
840	850	226.50	221.30	216.10	210.90	205.70	200.50	195.30	190.10	184.90	179.70	174.50
850	860	230.10	224.90	219.70	214.50	209.30	204.10	198.90	193.70	188.50	183.30	178.10
860	870	233.70	228.50	223.30	218.10	212.90	207.70	202.50	197.30	192.10	186.90	181.70
870	880	237.30	232.10	226.90	221.70	216.50	211.30	206.10	200.90	195.70	190.50	185.30
880	890	240.90	235.70	230.50	225.30	220.10	214.90	209.70	204.50	199.30	194.10	188.90
890	900	244.50	239.30	234.10	228.90	223.70	218.50	213.30	208.10	202.90	197.70	192.50
900	910	248.10	242.90	237.70	232.50	227.30	222.10	216.90	211.70	206.50	201.30	196.10
910	920	251.70	246.50	241.30	236.10	230.90	225.70	220.50	215.30	210.10	204.90	199.70
920	930	255.30	250.10	244.90	239.70	234.50	229.30	224.10	218.90	213.70	208.50	203.30
930	940	258.90	253.70	248.50	243.30	238.10	232.90	227.70	222.50	217.30	212.10	206.90
940	950	262.50	257.30	252.10	246.90	241.70	236.50	231.30	226.10	220.90	215.70	210.50
950	960	266.10	260.90	255.70	250.50	245.30	240.10	234.90	229.70	224.50	219.30	214.10
960	970	269.70	264.50	259.30	254.10	248.90	243.70	238.50	233.30	228.10	222.90	217.70
970	980	273.30	268.10	262.90	257.70	252.50	247.30	242.10	236.90	231.70	226.50	221.30
980	990	276.90	271.70	266.50	261.30	256.10	250.90	245.70	240.50	235.30	230.10	224.90
		36 percent of the excess over $990 plus—										
$990 and over		278.70	273.50	268.30	263.10	257.90	252.70	247.50	242.30	237.10	231.90	226.70

FIGURE 8.1 (Continued)

The steps in computing the income tax to be withheld under the percentage method are as follows:

1   Multiply the amount of *one* withholding exemption (see table above) by the number of exemptions claimed by the employee.
2   Subtract the amount thus determined from the employee's wages.
3   Determine amount to be withheld from appropriate table in Figure 8.2.

Example 5   **An unmarried employee has a weekly payroll period, for which he is paid $260 and has in effect a withholding exemption certificate claiming three exemptions. His employer, using the percentage method, computes the income tax to be withheld as follows:**

1	Total wage payment		$260.00
2	Amount of one exemption	$14.40	
3	Number of exemptions claimed on Form W-4	× 3	
4	Line 2 multiplied by line 3		−43.20
5	Line 4 subtracted from line 1		$216.80
6	Tax to be withheld on $216.80 from		
	Table 1—Single person (Figure 8.2)		
	Tax on $182.00	$27.52	
	Tax on remainder, $34.80 at 24 percent =	8.35	
	Total to be withheld		$ 35.87

In determining the amount of income tax to be deducted and withheld, the last digit of the wage amount may, at the election of the employer, be reduced to zero, or the wage amount may be computed to the nearest dollar. For example, if the weekly wage is $137.43, the employer may eliminate the last digit and determine the income tax withheld on the basis of a wage payment of $137.40 or he may determine the income tax withheld on the basis of a wage payment of $137.00.

It should be understood that the income tax withheld is not ordinarily the exact amount of income tax owed by the employee for the taxable year. The amounts withheld by the employer are remitted to the Internal Revenue Service and credited by them to the taxpayer's account. When the taxpayer files an income tax return for the year, the taxes withheld are claimed as a credit against the income tax liability and the taxpayer either pays an additional amount or is entitled to a refund.

Exercise 8.1

In all problems that follow, use the various payroll tax rates and the wage-base maximums that were in effect in 1977:

1   Patricia Packard, an accountant in California, earned $1220 per month. Find (a) the disability insurance premium deducted from her paycheck in each of the months January through September, (b) the disability insurance premium deducted in October, and (c) the total disability tax deductions for the year.

Tables for Percentage Method of Withholding

TABLE 1. WEEKLY Payroll Period

(a) SINGLE person—including head of household:

If the amount of wages is:		The amount of income tax to be withheld shall be:	
Not over $33 0			
Over—	But not over—		of excess over—
$33	—$76	.....16%	—$33
$76	—$143	.....$6.88 plus 18%	—$76
$143	—$182	...$18.94 plus 22%	—$143
$182	—$220	...$27.52 plus 24%	—$182
$220	—$297	...$36.64 plus 28%	—$220
$297	—$355	...$58.20 plus 32%	—$297
$355		...$76.76 plus 36%	—$355

(b) MARRIED person—

If the amount of wages is:		The amount of income tax to be withheld shall be:	
Not over $61 0			
Over—	But not over—		of excess over—
$61	—$105	....15%	—$61
$105	—$223	...$6.60 plus 18%	—$105
$223	—$278	...$27.84 plus 22%	—$223
$278	—$355	...$39.94 plus 25%	—$278
$355	—$432	...$59.19 plus 28%	—$355
$432	—$509	...$80.75 plus 32%	—$432
$509		...$105.39 plus 36%	—$509

TABLE 2. BIWEEKLY Payroll Period

(a) SINGLE person—including head of household:

If the amount of wages is:		The amount of income tax to be withheld shall be:	
Not over $65 0			
Over—	But not over—		of excess over—
$65	—$152	...16%	—$65
$152	—$287	...$13.92 plus 18%	—$152
$287	—$363	...$38.22 plus 22%	—$287
$363	—$440	...$54.94 plus 24%	—$363
$440	—$594	...$73.42 plus 28%	—$440
$594	—$710	...$116.54 plus 32%	—$594
$710		...$153.66 plus 36%	—$710

(b) MARRIED person—

If the amount of wages is:		The amount of income tax to be withheld shall be:	
Not over $121 0			
Over—	But not over—		of excess over—
$121	—$210	...15%	—$121
$210	—$445	...$13.35 plus 18%	—$210
$445	—$556	...$55.65 plus 22%	—$445
$556	—$710	...$80.07 plus 25%	—$556
$710	—$863	...$118.57 plus 28%	—$710
$863	—$1,017	...$161.41 plus 32%	—$863
$1,017		...$210.69 plus 36%	—$1,017

TABLE 3. SEMIMONTHLY Payroll Period

(a) SINGLE person—including head of household:

If the amount of wages is:		The amount of income tax to be withheld shall be:	
Not over $71 0			
Over—	But not over—		of excess over—
$71	—$165	...16%	—$71
$165	—$310	...$15.04 plus 18%	—$165
$310	—$394	...$41.14 plus 22%	—$310
$394	—$477	...$59.62 plus 24%	—$394
$477	—$644	...$79.54 plus 28%	—$477
$644	—$769	...$126.30 plus 32%	—$644
$769		...$166.30 plus 36%	—$769

(b) MARRIED person—

If the amount of wages is:		The amount of income tax to be withheld shall be:	
Not over $131 0			
Over—	But not over—		of excess over—
$131	—$227	....15%	—$131
$227	—$482	...$14.40 plus 18%	—$227
$482	—$602	...$60.30 plus 22%	—$482
$602	—$769	...$86.70 plus 25%	—$602
$769	—$935	...$128.45 plus 28%	—$769
$935	—$1,102	...$174.93 plus 32%	—$935
$1,102		...$228.37 plus 36%	—$1,102

TABLE 4. MONTHLY Payroll Period

(a) SINGLE person—including head of household:

If the amount of wages is:		The amount of income tax to be withheld shall be:	
Not over $142 0			
Over—	But not over—		of excess over—
$142	—$329	....16%	—$142
$329	—$621	...$29.92 plus 18%	—$329
$621	—$788	...$82.48 plus 22%	—$621
$788	—$954	...$119.22 plus 24%	—$788
$954	—$1,288	...$159.06 plus 28%	—$954
$1,288	—$1,538	...$252.58 plus 32%	—$1,288
$1,538		...$332.58 plus 36%	—$1,538

(b) MARRIED person—

If the amount of wages is:		The amount of income tax to be withheld shall be:	
Not over $263 0			
Over—	But not over—		of excess over—
$263	—$454	....15%	—$263
$454	—$965	...$28.65 plus 18%	—$454
$965	—$1,204	...$120.63 plus 22%	—$965
$1,204	—$1,538	...$173.21 plus 25%	—$1,204
$1,538	—$1,871	...$256.71 plus 28%	—$1,538
$1,871	—$2,204	...$349.95 plus 32%	—$1,871
$2,204		...$456.51 plus 36%	—$2,204

FIGURE 8.2

2 Craig Ralston, a supermarket manager, received a salary of $500 per week. A single person, he claimed two withholding exemptions. Use the wage-bracket withholding in Figure 8.1 to determine (a) the federal income tax withholding from his weekly pay check and (b) the total amount of FICA tax withheld for the calendar year.

TABLE 5. QUARTERLY Payroll Period

(a) SINGLE person—including head of household:

If the amount of wages is:	The amount of income tax to be withheld shall be:
Not over $425 0

Over—	But not over—		of excess over—
$425	—$988	16%	—$425
$988	—$1,863	$90.08 plus 18%	—$988
$1,863	—$2,363	$247.58 plus 22%	—$1,863
$2,363	—$2,863	$357.58 plus 24%	—$2,363
$2,863	—$3,863	$477.58 plus 28%	—$2,863
$3,863	—$4,613	$757.58 plus 32%	—$3,863
$4,613		$997.58 plus 36%	—$4,613

(b) MARRIED person—

If the amount of wages is:	The amount of income tax to be withheld shall be:
Not over $788 0

Over—	But not over—		of excess over—
$788	—$1,363	15%	—$788
$1,363	—$2,894	$86.25 plus 18%	—$1,363
$2,894	—$3,613	$361.83 plus 22%	—$2,894
$3,613	—$4,613	$520.01 plus 25%	—$3,613
$4,613	—$5,613	$770.01 plus 28%	—$4,613
$5,613	—$6,613	$1,050.01 plus 32%	—$5,613
$6,613		$1,370.01 plus 36%	—$6,613

TABLE 6. SEMIANNUAL Payroll Period

(a) SINGLE person—including head of household:

If the amount of wages is:	The amount of income tax to be withheld shall be:
Not over $850 0

Over—	But not over—		of excess over—
$850	—$1,975	16%	—$850
$1,975	—$3,725	$180.00 plus 18%	—$1,975
$3,725	—$4,725	$495.00 plus 22%	—$3,725
$4,725	—$5,725	$715.00 plus 24%	—$4,725
$5,725	—$7,725	$955.00 plus 28%	—$5,725
$7,725	—$9,225	$1,515.00 plus 32%	—$7,725
$9,225		$1,995.00 plus 36%	—$9,225

(b) MARRIED person—

If the amount of wages is:	The amount of income tax to be withheld shall be:
Not over $1,575 0

Over—	But not over—		of excess over—
$1,575	—$2,725	15%	—$1,575
$2,725	—$5,788	$172.50 plus 18%	—$2,725
$5,788	—$7,225	$723.84 plus 22%	—$5,788
$7,225	—$9,225	$1,039.98 plus 25%	—$7,225
$9,225	—$11,225	$1,539.98 plus 28%	—$9,225
$11,225	—$13,225	$2,099.98 plus 32%	—$11,225
$13,225		$2,739.98 plus 36%	—$13,225

TABLE 7 ANNUAL Payroll Period

(a) SINGLE person—including head of household:

If the amount of wages is:	The amount of income tax to be withheld shall be:
Not over $1,700 0

Over—	But not over—		of excess over—
$1,700	—$3,950	16%	$1,700
$3,950	—$7,450	$360.00 plus 18%	—$3,950
$7,450	—$9,450	$990.00 plus 22%	—$7,450
$9,450	—$11,450	$1,430.00 plus 24%	—$9,450
$11,450	—$15,450	$1,910.00 plus 28%	—$11,450
$15,450	—$18,450	$3,030.00 plus 32%	—$15,450
$18,450		$3,990.00 plus 36%	—$18,450

(b) MARRIED person—

If the amount of wages is:	The amount of income tax to be withheld shall be:
Not over $3,150 0

Over—	But not over—		of excess over—
$3,150	—$5,450	15%	—$3,150
$5,450	—$11,575	$345.00 plus 18%	—$5,450
$11,575	—$14,450	$1,447.50 plus 22%	—$11,575
$14,450	—$18,450	$2,080.00 plus 25%	—$14,450
$18,450	—$22,450	$3,080.00 plus 28%	—$18,450
$22,450	—$26,450	$4,200.00 plus 32%	—$22,450
$26,450		$5,480.00 plus 36%	—$26,450

TABLE 8. DAILY or MISCELLANEOUS Payroll Period

(a) SINGLE person—including head of household:

If the wages divided by the number of days in such period are:	The amount of income tax to be withheld shall be the following amount multiplied by the number of days in such period:
Not over $4.70 0

Over—	But not over—		of excess over—
$4.70	—$10.80	16%	—$4.70
$10.80	—$20.40	$.98 plus 18%	—$10.80
$20.40	—$25.90	$2.71 plus 22%	—$20.40
$25.90	—$31.40	$3.92 plus 24%	—$25.90
$31.40	—$42.30	$5.24 plus 28%	—$31.40
$42.30	—$50.50	$8.29 plus 32%	—$42.30
$50.50		$10.91 plus 36%	—$50.50

(b) MARRIED person—

If the wages divided by the number of days in such period are:	The amount of income tax to be withheld shall be the following amount multiplied by the number of days in such period:
Not over $8.60 0

Over—	But not over—		of excess over—
$8.60	—$14.90	15%	—$8.60
$14.90	—$31.70	$.95 plus 18%	—$14.90
$31.70	—$39.60	$3.97 plus 22%	—$31.70
$39.60	—$50.50	$5.71 plus 25%	—$39.60
$50.50	—$61.50	$8.44 plus 28%	—$50.50
$61.50	—$72.50	$11.52 plus 32%	—$61.50
$72.50		$15.04 plus 36%	—$72.50

FIGURE 8.2 *(Continued)*

3   Mr. and Mrs. Smith have three dependent children. Mr. Smith earns $285 per week and submitted a W-4 form to his employer as married, and claiming five exemptions. Mrs. Smith also is employed and submitted a W-4 form to her employer as married but claiming no exemptions. She earns $290 per week. Compute the total income tax deducted from their two wage checks for one week.

4 Find the federal income tax withheld per week by the percentage method.

	Gross weekly earnings	Exemptions	Married (M) or single (S)
(a)	$340	1	S
(b)	540	4	M
(c)	680	8	M
(d)	420	0	S

5 Acme Industries was subject to the federal and state unemployment tax. The federal rate is 3.4 percent on the first $4200 of gross earnings per employee; however, a credit is received of 2.7 percent for taxes paid the state on the first $4200 of each employee's earnings. The rate for the state is 3.6 percent on the first $7000 of gross earnings for each employee. Find the total unemployment tax of Acme Industries for the calendar year for the following employees:

Employee	Gross annual earnings
(a)	$ 3,000
(b)	5,000
(c)	6,500
(d)	10,000

6 Find the FICA (old-age and survivors tax) deduction from the gross pay of Evelyn Kay, who earned $809.47 in January.

7 For the calendar year, Frank Lewis earned $14,025. Find the total FICA deduction from his gross pay.

8 For the calendar year, James Granat earned $12,040 gross pay as a bookkeeper with the Barnes Construction Company and $5385 gross pay as a paymaster with the Apex Company. Find (a) total FICA deduction by the Barnes Construction Company, (b) total FICA deduction by the Apex Company, and (c) overpayment that he could apply as a payment on his federal income tax return.

9 For the calendar year, Roger Mason earned $3985 as a salesman in a men's furnishing store and $15,000 as a self-employed realty broker. Find (a) his FICA tax as a salesman, (b) his FICA self-employment tax, and (c) his total FICA tax for the year.

10 Chris Hake, a garage service manager, receives a gross monthly salary of $2100. Chris is single and claims three withholding exemptions. Use the percentage withholding tables and find the deduction for federal income tax.

11 Dr. Christine Sargent is a research director and receives an annual salary of $24,000 payable in four equal quarterly installments. Find the federal income tax withheld from each quarterly payment if Dr. Sargent is married and claims four withholding exemptions.

12 Dr. Robert Dickerson is a consultant employed by the Buckley Harriers and receives an annual salary of $18,000 payable in one payment. Dr.

Dickerson is married and claims five withholding exemptions. Find the deduction for federal income tax and FICA tax.

13 Forrest Waters, a substitute school teacher, substituted for 1 day at the Blue Lake elementary school. His gross earnings for the 1-day period were $45. Find the amount of federal income tax to be withheld by use of the daily or miscellaneous percentage rate withholding tables in Figure 8.2. Mr. Waters is married and claims two exemptions.

14 Thomas Joseph, a commercial pilot, was employed for 1 day by the Stover Air Service. His gross earnings for the 1-day period were $390. Find the amount of federal income tax to be withheld by use of the daily or miscellaneous percentage rate withholding tables. Mr. Joseph is married and claims three exemptions.

Unit 8.2

The Time Basis
for Wage Payments

The term *wages*, although technically including all forms of payment for all kinds of services, is generally used in a more restricted sense as applying to the compensation of labor.

Today, as in the past, most workers in this country are compensated for their efforts by means of an hour- or day-rate wage-payment plan. Output or performance is not considered in the wage calculation, although wages are varied in amounts in recognition of the differing degrees of time, effort, or skill required and the value of the services rendered.

STRAIGHT HOUR (OR DAY) RATE The method of payment by hour or day rate may be expressed by the following formula if overtime hours do not receive a higher rate of pay per hour:

$$W = R_h \times H_w$$

Wages equal rate per hour multiplied by hours worked.

Example 1 **George O'Reilly was paid $5.87 per hr. Find his gross pay for (a) a day during which he worked 7 hr, and (b) a week during which he worked 42 hr.**

(a) $W = \$5.87 \times 7 = \$41.09$
(b) $W = \$5.87 \times 42 = \$246.54$

SALARIED EARNINGS Salaries, a form of time payment for services, are paid usually on the basis of weekly, biweekly, semimonthly, or monthly periods. Expressed as a formula:

$$W = R_p$$

Wages equal a stipulated amount per period.

Example 2   **Leland Eisen received a weekly salary of $80; Roberta Madden received a biweekly salary of $150; John Lippitt received a semimonthly salary of $160; and John O'Shaughnessy received a monthly salary of $330. For each worker, find earnings (a) per year, (b) per month, and (c) per week.**

Leland Eisen:

(a) $80.00 × 52 = $4160.00 per year
(b) $4160.00 ÷ 12 = $346.67 per month
(c) $80.00 per week

Roberta Madden:

(a) $150.00 × 26 = $3900.00 per year
(b) $3900.00 ÷ 12 = $325.00 per month
(c) $150.00 ÷ 2 = $75.00 per week

John Lippitt:

(a) $160.00 × 24 = $3840.00 per year
(b) $160.00 × 2 = $320.00 per month
(c) $3840.00 ÷ 52 = $73.85 per week

John O'Shaughnessy:

(a) $330.00 × 12 = $3960.00 per year
(b) $330.00 per month
(c) $3960.00 ÷ 52 = $76.15 per week

Salaries *plus* commissions or bonuses (see Unit 8.5) are frequently employed as a method of incentive payment for the sale or purchase of goods, increased profits, decreased expenses, and other exceptional services performed. Workers in responsible executive or administrative positions are rewarded in many instances in such manner, the commissions or bonuses for high productivity often being equal to or many times greater than the nominal earnings from the base salaries.

OVERTIME PAY AND OVERTIME EXCESS PAY   Frequently it is provided that work after the usual working period is completed is paid at a higher rate than the regular rate. Many and differing arrangements are made, but ordinarily this higher rate is for work in excess of the standard workday (usually 8 hr) or the standard workweek (usually 40 hr). This higher rate is commonly half again or twice as much as the regular rate. In accordance with the Federal Wage and Hour Law, employees engaged in work or services that enter interstate commerce must be paid a rate not less than 50 percent greater than the regular hourly rate for all work in excess of 40 hr during a workweek.

Two general methods are used in computing total pay for employees who have worked longer than the stipulated standard time period. The original and still used method is to compute the pay for the regular work period and then add to it the *overtime pay*. A later and increasingly used method is to compute the pay for the total time at the regular rate and then add to it the *overtime excess (bonus) pay*.

Overtime pay The required computations in determining total pay including overtime pay may be expressed by the following formula:

$$W = R_h \times H_s + R_o \times H_o$$

Wages equal regular rate per hour times the number of standard hours worked plus the overtime rate per hour times the number of overtime hours worked.

Example 3 **James Callahan, an employee of the city of San Francisco, California, was paid $4.50 per hr for a standard workweek of 40 hr and time and a half for overtime. Find his (a) overtime pay and (b) total pay for a week in which he worked 47 hr.**

$H_o = 47 - 40 = 7$ overtime hours

$\qquad$ $\$4.50 \times 40 = \quad \$180.00$ Pay for standard workweek

(a) $\$4.50 \times 1\frac{1}{2} \times 7 = +\ 47.25$ Overtime pay

(b) $\qquad\qquad W = \overline{\$227.25}$ Total pay

Overtime excess pay The required computations in determining total pay including overtime excess pay may be expressed by the following formula:

$$W = R_h \times H_w + R_e \times H_o$$

Wages equal regular rate per hour multiplied by total hours worked plus *excess* rate per hour for overtime hours multiplied by the number of overtime hours worked.

Example 4 **Same problem as Example 3 except that it is required to find overtime excess pay (as distinguished from overtime pay) and total pay.**

$H_o = 47 - 40 = 7$ overtime hours

$\qquad$ $\$4.50 \times 47 = \$211.50$ Pay at regular rate

(a) $\$4.50 \times \frac{1}{2} \times 7 = +15.75$ Overtime excess pay

(b) $\qquad\qquad W = \overline{\$227.25}$ Total pay

$\qquad$ Example 4 on overtime excess pay illustrates the method most frequently used by private employers. In those states in which a workmen's compensation insurance law is in effect, the employer is required to carry workmen's compensation insurance (or post bond) so that, in the event an employee is injured on the job, the employee will receive disability compensation while unable to work. Such compensation must be paid to the injured worker (including hospital and medical costs) regardless of whether negligence on the part of the employer or employee contributes to the disability. In some occupations, the basis for the employer's insurance premium is the total pay earned minus overtime excess pay. Thus it is necessary for such employers to compute earnings at the regular rate for the total hours worked and the bonus or overtime excess pay as distinguished from overtime pay illustrated in Example 3.

Not only do workmen's compensation insurance laws necessitate the employer's computing overtime excess pay, but the provisions of the Wage and Hour Law (the Federal Fair Labor Standards Act) require for employees of concerns engaged in interstate commerce that earnings at the regular rate and overtime excess earnings be shown separately. Also, many states have enacted laws with similar provisions affecting *intra*state commerce.

The keeping of payroll records by computing overtime excess pay rather than overtime pay may also be chosen by employers for the following two reasons: (1) the employer regards such pay as a direct reduction in net profit and a penalty payment for poor management or unavoidable circumstances, it being to his or her advantage to keep such excess pay at a minimum; and (2) some labor unions, particularly those whose member dues or contributions by the employer to fringe benefits (such as health, welfare, pension, etc.) are based on earnings at the regular rate, require that the employer keep a separate account of such excess earnings.

Exercise 8.2

1 Jeff Bradley, a receiving clerk, was paid $6.25 per hr for a standard workweek of 40 hr and time and a half for overtime. During a week in which he worked 54 hr, find (a) his pay for the standard workweek, (b) his pay for overtime hours, and (c) his total gross pay.

2 Barry Anderson, a millwright, was paid $6.75 per hr for a standard workweek of 35 hr and time and a half for overtime. For a week in which he worked 42 hr, find (a) his pay for the standard workweek, (b) his pay for the overtime hours, and (c) his total gross pay.

3 Betty Murphy is paid $3.00 per hr, with time and a half for overtime beyond the standard 7-hr day. If she worked 10 hr on Monday, 6 hr Tuesday, 8 hr Wednesday, 7 hr Thursday, and 11 hr Friday, find (a) earnings at regular rate, (b) overtime excess earnings, and (c) total gross pay.

4 Lorraine Ball, a child psychologist, received gross earnings of $260 for a 5-day week. If Miss Ball receives $5.00 per hr and time and a half for any time over a regular 40-hr week, find (a) the number of regular hours worked, (b) the number of overtime hours worked, and (c) total hours worked.

5 Ruth Patterson, a fitter in a specialty shop, was paid $2.85 per hr for a standard 7-hr day and double time for overtime. For a day in which she worked $9\frac{1}{2}$ hr, find (a) her pay at the regular rate, (b) her overtime excess pay, and (c) her total gross pay.

6 Complete the payroll record of the Shaw Milling Company on the following page. Time and a half is paid for more than 40 hr per 7-day workweek. Deduct a 1 percent California disability insurance tax, a 5.85 percent FICA tax, and federal income tax withholding in the amounts as indicated by the weekly wage-bracket withholding table, Figure 8.1. Note

SHAW MILLING COMPANY Payroll for week ending Jan. 24, 19____

Employee number	S	M	T	W	Th	F	S	Total time, hours	Over-time, hours	Reg. rate per hour	Earnings at regular rate	Over-time excess earnings	Amount earned	Exemptions	Calif. disability tax	FICA tax	Income tax withholding	Total deductions	Net amount paid
81		8	8	8	8	3	8	48	8	$4.00	$192	$16	$208	M2	$2.08	$12.17	$19.50	$33.75	$174.25
82	7	10	7	9	11	11	2	57	17	4.80	273.60	40.80	314.40	S0	3.14	18.39	69	91.93	223.82
83	10	8	7	12	9	8	4	54	14	3.60	189.40	2.520	199.60	M4	2.19	12.85	16.10	50.96	128.84
84		8	8	8	8	8	4	44	4	4.20	160.80	8.40	192.20	S1	1.93	11.30	27.20	47.82	152.44
85			4	10	8	4	5	38		6.30	214.20	0	214.20	M3	2.14	12.53	18.70	52.66	180.83
86		9	8	8	9	9		44	8	3.30	138.40	13.20	151.60	M5	1.12	10.09	6.30	33.80	153.54
Total								2656	51	26.60	1271.40	103.60	1321		11.39	77.28	161.80	342.40	

that the amount earned is computed by adding overtime excess pay to the earnings at the regular rate.

7   Workers at the Evansville Bakery Company are paid a flat rate per hour. Find the weekly gross pay of William James, who was paid $3.125 per hr and worked 10 hr Monday, 5 hr Tuesday, 11 hr Wednesday, 10 hr Thursday, and 10 hr Friday.

8   Charles Robert received a weekly salary of $85; John Thomas received a biweekly salary of $165; Mary Ward received a semimonthly salary of $180; and Ronald Jarvis received a monthly salary of $365. For each worker, find gross earnings (a) per year, (b) per month, and (c) per week.

9   Burtis Bridges, a carpenter, was paid $4.95 per hr. Find his gross pay for a week in which he worked 8 hr Monday, 4 hr Tuesday, 8 hr Wednesday, 8 hr Thursday, and 5 hr Friday.

Unit 8.3

Task and Bonus, and Gain-Sharing Wage-Payment Plans

Many wage-payment plans over the years have been devised in the attempt to differentiate more accurately the value of the services rendered by the individual worker—services which were not taken into account in time-payment plans. Such different plans are based on productivity, the more skillful and speedy workers receiving more pay than their less efficient coworkers. Built into these different plans were opportunities for the worker to earn more money. With such incentives, workers were motivated to become more efficient and productive, the result being more earnings for the worker and more profit for the employer.

The oldest forms of incentive wage-payment plans were known as *piece-rate plans,* in which a fixed sum was paid per unit produced. Straight piece-rate plans no longer exist as such. The Fair Labor Standards Act has established certain minimum wages, and incentive plans must have a minimum (generally based on hours worked) base to them. Therefore, present-day incentive wage-payment plans combine the time basis and the piece-work basis in varying ratios.

Incentive wage-payment plans may be limited to the individual worker or may be designed to promote the productivity of the entire work force as a group.

Examples of Individual Wage Incentive Plans

THE GANNT TASK AND BONUS PLAN   This guarantees a base rate plus a high bonus for superior productivity and incorporates many of the advantages of assured minimum pay combined with the incentive features of piece-rate plans. Below task, wages equal the rate per hour multiplied by the hours worked:

$$W = R_h \times H_w$$

At or above task, wages equal 120 (up to 150) percent times the rate per hour multiplied by the hours standard (the hours of work accomplished):

$$W = 1.20 R_h \times H_s$$

Example 1   **If the rate per hour is $5.00, hours worked per day are 8, task is 32 pieces per day, and at task and above the pay is 120 percent times the rate per hour, find the gross wages of (a) Gerald Cresci, who completed 26 pieces, (b) Everett Silviz, who completed 32 pieces, and (c) James Hughes, who completed 36 pieces.**

(a) $W = \$5.00 \times 8 = \$40.00$

(b) $W = 1.20 \times \$5.00 \times 8 = \$48.00$

(c)   Standard hours $= 8 \times \dfrac{36}{32} = 9$-hr standard[1]

$$W = 1.20 \times \$5.00 \times 9 = \$54.00$$

or, directly, $W = 1.20 \times \$5.00 \times 8 \times \dfrac{36}{32} = \$54.00$

THE HALSEY PREMIUM PLAN   This plan provides for fractions of the time saved, usually 25 to 75 percent, to be paid to the worker at the wage rate. If the worker fails to save time, she or he is guaranteed a minimum pay. The Halsey plan is the first of the modern gain-sharing wage-payment plans. Task is usually set at approximately five-eighths to two-thirds of the normal accomplishment of efficient workers. At or below task, wages equal the rate per hour multiplied by the hours worked:

$$W = R_h \times H_w$$

Above task, wages equal the rate per hour multiplied by the hours worked plus 25 (to 75) percent of the rate per hour multiplied by the hours saved (hours standard accomplished less hours worked):

$$W = R_h \times H_w + .25 R_h (H_s - H_w)$$

Example 2   **If the rate per hour is $5.50, the hours worked per week are 40, task is 180 pieces per week, and the premium is 50 percent of the hours saved, find the gross earnings for a week in which (a) Charles Ohman completed 150 pieces and (b) Harold Friedman completed 198 pieces.**

(a) $W = 40.00 \times \$5.50 = \$220$

(b)   Standard hours $\dfrac{40 \times 198}{180} = 44$ hr

---

[1] By proportion: $\dfrac{8}{H_s} = \dfrac{32}{36}$ or $8 : Hs : : 32 : 36 = \dfrac{8 \times 36}{32} = 9.$

Regular earnings 40 × 5.50 = $220
Add premium earnings

$$H_s - H_w = 44 - 40 = 4$$

$$(4 \times .50) \times 5.50 = \underline{\quad 11}$$

Total earnings $231

GROUP-INCENTIVE GAIN-SHARING   *The Scanlon plan* is a group-incentive plan designed to promote efficiency by rewarding the employees as a group. A standard ratio or percentage of total labor cost to the adjusted sales is determined by reference to prior financial statements. The adjusted sales represents the sales amount adjusted for the sales value of the inventory increases or decreases. Current labor costs are then compared to the labor cost which would have resulted had the standard labor-cost percentage been applied to the current sales. If the current labor costs are less than this standard amount, an improvement has been made, and the *improvement difference* is then shared with the employees and the employer. If no labor-cost savings are made, there is no bonus for that period.

Example 3   **Twin Parks Lumber Company rewards its employees under the Scanlon plan. A standard percentage of total labor cost to the adjusted sales price has been determined to be 40 percent. Labor-cost savings are shared between employees and employer in the ratio of 7:3, respectively. The summary of operations for the first quarter of 1979 is as follows:**

Product sales	Sales value of change in inventory	Adjusted sales	Total labor cost
$80,000	+20,000	$100,000	$36,000

Find (a) the total bonus to be awarded the employees and (b) the percentage that each employee will receive.

(a)	Total adjusted sales for quarter	$100,000
	Standard labor-cost percentage	×0.40
	Total labor cost at standard	$ 40,000
	Less actual labor cost	$ 36,000
	Labor-cost savings to be allocated between employees and employer	$ 4,000
	Percentage allocated to employees	×0.70
	Amount allocated to employees	$ 2,800
(b)	Amount allocated to employees	$ 2,800
	Total labor cost	$ 36,000
	Percentage of cost savings to actual labor cost:	

$$\frac{\$2800}{\$36,000} = 7.78\%$$

Each employee would receive a bonus of 7.78 percent of wages earned in the first quarter.

There may be variations in the Scanlon plan regarding (1) how the standard cost ratio is computed, (2) frequency of calculating the bonus (monthly calculations are widely used), (3) proportion of labor-cost savings shared by employees, (4) the use of an "equalization reserve" which holds back a portion of the savings in more efficient periods and releases them in less efficient periods to avoid extremes in the amount of the bonus distributed each period, and (5) other variations such as method of payment (stock in company or cash), time of payment (currently or some deferred plan), etc.

Exercise 8.3

1 The Hog Iron Works Co., which pays its workers by the Halsey premium plan, gave a bonus of 40 percent for hours saved. If the rate per hour is $5.40, find the gross earnings for a $40-hr workweek of (a) Bob Beard, who accomplished 38.5 hr of standard work, and (b) Craig Rogers, who accomplished 47 hr of standard work.

2 The Anderson Bottling Co. paid its workers by the Halsey premium plan, giving a bonus of 75 percent for hours saved. If the rate is $4.55, find the gross earnings for a 36-hr workweek of (a) Jeff Boyer who accomplished 44.8 hr of standard work, and (b) Bill Turner who accomplished 35 hr of standard work.

3 The Silva Door Co. rewards its employees on the Scanlon plan. The standard labor-cost percentage is 45 percent. Seventy-five percent of the labor-cost savings are shared with employees. The operating results by months for the second quarter of 19/9 are as follows:

	Sales	Inventory change	Actual labor costs
April	$80,000	+$10,000	$38,100
May	90,000	+15,000	45,250
June	130,000	−20,000	46,700

Find (a) the labor-cost savings each month and (b) the amount of labor-cost savings distributed to the employees for each month.

4 The Ocean View Products Co. pays its employees a monthly bonus based on the Scanlon plan. The standard labor-cost percentage is 35 percent and the employees receive 80 percent of the cost savings. The operating results for the third quarter of 1979 are as follows:

	Sales	Inventory change	Actual labor costs
July	$140,000	+$10,000	$50,000
August	160,000	−20,000	49,000
September	150,000	−30,000	40,000

1. a. 4.60 × 8 = 36.80
2. 4.60 × 8 × 78/78 × 1.25 = 46.00
   c. 4.60 × 8 × 88/78 × 1.25 = 50.72.

6.
a. 6.15 × 40 = 246   91
b. 6.15 × 60 × 1.50 × 96
   102/96
= 369
c. 6.15 × 60 × 1.50
= 392.06.

Find (a) the bonus earned by the employees for each month, and (b) the bonus earned each month by employee Sally Urban, who earned $1200 in July, $1300 in August, and $1000 in September.

5 The W. F. Pickett Mfg. Co. paid its workers by the Gantt task and bonus plan, using 125 percent as the multiplier for work at or above task. If the rate per hour is $4.60 and task is 78 pieces for an 8-hr day, find the gross earnings of (a) George Post, who produced 73 pieces, (b) Frank Reidy, who produced 78 pieces, and (c) Sidney Sea, who produced 86 pieces.

6 The Stier Company paid its workers by the Gantt task and bonus plan, using 150 percent as their multiplier for work at or above task. If the rate per hour for a 40-hr workweek is $6.15, and weekly task is the completion of 96 articles, find the gross weekly earnings of (a) Sandra White, who completed 94 articles, (b) Bernhardt Jensen, who completed 96 articles, and (c) Arthur Hoge, who completed 102 articles.

a) 246.
b) 369
c) 392.06,

Unit 8.4   Labor-Cost Variance Analysis

To control labor costs, many firms compare their actual labor costs with a predetermined budget or standard. The amount of variance between the actual labor costs and the budget or standard labor cost is calculated from the accounting records. The variances from the budget or standard are then analyzed to determine the source of the variance and thus assist management in its task of controlling operations in order to achieve profitable results.

Example 1 **The Buckhorn Company produces a domestic air-conditioning unit. The budgeted labor costs per unit consisted of 5 hr at $3.50 per hour, or $17.50 labor costs per unit. Actual production for the month of September totaled 1000 units and actual labor costs were $19,800, consisting of 5500 hr at $3.60 per hour. (a) Calculate the labor-cost variance and (b) analyze the source of the variance.**

(a) Total amount of labor-cost variance:

Actual labor costs	$19,800
Budgeted or standard costs of producing	
1000 units (1000 × $17.50)	17,500
Total labor-cost variance	$ 2,300

(b) Analysis and calculation of separate causes of the $2300 variance: A scientific method of measuring or studying the effect of one variable in a total result is to attempt to hold all the factors involved in the result constant except that factor the effect of which you want to study or measure. This procedure is used to isolate the different causes in the $2300 total labor-cost variance. Thus:

1 The factors comprising the total budget and actual costs can be detailed as follows:

```
Units                    Hours   Price    Amount
Actual 1000 × 5.5 = 5500 × $3.60 = $19,800
Budget 1000 × 5   = 5000 ×  3.50 =  17,500
Actual over budget   500    $0.10    $ 2,300
```

2 The above detailed schedule shows that 500 more hours were used than were budgeted for 1000 units of product and that the labor price per hour was $0.10 higher than the budget.

3 To find the separate amount of the total variance caused from using 500 more hours than budgeted, we assume no change in the labor price and therefore isolate only the effect of the excess labor hours. Thus:

Excess hours × budget price = dollar amount of labor-quantity variance

```
   500      ×    $3.50    =              $1750
```

4 To find the separate amount of the total variance caused from the $0.10 increase in price, we assume no change in the number of labor hours and therefore isolate only the effect of the excess price. Thus:

Excess price per hour × budgeted hours = dollar amount of labor-price variance

```
   $0.10        ×      5000    =            $500
```

5 Because a change occurred in both labor hours and price per hour, there is a smaller part of the total variance that is a joint source and not a "pure" quantity factor or "pure" price factor. This is not isolated in (3) and (4) above and is calculated by:

Change in hours × change in price = dollar amount of joint quantity and price variance

```
   500      ×       $0.10    =              $50
```

6 Summarizing the causes of the total variance, the analysis shows:

```
Labor-quantity variance             $1750
Labor-price variance                  500
Jointly due to quantity and price      50
   Total variance                   $2300
```

The separate amounts are then further scrutinized by management to determine if the separate variances are *controllable* or *not controllable*. If controllable, steps should be taken to correct the condition. If not controllable, other areas in the total operations may have to be adjusted to offset the unfavorable labor-cost condition if the planned profit goals are to be achieved.

Example 2   **The Erica Johnson Industries manufactures a highway safety device. The labor-cost budget calls for each unit to be produced and packaged for delivery with 3 labor hours at an average price of $3.20. Actual production for June totaled 4000 units. Actual labor costs consisted of 11,000 hr at an average price of $3.25. (a) Calculate the labor-costs variance and (b) analyze the source of the variance.**

(a)   Actual labor costs:

11,000 hr × $3.25	$35,750
Less budgeted or standard costs:	
Budgeted hours = 4000 units × 3 hr = 12,000 hr	
12,000 budget hr × $3.20 budget price	(−)38,400
Labor-cost variance, actual (under) budget	$(2650)

(b)   1   Labor-quantity variance:

Actual hours	11,000		
Budget hours	12,000		
Actual (under) budget	(1,000)		
Decrease in hours × budget price:			
(1000)	×	3.20	= $(3200)

    2   Labor-price variance:

Actual price	$3.25		
Budget price	3.20		
Actual over budget	$0.05		
Increase in price × budget hours:			
$0.05	×	12,000	= $600

    3   Joint quantity and price variance:

Change in quantity × change in price			
(1000 hr)	×	$0.05	= (50)
Total variance, actual (under) budget			$(2650)

Rules for Determination If Source of Variance Is Favorable or Unfavorable

Careful observation of Examples 1 and 2 reveals the rules for determining if the quantity, price, or joint variance should be a favorable or unfavorable amount. The rules are the same as those in determining whether the product is positive or negative in the multiplication process:

1   If the multiplicand and the multiplier have the same sign [either (+) or (−)], then the product will be positive (+).
2   If the multiplicand and the multiplier have different signs [a (+) *and* a (−)], then the product will be negative (−).

Whenever the actual cost amounts are less than the budget cost amounts (favorable), represent the difference in parentheses (   ). Then assume that figures without parentheses are positive or (+), and figures within parentheses (   ) are negative or (−). In Example 1, the actual figures were in every case above the budget figures, so that no negative or figures in parentheses appeared. The products obtained by the various multiplication processes were all positive. In Example 2, however, note the following:

Labor-quantity variance:

Difference from actual × budget price
        (1000)   × $3.20   = $(3200)

Labor-price variance:

Difference from actual × budget quantity
        0.05   × $12,000   = $600

Joint variance:

Difference in actual quantity × Difference in actual price
        (1000)   × $0.05   =   (50)
   Total $(2650)

1 The quantity variance of $3200 is in parentheses because a figure in parentheses was multiplied by a figure not in parentheses.
2 The price variance of $600 is not in parentheses because two figures not in parentheses were multiplied together.
3 The joint variance of $50 is in parentheses because a figure in parentheses was multiplied by a figure not in parentheses.

The figures that appear in parentheses in the variance analysis then represent amounts where the actual results were under the budget estimates. Since we are considering costs, such a result is considered favorable. Although presented here in the context of labor-cost analysis, the above procedures have many applications in cost accounting and analysis of financial statements.

Exercise 8.4

Using the following price, quantity, and operating data, calculate for each case (a) total variance, (b) quantity variance, (c) price variance, and (d) joint variance. Indicate whether the variances would be favorable or unfavorable.

Units produced	Hours per unit		Price per hour	
	Budget	Actual	Budget	Actual
1	1000	7	6.80	$5.00	$5.10
2	1500	3	3.50	4.55	4.60
3	2000	5	4.75	4.00	3.80
4	1200	8	7.50	3.50	3.44
5	600	3	3.50	3.00	3.05
6	500	10	10.30	2.80	2.90

Unit 8.5   Commission Wage Payments

Employees whose productivity can be measured in terms of dollars or units of sales are often compensated for their efforts by means of commissions. Though there are many variations, the following methods of computation are perhaps the ones most frequently used:

1   Straight commission
2   Commission and bonus
3   Salary plus commission
4   Quota-bonus plan

STRAIGHT COMMISSION   Workers paid on a straight commission basis have no guaranteed wages but are paid only commissions earned. Commissions are computed as a percent of some base (usually sales), though sometimes they are a fixed number of dollars per item.

Example 1   **William Fox, a salesman of vacuum cleaners, receives $32.50 for each cleaner sold plus 25 percent commission for all accessories and supplies. Find his total income for a month in which he sells 14 cleaners and $237.40 worth of accessories and supplies.**

$$
\begin{array}{ll}
\$ \ 32.50 \times \ \ 14 = \$455.00 \\
\ \ \ 237.40 \times 0.25 = +59.35 \\
\hline
\text{Total earnings} = \$514.35
\end{array}
$$

COMMISSION AND BONUS   Salespersons whose travel expenses are paid by their employers may be given a bonus in the form of higher commission rates for increased productivity. Since travel expenses do not increase necessarily with increased sales, the employer may be able to offer higher rates of commission for sales beyond certain fixed minimums.

Example 2   **James Bryant, a salesman for Sara Walker Manufacturing Company, is compensated for all travel expenses, is allowed a drawing account of $600 per month, and receives a monthly commission of 2 percent of his first $30,000 of sales, 2.5 percent of the next $10,000 of sales, and 3 percent of all sales in excess of $40,000. Find the amount due him for a month in which his travel expenses paid out of pocket total $332.75, his drawings are $600, and sales total $41,180.**

$$
\begin{array}{lll}
\$30,000.00 \times 0.02 & = \$ \ 600.00 \\
\ \ \ 10,000.00 \times 0.025 & = \ \ \ \ 250.00 \\
\ \ \ \ \ 1,180.00 \times 0.03 & = \ +35.40 \\
\hline
\$41,180.00 & & \\
& \$ \ 885.40 & \text{Commissions} \\
& +332.75 & \text{Travel expenses} \\
\hline
\text{Total due} & = \$1218.15 \\
\text{Less drawing account} & = -600.00 \\
\hline
\text{Amount due} & = \$ \ 618.15
\end{array}
$$

SALARY PLUS COMMISSION Sales employees, particularly in the retail trade, are often paid a salary plus a commission based on sales.

Example 3 **Anka Perisich worked as a salesclerk in the dress department of a specialty shop. She received $160 semimonthly salary plus a commission of 1 percent of monthly sales. During the month of April, her sales were $3680. Find her total earnings for the month.**

Salary for month = $160.00 × 2   = $320.00
Plus commission =   3680 × 0.01 = +36.80
     Total earnings   = $356.80

QUOTA-BONUS PLAN A method frequently used by retail stores in computing the pay of sales employees is to pay a weekly salary plus a bonus (commission) on all sales in excess of a quarterly quota established on the basis of each employee's sales in the preceding quarter.

Example 4 **Jack Brady, a men's clothing salesman, was paid by the quota-bonus plan. It was the store policy to pay its salespersons a guaranteed weekly wage for each 13-week period (quarter-year). During the first quarter of the year, his sales had been $22,186, and this sum became his quota for the second quarter. His guaranteed pay for the second quarter was based on a 6 percent rate of commission, and so his weekly wage was computed as follows:**

$$\frac{\$22,186.00 \times 0.06}{13} = \frac{\$1331.16}{13} = \$102.40 \text{ per week wage guarantee}$$

If his sales for the second quarter were $25,690, find (a) his bonus at 6 percent of sales exceeding the quota, (b) his quota for the third quarter, and (c) his weekly wage guarantee during the third quarter.

(a) ($25,690.00 − $22,186.00) × 0.06 = $3504.00 × 0.06 = $210.24 bonus
(b) $25,690.00 is quota for third quarter

(c) $$\frac{\$25,690.00 \times 0.06}{13} = \frac{\$1541.40}{13} = \$118.57 \text{ per week wage guarantee}$$

If the sales made by Jack Brady in the third quarter were less than $25,690, he would fail to earn a bonus, this lower sales figure would become his quota for the fourth quarter, and his weekly wage guarantee would be reduced. Thus if his sales in the third quarter totaled $23,980, this sum would become his quota for the fourth period, and his weekly wage guarantee during the fourth quarter would be computed as follows:

$$\frac{\$23,980.00 \times 0.06}{13} = \frac{\$1438.80}{13} = \$110.68 \text{ per week wage guarantee}$$

Normally a quota will be sufficiently low so that the employee will be almost certain of attaining the quota considerably prior to the end of the quota period. Under such an arrangement, the employee is unlikely to quit his job until the quota period ends, and the employer can, by varying the terminating dates of quota periods, rather accurately control the times at which his labor turnover is likely to occur.

Exercise 8.5

1 Jane Ortiz, a saleswoman, was reimbursed for her travel expenses and received a commission of 11 percent on her first $50,000 of sales, 13 percent on the next $25,000, and 15 percent on all sales above $75,000. If her travel expenses for the year were $12,875 and her sales were $109,580, find the total of her expenses and commission.

2 Scott Ryder, a salesman of surgical supplies, receives 15 percent on sales up to and including $45,000 and 20 percent on all sales above $45,000. He is compensated for his traveling expenses and is allowed a drawing account of $500 per month. During the past year his sales were $91,580 and his unreimbursed travel expenses were $3225. He has withdrawn all of his drawing account. Find the gross amount due Mr. Ryder.

3 Nancy Roberts, a saleswoman in the ready-to-wear section of a large department store, was paid a semimonthly salary of $400 and a commission of 4 percent on all sales. Find her total gross earnings during a month in which her sales were $8000.

4 James Elder, a shoe salesman in a women's specialty store, was paid on the quota-bonus plan. His guaranteed weekly salary was $120 per week, and his bonus was 8 percent of all sales in excess of $15,600 during the 13-week quarter. If his sales were $20,000 for the quarter, find (a) his bonus and (b) his total earnings for the quarter.

5 Complete payroll record of Jog'n Shop (page 321). Deduct 80 cents from each employee's pay for union dues, 5.85 percent FICA tax, and federal income tax withholding in the amounts as indicated by the weekly wage-bracket withholding table (Figure 8.1). Note that the percent of commission on sales is variable.

6 For making a 10-year lease at $200 per month on a piece of business property, a real estate broker charged 3 percent of the first 4 years' rental income and 2 percent on the balance of the rental income. Find his total commission.

7 For obtaining an exclusive listing on property, a real estate saleswoman received 15 percent of half of the 5 percent selling commission charged by the realty firm, and if she made the sale herself, she was entitled to an additional half of the realty firm's commission charge. If she obtained an exclusive listing at $18,500, find (a) her listing commission if another member of the firm made the sale and (b) her total commissions if she made the sale.

8 A clothing salesman in a men's store was paid a commission of 6 percent of his sales. If his sales were $310 on Monday, $320 on Tuesday, $250 on Wednesday, $290 on Thursday, $335 on Friday, and $410 on Saturday, find his total commission for the week.

THE JOG'N SHOP (for Problem 5)

Name	Withholding exemptions	Net sales						Total sales	Com. rate	Total earned	Deductions				Net earnings
		M	T	W	Th	F	S				Union dues	FICA	Inc. tax	Total ded.	
Hunt, J.	M 4	$1209	$ 735	$903	$1578	$ 594	$1371	$5019	6%	301.14	80¢	$17.62	$33.30	$51.72	$249.42
Scoby, B.	S 2		846	768	1032	885	1806	4902	7	343.14	80¢	22.07	64.90	85.27	257.87
Ryan, J.	M 5	1299		975	1152	1233	975		5		80¢				
Elijah, R.	M 3	588	849		657	561	1206	5537	8	320.22	80¢	18.73	62.60	82.13	238.09
Anderson, B.	S 1	1014	855	795		1467	917		6		80¢				
Sodero, G.	M 0	1185	1068	981	1704				5		80¢				
Totals															

321

Unit 8.6   *Commission Accounts*

Sometimes it is impractical for manufacturers, wholesalers, retailers, and produce growers to assume all the selling or buying functions. Therefore they appoint others to act for them as selling or purchasing agents. The individuals or firms who act as the agents of others in selling or purchasing are known as commission merchants, agents, or brokers.

ACCOUNT SALES Many articles in daily use are not sold to wholesalers or retailers, but are delivered to them on consignment. When goods are "sold on consignment," the consignor (owner) retains title to the goods, can remove them at will, and merely delivers the goods to the consignee (wholesaler or retailer), who consummates the sale. When they are sold, the consignee pays the consignor for the goods, deducting a commission for selling and expenses such as freight, cartage, storage, insurance, etc. Most frequently sold under such an arrangement are food products, although manufacturers, wholesalers, and retailers of other types of goods will on occasion "sell" on a consignment basis.

As an example, a grower sends a carload of onions on consignment to a city commission merchant. The commission merchant pays the freight, cartage, storage, and other expenses, sells the goods for the highest obtainable price (gross proceeds), and after deducting these expenses and the agreed commission remits the net proceeds to the grower, together with an *account sales* in which all details of the transaction are recorded. An illustrative example of an account sales follows.

ACCOUNT SALES

February 24, 19____

GEORGE JOHNSON & SONS
Commission Merchants
St. Louis, Missouri

Sold for account of:

Sunkist Fruit Growers, Los Angeles, Calif.

19____ Feb.					
	18	245 crates oranges	@ $7.20	$1,764.00	
	21	125 crates oranges	@ 6.95	868.75	
	23	130 crates oranges	@ 7.05	916.50	
		Gross proceeds			$3,549.25
		Charges:			
		Freight		$ 109.85	
		Cartage		27.50	
		Storage		42.40	
		Commission, 7% of $3,549.25		248.45	428.20
		Net proceeds			$3,121.05

ACCOUNT PURCHASES A second type of commission agent buys rather than sells for his client. For example, if a large store wishes to secure a shipment of oriental rugs, it may commission an agent who will select and purchase the rugs (perhaps in Pakistan), send them by caravan to the nearest port, and then ship them by water and rail to the store. The agent will total the costs, including freight, insurance, commission, etc., add this sum to the purchase price of the rugs, and then bill the store accordingly for the gross cost in the form of an *account purchase*.

Commissions for this type of buying are based ordinarily on the purchase price (prime cost) of the goods, not on the purchase price plus expenses. The accompanying is an illustrative example of an account purchase.

ACCOUNT PURCHASE				
			June 15, 19____	
FREYBERG & COMPANY				
Commission Merchants				
San Francisco, California				
Bought for account of:				
Wellman Black, Salt Lake City, Utah				
19____		1500 lb Hill Bros. coffee @ $2.70	$ 4050.00	
June	14	2300 lb Folger coffee @ 2.58	5934.00	
		Prime cost		$9984.00
		Charges:		
		Insured freight	$ 114.60	
		Commission, 2% of $9984.00	199.68	314.28
		Gross cost		$10298.28

Exercise 8.6

1 Complete the following account sales:

ACCOUNT SALES				
			May 10, 19____	
BEN DRYDEN				
Commission Merchant				
San Francisco, Calif.				
Sold for account of:				
Acme Company, Chicago, Ill.				
19____		27 crates eggs @ $15.20		
May	5	32 crates eggs @ 15.70		
	7	55 crates eggs @ 12.30		
	8	22 crates eggs @ 12.00		
	9	Gross proceeds		
		Charges:		
		Express	$64.45	
		Storage	15.75	
		Commission, 4%		
		Net proceeds		*1698.7)*

2 Complete the following account sales:

<table>
<tr><td colspan="4" align="center">ACCOUNT SALES</td></tr>
<tr><td colspan="4" align="right">Sept. 7, 19____</td></tr>
<tr><td colspan="4" align="center">PACIOTTI & SONS
Commission Merchants
Latonia, Ky.</td></tr>
</table>

		ACCOUNT SALES		
		Sept. 7, 19____		
		PACIOTTI & SONS		
		Commission Merchants		
		Latonia, Ky.		
Sold for account of:				
		Goldstone Company, Cincinnati, Ohio		
19____ Sept.	5	25 crates cauliflower @ $7.50	*181.18*	
	5	235 bundles celery @ 2.60	*611 00*	
	6	85 crates cauliflower @ 7.86	*668.10*	*2913 10*
	6	550 bundles celery @ 2.63	*1444 50*	
		Gross proceeds		
		Charges:		
		Freight	$49.30	
		Storage	13.75	*150.44*
		Commission, 3%	*81.34*	*2762.66*
		Net proceeds		

3 Complete the following account purchase:

		ACCOUNT PURCHASE		
		Feb. 19, 19____		
		BEACH BAKER & COMPANY		
		Commission Merchants		
		Madison, Wisconsin		
Bought for account of:				
		Independent Grocers Association, Los Angeles, Calif.		
19____ Feb.	16	7500 lb Wisconsin Swiss @ $0.97		
	16	1575 lb American cheddar @ 0.885		
	19	2250 lb domestic blue @ 1.13		
		Prime cost		
		Charges:		
		Freight	$248.60	
		Cartage	56.25	
		Commission, 1½%		*11604.90*
		Gross cost		

4 Complete the following account purchase:

		ACCOUNT PURCHASE		
			June 9, 19____	
		JAMES E. HENRY CO.		
		Commission Merchants		
		San Francisco, California		
Bought for account of:				
		R. H. Green Company, Indianapolis, Ind.		

19____				
June	8	5800 lb White Bros. coffee @ $1.06		
	8	600 crates tomatoes @ 1.97		
	8	275 crates #1 cling peaches @ 2.08		
	9	430 crates #2 avocados @ 3.52		*9 4 5.60*
		Prime cost		
		Charges:		
		Freight, coffee	$186.80	
		Freight, refrigerator	334.50	*7 0 9. 5 1*
		Commission, 2%	*(8 8.3)*	
		Gross cost		*(0 / 2 1 . 2)*

Chapter 9

Purchase Discounts and Markup

Objectives To Be Achieved in This Chapter

1 *Solve problems involving chain trade discounts.*
2 *Become acquainted with the various cash discount terms and calculation of rate of interest earned by taking advantage of cash discounts.*
3 *Solve numerous problems in markup using the cost or sales price as the markup base.*
4 *Find terms in a retail operating statement for purposes of statement analysis, planning and budgeting, and finding unknown amounts.*

Intelligent business management requires an analysis of past operations and a shrewd forecasting of future business conditions. The methods of accomplishing this analysis and forecast are not within the province of this discussion, as our concern is with certain mathematical calculations necessary in the operation of most business enterprises.

It is obvious that the person in business must know the cost of the goods or services that he or she sells as well as the selling price that must be obtained to pay expenses and make a satisfactory profit.

Unit 9.1   *Trade Discounts*

Manufacturers and wholesalers distribute their goods largely through the agency of salespersons who call on customers and sell the various products by means of published catalogs containing accurate descriptions, illustrations, and prices of the products.

These catalogs are frequently large, bulky, and costly, sometimes numbering several thousands of pages of closely printed matter.

Products are also sold by the placing of catalogs in the hands of retailers who are thus able to continue ordering even in the absence of the salespersons.

When catalogs were not so large, different sections were printed and bound together in one volume. When a line was discontinued or added or when other changes were made, it was necessary to reprint an entire section of the catalog.

Today, with the loose-leaf system of binding, the making of changes has become much simpler. Single pages are sent for replacement or as additions to the catalogs and are inserted by the retailers or salespersons within the loose-leaf binders of the catalogs.

Prices quoted in the catalogs are not prices at which the goods are sold to the retailers. They are arbitrary prices, often suggested retail prices, from which discounts are taken in order to arrive at the actual net cost to the retailers. Rather than change pages in the catalog every time a price change takes place, the accepted practice is to mail replacement pages to the retailers, which give the new lists of discounts that are to be taken on the prices quoted in the catalog.

Extra discounts are often given for purchases in quantities or to secure the business of particularly desirable accounts. Frequently as many as a half-dozen discounts are given. When the price rises, a discount is reduced or dropped from the series; when the price goes down, a discount is increased or added to the series.

List or *catalog price* is the price quoted in the catalog.

Net price is the price after deduction of the trade discounts. This price is also known as the *seller's selling price*, the *purchaser's cost*, the *purchase price*, or the *cost price*.

Series or *chain discounts* are comprised of two or more discounts. *Trade discount problems* are problems in percentage. When more than one

LIST PRICE.
Trade discounts.
NET PRICE.
amount of each calculation . amount remitted

discount rate is allowed, each successive *difference* becomes the *base* for the next discount rate:

Example 1 Assume an initial list price of $100 and successive trade or chain discounts of 30, 15, and 5 percent (commonly written as 30/15/5) to be deducted.

	First		Second		Third	
	Number	%	Number	%	Number	%
Base	$100.00	100	$70.00	100	$59.50	100
Discount						
−(Percentage)	30.00	.30	10.50	.15	2.98	.05
Difference/D%	$ 70.00	.70	$59.50	.85	$56.52	.95

Example 2 The order in which the discounts are taken is immaterial. Assume the same data as Example 1, except that the trade or chain discounts are reversed to 5/15/30.

	First		Second		Third	
	Number	%	Number	%	Number	%
Base	$100.00	100	$95.00	100	$80.75	100
Discount	5.00	.05	14.25	.15	24.23	.30
Difference/D%	95.00	.95	80.75	.85	56.52	.70

Note that you cannot *add* the discounts and then multiply and make the subtraction. 30/15/5 is *not* equivalent to a 50 percent discount.

Calculating Trade Discounts

Computing the net price may be accomplished by either of two general methods:

1 By direct application of the discount series against the list price as illustrated in Examples 1 and 2 above
2 By trade discount equivalents

DISCOUNTING DIRECTLY AGAINST THE LIST PRICE Several arithmetical methods can be used to perform the operations in calculating the first discount, subtracting, and proceeding to the next discount.

Example 3 Discounting directly against the list price. Glassware with a list price of $1500 is subject to trade discounts of 25/20/10. What is the net price?

(a) *Multiplying by decimal equivalent of each rate of discount and subtracting:*

25% = 0.25   20% = 0.20   10% = 0.10

$1500.00
−375.00   ($1500.00 × 0.25)
————————
$1125.00
−225.00   ($1125.00 × 0.20)
————————
$ 900.00
−90.00   ($ 900.00 × 0.10)
————————
$ 810.00   Net price

(b) *Aliquot-parts method:*

$$25\% = \frac{1}{4} \quad 20\% = \frac{1}{5} \quad 10\% = \frac{1}{10}$$

To multiply by an aliquot fraction, divide by the fraction's denominator. Thus,

$1500
−375   (1500 ÷ 4)
————
$1125
−225   (1125 ÷ 5)
————
$ 900
−90   (900 ÷ 10)
————
$ 810   Net price

(c) *Multiplying by decimal complement of each rate of discount:*

Complement of 25% is 75% = 0.75; of 20% is 80% = 0.80; of 10% is 90% = 0.90

$1500.00 × 0.75 = $1125.00
$1125.00 × 0.80 = $ 900.00
$ 900.00 × 0.90 = $ 810.00   Net price

(d) *Multiplying by fractional complement of each rate of discount:*

Fractional complement of 25% or $\frac{1}{4}$ is $\frac{3}{4}$

Fractional complement of 20% or $\frac{1}{5}$ is $\frac{4}{5}$

Fractional complement of 10% or $\frac{1}{10}$ is $\frac{9}{10}$

$$\overset{\overset{30.00}{\cancel{150.00}}}{\cancel{\$1500.00}} \times \frac{3}{\cancel{4}} \times \frac{\cancel{4}}{\cancel{5}} \times \frac{9}{\cancel{10}} = \$810.00 \quad \text{Net price}$$

TRADE DISCOUNT EQUIVALENTS When more than one invoice is involved with the same series of chain discounts or when it is desirable or necessary to know the *net cost* of individual items, a single equivalent *net cost* rate is preferable because it is much faster.

To determine the single rate *to find the net cost* of an invoice with a series of chain discounts, *multiply the chain discount complements (the D%*

in Examples 1 and 2) by one another. Thus the single net cost rate of the series of chain discount rates of 30/15/5 is:

$$.70 \times .85 \times .95 = 56.53\%$$
$$\text{or} \quad .95 \times .85 \times .70 = 56.53\%$$

Example 4 **The net cost of an invoice with a list price of $100, with trade discounts of 30/15/5:**

List price	$100
Single equivalent cost rate	$\times .5653$
	56.53^1

Example 5 **Same problem data as Example 3. Find the net price.**

Single equivalent cost rate of the trade discounts of 25/20/10:

Complement of 25% = 75%
Complement of 20% = 80%
Complement of 10% = 90%

Single equivalent cost rate:

$$.75 \times .80 \times .90 = 54\%$$

List price	$1500
Single equivalent cost rate	$\times \quad 54$
Net cost	$ 810

TABLES OF NET COST FACTORS When certain combinations of trade discounts are frequently repeated, it is customary to tabulate the net cost factors for handy reference. Table 9.1 is an example of such a tabulation. In using the table, keep in mind that the same cost factor results no matter what the order of the chain discounts. Therefore the factor listed in any column that contains all the listed chain discounts will be the proper factor.

[1]$0.01 difference from Examples 1 and 2 is due to rounding.

TABLE 9.1 NET COST OF $1 LIST LESS TRADE DISCOUNTS

Trade discounts, %	Trade discounts in addition to series listed in first column			
	None	$33\frac{1}{3}\%$	20%	15%
Net	None	0.666 667	0.800 000	0.850 000
10	0.900 000	0.600 000	0.720 000	0.765 000
10, 5	0.855 000	0.570 000	0.684 000	0.726 750
20	0.800 000	0.533 333	0.640 000	0.680 000
20, 10	0.720 000	0.480 000	0.576 000	0.612 000
20, 10, 5	0.684 000	0.456 000	0.547 200	0.581 400
$2\frac{1}{2}$	0.975 000	0.650 000	0.780 000	0.828 750
10, $2\frac{1}{2}$	0.877 500	0.585 000	0.702 000	0.745 875
10, 5, $2\frac{1}{2}$	0.833 625	0.555 750	0.666 900	0.708 581

Example 6   **Find the net cost of an invoice of $565.43 list less trade discounts of 20/20/10/5.**

$565.43 × 0.547200 = $309.40

Example 7   **Find the list price of an invoice if the net price is $478.80 and the trade discounts allowed are 33⅓, 10, and 5 percent.**

$$\frac{\$478.80}{0.570000} = \$840.00$$

TO FIND THE SINGLE DISCOUNT RATE EQUIVALENT TO A SERIES OF CHAIN DISCOUNTS   If it is desired to know the *single discount rate* applicable to the price of an item or an invoice, find the single cost rate and then subtract this rate from 1.00 (100 percent).

Example 8   **Frisbees with a list price of $900 are subject to trade discounts of 30/20/5. Find the single discount rate equivalent to the trade discounts of 30/20/5.**

The single cost rate is found:

.70 × .80 × .95 = 53.2%

Single discount rate = 100% − 53.2% = 46.8%

List price	$900.00
Single discount rate	×.468
Total trade discount	$421.20

TO FIND LIST PRICE IF GIVEN NET COST AND A SERIES OF TRADE DISCOUNTS   Finding the list price when you know the net cost and the discount rates becomes the problem in percentage when the difference and its equivalent percent (the D%) are known and you want to find the base. The procedure is to divide the net cost (difference) by the cost rate (the D%). The procedure can be performed by using each successive trade discount complement or by using the single net cost rate.

Example 9   **Household furniture priced at $2700 net has been subject to trade discounts of 25/20/10. Find the list price by using the successive trade discounts.**

With decimals	With fractions
Complement of 25% = 75%	Complement of $\frac{1}{4} = \frac{3}{4}$
Complement of 20% = 80%	Complement of $\frac{1}{5} = \frac{4}{5}$
Complement of 10% = 90%	Complement of $\frac{1}{10} = \frac{9}{10}$

$$\frac{\$2700}{0.75} = \$3600$$

$$\frac{\$3600}{0.80} = \$4500$$

$$\frac{\$4500}{0.90} = \$5000$$

$$\frac{\overset{100}{\underset{1}{\cancel{\$2700}}}}{1} \times \frac{\cancel{4}}{\cancel{3}} \times \frac{5}{\cancel{4}} \times \frac{10}{\cancel{9}} = \$5000$$

Example 10 **Same problem data as Example 9. Find the list price using the single net cost rate.**

Net cost rate = .75 × .80 × .90 = 54%

$$\frac{\$2700}{0.54} = \$5000$$

TO FIND THE LIST PRICE IF GIVEN THE DISCOUNT IN DOLLARS AND THE SERIES OF DISCOUNTS If a model or map were drawn of the information provided in this type of problem, it would appear:

	Number	%
List price	_____	100
Less discounts of 20/15/5	−$424.80	___
Net cost	_____	___

Since we can find the single discount rate equivalent to 25/20/10 (see Example 9), we calculate it and place it in the model.

.80 × .85 × .95 = 64.6%
Single discount rate = 100% − 64.6% = 35.4%

When the 35.4 percent is placed in the model, it is seen that the discount of $424.80 is 35.4 percent of the list price. Since we now have a number and its equivalent percent of the base, the base or list price is found:

$$\frac{\$424.80}{0.354} = \$1200$$

	Number	%
List price	$1200.00	100
Less discount of 20/15/5	−424.80	35.4
Net cost	$775.20	64.6

Example 11 **An invoice for men's clothing received a total trade discount of $235.20. The invoices called for trade discounts of 15/15/5. Find (a) the list price and (b) the net cost.**

(a) $.85 \times .85 \times .95 = 68.64\%$ (Single cost rate)
$100\% - 68.64\% = 31.36\%$ (Single discount rate)

$$\frac{\text{Total discount}}{\text{Single discount rate}} = \frac{\$235.20}{.3136} = \$750.00$$

(b) List price $750.00
     Less total trade discount   − 235.20
     Net cost $514.80

Exercise 9.1

Discount <u>directly</u> against the list price and solve each problem by the following methods: (a) Multiplying by the decimal equivalent of each rate of discount and <u>subtracting</u>, (b) using aliquot parts, (c) multiplying by the decimal complement of each rate of discount, and (d) multiplying by the common-fraction complement of each rate of discount. *Note:* Answers for (a), (b), (c), and (d) in each problem will check, for the methods will obtain exactly the same answer.

1 A furniture dealer orders a dozen armchairs listed at $26 each less discounts of 25, 5, and 10 percent. What is the net price of the entire bill?

2 A millinery shop orders 6 gross of hats at $35 per doz, less discounts of 25/10/20. What is the net price of the entire bill? *Note:* A gross is 12 doz.

Discount directly against the list price in solving the following problems in trade discount. Solve by any method or combination of methods desired.

3 A record manufacturer offers to ship 5000 records to a retailer at $6.00 per record, less discounts of $33\frac{1}{3}$ percent, 20 percent, 15 percent, and 5 percent. Find the net cost of the entire shipment to the retailer.

4 A wholesaler offers to sell 10 flats of automobile batteries for $2200 at discounts of 25/5/15/10. Find the net price.

5 A nationally famous line of cosmetics is sold to retailers by the manufacturer at discounts of $33\frac{1}{3}$ percent, 5 percent, and 3 percent. Find the net price to the retailer on a <u>purchase</u> listed at $2748.60 by the manufacturer.

6 A manufacturer of furniture, who regularly sells furniture to retailers at discounts of 30 percent and 20 percent, offers an additional discount of 10 percent on some dining-room sets with a list price of $780.50. Find (a) the regular net price, and (b) the special price at the additional discount of 10 percent.

7 Two radio manufacturers offer comparable instruments at prices as follows: company X quotes $240 less 30 percent, 25 percent, and 10 percent. Company Y quotes $250 less 40 percent, 20 percent, and $6\frac{1}{4}$ percent. Which company has the lower net price and by how many dollars?

8   An electric refrigerator is offered at $640, less discounts of 40 percent, 20 percent, and 5 percent. What is the net price?

Express decimally the net cost of $1 list price less the following trade discounts. Do not drop any decimal places, and show any repetends as fractional endings reduced to lowest terms.

9   30 and 20 percent
10   42, 25, and 12 percent
11   25, 15, 2, and 10 percent

Express decimally the single-discount equivalents of the following trade discounts. Do not drop any decimal places, and show any repetends as fractional endings reduced to lowest terms:

12   25 and 20 percent
13   35, 25, and 5 percent
14   $33\frac{1}{3}$, 5, and $12\frac{1}{2}$ percent

Find in each of the following (a) present net price, (b) additional discount in percent that must be granted if the desired lower new net price is allowed, and (c) the new discount chain in percents.

15   List price $90.00, present discounts $33\frac{1}{3}$ and 20 percent, desired new net price $36.00.
16   List price $160.00, present discounts 40 and 10 percent, desired new net price $73.44.
17   List price $240.00, present discounts 30, 25, 5 percent, desired new net price $95.76.

Find the decimal equivalent of the net cost of $1 list in solving the following:

18   The buyer of a stationery department in a large store purchased several items at discounts of 20, $8\frac{1}{3}$, 25, and $12\frac{1}{2}$ percent. Find the net price of each item if the list prices were (a) $4.46, (b) $38.85, and (c) $895.27.
19   A merchant made purchases from a manufacturer whose list prices carried trade discounts of 20, $16\frac{2}{3}$, $8\frac{1}{3}$, and 2 percent. Find the net price of each of the following if the list prices were (a) $9.75, (b) $28.50, and (c) $750.68.

Find the list price in the following:

20   The net price of an invoice was $945.30. Trade discounts were 40, 20, and 10 percent.
21   The net prices of three invoices subjected to trade discounts of 25/$8\frac{1}{3}$/4 were (a) $330.33, (b) $21.06, and (c) $4.09. *Suggestion:* In solving, find the decimal equivalent of the net cost of $1 list.

Solve the following:

22   The trade discounts on an invoice were 40, 10, and 15 percent. If the total of the trade discounts was $335.48, find the list price of the invoice.

23 An invoice had a trade discount of $133.10. If the trade discount series was 25, 7$\frac{1}{2}$, and 4 percent, find (a) the list price and (b) the net price.

Use Table 9.1 (net cost of $1 list less trade discounts) in solving the following:

24 Find the net price of each of the following invoices: (a) $28.50 list, trade discounts 33$\frac{1}{3}$ and 2$\frac{1}{2}$ percent, (b) $320.00 list, trade discounts 15, 20, 10, and 5 percent, and (c) $830.50 list, trade discounts 20, 10, and 5 percent.

25 Find the list price in each of the following invoices: (a) $10.54 net price, trade discounts 20, 10, and 33$\frac{1}{3}$ percent, (b) $276.85 net price, trade discounts 33$\frac{1}{3}$, 10, and 5 percent, and (c) $5.44 net price, trade discounts 10, 2$\frac{1}{2}$, and 20 percent.

Unit 9.2   *Cash Discounts*

Practically all lines of merchandise are purchased with cash discount rates, such discounts ordinarily ranging between 1 and 10 percent.

Cash discounts are stipulated in the *terms of sale* included in the heading of an invoice. Trade discounts may be given on a catalog or list price, and these trade discounts are deducted to determine the net price. This net price or a directly quoted net price is usually subject to a cash discount.

Although the term "cash discount" implies that it is granted only upon the immediate payment of cash, this is not true in general business practice, as a period of several days from the date of the invoice or the receipt of the goods is usually granted within which period the stipulated percent of discount may be taken if a payment is made in full or in part. The exception to this statement is c.o.d. dating (collect-on-delivery), which indicates that the purchaser must make payment in full upon delivery of the goods.

Theoretically, cash discounts are given as an incentive to prompt payment. In practice, cash discounts vary greatly and the variance cannot be explained as simply a greater or lesser incentive to prompt payment. Whether the discount is 1 percent or 10 percent, it is imperative that the purchaser who wishes to resell the goods at a competitive price take advantage of the cash discount.

Custom within certain industries seems to be the determinant of the cash discount granted, although in general it may be said that rates of discount tend to be highest for lines of merchandise in which style risk or perishability is greatest.

TERMS OF SALE AND THEIR MEANING   Since there are various means of symbolizing cash discounts and various methods of calculating the time period within which the discount may be taken, the following examples are given as illustrative of the more common types of cash discounts found in the terms of sale.

Ordinary dating: 2/10, n/30 (also written as 2/10, net 30). The first digit is the discount rate of 2 percent. The second group of digits stipulates the number of days within which the discount may be taken, or 10 days. Thus if the invoice is paid in full within 10 days of the date of shipment, which corresponds to the date of the invoice, a 2 percent cash discount may be taken. After 10 days and up to 30 days, the full amount of the invoice is due. Net 30 or n/30 means that the invoice must be paid within *exactly* 30 days from the date of the invoice (not 30-day-month time) and that it will be considered overdue after 30 days and may from that time be considered as subject to a delinquency charge.

Example 1   **What payments are indicated on a $100 invoice shipped November 16 with terms of 3/10, n/30?**

    (a) If paid on or before November 26:
        $100.00 less 3 percent = $100.00 − $3.00 = $97.00
    (b) If paid on or between November 27 and December 16:
        The full amount of $100 is due.
    (c) If paid December 17 or later:
        The bill is past due and may be subject to a delinquency charge.

Example 2   **What payments are indicated on a $450 invoice dated October 28 with terms of 2/10, n/60?**

    (a) If paid on or before November 7:
        $450.00 less 2 percent = $450.00 − $9.00 = $441.00
    (b) If paid on or between November 8 and December 27:
        The full amount of $450 is due.
    (c) If paid December 28 or later:
        The bill is past due and may be subject to a delinquency charge.

    A similar type of cash discount occurs with such terms of sale as 5/10, 2/30, 1/60, n/90. This would signify 5 percent discount if paid within 10 days of the date of the invoice, 2 percent discount if paid within 11 to 30 days, 1 percent discount if paid within 31 to 60 days, net if paid within 61 to 90 days, and overdue and subject to a delinquency charge if paid on the ninety-first day or thereafter.

ADVANCE DATING OR POSTDATING   When the terms allow more time than date of shipment and time numerals (as 10 days in terms of 2/10) in the terms would indicate, the terms are said to be advance dated or postdated. In advance dating or postdating the invoice carries a later date than the actual date of the shipment, and the payment does not need to be made until the time indicated by both the terms and the advanced date of the invoice. Thus goods shipped on August 18 may be accompanied by an invoice dated August 18 as of October 1, with terms of 3/10, net 30. The cash discount may be earned by payment made on or before October 11, or the payment of the net invoice may be delayed until October 31.

END-OF-MONTH DATING   The abbreviation or symbol used to express end-of-month dating is e.o.m., which means that the days for allowing discount are counted from the end of the month following the date of the invoice, not from the date of the invoice.

Thus if an invoice dated March 17 has terms of 8/10 e.o.m., the discount of 8 percent is available up to and including the first 10 days of April, or through April 10. It is also business practice to grant a month's extension of time on e.o.m. terms if the invoice dating is on or after the twenty-sixth day of the month. For example, a bill dated May 26 with terms of 4/10 e.o.m. is subject to discount up to and including July 10.

After the cash discount period has elapsed, bills with e.o.m. dating are considered generally as having a 20-day net period following the cash discount period and thereafter being overdue and subject to a delinquency charge.

PROXIMO DATING   The abbreviation or symbol used to express proximo, defined as the next month after the present, is "prox." Invoices with proximo dating are usually treated as though they had e.o.m. dating.

Thus if an invoice dated August 24 has terms of 2/10 prox., the discount of 2 percent is available up to and including September 10. As with e.o.m. dating, invoices dated on or after the twenty-sixth day of a month are sometimes considered as being dated in the following month. For example, a bill dated December 28 with terms of 5/10 prox. may be subject to discount up to and including February 10.

Again as with e.o.m. dating, bills with proximo dating are considered generally as having a 20-day net period following the cash discount period and thereafter as being overdue and subject to a delinquency charge.

RECEIPT-OF-GOODS DATING   The abbreviation or symbol used to express receipt-of-goods dating, which means that the days for allowing discount are counted after receipt of the goods and not after the invoice date, is "r.o.g."

This type of dating is particularly useful when the time required for transportation is apt to be in excess of the number of days allowed in the discount period or when the time in transit is likely to be indefinite, as in shipments by water through the Canal Zone that may take 30 to 60 or more days, depending upon the frequency of the ship's ports of call.

Thus on an invoice dated April 4, with terms of 5/10 r.o.g. and received on April 16, the discount of 5 percent is available up to and including April 26. On an invoice dated September 26, with terms of 3/10 r.o.g. and received on October 26, the discount of 3 percent is available up to and including November 5.

When the net period is not stipulated, as is usual with r.o.g. terms, it may be assumed as being the 20 days following the cash discount period, and thereafter the invoice is overdue and subject to a delinquency charge.

EXTRA DATING   "Extra," "ex.," or "X," meaning extra dating, indicates that the discount is available for a period of time in addition to the number of days first specified in the terms. Thus 2/10–60X, or 2/10–60 extra, indicates 10 plus 60 or a total of 70 days from the date of the invoice as the period during which a 2 percent cash discount may be taken. In a bill the terms of which are 3/10–90 extra and the invoice date is June 7, 3 percent discount may be taken if payment is made on or before 100 days after June 7, or to and including September 15.

When the net period is not stipulated, as is usual with extra dating, it may be assumed as being the 20 days following the cash discount period, and thereafter the invoice is overdue and subject to a delinquency charge.

This type of dating is found most frequently in industries in which sales are likely to be seasonal. For example, a manufacturer of heating equipment who wishes to induce purchase in May or June is likely to offer extra dating with the final date for discount falling due in the normal fall selling season for heating equipment.

WHEN FINAL DATE OF DISCOUNT PERIOD IS A NONBUSINESS DAY If the last day of the discount period falls on a Sunday (or a Saturday in many states) or a legal holiday, the final date of allowable discount is extended to the first business day following.

Example 3 **An invoice with both trade and cash discounts:**

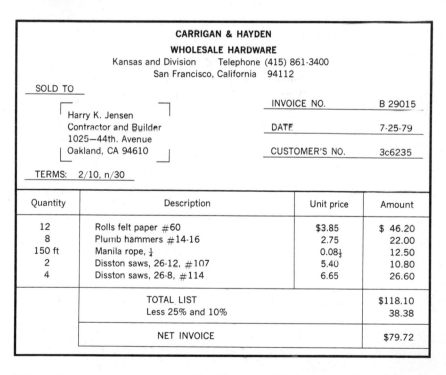

CARRIGAN & HAYDEN

WHOLESALE HARDWARE

Kansas and Division   Telephone (415) 861-3400

San Francisco, California   94112

SOLD TO

Harry K. Jensen
Contractor and Builder
1025—44th. Avenue
Oakland, CA 94610

INVOICE NO.	B 29015
DATE	7-25-79
CUSTOMER'S NO.	3c6235

TERMS: 2/10, n/30

Quantity	Description	Unit price	Amount
12	Rolls felt paper #60	$3.85	$ 46.20
8	Plumb hammers #14-16	2.75	22.00
150 ft	Manila rope, $\frac{1}{4}$	0.08$\frac{1}{4}$	12.50
2	Disston saws, 26-12, #107	5.40	10.80
4	Disston saws, 26-8, #114	6.65	26.60
	TOTAL LIST		$118.10
	Less 25% and 10%		38.38
	NET INVOICE		$79.72

If Harry K. Jensen, contractor and builder, pays this invoice in full within 10 days following July 25 (not later than August 4), he will deduct 2 percent from the net invoice of $79.72. Thus:

Net invoice $79.72

-1.59 Cash discount ($79.72 × 0.02) = $1.59

$\overline{\$78.13}$ Remittance necessary to pay invoice in full

If payment is made August 5 through August 24, a remittance of $79.72 will be required to pay the net invoice in full. In accordance with general business practice, it would be understood by both buyer and seller that any payments made *after* August 24 would be subject to a *delinquency charge*. The delinquency charge would generally be a stated monthly percentage rate applied to the delinquent balance. State laws may set maximum rates and disclosure requirements of the equivalent annual rate for such delinquency charges, but disclosure of the annual percentage rate charged for delinquent payments is not required under Federal Regulation Z (see Unit 7.1).

PARTIAL PAYMENT ON ACCOUNT   On occasions, the purchaser may make only a partial payment on account. If this payment is made within the discount period, the purchaser may be allowed a discount on the portion of the bill paid.

If terms are 2 percent 10 days, every 98 cents paid within the 10-day period entitles the purchaser to a credit of $1. If terms are 3 percent 10 days, a payment of 97 cents within the 10-day period entitles the purchaser to a credit of $1.

To find credit on a partial payment entitled to cash discount, divide the payment by the complement of the cash discount percent.

Cash discount earned on a partial payment equals the amount credited less the amount paid.

Example 4   **On a net invoice of $235 with terms of 4/10 e.o.m., dated May 22, a partial payment of $144 is made on June 10. Find (a) amount credited to the purchaser by the seller, (b) cash discount earned, and (c) balance due.**

Solution:

(a)   Cash discount is earned on $144.00 payment made on June 10.
   $100\% - 4\% = 96\% = 0.96$
   Amount credited $= \$144.00 \div 0.96 = \$150.00$
(b)   Cash discount earned $= \$150.00 - 144.00 = \$6.00$
(c)   Balance due $= \$235.00 - 150.00 = \$85.00$

Example 5   **A net invoice of $463.50 dated August 6 has terms of 5/10 r.o.g. The goods are received September 10, and payment of $265 is made on September 20. Find (a) amount credited to the purchaser by the seller, (b) cash discount earned, and (c) balance due.**

Solution:

(a)   Cash discount is earned on $265.00 payment made on September 20.
   $100\% - 5\% = 95\% = 0.95$
   Amount credited $= \$265.00 \div 0.95 = \$278.95$
(b)   Cash discount earned $= \$278.95 - \$265.00 = \$13.95$
(c)   Balance due $= \$463.50 - \$278.95 = \$184.55$

INTEREST RATE EQUIVALENT OF CASH DISCOUNT A comparison of cash discount rates with corresponding interest rates will further emphasize the necessity of the business person's taking advantage of cash discounts permitted in the terms of sale.

Example 6   **Elmer's Market purchased merchandise with an invoice price of $600 and terms of 2/10, n/60. Compute to the nearest $\frac{1}{10}$ percent the equivalent interest rate that can be earned by Elmer's Market if the invoice is paid in time to earn the cash discount.**

Elmer's Market has been given the opportunity to deduct 2 percent from the invoice price if it is paid 50 days prior to the due date. The first 10 days within which the 2 percent reduction is allowed is called the cash discount period, and the remaining 50 days is called the net period.

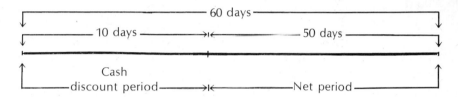

The above example relates to the problems of finding the interest rate *r* in ordinary simple interest as presented in Chapter 5.

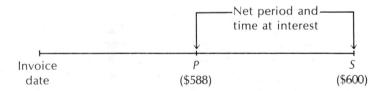

(a)   From the basic formula *I = Prt*, the formula to find *r* is:

1 $r = \dfrac{I}{Pt}$

r = unknown
P = $588 [$600 − ($600 × 2%)]
S = $600
I = $12 (*S* − *P* or $600 − $588)

$t = \dfrac{50}{360}$

2 $r = \dfrac{\$12}{\$588 \times \dfrac{50}{360}} = 0.147 = 14.7\%$

Example 7   **Lindstrand's Grocery purchased merchandise with an invoice price of $400 and terms of 2/10 e.o.m. Compute to the nearest $\frac{1}{10}$ percent the equivalent interest rate if Lindstrand's pays the invoice in time to earn the cash discount.**

Note: When the net period is not stipulated as in e.o.m., proximo, or extra dating, the net period is assumed to be 20 days.

$$r = \frac{I}{Pt}$$

r = unknown
P = $392 [$400 − (2% × $400)]
S = $400
I = $8 ($S$ − P or $400 − $392)

$$t = \frac{20}{360}$$

$$r = \frac{\$8}{\$392 \times \dfrac{20}{360}} = 0.367 = 36.7\%$$

Exercise 9.2

Solve the following:

1   An invoice of $560 has cash terms of 2/10, net 60, and is dated July 25. Find (a) the final date on which the cash discount may be taken and (b) the amount necessary to pay in full if the cash discount is earned.
2   An invoice for $2100 is dated January 15 and has cash terms of 4/30, 2/60, 1/120, n/150. Find the amount necessary to pay in full on February 15.
3   If cash terms are 3/10, net 60, as of April 10, the net invoice is for $1120.60, and the date of the invoice is March 17, find (a) the final date on which the discount may be taken, (b) the amount of the cash discount that may be taken, if earned, and (c) the amount necessary to pay in full if the cash discount is earned.
4   An invoice for $390 is dated February 22 and has cash terms of 6/10, e.o.m. Find (a) the final date on which the cash discount may be taken and (b) the amount necessary to pay in full if the cash discount is earned.
5   If an invoice for $3840 is dated May 1 and has cash terms of 5/10, prox., how much should be remitted by the purchaser to the seller if it is paid in full on June 10?
6   An invoice for $142 is dated March 16 and has cash terms of 3/30–60 extra. Find (a) the final date on which the cash discount may be taken, (b) the cash discount if paid in full on June 15, and (c) the amount necessary to pay the invoice in full on April 17.

Find (a) the cash discounts allowed, if earned, assuming that cash discounts are allowed on partial payments as well as payments in full, (b) the amounts remitted by purchaser, (c) the amounts credited by seller to purchaser, and (d) the balances due, if any. Assume that anticipation (see Unit 9.3) is not permitted.

Invoice	Date of invoice	Net invoice	Terms	Receipt of goods	Amount paid	Date of payment
7	February 8	$ 175.60	1/10, n/30		In full	February 18
8	December 15	75.85	2/30, 1/60, n/90		In full	February 13
9	June 8	560.75	3/10, 2/30, 1/60, n/90		$ 300.00	June 18
10	October 27	466.31	4/10, 2/30, n/60		$ 196.00	November 26
11	November 14	85.28	2/10, n/60 as of Dec. 1		In full	December 11
12	December 27	182.50	2/10, 1/30 as of May 15		$ 95.00	May 26
13	April 28	125.00	3/10, e.o.m.		In full	June 10
14	August 15	783.26	5/10, e.o.m.		$ 500.00	September 10
15	June 17	92.47	2/10, prox.		In full	July 10
16	May 27	1848.50	3/10, prox.		$1100.00	June 10
17	September 9	2784.00	4/30, r.o.g.	December 8	$1500.00	January 7
18	February 2	5.80	1/10, r.o.g.	May 9	In full	May 19
19	October 8	1780.00	6/10–90X		$ 900.00	January 16
20	January 19	311.25	2/15–45 extra		In full	March 20

21 An invoice to Arnold and Black, men's furnishers, is dated October 18 and itemizes 10 doz shirts at $25 per doz list less trade discounts of 40 and 5 percent with cash terms of 4/10, net 30, as of December 1. If payment in full is made on December 11, find the amount remitted by Arnold and Black.

22 An invoice dated July 12 for some merchandise is received on August 25 by the Botsford-King Company. The list totals $1428.50, with allowed trade discounts of 25, 15, and 20 percent. If the cash terms of sale are 2/30 r.o.g., find the amount necessary to pay in full on September 24.

23 Find the net price balance due from a purchaser who remits $375 on May 26 on an invoice of $850 dated May 11 and subject to trade discounts of $33\frac{1}{3}$ and $2\frac{1}{2}$ percent with cash terms of 1/15, net 45.

24 On May 25, a partial payment of $500 is made on an invoice of $1200 with cash terms of 5/10, 1/30, net 60, and dated May 15. Find the additional payment required to pay in full on June 14.

25 The Blue Lake Tire Shop purchased recapping supplies for the invoice price of $1600 and terms 2/10, n/60. Although ample cash will be available in 60 days, insufficient cash will be available in time to pay the invoice within the cash discount period. The proprietor can borrow the necessary cash at the local bank but will have to pay interest at the annual effective rate of $10\frac{1}{2}$ percent. (a) Should the Blue Lake Tire Shop borrow the money and pay the invoice in time to earn the cash discount? (b) State your reason.

26 The Buckhorn Cafe received supplies with an invoice price of $600 and terms of 3/10 e.o.m. Although cash will be available in 30 days, the Buckhorn Cafe will be unable to pay the invoice within the discount period. Cash can be borrowed at a bank which charges 9 percent interest. (a) Should the Buckhorn Cafe borrow the money? (b) State your reason.

27 An invoice of $480.50 net dated June 19 has terms of 3/10, 2/30, 1/60, net 90. Find the amount remitted by the purchaser if payment in full is made on (a) June 29, (b) July 18, (c) August 18, and (d) September 17.

28 A job lot of sport jackets priced at $932 has terms of 5/15 e.o.m. If the invoice is dated September 27, find (a) final date on which cash discount is earnable, (b) cash discount allowable, and (c) amount remitted by the purchaser if the invoice is paid in full and the cash discount is earned.

29 Hart and Company, wholesalers, offer wool hosiery at $15 per doz with terms of 4/10 e.o.m. A department store buyer is required to obtain 8/10 e.o.m. What must be the adjusted price per dozen if Hart and Company is not to lose and the buyer's required terms of 8/10 e.o.m. are allowed?

30 On the following invoice, find (a) extensions, (b) total list, (c) trade discount, (d) net invoice due, including prepaid freight, (e) net cost per unit not considering cash discount and prepaid freight, (f) cash discount if paid in full on July 2, and (g) amount necessary to pay in full on July 2. *Note:* A cash discount is not allowed on the prepaid freight.

BOOHER ELECTRIC CORPORATION
717 Sound Street
Seattle, Washington   98016

SOLD TO		INVOICE	4X-715
Stephen F. Shorb		DATE	June 2, 1979
11 Sequoia Way			
San Francisco, CA 94112		SHIPPED VIA	Prepaid freight
CUSTOMER ORDER 5-17-83		TERMS	2/30, n/60, F.O.B., Seattle

Quantity	Description	Unit Price	Amount
1	Receiver 214-21	$435.00	$
2	Receiver 218-24	621.00	
15	Receiver 50-5X	61.00	
9	Receiver 50-5Y	82.50	
1	Coil 802	6.25	
6	Condenser AY-43	2.95	
LIST TOTAL Less 40/10 trade discount			$
NET TOTAL Plus prepaid freight			$ 165.45
NET INVOICE DUE			$

In certain industries it is customary to deduct interest on accounts paid before the final due date. This deduction, known as "anticipation," is based on the prevailing rates of interest. Anticipation is taken in lieu of a cash discount when the terms of sale are net and is added to or taken in addition to any cash discount that may be permitted in the terms of sale.

In the examples that follow, note that anticipation is a percent per annum computed by counting the actual number of days (exact time) of prepayment and the use of a 360-day year as the base (denominator). When both a cash discount and anticipation are taken, count *only* the remaining days in which the cash discount percent earned is allowable.

The practice of taking anticipation is encouraged by many vendors, who feel that the additional discount for prompt payment is justified. Anticipation is computed in two ways:

1   On the basis of the net invoice *before* cash discounts have been taken
2   On the basis of the net invoice *after* cash discounts have been taken

It is obvious that, when the former method is used, the amount of anticipation will be slightly in excess of that which is computed by the latter method.

Example 1   **Based on net invoice. What is (a) the anticipation at 5 percent on an invoice of $500 dated June 10, terms of 90 days net, if paid in full on July 16 and (b) the amount remitted by the purchaser?**

Anticipation is for the 54 days prepayment of the final date of the net period.

(a) $\$500.00 \times \dfrac{54}{360} \times \dfrac{5}{100} = \$3.75$

(b) $\$500 - \$3.75 = \$496.25$

Example 2   **Based on net invoice. What is (a) the cash discount earned, (b) the anticipation at 6 percent, and (c) the amount remitted by the purchaser if payment in full is made on March 8 on an invoice for $240 and if the terms of sale are 2/30, 1/60, net 90, and the date of the invoice is February 26?**

Payment is made 10 days after date; therefore the 2 percent cash discount is earned and anticipation is for 20 days.

(a) $\$240.00 \times 0.02 = \$4.80$

(b) $\$240.00 \times \dfrac{20}{360} \times \dfrac{6}{100} = \$0.80$

(c) $\$240.00 - (\$4.80 + \$0.80) = \$240.00 - \$5.60 = \$234.40$

Note that (c) may be solved directly by combining both (a) and (b) as decimal fractions as shown in the following calculations.

$$\text{Cash discount } 2\% = \quad 0.02$$

$$\text{Anticipation } \frac{20}{360} \times \frac{6}{100} = \underline{+0.00\tfrac{1}{3}}$$

$$\text{Cash discount + anticipation} \quad 0.02\tfrac{1}{3}$$

$$\text{and } \$240.00 \times 0.02\tfrac{1}{3} = \$5.60$$

$$\$240.00 - \$5.60 = \$234.40$$

Example 3   **Based on net invoice less cash discount. Same problem as Example 2 except that anticipation is based on net invoice *after* cash discount has been taken.**

(a) $\$240.00 \times 0.02 = \$4.80$
(b) $\$240.00 - \$4.80 = \$235.20$

$$\text{and } \$235.20 \times \frac{20}{360} \times \frac{6}{100} = \$0.78$$

(c) $\$235.20 - \$0.78 = \$234.42$

Note that (c) may be solved directly by treating (a) and (b) as though they were chain discounts (which, in fact, they are).

Since anticipation is for 20 days, then $\frac{20}{360} \times \frac{6}{100} = 0.00\tfrac{1}{3}$. And 2 and $\tfrac{1}{3}$ percent in series discount equal a single-discount factor of $2.32\tfrac{2}{3}$ percent or a single-cost equivalent of $97.67\tfrac{1}{3}$ percent by any of the methods used in computing chain discounts (see Unit 9.1). Then:

$$\$240.00 \times 0.0232\tfrac{2}{3} = \$5.58$$

$$\$240.00 - \$5.58 = \$234.42$$

$$\text{or } \$240.00 \times 0.9767\tfrac{1}{3} = \$234.42$$

ANTICIPATION ON PARTIAL PAYMENTS   On partial payments there may be anticipation as well as cash discount to consider. If so, an additional calculation must be made. It is apparent that if anticipation is equivalent to $\tfrac{1}{2}$ percent, then every $99\tfrac{1}{2}$ cents paid entitles the purchaser to a credit of \$1 *before* computing the credit on a partial payment entitled to cash discount.

If only anticipation is to be considered (no cash discount being granted or earned), the steps in solution are as follows:

1   Find the decimal or fractional equivalent of the anticipation at the stipulated rate (usually 6 percent) for the number of days that anticipation is earned. Thus:

$$6\% \text{ anticipation for 45 days } \frac{6}{100} \times \frac{45}{360} = \frac{3}{400} = \frac{3}{4}\% = 0.0075$$

2   Divide the partial payment by the complement of the decimal or fractional equivalent. Thus to find the complement:

$$\text{Complement of } \frac{3}{400} = \frac{397}{400} \qquad \text{or} \qquad \text{of } 0.0075 = 0.9925$$

Example 4 **Considering only anticipation. A partial payment of $400 is made on a net invoice of $745. If no cash discount is granted but anticipation at 6 percent is allowed, find the amount credited to the purchaser by the seller if 36 days anticipation is earned.**

$$36 \text{ days at } 6\% = \frac{36}{360} \times \frac{6}{100} = \frac{6}{1000} = 0.006$$

$$\text{Complement} = 1.000 - 0.006 = 0.994$$

$$\text{Amount credited} = \frac{\$400.00}{0.994} = \$402.41$$

Proof: $\$402.41 \times 0.994 = \$400.00$

When both anticipation and cash discount are to be considered, the amount credited on a partial payment will vary, depending upon whether anticipation is based on (1) the net invoice before the cash discount has been taken or (2) the net invoice less the cash discount.

If anticipation is based on the net invoice before the cash discount has been taken, the steps in solution may be as follows:

1 Find the sum of the decimal or fractional equivalent of the percent of cash discount and percent of anticipation earned.
2 Divide the partial payment by the complement of this obtained sum.

Example 5 **Considering anticipation as based on the net invoice before the cash discount has been taken. A net invoice of $937.50 dated July 7 has terms of 3/10 e.o.m. A partial payment of $500 is made on July 11. If allowed anticipation of 6 percent is based on the net invoice before the cash discount has been taken, find the amount credited to the purchaser by the seller.**

Anticipation is 30 days.

$$30 \text{ days at } 6\% = \frac{30}{360} \times \frac{6}{100} = \frac{5}{1000} = 0.005$$

$$\text{Cash discount earned } 3\% = 0.03$$
$$\text{Anticipation} + \text{discount} = 0.005 + 0.03 = 0.035$$
$$\text{Complement} = 1.00 - 0.035 = 0.965$$

$$\text{Amount credited} = \frac{\$500.00}{0.965} = \$518.13$$

Proof: $\$518.13 \times 0.965 = \$500.00$

If anticipation is based on the net invoice less the cash discount, the problem of finding the amount credited is somewhat more difficult. The solution may be obtained as follows:

1 Divide the partial payment by the complement of the decimal or fractional equivalent of the anticipation earned.

2   Divide this obtained quotient by the complement of the decimal or fractional equivalent of the cash discount earned.

Example 6   **Considering anticipation as based on the net invoice less the cash discount. A net invoice of $500 dated June 20 has terms of 2/15–50 extra. A partial payment of $200 is made on June 25. If anticipation at 6 percent based on the net invoice less the cash discount is allowed, find the amount credited to the purchaser by the seller.**

Anticipation is 60 days.

$$60 \text{ days at } 6\% = \frac{60}{360} \times \frac{6}{100} = \frac{1}{100} = 0.01$$

Complement $= 1.00 - 0.01 = 0.99$ (or $100\% - 1\% = 99\%$)

Credit before cash discount is considered $= \dfrac{\$200.00}{0.99} = \$202.02$

Therefore anticipation is earned on $202.02.
    Cash discount complement $= 100\% - 2\% = 98\% = 0.98$

$$\text{Amount credited} = \frac{\$202.02}{0.98} = \$206.14$$

Proof: $206.14 \times 0.98 = \$202.02$; and $202.02 \times 0.99 = \$200.00$

Example 6 may also be solved by treating the cash discount percent and the anticipation percent earned as though they were chain discounts. Thus by any of the methods used in computing the single-cost equivalent of chain discounts (see Unit 9.1):

The single-discount equivalent of 1% and 2% = 2.98%
    The single-cost equivalent of 1% and 2% = 97.02%

$$\text{and } \frac{\$200.00}{0.9702} = \$206.14$$

Exercise 9.3

Solve the following problems in anticipation:

1   Find (a) anticipation taken at 6 percent and (b) amount remitted by the purchaser on an invoice of $703.56 dated June 17 with terms of net 15, 60-extra if payment in full is made on July 8.

2   On an invoice of $580 with terms of net 30 days as of September 1, find (a) anticipation allowed at 6 percent and (b) amount remitted by the purchaser if the date of the invoice is June 17 and payment in full is made on June 23.

3   On an invoice of $85.22 with terms of 3/10–45 extra, dated July 14, anticipation at 6 percent based on the net invoice is allowed. If payment in full is made on August 8, find (a) the cash discount earned, (b) the

anticipation earned, and (c) the amount received by the seller from the purchaser.

4 Based on the net invoice, if anticipation at 6 percent is allowed, find if paid in full (a) the cash discount earned, (b) the anticipation earned, and (c) the amount remitted by the purchaser to the seller on each of the following: Invoice no. 1, date March 28, net price $85.36, terms 5/10–90 extra, payment made on date; Invoice no 2, date September 2, net price $7450.50, terms 3/30, net 60, payment made September 5; Invoice no. 3, date July 27, net price $1009.82, terms 6/10 e.o.m., payment made August 11.

5 Based on the net invoice less the cash discount, if anticipation at 6 percent is allowed, find for the invoices in Problem 4 (a) the cash discount earned, (b) the anticipation earned, and (c) the amount received by the seller from the purchaser.

6 An invoice with trade discounts of 30, 20, and 10 percent has a total list of $1669.28. Cash terms are net 30, 60 extra. If the date of the invoice is July 28, $450 is paid on August 6, and anticipation at 6 percent is allowed, find the balance due to the seller.

7 Ms. Lowell, proprietor of a novelty store, purchased some goods at a net price of $3567.50 on terms of 3/10 e.o.m. If the invoice was dated May 6 and Ms. Lowell made a partial payment of $1200 on May 11, find the amount of credit that she received if anticipation at 6 percent is allowed based (a) on the net invoice and (b) on the net invoice less the cash discount.

8 On an invoice of $9875.23 with terms of 2/30, 1/60, n/90, dated September 18, a partial payment of $6000 is made on October 3. Compute the amount credited if anticipation at 6 percent is allowed, based (a) on the net invoice and (b) on the net invoice less the cash discount. *Note:* Anticipate only for the remaining number of days in which the cash discount percent earned is allowable.

Unit 9.4

Markup Percents Based on Cost and on Selling Price; Basic Markup Equations

The successful operation of any business depends in large part upon the proper pricing of its goods (or services). This requires that to the cost be added a markup sufficiently high so that the selling price will be large enough to pay the original cost plus all expenses incurred in making the final sale and still leave a satisfactory operating profit.

Markup, or markon, is the difference between cost and selling price.[1]

---

[1] In this text, the terms "markup" and "markon" are synonymous. In common usage, the terms "selling price," "sales," and "retail" have the same meaning.

PERCENTS BASED ON COST Since most manufacturers, many wholesalers, and some retailers take inventories at cost, such concerns are likely to compare sales, markup, expenses, profit or loss, etc., with cost.

Such businesses find that the records of their operations can be kept most easily and expressed best by means of what are known as "cost accounting systems." When a manufacturer quotes percents it may be assumed that the base is cost, not net sales. Since wholesalers and jobbers may use either cost or sales as a base, it is necessary to know whether percent comparisons refer to cost or to sales. Among retailers, the use of cost as a base for percent comparisons is found most commonly in such establishments as furniture stores and jewelry stores, where stock is limited in variety and number of pieces, thus simplifying the problem of keeping a cost inventory, and also in those establishments (notably jewelry stores) where extremely wide variations in the percent of markup of individual items are likely to occur, causing serious discrepancies in the valuation of stocks if a retail base is used.

PERCENTS BASED ON RETAIL Since most retailers find that it is much simpler for them to take inventories at retail (selling price), they are most likely to compare cost, markup, expenses, profit or loss, etc., with net sales.

In such retail establishments, the use of cost as a base for comparisons in percent would require that inventories be taken at cost, thus necessitating the coding of all price tickets or reference to original invoices, either method being slow and costly or necessitating use of electronic, programmed cash registers. Furthermore, among retailers, many expense items are determined by net sales, not by the cost of goods purchased or sold. As examples, salespersons are paid frequently by salary and/or commission or bonus based on net sales, administrative officers often receive salaries and/or bonuses based on net sales, and rental contracts often vary directly with net sales volume. Thus it is reasonable to assume that when a retailer quotes percents, the comparison is with net sales and is not based on cost.

THE BASIC EQUATION IN ALL MARKUP PROBLEMS The solution of all problems in markup on cost or on sales is dependent on an understanding of the following equation and the rules of percentage.

Let C = cost
M = markup
S = selling price

Then $C + M = S$

Example 1   **A pocket calculator cost a wholesaler $32.00. It was marked up $8.00 and a list price of $40.00 was placed on the calculator. If any two of the preceding three terms are known, the third can always be found:**

$$S = C + M \qquad S = 32 + 8 \qquad S = 40$$
$$C = S - M \qquad C = 40 - 8 \qquad C = 32$$
$$M = S - C \qquad M = 40 - 32 \qquad M = 8$$

When percents are attached to the equations, the *base number* may be either *cost* or *selling price*. It is absolutely essential that you know which term is serving as the base number. Thus:

When cost is the base or 100%	%		When selling price is the base or 100%	%
Cost	100		Cost	80
+ Markup	25		+ Markup	20
Selling price	125		Selling price	100

Once you can relate any given quantity to its equivalent percent of the base number, you can find the remainder of the terms in the equation.

WHEN COST IS THE BASE OR 100 PERCENT

Example 2   **To find markup, if cost and the markup percent are given. Find the markup if the cost is $32 and markup is 25 percent of cost.**

Construct a model and enter the given information:

	Number	%
Cost	$32.00	100
+ Markup	+ 8	25
Selling price		125

The base number (cost) and the markup percent of that base number are given. To find markup:

$M = \$32.00 \times .25 = \$8.00$

Example 3   **To find cost if given markup and the markup percent on cost. Find the cost if the markup is $8 and the markup percent is 25 percent of cost.**

	Number	%
Cost	$____	100
+ Markup	+8.00	25
Selling price		125

Since the markup of $8.00 is given along with its equivalent percent of the base number, find the cost (base number):

$$C = \frac{M}{M\%} = \frac{8.00}{.25} = \$32.00$$

Example 4   **To find cost if given selling price and the selling price as a percent of cost. If the selling price is $40.00 and is 125 percent of cost, find the cost.**

	Number	%
Cost	_____	100
+ Markup		25
Selling price	$40.00	125

Since the selling price and its equivalent percent of the base number (cost) are given, find the base number (cost):

$$C = \frac{S}{M\%} = \frac{\$40.00}{1.25} = \$32.00$$

WHEN SELLING PRICE IS THE BASE OR 100 PERCENT

Example 5   **To find markup if given selling price and markup as a percent of selling price. Find the markup if the selling price is $40.00 and the markup is 20 percent of selling price.**

	Number	%
Cost	_____	80
+ Markup		20
Selling price	$40.00	100

The base number (S) and the markup percent of that base number are given. To find markup:

$$M = 40 \times .20 = \$8.00$$

Example 6   **To find selling price if given markup and markup percent of selling price. Find selling price if the markup is $8.00 and the markup percent is 20 percent of the selling price.**

	Number	%
Cost		80
+ Markup	$8.00	20
Selling price		100

The markup is given along with its equivalent percent of the base number (selling price). To find the selling price (base number):

$$S = \frac{M}{M\%} = \frac{\$8.00}{.20} = \$40.00$$

Example 7   **To find selling price if given cost and the cost percent of selling price. If the cost is $32.00 and the cost percent is 80 percent of the selling price, find the selling price.**

	Number	%
Cost	$32.00	80
+ Markup		20
Selling price		100

The cost is given along with its equivalent percent of the base number (selling price). To find the selling price (base number):

$$S = \frac{C}{C\%} = \frac{32}{.80} = \$40.00$$

2. a) 31.50. (M)
   b) 30% (M%)
   c) 130 90 (S%) $\frac{M}{im\%} = \frac{X}{}$

Exercise 9.4

(f) 63.39 M   Solve the following problems:

$\frac{3\cancel{0.5}}{10\,5\cdot0}$ = .03

86.11 (C) **1** A furniture store put a markup of \$20 on a dressing table that cost \$80.
57.69.(C%)   Find (a) the selling price, (b) the markup percent on cost, and (c) the
   selling price as a percent of cost.

(6) a) 84 (c) **2** A jewelry store priced a set of silver-plated flatware at \$136.50. If the cost
   5.80 (S)   was \$105, find (a) the markup, (b) the markup as a percent of cost, and
   145%(S%)   (c) the selling price as a percent of cost.

3 A retailer put a markup of \$20 on a suit that he sold at \$60. Find (a) the
   cost, (b) the markup percent on the selling price, and (c) the cost as a
   percent of selling price.

(8) 75 (S) **4** A buyer in a store put a markup of 42.4 percent of the selling price on
   31.20 (M)   some women's coats that he sold at \$149.50. Find (a) the markup, (b) the
   41.60% 5   cost, and (c) the cost as a percent of selling price.

5 A manufacturer of games sold some decks of novelty playing cards that
   cost him \$12.00 per doz to produce at a price that was 250 percent of his
(6) 9/1 2 45.59   cost. Per dozen, find (a) the selling price, (b) the markup, and (c) the
   b). 2 45.59   markup percent on cost.

E) 13.35% **6** A jobbing house sold toys at a markup of 45 percent on cost. For a toy on
   which the markup was \$1.80, find (a) the cost, (b) the selling price, and
   (c) the selling price as a percent of cost.

7 A sporting-goods store sold golf balls at a markup of \$4.25 per doz. If the
(2) a) 45%   cost was 70 percent of the selling price, find (a) the markup as a percent
   b)/5   of selling price, (b) the selling price per dozen, and (c) the cost per
   c) 71.75 8   dozen.

8 A buyer of men's clothes paid \$43.80 each for a group of suits. If the cost
   was 58.4 percent of the selling price, find per suit (a) the selling price, (b)
   the markup, and (c) the markup as a percent of the selling price.

(4 a) 2 .30 **9** A wholesale house marked up wash dresses 25 percent on cost. If the
   b) 18.40%   selling price was \$20.30 per doz, find per dozen (a) the selling price as a
   c) 81.6%   percent of cost, (b) the cost, and (c) the markup.

10 A wholesaler purchased 600 sweaters for \$1540. If she sold 180 of the
   sweaters at \$2.75 each, 150 at \$2.95 each, 70 at \$3.25 each, 108 at \$3.50
(6 a) 0.63   each, and the remainder as a job lot for \$202.59, find (a) the total selling
   price, (b) the total markup, and (c) the markup percent on cost to nearest
   b) 4.13   hundredth percent.

11 Vicky Schweppe, a drugstore manager, sold a line of cosmetics at a
   c) 118%   markup of 30 percent on the selling price. For a bottle of cologne on
   which the markup was \$2.10, find (a) the selling price, (b) the cost, and
   (c) the cost as a percent of the selling price.

12 Robbie Walling, a seamstress, sold a certain style of dress at a price that was 145 percent of her cost. If the markup was $6.75, find (a) the markup percent on cost, (b) the cost, and (c) the selling price.

13 A merchant put a markup of $5.00 on some goods that cost $20.00. Find (a) the selling price, (b) the markup percent on selling price, and (c) the cost as a percent of selling price.

14 A wholesaler of plumbing supplies priced a faucet at $12.50. If the cost was $10.20, find (a) the markup, (b) the markup as a percent of selling price, and (c) the cost as a percent of selling price.

15 A manufacturer had a markup of $6.50 on some handbags that he sold at $37.50. Find (a) the cost, (b) the markup percent on cost, and (c) the selling price as a percent of cost.

16 A wholesaler put a markup of 18 percent on cost on some goods for which she paid $3.50. Find (a) the markup, (b) the selling price, and (c) the selling price as a percent of the cost.

17 A men's shop placed a selling price of $16.50 on hats that cost 70 percent of the selling price. Find (a) the cost, (b) the markup, and (c) the markup as a percent of selling price.

18 A drugstore sold a line of cosmetics at a markup of 33 percent on the selling price. For a bottle of lotion on which the markup was $1.65, find (a) the selling price, (b) the cost, and (c) the cost as a percent of selling price.

19 A manufacturer of automobile accessories sold rear-view mirrors at a price that was 110 percent of his cost. If the markup was 60 cents, find (a) the markup percent on cost, (b) the cost, and (c) the selling price.

20 A leather-goods manufacturer priced overnight bags at $28.08, which was 124.8 percent of the cost. Find (a) cost, (b) the markup, and (c) the markup as a percent of cost.

21 A store paid $38.00 for table radios. If the markup was 25 percent of the selling price, find (a) the cost as a percent of the selling price, (b) the selling price, and (c) the markup.

22 A buyer purchased a job lot of 240 linen tablecloths for $1920.10. If he sold 110 of the cloths at $16.50 each, 75 at $14.50 each, 30 at $12 each, and the remainder at $9.50 each, find (a) the total selling price, (b) the total markup, and (c) the markup percent on selling price to nearest hundredth percent.

Unit 9.5

Relating Markup Based on Cost to Markup Based on Selling Price

In business, it is frequently desirable to convert from a cost base to a selling-price base—or from a selling-price base to a cost base. Manufacturers who think in terms of a cost base for their own business find it necessary to understand the use of selling price as a base by those retailers and wholesalers who are their customers and who prefer to think in terms of a selling-price base. In like manner, it is helpful to such retailers and wholesalers to understand and to compare readily their operations with those of manufacturers who think in terms of a cost base.

TO CONVERT MARKUP PERCENT ON COST TO SELLING PRICE, OR ON SELLING PRICE TO COST   An article costing $2 and marked up $1 to a selling price (sales or retail) of $3 has a markup on cost of $1 ÷ $2 = $\frac{1}{2}$ = 0.50 = 50 percent, and a markup on selling price of $1 ÷ $3 = 0.33$\frac{1}{3}$ = 33$\frac{1}{3}$ percent. Thus a markup of 50 percent on cost is equivalent to a markup of 33$\frac{1}{3}$ percent on selling price.

Formulas to express the above conversion of the markup on cost to the equivalent markup on sales and vice versa are as follows:

To find the equivalent markup on sales from a given markup on cost:

$$\frac{\text{Markup on cost}}{1 + \text{markup on cost}} = \text{markup on sales}$$

(selling price)

Example 1   **If the given markup on cost is 50 percent, find the equivalent markup on sales.**

$$\frac{0.50}{1 + 0.50} = \frac{0.50}{1.50} = 33\frac{1}{3}\% \text{ markup on sales}$$

To find the equivalent markup on cost from a given markup on sales:

$$\frac{\text{Markup on sales}}{1 - \text{markup on sales}} = \text{markup on cost}$$

(cost price)

Example 2   **If the given markup on sales is 33$\frac{1}{3}$ percent, find the equivalent markup on cost.**

$$\frac{0.33\frac{1}{3}}{1 - 0.33\frac{1}{3}} = \frac{0.33\frac{1}{3}}{0.66\frac{2}{3}} = 50\% \text{ markup on cost}$$

Another relationship between markup based on cost and markup based on selling price can readily be seen in the following:

Markup based on cost price	Equivalent markup based on selling price
$\frac{1}{3}$	$\frac{1}{4}$
$\frac{1}{4}$	$\frac{1}{5}$
$\frac{1}{5}$	$\frac{1}{6}$
$\frac{2}{3}$	$\frac{2}{5}$
$\frac{3}{4}$	$\frac{3}{7}$

If you observe the preceding fractions, you will see that the numerators in the equivalents are the same; only the denominators vary. Furthermore, you will notice that the denominator of each markup on sales equals the sum of the numerator and denominator of the equivalent cost fraction. Thus a markup of $\frac{1}{8}$ on cost equals a markup of $\frac{1}{9}$ on selling price, $\frac{2}{5}$ markup on cost equals a markup of $\frac{2}{8}$ on retail, etc.

You will also observe that the denominator of each markup on cost equals the difference in the numerator and denominator of the equivalent sales fraction. Thus a markup of $\frac{1}{7}$ on selling price equals a markup of $\frac{1}{6}$ on cost, $\frac{3}{5}$ markup on retail equals a markup of $\frac{3}{2}$ (or $1\frac{1}{2}$ times) on cost, etc.

Percent markups may be converted to their equivalents in the same manner.

Exercise 9.5

Find markup based on sales, expressing as a fraction in lowest terms, when the markup based on cost is:

1 $\frac{1}{9}$ 2 $\frac{3}{5}$ 3 $\frac{2}{3}$ 4 $1\frac{5}{18}$

Find markup based on cost, expressed as a fraction in lowest terms, when the markup based on sales is:

5 $\frac{3}{8}$ 6 $\frac{2}{5}$ 7 $\frac{9}{10}$ 8 $\frac{5}{7}$

Find markup based on sales to nearest hundredth percent, when the markup based on cost is:

9 50%   10 20%   11 125%   12 30%

Find markup based on cost to nearest hundredth percent, when the markup based on sales is:

13 50%   14 42%   15 24%   16 64%

Complete the following models. Give dollar-and-cents answers to nearest cent, and percent answers to nearest hundredth percent. The first model is given as a sample.

#		Number	%		Number	%
17	Cost	$120	100	Cost	$120	60
	+ Markup	$ 80	66.67	+ Markup	$ 80	40
	Sales	$200	166.67	Sales	$200	100
18	C	$ 12.50	100	C	$ 12.50	18.82
	+ M	$ 8.25	70	+ M	$ 8.25	41.18
	S	$ 21.25	170	S	$ 21.25	100
19	C	$ 1.25	100	C	$ 1.25	.641
	+ M	$ 0.7	56	+ M	$ 0.7	35.90
	S	$ 1.95	156	S	$ 1.95	100
20	C	$ 1.86	100	C	$ 1.86	63.1
	+ M	$ 1.09	18.60	+ M	$ 1.09	36.90
	S	$ 2.95	158.60	S	$ 2.95	100
21	C	$ 2.55	100	C	$ 2.55	59.96
	+ M	$ 1.70	66.6)	+ M	$ 1.70	60.04
	S	$ 6.25	166.67	S	$ 6.25	100
22	C	$ 12.50	100	C	$ 12.50	62.86
	+ M	$ 7.45	59.60	+ M	$ 7.45	37.34
	S	$ 19.95	159.60	S	$ 19.95	100

$$\frac{C}{S} = e\%$$

#		Number	%		Number	%
23	C	$ 95.00	100	C	$ 95.00	56.29
	+ M	$ 80.00	84.21	+ M	$ 80.00	85.21
	S	$ 125.00	184.21	S	$ 125.00	100
24	C	$ 1.15	100	C	$ 1.15	57.5
	+ M	$ 0.85	23.91	+ M	$ 0.85	42.50
	S	$ 2	123.91	S	$ 2	100
25	C	$ 117.99	100	C	$ 117.99	62.00
	+ M	$ 71.51	60.86	+ M	$ 71.51	38.00
	S	$189.50	160.86	S	$189.50	100
26	C	$ 14.50	100	C	$ 14.50	64.44
	+ M	$ 8	55.17	+ M	$ 8	35.58
	S	$ 22.50	155.1	S	$ 22.50	100
27	C	$ 27.50	100	C	$ 27.50	61.11
	+ M	$ 17.50	63.64	+ M	$ 17.50	38.89
	S	$ 45.00	163.64	S	$ 45.00	100
28	C	$ 0.75	100	C	$ 0.75	53.96
	+ M	$ 0.64	81.33	+ M	$ 0.64	46.04
	S	$ 1.39	185.33	S	$ 1.39	100

$$\frac{x}{1+x} = \frac{3}{8}$$

$$8x = 3 + 3x$$

$$= \frac{3}{5}$$

$$\frac{x}{1-8} = \frac{1}{9}$$

$$9x = 1 - x$$

$$8x = 1$$

Unit 9.6   Retail Operating Statements[1]

In business, the primary purpose of an operating statement is to show the profit or loss for a given period of time.

In mercantile establishments, if there is to be a profit, it is apparent that sales must be in excess of cost of the merchandise sold plus the operating expenses. If sales are less than merchandise cost plus operating expenses, then the store will have operated at a loss. The equation is

Operating profit or loss = sales − (cost of goods sold + expenses)

This equation may be restated as follows:

$$\text{Sales} = \frac{\text{cost of}}{\text{goods sold}} + \frac{\text{operating}}{\text{expenses}} + \frac{\text{operating profit}}{\text{(or − loss)}}$$

In an operating statement, the main elements are (1) net sales, (2) cost of goods sold, (3) gross margin, (4) operating expenses, (5) operating profit or loss.[2]

Example 1   **Abbott Specialty Store.**

Operating statement for year ending Jan. 31, 19—

Gross sales	$27,500.00	
Less sales returns and allowances	−3,500.00	
Net sales		$24,000.00
Less cost of goods sold		−17,500.00
Gross margin		$ 6,500.00
Less operating expenses		− 4,200.00
Operating profit		$ 2,300.00

Net sales represent the actual dollars of income. *Gross sales* less merchandise returns, allowances to customers, and any discounts granted to customers equal net sales.

---

[1]See operating statement of the Carter Clothing Store on pp. 390–391 for a much more complete operating statement and a summary of the methods of computing the various items in dollars and in percents.

[2]The complete operating statement goes on from this point to include other income and expense, income taxes, extraordinary gains and losses, and earnings per share. However, the operating profit is an important stopping point for managers in assessing the effectiveness of the merchandising operations. Some of these items are presented in later chapters, and accounting courses deal with them in depth.

Example 2   **If gross sales are $102,673.50, merchandise returns $8674.20, customer allowances $975.38, and discounts to customers $1238.14, what are net sales?**

Gross sales		$102,673.50
Less:		
Merchandise returns	$8674.20	
Customer allowances	975.38	
Customer discounts allowed	1238.14	
		−10,887.72
Net sales		$ 91,785.78

     Cost of goods sold is the sum of the beginning inventory at cost plus
billed cost of purchases plus transportation in, less the cash discounts earned
on purchases from vendors, plus workroom or alteration costs, less final
inventory at cost.

Example 3   **If the beginning inventory is $42,682.34 at cost, purchases $75,614 at billed
cost with an average earned cash discount of 2 percent from vendors, freight
in $3842, alteration costs $1000 and final inventory $38,675.53 at cost, what is
the cost of goods sold?**

Beginning inventory		$ 42,682.34
Plus net cost of purchases:		
Net purchases	$75,614.00	
Freight in	+3,842.00	
Gross cost of purchases	$79,456.00	
Less 2% of net purchases	−1,512.28	
Net cost of purchases		77,943.72
Plus alteration costs		+ 1,000.00
Merchandise available for sale		$121,626.06
Less ending inventory		−38,675.53
Cost of goods sold		$ 82,950.53

     Gross margin (or gross profit) is the difference between net sales and
cost of goods sold. It is also the sum of the expenses plus operating profit or
minus operating loss.

Example 4   **If net sales are $32,398 and cost of goods sold is $24,865, what is the gross
margin?**

Net sales	$32,398.00
Less cost of goods sold	−24,865.00
Gross margin	$ 7,533.00

     Expenses are the cost of operating the business and must be paid out of
gross margin. If they exceed the gross margin, there is an operating loss; if
they are less than the gross margin, there is an operating profit.
     Operating profit or loss is the remainder after expenses have been
subtracted (or paid for) from the gross margin.

Example 5   **If expenses are $8534 and gross margin is $9096, what is the operating profit or loss?**

Gross margin	$9096.00
Less expenses	−8534.00
Operating profit	$ 562.00

Example 6   **If expenses are $5852 and operating loss is $938, what is the gross margin?**

Expenses	$5852.00
Less operating loss	−938.00
Gross margin	$4914.00

ATTACHING PERCENTS TO RETAIL OPERATING STATEMENTS[1]   Retail statements are usually presented with percent adjacent to the dollar amounts. Presenting the percents helps in communicating the data and facilitates comparison between different departments, different years of the same department, etc. The presence of the percents also assists in filling in statements with certain amounts missing or unknown.

Retail operating statements are presented with the net sales figure as representing the base number. All other major components of the operating statement are then percentages of the net sales base. Thus:

	Amount	Percent
Abbott Specialty Store		
Gross sales	$27,500	
Less sales returns and allowances	−3,500	
Net sales	$24,000	100.00%
Less cost of goods sold	17,500	72.92
Gross margin	$ 6,500	27.08
Less operating expenses	4,200	17.50
Operating profit	$ 2,300	9.58

FINDING MISSING QUANTITIES BY USE OF THE PERCENTS   In the analysis of operating statements, planning and budgeting, measuring merchandise losses by fire, theft or other casualty, etc., the knowledge and use of the inter- and intrarelationships of the percents in financial statements are most essential. A few of these uses are presented here, and others are presented in Chapter 11.

---

[1] A more intensive presentation of financial statements and percents is given in Chapter 11.

Example 7   **The sales department of G & S Manufacturing Co. forecasts net sales for 1980 at $1,400,000. Cost of sales will average 60 percent and operating expenses 25 percent. Construct the estimated operating statement of the G & S Manufacturing Co. for 1980.**

A sound procedure is to draft the income statement, place the known amounts and percents in the proper columns, and then proceed to fill in the blanks.

Estimated Operating Statement

	Amount	Percent
Sales	$1,400,000	100
Less cost of sales	*840,000*	60
Gross margin	$ *560,000*	*40*
Less operating expenses	*350,000*	25
Operating profit	$ *210,000*	*15*

The numbers and percents in *italic type* are the figures placed in the statement after the given information was entered.

Cost of sales	$1,400,000 × .60	= $840,000
Gross margin	$1,400,000 − 840,000	= $560,000
Operating expenses	$1,400,000 × .25	= $350,000
Operating profit	$560,000 − 350,000	= $210,000

Example 8   **An unfortunate riot during a power failure completely looted the ABC Men's Clothing Store. The books were posted up to the date of the catastrophe and disclosed the following:**

Net sales from Jan. 1 to date of looting	$460,000
Inventory of merchandise on hand Jan. 1 (at cost)	$50,000
Net cost of merchandise purchased from January 1 to date of looting	$310,000

The accounting records also disclosed that the ABC Men's Clothing Store had an average of a 35 percent gross profit margin over the past several years. There is no reason to believe that a 35 percent gross profit margin did not prevail up to the date of the looting. Find the estimated cost of the merchandise lost in the riot.

Draft the operating statement down to the *Gross margin* and fill in the given data:

	Amount	Percent
Sales	$460,000	100
Less cost of goods sold:		
Beginning inventory $ 50,000		
Add purchases 310,000		
Merchandise available for sale 360,000		
Less ending inventory 61,000		
Cost of goods sold	299,000	65.00
Gross margin	$161,000	35.00

The number and percents in *italic type* were placed in the statement after all the given information was entered in the statement.

Gross margin $460,000 × 35%   = $161,000
Cost of goods sold $460,000 − 161,000 = $299,000

Once the cost of goods sold is determined, it can then be subtracted from the merchandise available for sale and the estimated amount of the merchandise in the store at the time of the looting (ending inventory) determined.

$360,000 − 299,000 = $61,000

Exercise 9.6

1 Net sales were $182,520.20, purchases were $101,461 at billed cost with an average earned cash discount of 2 percent, freight was $4638.84, workroom and alteration costs were $3641.06, beginning inventory at cost was $48,341.72, and ending inventory at cost was $30,856.39. Find the gross margin in dollars.

2 Gross sales are $31,243.79, customer returns, allowances, and cash discounts are $3246.16, beginning inventory at cost is $11,005.42, purchases at billed cost are $17,824.34, freight in is $1230.40, workroom costs are $506.87, cash discounts earned from vendors average 1.5 percent, and ending inventory at cost is $13,348.51. What is the gross margin in dollars?

3 Gross sales are $65,724.48, customer returns and allowances are $7366.25, total merchandise available for sale is $85,274.40 at cost, ending inventory at cost is $48,720.84, and expenses are $21,835.59. What is the operating profit or loss in dollars?

4 Gross sales are $195,720, returns and allowances are $21,650, cash discounts granted customers are $2780, beginning inventory at cost is $57,230, workroom and alteration costs are $4675, cash discounts earned from vendors are $6520, freight in is $7975, purchases at billed cost are $119,358, ending inventory at cost is $55,209, and expenses are $39,481. What is the operating profit or loss in dollars?

5 If gross sales are $26,700.75, merchandise returns $8520.30, customer allowances $1362.65, and cash discounts to customers $2051.93, what are net sales?

6 Customer returns and allowances total $5704.34, cash discounts to customers are $1255.21, and net sales are $92,880.92. What are gross sales?

7 Beginning inventory is $32,600.00 at cost, purchases are $64,286.35 at billed cost with an average earned discount of 1.0 percent, freight in is $5201.79, and final inventory is $35,121.43 at cost. What is the cost of goods sold?

8 Beginning inventory was $36,208.85 at cost, purchases were $56,305.50 at billed cost with an average earned discount of 2.25 percent, freight in was $2833.46, and cost of goods sold was $48,993.52. What was the ending inventory at cost?

9 The Wright Welding Works desires a gross margin in 1980 of $120,000, which is normally 30 percent of sales. Operating expenses are budgeted for 25 percent of sales. Draft the estimated operating statement for 1980.

10 Hurricane Alice completely destroyed the Crunchy Taco Warehouse and all its merchandise. From books kept in the main office, the following was determined:

Sales from July 1, to date of destruction	$520,000
Inventory of merchandise July 1	80,000
Purchases of merchandise from July 1 to date of hurricane	330,000
Gross profit margin experienced for the last 5 years	40 percent

Find the amount of merchandise lost.

Chapter 10

Problems in Retailing

Objectives To Be Achieved in This Chapter

1 *Work with percents in solving the more complex problems in retail markup and pricing.*
2 *Calculate merchandise stock turnovers and other analytical retail operating relationships.*
3 *Work with ratios and formulas in analyzing and finding amounts in retail operating statements.*

Much of Chapter 9, Purchase Discounts and Markup, was an introduction to the subject of retail-store mathematics, and it is suggested that you refresh your memory, if necessary, with a few minutes review of that chapter before attempting work in the present chapter.

TERMINOLOGY OF RETAILING   To continue with the subject of retailing, it is necessary that you become acquainted with the terms that follow. The definitions for each of these terms, though some are perhaps difficult to understand at first reading, will be fully explained in this chapter.

Net cost is the price paid by the retailer to the manufacturer or distributor after trade discounts, cash discounts if earned, and anticipation if taken have been deducted from the invoice.

Net delivered cost is net cost plus transportation charges.

Gross delivered cost is the cost after trade discounts have been taken plus transportation charges, but *does not include* cash discounts earned or anticipation taken. Some stores do not treat cash discounts earned and anticipation taken as part of the store operating statement but classify them as "other income earned," thus adding them to the store operating statement in determining a total profit or loss statement of the business.

Original retail price is the first price placed on merchandise. It may be reduced by means of markdowns or increased by means of additional markons. *Note:* In this text, the terms "markon" and "markup" are synonymous.

Retail or *selling price* is the price of the merchandise at any given time; or after a sale has been completed, it is the net selling price.

Initial markup is the difference between the gross delivered cost and the original retail price. Expressed in dollars, it is ordinarily used in reference to a single purchase rather than a series of purchases. Expressed in percent, it is a predetermined optimum markup percent that the retailer attempts to secure on all purchases.

Cumulative markup is the difference between the total of the beginning inventory at cost plus the gross delivered cost of purchases less purchase returns at cost and the total of the beginning inventory at retail plus the purchases at retail less the purchase returns at retail plus any net additional markups.

Gross margin or *gross profit* is the difference between net sales and the cost of goods sold. It is equal to the maintained markup plus cash discounts earned and minus alteration costs.

Maintained markup is equal to the gross margin less cash discounts earned and plus alteration costs. It is equivalent to the initial markup in dollars less markdowns and shortages.

Markdown is a reduction in price below the original selling price. It is the difference between the original price and the reduced price.

Gross markdown is the total of one or a series of markdowns in the original selling price.

Markdown cancellation is a revision of a reduced price upward to, but not above, the original price.

Net markdown is the final amount of the markdown. It reflects the net downward change in the original selling price and is expressed in dollars or as a percent of net sales.

Additional markup is an increase above the original selling price. It is the difference between the original price and the increased price.

Additional markup cancellation is a revision of an increased price downward to, but not below, the original price.

Net additional markup is the final amount of the increase in the original selling price. It reflects the net upward change in the original selling price and is expressed in dollars or as a percent of net sales.

Shortages are losses at retail that occur through breakage, unrecorded markdowns and allowances, theft, or mysterious disappearance.

Reductions include both markdowns and shortages at retail.

Deductions include net sales, markdowns, and shortages at retail.

Inventory at retail is expressed either as a book inventory or as a physical inventory. The book inventory at retail is equivalent to merchandise available for sale at retail less net sales, less markdowns, less anticipated shortages. The physical inventory at retail is determined by an actual count of the goods in stock.

Inventory at cost is expressed either as a book inventory or as a physical inventory. It is found by multiplying the inventory at retail by the complement of the cumulative markup percent.

Unit 10.1   *Markup Based on Retail and the Use of Complements*

Standard practice among retailers is to base the markup percent on retail. Therefore whenever markup percent quoted by a retailer is given without a statement as to whether it is based on cost or on selling price, it is justifiable to assume that the markup percent is based on selling price.

The term "markup" may refer to an individual item, a group of items, or even an entire inventory of stock. Thus an item selling for $2 with a markup of 80 cents and an inventory at retail of $500,000 with a markup of $200,000 may both be referred to as having a markup of 40 percent.

USE OF COMPLEMENTS IN RETAIL CALCULATIONS   Since retailers consider the selling price as 100 percent and since cost plus markup equals the selling price, the cost percent and the markup percent total 100 percent and are complementary. Thus:

Markup 35%, cost is 65%   Cost 80%, markup is 20%
Markup 40%, cost is 60%   Cost $66\frac{2}{3}$%, markup is $33\frac{1}{3}$%
Markup 25%, cost is 75%   Cost 58%, markup is 42%
Markup 55%, cost is 45%   Cost 47%, markup is 53%

Therefore, if markup percent for a given inventory at retail is known, cost in dollars is readily found by multiplying the value of the inventory at retail by the decimal equivalent of the cost percent (complement of markup percent).

Example 1   **What is the cost in dollars of $230,000 worth of stock at retail if the markup is 30 percent of retail?**

$$100\% - 30\% = 70\%$$
$$70\% = 0.70$$
$$\$230,000.00 \times 0.70 = \$161,000.00 \quad \text{Cost}$$

If the cost percent on a given inventory at retail is known, the markup in dollars is found by multiplying the value of the inventory at retail by the decimal equivalent of the markup percent (complement of cost percent).

Example 2   **What is the markup in dollars on $230,000 worth of stock at retail if the cost is 70 percent of retail?**

$$100\% - 70\% = 30\%$$
$$30\% = 0.30$$
$$\$230,000.00 \times 0.30 = \$69,000.00 \quad \text{Markup}$$

FINDING THE VALUES OF RETAIL, COST, AND MARKUP   Whether determining dollars or percents, the following equation is basic:

Retail = cost + markup

From this equation the following are derived:

Cost = retail − markup
Markup = retail − cost

When any two of the values in dollars or percent are known, it is apparent that the third value is found readily. Perhaps the simplest form in which the problem of determining all three elements (in dollars and as percents of retail) may be presented is when any two are known in dollars. Thus in the following the missing dollar value is obvious:

Retail = cost   + markup
R = \$120.00 + \$80.00
\$200.00 = C + \$80.00
\$200.00 = \$120.00 + M

Once all three dollar values are known, the percent equivalents of retail may then be found as follows:

$$\text{Retail} \qquad = \text{cost} \qquad + \text{markup}$$

As percents of retail: $\dfrac{200}{200}$ or $100\% = \dfrac{120}{200}$ or $60\% + \dfrac{80}{200}$ or 40%

If only one of the elements (retail, or cost, or markup) is known in dollars *and a retail percent equivalent of the cost or of the markup is known,* then the solution for one of the missing dollar figures may be found.

In the schedules below, *italic type* represents desired figures. Given retail of $200 and cost 60 percent of retail:

	Amount	Percent
Retail	$200	100
Cost	$*120*	60
Markup	*80*	*40*
	$200	100

$C = $200 \times .60 = 120
$M = $200 \times .40 = 80

Given cost of $120 and cost 60 percent of retail:

	Amount	Percent
Retail	$*200*	*100*
Cost	120	60
Markup	*80*	*40*
	$200	100

$\text{Retail} = \dfrac{C}{C\%} = \dfrac{120}{.60} = 200

$M = $200 \times .40$

Given markup of $80 and cost 60 percent of retail:

	Amount	Percent
Retail	$*200*	*100*
Cost	*120*	60
Markup	80	*40*
	$200	*100*

$\dfrac{M}{M\%} = \dfrac{80}{.40} = 200

$C = $200 \times .60 = 120
$M\% = 100\% - 60\% = 40\%$

Note: Since *retail* is the *base number,* 100 percent can be entered immediately in the schedule opposite retail. Since cost + markup = retail, 100 percent can also be entered as the total percent for cost + markup. Once these numbers and the given numbers are entered in the schedule, the procedure to the completion of the schedule should be made clear.

Exercise 10.1

Complete the following schedules. Give dollars-and-cents answers to nearest cent, and percent answers to nearest hundredth percent. Retail is the base number or 100 percent in all cases.

		Amount	Percent
1	Retail	$175	
	Cost	$	60
	Markup		
		$	

		Amount	Percent
2	Retail	$225	
	Cost	$	
	Markup		30.24
		$	

		Amount	Percent
3	Retail	$	
	Cost	$125	40
	Markup		
		$	

		Amount	Percent
4	Retail	$	
	Cost	$ 3.51	
	Markup		41.50
		$	

	5 Retail	$____	___		6 Retail	$____	___
	Cost	$____	75		Cost	$____	
	Markup	$230	___		Markup	$104.15	41.66
		$____	___			$____	___

Solve the following, finding required percents to nearest hundredths. Unless otherwise stipulated, assume that percents are based on retail in this and all following exercises in this chapter.

7 A manufacturer of women's handbags wishes to obtain a profit of 15 percent on cost on some handbags that cost him $6.12 to produce. If he allows terms of 4/10 e.o.m., what price will he ask?

8 A buyer wishes to purchase sports coats to retail at $30.00. If she is required to obtain a minimum markup of 20 percent, what is the maximum price that she can pay for each coat?

9 A buyer purchases a group of shirts at $6.50 each. If the cost is 50.0 percent, what is his planned selling price per shirt?

10 A buyer purchases some dresses at $22.50. (a) What price must she mark the dresses to obtain a markup of 43 percent? (b) What would be the markup percent if the dresses are priced at $35? (c) What would be the markup percent if the dresses are priced at $42.50?

11 A buyer of men's furnishings paid $12.00 per doz for some wool neckties. If his markup was 20 percent, what was the selling price per necktie?

12 If the markup on a chair was $71.49 and the cost was 52.34 percent, find (a) retail and (b) cost.

13 A buyer purchases a job lot of 160 sweaters for $960. If he prices 60 of the sweaters at $7.31, 45 of the sweaters at $7.80, and the remainder at $8.58, what markup percent does he obtain on the entire job lot?

14 A buyer is offered a job lot of 96 robes on which she must obtain a minimum markup of 39.64 percent. If she intends to retail 40 of the robes at $34.95, 32 of the robes at $24.95, and the remainder at $19.95, what is the maximum total price she can afford to pay for the 96 robes?

Unit 10.2   Cumulative Markup[1]

The retail method of determining inventory at cost (and then cost of goods sold) is found by multiplying the inventory at retail by the complement of the cumulative markup percent. The cumulative markup in dollars is found by determining the difference between the total of the beginning inventory at cost plus the gross delivered cost of purchases less purchase returns at cost and the total of the beginning inventory at retail plus the purchases at retail plus the net additional markups. Additional markups are increases in original selling prices.

[1] It should be specially noted that cumulative markup at the end of any given period of time is thought of as initial markup (markup of beginning inventory) at the beginning of the next period of time.

The cumulative markup *percent* is found by dividing the cumulative markup in dollars by the value of the merchandise at retail.

Note particularly that the markup of a beginning inventory is the cumulative markup of the immediately preceding ending inventory. Note also that whereas net additional markups *are* taken into account in computing cumulative markup, earned cash discounts, markdowns, shortages, and alteration costs *are not* considered in computing cumulative markup.

The method used in determining cumulative markup in dollars and in percent is illustrated in the following examples.

Example 1 If the January 1 inventory at retail is $48,000 and its valuation at cost is $30,000, what is the cumulative markup (a) in dollars and (b) in percent (to nearest hundredths) on January 31, if purchases during the month cost $25,000 and were priced at $40,000 and net additional markups were $2000?

	Cost	Retail
January 1 inventory	$30,000.00	$48,000.00
Plus gross purchases	25,000.00	40,000.00
Plus net additional markups	+	+2,000.00
Total merchandise available	$55,000.00	$90,000.00

(a) Cumulative markup in dollars $= 90,000.00 - 55,000.00 = \$35,000$

(b) Cumulative markup in percent $= \dfrac{35,000}{90,000} = 38.89\%$

The cost valuation of inventory at any time may be determined by multiplying the inventory at retail by the complement of the cumulative markup percent. (The cost of goods sold at any time may be determined by subtracting the ending inventory at cost from the cost valuation of the total merchandise available.) This complement is also known as the cost equivalent and may be obtained directly. Thus in Example 1:

Complement of cumulative markup
percent or cost equivalent $= 1.0000 - 0.3889 = 0.6111 = 61\ 11\%$

or directly $= \dfrac{55,000.00}{90,000.00} = 0.6111 = 61.11\%$

Cumulative markup percent $= 1.0000 - 0.6111 = 0.3889 = 38.89\%$

Example 2 Stock on hand March 1 is $100,000 at retail with an initial markup of 40 percent (the cumulative markup on February 28), purchases during the month are $37,700 at cost with a markup of 35 percent, net additional markons total $4000, and the ending inventory on March 31 per actual count is $96,500 at retail. Find (a) the cumulative markup in dollars, (b) the cumulative markup percent, and (c) the cost valuation of the ending inventory, (d) the deduction at retail, and (e) the cost of goods sold.

Decimal equivalent of cost of beginning inventory $= 1.00 - 0.40 = 0.60$
Decimal equivalent of cost of purchases $\quad\quad = 1.00 - 0.35 = 0.65$

	Cost	Retail
Beginning inventory $100,000.00 × 0.60 = $60,000.00		$100,000.00

Plus gross purchases 37,700.00 $\dfrac{37,700.00}{0.65}$ = 58,000.00

Plus net additional markup   + 4,000.00

Total merchandise available $97,700.00 $162,000.00

Ending inventory (per actual count) $96,500.00

(a) Cumulative markup in dollars = $162,000.00 − $97,700.00 = $64,300.00

(b) Cumulative markup in percent = $\dfrac{\$64,300}{\$162,000}$ = 39.69%

(c) Cumulative valuation of ending inventory:

Cost percent = 100% − 39.691358   = 60.308642%

Cost percent if found directly $\dfrac{97,700}{162,000}$ = 60.308642%

Cost valuation in dollars = 96,500 × .60308642   = $58,197.84

(d) Deduction from total goods available at retail by net
sales, markdowns, and shortages: $162,000 − $96,500   = $65,500.00

(e) Cost of goods sold (actually cost of merchandise sold,
markdowns, and cost of shortages) $65,500 × .60308642 = $39,502.16

or

Cost valuation of goods available $97,700
Less cost valuation of ending
inventory   58,197.84 $39,502.16

In the above example, note the number of decimals in the percent calculated
for markup and cost. When the dollar amounts are large, use additional
decimal places to obtain the desired accuracy.[1]

In solving problems requiring determination of the cost valuation of
the ending inventory and/or the cost of goods sold, the following "setup
form" or model should be helpful.

	Cost	Retail
Beginning inventory	$____	$____
Add: Gross purchases	____	____
Net additional markups	x x x x	____
Total goods available	$____	$____
Less deductions:		
Net sales		($)
Markdowns		($)
Shortages		($)
Ending inventory at retail per actual count		$____
Less ending inventory at cost valuation	____	
Cost of goods sold	$____	

[1] The procedure for calculating retail inventory illustrated above determines the ending inventory by
what is known in accounting as the "cost or market, whichever is lower" method. Other ways of
calculating inventory by the retail method exist and can be found in accounting courses.

Exercise 10.2

In the following problems, assume that purchases means *gross* purchases. Unless otherwise stipulated, assume that percents are based on retail in this and the following exercises in retailing.

1   On August 1, inventory at retail is $95,000 and its valuation at cost is $45,000. If purchases during the month cost $28,600 and are priced at $54,000 and additional markups are $5000, what is the cumulative markup percent (to nearest hundredths) for the period ending August 31?

2   Beginning inventory on April 1 is $75,000 at retail, with a markup of 45 percent. Purchases at retail during the month total $96,000 and are marked up 41 percent. What is the cumulative markup percent (to nearest hundredths) on April 30?

3   On July 1, beginning inventory is $45,000 at cost, with a markup of 10.0 percent. *Note:* This is the cumulative markup percent for June 30. Purchases during the month are marked up 20 percent and total $60,000 at retail. What is the cumulative markup percent (to nearest hundredths) on July 31?

4   On October 1, inventory at retail of $35,724 had a cost valuation of $21,945. Purchases during October cost $18,276 and were priced to retail at $28,200. During the month, net additional markups were $1882. Deductions (sales + markdowns + shortages) were $38,827. What was the cost valuation of the ending inventory? (In solving, compute cumulative markup or its complement to eight decimal places.)

5   The records of the linen department of the Franklin Department Store contain the following information for the period from April 1 to June 30. Beginning inventory was $3775 at cost, $6250 at retail; purchases were $10,000 at cost, $16,900 at retail; gross additional markups were $750 at retail and additional markup cancellations were $150; deductions (net sales plus markdowns plus shortages) totaled $16,800. Find (a) the ending inventory at cost and (b) the cost of goods sold.

6   On July 1, stock at retail is $257,000 with cumulative markup to date of 39.32 percent. Purchases at retail during the following quarter total $552,000, with a markup of 43.75 percent. Net additional markups during the quarter are $11,000. On September 30, inventory at retail is $278,800. Find (a) the deductions at retail, (b) the cost valuation of the ending inventory, and (c) the cost of goods sold. (In solving, compute the decimal equivalent of the cumulative markup or its complement to eight decimal places.)

7   On December 1, the inventory at retail of the Reed Dress Shop was $7432.40, and cumulative markup on that date was 38.2 percent. Purchases during December totaled $4608.65 at retail, with an average markup of 43.8 percent. Sales and other deductions were $8057.95. What was the cost valuation of the ending inventory? (In solving, compute the decimal equivalent of the cumulative markup or its complement to eight decimal places.)

8   If beginning inventory of $18,360 cost $10,937, sales and other deductions totaled $14,500, and ending inventory of $16,725 cost $10,308, find the markup percent (to nearest hundredths) on purchases. (In solving,

compute the decimal equivalent of the cumulative markup or its complement to eight decimal places.)

Unit 10.3   *Initial Markup;*
                                                Averaging Markup

---

Unless the original or initial markup (M_i), the difference between cost and
original retail price, is sufficiently high to cover planned expenses and
planned operating profit, there will be a loss or profits will not be as large as
desired. Thus if planned expenses are 30 percent and planned operating
profit is 5 percent, the markup would need to be 35 percent.

Thus initial markup percent $(M_i\%)$ expressed as a formula would be

$$M_i\% = \frac{\text{expenses} + \text{planned profits}}{\text{sales}}$$

Example 1   **If expenses are estimated as 32 percent and planned operating profit is 6
percent, what should be the initial markup percent?** (*Note:* **Sales are 100
percent.**)

$$M_i\% = \frac{32 + 6}{100} = \frac{38}{100} = 0.38-= 38\%$$

Example 2   **If expenses are estimated at $27,500, planned operating profit at $5000, and
net sales at $92,500, what should be the initial markup percent?**

$$M_i\% = \frac{\$27,500.00 + \$5000.00}{\$92,500.00} = \frac{\$32,500.00}{\$92,500.00} = 0.3514 = 35.14\%$$

Furthermore, certain other elements must be considered, for they also
will affect the gross margin required. These are markdowns, shortages,
alteration expenses, and cash discounts earned.

Past experience enables the merchant to predetermine the amount of
markdowns, shortages, and alteration and/or workroom costs that will
probably occur on any given group of merchandise. These must be added to
the probable expenses and desired operating profit in determining a profitable selling price. Since markdowns and stock shortages also constitute a
deduction from the original price in addition to increasing the margin
required, they must be added to the probable net selling price.

Because cash discounts from vendors (on purchases) are deducted from
the cost of merchandise, the lowered cost increases the margin between cost
and selling price. In calculating the initial markup, it is therefore necessary to
subtract the amount of the cash discounts.

With these adjustments, the initial markup equation becomes

$$M_i\% = \frac{\begin{array}{c}\text{expenses} + \text{planned profit} + \text{markdowns} + \text{stock shortages} \\ + \text{alteration cost} - \text{purchase discounts}\end{array}}{\text{net sales} + \text{markdowns} + \text{stock shortages}}$$

The items in the denominator (e.g., net sales plus markdowns plus stock shortages) are called deductions.

Example 3   **What should be the initial markup percent if expenses are estimated at 30 percent, operating profit desired 5 percent, markdowns 9 percent, shortages 3 percent, alteration expenses 2 percent, and cash discounts earned 4.2 percent?**

$$M_i\% = \frac{30 + 5 + 9 + 3 + 2 - 4.2}{100 + 9 + 3} = 0.40 = 40\%$$

Example 4   **What should be the initial markup percent on sales of $200,000 if expenses are estimated at $56,000, markdowns at $15,000, shortages at $5000, alteration cost at $2500, and cash discounts earned from vendors at $4500, if an operating profit of $12,000 is desired?**

$$M_i\% = \frac{\$56,000.00 + \$12,000.00 + \$15,000.00 + \$5000.00 + \$2500.00 - \$4500.00}{\$200,000.00 + \$15,000.00 + \$5000.00}$$

$$= 0.3909 = 39.09\%$$

AVERAGING MARKUP   Merchants frequently have the opportunity of purchasing, at a low average cost, job lots of merchandise that should be marked at two retail prices because of the varying grades of quality within the assortment.

The problem confronting the merchant is to determine the number of units that should be placed at the lower price and at the higher price in order to maintain an average required initial markup.

Example 5   **Assume that a buyer for a dress department has the opportunity of purchasing a job lot of dresses at $6.75 that can be sorted into two groups to retail at $10.50 and $12.75. If the initial markup desired is 40 percent, what *ratio* of the dresses should be marked at each price?**

A solution procedure would be as follows:

1   Find the average retail price that needs to be maintained.
2   Establish ratio by relating retail prices of each group to average price.

Thus:

1   To find average retail price divide cost by its equivalent percent of sales:

Retail price % $- M_i\% = C\%$
$100\% - 40\% = 60\%$

$$\text{Retail price} = \frac{\$6.75}{.60} = \$11.25 = \text{average retail price}$$

2

	Group 1	Group 2
Average retail price	$11.25	$11.25
Desired prices	10.50	12.75
Desired prices over or (under)	($0.75)	$1.50

Ratio of group 2's excess over average to group 1's deficiency under average

$$\frac{150}{75} = \frac{2}{1} \text{ or 2 to 1}$$

Therefore, two dresses from group 2 should be sold for every one from group 1 to maintain the average markup of 40 percent.

Example 6 **A buyer purchases 100 hats at $3.25 each, 25 of which she marks for sale at $6. What is the minimum retail price that the buyer may place on the remainder if the average initial markup is to be 35 percent?**

1 Find the total retail valuation of entire lot (100 hats) to achieve average markup of 35 percent.

Total cost $= 100 \times \$3.25$ $= \$325$ Total cost

Retail price % $- M_i\% = C\%$

$100\% - 35\%$ $= 65\%$ C%

$$\text{Retail valuation} = \frac{\text{cost}}{C\%} = \frac{\$325}{65\%} = \$500 \quad \text{Retail}$$

2 Determine retail valuation of unpriced hats

Retail valuation of entire lot $= \$500$

Less retail valuation of 25 hats @ $6 $= \underline{\ 150}$

Retail valuation of remaining 75 hats $= \$350$

$$\text{Retail price per hat } \frac{\$350}{75} \qquad = \$4.67$$

A second type of averaging the markup is necessary when a merchant wishes to buy at two costs and to sell at one retail price. In this case the problem is to determine the ratio of items that must be purchased at each cost in order to maintain the average initial markup desired.

Example 7 **Wholesale costs are $5.25 and $6.50; retail selling price is $10. What ratio of items at each price must be purchased if an average initial markup of 40 percent is desired?**

If retail is $10 and average initial markup is 40 percent, then average cost should be 60 percent of $10, or $6.

$$
\begin{array}{lcc}
 & \text{Group 1} & \text{Group 2} \\
\text{Average cost} = & \$6.00 & \$6.00 \\
\text{Actual cost} \quad = & \underline{-5.25} & \underline{-6.50} \\
\text{Gain or loss} = & +\$0.75 & -\$0.50
\end{array}
$$

Ratio of group 1's gain to group 2's loss:

$$
\frac{75}{50} = \frac{1\frac{1}{2}}{1} \text{ or 3 to 2 ratio}
$$

Therefore, for every three hats purchased at the higher cost, two hats must be purchased at the lower cost.

Example 8 A merchant has a cumulative inventory at retail of $18,600 with a markup of $33\frac{1}{3}$ percent. His planned purchases during the month are $9000 at cost. What average initial markup must he place on the purchases if he wishes to increase his cumulative markup to 35 percent?

The inventory at cost would be $100\% - 33\frac{1}{3}\% = 66\frac{2}{3}\%$

$$
\$18,600.00 \times 0.66\frac{2}{3} = \$12,400.00
$$

$$
\begin{array}{ll}
\text{Inventory at cost} & = \$12,400.00 \\
\text{Purchases} & = \underline{\quad 9,000.00} \\
\text{Total merchandise} & = \$21,400.00
\end{array}
$$

If planned average markup is 35 percent, then average cost would be

$$
\begin{array}{l}
100\% - 35\% = 65\% \\
\quad\quad 65\% = \$21,400.00
\end{array}
$$

$$
\text{Total retail} = \frac{\$21,400.00}{0.65} = \$32,923.08
$$

$$
\begin{array}{ll}
\text{Less inventory at retail} = & \underline{18,600.00} \\
\text{Purchases at retail} = & \$14,323.08 \\
\text{Less purchases at cost} = & \underline{\quad 9,000.00} \\
\text{Markup in dollars} = & \$\ 5,323.08
\end{array}
$$

$$
\text{Purchases} \quad M\% = \frac{\$5,323.08}{\$14,323.08} = 0.3716 = 37.16\%
$$

Exercise 10.3

In solving, find percents to nearest hundredths:

1 If planned net sales are $100,000, estimated expenses are $25,000, and desired operating profit is $10,000, what should be the initial markup percent?

2　If planned net sales are $32,756, estimated expenses are $8240, and desired operating profit is $2875, what should be the initial markup percent?

3　What should be the initial markup percent if operating profit desired is 15 percent, expenses are estimated at 25 percent, markdowns 5 percent, shortages 2 percent, alteration expenses 2 percent, and cash discounts earned 3 percent?

4　What should be the initial markup percent on net sales of $40,000 if expenses are estimated at $12,300, markdowns $6240, shortages $200, alteration costs $225, cash discounts $1150, and a profit of $3600 is desired?

5　A buyer has planned net sales totaling $192,000. If estimated expenses are $48,700, markdowns $18,400, shortages $1800, workroom costs $2800, and cash discounts $5700, what initial markup should be obtained if an 8 percent profit is desired?

6　A buyer has the opportunity of purchasing a job lot of sweaters at $10.00 each that can be assorted into two groups retailing at $15.00 and $25.00. If the initial markup desired is 50 percent, what ratio of the sweaters should be marked (a) $15.00 and (b) $25.00?

7　A buyer purchases 165 blankets at $4.25 each, 75 of which the buyer prices at $7.45. What is the minimum price the buyer must place on the remainder of the blankets if he wishes the average initial markup to be at least 38.4 percent?

8　Wholesale prices are $5.45 and $6.65, retail selling price is $8.75. What is the ratio of items at (a) $5.45 and (b) $6.65 that must be purchased if an average initial markup of 32 percent is desired?

9　A buyer's May 1 inventory at retail is $7200, with a cumulative markup of 42 percent. Planned purchases for May are $4500 at cost. What average initial markup percent must be placed on the purchases if he wishes to reduce his cumulative markup to 39 percent?

Unit 10.4 　　　　　　　　　　　　Maintained Markup and Gross Margin

Frequently, original retail prices are lowered to induce the sale of slow-moving merchandise or to attract customers into the store through sales promotions at lowered prices. Regardless of the reason for such reductions (known as markdowns), the result is a smaller margin between cost and selling price.

　　　Maintained markup (M_m) is the margin after all reductions (including shortages as well as markdowns) have occurred.

　　　It represents the final difference between the *gross cost*[1] and the actual selling price. By formula, the maintained markup in dollars may be found:

---

[1] *Gross cost* is the cost computed without consideration of the following two elements: cash discounts earned on purchases, which decrease the actual cost; and alterations or workrooms, which usually operate at a loss and thus increase the actual cost.

$$M_m = \left(\begin{array}{c}\text{initial} \\ \text{selling price}\end{array}\right) + \left(\begin{array}{c}\text{net} \\ \text{additional markup}\end{array}\right) - \text{reductions} - \text{gross cost}$$

Ordinarily, maintained markup is expressed as a percent of the net sales and, if the initial selling price, net additional markup (if any) reductions, and gross cost in dollars are known, may be found as follows:

$$M_m\% = \frac{\left(\begin{array}{c}\text{initial} \\ \text{selling price}\end{array}\right) + \left(\begin{array}{c}\text{net} \\ \text{additional markup}\end{array}\right) - \text{reductions} - \text{gross cost}}{\text{initial selling price} + \text{net additional markup} - \text{reductions}}$$

Example 1   If goods with gross cost of $75 and priced at $125 are marked down $10, find (a) the initial markup percent and (b) the maintained markup percent.

(a) $M_i\% = \dfrac{\$125.00 - \$75.00}{\$125.00} = \dfrac{\$50.00}{\$125.00} = 0.40 = 40\%$

(b) $M_m\% = \dfrac{\$125.00 - \$10.00 - \$75.00}{\$125.00 - \$10.00} = \dfrac{\$40.00}{\$115.00} = 0.3478 = 34.78\%$

Example 2   If gross cost is $55, actual selling price is $85, there are no additional markups, and markdowns of $5 have already been taken, find (a) the maintained markup percent and (b) the initial markup percent.

(a) $M_m\% = \dfrac{\$85.00 - \$55.00}{\$85.00} = \dfrac{\$30.00}{\$85.00} = 0.3529 = 35.29\%$

(b) $M_i\% = \dfrac{\$85.00 + \$5.00 - \$55.00}{\$85.00 + \$5.00} = \dfrac{\$35.00}{\$90.00} = 0.3889 = 38.89\%$

When the *initial markup percent* and any net additional markup percent (or *cumulative markup percent*) and the reduction percent (expressed as a percent of the net sales) are known or may be found, the maintained markup percent may be computed readily through the use of the following equation:

$$M_m\% = M_i\% - (\text{reduction} \% \times \text{complement of } M_i\%)[1]$$

Example 3   If initial markup including any net additional markup (or cumulative markup) is 38 percent and markdowns are 7 percent, find the maintained markup percent.

Complement of initial markup percent $= 100\% - 38\% = 62\% = 0.62$

---

[1] The formula or equation as presented here has the weight of many years of use in retailing. It is invalid unless the initial markup is the same as the cumulative markup—and this is the way in which it is normally used, the initial markup being the same as the immediately preceding cumulative markup which has taken into account any net additional markups during past periods of time. Perhaps the following would be more acceptable:

$M_m\% = M_c\% - (\text{reduction} \% \times \text{complement of } M_c\%)$

$$M_m\% = 0.38 - (0.07 \times 0.62) = 0.38 - 0.0434 = 0.3366 = 33.66\%$$

If the markdowns or shortages do not occur, then the margin or markup remains constant and is the same for the cumulative markup and the maintained markup.

Maintained markup in dollars is equivalent to gross margin, less cash discounts earned on purchases, plus alteration or workroom costs. Thus:

$$M_m = \text{gross margin} - \text{cash discounts} + \text{alteration costs}$$

Example 4   **If gross margin is $45, cash discounts from vendors are $2.70, and alteration costs are $1, what is the maintained markup?**

$$M_m = \$45.00 - \$2.70 + \$1.00 = \$43.30$$

Gross margin (M_g), or the difference between net sales and the cost of goods sold, is the same as maintained markup except for cash discounts earned on purchases and alteration costs.

Cash discounts earned increase the size of the gross margin; alteration or workroom costs decrease it. Since cash discounts are almost always larger than alteration costs, gross margin usually exceeds maintained markup. The cost of goods sold (complement of the gross margin) is accordingly smaller than the gross cost of goods sold (complement of the maintained markup). Thus:

$$M_m = \text{net sales} - \text{gross cost of goods sold}$$
$$M_g = \text{net sales} - \text{cost of goods sold}$$

$$M_m\% = \frac{\text{net sales} - \text{gross cost of goods sold}}{\text{net sales}}$$

$$M_g\% = \frac{\text{net sales} - \text{cost of goods sold}}{\text{net sales}}$$

The distinction between gross cost of goods sold and cost of goods sold will be apparent from the following equations:

$$C \text{ of } GS = \text{gross } C \text{ of } GS - \text{cash discounts earned} + \text{alteration costs}$$
$$\text{Gross } C \text{ of } GS = C \text{ of } GS + \text{cash discounts earned} - \text{alteration costs}$$

The difference between maintained markup and gross margin may also be observed in the following equations:

$$M_m = \text{gross margin} - \text{cash discounts} + \text{alteration costs}$$
$$M_g = \text{maintained markup} + \text{cash discounts} - \text{alteration costs}$$
$$M_m = \text{net sales} - (C \text{ of } GS + \text{cash discounts} - \text{alteration costs})$$
$$M_g = \text{net sales} - (\text{gross } C \text{ of } GS - \text{cash discounts} + \text{alteration costs})$$

Example 5   If gross margin is $3660, cash discounts earned are $126, and alteration costs are $75, what is the maintained markup?

$$M_m = \$3660.00 - \$126.00 + \$75.00 = \$3609.00$$

Example 6   If maintained markup is $2320, vendors' discounts are $130, and alteration costs are $60, what is the gross margin?

$$M_g = \$2320.00 + \$130.00 - \$60.00 = \$2390.00$$

Example 7   If sales are $2500, gross cost of sales $1500, cash discounts earned on purchases $50, and alteration costs $20, find (a) the maintained markup in dollars, (b) the maintained markup percent, (c) the gross margin in dollars, and (d) the gross margin percent.

(a) $M_m = \$2500.00 - \$1500.00 = \$1000.00$

(b) $M_m\% = \dfrac{\$1000.00}{\$2500.00} = 0.40 = 40\%$

(c) $M_g = \$2500.00 - (\$1500.00 - \$50.00 + \$20.00) = \$1030.00$

(d) $M_g\% = \dfrac{1030.00}{2500.00} = 0.4120 = 41.20\%$

Example 8   If sales are $3200, cost of goods sold $1800, cash discounts from vendors $115, and alteration costs $65, find (a) the maintained markup in dollars, (b) the maintained markup percent, (c) the gross margin in dollars, and (d) the gross margin percent.

(a) $M_m = \$3200.00 - (\$1800.00 + \$115.00 - \$65.00) = \$1350.00$

(b) $M_m\% = \dfrac{1350.00}{3200.00} = 0.4219 = 42.19\%$

(c) $M_g = \$3200.00 - \$1800.00 = \$1400.00$

(d) $M_g\% = \dfrac{1400.00}{3200.00} = 0.4375 = 43.75\%$

The primary reason for distinguishing between maintained markup percent and gross margin percent is that some retailers do and some retailers do not consider cash discounts earned in computing gross margin in dollars and thus the gross margin percent. Since maintained markup percent does not include cash discounts earned (and alteration costs) in its determination, all retailers may directly compare the maintained markup percent of their own stores with the maintained markup percent of similar stores on the basis of figures available through statistics furnished by the Federal Reserve system and member stores of groups with which they may be affiliated. Comparisons of gross margin percents would be invalid unless all stores compared used the same accounting systems in determining gross margin percent.

Exercise 10.4

It is suggested that in solving Problems 5 and 6 of this exercise you make use of the setup form at the end of Example 2 in Unit 10.2. Find all required percents to nearest hundredths.

1   Goods with gross cost of $145 and priced at $250.00 are marked down $30. Find (a) the initial markup percent and (b) the maintained markup percent.

2   If gross cost is 75 percent of the original retail and reductions are 4 percent, what is the maintained markup percent?

3   If gross cost is $40.00, actual selling price is $55.00, and markdowns of $5 have already been taken, find (a) the maintained markup percent and (b) the initial markup percent.

4   If gross margin is $185, cash discounts from vendor are $11.50, and alteration costs are $3.50, what is the maintained markup in dollars?

5   Find the maintained markup percent from the following data: beginning inventory $12,581 at cost, $19,900 at retail; purchases at gross cost $31,500, at retail $49,000; ending inventory at cost $10,287; markdowns and shortages 15 percent (of net sales). Since there are neither alteration or workroom costs nor cash discounts in this problem, maintained markup is the same as gross margin, and gross cost of goods sold is the same as cost of goods sold.

6   Find the maintained markup percent from the following data: beginning inventory $4608 at cost, markup 36 percent; purchases at cost $7015, markup 39 percent; ending inventory at cost $4583.94, markdowns and shortages $600. Since there are neither alteration or workroom costs nor cash discounts in this problem, maintained markup is the same as gross margin, and gross cost of goods sold is the same as cost of goods sold. (In solving, compute the decimal equivalent of the cumulative markup or its complement to four decimal places.)

7   If maintained markup is $10,000, vendors' discounts are $500, and alteration costs are $1000, find the gross margin in dollars.

8   If sales are $23,483, gross cost of goods sold $14,028, cash discounts on purchases $535, and alteration costs $354, find (a) maintained markup percent and (b) gross margin percent.

9   If sales are $6300, cost of sales is $3200, cash discounts are $200, and workroom and alteration costs are $100, find (a) maintained markup percent and (b) gross margin percent.

10   If gross margin is $4851, gross cost of goods sold is $9476, cash discounts earned are $685, and alteration costs are $297, find (a) maintained markup percent and (b) gross margin percent.

Unit 10.5

Markdown and
Additional Markup

In every retail business, reduction in the selling price of some of the mer-chandise is necessary to stimulate the sale of slow-selling merchandise, to meet competitors' prices, and to attract customers to the store.

Such reduction in the original retail price is known as *gross markdown*. If the original price is restored or partially restored, the change is recorded as a *markdown cancellation*. The final amount of markdown is the *net mark-down*.

Markdown (M_d) may be expressed either in dollars or as a percent. Retail accounting practice is to base markdown percent on net sales, not as a percent of the original retail. Thus in percent:

$$\text{Net } M_d\% = \frac{\text{net markdown}}{\text{net sales}}$$

Example 1   **An item originally priced \$2.25 is marked down and sold at \$2.00. Find (a) the markdown and (b) the percent of markdown.**

(a) $M_d = \$2.25 - \$2.00 = \$0.25$

(b) $M_d\% = \dfrac{0.25}{?} - 0.125 = 12.5\%$

Example 2   **An item originally priced at \$6.75 is reduced to \$4.50 for the duration of a sale and is then re-marked and finally sold at \$5.50. Find (a) the gross markdown in dollars, (b) the markdown cancellation in dollars, and (c) the net mark-down in dollars and in percent.**

(a)   Gross $M_d = \$6.75 - \$4.50 = \$2.25$
(b) M_d cancellation $= \$5.50 - \$4.50 = \$1.00$
(c)   Net $M_d = \$2.25 - \$1.00 = \$1.25$

$$\text{Net } M_d\% = \frac{1.25}{5.50} = 0.2273 = 22.73\%$$

In some instances merchandise already in stock is re-marked upward in price. Such upward revision in price may occur because of increased cost of replacement or errors in original pricing, or in order that purposely low-priced sale merchandise may be restored to normal selling price.

Such increase in the original retail price is known as *gross additional markup*. If the original price is restored or partially restored, the change is recorded as an *additional markup cancellation*. The final amount of addi-tional markup is known as *net additional markup*.

Additional markups (M_a) may be expressed either in dollars or as a percent. Additional markup percent is based on net sales rather than being calculated as a percent of original retail. Thus in percent:

$$\text{Net } M_a\% = \frac{\text{net additional markup}}{\text{net sales}}$$

Example 3 **An item originally priced $2.25 is marked up and sold at $2.50. Find (a) the additional markup and (b) the percent of additional markup.**

(a) $M_a = \$2.50 - \$2.25 = \$0.25$

(b) $M_a\% = \dfrac{0.25}{2.50} = 0.10 = 10\%$

Example 4 **An item originally sale priced at $9.00 is marked up to the regular selling price of $12.00 and is later reduced and sold at $10.00. Find (a) the gross additional markup in dollars, (b) the additional markup cancellation in dollars, and (c) the net additional markup in dollars and in percent.**

(a)   Gross $M_a = \$12.00 - \$9.00 = \$3.00$
(b) M_a cancellation $= \$12.00 - \$10.00 = \$2.00$
(c)   Net $M_a = \$3.00 - \$2.00 = \$1.00$

$$\text{Net } M_a\% = \frac{1.00}{10.00} = 0.10 = 10\%$$

Take special note that additional markup cancellation is a revision of price downward to, but not below, the original selling price. Any further reduction constitutes a markdown. Likewise, markdown cancellation is a revision of price upward to, but not above, the original selling price. Any further increase in price is an additional markup.

As you already know (from Unit 10.4) maintained markup in dollars equals the original markup in dollars plus net additional markup in dollars less the reductions (markdowns and shortages) in dollars. If the initial markup percent including any net additional markup percent and the reduction percent on net sales are known, maintained markup percent can be determined readily by subtracting from the initial markup percent the product of the complement of the initial markup percent and the reduction percent. Repeating the equation from Example 2 in Unit 10.4:

$$M_m\% = M_i\% - (\text{reduction }\% \times \text{complement of } M_i\%)[1]$$

Example 5 **If the initial markup (including net additional markup) is 40 percent, markdowns 9 percent, and shortages 1 percent, what is the maintained markup percent?**

[1] See footnote, page 379.

Complement of initial markup % = 100% − 40% = 60%

Reduction % = 9% + 1% = 10%

$M_m\% = 0.40 - (0.10 \times 0.60) = 0.40 - 0.06 = 0.34 = 34\%$

When it is desired to know the reduction percent on sales that may be taken on a given initial markup to yield a desired maintained markup percent, the solution may be obtained readily by the use of the following equation:

$$\text{Reduction \%} = \frac{M_i\% - M_m\%}{\text{complement of } M_i\%}$$

Example 6   **Initial markup (including net additional markup) is 40 percent and desired maintained markup is 34 percent. Find the reduction (markdowns plus shortages) percent on sales that may be taken.**

Complement of initial markup percent = 100% − 40% = 60%

$$\text{Reduction \%} = \frac{0.40 - 0.34}{0.60} = \frac{0.06}{0.60} = 0.10 = 10\%$$

Example 7   **Initial markup is 35 percent, and desired maintained markup is 29.15 percent. Find the percent of reduction on sales that may be taken.**

Complement of initial markup % = 100% − 35% = 65%

$$\text{Reduction \%} = \frac{0.35 - 0.2915}{0.65} = \frac{0.0585}{0.65} = 0.09 = 9\%$$

Exercise 10.5

In solving, find all percents to nearest hundredths:

1   A buyer reduces 75 coats from $53.00 to $45.00 for a sale. After the sale, the remainder of 10 coats are marked back to the original price and sold at $53.00. Find (a) the markdown cancellation in dollars and (b) the net markdown percent.

2   A buyer marks down 20 robes from $20.00 to $12.00 for a sale during which 10 robes are sold at the reduced price. Those remaining after the sale are re-marked at the original price of $20.00. Three months later, 10 robes remaining are priced for clearance and sold at $15.00. What were the net markdowns (a) in dollars and (b) in percent?

3   A special purchase of 30 chairs that would have been marked regularly at $15.00 were priced at $10.00 for a special sale. After the sale, the 10 chairs that remained were re-marked and sold at their regular selling price. Find (a) the additional markup in dollars and (b) the net additional markup percent.

4   Of a group of 100 vases priced at $19.50, 50 were sold and the remainder marked up to $35.50. Three months later, 20 vases were still in stock and

were reduced to $21.00 and sold. Find (a) the additional markup cancellation in dollars and (b) the net additional markup percent.

5   One hundred and twenty pairs of wool gloves were specially priced at $3.00 per pair; 50 pairs were sold and the remainder were marked up to $4.00. At a later date, 15 pairs that remained were reduced to $1.30 per pair and sold in a year-end clearance. Find (a) the net additional markup percent and (b) the net markdown percent.

6   If the initial markup was 37 percent, markdowns are 6.2 percent, and shortages are 1.3 percent, what is the maintained markup percent?

7   In the men's furnishing department, the average initial markup for the season has been 41.3 percent. What is the maximum markdown percent that can be taken in order to end the season with a desired maintained markup of 36.6 percent?

8   The initial markup on a group of sweaters was $630, equaling 45 percent. If a maintained markup of 42.5 percent was desired on the sweaters, find the maximum markdown that could be made (a) in percent and (b) in dollars.

Unit 10.6

Average Inventory and Stock Turnover

The speed with which the average merchandise in a department or store is sold is a common criterion used by retailers to determine efficiency of operations.

If the stock is maintained at a minimum, less capital is required to operate the department or store, and the risk of carrying unseasonable merchandise that will require a high percent of markdown is greatly reduced.

Average inventory is determined by dividing the sum of the inventories by the number of times the inventory has been taken. Thus if inventory is taken for 1 month, that is, on the first and the last days of the month, the average inventory is found by dividing the sum of the two inventories by 2.

If the average inventory is to be found for 12 months, with inventories taken on the first day of each month and the final day of the last month, the average inventory is obtained by dividing the sum of the inventories by 13, the number of times inventory has been taken. The formula is

$$\text{Average inventory} = \frac{\text{sum of the inventories}}{\text{number of inventories taken}}$$

Example 1   **Inventory at retail in a shoe department was $12,600 on January 1, and $14,732 on January 31. What was the average inventory?**

$$\text{Average inventory at retail} = \frac{\$12,600.00 + \$14,732.00}{2} = \$13,666.00$$

Example 2 Inventory at cost in the lingerie department was $6076 on April 1, $5031.50 on May 1, $5256.50 on June 1, and $5805 on June 30. What was the average inventory at cost for the 3-month period?

$$\text{Avg. inv. at cost} = \frac{\$6076.00 + \$5031.50 + \$5256.50 + \$5805.00}{4} = \$5542.25$$

The *rate of stock turnover* (or stock turn) indicates the number of times the average stock has been sold for a given period. Usually this period of time is 1 year.

The rate of stock turnover may be determined at retail or at cost by the following formulas:

$$\text{Stock turnover at retail} = \frac{\text{sales}}{\text{average inventory at retail}}$$

$$\text{Stock turnover at cost} = \frac{\text{cost of goods sold}}{\text{average inventory at cost}}$$

Example 3 At retail. If sales are $86,234 and average inventory is $22,560 at retail, what is the rate of stock turnover?

$$\text{Stock turnover at retail} = \frac{\$86,234.00}{\$22,560.00} = 3.82$$

Example 4 At cost. If cost of goods sold is $28,672 and average inventory at cost is $11,593, what is the rate of stock turnover?

$$\text{Stock turnover at cost} = \frac{\$28,672.00}{\$11,593.00} = 2.47$$

Stock turnover at retail or at cost will be the same only if there are neither markdowns nor shortages. The greatest use of the rate of stock turnover is to compare department to department or store to store. Provided the same method is used, the comparative figures will express a true relationship.

Since the accepted store practice is to use the retail method rather than the cost method, the retail method is preferred. The fact that it is also slightly more conservative makes it more desirable from the viewpoint of most accountants.

Example 5 Sales in a store are $125,681. Inventory January 1 is $46,634 at retail; inventory on June 30 is $28,260 at cost. The cumulative markup is 40 percent. What is the rate of stock turnover for the 6-month period at retail?

$$\text{Inventory at retail June 30} = \frac{\$28,260.00}{0.60} = \$47,100.00$$

$$\text{Average inventory} = \frac{\$46,634.00 + \$47,100.00}{2} = \$46,867.00$$

$$\text{Stock turnover at retail} = \frac{\$125,681.00}{\$46,867.00} = 2.68$$

CONVERTING TURNOVERS TO AVERAGE DAYS   Merchants, store managers, and business analysts often convert various turnovers to average days to assist them in their decision-making functions. The procedure is to divide the calendar (or business) days in the year by the turnover. The quotient then represents the average number of days taken to "move," "turn," or sell the average inventory.

Example 6   **The stock turnover in a store was 2.68. Find the average number of days the merchandise remained in the store before being sold.**

$$\frac{\text{Days in calendar year}}{\text{Stock turnover}} = \frac{365}{2.68} = 136.19 \text{ or } 136 \text{ days}$$

With the help of computerized cash registers, stock turns and average days can be economically calculated on types of merchandise or even on each item of merchandise. This information can quickly identify slow movers and assist managers in their day-to-day merchandising decisions.

Exercise 10.6

1   The inventory at retail of a millinery department was $8542 on May 1 and $9248 on May 31. What was the average inventory at retail?

2   Cost valuation of inventories in a men's clothing shop was as follows: $13,592 on January 1; $11,947 on April 1; $14,337 on July 1; $14,876 on October 1; and $15,481 on December 31. What was the average inventory at cost?

3   Inventory on August 1 was $26,000 at retail, with a cumulative markup of 50.0 percent. Inventory on August 31 was $29,000 at retail, with a cumulative markup of 45.0 percent. (a) What was average inventory at retail? (b) What was the average inventory at cost?

4   Sales were $63,486 and average inventory at retail was $26,048. What was the rate of stock turnover at retail, to nearest hundredths?

5   Cost of goods sold was $91,740 and average inventory at cost was $18,348. What was the rate of stock turnover at cost, to nearest hundredths?

6   Sales for the quarter were $152,875. Inventory at retail was as follows: January 1, $89,225; February 1, $93,406; March 1, $101,362; March 31, $99,419. What was the rate of stock turnover at retail for the quarter, to nearest hundredths?

7   Cost of goods sold for the quarter was $125,000. Inventory at cost was as follows: July 1, $52,000; August 1, $54,000; September 1, $51,000; and September 30, $53,000. What was the rate of stock turnover at cost for the period, to nearest hundredths?

8 Find the average number of days merchandise remained unsold for the
   following:

	Sales	Average inventory at retail
(a)	600,000	100,000
(b)	420,000	68,000
(c)	215,000	110,000

9 In solving this problem, it is suggested that you refer to the operating
   statement of the Carter Clothing Store, pages 390–391. Find (a) reductions (markdowns + shortages) in dollars and as a percent of net sales,
   (b) markup percent of beginning inventory, (c) markup percent on gross
   cost of purchases, (d) cumulative markup percent (compute it or its
   complement to eight decimal places in determining ending inventory at
   cost), (e) gross margin in dollars and as a percent of net sales, (f) maintained markup percent, (g) average inventory at retail, (h) average inventory at cost, (i) stock turnover at retail, and (j) stock turnover at cost.
   (Give all answers to nearest hundredths.)

	Cost	Retail
Beginning inventory	$35,600.00	$ 53,000.00
Purchases, gross	$98,000.00	149,500.00
Less earned discounts	−4,200.00	
Net purchases		
Add: Net additional markup		2,000.00
Alteration cost	2,500.00	
Total goods available	_____	_____
Less deductions:		
Net sales		(131,000.00)
Reductions		(_____)
Ending inventory at retail per count		62,000.00
Ending inventory at cost	_____	
Cost of goods sold	_____	

AN OPERATING STATEMENT SHOWING HOW EACH ITEM IS COMPUTED AT THE CARTER CLOTHING STORE Operating Statement, Year Ending Jan. 31, 19—

	Cost	Percents of net sales	Retail
Gross sales	$113,670.00	113.67	(12.03% of gross sales)
Deduct returned sales and allowances	13,670.00	13.67	
Net sales	$100,000.00	100.00	
Deduct merchandise sold:			
Beginning inventory	$16,128.00		$ 24,200.00
Add net delivered cost of purchases:			
Purchases	$66,768.00		
Deduct returns and allowances	2,960.00		
Net purchases	$63,808.00		
Add freight and cartage in	4,736.00		
Gross cost of purchases	$68,544.00		126,000.00
Less earned cash discounts	2,500.00		
Net delivered cost of purchases	66,044.00		
Add alteration costs	1,396.00	1.40	1,000.00 (Add additional markup)
Total goods available for sale	$83,568.00		$151,200.00
Deduct ending inventory	23,520.00		42,000.00
Less cost of goods sold	60,048.00		$109,200.00 (Deductions)
Gross margin	$ 39,952.00	39.95	100,000.00 (Net sales)
			$ 9,200.00 (This is the sum of the net markdowns and shortages)
Deduct expenses:			
Administration	$ 5,650.00	5.65	
Occupancy	8,930.00	8.93	
Publicity	4,300.00	4.30	
Buying	4,120.00	4.12	
Selling	7,300.00	7.30	
Delivery	800.00	.80	
Total expenses	31,100.00	31.10	
Operating profit	$ 8,852.00	8.85	

COMPUTING CERTAIN FREQUENTLY USED PERCENTS

Markup of beginning inventory $= \dfrac{\$24,200.00 - \$16,128.00}{\$24,200\ 00} = 33.36\%$ { This is cumulative markup percent of 33.3553719% at end of preceding year

Markup on purchases (gross cost) $= \dfrac{\$126,000.00 - \$68,544.0C}{\$126,000.00} = 45.60\%$

Earned cash discount on purchases (net) $= \dfrac{\$2,500.00}{\$63,808.00} = 3.92\%$

Additional markup $= \dfrac{\$1,000.00}{\$100,000.00} = 1.00\%$ { Note that additional markup is not canceled by markdowns. It is included in cumulative markup base

Net markdowns (from markdown records) $= \dfrac{\$8,000.00}{\$100,000.00} = 8.00\%$ { Reductions totaling $9,200 are 9.20% of net sales and are deductions from stock in addition to net sales

Shortages ($9,200.00 − $8,000.00 = $1,200.00) $= \dfrac{\$1,200.00}{\$100,000.00} = 1.20\%$

Cumulative markup $= \dfrac{\$151,200.00 - (\$16,128.00 + \$68,544.00)}{\$151,200.00} = 44.00\%$ { Note that $151,200 includes additional markup of $1,000

Maintained markup $= \dfrac{\$39,952.00 - \$2,500.00 + \$1,396.00}{\$100,000.00} = 38.85\%$ { If there were neither earned cash discounts on purchases nor alteration costs, M_m would equal M_g

COMPUTING AVERAGE INVENTORY AND STOCK TURNOVER

Average inventory at retail $= \dfrac{\$24,200.00 + \$42,000.00}{2} = \$33,100.00$

Stock turnover at retail $= \dfrac{\$100,000.00}{\$33,100.00} = 3.02$ times (Stock turnover expressed as a decimal, not as a percent)

Average inventory at cost $= \dfrac{\$16,128.00 + \$23,520.00}{2} = \$19,824.00$

Stock turnover at cost $= \dfrac{\$60,048.00}{\$19,824.00} = 3.03$ times (Stock turnover expressed as a decimal, not as a percent)

Unit 10.7   *Percent of Return on Assets Employed; Stock Sales Ratio; Open-To-Buy*

COMPUTING PERCENT OF RETURN ON ASSETS EMPLOYED A prime motive in operating most retail establishments, as well as other businesses, is to earn as large a profit as possible on the assets employed or allocated for this particular use. To understand further some of the problems that confront the merchant and the decisions that must be made correctly to earn the maximum profit on the assets so allocated, consider the following equations:

1 (a) Percent of profit on sales $= \dfrac{\text{profit}}{\text{sales}}$

(b) Profit $=$ sales $\times$ percent of profit on sales

2 (a) Asset turnover $= \dfrac{\text{sales}}{\text{assets employed}}$

(b) Sales $=$ assets employed $\times$ asset turnover

(c) Assets employed $= \dfrac{\text{sales}}{\text{asset turnover}}$

3 (a) Percent return on assets employed $= \dfrac{\text{profit}}{\text{assets employed}}$

(b) Profit $=$ assets employed $\times$ percent return on assets employed

(c) Assets employed $= \dfrac{\text{profit}}{\text{percent return on assets employed}}$

In the above equations, the value amounts representing *sales* and *assets employed* are those amounts normally accumulated in the accounting records in accordance with generally accepted accounting principles. The amount for *sales* represents the sales value, less merchandise returned and price allowances, of the merchandise sold during the period. The amount for *assets employed* represents the *cost values,* or cost less accumulated depreciation where applicable, of the total assets of the business.

Turnover of certain types of assets is also a meaningful ratio. Hence, in the analysis of receivables, only those assets *directly employed or allocated* to receivables (i.e., the "Accounts Receivable" listed on the financial statements) are used. In merchandise turnovers (or stock turn), the assets *directly employed or allocated* to merchandise for resale ("Merchandise Inventory") are used.

A higher rate of asset turnover will result in a larger sales volume even though there is no increase in assets employed. If the percent of profit on sales remains constant, the net result will be a greater earning per asset dollar employed. *A higher rate of asset turnover with constant sales volume and percent of profit on sales* will result in a smaller required amount of assets employed and thus a greater earning per dollar of assets employed. *Finally, a higher percent of profit on sales* with a constant volume of sales, asset turnover, and amount of assets employed will result in a greater earning per dollar of assets employed.

Example 1   **Sales of a store are $100,000, profit on sales is 6 percent, and assets employed are $25,000. Find (a) dollar profit, (b) asset turnover, and (c) percent return on assets employed.**

(a)   Dollar profit = sales × percent of profit on sales
$$= \$100,000 \times 0.06 = \$6000$$

(b)   Asset turnover = $\dfrac{\text{sales}}{\text{assets employed}} = \dfrac{\$100,000}{\$25,000} = 4$

(c)   Percent return on assets employed:

$$\dfrac{\text{Profit}}{\text{Assets employed}} = \dfrac{\$6000}{\$25,000} = 24\%$$

Example 2   **If, in Example 1, asset turnover was increased to 5, and the assets employed and percent profit on sales remained constant, what would be the effect on (a) sales, and (b) percent of profit on assets employed?**

(a)   Sales would increase, thus:

Sales = assets employed × asset turnover
$$= \$25,000 \times 5 = \$125,000$$

(b)   Percent of profit on assets employed would increase; thus:

Profit = sales × percent of profit on sales
$$= \$125,000 \times 6\% = \$7500$$

Percent of profit on assets employed:

$$\dfrac{\text{Profit}}{\text{Assets employed}} = \dfrac{\$7500}{\$25,000} = 30\%$$

Example 3   **If, in Example 1, asset turnover was increased to 5, and sales and percent profit on sales remained constant, what would be the effect on (a) assets employed and (b) percent profit on assets employed?**

(a)   Assets employed would decrease; thus:

$$\text{Assets employed} = \dfrac{\text{sales}}{\text{turnover of assets}} = \dfrac{\$100,000}{5} = \$20,000$$

(b)   Percent profit on assets would increase; thus:

$$\text{Percent profit on assets} = \dfrac{\text{profit}}{\text{assets employed}} = \dfrac{\$6000}{\$20,000} = 30\%$$

The conclusions made in the preceding examples were based on the assumption that the rate of profit on sales would remain constant. In actual practice, this is rarely true. Thus a major merchandising problem arises from the tendency of the rate of profit to decrease with increase in asset turnover, since the increase is often brought about by lower prices or greater promotion expenses, or both. When inventory is purposely reduced in order to increase the rate of asset turnover, the profit rate tends to rise, but sales frequently will be less, because a lower inventory usually means less selection and consequent loss of sales. It is the problem of the merchant to determine an optimum rate of turnover for his business that will provide him with the most profitable dollar return.

COMPUTING STOCK SALES RATIOS   The successful management of a retail store necessitates not only careful estimation of future sales but also determination of the minimum inventories required to make planned future sales an accomplished fact. Estimates are usually made for each month, and the relationship between the beginning inventory (b.i.) and the planned sales for a particular month is known as the *stock sales ratio*.

Stock sales ratio is computed by dividing the beginning of the month (b.o.m.) inventory *at retail* by the planned sales for the month.

$$\text{Stock sales ratio} = \frac{\text{b.o.m. inventory}}{\text{planned sales}}$$

It is apparent that the larger the planned sales and the smaller the b.o.m. inventory, the smaller the stock sales ratio. Unlike stock turnover, in which a high ratio is ordinarily desirable, stock sales ratio should be as low as possible without causing a loss in sales because of insufficient inventories of goods. Estimations of future business conditions, together with records of past experience, enable the retailer to determine, for each month of the year, the stock sales ratio that will probably prove most profitable.

From the preceding equation, the following may be derived:

1   b.o.m. inventory = planned sales × stock sales ratio

2   Planned sales = $\dfrac{\text{b.o.m. inventory}}{\text{stock sales ratio}}$

Example 4   **Planned sales for November are $28,000, and planned retail stock on November 1 is $43,400. Find b.o.m. stock sales ratio.**

$$\text{Stock sales ratio} = \frac{\$43,400.00}{\$28,000.00} = 1.55$$

Example 5   **Planned sales for June are $15,000 and the planned b.o.m. stock sales ratio is 2.5. What should be the b.o.m. stock on June 1?**

b.o.m. inventory = $15,000.00 × 2.5 = $37,500.00

Example 6   **Planned b.o.m. inventory for April is $32,000. What are the planned sales for April if the desired stock sales ratio is 0.4?**

$$\text{Planned sales} = \frac{\$32,000.00}{0.4} = \$80,000.00$$

COMPUTING OPEN-TO-BUY   Profits in retailing are determined largely by the maintenance of a proper balance between inventories and sales. As you know, stock turnover and stock sales ratios are helpful guides in making a merchandise plan. However, actual sales and stock do vary from plan, and these variances necessitate adjustments in future purchases in order to keep the desired ratio between stock and sales.

The original monthly appropriations for purchases must be readjusted constantly with fluctuations in sales, for an increase in sales over planned figures results in a lowered inventory on hand, while a decrease in sales results in a larger than planned inventory.

Actual purchases at the end of any period of time may be found as follows:

Purchases = (ending inventory + sales + markdowns)
                           − (beginning inventory + purchases on order)

Open-to-buy (o.t.b.), or planned purchases for a period of time to follow, is determined as follows:

o.t.b. = (planned ending inventory
                     + planned sales + planned markdowns)
                           − (beginning inventory + purchases on order)

Example 7   **Find o.t.b. if planned ending inventory is $12,000, planned sales $25,000, planned markdowns $1000, beginning inventory $9000, and purchases on order $5000.**

o.t.b. = ($12,000.00 + $25,000.00 + $1000.00) − ($9000.00 + $5000.00)
         = $38,000.00 − $14,000.00 = $24,000.00

Note that all of the figures in the above example and o.t.b. are at retail. To determine planned purchases at cost, multiply o.t.b. at retail by the decimal complement of the planned initial markup percent on purchases. Thus, in this example, if the planned markup on purchases were 40 percent, planned purchases at cost would be

$24,000 × 0.60 = $14,400.00

The use of the stock sales ratio in determining open-to-buy is made apparent in the following example.

Example 8   **Planned sales for a department with an initial markup of 35 percent are $10,000 for May and $12,000 for June. If the desired b.o.m. stock sales ratio for May is 2 and for June is 1.5, what will be the May o.t.b. at cost?**

b.o.m. stock for May $10,000.00 × 2   = $20,000.00
b.o.m. stock for June $12,000.00 × 1.5 = $18,000.00

Therefore e.o.m. stock for May $18,000.00
Plus planned sales for May   +10,000.00
                                      $28,000.00
Deduct b.o.m. stock for May   −20,000.00
May o.t.b. at retail $ 8,000.00

Or stated as an equation:

May o.t.b. at retail = ($18,000.00 + $10,000.00) − $20,000.00 = $8000.00
    If initial markup = 35%, then cost = 65% of o.t.b. at retail
    May o.t.b. at cost = $8000.00 × 0.65 = $5200.00

     Purchases on order and planned markdowns are not included in this illustration. However, any purchases on order (at retail) would be added to the b.o.m. stock for May, and any planned markdowns would be added to planned sales for May. Note that b.o.m. stock for any month is the e.o.m. stock (or ending inventory) for the preceding month. Thus in Example 8, b.o.m. stock for June is also the ending inventory for May.

Example 9   **Same problem as Example 8 but with purchases on order at retail of $2500 and planned markdowns for May of $600.**

b.o.m. stock for May $10,000.00 × 2 = $20,000.00
  Plus purchases on order   +2,500.00 = $22,500.00
b.o.m. stock for June $12,000.00 × 1.5   = $18,000.00

Therefore e.o.m. stock for May $18,000.00

Plus: Planned sales for May $10,000.00
      Planned markdowns for May   +600.00   +10,600.00
                                                           $28,600.00
Deduct b.o.m. stock for May plus purchases on order   −22,500.00
May o.t.b. at retail $ 6,100.00

May o.t.b. at cost: $6100.00 × 0.65 = $3965.00

Exercise 10.7

Unless otherwise stipulated, given figures are at retail prices.

1   A store's sales are $220,000, profit on sales is 1.5 percent, and asset turnover is 11 times on assets employed of $20,000 (at cost). (a) Find percent return on assets employed. If sales and the amount of profit in dollars remained constant and asset turnover was reduced to 4, find (b) the amount of assets employed, and (c) the percent return on assets employed. If the assets employed and rate of profit on sales remained constant and the asset turnover was 8, find (d) the sales and (e) the percent of return on assets employed.

2   Hay Gulch Department Store has sales of $600,000, profit on sales of 2.5 percent, and an asset turnover (based on assets at cost) of 3. By a new policy of lower prices and more advertising, sales are increased to $1,800,000, profit on sales reduced to 2 percent, and the asset turnover increased to 6. Was the decision on the new merchandising policy profitable for the owners? Why or why not?

3   Planned sales for August are $19,500; planned retail stock on August 1 is $30,810. Find the planned b.o.m. stock sales ratio, to nearest hundredths.

4   Planned sales for January are $7520, and the b.o.m. stock sales ratio is 0.23. What should be the b.o.m. stock on January 1?

5   Planned stock for May 1 is $45,000. If the desired stock sales ratio is 1.5, what are the planned sales for May?

6   If a stock sales ratio of 2.0 for June is desired and if planned b.o.m. stock for June is $80,000, what are the planned sales for June?

7   If planned sales for December are $21,400 and the desired b.o.m. stock sales ratio is 0.65, what should be the planned b.o.m. stock for December?

8   Beginning inventory is $17,500, planned ending inventory is $15,000, planned sales are $11,000, planned markdowns are 6 percent, and purchases on order are $2200. What is the o.t.b. at retail?

9   What is the o.t.b. for July at cost if planned initial markup on purchases is 42 percent, beginning inventory is $8456, planned sales are $9600, planned markdowns are $615, purchases on order are $980, and planned ending inventory is $7950?

10   Planned sales are $354,000, planned markdowns are 12.2 percent, planned ending inventory is $192,000, purchases on order are $27,754, and beginning inventory is $171,000. What is the o.t.b. at cost if planned initial markup on purchases is 36.8 percent?

11   Planned sales for a department with a markup of 39.8 percent are $18,000 for January and $20,500 for February. The desired stock sales ratio for January is 1.6 and for February is 1.4. What will be the January o.t.b. (a) at retail and (b) at cost?

12   A department with an initial markup of 35 percent has planned sales of $27,400 for August and $32,800 for September. Purchases at retail on order August 1 are $3240, and planned markdowns are 8.4 percent of planned August sales. The desired b.o.m. stock sales ratio is 1.05 for August and 0.96 for September. Find the o.t.b. for August (a) at retail and (b) at cost.

Chapter 11

Income Statements;
Balance Sheets;
Measures of Central Tendency;
Business Graphs

Objectives To Be Achieved in This Chapter

1   Obtain significant information about a business by use of ratios developed from income statements and balance sheets.

2   Calculate various statistical averages and quartiles used in the communication of data and financial statement analysis.

3   Develop various types of graphs used in the presentation of business information.

Unit 11.1   *Income Statements*

The essential purpose of an income statement is to show the most important factors in the operation of a business for a stipulated period of time. *Income statements* (frequently called operating statements or profit and loss statements) are usually periodic summaries of income, costs of goods or services, expenses, etc., and resulting profit or loss for the stipulated period.

If income exceeds costs plus expenses, there will be a profit. If income is less than costs plus expenses, there will be a loss.

The income statement that follows is typical of income statements to the point of arriving at the net operating profit before income taxes, other income and expense, and extraordinary items.[1] Percents of net income are generally given as well as dollar figures not only to indicate what happened to income received for the specified period but also to compare differences or likenesses with similar previous periods of time. Percents of net sales are shown in accordance with the usual practice of comparing dollar figures with net sales for most entries on an income statement.

Example 1   **An income statement (partial).**

A. F. HEIDERICH SPECIALTY SHOP   Income statement for month ending June 30, 19____

Income from sales:				
Gross sales		$11,675.00	116.75%	
Less sales returns and allowances		1,675.00	16.75%	(of net sales)
Net sales		$10,000.00	100.00%	
Cost of goods sold:				
Inventory, June 1, 19____		$ 3,600.00		
Purchases	$7,295.00			
Less returns	945.00			
Net purchases	$6,350.00			
Plus freight in	327.00			
Gross purchase cost	$6,677.00			
Less cash discounts earned	127.00			
Net purchase cost		6,550.00		
Total cost of goods available for sale		$10,150.00		
Inventory, June 30, 19____		3,450.00		
Cost of goods sold		6,700.00	67.00%	
Gross margin on sales		$ 3,300.00	33.00%	
Expenses:				
Administration	$ 660.00		6.60%	
Occupancy	400.00		4.00%	
Selling	1,820.00		18.20%	
Miscellaneous	120.00		1.20%	
Total expenses		3,000.00	30.00%	
Operating net profit before income taxes, other income and expenses, and extra-ordinary items		$ 300.00	3.00%	

[1]Although the partial income statement as presented is adequate for the purposes intended in this text, it is not the complete statement as recommended by present-day accounting principles. The student should look to accounting courses for the preparation of more complete income statements.

COMMON INCOME STATEMENT RATIOS TO NET SALES Typical of useful ratios that may be determined from an income statement are certain percent comparisons between the major elements of the statement and net sales that may indicate the condition of the business. The following ratios (usually expressed in percents) are frequently shown:

1 Costs to net sales
2 Gross profit (margin) to net sales
3 Expenses to net sales
4 Operating profit to net sales
5 Net profit to net sales (assuming operating profit and net profit are in variance)

Thus, using as an illustration the preceding example of an income statement:

RATIO OF COST OF GOODS SOLD TO NET SALES Cost of goods sold may be expressed both in dollars and as a percent of net sales. Such a ratio may be for a stipulated period (usually but not necessarily the fiscal year) or for one or more similar previous periods. Thus, in the example,

$$\frac{\$6700.00}{\$10,000.00} = 0.6700 = 67.00\%$$

RATIO OF GROSS PROFIT TO NET SALES The percent that gross profit (or gross margin) is of net sales indicates the degree of spread between costs and net sales. It is of major importance, for out of gross profit must be paid all expenses before a net return (profit) can be realized. Thus, in the example,

$$\frac{\$3300.00}{\$10,000.00} = 0.3300 = 33.00\%$$

RATIO OF EXPENSES TO NET SALES Major expenses such as administration, occupancy, selling, etc., are usually expressed as percents of net sales as illustrated. The total of such expenses expressed as a percent of net sales is thus found in the example,

$$\frac{\$3000.00}{\$10,000.00} = 0.3000 = 30.00\%$$

RATIO OF OPERATING PROFIT TO NET SALES Not indicated in the simplified example is the possibility that net profit as distinguished from net operating profit of the business may be more or less depending upon additions to or deductions from the operating profit—resulting in higher or lower net income. However, since the example does not consider such factors,

$$\frac{\$300.00}{\$10,000.00} = 0.0300 = 3.00\%$$

RATIO OF NET PROFIT (OR LOSS) TO NET SALES   Had the preceding example of the A. F. Heiderich Specialty Shop statement of profit and loss included such items as workroom and/or alteration costs, and such additions to operating profits as interest earned, bad debts recovered, capital gains, or such deductions from overall net earnings as interest due, bad debts incurred, donations promised, capital loss incurred, the percent of final net profit or loss (to net sales) would vary from higher to lower as the dollars of net profit or loss would vary from higher to lower as income was added to or deductions were taken from operating profit (or loss).

VERTICAL AND HORIZONTAL ANALYSIS OF INCOME STATEMENTS   In comparing the items constituting an income statement, two general kinds of analysis may be made. This is also true of balance sheets.

1   Vertical analysis
2   Horizontal analysis

The example of the A. F. Heiderich Specialty Shop shows dollar amounts and their percent ratios to net sales for a single period of time. This makes possible *vertical analysis,* and the percents are helpful in telling what happened to each dollar of net sales. If in an adjacent column (or columns) an earlier similar period (or periods) of time is given, *horizontal analysis* is possible if similar dollar and percent ratios are given or can be computed. Dollar and percent figures from one or more similar time periods help make possible even more satisfactory vertical analysis.

Example 2   **Comparative income statements.**[1]

WILLIAM FOX, INC.   Comparative income statements for fiscal years ending May 31, 1979 and 1978

	1979	1978	Increase or (decrease) Dollars	Increase or (decrease) Percent	Percent of net sales 1979	Percent of net sales 1978
Net sales	$800,000	$600,000	$200,000	33.3	100.0	100.0
Cost of goods sold	480,000	390,000	90,000	23.1	60.0	65.0
Gross profit on sales	$320,000	$210,000	$110,000	52.4	40.0	35.0
Operating expenses	270,000	150,000	120,000	80.0	33.8	25.0
Net operating income	$ 50,000	$ 60,000	$(10,000)	(16.7)	6.3	10.0
Other income	22,800	31,400	(8,600)	(27.4)	2.9	5.2
Other expense	8,400	4,100	4,300	104.8	1.2	0.7
Net income before taxes	$ 64,400	$ 87,300	$(22,900)	(26.2)	8.5	14.6
Less income taxes	26,800	42,500	(15,700)	(36.7)	3.4	7.1
Net income	$ 37,600	$ 44,800	$ (7,200)	(16.1)	4.7	7.5

Even the most cursory inspection of the figures and percents given in Example 2 indicates, in the absence of other information, both desirable and

[1]See page 406 for similar analysis of comparative balance sheets of William Fox, Inc.

undesirable comparisons between the years 1978 and 1979. Both vertical and horizontal analysis may be employed. But if figures and percents from similar businesses indicated that they averaged twice the net profit and sales in 1979 as compared to 1978, or one-half the net profit and sales for 1979 as compared to 1978, etc., entirely different interpretations could be made. Comparable percents of both increase and decrease can be secured from industry averages, or perhaps from Federal Reserve district averages. In any event, the vertical and horizontal analyses of William Fox, Inc., are not completely valid unless information other than that supplied by the comparative income statements for the years 1978 and 1979 is obtained.

Exercise 11.1

1   Compute the missing entries in the following income statement. Find all percents to nearest hundredths.

STEWART MEN'S STORE   Operating income statement for month ended February 28, 19____

				Percent of Net Sales
Sales:				
Gross sales		$94,215.00		_____%
Less: Sales returns	$ 7,431.00			
Allowances	2,244.00	_____		_____%
Net Sales			$_____	100.00%
Cost of sales:				
Stock, February 1		$15,506.00		
Purchases	$48,322.00			
Plus: Freight in	3,106.00			
Purchases gross	$_____			
Less: Purchase rebates and				
allowances	2,480.00			
Net purchase cost	_____			
Cost of total goods for sale	$_____			
Stock, February 28	18,481.00			
Costs of goods sold			$_____	_____%
Gross margin on sales			$_____	_____%
Less: Expenses:				
Administration	$ 2,750.00			_____%
Occupancy	9,000.00			_____%
Publicity	940.00			_____%
Buying	1,680.00			_____%
Selling	12,320.00			_____%
Delivery	440.00			_____%
Miscellaneous	760.00			_____%
Total operating expenses	_____		_____	_____%
Net operating income			$_____	_____%

2 Compute the missing entries in the following comparative income statements. Find percent answers to nearest tenths.

BURT BOLLES MANUFACTURING COMPANY Condensed comparative income statements for fiscal years ending August 31, 1979 and 1978

	1979	1978	Increase or (decrease) Dollars	Increase or (decrease) Percent	Percent of net sales 1979	Percent of net sales 1978
Net sales	$740,000	$694,000	$_____	_____	100.0	100.0
Cost of goods sold	340,000		_____	_____	_____	_____
Gross profit on sales	$_____	$248,000	$_____	_____	_____	_____
Operating expenses	224,000		_____	_____	_____	_____
Net operating income	$_____	$ 59,000	$_____	_____	_____	_____
Other income	28,400		_____	_____	_____	_____
Other expense		8,100	_____	_____	_____	_____
Net income before taxes	$ 78,000	$ 84,900	$_____	_____	_____	_____
Less income taxes	20,200	22,300	_____	_____	_____	_____
Net income	$_____	$_____	$_____	_____	_____	_____

Unit 11.2   *Balance Sheets*

The essential purpose of a balance sheet is to show the *financial position* of a business (or of an individual) as of a certain specific date. Balance sheets are financial statements presenting the total amounts for assets, liabilities, and proprietorship in the framework of the basic accounting equation:

Assets = liabilities + proprietorship

Assets represent *future benefits* to be received by the business entity or the individual. The assets are recorded at their cost to the business entity. In the case of personal balance sheets prepared by individuals, the assets usually reflect the presumptive values as of the balance sheet date. Assets for a business entity are normally segregated into subgroups depending on the intent of the business entity for their use.

Current assets, such as cash, notes and accounts receivable, and inventories are either in liquid form (i.e. cash) or by intent will become liquid within a year.

Fixed assets, such as buildings, fixtures and equipment (all less depreciation or that portion of the initial cost which has been allocated to expense or "expired benefits"), and land (nondepreciable) are by intent to be used by the business and not to be sold or converted to liquid form within a year.

Liabilities are the amounts owed by the entity to persons outside the entity in a debtor-creditor relationship. As with assets, the liabilities are segregated into subgroups depending on when they must be paid. *Current liabilities,* such as notes and accounts payable, accrued expenses, etc., will normally be paid within 1 year. Long-term liabilities, indebtedness, etc., are those liabilities which will be paid beyond the next year. The portion of the long-term liabilities that falls due within the next year is included with the current liabilities.

Proprietorship is the residual amount that remains after deducting the liabilities from the assets. Proprietorship represents the equity or interest in the total assets by the ownership group. Other terms having the same meaning in business as proprietorship are *net worth, net capital, net owner-ship, net investment, net assets, total stockholders' equity,* etc.

Example 1   **A balance sheet.**

HYMAN BERSTON   Balance sheet, February 29, 19____

Assets		
Cash on hand	$ 278.50	
Cash in bank	1,065.80	
Merchandise inventory	9,720.00	
Accounts receivable	2,852.50	
Notes receivable	1,048.20	
Current assets		$14,965.00
Land	$ 4,000.00	
Building (less depreciation)	26,800.00	
Fixtures (less depreciation)	6,500.00	
Fixed assets		37,300.00
Total assets		$52,265.00

Liabilities and Proprietorship		
Accounts payable	$ 5,534.60	
Notes payable	2,035.00	
Current liabilities		$ 7,569.60
Land mortgage	$ 1,450.00	
Building mortgage	12,640.00	
Long-term liabilities		14,090.00
Total liabilities		$21,659.60
Hyman Berston, net worth		30,605.40
Total liabilities and proprietorship		$52,265.00

As is apparent from the balance sheet of Hyman Berston, the following is true:

Assets   = liabilities + net worth
$52,265.00 = $21,659.60 + $30,605.40

Liabilities = assets   − net worth
$21,659.60 = $52,265.00 − $30,605.40

Net worth = assets   − liabilities
$30,605.40 = $52,265.00 − $21,659.60

COMMON BALANCE SHEET RATIOS   As with income statement ratios, a number of useful ratios can be determined from balance sheets. Most ratios are expressed in percents; others are usually expressed decimally. Comparative balance sheets for similar time periods may be necessary as well as income statements for the same time periods. Both vertical and horizontal analysis may be made, and again, as with income statements, it is desirable that comparable average increases and decreases in similar businesses be available so that reasonable conclusions can be determined.

Example 2   **Comparative balance sheets.**[1]

WILLIAM FOX, INC.   Condensed comparative balance sheets for fiscal years ending May 31, 1979 and 1978

	1979	1978	Increase or (decrease) Dollars	Increase or (decrease) Percent	Percent of total assets 1979	Percent of total assets 1978
Assets						
Current assets	$350,000	$296,000	$ 54,000	18.2%	50.2%	45.5%
Buildings, equipment (less						
depreciation) plus land	320,000	335,000	(15,000)	(4.5)	45.9	51.5
Other assets	27,000	19,600	7,400	37.8	3.9	3.0
Total assets	$697,000	$650,600	$ 46,400	7.1%	100.0%	100.0%
Liabilities and						
Stockholders' Equity						
Liabilities						
Current liabilities	$128,600	$ 95,200	$ 33,400	35.1%	18.5%	14.6%
Long-term liabilities	210,000	238,000	(28,000)	(11.8)	30.1	36.6
Total liabilities	$338,600	$333,200	$ 5,400	1.6%	48.6%	51.2%
Stockholders' Equity						
7% preferred stock	$120,000	$120,000			17.2%	18.4%
$4 par common stock	95,600	88,000	$ 7,600	8.6%	13.7	13.5
Paid-in capital in excess of						
par	40,200	36,000	4,200	11.7	5.8	5.5
Retained earnings	102,600	73,400	29,200	39.8	14.7	11.3
Total stockholders' equity	$358,400	$317,400	$ 41,000	12.9%	51.4%	48.8%
Total liabilities and stock-						
holders' equity	$697,000	$650,600	$ 46,400	7.1%	100.0%	100.0%

CERTAIN OTHER USEFUL RATIOS   A number of ratios other than those indicated in the comparative income statements and comparative balance sheets of William Fox, Inc. (see also page 402) are of considerable importance in determining not only the efficiency but also the general financial position

[1]See page 402 for similar analysis of comparative income statements of William Fox, Inc.

of the company and operating policies of the management. Omitted in the following brief discussion are what may be some vital statistics, such as average wages, labor turnover, pension funds, and stock purchase rights. Again, similar ratios of like businesses or perhaps entirely different businesses in other industries may prove to be of great importance to a potential investor.

Among the usual ratios considered in analysis of a business are:

1   Net income to average net worth
2   Times preferred dividend is earned (same for bonds if such indebtedness)
3   Earnings per share of common stock
4   Return on average of common stockholders' equity
5   Return on average total assets
6   Working capital ratio
7   Acid-test ratio
8   Total capital turnover
9   Average age of accounts receivable
10   Fixed property turnover
11   Stock turnover and stock sales ratios (see Units 10.6 and 10.7)

Again utilizing the statements of William Fox, Inc. (pages 402 and 406), for the fiscal year 1979 (and in some instances the fiscal year 1978), the ratios other than stock turnover and stock sales ratios can be determined as illustrated in the following examples.

NET INCOME TO AVERAGE NET WORTH   A primary objective of most businesses is to earn income. If variances in net worth throughout the year are not available, then the average capital at the beginning and end of the year may be utilized.

Example 3   **Net income to average net worth.**

Stockholders' equity, beginning of year $317,400.00
Stockholders' equity, end of year $\underline{+358,400.00}$
                                             $675,800.00

Average equity: $\dfrac{\$675,800.00}{2} = \$337,900.00$

$\dfrac{\text{Net income, 1979}}{\text{Average equity}} : \dfrac{\$37,600.00}{\$337,900.00} = 0.111 = 11.1\%$

TIMES PREFERRED DIVIDEND IS EARNED   Preferred stockholders (particularly, if as is usual, the preferred stock is nonparticipating in earnings distributed to the common stock) are concerned with a ratio that the net income of the business is to the stipulated par or stated dollars due the owner of preferred shares.

Example 4   **Times preferred dividend is earned.**

$$\frac{\text{Net income, 1979}}{0.07 \times \$120,000.00} : \frac{\$37,600.00}{\$8400.00} = 4.48 \text{ times}$$

EARNINGS PER SHARE OF COMMON STOCK   The net income available to the stockholders for the year 1979 was $37,600. Again, assuming the preferred stock to be nonparticipating, earnings per share of common stock may be computed as follows.

Example 5   **Earnings per share of common stock.**

Net income, 1979 $37,600.00
Less preferred dividend requirements (0.07 × $120,000.00)   −8,400.00
    Net income available for common stock $29,200.00

Average number of
    dollars common stock: $\dfrac{\$88,000.00 + \$95,600.00}{2} = \$91,800.00$

Average number of shares common stock: $\dfrac{\$91,800.00}{\$4.00 \text{ par}} = 22,950 \text{ shares}$

$\dfrac{\text{Net income available for common stock}}{\text{Average number of shares common stock}} : \dfrac{\$29,200.00}{22,950} = \$1.27$

RETURN ON AVERAGE OF COMMON STOCKHOLDERS' EQUITY   Assuming that the par of $120,000 represents the preferred stockholders' equity, the return on the common stockholders' average equity may be computed as follows.

Example 6   **Return on average of common stockholders' equity.**

Total stockholders' equity, beginning of year $317,400.00
Less preferred stockholders' equity   −120,000.00
Common stockholders' equity, beginning of year $197,400.00
Total stockholders' equity, end of year   358,400.00
Less preferred stockholders' equity   −120,000.00
Common stockholders' equity, end of year $238,400.00

Common stockholders'
    average equity: $\dfrac{\$197,400.00 + \$238,400.00}{2} = \$217,900.00$

As illustrated in Example 5, net income available for common stock was $29,200. Hence,

Return on common
    stockholders' average equity: $\dfrac{\$29,200.00}{\$217,900.00} = 0.134 = 13.4\%$

RETURN ON AVERAGE TOTAL ASSETS The income earned on all funds used by the business is considered an important test of management's competency. The income figure used in this computation should be income before payment of any interest expense (e.g., net income plus interest paid). If we assume 5 percent interest paid on the long-term liabilities, the computation may be as follows.

Example 7   **Return on average total assets.**

$$\text{Average long-term liabilities: } \frac{\$238,000.00 + \$210,000.00}{2} = \$224,000.00$$

Net income, 1979	$37,600.00
Plus interest paid ($224,000.00 × 0.05)	11,200.00
Net income before interest expense	$48,800.00

$$\text{Average total assets: } \frac{\$650,600.00 + \$697,000.00}{2} = \$673,800.00$$

$$\text{Return on average total assets: } \frac{\$48,800.00}{\$673,800.00} = 0.072 = 7.2\%$$

WORKING CAPITAL RATIO Perhaps the best known test of financial statements is the working capital ratio, often called the current ratio. This ratio compares the current assets with the current liabilities. Depending upon the industry, borrowers on commercial paper are often expected to maintain a ratio of not less than 2:1 (e.g., not less than $2 of current assets for each $1 of current liabilities).

Example 8   **Working capital ratio.**

$$\text{Ratio at beginning of year} = \frac{\text{current assets}}{\text{current liabilities}} = \frac{\$296,000.00}{\$95,200.00} = \frac{3.1}{1} \text{ or } 3.1$$

$$\text{Ratio at end of year} = \frac{\text{current assets}}{\text{current liabilities}} = \frac{\$350,000.00}{\$128,600.00} = \frac{2.7}{1} \text{ or } 2.7$$

ACID-TEST RATIO Certain current assets such as inventories and prepaid expenses are not readily convertible into cash. To distinguish the ratio of all current assets to current liabilities (working capital ratio), a ratio known as the quick ratio or acid-test ratio is frequently computed. Thus cash and assets readily convertible to cash such as accounts receivable, short-term notes receivable, listed marketable securities, etc., are compared with current liabilities to compute the quick ratio or acid-test ratio. Normally, a ratio of at least 1:1 is considered desirable (1.0 or more).

    The condensed comparative balance sheet of William Fox, Inc., does not state the items constituting current assets at the end of the fiscal year 1979. However, assume that finished goods, goods in process, raw materials, and prepaid expenses totaled $206,000 of the $350,000 of current assets and that cash, accounts receivable, and notes receivable in an amount of $144,000 comprised the balance of the current assets, then the acid-test ratio at the end of the fiscal year 1972 would be found as follows.

Example 9   **Acid-test ratio.**

$$\text{Acid-test ratio} = \frac{\text{quick current assets}}{\text{current liabilities}} = \frac{\$144,000.00}{\$128,600.00} = \frac{1.12}{1} \text{ or } 1.12$$

TOTAL CAPITAL TURNOVER   This ratio expresses the relationship between net sales and the average total assets used or employed in the operation of the business. Thus, if we assume that "other assets" as shown on the comparative balance sheets for William Fox, Inc., are not essential to the conduct of the business, the total capital turnover may be computed as follows.

Example 10   **Total capital turnover ratio.**

Total assets, beginning of year	$650,600.00
Less other assets not used in operating the business	−19,600.00
Total capital used in operating the business	$631,000.00
Total assets, end of year	$697,000.00
Less other assets not used in operating the business	−27,000.00
Total capital used in operating the business	$670,000.00

$$\text{Average capital used in operating the business: } \frac{\$631,000.00 + \$670,000.00}{2} = \$650,500.00$$

$$\text{Total capital turnover: } \frac{\$800,000.00}{\$650,500.00} = 1.23 \text{ times}$$

AVERAGE AGE OF ACCOUNTS RECEIVABLE   This computation is used to indicate whether overdue accounts are present. The normal credit period, whether it is 10 days, 30 days, 60 days, etc., is compared with the age of accounts receivable to judge the efficiency of collections. A formula that may be used is as follows:

$$\text{Average age of accounts receivable: } \frac{\text{accounts receivable at end of year} \times 365}{\text{net sales for the year}}$$

Example 11   **Average age of accounts receivable.**

The condensed comparative balance sheets of William Fox, Inc., do not show the accounts receivable at the end of the fiscal year 1979. Assume accounts receivable were $76,500 and the normal credit period was 30 days. Then,

$$\text{Average age of accounts receivable: } \frac{\$76,500.00 \times 365}{\$800,000.00} = 34.9 = 35 \text{ days}$$

And, with a normal credit period of 30 days, the presence of overdue accounts is indicated.

FIXED PROPERTY TURNOVER This ratio compares net sales with the assets employed in fixed property, such as buildings, equipment, and land. If such fixed assets are too large, their costs, such as interest, insurance, maintenance, taxes, may result in an unfavorable income statement.

Example 12 **Fixed property turnover.**

$$\text{Fixed property turnover:}\ \frac{\$800{,}000.00}{\$320{,}000.00} = 2.50 \text{ times}$$

Exercise 11.2

1 Compute the missing entries in the following comparative balance sheets. Find percent answers to nearest tenths.

BURT BOLLES MANUFACTURING COMPANY   Condensed comparative balance sheets for fiscal years ending December 31, 1979 and 1978

	1979	1978	Increase or (decrease) Dollars	Increase or (decrease) Percent	Percent of total assets 1979	Percent of total assets 1978
Assets						
Cash	$ 62,100	$ 75,500	$_____	_____%	_____%	_____%
Accounts receivable	81,300	68,700	_____	_____	_____	_____
Notes receivable, short term	24,600	21,800	_____	_____	_____	_____
Inventory	164,900	143,400	_____	_____	_____	_____
Prepaid expenses	4,100	3,600	_____	_____	_____	_____
Current assets	$327,000	$313,000	$_____	_____%	_____%	_____%
Land	$ 30,300	$ 30,300	$_____	_____%	_____%	_____%
Buildings, less depreciation	210,500	215,300	_____	_____	_____	_____
Equipment, less depreciation	26,200	29,400	_____	_____	_____	_____
Fixed assets	$267,000	$275,000	$_____	_____%	_____%	_____%
Total assets	$594,000	$588,000	$_____	_____%	100.0%	100.0%
Liabilities and Stockholders' Equity						
Liabilities						
Current liabilities	$136,700	$142,900	$_____	_____%	_____%	_____%
Long-term liabilities	202,300	220,100	_____	_____	_____	_____
Total liabilities	$339,000	$363,000	$_____	_____%	_____%	_____%
Stockholders' Equity						
6% preferred stock, nonparticipating, redeemable at $25 par	$130,000	$130,000	$_____	_____%	_____%	_____%
$1 par common stock	53,600	51,200	_____	_____	_____	_____
Paid-in capital in excess of par	18,300	15,100	_____	_____	_____	_____
Retained earnings	53,100	28,700	_____	_____	_____	_____
Total stockholders' equity	$255,000	$225,000	$_____	_____%	_____%	_____%
Total liabilities and stockholders' equity	$594,000	$588,000	$_____	_____%	100.0%	100.0%

Compute the following ratios for the Burt Bolles Manufacturing Company. Use the preceding comparative balance sheets and, when necessary, refer to the comparative income statements, page 404:

2   Net income to average net worth.
3   Times preferred dividend is earned.
4   Earnings per share of common stock.
5   Return on average common stockholders' equity.
6   Return on average total assets, assuming 5 percent interest paid on long-term liabilities.
7   Working capital ratio (a) at beginning of year 1979 and (b) at end of year 1979.
8   Acïd-test ratio at end of year 1979.
9   Total capital turnover, all assets used in the business.
10 (a) Average age of accounts receivable, and (b) if the normal credit period is 40 days, does the computation indicate the presence of overdue accounts?
11 Fixed property turnover.

Unit 11.3   *Measures of Central Tendency*

One of the better methods to promote sleep is to have to listen to or read vast arrays of numbers in order to receive some type of message. Most of us have neither the ability nor the desire to "digest" and understand the importance of a large volume of numbers or statistical data. We would rather look at some picture, cartoon, graph, or just a few figures cited to depict the entire collection and thus communicate the message to us. The old Chinese proverb, "One picture is worth one thousand words" suggests that people have not changed much in this regard over time. Successful communication involves holding your listener's attention, and the attention span of most of us is not very long. Therefore, messages must be communicated briefly yet be honest and not misleading.

Measures of central tendency are used to describe "typical values" of a set of data. We have already mentioned and used such terms as "average inventory," "average total assets," "average outstanding principal," etc. Measures of central tendency, *or averages,* attempt to give the measurement of value on which all of the data of a group tend to center. Averages attempt to describe a set of data by means of a single representative number.

Actually, there are three "averages." To most people the word "average" means the sum of all the items in a group, divided by the number of items. However, this is just one type of average, the arithmetic mean. There are two other common types of averages, the *median* and the *mode.* In business, we also make use of adaptations of the arithmetic mean in moving, progressive, and weighted averages.

The Arithmetic Mean, Median, and Mode

These averages are defined as follows:

The *arithmetic mean* is the sum of all the items in a group, divided by the number of items. It is perhaps the most popular and considers all the items in a group. However, it may miss the objective of being the number that best represents the group.

Example 1   **The annual salaries and wages of the Marvin Wright Construction Co. are as follows:**

1	President	$125,000
1	V. President	40,000
1	Secretary-Treasurer	25,000
2	Foremen @ $20,000	40,000
5	Carpenters @ $15,000	75,000
10	Laborers @ $9000	90,000
Totals	20	$395,000

Arithmetic mean salary: $\dfrac{\$395,000}{20} = \quad \$19,750$

To say that the average salary of the Marvin Wright Construction Co. is $19,750 would not be representative because of the higher salaries of the three officers at one end, and the lower salaries of 17 people on the other end. This is very similar to the observation that a person who is unable to swim could drown wading across a river that was an *average of only 2 feet deep*.

The *median* is that number above which and below which there are 50 percent of the items. The median is the "middle value" where the number of items is considered. The median has the advantage of being simple to calculate. Merely arrange the values in either ascending or descending order and select the value halfway down the list. If there is an even number of items in a set of data, no single item divides the group in two equal parts, and the two middle items must be selected. If they are numerically the same, they may be used as the median. If they are not numerically the same, then they are written as the median with a dash between them, thus 25–26, 54–55, etc.

The median also has the advantage of not being influenced by very high or very low values. However, there are still certain types of distribution in which it, too, does not reach the objective of being the number most representative of the group.

Example 2   The inventories of $15,000
             merchandise at the end of   15,000
             each month are shown   18,000
             arranged in ascending   19,500
             order.   20,000
                                           22,000
                                           23,000   median = between 22,000–23,000
                                           45,000
                                           46,000
                                           50,000
                                           60,000
                                           75,000

To say that $22,000–$23,000 represents the inventory for the year could cause erroneous observations on inventory turnovers, capital requirements, etc.
     The *mode* is the easiest average to find as it involves the discovery of the value that occurs most often. A disadvantage is that it is not at all affected by the other values, and if no two values are the same, may even be nonexistent. In Example 2 above, the mode is $15,000.

Example 3   **During the 27 business days of October, 1979, the following number of people sought employment from the Peerless Employment Agency:**

October 1–54	**Find**	71
October 2–38	**(a) the mean,**	68
October 3–47	**(b) the median, and**	65
October 4–56	**(c) the mode.**	63
October 5–71		60
October 6–53		59
October 8–56		59
October 9–50		58
October 10–52		56
October 11–51		56
October 12–48		56
October 13–53		56
October 15–59		56
October 16–65		54
October 17–56		54
October 18–54		54
October 19–59		54
October 20–50		53
October 22–58		53
October 23–49		52
October 24–63		51
October 25–60		50
October 26–56		50
October 27–56		49
October 29–54		48
October 30–68		47
October 31–54		38

Sum or total   = 1490
Total number of items =   27

(a) Mean = total divided by number of items = $1490 \div 27 = 55.19-$

(b) Median = middle of the 27 numbers, or fourteenth number from either end of the array = 54

(c) Mode = most frequently occurring number = 56

QUARTILES *Quartiles* are the items, or values, which, with the median, best separate a group of items, placed in order of magnitude from largest to smallest or from smallest to largest, into four groups.

The *first quartile* separates the lower one-fourth of the items from the upper three-fourths of the items.

The *second quartile* is the median; half of the items lie above it and half lie below it.

The *third quartile* separates the lower three-fourths of the items from the upper one-fourth of the items.

To find the quartiles, divide the number of items by 4; take the nearest whole number to this quotient; then count that number of items from the lower and upper ends of the array of items to find the first and third quartiles, respectively.

Example 4 **Find the first and third quartiles of the numbers of people in Example 3 who sought employment on each business day of October, 1979, with the Peerless Employment Agency.**

$27 \div 4 = 6\frac{3}{4}$

The nearest whole number is 7

Therefore first quartile is seventh number from lower end = 51
Third quartile is seventh number from upper end = 59

The positions of the first and third quartiles indicate the distribution of the items in the array. If the values (or quantities) of these quartiles are close together, the items in the group of data tend to be confined within a small distance on the entire scale of values (as in the example of the Peerless

Employment Agency). However, if these quartiles are far apart, the items in the group are widely separated on the entire scale of values.

When four divisions, or quartiles, do not satisfactorily segregate a large number of items, *deciles,* or 10 groupings, may be used. In an extremely large array of items, *percentiles,* or divisions of the grouping into 100 separations, are frequently desirable.

WHICH AVERAGE TO USE?   The decision as to which of the above averages to use is not an easy one. A subjective judgment must be made which could involve all three. Unfortunately, from the same set of data, different groups will accept that statistical measure which best serves their purpose, even though they know it does not tell the whole story. As members of the business community, we should attempt to communicate the data as honestly as we know how. As consumers and citizens, we should be aware of "deceptive devices"—the "well-chosen average"—so that we will not be misled.[1]

Moving, Progressive, and Weighted Averages

In inventory pricing and various aspects of sales and cost analysis, use is made of what are labeled moving, progressive, and weighted averages.

MOVING AVERAGES   Moving averages are a series of simple averages of groups of statistics of equal time units. Each successive group excludes the data of the first time unit of the preceding group and includes the data for the time unit immediately following. Thus a 6-month moving average might include the data from January through June; the next group would exclude the data from January but would include the data for July; the next group would exclude the data from February but would include the data for August; etc.

Example 5   **Sales for the four quarters of the year were: first quarter, $18,000; second quarter, $21,000; third quarter, $19,600; fourth quarter, $22,200. Sales the following two quarters (fifth and sixth quarters) were $23,800 and $23,400, respectively. Find the average sales per quarter for each successive four-quarter period.**

$$\frac{\$18,000.00 + \$21,000.00 + \$19,600.00 + \$22,200.00}{4} = \frac{\$80,800.00}{4} = \$20,200.00$$

$$\frac{\$80,800.00 - \$18,000.00 + \$23,800.00}{4} = \frac{\$86,600.00}{4} = \$21,650.00$$

$$\frac{\$86,600.00 - \$21,000.00 + \$23,400.00}{4} = \frac{\$89,000.00}{4} = \$22,250.00$$

---

[1] Your courses in statistics should prove most interesting and informative. These measures, plus many more, are presented and developed in the attempt to analyze raw data and use them in the decision-making process.

PROGRESSIVE AVERAGE   A progressive average is a cumulative simple average in which results of the latest period are added to the sum previously computed and the total is divided by the previous divisor + 1.

Example 6   **Find the progressive averages beginning with the first four quarters from the data given in the preceding example of a moving average.**

$$\frac{\$18,000.00 + \$21,000.00 + \$19,600.00 + \$22,200.00}{4} = \frac{\$80,800.00}{4} = \$20,200.00$$

$$\frac{\$80,800.00 + \$23,800.00}{4 + 1} = \frac{\$104,600.00}{5} = \$20,920.00$$

$$\frac{\$104,600.00 + \$23,400.00}{5 + 1} = \frac{\$128,000.00}{6} = \$21,333.33$$

WEIGHTED AVERAGE   A weighted average considers not only the number of units to be averaged but also any differences in the values of the units.

Example 7   **During the month, the purchases of a certain chemical were: 800 lb at 80 cents per lb; 1500 lb at $1 per lb; and 1100 lb at 90 cents per lb. Find the (weighted) average price paid per pound.**

$$\begin{array}{ll}
\$0.80 \times 800 & = \$\ 640.00 \\
1.00 \times 1500 & = \ \ 1500.00 \\
0.90 \times 1100 & = \ \ \ \ 990.00 \\
\hline
3400\ \text{lb} & = \$3130.00
\end{array}$$

Average price per pound $= \dfrac{\$3130.00}{3400} = \$0.9206$

Exercise 11.3

1   In a manufacturing plant, a number of individual workers accomplished the following numbers of pieces of work on Monday: 160, 163, 145, 129, 152, 173, 155, 138, 157, 153, 149, 167, 158, 166, 152, 150, 127, 151, and 168. Find the following average numbers of pieces of work accomplished: (a) the mean to nearest hundredths, (b) the median, and (c) the mode.

2   A class of students received the following grades in an arithmetic test: one received 95, one received 40, three received 65, four received 80, one received 55, seven received 75, three received 90, five received 85, five received 70, two received 50, and three received 60. Find the following average grades received: (a) the mean, (b) the median, and (c) the mode.

3   The Halsey Insurance Company gave its typists a test to determine their speed and accuracy. The grades assigned to the papers were as follows: 46, 83, 49, 57, 42, 63, 81, 31, 54, 59, 64, 61, 68, 54, 51, 50, 61, 58, 65, 61, 62, 61, 63, 54, 60, 27, 58, 60, 25, 57, 58, 56, and 62. Find (a) the mean to nearest tenths, (b) the median, and (c) the mode.

4 Some of the fastest railway runs in the United States accomplish the following mean average speed in miles per hour: 67, 63, 81, 93, 75, 78, 120, 81, 93, 64, 66, 87, 84, 59, 73, 81, 66, 59, 113, 99, 102, 72, 60, 75, 79, 115, and 105. For the entire group, find (a) the mean to the nearest miles per hour, (b) the median, (c) the mode, (d) the first quartile, and (e) the third quartile.

5 The labor costs in a manufacturing plant for the first 6 months of the year were $4087 for January, $3825 for February, $4264 for March, $3990 for April, $4502 for May, and $4178 for June. During the next 3 months the labor costs were $4829 for July, $4653 for August, and $4485 for September. Find the average labor cost per month for each 6-month period following January 1.

6 Sales of the Lucero, Taddei Company were $85,000 for July, $93,680 for August, $81,591 for September, $78,364 for October, $87,809 for November, and $110,545 for December. Find the average sales per month for each successive 3-month period following July 1.

7 Using the data from Problem 5, find the progressive (cumulative) averages as of June 30, July 31, August 31, and September 30.

8 Using the data from Problem 6, find the progressive (cumulative) averages as of August 31, September 30, October 31, November 30, and December 31.

9 The materials used in the manufacture of a product are combined as follows in each unit produced: material A, 12 lb at $1.20 per lb; material B, 2 lb at $2.00 per lb; material C, 8 lb at 40 cents per lb; and material D, 4 lb at $3.00 per lb. Find the percent of increase or decrease in the cost of the product if material prices change as in the following: material A, increase of 25 percent; material B, decrease of 30 percent; material C, decrease of 45 percent; and material D, increase of 20 percent.

Unit 11.4   *Business Graphs*

In business, statistical data are ordinarily presented either as a table or as a graph. When it is desirable to visualize the relationships existing among the various items, a graph is usually prepared, for it is a pictorial presentation enabling one to interpret more readily the comparative facts within the data.

Types of Graphs

A wide variety in types of graphs may be used to express relationships. Among the more commonly used are horizontal or vertical bar graphs, single-line or rectangle graphs, circle graphs, and broken-line or curved-line graphs.

Pictorial graphs are also used to present relationships by means of illustrations in varying sizes or quantities. Thus the various armed forces in the world might be represented by the figures of soldiers, the size of the figures or number of figures representing the varying sizes of the armed forces of each country.

HORIZONTAL OR VERTICAL BAR GRAPHS In a horizontal bar graph, the bars are drawn horizontally; in a vertical bar graph, the bars are vertical. The procedure in forming either is much the same. Figure 11.1 is a vertical bar graph. The following procedure is recommended:

1 Assemble the data, usually in order from lowest to highest or from first to last.
2 Use graph paper, selecting scales that will make interpretation easy.
3 If one element is time, always locate it on the *X* axis (the horizontal line as at the base of the graph, also known as the "axis of abscissas"). If one element is quantity and the other is value, locate quantity on the *X* axis.
4 Place the data on the graph and draw the bars to the places indicated.
5 Title the graph.

Example 1 **Make a vertical graph of the sales volume of the White Company for the years 1971 to 1980.**

Year	Sales
1971	$150,000
1972	130,000
1973	115,000
1974	90,000
1975	95,000
1976	105,000
1977	110,000
1978	125,000
1979	120,000
1980	140,000

This type of graph is ordinarily used to compare quantity in relation to value or quantity, value in relation to time, or quantity in relation to time.

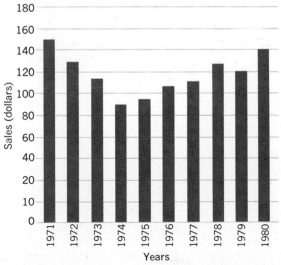

FIGURE 11.1 *White Company sales, 1971–1980 (in thousands of dollars).*

SINGLE-LINE OR RECTANGLE GRAPHS The recommended procedure in forming a single-line (Figure 11.2) or rectangle graph (Figure 11.3) is given below. Graph paper, while helpful, is not essential.

1 Assemble the data, usually in order from lowest to highest.
2 Scale so that smallest item is readily visible and comparable to the largest item.
3 Total the items. This total determines the length of the vertical line or the height of the rectangle. The value of each item to the whole (total) is indicated by the distance between each in the single-line graph and by the area in the rectangle graph. The items are usually placed in ascending or descending order, but this is not necessary or always advisable.
4 Title the graph.

Example 2   **In 1980 the Black Company's sales were $200,000. Expenses were the following percent of sales: administrative 8, occupancy 12, buying 6, selling 7.5, publicity 5, delivery 1.5. Express the relationship of each expense item to the total expense in dollars and as a percent of the total expense in a single-line graph and as a rectangle graph.**

Single-line and rectangle graphs are used to show relationships of various items to each other and to a whole quantity.

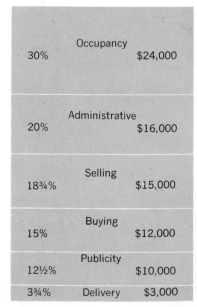

30%	Occupancy $24,000
20%	Administrative $16,000
18¾%	Selling $15,000
15%	Buying $12,000
12½%	Publicity $10,000
3¾%	Delivery $3,000

FIGURE 11.2 Single-line graph. *Black Company expenses, 1980, $80,000.*

FIGURE 11.3 Rectangle graph. *Black Company expenses, 1980, $80,000.*

Item	Expense	Percent of total expense
Occupancy	0.12 × $200,000.00 = $24,000.00	30
Administrative	0.08 × 200,000.00 = 16,000.00	20
Selling	0.075 × 200,000.00 = 15,000.00	18¾
Buying	0.06 × 200,000.00 = 12,000.00	15
Publicity	0.05 × 200,000.00 = 10,000.00	12½
Delivery	0.015 × 200,000.00 = 3,000.00	3¾
Total expense	$80,000.00	100

BROKEN-LINE OR CURVED-LINE GRAPHS   The recommended procedure in forming a broken-line or curved-line graph is as follows:

1   Assemble the data in order from lowest to highest or from earliest to latest.
2   Place time periods on the X axis, quantity or value on the Y axis (the vertical line at the left of the graph, also known as the "axis of ordinates").
3   When only quantity and value are involved, ordinarily place quantity on the X axis.
4   Locate points where vertical lines from the X axis and corresponding horizontal lines from the Y axis intersect.
5   Connect these points by straight or curved lines.
6   Title the graph.

Example 3   **The Smith Department Store had sales, cost of goods sold, expenses, and profit or loss for the years 1971 to 1980 as shown in the table that follows. Figures are in thousands of dollars.**

Year	Sales	Cost of goods sold	Expenses	Profit and loss
1971	$200	$110	$ 95	−$5
1972	240	120	95	25
1973	220	125	110	−15
1974	260	125	105	30
1975	290	140	110	40
1976	290	150	115	25
1977	300	150	105	45
1978	320	160	130	30
1979	345	170	120	55
1980	360	180	140	40

Express the relationship of the amounts of these items in a multiple broken-line graph (see Figure 11.4).

Note: The time factor is placed on the X axis.

Broken-line or curved-line graphs express proportions including quantity or value in relation to time, quantity in relation to value, and parts in relation to the whole or each other over a series of time periods.

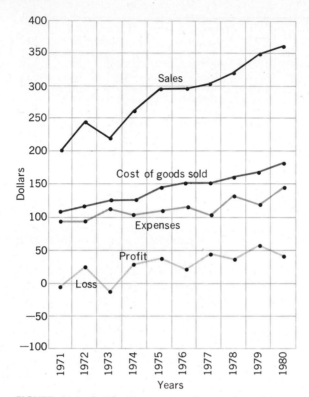

FIGURE 11.4 *Smith Department Store, 1971–1980 (in thousands of dollars).*

Curved lines instead of straight lines could have been used for the graph in Figure 11.4.

CIRCLE GRAPHS   The recommended procedure in forming a circle graph is given below. Graph paper is helpful but not essential.

1   Assemble the data, usually in order from lowest to highest.
2   Make a circle of the desired size.
3   The circumference of the circle or 360° represents 100 percent if a percent basis is used, or $1 if 100 cents is the basis. Each percent or cent must be changed to its equivalent of 3.6°.
4   Complete the graph. The number of degrees in the arcs and the areas of the sections show the relationship of the data presented in the graph.
5   Title the graph.

Example 4   **The Kinkade family with net income after taxes of $17,200 in 1977 made the following expenditures:**

Item	%	Amount	Degrees
Food	25	$ 4300	90
Home occupancy	25	4300	90
Clothing	9	1548	32
Savings	8	1376	29
Recreation	8	1376	29
Contributions	5	860	18
Health	8	1376	29
Auto expense	10	1720	36
Miscellaneous	2	344	7
Total expense	100	$17,200	360

Circle graphs are frequently used to show the relationships between quantities or values in percents or number of cents in $1.

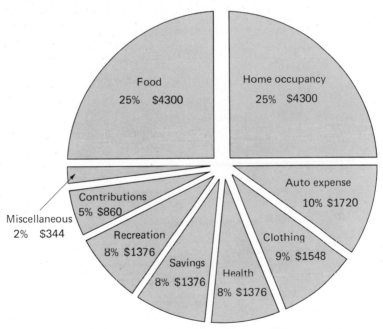

FIGURE 11.5 *Kinkade family expenditures—1977 net income after taxes, $17,200.*

Selection of Proper Scales and Location of Each Axis and Point of Origin

Unless the statistical data have been accurately collected and properly assembled, it is impossible to construct a graph that will give a true pictorial presentation. Further, even though the statistical facts contained within the graph are true, it is still possible to so present this information that the graph is misleading.

Scales for both the X axis and Y axis should be carefully selected in order that interpretation of the data may be read easily and conclusions made logically.

It is essential that each axis should be located on the O or zero line. If for any reason a portion of the graph has been left out, this fact must be clearly indicated.

If you will observe graphs prepared for business or political purposes, you will frequently find that they have been accidentally or purposely so constructed as to minimize or maximize interpretation. When this occurs, the graphs are misleading to the unwary or uninformed. Such graphs do not accomplish what should be the primary purpose of every graph, that is, to present a truthful, vivid, and easily understood conception of the relationships existing in the statistical data.

As a simple illustration of how improperly constructed graphs may lead to incorrect interpretation of the data presented, consider the following:

Through solicitation of personal friends of President Jones of the ABC Company, Mr. Brown obtained a job as salesman despite the protests of Sales Manager Smith. Mr. Brown's sales during his first week of employment were as follows: Monday, $50; Tuesday, $60; Wednesday, $55; Thursday, $70; Friday, $65; and Saturday, $60.

On Monday of the following week, Sales Manager Smith in an audience with President Jones requested the immediate dismissal of Mr. Brown and included a graph (Figure 11.6) in support of his request. President Jones called Mr. Brown to his office and Mr. Brown in defending his position also presented a graph (Figure 11.7).

As each graph apparently presented an entirely different picture of Mr. Brown's sales performance, President Jones requested his statistician to help him properly interpret the two graphs.

The statistician pointed out that the scale of values used for the X axis and Y axis varied in both graphs, and even more important, that both graphs failed to indicate the point of origin O and thus properly locate the X axis.

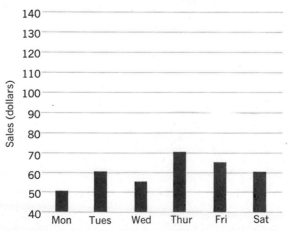

FIGURE 11.6   *Sales of Mr. Brown (as prepared by Sales Manager Smith).*

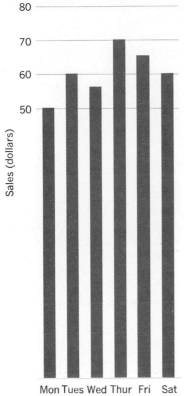

FIGURE 11.7 *Sales of Mr. Brown (as prepared by Mr. Brown).*

FIGURE 11.8 *Sales of Mr. Brown (vertical bar graph as prepared by statistician).*

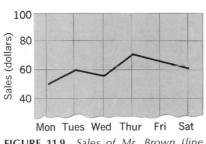

FIGURE 11.9 *Sales of Mr. Brown (line graph as prepared by statistician).*

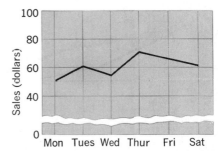

FIGURE 11.10 *Sales of Mr. Brown (line graph as prepared by statistician).*

The statistician then prepared graphs (Figures 11.8 through 11.10) with properly located points of origin O.

In the vertical bar graph (Figure 11.8), the point of origin O is properly located. In the line graphs (Figures 11.9 and 11.10) the point of origin is indicated as being some distance below the lower portion of the graphs, by the use of the jagged lines at the bottoms of the graphs. When it is desired to save space by reducing the height required to present the data properly, the use of a broken or jagged line at the bottom as in Figures 11.9 and 11.10 is permissible, but the method used in Figure 11.10 is preferable.

Exercise 11.4

Two pages of graph paper in arithmetic grid are required for Problems 1 to 4.

1   Use the top portion of one page of the graph paper to make a horizontal bar graph of the net sales of the clerks employed by the Ingram Hardware Store during the period September 1 through September 15, 1979. (Arrange in order from highest sales to lowest sales.)

Ayers	$2350	Quinton	$ 900
Holden	1700	Baker	2780
Pierce	1925	French	2250
Watson	2100	Nelson	1400
Dean	1400	Miller	1875

2   Use the lower portion of the same page of graph paper to make a vertical bar graph of the stock of men's $25.00 shoes in the Oliver Department Store, December 31, 1979. Note: In a stock-record graph of this kind, sizes 1 to $6\frac{1}{2}$ need not be indicated.

Size	No. pairs	Size	No. pairs	Size	No. pairs
7	63	9	135	11	146
$7\frac{1}{2}$	90	$9\frac{1}{2}$	178	$11\frac{1}{2}$	118
8	129	10	160	12	84
$8\frac{1}{2}$	146	$10\frac{1}{2}$	182	$12\frac{1}{2}$	37

3   On the second page of the graph paper, use the top portion to make (a) single-line graph and (b) a rectangle graph, showing relationship of the following in dollars and in percents. These items represent the monthly expenditure of the James Vincent family in May, 1979.

Savings	$133.00
Food	$312.00
Shelter	$296.00
Clothing	$103.00
Operating	$ 96.00
Advancement	$ 60.00

4   On the bottom portion of the second page of the graph paper, make a circle graph of the planned monthly budget of the Carol Eaton family for July, 1979. Express the following items in both dollars and percents:

Savings	14%
Food	24%
Shelter	22%
Clothing	18%
Operating	12%
Advancement	10%
100%	= $1800

Two pages of graph paper in arithmetic grid are required for Problems 5 and 6.

5   On one page of graph paper, prepare a broken-line or curved-line graph showing sales by months of the various departments in the basement store of Upson Brothers, 1979.

	Men's shop	Millinery	Shoes	Dresses	Coats
January	$28,962	$ 5,672	$ 8,745	$15,840	$12,384
February	31,504	5,813	8,450	12,360	10,784
March	35,655	7,534	9,800	19,834	13,362
April	40,006	11,476	14,176	28,432	16,439
May	38,760	8,285	12,008	22,386	14,365
June	34,200	7,988	11,460	18,549	9,840
July	38,677	6,345	8,738	17,300	8,365
August	24,932	7,893	7,222	21,847	11,483
September	32,473	7,946	9,306	26,500	16,781
October	38,741	9,001	12,845	24,279	21,325
November	48,254	8,885	8,255	18,951	20,403
December	64,920	4,275	6,905	14,378	15,379

6   On the other page of graph paper, prepare a broken-line or curved-line graph showing sales, cost of goods sold, expenses, and net profit or loss of the Anderson Clothing Store for the years 1971 to 1980.

Year	Sales	Cost of goods sold	Expenses
1971	$ 624,000	$420,000	$310,000
1972	725,000	460,000	295,000
1973	780,000	480,000	275,000
1974	700,000	400,000	240,000
1975	830,000	510,000	265,000
1976	900,000	550,000	310,000
1977	980,000	580,000	320,000
1978	1,070,000	660,000	345,000
1979	1,345,000	770,000	405,000
1980	1,223,000	700,000	385,000

Chapter 12

Sales and Property Taxes; Depreciation; Overhead Distribution; Distribution of Ownership and Profits

Objectives To Be Achieved in This Chapter

1 Work with sales and property taxes. Finding assessed valuation and property tax rates from various given data.

2 Determination of the charge for depreciation by the most commonly used depreciation formulas.

3 Calculation of the overhead allocation to different service or production departments.

4 Determination of the book value or net worth of a business enterprise and its allocation to partners or stockholders.

5 Allocation of the profits in a partnership by the more common methods.

6 Work with corporation ownership terms of preferred and common stock, retained earnings, dividends, and book value per share.

7 Become acquainted with the concept of leverage and trading on the equity.

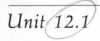

Unit 12.1

*Sales Taxes
and Property Taxes*

A sum of money assessed by government authority for any public use or service such as for the support of municipal, state, or federal undertakings or for the support of government is a *tax*.

Taxes on tobacco, liquor, luxuries, transportation, imports, communication, etc., are *indirect taxes*. Taxes on the person, property, or income of an individual are *direct taxes*.

Deductions from employees' gross earnings for federal old-age and survivors insurance, state disability taxes, and federal income taxes have already been discussed (see Unit 8.1). Among other important taxes paid by most individuals are sales and property taxes.

Sales Taxes

Many state, county, and/or municipal governments now levy taxes on the sale of merchandise, known as *sales taxes*. Usually a percent of the amount of the transaction is charged the purchaser by the seller, who acts as an agent, periodically turning over such collections to the state, county, and/or municipal governments.

To avoid charges of fractional cents, sales taxes are usually assessed in arbitrary amounts on sales involving fractional parts of a dollar, although in some states more accurate collections are made through the issuance of stamps or tokens representing fractions of a cent.

Table 12-1 is a typical schedule of arbitrary rates of sales tax charged by a state government which includes the additional rate charged by a municipality in the same state. The tax is collected from the consumer by the retailer. Periodic reports and remission of all the taxes collected are made by the retailer to the state government. The reports filed by the retailer contain information for the state to return to the municipality the sales taxes allocable to the municipality.

**TABLE 12.1   STATE AND MUNICIPALITY
6 PERCENT COMBINED SALES TAX
SCHEDULE FOR SALES INVOLVING
FRACTIONAL PARTS OF $1[1]**

Transaction amount	Tax
$0.01–$0.09	$0.00
0.10– 0.24	0.01
0.25– 0.41	0.02
0.42– 0.58	0.03
0.59– 0.74	0.04
0.75– 0.91	0.05
0.92– 1.08	0.06

[1] Plus 6 percent of the number of full dollars in the transaction.

Example 1   **Using the preceding tax schedule, find the sales taxes paid by John Edens on the following purchases made within the municipality: (a) $10.00, (b) $24.93, (c) $8.73, (d) $464.32.**

(a) $10.00 × $0.06   = $0.60

(b) $24.00 × $0.06   = $1.44
      Tax on $0.93   = $\underline{0.06}$
      $1.50

(c) $8.00 × $0.06   = $0.48
      Tax on $0.73   = $\underline{0.04}$
      $0.52

(d) $464.00 × $0.06 = $27.84
      Tax on $0.32 = $\underline{0.02}$
      $27.86

Property Taxes

Real- and personal-property taxes are imposed by state, county, and/or municipal governments for the operation and maintenance of their services and institutions. Real-property taxes are levied against land and fixed improvements thereon, such as buildings; personal-property taxes are levied against all other property, tangible or intangible, such as cash, radios, television sets, household furnishings, etc.

Although real- and personal-property taxes vary from state to state, county to county, and incorporated municipality to incorporated municipality, the method of computation is the same.

Three factors are involved: (1) assessed valuation, an arbitrary value placed on property for tax purposes; (2) the tax rate applied by the state, county, and/or municipality expressed as a percent, in mills (tenths of a cent) and fractions thereof, or in dollars and cents and fractions thereof; (3) the tax itself. Note that assessed valuations (arbitrary values) made by state, county, and/or municipality may be the same or different. In some states, real- and personal-property taxes are collected only by counties and/or municipalities. The formulas for property tax computations are

$$\text{Tax rate} = \frac{\text{tax}}{\text{assessed valuation}}$$

$$\text{Tax} = \text{assessed valuation} \times \text{tax rate}$$

$$\text{Assessed valuation} = \frac{\text{tax}}{\text{tax rate}}$$

To determine the amount of tax that must be raised to pay the expenses of a municipality, the general procedure is for the various divisions or departments to prepare a budget. This budget of estimated expenses is then subject to inspection and analysis by the legally authorized representatives of the citizens of the municipality. Upon acceptance or upon modification and subsequent acceptance, the property tax for the municipality is determined.

To this must be added the municipality's share of county and state taxes. Thus:

Total tax = municipal tax + county tax + state tax

Assessed valuation is determined by an appointed or elected representative of the citizens. The assessor or assessors place a valuation known as "assessed valuation" on the various real properties contained within the areas of the municipality. This valuation varies between communities, but it is usually 25 to 60 percent of the current market valuation of the real properties. Within a community, the assessed valuation is supposedly calculated on the previously agreed upon percent. Thus if a 50 percent assessed valuation is to be used, a $10,000 piece of property would be valued at $5000, a $15,000 property at $7500, and an $8000 property at $4000.

Residents of unincorporated municipalities do not pay a municipal tax, their tax being the sum of the county and state taxes, if any.

TO FIND TAX RATE When the total assessed valuation and the tax budget are known,

$$\text{Tax rate} = \frac{\text{tax}}{\text{assessed valuation}}$$

Custom varies as to the number of decimal places of accuracy used in setting the tax rate, *but in no instance is even the smallest fraction rounded off,* the practice being to raise the final digit. Thus if computations indicate the necessary tax rate to be 0.043521+, the rate might be set and expressed as $4.3522 per $100, $4.353 per $100, or $4.36 per $100 of assessed value.

Example 2   **The assessed valuation of the taxable property in a certain municipality is $52,384,600, and the taxes to be raised are $123,475 by the state, $931,442.75 by the county, and $319,878 by the municipality. If the county collects the taxes and then reimburses the state and the municipality, find the combined tax rate if expressed (a) to thousandths percent, (b) in mills (tenths of a cent) per $1 of assessed value, (c) to cents per $100 of assessed value, and (d) to mills per $1000 of assessed value.**

Total tax = $123,475.00 + $931,442.75 + $319,878.00 = $1,374,795.75

$$\frac{\$1,374,795.75}{\$52,384,600.00} = 0.0262442+$$

(a) To thousandths percent   2.625%
(b) In mills per $1.00 of assessed value   27 mills (or $0.027)
(c) To cents per $100.00 of assessed value $2.63
(d) To mills per $1000.00 of assessed value $26.245

Note: In each instance the final digit retained is raised, no matter how small the remainder.

TO FIND TAX When the assessed valuation and the tax rate are known:

Tax = assessed valuation × tax rate

Example 3   **Ms. Smith owns a home with an assessed value of $3250. On November 10 the tax rate for the fiscal year beginning February 1 is announced as 2.351 percent. What tax will she be required to pay?**

$$2.351\% = \$0.02351 \text{ per dollar of assessed valuation}$$
$$\$3250 \times 0.02351 = \$76.4075 = \$76.41$$
$$\text{or } 2.351\% = \$2.351 \text{ per } \$100.00 \text{ of assessed valuation}$$
$$\text{and } \$3250 = 32.5 \text{ hundreds}$$
$$\$2.351 \times 32.5 = \$76.4075 = \$76.41$$

Sometimes a collector's fee, usually a percent of the tax itself, is added to the tax payment collected.

Example 4   **Mr. Rose owned a store with an assessed valuation of $6640. The tax rate was $3.87 per $100, and the collector charged 2 percent of the tax for collecting. What was the total amount paid by Mr. Rose?**

$6640.00 = 66.4$ hundreds

$$\text{Tax} = \$3.87 \times 66.4 \qquad\qquad = \$256.97$$
$$\text{Collector's fee} = \$256.97 \times 0.02 = \quad +5.14$$
$$\text{Total amount paid} = \overline{\$262.11}$$

Usually, failure to pay property taxes when they are due subjects the owner to interest charges and sometimes to other penalties. Ordinarily, if taxes on property are in default for a stipulated period of years, the property is sold under court order; and the accumulated taxes, interest, penalties, and costs are deducted, with the remainder, if any, remitted to the owner. In practice, the selling price is unlikely to exceed the obligation, and tax-defaulted property often brings no return to the owner.

TO FIND ASSESSED VALUATION When the total tax budget and the tax rate are known:

$$\text{Assessed valuation} = \frac{\text{tax}}{\text{tax rate}}$$

Example 5   **A city has a municipal, county, and state tax budget totaling $2,455,335. The tax rate is comprised of a state tax of 52 cents per $100, a county tax of 31 cents per $100, and a municipal tax of $1.42 per $100. What is the total assessed valuation?**

Total tax rate = $0.52 + $0.31 + $1.42 = $2.25 per $100.00
$2.25 per $100.00 = 2.25% = 0.0225

$$\frac{\$2,455,335.00}{0.0225} = \$109,126,000.00 \qquad \text{Total assessed valuation}$$

Example 6   **Mr. Eyre pays a tax and collector's fee totaling $70.62 on his home. What is the assessed valuation if the tax rate is 2.432 percent and a collection fee of 1 percent of the tax is charged?**

Tax + 1% collector's fee = $70.62
100% tax + 1% tax = $70.62
101% or 1.01 tax = $70.62

Therefore, tax = $\dfrac{\$70.62}{1.01} = \$69.92$

$$2.432\% = 0.02432$$
$$\frac{\$69.92}{0.02432} = \$2875.00 \qquad \text{Assessed valuation}$$

Exercise 12.1

Solve the following problems in computing sales taxes. All sales were made in and for delivery within a municipality whose 1 percent sales tax is included in the combined state and municipality 6 percent arbitrary sales tax schedule on page 430.

1 Bill Johnson made a purchase of $21.46. Find the sales tax that he paid.
2 Chris Carmichael bought a motorcycle for $229.99. Find the sales tax she paid.
3 Wendy Sibray paid $306.87, including sales tax, for a couch. Find (a) the invoice price of the couch and (b) the amount of sales tax paid.
4 Sheila Benson bought a new motorbike for $4060.00 including sales tax and $85 license fee. No sales tax is charged on license fees. Find (a) the invoice price of the motorbike and (b) the amount of sales tax.

Solve the following problems in property taxes:

5 The assessed valuation of the taxable property in a certain municipality is $32,556,000. If planned expenditures require that $1,182,000 be raised through property taxes, find the tax rate to cents per $100 of assessed value. *Reminder:* In establishing a tax rate, raise the last digit retained if there is any remainder, regardless of how small the remainder may be.
6 The assessed valuation of the taxable property in a certain county is $36,847,000 and annual property taxes to be raised are $284,815 for the state and $160,419 for the county. Find the combined tax rate (a) if quoted in percent to thousandths or (b) if quoted to cents per $1000 of assessed value.
7 The assessed valuation of the taxable property in a certain incorporated municipality is $152,785,960. The property taxes to be raised are $601,524 for the state, $422,358 for the county, and $3,258,483 for the municipality.

Find the combined tax rate if quoted (a) in percent to thousandths, (b) to hundredths of a mill per dollar of assessed value, (c) to tenths of a cent per $100 of assessed value, and (d) to cents per $1,000 of assessed value.

8   The Phi Kappa Tau Fraternity's chapter house has an assessed valuation of $17,951, and the tax rate is $0.0947 per dollar of assessed value. What annual property tax is the Phi Kappa Tau Fraternity required to pay?

9   Mrs. Alder has a home with an assessed valuation of 25 percent of its cost of $24,800. If the tax rate is $9.58 per $100 of assessed value, find the annual property tax that she must pay.

10   Mr. Hughes owns a store building with an assessed valuation of $52,500. If the tax rate is $96.90 per $1000 of assessed value and a collector's fee of 1 percent of the tax is charged, what total annual property tax and collector's fee does he pay?

11   A city has a combined municipal, county, and state property tax budget totaling $2,589,761.16. Per $100 of assessed value, the municipal tax rate is $2.80, the county tax rate is $5.60, and the state tax rate is $1.29. Find the total assessed valuation of the taxable property in the city.

12   If the total annual tax payment on a building lot, including a collector's charge of 2 percent of the property tax, is $221.43 and the tax rate is $0.1042 per dollar of assessed value, find the assessed value of the lot.

13   Ms. DeWitt pays an annual total of $2130.49 tax and collector's fee on her apartment house, a sum determined by a tax rate of 8.68 percent of assessed value plus a collector's fee of 1 percent of the tax. Find the assessed valuation of the apartment house.

Unit 12.2   *Depreciation*

Whenever a business asset contributes services beyond one fiscal period (usually a year), its cost, less any salvage value, is distributed over the years of its useful economic life. The allocation of this cost is what is known in accounting as *depreciation*.[1]

General Characteristics of Depreciation

LIMITED LIFE   Business assets that are subject to depreciation must have a limited life. There must be a limit to the time when future benefits will cease. Useful lives are determined by the nature of the asset and the intentions of management for its use. The Internal Revenue Service has published guidelines and ranges within which they will readily accept a

---

[1]Depreciation *per se* is the decline in value of any item due to its use, obsolescence, decay, etc. However, this is not what is being measured and charged to expense in accounting statements. Depreciation, as used in accounting, is a *cost allocation* process which may or may not have any correlation with its decline in value due to wear and tear, decay, obsolescence, etc.

depreciation life for income tax purposes. Useful lives outside of this range may have to be proven by management before a deduction is allowable.

Example 1   **A farmer purchased a farm which included the following:**

160 acres of land
Barns and sheds
50 head breeding stock (cattle)
Farm machinery
Personal residence

Except for the 160 acres of land, all of the above would have limited useful lives. The personal residence is not considered a business asset by the Internal Revenue Service, therefore allocation of its cost could not be taken for income tax purposes.

DEPRECIATION BASIS The costs that are to be allocated over the depreciable assets' useful life are all those costs incurred to place the asset in the use for which it was intended. These costs include not only the initial invoice price, but also freight, installation, and setup costs, and even expenditures for breaking-in. From these total costs are subtracted the estimated value, if any, that the asset may have at the end of its useful life.

Example 2   **A logging contractor purchased a tractor. The invoice price was $125,000. The logger added winches, canopy, and an angle blade for an additional $25,000. Freight on the machine to the contractor's place of business was $2500. The tractor was expected to have a value of $30,000 at the end of its useful life in the woods. Find the depreciation basis of the tractor.**

The depreciation basis of the tractor would be:

Invoice price	$125,000
Additional equipment	25,000
Freight	1,500
Subtotal	$151,500
Less salvage value	30,000
Basis for depreciation	$121,500

The depreciation basis illustrated above depicts a newly acquired asset and is relatively simple. The calculation of the basis for depreciation purposes can become complex when assets are traded, received by gift or inheritance, converted from personal use, repossessed, etc. The presentation of these basic rules will be left to your courses in accounting and income taxes.

METHODS FOR ALLOCATING BASIS OF DEPRECIABLE ASSETS Numerous methods exist for allocating costs of depreciable assets over their useful lives. In general, the methods used in industry and allowable for income tax purposes parallel each other, although there are important differences. These common methods are described in the next section.

Twenty percent first-year depreciation is a feature which is unique in the present income tax law. To encourage investment in new equipment, the federal government passed a law which allows taxpayers to deduct 20 percent of the cost of a new or used business asset the first year. The 20 percent first-year depreciation is limited to $10,000 cost of all eligible property of a corporation or a taxpayer filing a separate return. The limit is $20,000 cost if taxpayers are married and filing a joint return. The asset must be tangible personal property (as defined by the law) and have a useful life of at least six years. The 20 percent is applied to the total cost of the asset before any salvage is deducted. The 20 percent first-year depreciation is then subtracted from the asset's total cost along with any salvage value, and the remainder then becomes the basis for depreciation by the other depreciation methods.

Example 3   **Same problem data as Example 2. Assume the useful life of the tractor is 8 years and the taxpayer is a corporation. The 20 percent first-year depreciation for income tax purposes and the calculation of the remaining depreciation base are as follows:**

Total cost before salvage value = $151,500
First-year depreciation limited
    to eligible property of   = $10,000
    20% thereof   = $2,000

Calculation of basis for regular
depreciation:

Cost	=		$151,500
Less: First-year depreciation	=	$2,000	
Salvage value	=	$30,000	− 32,000
Basis for regular depreciation			$119,500

Methods of Depreciation

STRAIGHT-LINE METHOD OF COMPUTING DEPRECIATION   The most frequently used of all methods of computing depreciation is the straight-line method. Cost or other basis of property, less estimated salvage value, is the basis. However, if additional first-year depreciation is taken, it must be subtracted from this basis to determine a new and lower basis for computing depreciation.

Annual depreciation can be found by dividing the established basis by the estimated life in years. Or, the depreciation for each year can be determined by dividing that portion of the asset, less salvage value, not yet depreciated by the remaining useful life of the property.

If the assumptions are correct, the actual selling price or trade-in value (or junk value at the end of the useful life) will be equivalent to the remaining cost including salvage value not yet recovered through depreciation.

Example 4   **Straight-line method.**[1] **Find the ordinary depreciation allowable for (a) the first year and (b) the second year for an asset with depreciable basis of $2200 acquired on May 12, if the estimated life is 8 years and the salvage value is estimated at $200.**

$$\text{Depreciable basis} = \$2200.00 - \$200.00 = \$2000.00$$

$$\text{Annual depreciation} = \frac{\$2000.00}{8} = \$250.00$$

(a)   May 12 is considered as May 1, and 8 months' or $\frac{8}{12}$ of a full year's depreciation is claimed:

$$\$250.00 \times \frac{8}{12} = \$166.67$$

(b)   The full year's depreciation of $250 is claimed.

Example 5   **Straight-line method. If additional first-year depreciation of 20 percent is elected, find the depreciation allowable for (a) the first year and (b) the second year for a depreciable asset that cost $7500 on October 26, if the estimated life is 6 years and the salvage value is estimated at $900.**

$$\text{Additional first-year depreciation} = \$7500.00 \times 0.20 = \$1500.00$$
$$\text{Depreciable basis} = \$7500.00 - \$1500.00 - \$900.00 = \$5100.00$$

$$\text{Annual depreciation} = \frac{\$5100.00}{6} = \$850.00$$

(a)   October 26 is considered as November 1, and 2 months' or $\frac{2}{12}$ of a full year's depreciation is claimed:

$$\$850.00 \times \frac{2}{12} = \$ \ 141.67$$

$$\text{Additional first-year depreciation} = \$1500.00$$
$$\text{Depreciation for first year} \qquad = \overline{\$1641.67}$$

(b)   The full year's depreciation of $850 is claimed.

DECLINING-BALANCE METHOD OF COMPUTING DEPRECIATION   Under the declining-balance method of depreciation, the amount of depreciation taken each year is subtracted from the cost or other basis of the property before computing the next year's depreciation, so that the depreciation applies to a smaller or declining balance in each succeeding year. Since the declining-balance method results in high depreciation in the earlier years of an asset's life, it offers possible income tax advantages to the user.
  Salvage value is not deducted from basis in the calculations for declin-

---

[1]In this example and all others in this unit, it is assumed that dates of acquisition are the nearest first-of-month and that the fiscal year is the calendar year.

ing-balance method of depreciation. The original basis, less first-year depreciation, if any, is used as the starting point. However, while salvage value is not taken into account in the calculations, the Internal Revenue Code (IRC) does not allow the property to be depreciated below its reasonable salvage value. The IRC as currently amended, has established maximum declining-balance rates on the various types of property. The rates vary from $1\frac{1}{4}$ times the straight-line rate for used residential rental property to twice the straight-line rate for new personal property and new residential rental property. The estimated useful life must be a minimum of 3 years.

PROCEDURE FOR DECLINING-BALANCE DEPRECIATION METHOD The calculations for the declining-balance method are similar to problems in percentage. A constant rate (percent) is applied to the difference between the preceding year's basis and the preceding year's depreciation. Thus:

Example 6 **Assume an asset with a basis of $1200 and a useful life of 3 years being depreciated at twice the straight-line rate.**

	Year 1	Year 2	Year 3
Previous year's basis	$1200	$1200	$400.00
Less previous year's depreciation	0	800	266.67
Current year's basis	$1200	$400	$133.33
Constant rate	0.6667	0.6667	0.6667
Current year's depreciation	$800	$266.67	$88.89

Example 7 **Declining-balance method. If additional first-year depreciation is elected, find the maximum depreciation allowable for (a) the year 5 and (b) the year 6 for a new truck purchased on October 10, year 5 by George and Agnes Michaels at a cost of $18,000. The truck has an estimated useful life of 6 years and an estimated salvage value of $4000 at that time. The declining-balance method of depreciation at twice the straight-line rate is to be used. A joint tax return is filed.**

   Note: Since the declining-balance is elected, salvage value need not be considered in the calculation.

(a) Cost of asset $18,000

      20% additional first-year depreciation   ×0.20

         Additional first-year depreciation $3600

      Depreciation basis:

        Cost $18,000

        Less additional first-year depreciation   3600

        Depreciation basis $14,400

      Declining-balance method of depreciation:

        Straight-line rate $= \dfrac{1}{6}$

$$\text{Twice the straight-line rate} = \frac{1}{6} \times 2 = \frac{1}{3} \qquad \times \frac{1}{3}$$

Annual depreciation	$4800

$$\frac{3}{12} \text{ of year 5 (From October 1)} \qquad \times \frac{1}{4}$$

Regular depreciation for year 5	$1200
Total depreciation for year 5	$4800

(b)

Depreciation basis year 5	$14,400
Less regular depreciation taken in year 5	1200
Depreciation basis, January 1, year 6	$13,200
Declining-balance rate	$\times \frac{1}{3}$
Depreciation, year 6	$4400

SUM-OF-THE-YEARS'-DIGITS METHOD OF COMPUTING DEPRECIATION

The sum-of-the-years'-digits method applies a fraction of constantly decreasing value against the total cost of the property decreased by first-year depreciation and salvage, if any. As with the declining-balance method of depreciation, the Internal Revenue Code has restricted the use of this method to property with a useful life of 3 years or more and other types of restrictions.

PROCEDURE FOR SUM-OF-THE-YEARS'-DIGITS DEPRECIATION METHOD

In the sum-of-the-years'-digits method, the constant denominator of the fractions used as multipliers is the sum of all the years of estimated useful life of the property. The declining numerators of the fractions used as multipliers are 1 smaller each year and begin with the original number of years of estimated life. Thus, if the useful life is 4 years, the fractions to be applied to the cost or other basis of the property, less salvage value, will have a constant denominator of $4 + 3 + 2 + 1 = 10$; and the declining numerators will be 4, 3, 2, and 1 for each of the successive 4 years of life. The denominator can be obtained by applying the formula for an arithmetic progression introduced in other chapters (see Unit 7.3). Thus the sum of the digits and the denominator for the fraction for an asset with a 4-year life is

$$4 \times \frac{4 + 1}{2} = 10$$

Example 8   **Assume an asset with a depreciation basis of $1200 and a 4-year life. The sum-of-the-years'-digits depreciation for each year would be as follows:**

Year	Depreciation basis	Fraction	Depreciation
1	$1200	$\frac{4}{10}$	$480
2	1200	$\frac{3}{10}$	360
3	1200	$\frac{2}{10}$	240
4	1200	$\frac{1}{10}$	120
Total depreciation			$1200

A problem arises when the sum-of-the-years'-digits method is started after the beginning of a fiscal year. The amounts for each full-year depreciation calculated under the procedure above must be re-allocated to the proper fiscal years. Thus:

Example 9   **Same problem data as Example 1 except the asset was acquired on August 1 and the fiscal year closes December 31.**

Depreciation (12-month period) Example 8			Depreciation for fiscal year ending December 31	
Year	Amount	Allocated	Amount	Year
1	$ 480	$\frac{5}{12}$ = \$280	$ 280	1
		$\frac{7}{12}$ = 200	350	2
2	360	$\frac{5}{12}$ = 150		
		$\frac{7}{12}$ = 210	310	3
3	240	$\frac{5}{12}$ = 100		
		$\frac{7}{12}$ = 140	190	4
4	120	$\frac{5}{12}$ = 50		
		$\frac{7}{12}$ = 70	70	5
Totals	$1200		$1200	

Example 10   **Sum-of-the-years'-digits method. If additional first-year depreciation of 20 percent is elected, find the depreciation allowable for (a) the first year and (b) the second year for a machine acquired April 1 that cost $9781.25, with estimated life of 6 years and estimated salvage value of $1000.**

(a)   Additional first year depreciation:

20% × $9781.25 = $1956.25

Regular depreciation:

Depreciation basis:

Cost $9781.25

Less:

Salvage   1000.00

First-year depreciation   1956.25   2956.25

Basis $6825.00

Sum of digits:

$$6 \times \frac{6+1}{2} = 21$$

Depreciation 1st twelve months:

$$\frac{6}{21} \times \$6825 = \$1950.00$$

Regular depreciation for first fiscal year

$$\frac{9}{12} \times \$1950 = \qquad\qquad \$1462.50$$

Total depreciation, first year $\$3418.75$

(b) $\$6825 \times \dfrac{6}{21} \times \dfrac{3}{12} = \$\ 487.50$

$\$6825 \times \dfrac{5}{21} \times \dfrac{9}{12} = \underline{\ 1218.75}$

Total depreciation, second year $\$1706.25$

A SUMMARY WITH TABLE ILLUSTRATING THE THREE METHODS OF DE-PRECIATION   Suppose that new refrigerators costing a total of $2625 and having an estimated life of 10 years are bought on January 2, and that their salvage value is estimated to be $100. Also, it is elected to claim additional first-year depreciation on the refrigerators since they qualify as tangible personal business property, with an estimated life of 6 years or more. The deduction for first-year depreciation is 20 percent of the cost of $2625 (disregarding salvage value), or $525.

Under the straight-line method, the annual ordinary depreciation is $200, computed as follows: Deduct salvage value of $100 and additional first-year depreciation of $525 from $2625 (cost of refrigerators), leaving $2000. Then divide $2000 by 10 (the number of years of estimated useful life) to arrive at the annual depreciation of $200.

Under the declining-balance method, the annual ordinary depreciation may not exceed $\frac{1}{5}$, or 20 percent, that is, twice the straight-line rate of $\frac{1}{10}$, or 10 percent, as indicated in the preceding. The maximum ordinary depreciation the first year is $420, or 20 percent of $2100 (cost of $2625 less additional first-year depreciation of $525). The depreciation for the second year is $336 (20 percent of $1680, the unrecovered cost).

Under the sum-of-the-years'-digits method, the ordinary depreciation would be $363.64 the first year. This is $\frac{10}{55}$ of $2000 (cost of $2625 less both $525 additional first-year depreciation and $100 salvage value). The numerator of this fraction represents the 10 years of useful life remaining at the beginning of the year and the denominator of the fraction is the sum of the numbers 1 through 10. The depreciation the second year would be $\frac{9}{55}$ of $2000; the third year, $\frac{8}{55}$ of $2000; and so on.

Exercise 12.2

Solve the following, assuming all dates of acquisition are the nearest first-of-month and that the calendar year is the fiscal year.

1   An asset costing $3000 was acquired on January 2, year 8. It had an estimated life of 5 years with no salvage value at the end of that time. Prepare a schedule of comparison (similar to Table 12.2) of the deprecia-

TABLE 12.2 COMPARISON TABLE OF THE THREE METHODS OF DEPRECIATION

Year	Annual depreciation		
	Straight line ($\frac{1}{10}$ or 10%)	Declining balance ($\frac{1}{5}$ or 20%)	Sum of the years' digits (in 55ths)
First-year additional depreciation	$ 525.00	$ 525.00	$ 525.00
First-year ordinary depreciation	200.00	420.00	363.64
Total depreciation—first year	$ 725.00	$ 945.00	$ 888.64
Second-year depreciation	200.00	336.00	327.27
Third-year depreciation	200.00	268.80	290.91
Fourth-year depreciation	200.00	215.04	254.55
Fifth-year depreciation	200.00	172.03	218.18
Sixth-year depreciation	200.00	137.63	181.82
Seventh-year depreciation	200.00	110.10	145.45
Eighth-year depreciation	200.00	88.08	109.09
Ninth-year depreciation	200.00	70.46	72.73
Tenth-year depreciation	200.00	56.37	36.36
Total	$2,525.00	$2,399.51	$2,525.00
Salvage value or unrecovered cost	$ 100.00	$ 225.49	$ 100.00

tion by the straight-line method, the declining balance method at $1\frac{1}{2}$ times the straight-line rate, and the sum-of-the-years'-digits method. Round to the nearest dollar.

2 By the straight line method, find the depreciation allowed for (a) the first year and (b) the second year on business equipment purchased at a cost of $14,770 on June 23, if the estimated life is 5 years and the salvage value is estimated at $1350.

3 Find the depreciation allowable by the straight-line method for (a) the first year and (b) the second year for an automobile that cost $4260, with estimated life of 4 years, salvage value of $700 and 75 percent business use (25 percent personal use), if purchased on May 25.

4 Using the straight-line method, find the total depreciation allowed for (a) the first year and (b) the second year if the cost of a used printing press is $14,600 when purchased on November 23, estimated life is 8 years, salvage value is $2300, and additional first-year depreciation of 20 percent is elected.

5 By the declining-balance method, find the maximum depreciation allowed for (a) the first year and (b) the second year for a new depreciable asset at twice the straight-line rate if the cost was $3245, estimated life 3 years, and the purchase date February 20.

6 If additional first-year depreciation of 20 percent is elected, find the maximum depreciation allowable by the declining-balance method at $1\frac{1}{2}$ times the straight-line rate for (a) the first year and (b) the second year for used equipment with estimated life of 12 years, purchased on April 8 with a basis of $26,810.

7 By the sum-of-the-years'-digits method, find the maximum depreciation allowable (a) the first year, (b) the second year, and (c) the third year for new furnishings in an apartment house that cost $12,400 on January 2, if

the estimated life was 9 years, estimated salvage value was $600, and if it was elected to claim 20 percent additional first-year depreciation.

8 A new, unused house and lot were purchased on May 8 at a cost of $24,200. If the lot was valued at $6000, the estimated life of the house was 15 years, and the salvage value of the house (exclusive of the lot) was $1500, find by the sum-of-the-years'-digits method the maximum depreciation allowable for (a) the first year and (b) the second year.

9 Suppose that new stoves costing $8600 for an apartment house were purchased on January 2 and that the estimated life was 7 years with a salvage value of $880. If it was elected to claim additional first-year depreciation of 20 percent, prepare a complete comparison table of the three methods of depreciation similar to that shown in Table 12.2.

Unit 12.3   *Distribution of Overhead*

Certain expenses of every manufacturing plant and trading concern are costs that cannot be allocated directly against individual items that are manufactured and sold or purchased and sold. To determine whether individual items are being sold at a profit or a loss, it is necessary to add to the direct costs of material and labor a fair share of all the indirect costs known as *overhead*.

Overhead consists of such indirect labor costs as the salaries and wages of the administrative staff, department supervisors, inspectors, janitors, warehousepersonnel, deliverers, and all others whose work is necessary to the business but who do not contribute directly to the manufacture or sale of goods. Additional charges to overhead must be made for such expenses as rent, supplies, depreciation, insurance, taxes, and utility costs.

The methods of apportionment of overhead to individual items and to departments may vary greatly. (1) The use of square feet of space occupied and (2) the use of net sales as bases are common methods of distributing overhead costs equitably. Other bases frequently used in apportioning overhead are (3) the ratio of overhead to the direct labor cost and (4) the ratio of overhead to the combined costs of direct labor and materials (known as prime cost).

Example 1 **Distribution of overhead based on floor space. Department A occupied 8100 sq ft of the 121,500 sq ft of space used by Harrison Manufacturing Company. Find (a) department A's share of overhead based on floor footage for a month in which the total overhead of the Harrison Manufacturing Company was $97,500 and (b) the overhead charged to each of a total of 13,000 similar items produced by department A during the month.**

(a) $\dfrac{8100}{121,500} \times \$97,500.00 = \$6500.00$

(b) $\dfrac{\$6500.00}{13,000} = \$0.50 \text{ per item}$

Example 2   **Distribution of overhead based on sales. The lingerie department of the Redding Department Store had $10,200 of sales during a month in which the sales for the entire store were $408,000. If administrative expenses for the store were $22,600 for the month, find (a) the share of administrative expenses based on sales to be borne by the lingerie department and (b) the administrative expense as a percent of sales (to nearest hundredths).**

(a) $$\frac{\$10,200.00}{\$408,000.00} \times \$22,600.00 = \$565.00$$

or $$\frac{\$10,200.00}{\$408,000.00} = 0.025 \text{ and } \$22,600.00 \times 0.025 = \$565.00$$

(b) $$\frac{\$22,600.00}{\$408,000.00} = 0.0554 = 5.54\% \text{ of sales}$$

Example 3   **Distribution of overhead based on total direct labor cost. The total overhead of a factory for 1 month was $4200, and the total direct labor cost was $35,000. If each department was charged overhead based on the percent (ratio) of total overhead to the total direct labor cost of the factory, find (a) the overhead percent of direct labor cost charged each department and (b) the cost of overhead for a department with direct labor cost of $5340 for the month.**

(a) $$\frac{\$4200.00}{\$35,000.00} = 0.12 = 12\%$$

(b) $\$5340.00 \times 0.12 = \$640.80$

Example 4   **Distribution of overhead based on total prime cost. If total overhead is $44,733, total direct labor is $185,600, and total materials used are $54,900 and overhead is based on the percent (ratio) of total overhead to total prime cost (total labor + total materials used), find (a) the overhead percent of prime cost charged each department and (b) the cost of overhead for a department with prime cost of $32,600.**

(a) $\$185,600.00 + \$54,900.00 = \$240,500.00$ Prime cost

$$\frac{\$44,733.00}{\$240,500.00} = 0.186 = 18.6\%$$

(b) $\$32,600.00 \times 0.186 = \$6063.60$

Exercise 12.3

1   The lathe department occupied 10,375 sq ft of the 166,000 sq ft of space used by the Kirby Manufacturing Company. Based on floor footage for a month in which the total overhead of the company is $41,144, find (a) the lathe department's share of overhead and (b) the overhead charged to each of a total of 6950 similar items produced by the lathe department during the month.

2   The toiletry department occupied 1620 sq ft of the 12,960 sq ft of space on the first floor of the three-floor Jelinek Department Store. If space on the first floor was charged 45 percent of the total overhead for the store, for a year during which overhead costs for the store totaled $135,720, find (a) overhead cost borne by the first floor and (b) overhead cost borne by the toiletry department.

3   The clothing department of the Weidman Men's Store had $56,400 of sales during a month in which sales for the entire store were $197,400. If administrative expenses for the store were $9573.90, find (a) the share of administrative expenses based on sales to be borne by the clothing department and (b) administrative expense as a percent (to nearest hundredths) of sales.

4   Under a lease agreement, the Lucky Market paid its landlord 5.8 percent of its monthly net sales. In addition to its share of the rent based on sales, each department of the Lucky Market paid its share of utilities, janitorial expense, and maintenance—also based on sales and all charged under the general heading of occupancy. During a month in which store sales were $108,000, utilities $492, janitorial expense $624, and maintenance $928, find (a) occupancy expense for the store, (b) occupancy expense for the meat department that had $34,560 of sales, and (c) occupancy expense as a percent (to nearest hundredths) of sales.

5   The total overhead of a factory for 1 month was $6552.00, and the total direct labor cost was $54,600. If each department was charged overhead based on the percent (ratio) of total overhead to the total direct labor cost of the factory, find (a) the overhead percent of direct labor cost charged each department and (b) the cost of overhead for a department with direct labor cost of $7300 for the month.

6   The Garibaldi Ornamental Iron Company had a total overhead for the year of $81,797 and a total direct labor cost of $208,400. If each department and job was charged overhead based on the percent (ratio) of total overhead to the total direct labor cost of the company, find (a) the overhead percent of direct labor cost charged each department, (b) the cost of overhead for the paint and finishing department with a direct labor cost of $27,080, and (c) the cost of overhead that should have been charged to a job with direct labor cost of $1400.

7   The total overhead is $62,376, total direct labor $94,600, and total materials used $329,150, and overhead is based on the percent (ratio) of total overhead to total prime cost (total direct labor + total materials used). Find (a) the overhead percent of prime cost charged each department and (b) the cost of overhead for a department with a prime cost of $67,800.

8   The Linville Corporation had a total overhead of $13,425 and total prime cost of $161,100. If overhead is based on the percent (ratio) of total overhead to total prime cost, find (a) the overhead percent of prime cost charged each department and (b) the cost of overhead for a department with total direct labor cost of $2108 and total materials used costs of $6132.

Unit 12.4   *Determination of Net Worth and Distribution of Ownership*

The ownership of business enterprises may be classified in three general groupings: (1) sole proprietorships, (2) partnerships, and (3) corporations.

A business in which a single individual supplies all the capital, assumes all the liabilities, and receives all the profits or bears all the losses is known as a *sole proprietorship* or as an *individual enterprise*. The limitation in capital and management that could be supplied by one individual led to the formation of a type of business enterprise known as a partnership.

A business owned by two or more individuals who together supply the capital, assume jointly and separately all the liabilities, and share in the profits and losses is known as a *partnership*. Unless formed in states where liability may be limited, partnerships place complete responsibility for the acts and debts of the partnership upon each partner; that is, the partners may be held responsible separately or jointly for all liabilities incurred by the partnership. Limitation of capital, legal liabilities for debt, dissolution through death, and the difficulties that often arose in withdrawing from a partnership without excessive loss led to the creation of a third form of business organization known as a corporation.

A business organization authorized by law to act as a single entity conducting an enterprise with the ownership consisting of transferable shares (stock) is known as a *corporation*. Liability is usually limited to what has been invested in the corporation by the shareholders, and neither creditors nor the corporation itself may make additional assessments on the shareholders. Earnings belong to the shareholders in the ratio that their shares bear to the total outstanding shares of the same class of stock (e.g., preferred, class A common, class B common, etc.).

Determination of Net Worth

As you already know (see Unit 11.2), the net worth of any form of business enterprise may be found by subtracting the sum of its liabilities (amounts owed) from the sum of its assets (future benefits). From the basic accounting equation:

Assets = liabilities + proprietorship (net worth)
Net worth = assets − liabilities

Example 1   **The Smith Drug Store is a sole proprietorship with the following assets: building and land at book value (cost less depreciation) of $36,000, furniture and fixtures at book value of $12,000, merchandise at cost $23,500, accounts receivable (money owed by customers) of $3675, and cash $3150. Liabilities are: mortgage owed on the building and land of $14,250, a note owed to the bank for $1820, and accounts payable (money owed to suppliers) of $6085. Find the net worth of the Smith Drug Store.**

	Assets		Liabilities	
Cash	$ 3,150.00	Note to bank	$ 1,820.00
Merchandise	23,500.00	Accounts payable	6,085.00
Accounts receivable	3,675.00	Mortgage	14,250.00
Furniture and fixtures	12,000.00		
Building and land	+36,000.00		+
Total assets	$78,325.00	Total liabilities	$22,155.00

Net worth = $78,325.00 − $22,155.00 = $56,170.00

Distribution of Ownership

In a sole proprietorship, the entire net worth of the business belongs to the individual owner.

In a partnership, increases or decreases in the net worth of the partnership are shared equally in the absence of an agreement, usually written, dividing changes in the ownership in some other manner.

In a corporation, the net worth of the business belongs to the stockholders in the ratio that each stockholder's shares bear to the total number of shares issued.

Example 2   **In the preceding example of the Smith Drug Store, what is the net worth belonging to Harriet Smith, owner?**

Since this is a sole proprietorship, the entire net worth of $56,170 belongs to Harriet Smith, owner.

Example 3   **Mr. Hill and Mr. Latham enter into a partnership investing $30,000 and $15,000, respectively. Four years later the partnership is sold for $39,000. How much does each partner receive?**

Since there is no agreement otherwise, each partner is an equal partner and ($30,000 + $15,000) − $39,000 = $6000 loss is shared equally.

Mr. Hill receives $30,000.00 − $\dfrac{\$6000.00}{2}$ = $30,000.00 − $3000.00

$$= \$27,000.00$$

Mr. Latham receives $15,000.00 − $\dfrac{\$6000.00}{2}$ = $15,000.00 − $3000.00

$$= \$12,000.00$$

Example 4   **If in Example 3 there had been a written agreement that in the event of dissolution of the partnership each partner should receive a share of the net worth (selling price) in the ratio that his original investment bore to the total original investment of the partners, what would each partner receive?**

$$\begin{aligned}
\text{Investment by Mr. Hill} &= \$30{,}000.00 \\
\text{Investment by Mr. Latham} &= +15{,}000.00 \\
\text{Total investment} &= \$45{,}000.00
\end{aligned}$$

$$\text{Mr. Hill's share} = \frac{\$30{,}000.00}{\$45{,}000.00} \times \$39{,}000.00 = \$26{,}000.00$$

$$\text{Mr. Latham's share} = \frac{\$15{,}000.00}{\$45{,}000.00} \times \$39{,}000.00 = \$13{,}000.00$$

Example 5   **The Universal Corporation with 500,000 issued shares of stock had a net worth of $3,200,000. Mr. Brugh owned 200 shares of stock. What was Mr. Brugh's share of the net worth of the company?**

$$\frac{200 \times \$3{,}200{,}000.00}{500{,}000} = \$1280.00$$

Exercise 12.4

Find the missing quantities in the following:

Net worth =   assets   − liabilities

1. $\$\underline{2421}$ = $ 9,841.00 − $ 7,420.00
2. $20,000.00 − $45,480.00 − $\underline{25480}$
3. $ 2,871.00 = $\underline{11,195}$ − $ 8,324.00
4. $\underline{(\,506\,)}$= $ 2,541.00 − $ 3,047.00
5. $ 846.00 = $ 8,096.00 − $\underline{7,250}$
6. $ 7,849.00 = $\underline{31,336}$ − $23,487.00

Solve the following:

7.   Ms. Aggeler owns a drugstore. The building has a book value of $33,000, fixtures have a book value of $6200, and the stock at cost is $7834. There is a $5200 mortgage on the building, $2015 is owed on the fixtures, a note of $550 is owed to the bank, and $824 is owed to manufacturers and wholesalers. What is the net worth of Ms. Aggeler's proprietorship in the drugstore and building?

8.   Mr. Allman is the sole owner of a small manufacturing concern. The book value of the land and building is $45,000 and has a $17,000 mortgage against it. The machinery and equipment have a book value of $12,740; the inventory includes $3030 worth of raw materials at cost and $6725 worth of finished products at cost; and accounts receivable (money owed by customers) total $2568. Accounts payable (money owed to suppliers) total $4746 and the bank holds Mr. Allman's note for $2000. What is Mr. Allman's proprietorship (net worth) in the manufacturing company?

9.   Ms. Cloud, Mr. Mohr, and Ms. Redford formed a partnership with investments of $4800, $6000, and $7200, respectively. After 2 years of operation, the partnership had a net worth of $15,300. What was the

value of each partner's share in the business if it was agreed that each partner's share of any increase or decrease in net worth should be in the ratio that the original investment of each bore to the total investment of the partners?

10 Mr. Houston, Ms. Strong, Ms. Nagel, and Mr. Plummer formed a partnership with investments of $2100, $2700, $1800, and $1500, respectively, each partner's share in the ownership to be in the ratio that his original investment bore to the total investment of the partners. Eight years later, Ms. Nagel died, automatically dissolving the partnership. At that time, the capital worth (net worth) of the partnership was $39,000. What share in the net worth belonged to the estate of Ms. Nagel, to Mr. Houston, to Ms. Strong, and to Mr. Plummer?

11 Mr. Nichols, Mr. Selig, and Mr. Harris formed a partnership with the agreement that each partner's share in the ownership and in any profit or loss should be in the ratio that his original investment bore to the total investment of the partners and also that if any one of the partners withdrew, the remaining partners were privileged to purchase the withdrawing partner's share in such amount that the remaining partners' shares would be equal. The original investments were $6200, $10,300, and $8500, respectively. After 3 years' time, Mr. Nichols decided to withdraw. Assets at that time were $35,200 and liabilities $9400. Mr. Selig and Mr. Harris purchased Mr. Nichols's share in amounts according to the agreement, which made them equal partners in the business. How much did Mr. Nichols receive (a) from Mr. Selig, (b) from Mr. Harris?

12 The Moynihan Corporation with 800,000 issued shares of stock had a net worth of $7,200,000. Ms. Wilson owned 320 shares of stock. What was her share of the net worth of the company?

13 The Griffing Company with 18,000 issued shares of stock had assets of $2,440,000 and liabilities of $1,756,000. Ms. Schoon owned 465 shares. Find (a) the net worth of the company and (b) the net worth of Ms. Schoon's shares.

14 The Cook Corporation had a net worth of $1,462,781. Of this sum, first claim to ownership of the net worth was reserved for the preferred stock in an amount of $478,781. The balance of the net worth belonged to 32,800 shares of common stock of which Mr. Gaddy owned 240 shares. What was the net worth of Mr. Gaddy's shares of common stock?

Unit 12.5   Distribution of Profit and Loss in a Partnership

Unless the partnership contract specifies otherwise, profits and losses are shared equally by the partners, regardless of how disproportionate may be the capital invested or the time or the value of the services rendered by the individual partners.

The division of future profits or losses is usually agreed upon at the time of formation of the partnership, and any method of distribution mutually satisfactory to the partners may be used. Several of the more common methods are illustrated in the following examples.

Example 1   **Shared equally. Foster and Seldon enter into a partnership, investing $6000 and $4000, respectively. It is agreed in writing that they are to be equal partners. The first year they lose $3000; the second year they gain $6500. Find each partner's share of gain or loss (a) the first year and (b) the second year.**

Since they are to share gains and losses equally:

(a) $\dfrac{\$3000.00}{2} = \$1500.00$ Loss by each partner

(b) $\dfrac{\$6500.00}{2} = \$3250.00$ Gain by each partner

Example 2   **Shared according to original investment. A and B enter into a partnership, investing $5000 and $4000, respectively. Profits are to be shared in the ratio that each partner's original investment bears to the total original capital. Profits are $2250 for the first year and $3375 for the second year. A withdraws his entire share of the profits both years. B withdraws his share of the profits only in the second year. Find the profit to which each partner is entitled (a) for the first year and (b) for the second year.**

(a)   Original capital $= \$5000.00 + \$4000.00 = \$9000.00$

$$A's\ share = \frac{\$5000.00}{\$9000.00} \times \$2250.00 = \$1250.00$$

$$B's\ share = \frac{\$4000.00}{\$9000.00} \times \$2250.00 = \$1000.00$$

(b)   Notice that B's ratio the second year remains the same and does not equal A's, even though his total investment is then $4000 + $1000, equivalent to A's original investment of $5000.

$$A's\ share = \frac{\$5000.00}{\$9000.00} \times \$3375.00 = \$1875.00$$

$$B's\ share = \frac{\$4000.00}{\$9000.00} \times \$3375.00 = \$1500.00$$

Example 3   **Shared according to investment at beginning of each year. A and B enter into a partnership, investing $8000 and $6000, respectively. Profits and losses are to be shared in the ratio that each partner's investment at the beginning of each year bears to the total investment at that time. Profits the first year are $10,500, A withdrawing his entire share, B withdrawing only $1500. Profits the second year are $3400, each partner withdrawing his full share. The third year a loss of $2550 occurs. Find the profit or loss of each partner (a) the first year, (b) the second year, and (c) the third year.**

(a) First year investment = $8000.00 + $6000.00 = $14,000.00

A's share = $\dfrac{\$8000.00}{\$14,000.00} \times \$10,500.00 = \$6000.00$

B's share = $\dfrac{\$6000.00}{\$14,000.00} \times \$10,500.00 = \$4500.00$

(b) Since B withdraws only $1500, investing the remainder, or $3000: Second year investment = $8000 + $6000 + $3000 = $17,000

A's share = $\dfrac{\$8000.00}{\$17,000.00} \times \$3400.00 = \$1600.00$

B's share = $\dfrac{\$6000.00 + \$3000.00}{\$17,000.00} \times \$3400.00$

$= \dfrac{\$9000.00}{\$17,000.00} \times \$3400.00 = \$1800.00$

(c) Since each partner withdrew his entire share of the profits the second year, the share of each in the loss for the third year is in the same ratio as was the share of each in the profit for the second year:

A's loss = $\dfrac{\$8000.00}{\$17,000.00} \times \$2550.00 = \$1200.00$

B's loss = $\dfrac{\$9000.00}{\$17,000.00} \times \$2550.00 = \$1350.00$

Example 4   **Shared equally with interest on his investment paid to each partner before division of profit or loss. A invests $10,000 and B $6000 in a partnership. Interest at 6 percent on his invested capital is to be paid each partner, the remaining profit or loss to be shared equally. Find each partner's share including interest on his investment if, before payment of interest, (a) profits the first year are $4200 and (b) profits the second year are $400.**

A's interest = $10,000.00 × 0.06 = $600.00
B's interest = $6000.00 × 0.06 = +$360.00
                         Total interest $960.00

(a) Profit exceeds interest due. Therefore after payment of interest,

$4200.00 − $960.00 = $3240.00   Net profit to be divided

$\dfrac{\$3240.00}{2} = \$1620.00$

A's share = $600.00 + $1620.00 = $2220.00
B's share = $360.00 + $1620.00 = $1980.00

(b) Profit is less than interest due. Therefore if interest is to be paid,

$960.00 − $400.00 = $560.00   Net loss to be divided

$$\frac{\$560.00}{2} = \$280.00$$

A's share = $600.00 − $280.00 = $320.00
B's share = $360.00 − $280.00 = $ 80.00

Example 5   Shared according to average investment. A and B enter into a partnership. A invests $5000 on January 1, $1000 on March 31, and $3000 on May 20. B invests $6000 on January 1, withdraws $2000 on April 10, and invests $4000 on August 28. If the profits for the calendar year are $4800, find each partner's share if they agree to share profits in ratio to their average capital invested (a) computed by months to the nearest first-of-month (12-month year) or (b) computed to the exact number of days (365-day year).

(a)   To the nearest number of months:

A invests:

$5000.00 × 3 (months to April 1)   = $15,000.00
+ 1000.00 March 31 investment
  $6000.00 × 2 (months to June 1)   =   12,000.00
+ 3000.00 May 20 investment
  $9000.00 × 7 (months to year-end)   = +   63,000.00
                                             $90,000.00 dollar-months

B invests:

$6000.00 × 3 (months to April 1)   = $18,000.00
− 2000.00 April 10 withdrawal
  $4000.00 × 5 (months to September 1) =   20,000.00
+ 4000.00 August 28 investment
  $8000.00 × 4 (months to year-end)   = +   32,000.00
                                             $70,000.00 dollar-months

The average investment of each partner may be found by dividing the total dollar-months by 12. Thus:

$$\frac{\$90,000.00}{12} = \$\ 7500.00 \quad \text{Average investment of A}$$

$$\frac{\$70,000.00}{12} = +\ 5833.33 \quad \text{Average investment of B}$$
$$\phantom{\frac{\$70,000.00}{12} =}\ \$13,333.33 \quad \text{Total average investment of partners}$$

$$\text{A's share} = \frac{\$7500.00}{\$13,333.33} \times \$4800.00 = \$2700.00$$

$$\text{B's share} = \frac{\$5833.33}{\$13,333.33} \times \$4800.00 = \$2100.00$$

However, it is needless to determine the average investment by each partner, for the dollar-months credited to each partner may be compared more readily. Thus:

$ 90,000.00	Dollar-months credited to A
70,000.00	Dollar-months credited to B
$160,000.00	Total dollar-month investment of partners

$$\text{A's share} = \frac{\$90,000.00}{\$160,000.00} \times \$4800.00 = \$2700.00$$

$$\text{B's share} = \frac{\$70,000.00}{\$160,000.00} \times \$4800.00 = \$2100.00$$

You will recall the dollar-day product method of computing interest in which principal × days = 36,000 percent interest (see Unit 5.2). In like manner, interest may be computed by a dollar-month product method in which principal × months = 1200 percent interest. By moving the decimal point in the product two places to the left, 12 percent interest is obtained. Thus in the preceding, $900 would be 12 percent interest on A's average investment; and $700 would be 12 percent interest on B's investment. And, of course, once 12 percent interest is known, conversion may be made to other rates of interest. At 6 percent interest on the average investment, A would be entitled to $450 and B would be entitled to $350, etc.

If interest is to be paid to the partners on the average capital invested to the nearest first-of-month, a knowledge of the dollar-month product method is highly desirable since only one interest computation need be made for each partner. If each withdrawal or investment is treated as a separate interest computation and if it is the policy of the partners to make frequent withdrawals (perhaps weekly or oftener) and occasional investments, the determination of the interest owed or due each partner at the end of the year could be a laborious and lengthy task unless the dollar-month product method of computing interest is used.

(b) To the exact number of days:

A invests:

$5000.00 × 90 (days exactly to March 31)	=	$ 450,000.00
+ 1000.00 March 31 investment		
$6000.00 × 50 (days exactly to May 20)	=	300,000.00
+ 3000.00 May 20 investment		
$9000.00 × 225 (days exactly to year-end)	=	+2,025,000.00
		$2,775,000.00 dollar-days

B invests:

$6000.00 × 100 (days exactly to April 10)	=	$ 600,000.00
− 2000.00 April 10 withdrawal		
$4000.00 × 140 (days exactly to August 28)	=	560,000.00
+ 4000.00 August 28 investment		
$8000.00 × 125 (days exactly to year-end)	=	+1,000,000.00
		$2,160,000.00 dollar-days

Again, as with dollar-months, it is not necessary to determine the average investment of each partner (e.g., dividing by 365), for the dollar-days may be compared more readily. Thus:

$2,775,000.00   dollar-days credited to partner A
+2,160,000.00   dollar-days credited to partner B
$4,935,000.00   total dollar-day investment of partners

$$\text{A's share} = \frac{\$2,775,000.00}{\$4,935,000.00} \times \$4800.00 = \$2699.09$$

$$\text{B's share} = \frac{\$2,160,000.00}{\$4,935,000.00} \times \$4800.00 = \$2100.91$$

As with the dollar-month investments by the partners, if interest is to be paid the partners, before division of profit or loss, utilize the dollar-day product method. Thus in the preceding, at 6 percent interest, A would be entitled to $462.50 and B would be entitled to $360.

The number of ways in which profits and losses in a partnership may be divided is almost unlimited, as the five preceding examples show. Combinations of these methods may be used, or entirely different arrangements may be made. The important point is that the method used should be mutually decided and agreed upon in writing at the time the partnership is formed. Unless otherwise specified, it may be assumed that partners share equally in the ownership and in all profit or loss.

Exercise 12.5

1   Ms. Beswick and Mr. Lillard enter into a partnership, investing $5000 and $4000, respectively. Profits the first year are $4560, the second year $2340. If profits are to be shared equally, what would each partner be entitled to receive (a) the first year and (b) the second year?

2   If in Problem 1, profits are to be shared in the ratio that each partner's original investment bears to the total original investment and Ms. Beswick withdraws her entire share of profits the first year but Mr. Lillard makes no withdrawal of his profits for the first year, find the profit earned by each partner (a) the first year and (b) the second year.

3   If in Problem 1, profits are to be shared according to the investment at the beginning of each year and Ms. Beswick withdraws her entire share of profits for the first year but Mr. Lillard makes no withdrawal of his profits for the first year, find the profit earned by each partner the second year.

4   Ms. MacGregor and Ms. Houser enter into a partnership, investing $13,500 and $10,668, respectively. Profits or losses are to be shared in the ratio that each partner's investment at the beginning of each year bears to the total investment at that time. Profits the first year are $12,084, Ms. MacGregor withdrawing her full share and Ms. Houser only $1710. The second year, a loss of $4800 occurs. Find (a) the profit of each partner the first year and (b) the loss of each partner the second year.

5   Luckmann and Tarnopol form a partnership, investing $12,500 and $10,000, respectively. Profits the first year are $8100, the second year $9900. It is

6.

$c = 2842.30$

$c = 2784.70$

$M = 2784.70$

$= 2358.70$

7.

agreed that profits are to be shared equally after payment of 8 percent interest on each partner's investment remaining in the partnership. If Luckmann withdraws both interest and profit at the end of the first year but Tarnopol withdraws only interest at the end of the first year, find the total (including interest) each partner would be entitled to (a) the first year and (b) the second year.

6 On January 1, Mr. Carpenter invested $6300 and Mr. Manning invested $7100 in a partnership, mutually agreeing that 6 percent ordinary interest at 30-day-month time computed to the nearest first-of-month was to be allowed each partner on his invested capital, the remaining profit or loss to be divided equally. On April 6, Mr. Carpenter invested an additional $2400. At the end of the year, profits before payment of interest were $5627. Find the share of profits (including interest) to which each partner was entitled.

7 Ms. French, Ms. Muscio, and Ms. Booher enter into a partnership, agreeing that 6 percent ordinary interest at 30-day-month time computed to the nearest first-of-month is to be allowed each partner on her invested capital, the remaining profit or loss to be divided equally. On January 1, each partner invests $9000; April 22, Ms. Muscio invests an additional $4000; on July 14, Ms. Booher withdraws $3000. At the end of the year, profits before payment of interest are $1465. Find the share of profits (including interest) to which each partner is entitled.

8 Mr. Allen and Ms. Roberts enter into a partnership. Mr. Allen invests $8000 on January 1, $4500 on April 10, $2500 on September 7, and $1000 on November 26. Ms. Roberts invests $12,000 on January 1, withdraws $2500 on March 21, invests $3500 on June 29, invests $1500 on August 8, and withdraws $9500 on September 27. If the profits for the calendar year are $14,894, find each partner's share if they agree to share profits in ratio to their average capital invested (a) computed by months to the nearest first-of-month (12-month year) or (b) computed to the exact number of days (365-day year).

8.

a 8166.78

$s \; 727.22$

Unit 12.6   *Corporate Ownership*

A corporation is authorized by law to operate and act as a single entity in conducting a specified enterprise, the ownership or capital consisting of transferable shares.

Legal authority to organize a corporation is conferred by the state in which the charter or certificate of organization is granted. Ordinarily, this charter will include the name under which the enterprise will operate, the business in which it is to engage, the quantity and kind of capital stock that it is authorized to issue, and the life of the charter.

Shareholders of the corporation participate in the ownership and in any profits earned by the business in the ratio that their shares are to the total capital stock issued. Ordinarily, liability is limited to what has been invested in such stock, and neither creditors nor the corporation itself may make additional assessments on the stockholders. Further, the shares may be sold or transferred at any time without affecting the organization of the company, and the value of each share is ordinarily low enough to allow ready sale to a large number of people; whereas in a partnership the value of any partner's holding may be so large as to limit the number of prospective purchasers.

Finally, since the value per share is usually low, a great number of people may participate in the ownership, and these accumulated savings allow the formation of capital investments far exceeding in size the capital investment possible in an individual enterprise or in a partnership.

Stocks

The capital stock of a corporation is the value placed on the shares issued for the net assets invested by the ownership group. A corporation may be authorized to issue many more shares than it actually has issued. The holders of the issued shares of stock represent the ownership of the corporation.

Certificates of stock are the documents on which the number of shares owned by the shareholder are indicated. Certificates of stock are usually issued for each 100 shares or fraction thereof.

Stated capital is that amount of net assets invested by the shareholders which has been designated by state law and the corporation to represent the legal capital paid in by the shareholders. In some states, stated capital may be less than the total net assets paid in by the shareholders.

Paid-in capital is the total net assets paid in by the shareholders. It consists of the legal stated capital plus any net assets paid in by the shareholders over and above the legal stated capital.

Authorized stock is the number of shares of stock that the corporation's charter entitles it to issue.

Outstanding stock is the number of shares of stock presently in the possession of the shareholders.

Treasury stock is stock issued and reacquired by the corporation. It remains within the company and does not share in the earnings, nor does it have voting power. It may be reissued.

Deficit is the amount by which the sum of the liabilities and the paid-in capital exceeds the total assets of the business.

Par value is the nominal value placed by the issuing corporation on its stock. It usually gives no true indication of the real worth of common stock. For *no-par* or *nonpar* stock an arbitrary and usually nominal figure called *stated value* or *issue price* may be placed by the issuing corporation.

The *book value* of a share of stock is its pro rata part in the net assets (net worth) of the corporation. It is frequently termed *net asset value* per share, *net worth* per share, *liquidation value* per share, or *redemption value* per share. Ordinarily, the book value of a par-value preferred share is its par value or its redemption value if callable within a specified period of time or upon liquidation of the corporation. If the preferred stock has no-par value (such as a $5 preferred), then its book value will be that as stated in the charter granted to the corporation or as stipulated on issued certificates of stock. If the net assets are less than the total par (or redemption) value of the preferred, the book value of a preferred share may be found by dividing the net assets by the number of outstanding shares of preferred. The book value per share of the common stock is found by dividing the net assets less the total par (or redemption value) of any outstanding preferred shares by the number of outstanding shares of common stock.

Stockholders' equity is a term commonly used to describe the corporate net worth (or net asset values) belonging to the holders of outstanding stock.

The *market value* of a share of stock is the price at which the stock may be purchased or sold on the open market or in a stock exchange. It is the current price, usually fluctuating, and it may be more or less than either the par value or the book value.

COMMON STOCK   Stock without preference as to dividends or to assets in the event of dissolution of the corporation, each share usually entitling its holder to one vote in the election of directors of the corporation, is known as *common stock*. Expenses, interest on bonds or notes, and dividends to preferred stock must be paid before any dividends may be declared on the common stock.

No-par (or *nonpar*) *common* stock is issued without any nominal value.

Par-value common stock is issued with a nominal value placed on it by the authority of the state in which the corporation is chartered. It may be assumed that the par value of a common stock has no significance insofar as the real value of the stock is concerned.

Thus, a $50 par-value common stock might be valueless or might be worth $1, $1000, or any amount. A no-par common stock might likewise be worthless or valuable.

Because par valuation had a tendency to confuse some investors, it became common practice to issue no-par common stock. However, among other reasons, since some states arbitrarily consider no-par stock to have a $100 valuation for certain liabilities and tax charges, the issuance of low-par common stock with a nominal valuation of less than $10 is now a frequent practice.

PREFERRED STOCK   Stock that has certain preferences over the common stock, as stipulated in the charter granted to the corporation or on the certificate of stock, is known as *preferred stock*. These preferences usually take the form of a fixed rate of dividends per annum on the specified par value or a fixed rate of dividends per annum in dollars per share. Also, preferred stock usually has prior rights over the common stock to the assets of the company in the event of dissolution, usually limited to the par value (if any). Ordinarily, preferred stock is nonvoting and does not share in earnings in excess of the stipulated fixed dividends. However, both these privileges and many others may be granted to preferred shares.

Retained Earnings

When the net assets of a corporation exceed the paid-in capital, the amount of net assets remaining represents the *earned capital* of the corporation and is generally known as *retained earnings*. Retained earnings can also be defined as the net assets *earned* by the operations of the corporation and *retained* in the corporation instead of being distributed to the shareholders as dividends.

BOOK VALUE PER SHARE   As stated earlier, the book value per share of a *preferred stock* is its par value or its stipulated redemption value. The book value per share of a *common stock* is determined by dividing the net assets of the corporation, less the book value of any preferred stock, by the number of outstanding shares of common stock. Thus:

$$\frac{\text{Net assets} - \text{book value of preferred stock}}{\text{Number of outstanding shares of common stock}}$$

$$= \text{book value per share of common stock}$$

Example 1   **From the statement of stockholders' equity of the Street Corporation, determine (a) the amount of stockholders' equity belonging to the preferred stock, (b) the book value per share of preferred stock, (c) the amount of stockholders' equity belonging to the common stock, and (d) the book value per share of the common stock.**

The Street Corporation   Statement of stockholders' equity, December 31, 19____

Paid-in capital:		
Capital stock:		
Preferred stock:		
50,000, 6%, $50 par-value shares authorized; 30,000 shares issued and outstanding	$1,500,000	
Common stock:		
500,000, $10 par value shares authorized; 219,000 shares issued and outstanding	2,190,000	
Other paid-in capital:		
'Premium received on preferred stock	301,000	
Total paid-in capital		$3,991,000
Retained earnings		3,860,000
Total stockholders' equity		$7,851,000

(a)   Stockholders' equity belonging to preferred stock = $1,500,000
(Even though the preferred shareholders paid a premium of $301,000 for the preferred stock, the preferred shareholders are entitled to only the par value or other stipulated and disclosed value.)

(b)   Book value per share of preferred stock is its par value, or

$$\frac{\$1{,}500{,}000}{30{,}000 \text{ shares}} = \$50$$

(c)   Stockholders' equity belonging to common stock:

$$\$7{,}851{,}000 - \$1{,}500{,}000 = \$6{,}351{,}000$$

(d) Book value per share of common stock:

$$\frac{\$6,351,000}{219,000 \text{ shares}} = \$29$$

The examples that follow illustrate the determination of various amounts included in the proprietorship section of a corporation's financial statement and the interrelationship of the amounts involved in the basic accounting equation of:

Assets = liabilities + proprietorship (stockholders' equity).

Example 2   **To determine stockholders' equity; paid-in capital; retained earnings; and book value per share of stock. The Muffin and Margie Company, Inc., has 4000 shares of $5 par-value common stock outstanding. The balance sheet data show assets of $125,000 and liabilities of $50,000. Find (a) stockholders' equity (b) total paid-in capital, (c) retained earnings, and (d) book value per share of stock.**

(a)   Assets − liabilities = proprietorship (stockholders' equity)
         $125,000 −   50,000   = $75,000 stockholders' equity

(b)   Number of shares × par value per share = paid-in capital
              4000   × $5   = $20,000 paid-in capital

(c)   Stockholders' equity − paid-in capital   = retained earnings
              $75,000   −   20,000   = $55,000 retained earnings

(d) $\dfrac{\text{Equity of common stock, \$75,000}}{\text{Shares of common stock, 4000}}$ = $18.75 book value per share of common stock

Example 3   **To determine net worth per share. The Bill Jr. and Sherry Manufacturing Company in its statement of stockholders' equity indicates that it has $20,000 of $100 par preferred stock and a total stockholders' equity of $110,000. The common stock has a $50 par value, and the total of the retained earnings is $30,000. Find (a) the number of shares of preferred stock, (b) number of shares of common stock, (c) net worth per share of preferred stock, and (d) net worth per share of common stock.**

(a) $\dfrac{\text{Par value of preferred, \$20,000}}{\text{Par value per share, \$100}}$ = 200 shares of preferred stock

(b)   Total stockholders' equity $110,000
          Less retained earnings   30,000
          Paid-in-capital   80,000
          Less par value of preferred   20,000
          Par value of common $ 60,000

$\dfrac{\text{Par value of common, \$60,000}}{\text{Par value per share, \$50}}$ = 1200 shares of common stock

(c) $\dfrac{\text{Equity of preferred, \$20,000}}{\text{Shares of preferred, 200}}$ = \$100 net worth per share (book value) of preferred stock (same as its par value)

(d) Stockholders' equity   \$110,000
     Less equity of preferred stock   20,000
          Equity of common stock $ 90,000

$\dfrac{\text{Equity of common stock, \$90,000}}{\text{Shares of common, 1200}}$ = \$75 net worth per share (book value) of common stock

---

Example 4   **To determine stockholders' equity in excess of paid-in capital, stockholders' equity, and total assets. The Agnes, George, and Catherine Co., Inc., with liabilities of $109,500 has 2400 issued shares of $25 par preferred stock and 30,000 shares of $2.50 par common stock with a book value of $4.20 per share. Find (a) total par value of the preferred stock, (b) total par value of the common, (c) stockholders' equity, (d) stockholders' equity in excess of paid-in capital (retained earnings), and (e) total assets.**

(a)   2400 × \$25   = $ 60,000   Par value of preferred
(b)   30,000 × \$2.50   = $ 75,000   Par value of common
(c)   Number of shares of common stock   30,000
     Book value per share   ×\$4.20
     Equity applicable to common stock $126,000
     Equity applicable to preferred
     stock (same as par value of
     preferred stock)   +60,000 = \$186,000   Stockholders' equity

(d)   Total stockholders' equity   \$186,000
     Less paid-in capital:
       Par value of preferred   \$60,000
       Par value of common   75,000
         Total paid-in capital   −135,000
                                  $ 51,000   Stockholders' equity in excess of paid-in capital (retained earnings)

(e)   Total stockholders' equity   \$186,000
     Liabilities   +109,500
                           \$295,500   Total assets

Exercise 12.6

1 The Ward Manufacturing Company has 800 shares of $45 par-value stock outstanding. Its balance sheet shows assets of $85,400 and liabilities of $36,000. What is (a) the proprietorship of the company and (b) the book value per share of stock?

2 The balance sheet of the Barry Company shows the following items: cash, $8700; notes receivable, $5740; accounts receivable, $8420; furniture and fixtures, $3850; inventory at cost, $47,224; land and buildings, $35,000; notes payable, $10,975; accounts payable, $12,479; mortgage on land and buildings, $19,800. The Barry Company has issued 1800 shares of $5 par-value stock. What is (a) the net worth of the company and (b) the net asset value per share of stock?

3 The Page Manufacturing Company in its statement of proprietorship indicates that it has 540 issued shares of $100 par-value preferred stock, and 6300 issued shares of no-par common stock and that its total stockholders' equity is $202,500. Find (a) the equity of the total preferred stock and (b) the equity per share of the common stock.

4 The Sutton Dry Goods Company has issued $45,000 of $100 par-value preferred shares and a total capital stock, including $25 par-value common, of $75,000. Also, the Sutton Dry Goods Company has retained earnings of $24,300. Find (a) the number of shares of preferred, (b) the number of shares of common, (c) the equity per share of the preferred, and (d) the equity per share of the common stock.

5 The Minor Company has the following assets and liabilities: cash, $24,000; notes receivable, $15,600; accounts payable, $31,200; notes payable, $17,280; land and building, $95,600; raw inventory, $10,400; inventory of goods in process of manufacture, $5300; finished inventory at cost, $7110; mortgages owed $40,800; equipment, $5940; accounts receivable, $16,500. Outstanding are 500 shares of $50 par-value preferred and 1500 shares of $8 par-value common. What is (a) the net asset value of the outstanding common stock and (b) the net asset value of the common stock per share?

6 The Duncan Company with liabilities of $210,000 has 5000 issued shares of $40 par cumulative preferred, 2000 issued shares of $50 par noncumulative preferred, and 30,000 issued shares of $3 par common with a book value per share of $6.40. Find (a) total par value of cumulative preferred, (b) total par value of noncumulative preferred, (c) total par value of common, (d) total book value of common, (e) retained earnings, (f) stockholders' equity, and (g) total assets.

7 The Rider Wholesale Company has outstanding 3000 shares of $50 par-value preferred stock and 18,600 shares of $4 par-value common stock with a book value per share of $16.40. If total assets are $930,040, what are (a) the retained earnings and (b) the total liabilities?

Unit 12.7   *Allocation of Corporate Dividends*

Distributions to the shareholders of portions of the net assets earned by the operations of the corporation are known as *dividends*. The *board of directors* of the corporation makes the decision on how much of the accumulated earnings (retained earnings) they wish to declare as a dividend. If and when dividends are declared by the board of directors, the first moneys set aside for such purpose must be allocated to the owners of the preferred stock. Dividends in excess of the amount to meet the rights to earnings by the preferred stock may then be allocated to the common stock.

Preferred stock frequently has a specified par of $100, although $25, $50, and other par valuations are not unusual. Thus a 5 percent, $100 par preferred would be expected to pay dividends of $5 per share each year; a 6 percent, $25 par preferred would be expected to pay dividends of $1.50 per share each year; etc. If the preferred stock has no-par valuation, then the amount of the yearly dividends per share that may be expected will be stated in dollars, as $6, $3.50, or $5 preferred.

Cumulative preferred stocks are stocks the unpaid dividends of which are accumulated and must be paid in full before any dividends may be declared to the common stock. Thus if a 6 percent cumulative preferred stock with par value of $50 had failed to pay dividends for 3 years, an accumulated dividend of $12 would have to be paid at the end of the fourth year before any dividend to the common stock could be paid.

Noncumulative preferred stocks are stocks the unpaid dividends of which do not accumulate and payment of the dividend for any year permits the declaration of a dividend to the common stock. Thus, if a 7 percent, $20 par-value, noncumulative stock failed to receive dividends for 3 years, a dividend of $1.40 at the end of the fourth year to each share of the noncumulative preferred would permit the payment of a dividend at that time to the common stock.

Participating preferred stocks are stocks that receive some portion of whatever dividends may be paid to the common stock. In addition to the stipulated dividend due as a preferred stock, participating stocks may receive dividends equal to, more than, or less than the dividends paid to the common stock. Neither noncumulative nor participating preferred stocks are usual; cumulative preferred stocks without participation in common stock dividends are much more frequently issued.

Example 1 **Allocation of dividends. The Peter Darrel Company's capital consisted of 2000 shares of no-par common and 1000 shares of 6 percent cumulative preferred with a par value of $100. During 1977, 1978, and 1979 no dividends were declared. At the end of the year 1980, the directors determined to distribute $20,000 in earnings. How much was received (a) by each share of preferred stock and (b) by each share of common stock?**

(a)   Par value of 1000 pfd. shares $100.00 × 1000 = $100,000.00
Dividends due yearly $100,000.00 × 0.06 = $6000.00
Accumulated 1977 through 1980 $6000.00 × 4 = $24,000.00

Since only $20,000 in dividends was declared, the cumulative preferred received it all.

Each preferred share received $\dfrac{\$20,000.00}{1000} = \$20.00$ per share

(b) Since there were no remaining dividends, common stockholders received nothing, and there remained a cumulative balance of

$24,000.00 − $20,000.00 = $4000.00

still due the preferred stockholders which had to be paid before the common stockholders could receive dividends.

Example 2   **Allocation of dividends. Same problem as Example 1, except that preferred stock is noncumulative.**

(a)   Par value of 1000 pfd. shares $100.00 × 1000 = $100,000.00
Dividends due yearly $100,000.00 × 0.06 = $6000.00
1977 to 1979 not paid but noncumulative

Dividends declared $20, 000.00
To preferred shares −6,000.00
To common shares $14,000.00

Each preferred share received $\dfrac{\$6000.00}{1000} = \$6.00$ per share

(b)   Since 2000 common shares received $14,000, each share received

$\dfrac{\$14,000.00}{2000} = \$7.00$ per share

Exercise 12.7

1   The Wilbur Company capital consisted of 2640 shares of no-par common stock and 1800 shares of 6 percent cumulative preferred stock with a par value of $100. During 1978 and 1979 no dividends were declared. At the end of 1980, the directors distributed $18,000 in dividends. What dividends were received by (a) each share of preferred stock and (b) each share of common stock?

2   The Atwood Manufacturing Company directors announce yearly dividends of $37,880.80. There are issued 1700 shares of 5 percent, $100 par-value, cumulative preferred stock and 4872 shares of $50 par-value common stock. Assuming that no dividends have been passed (are not in default, not in arrears) on the preferred stock, what dividends will be received by (a) each share of preferred stock and (b) each share of common stock?

3   The Taylor Manufacturing Company had a total capital stock of $180,000 consisting of $60,000 of $4\frac{1}{2}$ percent, $50 par-value, cumulative preferred stock and $120,000 of $5 par-value common stock. In 1979, dividends of $1800 had been paid. At the end of 1980, dividends of $9600 were distributed. How much was received for 1980 by (a) each share of preferred stock and (b) each share of common stock?

4 The Miller Company's capital stock consisted of 4400 shares of $20 par-value common stock and 1400 shares of 5 percent, $100 par-value, noncumulative preferred stock. During 1978, 1979, and 1980 no dividends were declared. At the end of 1981 the directors distributed $43,080 in dividends. What dividends were received by (a) each share of preferred stock and (b) each share of common stock?

5 The Walker Manufacturing Company, Inc., had a capital consisting of $70,000 worth of 5 percent, $50 par-value, noncumulative preferred stock and $90,000 worth of $12 par-value common stock. Dividends of $1.25 were declared to each preferred share in 1978 and 1979. In 1980, dividends of $9650 were declared. How much was received for 1980 by (a) each share of preferred stock and (b) each share of common stock?

6 The Osler Company had a capital consisting of 4000 shares of 6 percent, $100 par-value, cumulative preferred; 2500 shares of 7 percent, $100 par-value, noncumulative preferred; and 36,000 shares of $10 par-value common stock. In 1978, full dividends were paid to the cumulative preferred but not to the noncumulative preferred or common stock. In 1979, a $3 dividend was paid to each share of the cumulative preferred. At the end of 1980, a dividend of $76,540 was declared. How much was received for 1980 by (a) each share of cumulative preferred, (b) each share of noncumulative preferred, and (c) each share of common stock?

7 The Gilfert Company had the following number of outstanding shares, each with a par value of $50: 85,000 shares of 5 percent cumulative preferred, 36,000 shares of 6 percent noncumulative preferred; and 142,000 shares of common. During the year ending December 31, 1978, the Gilfert Company earned a profit of $200,000 but no dividends were declared. At the year ending December 31, 1979, the board of directors declared a dividend of 4 percent of its par value to the common stock. For 1979, what *total* dividends were received by (a) the cumulative preferred, (b) the noncumulative preferred, and (c) the common stock? If the $200,000 profit earned in 1978 was added to the profit earned in 1979, (d) what amount of profit was necessary in 1979 to cover the dividends?

Unit 12.8 Trading on the Equity by Individuals, Partnerships, and Corporations

---

Individuals in business and partnerships borrow money frequently by means of notes or mortgages so that they may expand their businesses, with the expectation that the borrowed capital will increase earnings by more than it costs in interest. In so borrowing, the assets of the business are usually pledged as security to the lender to insure payment of interest and principal when due.

In like manner, to increase net earnings, corporations borrow money by means of notes, mortgages, and bonds. A *bond* is a written promise to pay a specified sum of money at maturity and interest at specified times.

The essential distinction between stocks and bonds is simply that stocks represent ownership, while bonds represent a particular kind of debt incurred. A stockholder is a part owner; a bondholder is a creditor.

Because of the many types of so-called compromise securities, it is sometimes difficult to distinguish certain types of stocks from certain types of bonds. For example, preferred stocks sometimes carry conditions of preference that in many respects make them more like a bond than like a common stock.

A *note* is usually the term applied to a written promise to pay if its duration is less than 10 years.

As the above definitions indicate, notes and bonds are quite similar in nature, the difference largely being the length of time from date of origin to maturity. Bonds are usually issued in $1000 denominations, although other denominations, such as $10,000, $5000, $2000, $500, $100, $25, are not uncommon.

Interest payments on both bonds and notes must be made when due, regardless of earnings. Since bonds ordinarily have a prior lien over preferred or common stocks to the assets of a business, failure to meet fixed charges (interest due on bonds) may result in insolvency proceedings being forced in court by the bondholders, followed by liquidation (sale of the assets in order to meet the claims of the bondholders).

Since this risk occurs, the question naturally arises as to why corporation bonds are issued. The answer is to be found in the principle of *trading on the equity*. It is advantageous for a corporation (or individual) to borrow if the average rate of earnings on the borrowed capital is in excess of the interest charges for the use of the borrowed capital.

The issuance of preferred stock by a corporation offers common stockholders the opportunity to gain by trading on the equity without the risk of borrowing through notes, mortgages, or bonds, for payment of dividends even to cumulative preferred may be indefinitely delayed at the discretion of the board of directors of the corporation. However, the amount of gain will usually be somewhat less, for preferred dividends ordinarily must be at a higher rate to induce investors' capital than the rates of interest necessary to induce the more secure investments offered by notes, mortgages, and bonds.

Example 1   **Gain in dollars. Sara Harney, owner of a small variety store, earns 12 percent on her investment of $35,000. If additional capital of $15,000 that she can borrow at 5 percent interest will earn 14 percent before payment of interest, find the yearly increase in income.**

$$14\% - 5\% = 9\% \qquad \text{Net gain on borrowed capital}$$
$$\$15,000.00 \times 0.09 = \$1350.00 \qquad \text{Net increase in income}$$

Or, solve:

$$\$15,000.00 \times 0.14 = \$2100.00 \qquad \text{Gross gain}$$
$$\$15,000.00 \times 0.05 = \underline{-750.00} \qquad \text{Less interest cost}$$
$$\$1350.00 \qquad \text{Net increase in income}$$

Example 2   **Percent of increase in earnings and percent of return on original capital. The Lang-Grant Electrical Suppliers, a partnership, earns $35,200 on a capital investment of $220,000. The partners estimate that they can make the same rate of gain on an additional investment of $80,000. If this $80,000 is borrowed at $5\frac{1}{2}$ percent, find (a) the expected percent of increase in income, and (b) the expected percent of return on their original capital investment.**

$$\frac{\$35,200.00}{\$220,000.00} = 0.16 = 16\%$$ Original rate of return

$$16\% - 5.5\% = 10.5\%$$ Net gain in percent on borrowed capital
$$\$80,000.00 \times 0.105 = \$8400.00$$ Net gain in dollars

(a) $$\frac{\$8400.00}{\$35,200.00} = 0.2386 = 23.86\%$$ Percent increase in income

(b) $$\frac{\$35,200.00 + \$8400.00}{\$220,000.00} = \frac{\$43,600.00}{\$220,000.00} = 0.1982 = 19.82\%$$ Percent return on original capital

Example 3   **Dollar and percent gains from trading on the equity. The Barlow Company, Inc., has a capital of $400,000 all financed by common stock. Its present earnings are 9 percent on the investment. The board of directors believe that an additional investment of $120,000 would earn 12 percent. If their estimate is true and the additional capital is raised by means of a 4 percent bond issue, find (a) original earnings, (b) dollar gain in net earnings, (c) total net earnings, including the increase, (d) percent of gain in earnings, and (e) new percent of return on the original capital investment.**

(a) $\$400,000.00 \times 0.09 = \$36,000.00$ Original earnings
(b) $12\% - 4\% = 8\%$ Net gain in percent on borrowed capital

$\$120,000.00 \times 0.08 = \$9600$ Dollar gain in net earnings
(c) $\$36,000.00 + \$9600.00 = \$45,600.00$ Total net earnings, including increase

(d) $$\frac{\$9600.00}{\$36,000.00} = 0.2667 = 26.67\%$$ Percent gain in earnings

(e) $$\frac{\$45,600.00}{\$400,000.00} = 0.1140 = 11.40\%$$ New return in percent on original capital

There are two main classifications for bonds: (1) bonds secured by property and (2) bonds issued on the strength of the general credit of the corporation.

Bonds secured by property may take the form of mortgages on the real property or equipment of the issuing company, or they may be secured by the deposit of other securities, such as stocks and bonds, which are pledged as collateral.

Both interest rate and date of maturity are used frequently to describe particular bond issues. As an example: Bell Telephone of Pennsylvania debenture bonds bearing interest at 3 percent and maturing in 1974 may be known as "Bell Telephone of Pa. Deb. 3's 74," "Bell Tel. of Pa. Deb. 3's," or as "Bell Tel. of Pa. 74's" (the ticker tape symbol is "BLP 3's"), or any other simple contraction of the complete name that will distinguish the bonds from other companies' bonds or other bonds issued by the same company.

The terminology of bonds is complex, but following are a few of the more common expressions and definitions with which you may wish to be familiar.

Registered bonds are carried on the books of the registrar or trustee in the name of the bond owner so that loss of the bond itself will not mean loss of the investment. Payment of interest is made to the registered holder.

Coupon bonds, which are the more frequent, are rarely registered but carry a separate coupon for each interest payment, and each coupon when detached entitles the bearer to the interest when due. Loss of the bond, unless it is recovered, means loss of the investment.

Mortgage bonds are secured by real property, equipment, or collateral. They may be issued as first mortgage, second mortgage, etc., the first-mortgage bonds having prior lien over the later issues.

Debentures are bonds secured solely by the general credit of the issuing company. This does not necessarily mean that they are undesirable, for a debenture in a strong company is preferable to a first-mortgage bond in a weak company.

Convertible bonds may be converted to stocks within a specified period of time. The speculative element created by this privilege may help in the original sale of the bonds by the issuing company.

Collateral trust bonds are secured not by tangible physical property but by the securities of other corporations pledged as collateral. This type of bond is most frequently issued by holding corporations.

Income bonds are ordinarily undesirable, for they are not required to pay interest at stated periods but pay only if earnings are sufficient to meet the interest charges. They are issued often by companies that have gone through insolvency proceedings, and in such instances the bond interest payment is frequently in default.

Exercise 12.8

Solve the following, finding all percent answers to nearest hundredths:

1   Mr. Beach owns a service station that cost him $15,000 and that earns an average yearly net profit of $3000. He estimates that improvements costing $6000 will bring an additional return at the same rate of profit. If his estimate is correct and he borrows $6000 from his bank at 5 percent interest, find (a) the net annual increase in income that he would make in dollars, (b) his percent of increase in income, and (c) his new percent of return on his original investment.

2 Ms. Rowe and Mr. Tyler have a partnership in which profits are divided in the ratio that each partner's original investment bears to their total original investment. Ms. Rowe's investment is $8000; Mr. Tyler's, $7000. Earnings have been 15 percent on the total investment. If the same percent of earnings could be made on an additional investment of $5000, find (a) the yearly increase in income that each partner would make if $5000 is borrowed by the partnership at 5.5 percent interest, (b) the percent of increase in income by the partnership, and (c) the new percent of profit that the partnership would make yearly on the original investment.

3 The Webster Company with a capital of $90,000, all financed by the sale of common stock, earns 10 percent on the investment. It is estimated that the same percent of earnings could be made on an additional capital of $120,000. If this $120,000 can be raised by the sale of cumulative 6 percent preferred stock, find (a) the net increase in dollars of yearly income that the total common stock would make, (b) the percent of increase in earnings by the common stock, and (c) the percent of profit the common stock would then earn annually on the original capital of $90,000.

4 The Stuart Corporation capital consists of $400,000 of $50 par-value common stock earning 8 percent on its par value. It is estimated that an additional capital of $150,000 will earn 7 percent. If this additional capital can be raised by the sale of bonds bearing $3\frac{3}{4}$ percent interest, find (a) the expected increase in income (to nearest cents) that would be made by each share of common stock, (b) the expected percent of increase in earnings by the common stock, and (c) the expected percent of profit that the common stock would earn annually on its par value.

5 The Andrews Manufacturing Company capital stock consists of 15,000 shares of $100 par-value common stock and 3000 shares of $6 cumulative preferred stock. Bonded indebtedness consists of $180,000 worth of 3 percent interest-bearing bonds. Earnings by the common stock are $11 per share. If additional capital of $500,000 raised by the sale of 4 percent interest-bearing bonds will earn 9 percent before payment of interest in addition to the present earnings of the company, find (a) what the total annual earnings would be per share of common stock, (b) the percent of increase in annual earnings by the common stock, and (c) the percent of earnings the common stock would then be making on its par value.

6 The Carlsen Company capital stock consisted of 50,000 shares of $2 par-value common. Earnings were $14,500 per year. Then 1800 shares of 5 percent, $50 par-value cumulative preferred shares are sold. Earnings increase to $25,000 per year before payment of dividends to the preferred stock. Find the per year (a) original earnings in dollars per share of common stock, (b) present earnings in dollars per share of common stock, (c) original percent of earnings by common stock on par value, and (d) present percent of earnings by common stock on par value.

7 Perry and Company, Inc., has a capital of $480,000, all financed by common stock. Its present earnings are 9 percent on the investment. The board of directors believe that an additional investment of $150,000 would earn 11 percent. If their estimate is true and the additional capital is raised by means of a 4 percent bond issue, find (a) original earnings, (b) dollar gain in net earnings, (c) total net earnings, including the increase, (d) percent of gain in earnings, and (e) new percent of return on the original capital investment.

8 The Regent Corporation earned 11 percent on its capital of $550,000. After borrowing $240,000 at 6 percent interest, earnings before payment of interest are $70,000. Find (a) the net gain or loss in earnings, (b) the new percent of earnings on the original capital, and (c) the percent of gain or loss on the original earnings.

Chapter 13

Transactions in Corporate Securities

Objectives To Be Achieved in This Chapter

1   *Read and interpret stock and bond price quotations printed in newspapers.*
2   *Determine stock brokerage commission costs, state transfer taxes, and other costs to arrive at the net cost of a security purchase or net proceeds of a security sale.*
3   *Allocate costs to stock rights and determine gain or loss on the sale of securities.*
4   *Calculate current yield rates on stocks and bonds.*
5   *Calculate yield-to-maturity rates on bonds by an approximation method and by compound-interest methods.*

Corporate securities may be purchased and sold by direct negotiation between buyer and seller, but such transactions frequently take place through the medium of a broker or dealer whose facilities are organized to provide such service for the general public.

Stocks and bonds bought and sold on established exchanges are known as *on-board* or *listed* securities. Stocks and bonds not sold on established exchanges are known as *off-board, unlisted,* or *over-the-counter* securities.

STOCK EXCHANGES Stock exchanges operate in most of the principal cities of the United States. The New York Stock Exchange (NYSE) and the American Stock Exchange (AMEX), both located in New York City, are the two largest in both volume of sales and value of transactions. Aside from mining, oil, and commodity exchanges to be found in a number of cities, the other principal exchanges in North America are the Canadian stock exchanges. Because of its importance in size and leadership, illustrative examples and all problem material will be confined to the NYSE.

Unit 13.1 — Odd-Lot Differentials and Commission Rates

For their services, brokers charge a fee or commission called *brokerage*. As of May 1, 1975, all security brokerage firms were allowed to set their own competitive commission rate schedules, rather than having them set by the various exchanges. Additional expenses to the purchaser or seller of stocks may include Federal Securities and Exchange Commission charges, state transfer taxes, postage, and other fees. Such expenses are added to the cost to the purchaser and are deducted from the remittance to the seller.

ODD-LOT DIFFERENTIALS The unit of trading used most commonly on the NYSE is 100 shares. A limited number of usually inactive issues is traded in units of 10 shares instead of 100 shares. Therefore in 100-share-unit stocks, odd lots are any number of shares from 1 to 99; and in 10-share-unit stocks, odd lots are any number of shares from 1 to 9 (on the AMEX, stocks are traded in units of 100, 50, 25, and 10 shares).

When an individual places an order with his broker to buy or sell an odd lot of stock, the broker *must* buy that stock from an odd-lot dealer who performs a kind of wholesaling function by breaking up round lots of securities into smaller groupings. Such odd-lot dealers do business only with brokers on the exchange floor, not with the general public. For this service the odd-lot dealer charges a *differential,* an additional cost to the individual buyer or charge to the seller.

THE ODD-LOT DEALER'S DIFFERENTIAL The amount of differential charged by an odd-lot dealer depends upon the price of the round-lot transaction in that security executed on the floor of the Exchange after receipt of the odd-lot order by the odd-lot dealer. This qualifying round-lot transaction is called an *effective sale*. The odd-lot differential is then:

	If the effective sale is	The odd-lot differential is
NYSE		
	$\frac{1}{8}$ or below ($0.125)	$\frac{1}{2}$ the price of the effective sale
	$\frac{5}{32}$ ($0.15625)	$\frac{3}{32}$ ($0.09375) for sell orders
		$\frac{1}{8}$ ($0.125) for buy orders
	above $\frac{5}{32}$ ($0.15625)	$\frac{1}{8}$ ($0.125)
AMEX		
	Below $40 per share	$\frac{1}{8}$ ($0.125)
	$40 and above	$\frac{1}{4}$ ($0.25)

Since almost all round-lot transactions on the NYSE are above $\frac{5}{32}$ ($0.15625), for practical purposes the odd-lot differential is $\frac{1}{8}$ point ($0.125) on the NYSE.

On purchase (buying) orders, the odd-lot differential is added to this round-lot transaction price. On sales (selling) orders, the odd-lot differential is subtracted from the round-lot transaction price.

The statement of price, known as the *execution price,* by the broker to the individual purchaser or seller of an odd lot includes the differential.

Example 1 **Execution price on an odd lot when effective round-lot price is more than $0.16 per share. Find the execution price on an odd lot of a 100-share unit stock if the effective round-lot price is 28 to (a) the individual buyer and (b) the individual seller.**

(a) Execution price per share $28 + \frac{1}{8} = 28\frac{1}{8} = \$28.125$ per share
(b) Execution price per share $28 - \frac{1}{8} = 27\frac{7}{8} = \$27.875$ per share

COMMISSION RATES Since all security brokers can now set their own competitive commission rates, the rates listed below are not necessarily those of any one brokerage firm; nor do they purport to include rates for all types of transactions. They are listed for purposes of illustrating the total cost and/or net proceeds of a normal purchase or sale of a security by an investor.

On stocks, rights, and warrants selling at $1.00 per share and above:

Principal amount	Basic rates
$300 or less	10% or $6, whichever is greater
$ 301– $800	2.000% + $11
$ 801– $2500	1.500% + $15
$ 2501– $5000	1.120% + $27
$ 5001–$20,000	1.100% + $30
$20,001–$30,000	0.750% + $103
Over $30,000	0.495% + $182

Plus:

Multiple round-lot orders up to and including 1000 shares, add $7.50 per round lot.

Multiple round-lot orders involving more than 1000 shares, add $5.00 per round lot in excess of 1000 shares.

Subject to minimum and maximum charges of:

Minimum of $30 on orders involving a principal amount in excess of $300.
Maximum of $85 per order on odd-lot orders.
Maximum of $85 per round-lot or $0.85 per share on orders involving 100 shares or more

On stocks, rights, and warrants selling at under $1.00 per share:

Principal amount	Rate
Under $1000	10%
$1001–$10,000	6% + $40
Over $10,000	5% + $140

Subject to minimum and maximum charges of:

Minimum of $6 per order.
Maximum of $80 per round-lot or $0.80 per share on orders involving over 100 shares.

Example 2   **Odd-lot number of shares of trading. Find the commission charge in transactions of (a) 54 shares if round-lot price was $23\frac{3}{8}$, (b) 12 shares if round-lot price was $10\frac{1}{8}$.**

(a)   Money value of shares:

Round-lot price	$23\frac{3}{8}$
Add odd-lot differential	$\frac{1}{8}$
Total price	$23\frac{1}{2}$ ($23.50)
Value = 54 shares $\times$ $23\frac{1}{2}$ =	$1269.00
Commission:	
$15.00 + 1.5% $\times$ $1269.00	= $34.04

(b)   Money value of shares:

Round-lot price	$10\frac{1}{8}$
Add odd-lot differential	$\frac{1}{8}$
Total price	$10\frac{1}{4}$ ($10.25)
Value = 12 shares $\times$ $10\frac{1}{4}$ =	$123
Commission:	
10% of $123 =	$12.30

Example 3   **Round lots in 100-share units of trading. Find the commission charge on transactions of (a) 100 shares at 28¾, (b) 10,000 shares at 34, (c) 400 shares at 18⅛.**

(a)   Money value of shares:

$$100 \times 28\frac{3}{4} = \qquad\qquad\qquad\qquad \$2875.00$$

Commission:
$27.00 + 1.12% × $2875   = $59.20

(b)   Money value of shares:
10,000 × 34 = $340,000
Commission:
$183.00 + .495% of $340,000   = $1866.00
Add: 10 round-lot units at $7.50   =   75.00
90 round-lot units in excess
of first 1000 shares at $5.00   =   450.00
Total commission: $2391.00

(c)   Money value of shares:

$$400 \times 18\frac{1}{8}(\$18.125) = \qquad\qquad\qquad \$7250$$

Commission:
$30.00 + 1.1% × $7250   − $109.75
Add $7.50 per round lot:
4 × $7.50   =   30.00
Total commission: = $139.75

Example 4   **Odd-lot number of 100-unit shares of trading in stocks of less than $1.00. Find the commission charge on (a) 85 shares at ¾ ($0.75), and (b) 25 shares at ⅝ ($0.625).**

(a)   Money value of shares:

Round-lot price $\frac{3}{4}$

Odd-lot differential $\frac{1}{8}$

Total price: $\frac{7}{8}$ ($0.875)

Value = 85 shares × $\frac{7}{8}$ = $74.38

Commission:
10% × $74.38   = $7.44

(b) Money value of shares:

Round-lot price $\qquad \dfrac{5}{8}$

Odd-lot differential $\qquad \dfrac{1}{8}$

Total price $\qquad \dfrac{3}{4}$ ($0.75)

Value = 25 shares at $\dfrac{3}{4}$ = \$18.75

Commission:
10% of \$18.75 = \$1.88
However, subject to minimum fee $\qquad\qquad\qquad$ = \$6.00

Example 5 **Round-lots of 100-unit shares of trading in shares of less than \$1.00. Find the commission charge on (a) 200 shares at $\frac{1}{2}$, (b) 10,000 shares at $\frac{7}{8}$.**

(a) Money value of shares:

$$200 \times \frac{1}{2} = \qquad\qquad \$100.00$$

Commission:
10% × \$100.00 $\qquad\qquad$ = \$10.00

(b) Money value of shares:

$$10,000 \times \frac{7}{8}(\$0.875) = \qquad \$8750.00$$

Commission:
\$40.00 + 6% × \$8750.00 $\qquad\qquad$ = \$565.00

Example 6 **Round-lots and an odd-lot of 100-unit shares of trading. Find the commission charge on 630 shares at $25\frac{1}{4}$.**

This is calculated as a round-lot transaction for 600 shares and an odd-lot transaction of 30 shares.

(a) Round-lot transaction:
Money value of shares:

$$600 \times 25\frac{1}{4} = \$15,150.00$$

Commission:
\$30.00 + 1.1% × \$15,150 $\qquad\qquad$ = \$196.65
Add \$7.50 per round lot
$\qquad$ 6 × \$7.50 $\qquad\qquad$ = 45.00
$\qquad$ Total commission on round lots $\qquad$ = \$241.65

(b) Odd-lot transaction:
Money value of shares:

Round-lot price	$25\frac{1}{4}$
Odd-lot differential	$\frac{1}{8}$
Total price	$25\frac{3}{8}$

$$\text{Value} = 30 \text{ shares} \times 25\frac{3}{8} = \$761.25$$

Commission:
$11.00 + 2% × $761.25 = $26.23
Subject to a minimum of   30.00
Total commission $271.65

Exercise 13.1

1 Find the execution price per share to the purchaser on odd lots of 100-share units if the effective round-lot prices are (a) $\frac{5}{8}$, (b) $15\frac{1}{4}$, (c) $120\frac{3}{8}$, and (d) $52\frac{7}{8}$.

2 Find the execution price per share to the seller on odd lots of 100-share units if the effective round-lot prices are (a) $\frac{3}{4}$, (b) 14, (c) $180\frac{1}{8}$, and (d) $62\frac{1}{4}$.

3 Find the commission charges in the purchase or sale in transactions of (a) 100 shares at $28\frac{1}{4}$, (b) 100 shares at $\frac{7}{8}$, (c) 500 shares at 28, and (d) 5000 shares at $15\frac{3}{4}$.

4 Find the commission charges in the purchase or sale in transactions of (a) 100 shares at $\frac{5}{8}$, (b) 100 shares at $23\frac{1}{4}$, (c) 800 shares at $16\frac{1}{8}$, and (d) 8000 shares at $22\frac{1}{8}$.

5 Find the commission charges in the purchase of 100-share units of (a) 123 shares at $24\frac{1}{8}$, (b) 619 shares at $9\frac{1}{4}$, (c) 246 shares at 43, and (d) 2315 shares at $16\frac{1}{2}$.

6 Find the commission charges in the sale of 100-share units of (a) 180 shares at $16\frac{1}{4}$, (b) 215 shares at 43, (c) 2040 shares at $20\frac{5}{8}$, and (d) 942 shares at $8\frac{1}{2}$.

7 Find the commission charges in the purchase of 100-share units of (a) 20 shares at $\frac{5}{8}$, (b) 60 shares at $10\frac{1}{4}$, (c) 90 shares at $3\frac{5}{8}$, and (d) 80 shares at 200.

8 Find the commission charges in the sale of (a) 25 shares of 100-share units of trading sold at the effective round-lot price of $68\frac{5}{8}$ and (b) five shares of 100-share units of trading sold at the effective round-lot price of $31\frac{7}{8}$.

9 Find the commission charges in purchases of the following 100-share unit of trading stocks for (a) 360 shares bought at the effective round-lot price of $17\frac{1}{2}$ and (b) 155 shares bought at the effective round-lot price of $102\frac{1}{8}$.

10 Find the commission charges in sales of the following 100-share unit of trading stocks for (a) 225 shares sold at the effective round-lot price of $91\frac{7}{8}$ and (b) 140 shares sold at the effective round-lot price of 40.

Unit 13.2   *Stock Purchases*

The day on which a transaction takes place is known as the *trade date*.
    The day on which the purchaser is expected to make payment in full to his broker for the securities he has ordered bought and the seller is expected to deliver to his broker the securities that he has ordered sold is known as the *settlement date*.

    Ordinarily, the settlement date is the fifth business day following the trade date. When the settlement date is to be longer than the fifth business day following the trade date, the seller must have so stipulated and a later settlement date known and agreeable to the buyer must have been determined.

Example 1   **A stock purchase. Find the total cost to the purchaser of 160 shares of Square D Company common stock (100-share unit of trading) purchased through a broker on the NYSE, if the effective round-lot price is $52\frac{1}{2}$. The stock was purchased Monday, October 3, 19___.**

Trade date, October 3, 19___   **Settlement date,** October 10, 19___

Exc.	Bot	Description	Price	Amount	Commission	Total
NYSE	100	Square D	52 1/2	$5250.00	$ 87.75	$5337.75
NYSE	60		52 5/8	3157.50	62.36	3219.86
Totals				$8407.50	$150.11	$8557.61

Explanation

Trade date: October 3, 19___. The date on which the broker made the purchase.

Settlement date: October 10. As is ordinarily the case, the fifth business day following the trade date.

Exc.: NYSE. The transaction took place on the New York Stock Exchange.

Bot.: 100.   A full unit of trading in this instance.
       60.   An odd lot.

Description: Square D.   The abbreviation for Square D Company common stock.

Price: $52\frac{1}{2}$.   Purchase price per share on full unit of trading.
       $52\frac{5}{8}$.   Purchase price per share including differential on odd lot.

Amount: 5250.00. $52\frac{1}{2} \times 100 = \$5250.00$

       3157.50. $52\frac{5}{8} \times 60 = \$3157.50$

Commission: Computed as follows on (a) *round lot* and (b) *odd lot.*

(a) *Round lot:*

Money value of shares:

$$100 \times 52\tfrac{1}{2} = \qquad\qquad\qquad \$5250.00$$

Commission:
$$\$30.00 + 1.1\% \times \$5250 = \qquad\qquad \$87.75$$

(b) *Odd lot:*

Money value of shares:

$$60 \text{ shares} \times 52\tfrac{5}{8} = \qquad\qquad \$3157.50$$

Commission:
$$\$27.00 + 1.12\% \times \$3157.50 = \qquad\qquad \underline{\$62.36}$$

Total column: The sum of the amount and commission for the 100 shares and the 60 shares.

Totals line: The sum of the items placed in the *amount,* commission, and total column.

Exercise 13.2

In solving the following problems involving stock purchases on the New York Stock Exchange, use the stock listings in Table 13.1. For each purchase find (a) execution price per share, (b) the commission, (c) total cost to the purchaser.

TABLE 13.1   EFFECTIVE ROUND-LOT PRICES FOR CERTAIN STOCKS ON THE NYSE[1]

1977 High	Low	Stock	Sales in 100's	Open	High	Low	Close	Net change[2]
$5\frac{1}{4}$	$3\frac{3}{4}$	Am Motors	129	$3\frac{7}{8}$	4	$3\frac{7}{8}$	4	$+\frac{1}{8}$
$11\frac{1}{4}$	$7\frac{3}{4}$	Ampex	186	$10\frac{1}{2}$	$10\frac{1}{2}$	$10\frac{1}{8}$	$10\frac{1}{4}$	$-\frac{1}{8}$
$20\frac{5}{8}$	16	Avnet	148	$18\frac{1}{4}$	$18\frac{3}{4}$	18	$18\frac{1}{4}$	—
$3\frac{5}{8}$	$1\frac{1}{2}$	BengtB	115	$2\frac{1}{8}$	$2\frac{1}{2}$	$2\frac{3}{8}$	$2\frac{1}{2}$	$+\frac{1}{8}$
$17\frac{5}{8}$	$12\frac{3}{4}$	Brunswk	204	$13\frac{7}{8}$	14	$13\frac{3}{4}$	$13\frac{7}{8}$	—
$62\frac{1}{4}$	55	CBS	158	$55\frac{7}{8}$	$56\frac{1}{4}$	$55\frac{7}{8}$	$56\frac{1}{4}$	$+\frac{3}{8}$
$37\frac{3}{8}$	$29\frac{3}{8}$	Comsat	250	$33\frac{3}{8}$	$33\frac{1}{2}$	$33\frac{1}{4}$	$33\frac{1}{4}$	$-\frac{1}{8}$
$43\frac{1}{2}$	$30\frac{3}{8}$	Dow Ch	882	$30\frac{5}{8}$	$30\frac{7}{8}$	30	$30\frac{7}{8}$	$+\frac{1}{4}$
$13\frac{3}{8}$	$9\frac{3}{4}$	GAF CP	154	$9\frac{3}{4}$	10	$9\frac{3}{4}$	$9\frac{3}{4}$	—
$6\frac{3}{4}$	$3\frac{3}{4}$	Genesco	38	$4\frac{1}{8}$	$4\frac{1}{8}$	$4\frac{1}{8}$	$4\frac{1}{8}$	$+\frac{1}{8}$
$14\frac{3}{4}$	$11\frac{1}{8}$	Holiday Inn	668	$13\frac{1}{2}$	$13\frac{7}{8}$	$13\frac{1}{2}$	$13\frac{3}{4}$	$+\frac{1}{4}$
$27\frac{7}{8}$	$23\frac{1}{8}$	Kellog	32	$24\frac{3}{4}$	$24\frac{7}{8}$	$24\frac{3}{4}$	$24\frac{7}{8}$	$+\frac{1}{8}$
$3\frac{7}{8}$	$2\frac{1}{4}$	Lionel	36	$3\frac{5}{8}$	$3\frac{5}{8}$	$3\frac{1}{2}$	$3\frac{5}{8}$	—
$6\frac{1}{8}$	$3\frac{5}{8}$	Pan Am	287	$5\frac{3}{8}$	$5\frac{1}{2}$	$5\frac{3}{8}$	$5\frac{3}{8}$	—
$21\frac{3}{8}$	$15\frac{1}{2}$	Pitney B	286	$19\frac{1}{4}$	$19\frac{1}{4}$	19	19	$-\frac{1}{4}$

[1] Prices were taken from the *Wall Street Journal,* Monday, August 22, representing prices as of Friday, August 19, 1977.
[2] Net change is the increase or decrease in today's closing quotation from yesterday's closing quotation.

1 100 shares of AM Motors at yesterday's last effective round-lot quotation.
2 100 shares of Holiday Inn at today's high effective round-lot quotation.
3 100 shares of Pitney B at today's low effective round-lot quotation.
4 100 shares of Dow Ch at today's last effective round-lot quotation.
5 30 shares of a 100-share unit of Pan American Airlines at today's last effective round-lot quotation.
6 600 shares of Comsat at today's opening quotation.
7 10,000 shares of Ampex Corporation at the 1977 low quotation.
8 225 shares of a 100-share unit of CBS at the 1977 high quotation.

Unit 13.3   *Stock Sales*

All stock sales and transfers of stocks made through registered exchanges, whether full units of trading or odd lots, are liable for a Federal Securities and Exchange Commission charge. Additionally, all stock sales made on registered exchanges in the states of New York, Florida, South Carolina, and Texas require the payment of city and/or state transfer taxes.

FEDERAL SECURITIES AND EXCHANGE COMMISSION CHARGE To help defray the expenses of the Securities and Exchange Commission (SEC), 1 cent per $500 or fraction thereof is charged the seller for all transactions on any registered exchange.

Example 1 **Find the SEC charge on sales (excluding commissions or any taxes) totaling $300, $501, and $2735.**

SEC charge on $ 300.00: $0.01 $\times$ 1 = $0.01
SEC charge on $ 501.00: $0.01 $\times$ 2 = $0.02
SEC charge on $2735.00: $0.01 $\times$ 6 = $0.06

NEW YORK TRANSFER TAX ON STOCK SALES Since the discussion in this text is limited to transactions on the NYSE, transfer taxes levied by other states are omitted.

The combined transfer tax charged by New York State and New York City on stock sales or transfer is computed as follows:

Selling price per share	Residents	Nonresidents
Less than $5	$0.0125	$0.00625
$5, less than $10	0.025	0.0125
$10, less than $20	0.0375	0.01875
$20 or more	0.05	0.025

Example 2   **Find the New York transfer tax for a New York resident on (a) 60 shares selling at $3\frac{1}{2}$, (b) 100 shares selling at 7, (c) 25 shares selling at $16\frac{1}{4}$, and (d) 240 shares selling at 83.**

(a) $\$0.0125 \times 60 = \$\ 0.75$
(b) $\$0.025\ \ \times 100 = \$\ 2.50$
(c) $\$0.0375 \times 25 = \$\ 0.94$
(d) $\$0.05\ \ \ \ \times 240 = \$12.00$

Example 3   **A stock sale. Find the net proceeds to the seller of 215 shares of Safeway Stores, Incorporated (100-share unit of trading) sold through a resident broker on the NYSE, if the effective round-lot price is 44.**

Trade date, November 9, 19___   **Settlement date,** November 17, 19___

Exc.	Sold	Description	Price	Tax	Amount	Commission	Proceeds
NYSE	200	Safewy	44	$10.18	$8789.82	$141.80	$8648.02
NYSE	15		$43\frac{7}{8}$	0.79	657.34	30.00	627.34
Totals					$9447.16	$171.80	$9275.36

Explanation

Trade date: November 9, 19___. The date on which the broker made the sale.

Settlement date: November 17. As is ordinarily the case, the fifth business day following the trade date. November 11 was a legal holiday; November 12 and 13 were Saturday and Sunday, always nonbusiness days; and thus the fifth business day following November 9 was November 17.

Exc.: NYSE. The transaction took place on the New York Stock Exchange.

Sold: 200. Two full units of trading in this instance.
            15. An odd lot.

Description: Safewy. The abbreviation for Safeway Stores, Incorporated.

Price: 44. The selling price per share per full unit of trading.

Tax: 200 round-lot shares:

NY transfer tax: 200 sh at $0.05   = $10.00
SEC charge: 200 sh at 44 = $8800
   $8800 \div 500 = 17.6$ $500s;
      $18 \times \$0.01 =$ =   .18 $10.18
15 odd-lot shares:
NY transfer tax: 15 sh at $0.05   =   .75

SEC charge: 15 sh at $43\frac{7}{8} = \$658.13$

   $\$658.13 \div 500 = 1.32$; $2 \times \$0.01$ =   .02 $.77

Amount:	200 round-lot shares:		
	200 at 44	=	$8800.00
	Less taxes:		−10.18 $8789.82
	15 odd-lot shares:		
	15 at $43\frac{7}{8}$	=	$658.13
	Less taxes:		−.77 $657.36

Commission:	200 round-lot shares:		
	Money value of shares:		
	200 at 44	=	$8800.00
	Commission:		
	$30.00 + 1.1% × $8800.00	=	$126.80
	Add $7.50 per round-lot; 2 at $7.50		15.00
	Total commission	=	$141.80
	15 odd-lot shares:		
	Money value of shares:		
	$15 × 43\frac{7}{8}$	=	$658.13
	Commission:		
	$11.00 + 2% × $658. 13	=	$24.16
	Subject to minimum charge		$30.00
Proceeds:	Round-lot transaction: $8789.82 − $141.80 =		$8648.02
	Odd-lot transaction: $657.36 − $30.00 =		$627.36

Exercise 13.3

Solve the following problems in transfer taxes in the sale of stocks:

1 Compute (a) the SEC charge, (b) the New York transfer tax, and (c) the total transfer taxes on the sale of 100 shares of stock if the selling price is $12\frac{1}{4}$.

2 Compute (a) the SEC charge, (b) the New York transfer tax, and (c) the total transfer taxes on the sale of 200 shares of stock if the selling price is $31\frac{3}{4}$.

3 Compute (a) the SEC charge, (b) the New York transfer tax, and (c) the total transfer taxes on the sale of an odd lot of 58 shares of a 100-share unit of trading stock if the effective round-lot price is $17\frac{1}{4}$.

4 Compute (a) the SEC charge, (b) the New York transfer tax, and (c) the total transfer taxes on the sale of 80 shares of a 100-share unit of trading stock if the effective round-lot price is $113\frac{1}{4}$.

Solve the following stock sales on the NYSE, using the stock listings in Table 13.1. For each sale, find (a) execution price per share, (b) total SEC and New York transfer taxes, (c) commission, and (d) net proceeds to seller.

5 100 shares of Avnet at yesterday's closing round-lot quotation.

6 100 shares of Dow Chemical at yesterday's closing round-lot quotation.

7   100 shares of GAF Corporation at today's low round-lot quotation.
8   300 shares of Comsat at today's closing round-lot quotation.
9   25 shares of a 100-share unit of Genesco at today's high round-lot quotation.
10 200 shares of Lionel at today's opening round-lot quotation.

Unit 13.4 — *Purchase and Sale of Bonds*

Corporate bonds as well as stocks are usually purchased or sold through the medium of a broker who charges a commission for his services. If the bonds are coupon bonds and delivered by mail, there may also be an insured postage charge made to the buyer. SEC charge is an additional expense to the seller, but there are no transfer taxes on bond sales and there are no transfer taxes (SEC or state or city) on bond purchases.

Unlike most stock transactions, a bond transfer may include an element other than market price. In stocks, the market price ordinarily reflects (includes) the value of any earnings accruing since the last dividend payment. In the case of bonds, accrued interest is not included in the market price, and thus accrued interest is added to the cost to the purchaser and to the remittance to the seller.

INTEREST ON BOND TRANSFERS   Since the market price of a bond does not include any interest which may have accumulated, it is usually necessary to make this calculation in bond transfers. Exceptions to this statement are:

1   Registered bonds in which the settlement date is after the final date of record for any given payment. If a bond is registered, the holder's name is recorded by the registrars or trustees who make payment of interest to the holder of record. A final date is set, usually about 1 month prior to the interest date for change of registration of holders for the next interest payment. It is obvious that a certain amount of time is required to complete the accounting processes necessary in transferring ownership from one party to another.
2   If the settlement date of a coupon bond is the interest date, it is required that the coupon due on the settlement date be attached, and thus an interest computation is not necessary. The new holder presents the coupon due for payment. In such instance, the bond is sold *flat* (see Exception 3 following).
3   Perhaps the most frequent exception to the need to make interest calculations occurs when a bond is flat and is in default, that is, interest payments are in arrears and one or more interest payments have not been made when due. In such instance, on a registered bond all interest payments due are accumulated and on a coupon bond all coupons unpaid when due are attached, and the accumulated interest if paid in the future goes to the registered holder of record at that time if a registered bond, and to the bearer at that time if a coupon bond.

COMPUTING INTEREST ON BOND TRANSFERS Assuming that the three exceptions as noted in the preceding do not obtain, bond interest due to the seller and owed by the buyer in addition to the selling price is computed on the following basis.

Bond interest is based on the par (redemption) value of the bond at the specified interest rate for the number of days including the date of the last interest payment up to and including the day before the settlement date. As with stocks, the settlement date of a bond transaction is ordinarily the fifth business day following the trade date. When the settlement date is to be longer than 5 full business days following the trade date of the transaction, the seller must have so stipulated and a later date known and agreeable to the buyer must have been determined.

In making interest calculations, note that nonbusiness days are not considered in counting the number of days to the settlement date. Thus a bond transaction with a trade date on a Thursday has a settlement date on the following Thursday, and if Friday, Monday, Tuesday, or Wednesday is a legal holiday (nonbusiness day), the settlement date would be delayed until the following Friday.

On corporate bonds, the interest is computed as ordinary interest at 30-day-month time (on U.S. bonds exact interest is used)—the numerator of the time element being computed at 30-day-month time with a denominator of 360 days. Thus it is obvious why ordinary interest at 30-day-month time is frequently called *ordinary interest at bond time*.

Bond interest payments are usually made semiannually. Interest dates and redemption (maturity) dates of bonds are usually symbolized as follows: *MS 70, AO* 78, *JJ 80; the capital letters indicate the months in which semiannual interest payments are due (the first day of the month unless otherwise indicated); the asterisk (*) indicates the month of maturity; and the figures indicate the year of maturity. Thus the preceding symbols mean: *MS 70, semiannual interest payable March 1 and September 1, maturity date of March 1, 1970; AO* 78, semiannual interest payable April 1 and October 1, maturity date of October 1, 1978, and *JJ 80, semiannual interest payable January 1 and July 1, maturity date of January 1, 1980.

Example 1   **Compute the accrued interest on a 4 percent, $1000 par corporate bond FA* 72 with trade date of April 8.**

The time period is from and including February 1, the date of the last interest payment, to and including April 14, the day preceding the settlement date of April 15: 2 months 14 days = 74 days.

$$\$1000.00 \times \frac{74}{360} \times \frac{4}{100} = \$8.22 \quad \text{Accrued interest}$$

Example 2   **Compute the accrued interest on six $1000 par, $4\frac{1}{2}$ percent corporate bonds *JD 75 with trade date of October 28.**

The time period is from and including June 1, the date of the last interest payment to and including November 3, the day preceding the settlement date of November 4 (note that the exact number of days following October 28 including October 31 are counted in determining the settlement date): 5 months 3 days = 153 days.

$$\$1000.00 \times 6 = \$6000.00$$

$$\$6000.00 \times \frac{153}{360} \times \frac{45}{1000} = \$114.75 \quad \text{Accrued interest}$$

Example 3   **Compute the accrued interest, if any, that is added to the purchaser's cost or to the seller's proceeds on a bond that is flat.**

When a bond is purchased or sold flat, it means that interest payments due have not been made and the market price reflects the value of the bond including all interest payments not yet paid. Therefore interest is not computed.

BOND QUOTATIONS   Bond quotations are per bond, there being no such thing as an odd lot. Quotations are a percent of par, not in dollars. Most corporate bonds are $1000 par, though a few are in denominations of $100 to $500. Bonds of $1000 par value are referred to by the capital letter M, the roman numeral for 1000. Thus five $1000 bonds would be referred to as 5 M.

Example 4   **Quotations on $1000 par bonds.**

$$110\frac{1}{8} = \$1000.00 \times 1.10\frac{1}{8} = \$1101.25 \text{ per bond}$$

$$83\frac{1}{4} = \$1000.00 \times 0.83\frac{1}{4} = \$\ 832.50 \text{ per bond}$$

$$22\frac{5}{8} = \$1000.00 \times 0.22\frac{5}{8} = \$\ 226.25 \text{ per bond}$$

SEC CHARGE ONLY ON BOND TRANSFERS   The seller of bonds (except for federal, state, and municipal bonds) on a recognized exchange must pay an SEC charge of 1 cent for each $500 or fraction thereof of the amount involved.

There are no taxes on bond sales or purchases, nor are there SEC charges on bond purchases.

The SEC charge paid by the broker on bond sales is deducted by the broker from the remittance to the seller.

Example 5   **Find the SEC charge on the sale of four $1000 par bonds at 91½.**

$$\$1000.00 \times 0.91\frac{1}{2} = \$915.00 \quad \text{Selling price per bond}$$

$$\$915.00 \times 4 = \$3660.00 \quad \text{Total selling price of 4 bonds}$$
$$\$3660.00 = \text{seven and a fraction } \$500\text{s}$$
$$\$0.01 \times 8 = \$0.08 \quad \text{SEC charge}$$

COMMISSION RATES ON PURCHASE OR SALE OF BONDS Brokers have also been allowed to set competitive rates for bonds. The following rates for listed and over-the-counter bonds do not reflect those of any one broker, but should be fairly representative.

Principal amount	Maturity	Rate per $1000
Any amount	Up to 2 years	$5.00
1 M–25 M	2 years and longer	$7.50
26 M–99 M	2 years and longer	$5.00
100 M or more	2 years and longer	$2.50

A minimum of $25 will be maintained on all trades. For bonds less than 1 M, the charge is approximately $2.50 per $100 par with a $5.00 minimum charge per transaction.

Government bonds and other miscellaneous notes, commercial paper, bankers acceptances, etc., carry commission charges that vary from slightly less than $1.00 per $1000 to approximately $5.00 per $1000. All such transactions usually include at least a $25.00 minimum charge.

Example 6 **Find the commission charges on bonds purchased or sold in quantities and prices as follows: (a) 1 M at 91, due in 5 years, (b) 30 M at $96\frac{1}{4}$, due in $1\frac{1}{2}$ years, (c) 125 M due in 20 years at $42\frac{1}{2}$.**

(a) 1 M at 7.50 = $7.50.

Subject to minimum charge of $ 25.00

(b) 30 M at $5.00   = $150.00
(c) 125 M at $2.50   = $312.50

Example 7 **A bond purchase. Find the cost to a purchaser of 5 M Exxon 6 percent bonds, MN*97 at $83\frac{1}{4}$. Trade date was Monday, August 22, 19___, and the settlement date was Monday, August 29, 19___.**

Trade date, August 22, 19___   **Settlement date,** August 29, 19___

Exc.	Bot	Description	Price	Interest	Amount	Commission	Total
NYSE	5 M	Exxon 6s MN*97	$83\frac{1}{4}$	$98.33	$4260.83	$37.50	$4298.33

Explanation

Trade date: August 22, 19___. The date the broker made the purchase.

Settlement date: August 29, 19___. The fifth business day after the trade date. The date that the buyer is to make payment and the seller is to deliver the bond.

Bot: 5 M. Purchased $5000 par value of bonds.

Description: Exxon 6s MN*97. Abbreviation for Exxon Corporation 6 percent bonds. The bonds are due on November 1, 1997 and interest is payable May 1 and November 1 of each year.

Price: $83\frac{1}{4}$. The percent of par value at which the bonds were purchased.

Interest: $98.33. Ordinary interest computed at 30-day-month time from the date of the last interest payment, May 1, to and including August 28, the day before the settlement date of August 29.

$$5/1 - 8/28 = 3 \text{ months } 28 \text{ days } = 118 \text{ days}$$

$$\$5000 \times \frac{6}{100} \times \frac{118}{360} = \$98.33$$

Amount: $4260.83. The sum of 5 M bonds at $83\frac{1}{4}$ plus accrued interest.

($5000 × 0.8325 = $4162.50 + $98.33 = $4260.83)

Commission: $37.50. 5 M bonds at $7.50 = $37.50.

Total: $4298.33. The cost to the purchaser.

($4260.83 + $37.50 = $4298.33)

Example 8   **A bond sale. Find the proceeds to the seller of 4 M, $10\frac{1}{2}$ percent mortgage bonds of the Acme Railroad, *FA, 87, if sold through a member of the NYSE at $112\frac{1}{4}$.**

Trade date, November 29, 19____   **Settlement date,** December 6, 19____

Exc.	Sold	Description	Price	Interest	Tax	Amount	Comm.	Proceeds
NYSE	4 M	Acme RR $10\frac{1}{2}$s *F A 87	$112\frac{1}{4}$	$145.83	0.09	$4635.74	$30.00	$4605.74

Explanation

Trade date: November 29, 19___. The date the broker made the sale.

Settlement date: December 6. The fifth business day after the trade date. The day the seller is to deliver the bonds and receive payment.

Exc: NYSE. Transaction took place on the NYSE.

Sold: 4 M. Sold $4000 par value.

Description: Acme RR $10\frac{1}{2}$ *FA 87. Abbreviation of Acme Railroad $10\frac{1}{2}$ percent bonds, interest payable on February 1 and August 1. Bonds mature on February 1, 1987.

TABLE 13.2 A LISTING AND QUOTATIONS OF CERTAIN $1000 PAR CORPORATE BONDS[1]

Today's sales (M)	Description	Current yield[2]	Interest and maturity dates	Today's quotations High	Low	Close	Net change[3]
4	Ala P 9s	8.8	*MS 2000	102	102	102	—
13	Amfac $5\frac{1}{4}$ CV[4]	—	FA* 1994	$67\frac{1}{4}$	67	$67\frac{1}{4}$	$+\frac{1}{4}$
28	Beth St 9s	8.7	*MN 2000	$103\frac{5}{8}$	$103\frac{3}{8}$	$103\frac{3}{8}$	$+\frac{3}{8}$
9	Chryslr 8s	9.1	*JD 1998	$88\frac{3}{8}$	$88\frac{3}{8}$	$88\frac{3}{8}$	—
30	Frd C $7\frac{1}{2}$ Debs[5]	7.9	JJ* 1992	$95\frac{1}{2}$	$95\frac{1}{2}$	$95\frac{1}{2}$	-2
10	PGE 8s Mtge[6]	8.3	*FA 2003	$98\frac{1}{4}$	$96\frac{5}{8}$	$96\frac{5}{8}$	$-1\frac{3}{8}$
20	Sears $8\frac{5}{8}$	8.3	*MS 1995	104	104	104	$+\frac{1}{2}$
5	ShellO $4\frac{5}{8}$	5.3	*JJ 1986	$87\frac{3}{8}$	$87\frac{3}{8}$	$87\frac{3}{8}$	$-1\frac{1}{8}$
3	TVA 7s	7.5	AO* 1997	93	93	93	$+1$
30	Xerox 8.2s	8	*MS 1982	$103\frac{3}{8}$	$102\frac{5}{8}$	$102\frac{5}{8}$	$+\frac{1}{2}$

[1] All data presented in this listing are not factual as of any date.
[2] Current yield is annual returns on present market price.
[3] Net change is change from yesterday's close.
[4] CV is abbreviation for convertible bond. Yield percent not entered as price tends to follow stock into which it is convertible.
[5] Debs is abbreviation for debenture bond.
[6] Mtge is abbreviation for mortgage bond.

Price: $112\frac{1}{4}$. The percent of par value at which the bonds were sold.

Interest: \$145.83. Four months, 5 days (125 days) at 30-day-month time from August 1 to December 5 (the day before the settlement date) at $10\frac{1}{2}$ percent.

$$\$4000 \times \frac{10.5}{100} \times \frac{125}{360} = \$145.83$$

Tax: \$0.09. The SEC charge of \$0.09 computed as follows: money value of 4 M bonds at $112\frac{1}{4}$ = \$4490 and contains eight and a fraction \$500s.

$$9 \times \$0.01 = \$0.09$$

Amount: \$4635.74. Money value plus interest minus tax

$$\$4490.00 + \$145.83 - \$0.09 = \$4635.74$$

Proceeds: \$4605.74. Proceeds to the seller.

$$\$4635.74 - \$30.00 = \$4605.74$$

Exercise 13.4

For each of the following bond purchases, find (*a*) dollars of par purchased, (*b*) price in percent, (c) interest, if any, (*d*) amount, (e) commission at rates on page 486, and (*f*) total cost to purchaser. Use bond listings from Table 13.2 and assume that quantities purchased are as indicated under the column "Today's sales (M)" and that settlement dates are five days after trade dates.

1   Ala P 9s at today's low quotation, trade date October 7.
2   Amfac 5¼ CV at today's high quotation, trade date July 11.
3   Beth St 9s at today's last quotation, trade date June 18.
4   Chrysler 8s at today's high quotation, trade date November 13.
5   Frd C 7½ debs at today's last quotation, trade date March 28.
6   PGE 8s mtge at today's low quotation, trade date December 17.
7   Sears 8⅝ at today's high quotation, trade date March 30.
8   ShellO 4⅝ at today's last quotation, trade date December 3.

For each of the following bond sales, find (a) dollars of par sold, (b) price in percent, (c) interest, if any, (d) SEC transfer tax, (e) amount, (f) commission at rates on page 486, and (g) net proceeds to the seller. Use bond listings from Table 13.2 and assume that quantities sold are as indicated under the column "Today's sales (M)" and that settlement dates are five days after trade dates.

9   Alabama Power Co. Mtg. 9s at today's last quotation, trade date August 2.
10   Xerox 8.2s at today's low quotation, trade date July 20.
11   TVA 7s at today's high quotation, trade date August 10.
12   PGE 8s mtge at today's last quotation, trade date November 9.
13   Frd C 7½s debs at today's low quotation, trade date July 29.
14   ShellO 4⅝s at today's high quotation, trade date May 11.
15   Amfac 5¼s CV at today's high quotation, trade date September 16.
16   Sears 8⅝s at today's last quotation, trade date October 20.

Unit 13.5   Stock Rights; Dollar and Percent Gain or Loss on Securities

---

STOCK RIGHTS The laws of most states require that a corporation increasing the amount of its common stock allow the existing stockholders a right known as *stockholder's right* to purchase such new stock in the ratio that their present holdings are to the total shares of the corporation.

Such rights, known as "stock rights," may be exercised by all persons who are shown on the records of the company to be stockholders at the close of business on the "record date," a date ordinarily set several weeks after the board of directors have declared their intent to issue such rights. Since the subscription price of the new stock is usually offered at less than the current market price in order to ensure its sale, stock rights are valuable, but they must be exercised or sold before their expiration date or they become worthless.

Between the declaration date and the time when the stockholders actually have possession of the certificate representing their rights, such rights may be sold on a "when issued" basis. From the date of delivery of the rights to the expiration date, the actual certificates for the rights may be exercised or sold.

Prior to the delivery of the rights (during this period the stock is quoted "cum-rights" or "rights-on"), the value of a right may be computed as follows:

$$\text{Value of a right} = \frac{\text{market price} - \text{subscription price}}{\text{number of rights to purchase one share} + 1}$$

Example 1 **A corporation offered, at $120 a share, one share of its new stock for each five shares held. The stock was selling at $150 following the declaration date. Find the value of a right.**

$$\frac{\$150.00 - \$120.00}{5 + 1} = \frac{\$30.00}{6} = \$5.00$$

After delivery of the certificate of rights (during this period the stock is quoted "ex-rights" or "rights-off"), the value of a right may be computed as follows:

$$\text{Value of a right} = \frac{\text{market price} - \text{subscription price}}{\text{number of rights to purchase one share}}$$

Example 2 **Following the delivery of the certificates representing the stock rights in the preceding example (the stock was then ex-rights), the market price of the stock dropped to $145. Find the value of a right.**

$$\frac{\$145.00 - \$120.00}{5} = \frac{\$25.00}{5} = \$5.00$$

Note that the rights in both examples have the same value. Assuming that the general market for this stock was unchanged between the rights-on price of $150 and the ex-rights price of $145, the market values of the rights for both periods tend to coincide for any appreciable difference would create an opportunity for profit. It should also be apparent that such rights offer a buyer considerably more opportunity for speculation than does the stock itself. Thus, if the market price of the stock should fall to $120, the rights would be worthless; if the market price should rise to $180 during the rights-on period or to $170 during the ex-rights period and before their expiration date, the value of the rights would double.

TO FIND GAIN OR LOSS ON SECURITIES   Gain on stocks or bonds may be derived from two sources: (1) dividends or interest and (2) increment in value. Loss may occur through decline in value. The calculations in dollars and cents are very simple.

Example 3   **Continental Insurance Co. common stock is purchased at 105 and is sold for 115, dividends received being $6. What was gain per share?**

$$
\begin{aligned}
\text{Gain from dividends} &= \ \$\ 6.00 \\
\text{Gain through increment} = \$115.00 - \$105.00 &= +10.00 \\
\hline
\text{Total gain} &= \ \$16.00
\end{aligned}
$$

Example 4   **Florida Power Corp. 1st Mtg. 4s 76 purchased at $106\frac{1}{2}$ are sold for $98\frac{1}{4}$, 1 year's interest being received. What is the gain or loss per bond?**

$$
\begin{aligned}
\text{Gain from interest} = \$1000.00 \times 0.04 &= \ \$40.00 \\
\text{Loss from depreciated value} = \$1065.00 - \$982.50 &= -82.50 \\
\hline
\text{Net loss} &= \ \$42.50
\end{aligned}
$$

TO FIND PERCENT OF GAIN OR LOSS ON SECURITIES   Percent of gain or loss on stocks and bonds is also computed easily. To express the relationship of gain or loss to cost, divide gain or loss by cost.

Example 5   **Southern California Edison common stock purchased at $23\frac{1}{4}$ is sold for $30\frac{1}{2}$, no dividends having been received. What is the percent of gain or loss on cost per share?**

$$
\begin{aligned}
\text{No gain from dividends} &= \ \$0.00 \\
\text{Gain from increment} = \$30.50 - \$23.25 &= +7.25 \\
\hline
\text{Total gain} &= \ \$7.25
\end{aligned}
$$

$$
\text{Percent gain on cost} = \frac{\$7.25}{\$23.25} = 0.3118 - 31.18\%
$$

Example 6   **Iowa Public Service Co. Deb. 6s 72 purchased at 108 are sold at 100, 5 years' interest being received. What is the percent of gain or loss on cost per bond?**

$$
\begin{aligned}
\text{Gain from interest} = \$1000 \times 0.06 \times 5 &= \$300.00 \\
\text{Loss from depreciated value} = \$1080.00 - \$1000.00 &= -80.00 \\
\hline
\text{Net gain} &= \$220.00
\end{aligned}
$$

$$
\text{Percent gain on cost} = \frac{\$220.00}{\$1080.00} = 0.2037 = 20.37\%
$$

Exercise 13.5

Solve the following problems in stock rights:

1   A corporation offered at $50 per share, one share of its new stock for each five shares held. The stock was selling at $86 per share following the declaration date. Find the value of a right.

2   Following the delivery of the certificates representing the stock rights, a stock selling at $42 per share was quoted ex-rights. If five rights entitled the possessor to purchase one share of new stock at $12, find the value of a right.

3   The issued capital stock of a company was $500,000 divided into 20,000 common shares with a par value of $25 per share. Finding that $100,000

of additional capital is needed, the board of directors determine to issue 4000 shares of new common stock at par. If the market price of the stock is then $42 per share, find (a) the number of rights required to subscribe for each new share, (b) the value of a right during the rights-on period, and (c) the market price per share that the stock may be expected to sell for during the ex-right period.

4   A corporation has a capital stock consisting of 30,000 issued shares of $10 par common stock with a then market quotation of 59. The board of directors determine to issue 6000 new shares, permitting present stock-holders to purchase at $50 per share one share of new stock for each five shares of the old stock held on date of record. Find (a) the total dollars of new capital the directors expect the company to obtain, (b) the value of a stock right during the rights-on period, and (c) the market price per share that the stock may be expected to sell for during the ex-right period.

Solve the following without consideration of taxes, odd lots, commissions, or any brokerage costs:

5   100 shares of American Tel. and Tel. common stock were purchased on May 1, 1970, at $178\frac{1}{4}$ and sold on November 1, 1977, at $165\frac{7}{8}$. If dividends per quarter per share were $2.25, find (a) gain from dividends, (b) loss from depreciated value, and (c) net gain considering both dividends and loss from depreciated value.

6   80 shares of Pacific Gas & Electric Co. 6 percent $100 par-value preferred stock were purchased on June 1, 1969, at $102\frac{1}{2}$ and sold on December 1, 1977, at $108\frac{3}{4}$. If dividends payable quarterly were not in arrears, find (a) gain from dividends, (b) gain from increment in value, and (c) net gain considering both dividends and gain through increment.

7   Five 4 percent interest-bearing, $1000 mortgage bonds of the Southern Pacific Railway Company were purchased on May 15, 1969, at $102\frac{1}{2}$ and sold on November 15, 1969, at $98\frac{1}{8}$. If the interest was not flat (not in default), find (a) gain from interest, (b) loss from depreciated value, and (c) net gain considering both interest and loss from depreciated value.

Solve the following to nearest hundredth percent without consideration of taxes, odd lots, commissions, or any brokerage costs:

8   300 shares of Rheem Company common stock were purchased on March 8, 1972, at $22\frac{3}{4}$ and sold on September 8, 1978, at $19\frac{7}{8}$. If total dividends received over the period had been $7.80 per share, find the percent of gain on cost.

9   200 shares of Raphael Weill & Company, Inc., 7 percent $100 par-value, cumulative preferred stock were bought on June 19, 1974, at $102\frac{1}{8}$ and sold on June 19, 1979, at $75\frac{1}{2}$. If dividends became in arrears $42 per share, find the percent of loss on cost.

10 Eight Canada Dry Ginger Ale Deb. 9s, $1000 par value, were purchased on June 2, 1975, at $99\frac{7}{8}$ and sold on December 2, 1978, at $104\frac{1}{2}$. If the interest, payable semiannually, was not flat (not in default), find the percent of gain on cost.

Unit 13.6   *Rate of Gain or Loss*
on Securities

Finding the rate of gain or loss on stocks or bonds introduces the factor of time into the calculations, making the computation more complex than simply finding the gain or loss in dollars and percent of gain or loss.

Rate of current yield is the term used to express the percent of annual return at the present market price.

Rate of yield to maturity is the term used to express the percent of average annual return with not only present market price but also future selling price considered. The term is used most frequently in reference to bonds selling at a premium or discount that presumably will be redeemed at par on their maturity date.

The dividend rates on preferred stocks and the interest rates on bonds are usually nominal rates, since the market or purchase price is rarely exactly at par. Thus a 5 percent, $100 par share of preferred stock pays dividends of $5 per year, and a 7 percent, $1000 bond pays interest of $70 per year; but the real rate of return on the preferred share will be more or less than 5 percent as the market price is less or more than $100, and the real rate of return on the bond will be more or less than 7 percent as the market price is less or more than $1000.

TO FIND RATE OF CURRENT YIELD   To find the rate of current yield on a common stock, preferred stock, or bond, divide the annual return (dividend or interest) by the market price.

Example 1   **What is the rate of current yield on a 6 percent, $100 par share of preferred stock selling at 105?**

$$\text{Current yield} = \$100.00 \times 0.06 = \$6.00$$

$$\text{Rate of current yield} = \frac{\$6.00}{\$105.00} = 0.0571 = 5.71\%$$

Example 2   **What is the rate of current yield on a 9 percent, $1000 bond if the market price is quoted at 102?**

$$\text{Current yield} = \$1000.00 \times 0.09 = \$90.00$$

$$\text{Rate of current yield} = \frac{\$90}{\$1020} = 0.0882 = 8.82\%$$

TO FIND RATE OF YIELD TO MATURITY   Rate of yield to maturity on bonds *purchased on an interest date*[1] is found by use of compound interest and annuity formulas and interpolation in the tables, by use of prepared bond tables, or by a method which calculates an *approximate* yield rate.

[1]When bonds are purchased between interest dates, the calculation of the yield to maturity is more complex. The presentation here will be limited to purchase on an interest date.

TO FIND APPROXIMATE RATE OF YIELD FOR BONDS SOLD AT A PRE-MIUM   If the bond is purchased at more than the redemption value (par value), the *approximate rate of yield to maturity* is found by dividing the *average yield* by the *average investment*. The procedure is as follows:

1   Subtract the par value from the cost to obtain the *premium*.
2   Divide the premium by the number of years to maturity to obtain ap-proximate *annual amortization* (straight-line method) of the premium.
3   Find the *approximate effective annual yield* by subtracting the annual amortization of the premium from the annual yield.
4   Find the *approximate average investment* in the bond by adding the cost and the par value and dividing the sum by 2.
5   Divide the *approximate effective annual yield* by the *approximate average investment*.

Example 3   **Approximate yield to maturity on premium bonds. Find the approximate yield to maturity of a $1000, 12 percent bond purchased February 2 at $119\frac{1}{2}$. The bond pays interest semiannually on February 1 and August 1, and matures 10 years from date of purchase.**

Cost: $119\frac{1}{2}$ 1.195 × $1000 = $1195.00.
Years to maturity: 10.
Annual yield: $1000 × 0.12 = $120.00.

Steps in solution:

1   $1195 − $1000 = $195.00   Premium

2   $\dfrac{\$195}{10}$ = $19.50   Annual amortization of premium

3   $120 − $19.50 = $100.50   Approximate effective annual yield

4   $\dfrac{\$1195 + \$1000}{2}$ = $1097.50   Approximate average investment

5   $\dfrac{\$100.50}{\$1097.50}$ = 9.16%   Approximate rate of yield to maturity

TO FIND APPROXIMATE RATE OF YIELD FOR BONDS SOLD AT A DIS-COUNT   The procedures followed for a bond purchased at a discount are the same as those for a bond purchased at a premium, except for the difference in the first step which establishes the discount as opposed to the premium. The third step also differs since the discount is added in rather than sub-tracted as the premium is.

1   Subtract the cost from the par value to obtain the *discount*.
2   Divide the discount by the number of years to maturity to obtain ap-proximate *annual amortization* (straight-line method) of the discount.
3   Find the *approximate effective annual yield* by adding the annual amorti-zation of the discount to the annual yield.
4   Find the *approximate average investment* in the bond by adding the cost and the par value and dividing the sum by 2.

5   Divide the *approximate effective annual yield* by the *approximate average investment.*

Example 4   **Approximate yield to maturity on discount bonds. Find approximate yield to maturity of $1000, 6 percent bond purchased April 2 at 80½. The bond pays interest semiannually on April 1 and October 1. The bond matures 10 years from date of purchase.**

Cost: 80½.   80½ × $1000 = $805.00.
Years to maturity: 10.
Annual yield: $1000 × 0.06 = $60.00.

Steps in solution:

1   $1000 − $805.00 = $195.00   Discount

2   $\dfrac{\$195}{10}$ = $19.50   Annual amortization of discount

3   $60.00 + $19.50 = $79.50   Approximate effective annual yield

4   $\dfrac{\$1000 + \$805}{2}$ = $902.50   Approximate average investment

5   $\dfrac{\$79.50}{\$902.50}$ = 8.81%   Approximate rate of yield to maturity

TO FIND YIELD TO MATURITY BY COMPOUND INTEREST AND INTERPO-LATION IN THE TABLES   To find the yield by compound interest, an "edu-cated guess," or approximation, is made of what the yield rate might be. The procedures illustrated above serve this purpose extremely well. Using one rate below this approximation, a calculation is made of the present value (cost) of the bond. Using another rate (usually above the approximate rate), we again calculate the present value (cost) of the bond. If the two calculated values for the present value bracket the actual cost, then we can find the more precise rate by interpolation. If the two values do not bracket the cost, keep experimenting with other rates until you find two rates which do bracket the cost.[1] First, however, note the procedure to find the present value, or cost, of a bond.

To find the present value of a bond by compound-interest formulas, the following procedure is the shortest and most convenient.

(a)   *If the bond sells for a premium.* The bond will sell for a premium if the bond rate is *higher* than the *yield rate.*
1   Find the difference between the interest payment as determined by the bond rate of interest and the interest payment *as if* it were determined by the yield rate of interest.
2   Find the present value of an ordinary annuity whereby the periodic

---

[1]If you desire to *lower* your calculated cost, use a *higher* rate; if you want to *raise* your calculated cost, use a *lower* rate.

payment (R) is the difference found in (1) for the number of payments to maturity, and at the *yield rate* of interest per period.

   3 Add the present value of the annuity in (2) to the par value.

(b) *If the bond sells for a discount.* The bond will sell for a discount if the
bond rate is *lower* than the *yield rate.*

   1 Same as step (1) for a bond selling at a premium.

   2 Same as step (2) for a bond selling at a premium.

   3 Subtract the present value of the annuity in (2) from the par value.

Example 5 **Find the cost of a $1000, 10 percent bond, maturing in 5 years, interest
payable twice a year to yield (a) 8 percent and (b) 12 percent.**

(a) Since the yield rate is *lower* than the 10 percent bond rate, a *premium*
will result.

   1 Semiannual interest payment at bond rate $1000 $\times$ 10% ÷ 2 = $50

      Semiannual interest payment at yield rate $1000 $\times$ 8% ÷ 2 = $40

      $R = \$50 - \$40 = \$10$

$$i = \frac{8\%}{2} = 4\%$$

$$n = 10(2) = 20$$

   2 $P = R(a_{\overline{n}|i})$

      $P = 10(a_{\overline{20}|4}) = 10(13.5903263)$(Table 6.5)

      $P = \$135.90$

   3 $1000 + \$135.90 = \$1135.90$ Present value (cost) of bond

(b) Since the yield rate is higher than the 10 percent bond rate, a *discount*
will result.

   1 Semiannual interest payment at bond rate $1000 $\times$ 0.10 ÷ 2 = $50

      Semiannual interest payment at yield rate $1000 $\times$ 0.12 ÷ 2 = $60

      $R = \$60 - \$50 = \$10$

$$i = \frac{12\%}{2} = 6\%$$

$$n = 10(2) = 20$$

   2 $P = R(a_{\overline{n}|i})$

      $P = 10(a_{\overline{20}|6}) = 10(11.4699212)$ (Table 6.5)

      $P = \$114.70$

   3 $1000 - \$114.70 = \$885.30$ Present value (cost) of bond

    To find the yield to maturity by compound interest, we use the present
value calculation in step (2) above to serve as the basis for interpolation.

Example 6 **Same factual data as Example 3. Find the yield rate by compound interest and
interpolation.**

Since we already know the approximate rate is 9.16 percent, we should
choose 9 percent and 10 percent, $m = 2$, as our trial rates. However, Table 6.5

does not have factor tables for $\dfrac{9\%}{2} = 4.5$ percent, so we will choose 8 percent and 10 percent.

Trial at 8 percent, $m = 2$:

1 Semiannual interest payment at *bond rate* of 12 percent:

$$\frac{\$1000 \times 0.12}{2} = \$60.00$$

Semiannual interest payment *as if* rate were 8 percent:

$$\frac{\$1000 \times 0.08}{2} = \$40.00$$

$R = \$60.00 - \$40.00 = \$20.00$

$i = \dfrac{8}{2} = 4$

$n = 10(2) = 20$

2 $P = \$20(a_{\overline{20}|4}) = \$20(13.5903263)$ (Table 6.5)
$P = \$271.81$

3 $\$1000 + \$271.81 = \$1271.81$ Cost of bond to yield 8%

Trial at 10 percent, $m = 2$:

1 Semiannual interest payment at *bond rate* of 12 percent:

$$\frac{\$1000 \times 0.12}{2} = \$60.00$$

Semiannual interest payment *as if* rate were 10 percent:

$$\frac{\$1000 \times 0.10}{2} = \$50.00$$

$R = \$60.00 - \$50.00 = \$10.00$

$i = \dfrac{10\%}{2} = 5\%$

$n = 10(2) = 20$

2 $P = 10(a_{\overline{20}|5}) = 10(12.4622103)$
$P = \$124.62$

3 $\$1000 + \$124.62 = \$1124.62$ Cost of bond to yield 10%

The cost of the bond ($1195.00) is now bracketed between the values for 8 percent, $m = 2$ ($1271.81) and 10 percent, $m = 2$ ($1124.62). By interpolation (see Unit 6.5):

$$4\% + \frac{7681}{14719}(1\%) = 4\% + .52\% = 4.52\%$$

Annual yield rate $= 2(4.52\%) = 9.04\%$[1]

Example 7   **Same factual data as Example 4. Find a more precise rate by interpolation in the compound-interest tables.**

Since we know the approximate rate is 8.81 percent, we should choose the rates of 8 and 9 percent. However, Table 6.5 does not have factors for $\frac{9\%}{2} = 4.5$ percent, so we shall choose 10 percent.

Trial at 8 percent:

Semiannual interest payment *as if* interest rate were 8 percent:

$$\frac{\$1000 \times 0.08}{2} = \$40.00$$

Semiannual interest payment at *bond rate* of 6 percent:

$$\frac{\$1000 \times 0.06}{2} = \$30.00$$

$R = \$40.00 - \$30.00 = \$10.00$

$i = \dfrac{8\%}{2} = 4\%$

$n = 10(2) = 20$
$P = 10(a_{\overline{20}|4}) = 10(13.5903263)$ (Table 6.5)
$P = \$135.90$
Cost $= \$1000 - \$135.90 = \$864.10$ Cost of bond to yield 8%

Trial at 10 percent:

Semiannual interest payment *as if* interest rate were 10 percent:

$$\frac{\$1000 \times 0.10}{2} = \$50.00$$

Semiannual interest payment at *bond rate* of 6 percent:

$$\frac{\$1000 \times 0.06}{2} = \$30.00$$

$R = \$50.00 - \$30.00 = \$20.00$

$i = \dfrac{10\%}{5} = 5\%$

$n = 20$
$P = 20(a_{\overline{20}|5}) = 20(12.4622103)$ (Table 6.5)
$P = \$249.24$
Cost $= \$1000.00 - \$249.24 = \$750.76$ Cost of bond to yield 10%

---

[1] The true yield rate for this bond is 9 percent. Interpolation procedures tend to be high.

The cost of the bond ($805.00) is now bracketed between the values for 8 percent, $m = 2$ ($864.10) and 10 percent, $m = 2$ ($750.76) By interpolation:

$$1\% \left[\begin{array}{l} 4\% \\ \leftarrow \text{yield rate} \\ 5\% \end{array} \right. \qquad \left. \begin{array}{l} 864.10 \\ 805.00 \\ 750.76 \end{array} \right\} \rightarrow 59.10 \left] \rightarrow 113.34 \right.$$

$$i = 4\% + \frac{59.10}{113.34}(1\%) = 4\% + .52\% = 4.52\%$$

$$2i = 9.04\%^1$$

The same method of determining yield to maturity could be used for stock transactions if dividend returns are fairly constant in amount each year. However, in the preceding examples, the assumption has been made that the bonds would continue to pay interest and would be held to maturity, when they would be redeemed at par. Ordinarily, neither the price of a stock nor its dividends at some given date in the future can be readily forecast, and so such a computation is impractical with stocks. If it is desired to determine the true annual yield earned on a stock transaction over a preceding period of time, the same method of computation may be used.

Exercise 13.6

Find rate of current yield (in percents to nearest tenths) on each of the following stocks and bonds. Use today's last quotations from the stock listings in Table 13.1 and from the bond listings in Table 13.2. Assume that the following indicated dividends and interest payments are annual. *Do not consider any taxes or brokerage costs.*

1	Am Motors	($0.26 dividend)
2	Avnet	($0.96 dividend)
3	CBS	($3.52 dividend)
4	Dow Ch	($1.48 dividend)
5	Ala P 9s	
6	Chryslr 8s	
7	PGE 8s	
8	Xerox 8.2s	

Determine the approximate rate of yield to maturity (in percents to nearest tenths) on the following bonds listed in Table 13.2. Use today's last quotation and assume date of settlement on purchase to be the day immediately following the first interest payment due on each bond in 1979. *Do not consider any tax or brokerage costs.*

9	Beth St 9s
10	Frd C $7\frac{1}{2}$
11	PGE 8s
12	Sears $8\frac{5}{8}$

[1] The true yield of this bond is 9 percent. Interpolation procedures tend to give high answers.

13 ShellO $4\frac{5}{8}$
14 TVA 7s
15 Xerox 8.2s
16 Ala P 9s

By interpolation, compute the following yields to maturity:

	Par	Cost	Bond rate %	Interest payments	Frequency	Years to maturity
17	1000	$87\frac{1}{2}$	4	40	annual	20
18	1000	$112\frac{3}{4}$	5	50	annual	15
19	1000	$91\frac{3}{4}$	6	30	semiannual	5
20	1000	$119\frac{1}{2}$	12	60	semiannual	10

Chapter 14

Personal and Business Insurance

Objectives To Be Achieved in This Chapter

1 *Become acquainted with different types of life insurance policies and calculate the premium cost, net cost, and cash surrender values from value tables.*

2 *Calculate premiums for fire and other hazard insurance policies from prepared tables.*

3 *Determine loss recovery under policies with coinsurance clauses.*

4 *Calculate premium cost under workmen's compensation, business interruption, and other types of insurance coverage.*

GENERAL CHARACTERISTICS AND DEFINITION OF TERMS Insurance is a form of financial protection against loss or damage caused by a contingent or unforeseen event. The cost of insurance to the consumer is viewed as a *definite smaller expense* to defray a *possible larger loss* if the contingency or unforeseen event occurred. Insurance is based on the principle of spreading, or dividing, the risk of loss over many participants. If a loss to any one or several individuals is spread over a large number of individuals, the loss will not be an excessive burden on any one. The larger the number of people participating, the greater the division of risk and losses resulting therefrom. For example, the financial loss by fire, hurricane, or earthquake to any one individual could be economically fatal, unless this loss was reimbursed by the funds contributed by many individuals via the medium of insurance.

The determination of the cost of protection against a possible loss is based on the statistical probability of the occurrence of the loss and the rate of earnings on the funds and investments accumulated by the insurance companies to pay for the losses. Insurance is meant to protect the consumer against a possible loss, not to give the opportunity of making a profit should a casualty occur. The amount reimbursed is limited to the loss, or the amount of insurance carried, whichever is smaller. If the amount of insurance carried is less than the amount of the loss, the excess loss must be borne by the individual suffering the loss.

DEFINITION OF GENERAL INSURANCE TERMS The *insured* is the one who carries the insurance or financial protection against loss.

Insurer or underwriter is the carrier (the insurance company) who assures payment of the stipulated loss according to contract provisions if the specified contingency occurs.

Policy is the contract whereby the insurer agrees to indemnify the insured for the loss caused by the risks covered. The policy includes all the terms and conditions agreed upon between the insured and the insurer.

Risk is the contemplated or unforeseen hazard for which the policy provides indemnification.

Face is the limit of protection afforded for the one or several risks covered by the policy.

Parties to the insurance policy are the insured and the insurer.

Premium is the amount paid (usually monthly, quarterly, semiannually, or annually) by the insured for the protection provided by the policy. The calculation of the premium is similar to finding percentage, whereby the face of the policy is the *base,* the rate of premium (usually quoted in terms of $100, $1000, $5000, or $10,000 units) is equivalent to the *rate,* and the premium is equivalent to the *percentage.*

Beneficiary is the one to whom the proceeds of the policy are payable. This may be the insured or one or several others whom the insured designates.

Unit 14.1   *Life Insurance*

In most types of insurance, the underwriter makes payment upon the occurrence of a contingency which may or may not occur. In many instances, since losses do not occur, no payments are made; if losses do occur, they may be in an amount considerably less than the face of the policy. For example, a house may not burn, it may burn partially, or it may be a total loss.

It is obvious that life insurance is essentially different, for death of the insured and payment of the entire face of the policy by the insurer will eventually occur (provided, of course, the policy is in force at the time of the insured's death). The uncertainty in life insurance is not whether the contingency insured against will ultimately occur and the face of the policy must be paid in full but rather when this eventuality will occur. Furthermore, the risk increases progressively with the age of the insured. Also, the contract is not an indemnity contract but provides for payment as specified; that is, the economic value of the deceased is not material to the payment.

ADDITIONAL PROTECTION AVAILABLE IN LIFE INSURANCE POLICIES   A wide range of supplementary risks may be included in life insurance contracts, each, of course, resulting in an increase in the amount of the premium. In comparing policies offered by different companies, among other considerations it is necessary to consider the value of the additional protection that may be offered by some of the policies. Thus a policy for which the premiums seem to be lowest may be highest if the optional protection afforded by other policies is also purchased.

Some of the more commonly included additional protections are

1   Double indemnity in event of death by accidental means
2   Waiver of premium in event of total disability
3   Periodic payments (usually monthly) in the event of total disability
4   Annuities or lump-sum payments upon attainment of a predetermined age or stipulated number of premium payments

OWNERSHIP OF LIFE INSURANCE COMPANIES   Ownership of life insurance companies may be classified as of two kinds:

1   *Stock companies* are life insurance companies owned by stockholders (just as in any corporation) who have supplied capital or purchased stock as an investment. Ordinarily, in companies of this type all earnings from investments, excess premium charges, and other savings belong to the stockholders. However, in some stock companies provision is made for limited participation in earnings by the policyholders.
2   *Mutual companies* are life insurance companies owned by the policyholders. Earnings from investments, excess premium charges, and other savings belong to the policyholders and are used as additional reserves against possible future loss or are returned to the participating policyholders in the form of dividends. These dividends may be withdrawn by the insured, applied as part payment on the next premium, or left with the insurance company to purchase additional insurance or to pay up the policy.

DIVIDENDS FROM LIFE INSURANCE POLICIES   Insurance policies are commonly classified as to participation in earnings:

1   *Participating policies* entitle the holder to share in the earnings of the company.

2 *Nonparticipating policies* do not entitle the holder to share in the earnings of the company.

Premiums for life insurance policies are based on actuarial tables, that is, tables of life expectancy. From these tables is determined the amount of premium (and/or number of premiums) that individuals of given ages must contribute in order to build funds equivalent to the face of the policies at the time of probable death of the insured.

Conservative practice among insurance companies is to charge higher rates than actuarial tables would indicate. This is particularly true in participating policies.

Therefore, in comparing the costs of participating and nonparticipating policies, it is necessary to consider the factor of dividends as a decrease in the gross cost of the participating policies. Thus the net cost of a participating policy in a company that has paid in the past (and probably will pay in the future) a comparatively high rate of dividend may be lower than the net cost of a participating policy with a company offering a lower annual premium but also a lower rate of dividend. And the net cost of a participating policy may be less than a nonparticipating policy in which the yearly premium is considerably smaller.

KINDS OF LIFE INSURANCE POLICIES Among the many available types of life insurance policies, the most frequently selected, in order of premium cost from lowest to highest, are (1) term, (2) ordinary life (also known as whole life or straight life), (3) limited payment, and (4) endowment.

Term Insurance. Term life insurance is sold for a fixed term of years, usually for periods of 1, 5, 10, 15, or 20 years. It is usually nonparticipating and at maturity has no cash or paid-up value. Protection other than life insurance is rarely included, and ordinarily no return is made by the insurer unless the insured dies within the specified term of years the contract is in force.

At the expiration of the term of the insurance, both premiums and insurance cease. Frequently, term insurance is convertible to other types of insurance, within a limited and specified period of time, by payment of higher premiums at the attained age.

Of all the life insurance availabe, term insurance premiums are the lowest as they usually do not combine savings with protection.

Ordinary Life. Ordinary life policies are those in which the insured agrees to pay the insurer a specified premium each year until death, the insurer agreeing to pay the face of the policy to the estate of the insured or to the person or persons designated as beneficiaries.

In this type of policy, the insured combines a moderate amount of saving with protection. Excess of premiums over actual cost to the insurer builds for the insured a cash surrender value, a paid-up value, a borrowing collateral, or the right to purchase extended term insurance.

Limited Payment. Limited-payment policies are those in which the insured agrees to make premium payments for a specified number of years, usually 20, although 10-, 15-, and 30-year payments are not uncommon. They may also be purchased with maturity dates at some designated age of the insured, such as fifty-five, sixty, or sixty-five years.

In this type of policy the insured usually selects, as a specified number of years, the time during which his earnings will probably be the greatest and premium payments will be the easiest to meet without undue sacrifice.

Premiums are sufficiently higher than ordinary life premiums to accumulate a sum sufficient to mature the policy in the time specified. Upon completion of premium payments for the specified number of years, the premium ceases and the policy remains in force until death. Cash surrender value, paid-up value, borrowing collateral, and the amount of extended term insurance accumulate more rapidly than in ordinary life policies because of the higher premium rate.

Endowment. As in limited-payment policies, endowment policies are purchased with maturity dates of 10, 15, 20, 30, or even 35 years. They may also be purchased with maturity dates at some designated age of the insured, such as fifty-five, sixty, or sixty-five years.

If death occurs before the maturity date, the estate or beneficiaries receive the face of the policy. If the insured is alive at maturity date, the insured receives the face of the policy.

Premiums are considerably higher for this type of life insurance, for they must include not only protection but also an amount sufficient to create a fund during the maturing period that is equivalent to the face of the policy. Cash surrender value, paid-up value, borrowing value, and the amount of extended term insurance also accumulate rapidly.

Premiums. The following are excerpts from premium tables of large insurance companies. Rates vary slightly from company to company, and these given here are simply close approximations of those offered by most life insurance companies.

TABLE 14.1   ANNUAL PREMIUM RATES FOR $1000 POLICIES IN COMPANIES A AND B[1]

Age at issue	Co. A and Co. B 10-year term	Ordinary life		20-payment life		20-year endowment	
		Co. A partici-pating	Co. B nonpar-ticipating	Co. A partici-pating	Co. B nonpar-ticipating	Co. A partici-pating	Co. B nonpar-ticipating
18	$ 8.17	$18.44	$13.80	$28.53	$22.40	$48.18	$42.82
19	8.25	18.81	14.14	28.95	22.80	48.33	42.85
20	8.33	19.21	14.49	29.39	23.20	48.48	42.89
21	8.39	19.62	14.86	29.84	23.61	48.63	42.92
22	8.44	20.06	15.23	30.31	24.04	48.79	42.96
23	8.49	20.51	15.63	30.80	24.48	48.96	42.99
24	8.53	20.99	16.04	31.31	24.93	49.14	43.03
25	8.58	21.49	16.47	31.83	25.40	49.33	43.07
30	8.96	24.38	18.95	34.76	28.02	50.43	43.41
35	10.00	28.11	22.19	38.34	31.34	51.91	44.18
40	12.13	33.01	26.48	42.79	35.51	54.06	45.60
45	15.83	39.55	32.09	48.52	40.76	57.34	48.01
50	21.59	48.48	39.52	56.17	47.91	62.55	51.94
55	30.89	60.72	49.39	66.69	56.31	70.81	58.71
60	44.88	77.69	62.55	81.60	72.60	83.82	68.40

Note: Semiannual rate, 52 percent of annual; quarterly rate, 26.5 percent of annual; monthly rate, 8.875 percent of annual. The above rates and multipliers will vary between companies and over time. These rates should not be considered as rates in effect in any year.

[1] This is a table for males. Because of their longer life expectancy, rates for females are slightly higher.

To read the table, find in the first column the age of the insured to nearest birthday. The horizontal amount in dollars and cents is the annual premium on $1000 units (for the age indicated in the first column) for the type of insurance specified at the head of each column.

Example 1   **Mr. Arnold is twenty-two years old on his nearest birthday. What annual premium will he pay for $5000 worth of (a) 10-year term, (b) company A participating ordinary life, (c) company B nonparticipating 20-payment life?**

   (a) Annual premium per $1000, 10-year term = $8.44
          Annual premium for $5000 = $8.44 × 5 = $42.20
   (b) Annual premium per $1000, participating ordinary life = $20.06
                Annual premium for $5000 = $20.06 × 5 = $100.30
   (c) Annual premium per $1000, nonparticipating 20-payment life = $24.04
                Annual premium for $5000 = $24.04 × 5 = $120.20

Example 2   **Mr. Beddow is twenty-one years of age on his nearest birthday. If he purchases $6000 worth of company B nonparticipating 20-year endowment insurance, what will be the (a) annual premium, (b) semiannual premium, (c) quarterly premium, (d) monthly premium?**

   Annual premium $1000, nonparticipating, 20-year endowment = $42.92

   (a)   Annual premium for $6000 = $42.92 × 6 = $257.52
   (b) Semiannual premium for $6000 = $257.52 × 0.52 = $133.91
   (c)   Quarterly premium for $6000 = $257.52 × 0.265 = $68.24
   (d)   Monthly premium for $6000 = $257.52 × 0.08875 = $22.85

PRIVILEGES ATTACHED TO MOST LIFE INSURANCE POLICIES In casualty insurance, if the insured cancels a policy, she or he receives a refund.

     In life insurance, each policyholder (except in the usual term policy) is theoretically accumulating with the insurer a fund sufficient in size to pay the beneficiary the face of the policy at the time of the insured's death or upon maturity of the policy. Because this fund does accumulate, life insurance contracts (except in term insurance) ordinarily provide for reimbursement of the insured if he or she decides to discontinue his policy.

     Because of selling costs, these values are ordinarily not considered as having accumulated until 2 or 3 years' premiums have been paid. However, this period of time varies among companies and policies, and in a few instances value is considered as having accumulated after payment of the first premium.

     At the end of the specified time, insurance policies may be surrendered with the following optional privileges of the policyholders: (1) cash surrender value, (2) paid-up value, or (3) extended term insurance.

     Cash surrender value is the amount of money the policyholder receives as a lump sum on surrendering the policy. The amounts vary with the types of policies and amounts and numbers of premiums paid.

Paid-up value is the amount of the paid-up insurance for life the insured will receive on surrendering the policy.

Extended term insurance is the length of time during which the face of the policy will continue as term insurance. If the policyholder allows his premiums to become in default, most insurance companies arbitrarily purchase extended term insurance unless state laws require otherwise.

An additional privilege attached to most insurance policies (but not usually to term insurance) is the right of the holder to borrow without surrendering the policy or the protection afforded by the policy.

Borrowing may be done by the policyholder in an amount up to but not in excess of the cash surrender value of the policy. The usual interest charge paid by the insured for borrowing against the cash surrender value is usually less than the insured could obtain from other financial institutions.

CASH SURRENDER VALUE   Tables 14.2 to 14.4 are excerpts from tables of certain large companies giving cash surrender values on ordinary life, 20-payment life, and 20-year endowment policies, both participating and non-participating. Term insurance policies rarely have cash surrender values. Only ages twenty, twenty-five, thirty, thirty-five, and forty for origin of the policies and cash surrender values after 5, 10, 15, and 20 years are included in these tables. The amounts given here will vary slightly from company to company, these being simply close approximations.

TABLE 14.2   CASH SURRENDER VALUE, ORDINARY LIFE, $1000 POLICIES IN COMPANIES A AND B

Age at issue	Premiums		Co. A participating				Co. B nonparticipating			
	Co. A partici-pating	Co. B nonpartic-ipating	5 yr	10 yr	15 yr	20 yr	5 yr	10 yr	15 yr	20 yr
20	$19.21	$14.49	$27	$ 71	$122	$192	$29	$ 77	$131	$192
25	21.49	16.47	35	88	150	230	36	94	157	230
30	24.38	18.95	44	108	183	276	44	114	190	276
35	28.11	22.19	54	131	221	327	54	138	229	328
40	33.01	26.48	66	159	264	383	67	167	273	383

TABLE 14.3   CASH SURRENDER VALUE, 20-PAYMENT LIFE, $1000 POLICIES IN COMPANIES A AND B

Age at issue	Premiums		Co. A participating				Co. B nonparticipating			
	Co. A partici-pating	Co. B nonpartic-ipating	5 yr	10 yr	15 yr	20 yr	5 yr	10 yr	15 yr	20 yr
20	$29.39	$23.20	$ 69	$170	$297	$459	$ 70	$180	$307	$459
25	31.83	25.40	76	188	326	504	77	198	338	505
30	34.76	28.02	84	207	360	555	86	219	373	555
35	38.34	31.34	94	231	397	609	96	242	411	610
40	42.79	35.51	106	259	436	666	107	268	451	667

TABLE 14.4 CASH SURRENDER VALUE, 20-YEAR ENDOWMENT, $1000 POLICIES IN COMPANIES A AND B

Age at issue	Premiums		Co. A participating				Co. B nonparticipating			
	Co. A partici- pating	Co. B nonpartic- ipating	5 yr	10 yr	15 yr	20 yr	5 yr	10 yr	15 yr	20 yr
20	$48.48	$42.89	$161	$384	$652	$1,000	$157	$388	$666	$1,000
25	49.33	43.07	161	383	651	1,000	155	387	665	1,000
30	50.43	43.41	161	383	650	1,000	154	385	663	1,000
35	51.91	44.18	161	383	649	1,000	152	384	662	1,000
40	54.06	45.60	162	383	648	1,000	151	383	661	1,000

DIVIDENDS Table 14.5 shows excerpts from the tables of company A that illustrate cash surrender values of participating policies.

TABLE 14.5 ACCUMULATED DIVIDENDS ON COMPANY A, $1000 PARTICIPATING POLICIES

Age at issue	Ordinary life				20-payment life				20-year endowment			
	Pre- mium	5 yr	10 yr	20 yr	Pre- mium	5 yr	10 yr	20 yr	Pre- mium	5 yr	10 yr	20 yr
20	$19.21	$20.99	$53.94	$150.07	$29.39	$24.22	$64.91	$173.05	$48.48	$24.21	$67.68	$173.39
25	21.49	22.58	57.66	155.64	31.83	25.40	66.74	176.90	49.33	25.78	72.41	182.09
30	24.38	24.32	61.09	160.46	34.76	27.77	77.00	184.61	50.43	28.93	77.87	191.50
35	28.11	25.94	64.62	166.37	38.34	30.14	75.26	192.33	51.91	32.08	83.34	200.92
40	33.01	28.21	69.20	175.92	42.79	32.31	79.61	202.18	54.06	35.13	88.99	211.71

Note: Insurance underwriters have complete tables similar to this for all ages, all types of participating policies, and all dividend periods—both past and estimated in the future.

FINDING NET COST, NET RETURN, AND REFUND OR PREMIUM EARNED IN EXCESS OF COST Assuming that consideration is not given to interest that may be earnable on premiums, if premium costs, cash surrender values, and estimated accumulated dividend payments are known it is possible to compare readily various participating and/or nonparticipating policies as to net cost or net return (at maturity or at date of surrender). Net return is sometimes considered as a refund or premium earned in excess of total premiums paid. Thus:

For a nonparticipating policy:

Total premiums — cash surrender value

For a participating policy

Total premiums — (cash surrender value + accumulated dividends)

Example 3   Mr. Nardi, twenty-five years old on his nearest birthday, wishes to compare the net cost (not including interest that may be earnable on premiums) of company B nonparticipating and company A participating ordinary life policies for $1000 after a duration of 5 years.

From Table 14.2, company B nonparticipating policy of $1000, age 25, is as follows:

```
Annual premium = $16.47
Premiums, 5 years = $16.47 × 5 =   $82.35
Less cash surrender value:        − 36.00
                    Net cost =     $46.35
```

From Table 14.2, company A participating policy for $1000, age twenty-five, is as follows:

```
Annual premium = $21.49
Premiums, 5 years = $21.49 × 5 = $107.45
Less
  Cash surrender value: $35.00
  Dividends for 5 years:  22.58
              Total deduction =  − 57.58
              Net cost = $  49.87
```

Example 4   **Mr. Motley, insurable age thirty, wishes to compare the costs (not including interest that may be earnable on premiums) of company B nonparticipating and company A participating 20-payment life policies for $1000 after 20 years.**

From Table 14.3, company B nonparticipating policy for $1000, age thirty, is as follows:

```
Annual premium = $28.02
Premiums, 20 years = $28.02 × 20 =   $560.40
Less cash surrender value:          − 555.00
                    Net cost =       $   5.40
```

From Table 14.3, company A participating policy for $1000, age thirty, is as follows:

```
Annual premium = $34.76
Premiums, 20 years = $34.76 × 20 =   $695.20
Less
  Cash surrender value:  $555.00
  Dividends for 20 years:  184.61
            Total deduction =  − 739.61
            Net return =  $  44.41
```

The net return of $44.41 may be considered as a refund due (in excess of dividends) or as a premium earned in excess of cost.

PAID-UP AND EXTENDED TERM INSURANCE   Table 14.6 shows the difference in cash surrender value and paid-up value. It also shows the extended term insurance for $1000 that may be purchased at the option of the insured when he surrenders his policy.

TABLE 14.6 CASH SURRENDER VALUE, PAID-UP VALUE, AND EXTENDED TERM INSURANCE FOR COMPANY B, $1000 NONPARTICIPATING ORDINARY LIFE POLICIES (TO NEAREST DOLLARS)

Age 20, premiums $14.49				End of policy year	Age 30, premiums $18.95			
Cash surren- der value	Paid-up value	Extended term insurance			Cash surren- der value	Paid-up value	Extended term insurance	
		Years	Days				Years	Days
$ 10	$ 30	1	129	3	$ 18	$ 44	2	47
19	55	2	205	4	31	74	3	253
29	81	3	302	5	44	105	5	107
38	106	5	57	6	57	135	6	332
48	131	6	199	7	71	164	8	190
58	156	7	358	8	86	194	10	27
68	178	9	114	9	100	221	11	149
77	201	10	241	10	114	247	12	223
87	223	12	7	11	128	274	13	244
98	245	13	139	12	143	300	14	210
108	267	14	243	13	158	326	15	185
119	289	15	325	14	174	351	15	359
131	311	16	364	15	190	377	16	183
142	333	17	354	16	207	402	16	334
154	354	18	298	17	223	426	17	85
166	376	19	198	18	241	450	17	172
179	397	20	44	19	258	474	17	231
192	418	20	217	20	276	497	17	267

Such tables are available for all kinds of policies (though normally not for term insurance). However, for purposes of illustration, only excerpts from tables for $1000 nonparticipating ordinary life policies issued at ages twenty and thirty are shown here. Cash surrender value, paid-up insurance value, and extended term insurance would of course be greater in limited-payment and endowment policies.

Example 5   **Mr. Schulman purchased an $8000 company B nonparticipating ordinary life policy 6 years ago at the age of twenty. What is (a) the cash surrender value, (b) the paid-up value, and (c) for how many days can he select extended term insurance at the same face?**

(a)   From Table 14.6
   Cash surrender value of $1000 policy after 6 years = $38.00
   Therefore
   Cash surrender value of $8000 policy = $38.00 × 8 = $304.00

(b)   From Table 14.6
   Paid-up value of $1000 policy after 6 years = $106.00
   Therefore
   Paid-up value of $8000 policy = $106.00 × 8 = $848.00

(c)   From Table 14.6
   Extended term insurance on $1000 after 6 years = 5 years 57 days
   Therefore
   Extended term insurance on $8000 policy is also 5 years 57 days

When the insured defaults on premiums and fails to specify cash or paid-up insurance in some other form, the insurer usually elects extended term insurance at the same face as the original policy.

SOCIAL SECURITY BENEFITS A discussion of life insurance should make some mention of the benefits provided by the Social Security Act of 1935 and its amendments.

The basic idea of social security is a simple one: During working years employees, their employers, and self-employed people pay social security contributions, which go into special funds; and when earnings stop or are reduced because the worker retires, dies, or becomes disabled, monthly cash benefits are paid from the funds to replace part of the earnings the family has lost.

Part of the contributions made during the working years go into a separate hospital insurance trust fund so that when workers or their dependents reach sixty-five they will have paid-up hospital insurance to help pay their hospital bills.

A program of supplementary medical insurance, which is available to people sixty-five or over, helps them pay doctors' bills and other medical expenses. This program is voluntary and, instead of being paid for out of social security contributions, is financed out of premiums shared half-and-half by the older people who sign up and the federal government.

Nine out of ten working people in the United States are now building protection for themselves and their families under the social security program.

It should be noted that the Social Security System is not a *fully funded system*. This means that a fund is *not maintained* to cover the benefits that are payable from the fund. The source of these benefits will depend upon the economic health and the taxing power of the United States.

Since social security benefits are a part of any retirement plan, for the determination of the amount of insurance needed, Table 14.7 provides data in simplified form for your information. Generally, average earnings are figured over the period starting in 1951 until the worker reaches retirement age, becomes disabled, or dies. Up to 5 years of low earnings, or no earnings, can be excluded. The maximum earnings creditable for social security after 1950 have been:

1951–54	$3600	1973	$10,800
1955–58	4200	1974	13,200
1959–65	4800	1975	14,100
1966–67	6600	1976	15,300
1968–71	7800	1977	16,500
1972	9000	1978	17,700

The maximum amount of annual earnings that count for social security will rise automatically in future years as earnings levels increase. The premium paid for these benefits is 13.10 percent in 1978 of the actual earnings up to the

TABLE 14.7   EXAMPLES OF MONTHLY RETIREMENT BENEFITS UNDER THE SOCIAL SECURITY SYSTEM (Effective June 1976)

Average yearly earnings	For workers				For dependents[1]				
	Retirement				Wife at 65; child	Wife at 64	Wife at 63	Wife at 62	Family[2] benefits
	at 65	at 64	at 63	at 62					
$923 or less	$107.90	$100.80	$ 93.60	$ 86.40	$ 54.00	$ 49.50	$ 45.00	$ 40.50	$161.90
1200	138.90	129.70	120.40	111.20	69.50	63.80	58.00	52.20	208.40
2000	180.70	168.70	156.70	144.60	90.40	82.90	75.40	67.80	271.10
2600	203.90	190.40	176.80	163.20	102.00	93.50	85.00	76.50	305.90
3000	223.20	208.40	193.50	178.60	111.60	102.30	93.00	83.70	341.20
3400	239.30	223.40	207.40	191.50	119.70	109.80	99.80	89.80	385.50
4000	262.60	245.10	227.60	210.10	131.30	120.40	109.50	98.50	448.80
4400	281.30	262.60	243.80	225.10	140.70	129.00	117.30	105.60	498.60
4800	297.80	278.00	258.10	238.30	148.90	136.50	124.10	111.70	543.20
5000	304.50	284.20	263.90	243.60	152.30	139.70	127.00	114.30	561.90
5200	313.10	292.30	271.40	250.50	156.60	143.60	130.50	117.50	587.50
5400	319.80	298.50	277.20	255.90	159.90	146.60	133.30	120.00	597.00
5600	328.50	306.60	284.70	262.80	164.30	150.70	137.00	123.30	609.10
5800	337.40	315.00	292.50	270.00	168.70	154.70	140.60	126.60	622.00
6000	344.10	321.20	298.30	275.30	172.10	157.80	143.50	129.10	631.30
6200	352.80	329.30	305.80	282.30	176.40	161.70	147.00	132.30	644.20
6400	359.50	335.60	311.60	287.60	179.80	164.90	149.90	134.90	653.50
6600	368.10	343.60	319.10	294.50	184.10	168.80	153.50	138.10	666.30
6800	376.00	351.00	325.90	300.80	188.00	172.40	156.70	141.00	675.80
7000	385.60	359.90	334.20	308.50	192.80	176.80	160.70	144.60	687.20
7400	403.10	376.30	349.40	322.50	201.60	184.80	168.00	151.20	708.80
7600	412.70	385.20	357.70	330.20	206.40	189.20	172.00	154.80	722.20
8000	427.80	399.30	370.80	342.30	213.90	196.10	178.30	160.50	748.70

[1] If a woman is eligible for both a worker's benefit and a wife's benefit, the check actually payable is limited to the larger of the two.
[2] Worker 65 or older, wife under 65, and one or more children.
Source: U.S. Department of Health, Education, and Welfare. *HEW Publication No.* (SSA) 76-0047 May, 1976.

above maximum amounts. The premium is paid one-half by the worker and one-half by the worker's employer (see Unit 8.1).

Conveniently located district offices of the Social Security Administration of the U.S. Department of Health, Education, and Welfare will provide additional information if requested in person, by telephone, or by mail.

Exercise 14.1

Use the tables given in the preceding unit in solving the following problems:

1   If ages at issue are twenty-four, thirty-five, and fifty-five, find the cost of the following $8000 policies at each age: (a) 10-year term, (b) company A

participating ordinary life, (c) company B nonparticipating ordinary life, (d) company A participating 20-payment life, (e) company B nonparticipating 20-payment life, (f) company A participating 20-year endowment, and (g) company B nonparticipating 20-year endowment.

2   On May 14, Mike Doyle, who is age twenty-two, purchases a $15,000 company A participating ordinary life policy. How much will he save yearly on premiums if he makes semiannual instead of monthly payments?

3   Scott Ryder's birthday is October 15. The first week of April preceding his becoming twenty-five years of age, he considers taking out a company A participating 20-payment life policy for $12,000. How much will he save (a) on each annual premium and (b) over a 20-year period on annual premiums if the policy is dated prior to April 16?

4   John Edminston, at the insurable age of forty, purchases an $18,000 company A participating ordinary life policy. What is the maximum amount that he can borrow (dividends are excluded since they are payable on demand) on the policy 15 years later?

5   If purchased at the insurable age of thirty, what is the cash surrender value 20 years later of company A policies, each for $12,000: (a) participating ordinary life, (b) participating 20-payment life, and (c) participating 20-year endowment?

6   At insurable age thirty, Mr. Caldron purchased a $5000 company B nonparticipating 20-payment life policy. At the same time, Mr. Gates, who was the same age, purchased a $5000 company A participating 20-payment life policy. After 5 years, what was the net cost or premium earned in excess of cost (not including interest that may have been earnable on annual premiums paid) of (a) Mr. Caldron's policy and (b) of Mr. Gates's policy?

7   Mr. Irving, who is twenty, is undecided between company A's $10,000 participating and company B's $10,000 nonparticipating 20-year endowment policies. After 20 years what would be the total cost (a) of the participating policy, (b) of the nonparticipating policy?

8   Find the net cost or net return on the following (a) company A participating and (b) company B nonparticipating policies. (Do not consider interest that may have been earnable on annual premiums paid.)

Face of policy	Age at issue	Kind of policy	Years in force
$15,000	35	20-payment life	20
7,000	25	20-year endowment	20
5,000	30	Ordinary life	10

9   Mr. Castenada purchased company B's $18,000 nonparticipating ordinary life policy 10 years ago, when he was twenty. Find (a) the cash surrender value, (b) the paid-up value, and (c) the period for which he may select extended term insurance of the same face.

10 Mr. Cordeiro purchased company B's $28,000 nonparticipating ordinary life policy 18 years ago, when he was thirty. Find (a) the cash surrender value, (b) the paid-up value, and (c) the period for which he may select extended term insurance of the same face.

Unit 14.2   *Fire Insurance*

Fire insurance insures against loss by fire and certain other damage that may result directly from attempts to extinguish a fire, such as loss caused by water and chemical extinguishers or breakage of property by fire fighters. Many kinds of property may be insured against loss from fire, including crops, automobiles, homes, commercial buildings, inventories, equipment, furnishings, etc.

Fire insurance for homes and/or contents is a subject that should be of interest to you in the future, if not at present. Insurance against loss by fire or other casualty normally requires that the insured pay premiums in advance, and for dwelling properties as well as their contents, these are determined from premium tables. Unlike life insurance, the underwriter makes payment only upon the occurrence of a contingency that may or may not occur. In most instances, since losses do not occur, payments are not made. If losses do occur, they frequently are in an amount considerably less than the face or specified limitations of the policy. Thus a house and its contents may be fully or partially insured and it may not burn, it may burn partially, or it may burn completely.

PREMIUM TABLES AND RATES   Fire insurance premium tables and rates are presented in Tables 14.8 and 14.9 for class D buildings and contents. The rates presented in the tables are annual rates. Three-year policies may be written and if so, the rate is three times the annual rate, even if paid in advance. Most insurance companies are limiting the issuance of policies to one year so they may take advantage of the current rate increase due to inflation. Fire insurance premiums may be rounded to the nearest dollar.

The premium rates are based upon the risk exposure inherent in the property insured. The risk exposure is based primarily on three factors:

1   Type of building construction and its resistance to fire. For this factor, the buildings are given a classification starting with A for the most resistant to fire. A class D building is a "frame" building (constructed of wood).
2   Quality of fire protection available in the area. For this factor, fire protection districts are given a classification starting with I for the highest quality.
3   The geographical district in which the property is located. Most states divide the state by counties and establish districts based upon the relative fire risk.

TABLE 14.8 ANNUAL FIRE PREMIUMS. DWELLING BUILDING (OWNER-OCCUPIED). ONE- AND TWO-FAMILY UNITS, CLASS D, DISTRICT I

Amount of insurance	Fire protection class								
	2	3	4	5	6	7	8	9	10
$ 1,000	$11	$12	$13	$14	$16	$ 18	$ 21	$ 32	$ 37
2,000	12	13	15	16	17	20	24	36	41
3,000	14	15	16	18	19	22	26	40	46
4,000	15	16	18	19	21	24	29	43	49
5,000	16	18	20	21	23	26	31	48	54
6,000	17	19	21	23	25	28	34	51	58
7,000	19	21	23	25	27	31	36	55	63
8,000	20	22	24	26	28	32	39	59	67
9,000	21	24	26	28	30	35	41	63	72
10,000	23	25	27	30	32	37	44	66	76
11,000	22	23	26	28	31	35	41	63	72
12,000	23	25	27	30	32	37	44	67	76
13,000	24	26	29	32	34	39	47	70	80
14,000	25	28	31	32	35	41	49	74	84
15,000	26	29	32	34	37	42	50	77	87
16,000	27	30	32	36	39	44	52	79	91
17,000	28	32	34	37	40	46	54	83	95
18,000	29	32	35	39	41	48	57	86	98
19,000	31	33	37	40	43	50	59	89	102
20,000	32	34	38	41	44	50	60	92	104
21,000	32	36	39	42	46	52	62	95	108
22,000	33	37	41	44	47	54	65	98	112
23,000	34	38	41	45	49	56	67	101	115
24,000	35	40	43	47	50	58	68	104	119
25,000	37	41	44	48	51	59	70	107	122
26,000	38	41	45	50	53	61	73	110	126
27,000	39	42	47	50	55	63	75	113	130
28,000	40	44	48	52	56	64	77	116	132
29,000	41	45	50	53	58	66	78	120	136
30,000	41	46	50	55	59	68	81	122	140
35,000	47	52	57	61	67	77	91	138	158
40,000	52	58	63	68	74	85	101	153	175
45,000	58	63	69	76	81	93	111	168	192
50,000	63	69	76	82	88	102	121	184	210
Each additional $10,000	10.8	11.7	12.6	13.5	14.4	17.1	19.8	30.6	35.1

Note: If dwelling building is occupied by a tenant, increase building fire premium by 25 percent (rounded to nearest dollar).
If dwelling building is of masonry construction (class C), decrease frame fire premium by 20 percent (rounded to nearest dollar).
For three- and four-family units, increase above rates 10 percent (rounded to nearest dollar).
Source: Printed by permission of the Pacific Fire Rating Bureau, 465 California Street, San Francisco, CA.

TABLE 14.9   ANNUAL FIRE PREMIUMS. DWELLING CONTENTS (OWNER- OR TENANT-OCCUPIED). ONE- AND TWO-FAMILY UNITS, CLASS D, DISTRICT I

Amount of insurance	Fire protection class								
	2	3	4	5	6	7	8	9	10
$ 1,000	$ 3	$ 3	$ 4	$ 4	$ 4	$ 5	$ 5	$ 8	$ 9
2,000	4	4	5	5	5	6	7	11	12
3,000	5	5	6	6	7	8	9	14	16
4,000	6	7	7	7	8	10	11	17	19
5,000	7	8	9	9	10	11	13	20	23
6,000	8	9	10	10	11	13	15	23	26
7,000	9	10	11	11	12	15	17	26	29
8,000	10	11	13	13	14	16	19	29	33
9,000	11	13	14	14	15	18	21	32	36
10,000	12	14	15	15	17	20	23	35	40
11,000	13	15	17	17	18	21	25	38	43
12,000	14	16	18	18	20	23	27	41	46
13,000	15	17	19	19	21	25	29	44	50
14,000	16	18	20	20	22	27	31	47	53
15,000	17	20	22	22	24	28	33	50	56
16,000	18	21	23	23	25	30	35	53	60
17,000	19	22	24	24	27	32	36	56	63
18,000	20	23	26	26	28	33	38	59	67
19,000	22	24	27	27	30	35	40	62	70
20,000	23	25	28	28	31	37	42	65	73
21,000	24	27	30	30	32	38	44	68	77
22,000	25	28	31	31	34	40	46	71	80
23,000	26	29	32	32	35	42	48	74	83
24,000	27	30	33	33	37	43	50	77	87
25,000	28	31	35	35	38	45	52	80	90
26,000	29	32	36	36	40	47	54	83	94
27,000	30	34	37	37	41	48	56	86	97
28,000	31	35	39	39	42	50	58	89	100
29,000	32	36	40	40	44	52	60	92	104
30,000	33	37	41	41	45	54	62	95	107
35,000	38	43	48	48	52	62	72	110	124
40,000	43	49	54	54	60	70	81	125	141
45,000	49	55	61	61	67	79	91	140	158
50,000	54	60	67	67	74	87	101	155	175
Each additional $10,000	10	12	13	13	14	17	20	30	34

NOTE: If dwelling building is of masonry construction (class C), decrease frame fire premium by 20 percent (rounded to nearest dollar).

For three- and four-family units, increase above rates by 10 percent (rounded to nearest dollar).

Source: Printed by permission of the Pacific Fire Rating Bureau, 465 California St., San Francisco, CA.

Note the adjustments of the basic annual rate listed at the bottom of the premium rate tables.

Example 1　**From the premium tables, find (a) the annual premium for an owner-occupied dwelling, in fire protection class 3 for (a) dwelling insurance coverage of $30,000 and (b) contents coverage of $5000.**

(a) Dwelling premium for $30,000　　　　　　= $46
(b) Contents premium for $5000　　　　　　= $8

AMOUNT OF INSURANCE NOT GIVEN IN PREMIUM TABLES The premium for an intermediate amount of fire insurance not shown in the premium table must be determined by interpolation. Where coverage is in excess of $50,000 or for a three- or four-unit family dwelling, apply the adjustment factors given at the bottom of the table.

Example 2　**Find the annual fire insurance premium of a *tenant-occupied* one-family dwelling for insurance coverage of $42,000 in fire protection class 5.**

Premium for an owner-occupied dwelling for insurance coverage of:

	$45,000		$76
	40,000		68
Difference	$ 5,000		$ 8

Premium for $42,000 coverage:

$$\$68 + \frac{2000}{5000} \times \$8 = \$68 + 3.20 \qquad\qquad = \$71 \quad \text{(Rounded)}$$

Add 25 percent increase for tenant-occupied
25% × $71　　　　　　　　　　　　　　　　= $18　(Rounded)

Fire insurance premium for a tenant-
occupied dwelling for $42,000　　　　　　　= $89

Example 3　**Find the premium for an owner-occupied one-family dwelling for insurance coverage of $90,000 in fire protection class 4.**

Insurance for $50,000　　　　　　　　　　= $ 76

$$\text{Add } \frac{40,000}{10,000} \times \$12.60 \qquad\qquad\qquad = \underline{\quad 50} \quad \text{(Rounded)}$$

Fire insurance for $90,000　　　　　　　　= $126

Example 4　**Find the premium for a tenant-occupied four-family dwelling for insurance coverage of $100,000 in fire protection class 6.**

$100,000 insurance for owner-occupied dwelling for one-family unit:

Insurance for $50,000	$ 88
Add additional $50,000:	
$\dfrac{\$50,000}{\$10,000} \times \$14.4$	72
Subtotal	$160
Add 25 percent for tenant-occupied	40
Subtotal	$200
Add 10 percent for four-family tenant-occupied dwelling	20
Total	$220

Note: There is no difference in which order you multiply the insurance premium for $100,000 for an owner-occupied dwelling of one-family unit ($160) for the adjustments indicated ($160 \times 1.25 \times 1.10 = 160 \times 1.10 \times 1.25$).

EXTENDED COVERAGE AND OTHER ENDORSEMENTS If the insured desires additional hazards other than fire to be included in the basic fire insurance policy, she or he may add one or several "endorsements" to the policy which in turn adds reimbursement for loss caused by hazards other than fire. The endorsements do not increase the amount of insurance, just the hazards which may cause the loss.

Extended coverage endorsement (ECE) includes the additional hazards such as windstorm, hail, water, and smoke.

Vandalism and malicious mischief endorsement (VMM) adds still more hazards to the basic policy from which losses will be reimbursed.

Broad form (BF) and special form endorsements (SF) add still more hazards and include just about complete coverage for loss from all possible hazards.

Premium additions for these endorsements are presented in Table 14.10.

Example 5 **Find the total premium for an owner-occupied dwelling of one-family unit for $50,000 of insurance on the dwelling and $15,000 insurance on the contents in fire protection class 3 and with an ECE and VMM endorsements.**

Dwelling, $50,000	(Table 14.8)	$69	
ECE	(Table 14.10)	20	
VMM	(Table 14.10)	6	
Total dwelling			$ 95
Contents, $15,000	(Table 14.9)	20	
ECE	(Table 14.10)	3	
VMM	(Table 14.10)	2	
Total contents			$ 25
Total premium			$120

HOMEOWNERS' POLICY Most policies in force for the average home are not just fire policies with specified endorsements, but "package policies" known as homeowners' policies. Homeowners' policies start with HO-1

TABLE 14.10   ANNUAL PREMIUMS. EXTENDED COVERAGE (ECE), ETC., ONE- THROUGH FOUR-FAMILY UNITS, CLASS D, DISTRICTS I AND II

Amount of insurance	Dwellings — Over $10,000 and located in protection classes 2 through 9				Dwellings — All others				Contents — All contents		
	ECE	VMM	BF	SF	ECE	VMM	BF	SF	ECE	VMM	BF
$ 1,000					$ 2	$ 1	$ 1		$ 1	$ 1	$ 1
2,000					2	1	1		1	1	1
3,000					3	1	2		1	1	2
4,000					3	1	2		1	1	2
5,000					4	1	3		1	1	3
6,000					4	1	4		1	1	4
7,000					4	1	4		1	1	4
8,000					5	1	5	$ 6	1	2	5
9,000					5	1	5	6	2	1	5
10,000					6	1	6	7	2	1	6
11,000	$ 5	$ 1	$ 6	$ 7	6	2	7	8	2	2	7
12,000	6	2	6	8	7	2	7	8	2	2	7
13,000	6	2	7	8	7	2	8	9	2	2	8
14,000	7	2	8	9	8	2	8	10	2	2	8
15,000	7	2	8	9	8	2	9	11	3	2	9
16,000	7	2	9	10	8	2	10	11	3	2	10
17,000	8	2	9	11	9	2	10	12	3	2	10
18,000	8	2	10	11	9	3	11	13	3	3	11
19,000	9	2	10	12	10	3	11	13	3	3	11
20,000	9	3	11	13	10	3	12	14	3	3	12
21,000	10	3	11	13	11	3	13	15	4	3	13
22,000	10	3	12	14	11	3	13	15	4	3	13
23,000	10	3	12	15	11	3	14	16	4	3	14
24,000	11	3	13	15	12	3	14	17	4	3	14
25,000	11	3	14	16	12	4	15	18	4	1	15
26,000	12	3	14	16	13	4	15	18	4	4	15
27,000	12	3	15	17	13	4	16	19	5	4	16
28,000	13	4	15	18	14	4	17	20	5	4	17
29,000	13	4	16	18	14	4	17	20	5	4	17
30,000	13	4	16	19	14	4	18	21	5	4	18
35,000	14	4	19	22	16	5	21	25	6	5	21
40,000	16	5	22	25	18	6	24	28	7	6	24
45,000	18	6	24	28	20	6	27	32	8	6	27
50,000	20	6	27	32	22	7	30	35	8	7	30
Each additional $10,000	3.6	1.26	5.4	6.3	4.	1.4	6.	7.	2	1.4	6.

Source: Printed by permission of the Pacific Fire Rating Bureau, 465 California Street, San Francisco, CA.

(basic form), which includes the hazards of fire, ECE, VMM, glass (limit $50), theft, and liability. A very important feature of this policy is that it will reimburse loss of the dwelling at its *replacement cost,* rather than the conventional depreciated value based on age, condition, etc. This feature eliminates discussion as to the value of that which was lost, and makes for a much smoother and happier reimbursement for the insured. The home-owners' policies range from HO-1 on up to HO-6, each covering additional hazards. The HO-4 policy covers contents only and is designed for the renter or tenant. All homeowners' policies have a limit on money and securities (usually $100) and jewelry and furs ($500). Higher amounts of insurance can be obtained for these items for additional premiums. Table 14.11 presents rates for homeowners' policy number 3 (HO-3) with adjustment multipliers for HO-1 and HO-2 policies.

Example 6   **Find the insurance premium for an insurance coverage of $65,000 in basic premium group 3 for (a) HO-1 policy, (b) HO-2 policy, and (c) HO-3 policy.**

(a) HO-1 = $335 × 85% = $285   (Rounded)
(b) HO-2 =   335 × 95% = $318   (Rounded)
(c) HO-3   = $335

CANCELLATION BY INSURER   In all fire and in most casualty policies, both the insurer (underwriter) and the insured (policyholder) have the right to cancel. If the insuring company wishes to cancel, most state laws require that the policyholder be given at least 5 days' advance notice so that the insured may have sufficient time to obtain insurance coverage from the same or some other underwriter. As additional protection to the insured, most state laws require that the insuring company retain not more than an exact pro rata portion of the premium for the length of time that the policy has been in force, the remainder of the prepaid insurance being refunded to the insured. Thus if an insurer cancels a 1-year policy after 172 days (exact time), during which period the policy has been in effect, the insurer may retain $\frac{172}{365}$ of the 1-year premium, the balance, or $\frac{193}{365}$ of the prepaid 1-year premium, being refunded to the insured. If the insurer cancels a 3-year policy that has been in force for 1 year and 17 days (365 + 17 = 382 days), the insurer may retain not more than $\frac{382}{1095}$ of the premium paid, the balance of the prepaid 3-year premium being refunded to the insured.

Note that in determining the pro rata portion of the premium that may be retained by the insurer, it is customary to count the actual number of days for both numerator and denominator since 30-day-month time would not usually provide an exact pro rata of the premium for the length of time that the policy has been in force.

Example 7   **Cancellation by insurer. On April 30, 1979, Mr. Herman purchased a 1-year fire insurance policy on his store building, paying a premium of $132. On July 12, 1979, the insurer canceled the policy. Find (a) the premium retained by the insurer and (b) the refund paid to Mr. Herman.**

TABLE 14.11 ANNUAL PREMIUM RATES. HOMEOWNERS POLICY 3 (HO-3) (FOR HO-1, USE 85 PERCENT; FOR HO-2, USE 95 PERCENT)

Coverage A dwelling amount	Basic premium groups								
	1/2	3/4	5/6	7	8	9/10	11/12	13/14	15
$ 15,000	$ 65	$ 71	$102	$117	$ 60	$ 60	$ 66	$101	$ 123
16,000	68	75	107	122	63	62	69	106	129
17,000	71	79	112	129	66	66	72	111	136
18,000	74	81	116	133	68	68	75	116	140
19,000	77	85	122	139	71	71	78	121	147
20,000	80	89	127	145	74	74	82	126	153
21,000	84	93	133	152	78	78	85	132	161
22,000	87	96	138	158	81	81	89	137	167
23,000	91	101	144	165	85	84	93	143	173
24,000	95	106	151	173	89	88	97	150	183
25,000	100	110	158	181	93	92	102	156	191
26,000	104	116	165	190	98	97	106	164	200
27,000	109	121	173	198	101	101	111	171	208
28,000	113	125	179	206	106	105	116	178	217
29,000	118	131	187	214	110	109	120	185	225
30,000	122	136	194	222	114	113	124	192	235
31,000	128	141	202	231	119	118	130	201	244
32,000	133	147	210	241	124	123	136	208	254
33,000	138	152	218	250	128	127	141	217	264
34,000	143	158	226	259	134	132	146	224	274
35,000	149	164	235	269	138	137	151	233	284
36,000	154	170	243	278	143	141	157	241	293
37,000	159	176	251	287	148	146	162	249	303
38,000	164	181	259	297	152	151	167	257	313
39,000	169	187	267	306	158	156	172	265	323
40,000	174	193	275	315	162	161	178	273	333
41,000	179	198	284	325	167	165	183	281	343
42,000	185	204	292	334	172	170	188	289	353
43,000	190	209	305	343	176	175	193	298	362
44,000	195	215	308	353	182	180	199	305	372
45,000	200	221	316	362	186	185	204	314	383
46,000	205	227	325	371	191	189	209	321	392
47,000	210	233	332	381	196	194	214	330	402
48,000	215	238	341	390	200	199	220	337	411
49,000	221	244	349	399	206	204	225	346	422
50,000	226	250	357	409	210	209	230	354	432
51,000	231	256	366	418	215	214	236	363	442
52,000	236	261	373	427	220	218	241	371	451
53,000	242	267	382	437	224	223	246	379	462
54,000	247	272	389	446	230	228	251	387	471
55,000	252	278	398	455	234	232	257	395	481
56,000	257	284	406	465	239	237	263	404	491
57,000	263	290	414	474	244	242	267	411	501
58,000	268	296	422	483	248	246	273	420	511
59,000	273	301	430	492	254	251	278	428	520
60,000	278	307	439	502	258	256	284	436	530
61,000	284	313	447	511	263	261	289	445	541
62,000	289	318	455	520	268	266	294	452	550
63,000	294	324	463	530	272	270	300	461	560
64,000	299	329	471	538	278	275	305	468	570

(Continued)

TABLE 14.11   ANNUAL PREMIUM RATES. HOMEOWNERS POLICY 3 (HO-3) (FOR HO-1, USE 85 PERCENT; FOR HO-2, USE 95 PERCENT) (Continued)

Coverage A dwelling amount	1/2	3/4	5/6	7	8	9/10	11/12	13/14	15
						Basic premium groups			
$65,000	305	335	479	548	282	280	310	477	580
66,000	310	341	488	558	287	285	316	485	590
67,000	315	347	496	566	292	290	321	493	599
68,000	320	353	504	576	296	294	326	502	609
69,000	326	358	512	585	302	299	331	509	619
70,000	331	364	520	594	306	304	337	518	629
71,000	336	370	529	604	311	309	342	526	639
72,000	341	375	536	613	316	314	347	534	649
73,000	347	381	545	622	320	318	353	542	659
74,000	352	386	553	631	326	323	358	550	668
75,000	357	392	561	641	330	328	363	558	678
80,000	383	421	602	687	354	351	390	599	728
85,000	410	449	643	734	378	375	417	640	777
90,000	436	478	683	780	402	399	443	681	826
95,000	462	506	724	826	426	423	470	722	876
100,000	488	535	765	873	450	447	496	762	925
105,000	515	563	806	919	474	470	523	803	974
110,000	541	592	847	966	498	494	550	844	1023
Each additional $5,000	26	28	41	46	24	23	27	41	49

Source: Printed by permission of the Pacific Fire Rating Bureau, 465 California Street, San Francisco, CA.

Policy is for 1 year = 365 days.
April 30, 1979, to July 12, 1979, is 73 days.

(a) $132.00 × $\dfrac{73}{365}$ = $26.40

(b) $132.00 − $26.40 = $105.60

SHORT-TERM POLICIES AND CANCELLATION BY INSURED   On occasion, the insured may find it desirable to purchase insurance for a period of less than 1 year or may wish to cancel a 1-year policy prior to its expiration and receive a refund for the period of time between the cancellation date and the expiration date of the policy. In either event, the underwriter will short-rate the policy, that is, make a higher charge than an exact pro rata of the annual premium for the period that the policy is in force.

Table 14.12 is a short-rate table for a one-year policy.

Example 8   **Short-term policy. Mr. Jordan wants a 90-day fire insurance policy with a face of $20,000 on a dwelling in protection class 7. Find the cost of the short-term policy.**

TABLE 14.12 CANCELLATION OR SHORT-RATE PREMIUM CHARGES

Policy in force, days	Policy term and multiples 1 year 1 ann. Percent of earned premium	Policy in force, days	Policy term and multiples 1 year 1 ann. Percent of earned premium	Policy in force, days	Policy term and multiples 1 year 1 ann. Percent of earned premium
1	5	106–109	40	224–228	70
2	6	110–113	41	229–232	71
3–4	7	114–116	42	233–237	72
5–6	8	117–120	43	238–241	73
7–8	9	121–124	44	242–246	74
9–10	10	125–127	45	247–250	75
11–12	11	128–131	46	251–255	76
13–14	12	132–135	47	256–260	77
15–16	13	136–138	48	261–264	78
17–18	14	139–142	49	265–269	79
19–20	15	143–146	50	270–273	80
21–22	16	147–149	51	274–278	81
23–25	17	150–153	52	279–282	82
26–29	18	154–156	53	283–287	83
30–32	19	157–160	54	288–291	84
33–36	20	161–164	55	292–296	85
37–40	21	165–167	56	297–301	86
41–43	22	168–171	57	302–305	87
44–47	23	172–175	58	306–310	88
48–51	24	176–178	59	311–314	89
52–54	25	179–182	60	315–319	90
55–58	26	183–187	61	320–323	91
59–62	27	188–191	62	324–328	92
63–65	28	192–196	63	329–332	93
66–69	29	197–200	64	333–337	94
70–73	30	201–205	65	338–342	95
74–76	31	206–209	66	343–346	96
77–80	32	210–214	67	347–351	97
81–83	33	215–218	68	352–355	98
84–87	34	219–223	69	356–360	99
88–91	35			361–365	100
92–94	36				
95–98	37				
99–102	38				
103–105	39				

Annual premiums: $50.00
90-day short-rate table: 35% of annual premium
90-day premium: $50.00 × 0.35 = $17.50, rounded off to $18.00

Example 9   **Cancellation by insured. Mr. Jorgensen notified his fire insurance underwriter that he wished to cancel as of November 15 his 1-year fire policy dated
July 15. If the annual premium was $84, find (a) the amount of the premium
retained by the insurance company and (b) the refund received by Mr.
Jorgensen.**

July 15 to November 15 by exact time = 123 days
123-day short-rate table = 44%

(a) $84.00 × 0.44   = $36.96   Premium retained
(b) $84.00 − $36.96 = $47.04   Refund to Mr. Jorgensen

Exercise 14.2

Find the total premium for the following fire insurance policies for class D
structures (use Tables 14.8 through 14.11).

	Insurance amount		Fire protection	**Endorsements**			
	Building	Contents	class	ECE	VMM	BF	SF
1	$28,000		3	yes	yes	no	no
2	$45,000	$12,000	7	yes	yes	no	no
3	$50,000	$15,000	6	yes	yes	yes	yes
4	$70,000	$20,000	5	yes	yes	no	no
5	$38,000	$11,000	4	yes	yes	no	no
6	$85,000	$32,000	6	yes	yes	yes	yes

7   Determine the annual premium for a $40,000 fire insurance policy on the
building, $10,000 on the contents, with ECE and VMM endorsements, for
a four-unit dwelling in protection class 8.

8   Determine the annual premium for a fire insurance policy for a four-unit
dwelling in fire protection class 7 for the following amounts: $60,000 on
the building, $20,000 on the contents, and ECE and VMM endorsements.

9   Herbert and Fritzie Urban took out a homeowners' policy (HO-3) for
$60,000 in basic premium group 3. Find the premium.

10   Richard Urban took out a homeowners' policy (HO-1) for $45,000 in
premium group 6. Find the premium.

11   Barbara Brewer took out a $40,000 homeowners' (HO-2) policy in pre-
mium group 5 on June 8. On August 10 the insurer canceled the policy.
Find (a) the amount of the premium and (b) the amount of the refund
due Barbara.

12   On September 8, Sheila Kurwitz, took out a $60,000 homeowners' policy
(HO-3) in premium group 6. On January 15 of the following year, the
insurer canceled the policy. Find (a) the premium and (b) the amount of
the refund due Sheila.

13 On August 16 Bob Thompson took out a 1-year fire insurance policy in fire protection class 5 on a four-unit dwelling for $50,000 on the building and $15,000 on the contents, both with ECE and VMM endorsements. On December 3, Bob sold the property and canceled the insurance. Find (a) the total premium and (b) the refund due Mr. Thompson.

14 Richard George completed a four-unit dwelling and listed it for sale. On August 28 he obtained a 90-day fire insurance policy in fire protection class 6 with ECE and VMM endorsements. The face of the dwelling policy was $75,000. Find the total premium.

Unit 14.3

Two or More Fire Underwriters Insuring the Same Property; Coinsurance

---

Multiple Underwriters

On occasions, more than one fire underwriter insures the same piece of property. This may occur for a number of reasons: the value of the property may be so large that no one company wishes to assume all of the risk; a lending agency holding a mortgage on the property may require more than one insurer; the insured may wish to divide his policies among two or more friendly agents or brokers; or the insurance agent transfers from one company to another and the insured, when raising the total amount of his insurance because of increased value of the property, may prefer to retain the same agent for all his policies.

Whenever more than one underwriter insures the same property, if a loss occurs, each company pays the pro rata share that its policy bears to the total insurance carried. Thus if company A's policy is 50 percent, company B's policy is 30 percent, and company C's policy is 20 percent of the total insurance carried by the insured, the total of any loss to be paid by the three insurers is ascertained as follows: company A will pay 50 percent; company B will pay 30 percent; and company C will pay 20 percent. Loss is limited to the value of the property damaged, but in no case will the loss paid be in excess of the face of the policies. Expressed as a formula:

$$\text{Each insurer's share of loss payable} = \underbrace{\text{loss}}_{\substack{\text{Actual loss or total faces of} \\ \text{policies, whichever is smaller}}} \times \frac{\text{the face of its policy}}{\text{total insurance carried}}$$

Example 1 **The Georgetown Corporation carries the following fire insurance policies: Aetna Insurance Co., $30,000; Fireman's Fund Insurance Co., $20,000; Phoenix Insurance Co., $15,000; Southwestern Insurance Co., $10,000. A loss through fire occurs amounting to $27,000. What is the amount of loss borne by each company?**

Insurer	Face of policy
Aetna	$30,000.00
Fireman's Fund	20,000.00
Phoenix	15,000.00
Southwestern	10,000.00
Total insurance	$75,000.00

Loss sustained by Aetna $= \$27{,}000.00 \times \dfrac{\$30{,}000.00}{\$75{,}000.00} = \$10{,}800.00$

Loss sustained by Fireman's Fund $= \$27{,}000.00 \times \dfrac{\$20{,}000.00}{\$75{,}000.00} = \$\ 7200.00$

Loss sustained by Phoenix $= \$27{,}000.00 \times \dfrac{\$15{,}000.00}{\$75{,}000.00} = \$\ 5400.00$

Loss sustained by Southwestern $= \$27{,}000.00 \times \dfrac{\$10{,}000.00}{\$75{,}000.00} = \$\ 3600.00$

Coinsurance

Since few fires result in total loss of the insured property, many owners of large properties insure their holdings for only a fractional part of their value. To adjust fire insurance costs equitably for those property owners who desire less than full coverage, the principle of coinsurance has been developed. In coinsurance, the insured agrees to carry insurance to cover a stated percent of the property's value—frequently 80 percent, although this percent varies.

If the insured fails to carry insurance equivalent to the stated percent, he is considered a coinsurer for the difference between the percent he carries and the stated percent of the policy. If a loss is sustained, the insured is reimbursed in full up to the face value of his policy if his insurance is at least the stipulated percent of the value of the property at the time of the loss. Usually the insurance need not be taken wholly with one company, but the total or aggregate insurance must equal or exceed the required amount. If the total insurance is less than the required amount, the insured shares pro rata with the insurers in any loss sustained. Regardless of the amount of total loss, in no case will the loss paid be in excess of the actual loss or of the face of the policies.

Coinsurance clauses become inoperative if the loss is equal to or exceeds the stipulated percentage of value. Thus if the insurance required is $8000, the insurance taken $2000, and the loss $8000 or more, the insurer pays the loss in the ratio that $2000 bears to $8000 times the loss, or to the extent of $2000. The formula for computing the insurer's share of the loss may be stated as follows:

$$\text{Insurance required} = \text{actual value} \times \text{stipulated percent of value}$$

$$\text{Insurer's share of loss} = \underbrace{\text{actual loss} \times \dfrac{\text{insurance carried}}{\text{insurance required}}}_{}$$

Not to exceed actual loss or face
of policy, whichever is smaller

Example 2   Mr. Abbott carried $10,000 insurance with an 80 percent coinsurance clause on the stock of his men's clothing store. At a time when his inventory showed $15,000 as the value of his merchandise at cost, a fire destroyed $3600 worth of the goods. How much insurance settlement did Mr. Abbott receive?

80% insurance required = $15,000.00 × 0.80 = $12,000.00
But Mr. Abbott carried only $10,000 insurance. Therefore,

$$\text{Settlement} = \$3600.00 \times \frac{\$10,000.00}{\$12,000.00} = \$3000.00$$

Example 3   Mr. Plaskett carries $18,000 insurance with a 90 percent coinsurance clause on a stock of hardware. At a time when his inventory shows $19,000 as the value of his merchandise at cost, a fire completely destroys the store and contents. How much insurance settlement will Mr. Plaskett receive?

90% insurance required = $19,000.00 × 0.90 = $17,100.00
Mr. Plaskett carries $18,000 insurance (in excess of required amount).

Therefore the settlement is face of policy = $18,000.00

Example 4   Mr. Pribble carries $12,000 insurance with an 80 percent coinsurance clause on his stock of merchandise. At a time when the value of the merchandise is $20,000, a fire destroys $18,000 worth of the stock. How much insurance settlement will Mr. Pribble receive?

80% insurance required = $20,000.00 × 0.80 = $16,000.00
Mr. Pribble carries only $12,000 insurance. Therefore,

$$\text{Settlement} = \$18,000.00 \times \frac{\$12,000.00}{\$16,000.00} = \$13,500.00$$

but loss is limited to face of policy = $12,000.00

Exercise 14.3

Solve the following problems in fire insurance:

1   A loss of $70,000 occurred on an apartment building. The insurance was carried by three companies, A for $20,000, B for $30,000, and C for $50,000. How much did each company have to pay to the insured?

2   Fire insurance policies for $10,000, $20,000, and $30,000 were carried with companies A, B, and C, respectively. The insured building, valued at $55,000, was completely destroyed by fire. What loss was assumed by each company?

3   Mr. Lenz carries $13,000 insurance with a 90 percent coinsurance clause on his stock of electrical appliances. At a time when his inventory shows $17,000 as the value of the merchandise at cost, a fire completely destroys the store and contents. What insurance settlement does Mr. Lenz receive?

4 Ms. Franklin carries $15,000 insurance with a 90 percent coinsurance clause on the stock of her grocery store. At a time when her inventory shows $20,000 as the value of the merchandise at cost, a fire destroys $7500 worth of goods. What insurance settlement does Ms. Franklin receive?

5 A factory was valued at $500,000. The insurance with 80 percent coinsurance clauses was carried by four companies. Company A carried $150,000; B, $90,000; C, $100,000; and D, $80,000. A loss of $290,000 occurred. How much did each company pay?

6 A fire loss of $150,000 occurred. Four companies had sold policies with 80 percent coinsurance clauses. Company A held $50,000, B held $70,000, C held $85,000, and D held $110,000. The building was valued at $450,000. How much did each pay?

Find the fire insurance settlement in each of the following:

	Face of policy	Coinsurance clause, %	Value at time of loss	Actual loss sustained
7	$ 10,000.00	80	$ 12,000.00	$ 8,000.00
8	35,000.00	90	40,000.00	40,000.00
9	5,600.00	60	8,000.00	7,000.00
10	7,200.00	80	10,000.00	7,500.00
11	900,000.00	80	1,200,000.00	850,000.00
12	78,000.00	90	90,000.00	90,000.00

Unit 14.4   Business Insurance

A great number of business risks in addition to the possibility of loss through fire need to be protected against by the businessman. Some of these are purely for his own protection, others are for the protection of his employees and may be provided, among other reasons, as a contribution by the employer to the well-being of his working force or to increase their loyalty and efficiency.

BUSINESS INTERRUPTION INSURANCE This form of insurance is a means of protecting a business from the losses that would occur if an event such as fire, tornado, or earthquake should interrupt the normal activities of the business.

Business interruption insurance provides indemnity for expenses that will continue and for the net profit that would have been made during the suspension of business. Among the expenses that may continue in whole or in part are taxes, insurance, interest, advertising, leaseholds, utilities, and the wages and salaries of key employees who must be retained.

Example 1   **For a given month, net sales of a business are estimated to be $60,000, cost of sales $38,000, and expenses $15,000. Find the estimated amount of business interruption insurance that needs to be carried for each working day if the average number of working days each month is 25 and expenses that must continue during suspension of business are $11,000 per month.**

Net sales	$60,000.00
Less cost of sales	−38,000.00
Gross profit	$22,000.00
Less expenses	−15,000.00
Net profit	$ 7,000.00
Add expenses that must continue	+11,000.00
Business interruption value for month	$18,000.00

$$\text{Business interruption insurance value per day} = \frac{\$18,000.00}{25} = \$720.00$$

WORKMEN'S COMPENSATION INSURANCE   This form of insurance provides financial protection for the loss of earnings by the worker due to accidental or occupational sickness incurred while on duty.[1]

    Workmen's compensation insurance policies may be purchased from casualty insurance companies, although a few states also have their own workmen's compensation insurance funds that provide insurance protection for the employer (and for the employee). Such policies usually include death benefit as well as wage compensation in limited amounts per pay period.

    Rates vary with the occupational hazards of the differing types of work covered. Premiums are then determined by the number of dollars of wages at regular rates (overtime excess pay is not usually considered) paid by the employer.

Example 2   **If the workmen's compensation insurance rate for clerical workers was $3.50 per $100 of wages, find the total premium paid by an employer whose clerical staff earned $9000.**

$$\$9000 = 90.00 \quad \text{(hundreds of dollars)}$$
$$\$3.50 \times 90.00 = \$315.00 \quad \text{Premium}$$

Example 3   **A deposit of $1000.00 on his workmen's compensation insurance premium was made by a logging contractor to cover expected wage payments during a 3-month period. If the rate was $23.00 per $100 of wages and the total wages paid for the period was $10,000, find the amount owed or the refund due on the policy.**

---

[1]The State of California is one of the few states (if not the only one) to include the injury of cumulative trauma, caused by a job-related condition in those injuries compensated by workmen's compensation insurance. For example, a high noise exposure in a job could cause a hearing impairment. If just before retirement a worker filed a claim for a job-related hearing loss, benefits would be paid if the job-related hearing loss could be established. This feature has caused workmen's compensation insurance premiums to be quite high in California.

$$\$10{,}000 = 100 \quad \text{(hundreds of dollars)}$$
$$\$23.00 \times \$100 = \$2300.00 \quad \text{Premium}$$
$$\text{Amount owed on policy} = \$2300.00 - \$1000.00 = \$1300.00$$

HEALTH AND ACCIDENT INSURANCE This form of insurance is provided to compensate employees for loss of earnings due to sickness and accidents not covered by workmen's compensation insurance. The costs of health and accident insurance plans are usually paid in part by the employees, though in some businesses the employer pays the full amount. Contributions by employees are limited to a small charge which is deducted from wages. In some states, health and accident insurance for nonoccupational illnesses or accidents is provided through disability insurance funds contributed to by both employer and employee.

In most instances, length of service by the employee is a major factor in determining the amount that he may receive.

Example 4 **The Eaton Company disability plan provided that workers with less than 1 year of service received no benefits; 1 but less than 5 years received 4 weeks full pay plus half-pay for the next 6 weeks; 5 but less than 10 years received 8 weeks full pay plus half-pay for the next 8 weeks; 10 years and over received 13 weeks full pay plus half-pay for the next 13 weeks. Find the maximum disability benefits to which an employee with 7 years' service was entitled if his weekly wage was $65.50.**

$$\text{Full pay for 8 weeks} = \$65.50 \times 8 \qquad = \$524.00$$
$$\text{Half-pay for 8 weeks} = \frac{\$65.50}{2} \times 8 \qquad = \$262.00$$

$$\text{Maximum disability benefits} = \$524.00 + \$262.00 = \$786.00$$

Example 5 **The Hicks Company health and accident plan provided 50 percent of wages to employees in service up to 5 years, and 75 percent of wages to employees in service more than 5 years, and maximum benefits of $55 per week for 26 weeks. Mr. Robert Merritt, who had been employed for 3 years at $65 per week, became incapacitated for 30 weeks. Find his total benefit.**

$$\$65.00 \times 0.50 = \$32.50 \quad \text{(per week benefit)}$$
$$\$32.50 \times 26 = \$845.00 \quad \text{Total benefit (maximum time, 26 weeks)}$$

GROUP LIFE INSURANCE Such insurance provides the worker with low-cost life insurance (usually term insurance with no accumulating values), for a portion of the premium is paid by the employer. If the employee leaves the services of the particular employer, the insurance usually ceases, although some group life insurance plans provide that the employee may in such case optionally convert his group policy to an ordinary life insurance policy without medical examination.

The simplest form of group life insurance is for a fixed face (for example, $1000) provided to all employees for a small monthly payment. In other instances the face of the policy increases with any increase in the employee's annual income. In this latter case, the monthly contribution by the employee usually increases pro rata both with any increased coverage and with increasing age.[1]

Example 6   **Employees of the Halsey Corporation earning less than $10,000 per year may obtain $1000 of life insurance. For workers earning more than $10,000.00 per year, an additional $300 of life insurance may be obtained for each additional $500 or fraction thereof of earnings. The contribution schedule by the employees per $1000 of insurance is based on age. If Ms. Carol Cook, age 36, whose yearly earnings are $14,200.00, has a contribution schedule rate of $1.70 per month per $1000 of insurance, find the monthly deductions that will be made from her salary for life insurance.**

Excess earnings over $10,000.00 = $14,200.00 − $10,000.00 = $4200.00

Insurance available in addition to the base of $1000 is:

$$\frac{\$4200.00}{\$500.00} = 8+, \text{ or 9 additional units of \$300 each}$$

Total insurance = $1000.00 + ($300.00 × 9) = $1000.00 + $2700.00 = $3700.00

Monthly deduction = $1.70 × 3.7 = $6.29

Exercise 14.4

Solve the following:

1   A retail business had average monthly sales of $130,000, cost of goods sold of $74,000, and expenses of $46,000. If fire should cause a complete suspension of business, find the estimated amount of business interruption insurance that should be carried for each working day if the average number of working days per month is 25 and the expenses that will continue are $11,000 per month.

2   Assuming that it would require 152 working days to reconstruct the Risso Manufacturing Co. plant in the event of complete loss from fire, from the planned data for the period that follows compute the business interruption insurance required (a) in total amount, (b) per workday, and (c) the 3-year insurance premium if the rate is $2.65 per $100 for a 3-year policy. Beginning inventory is $85,652; ending inventory, $86,305; manufacturing costs and operating expenses, $1,745,868; net sales, $1,820,500. Fixed

---

[1] Under present provisions of the Internal Revenue Code, an employer can pay the premiums of life insurance up to $50,000 per employee without the employee receiving any "taxable income," and the employer is allowed to deduct the premiums as an expense.

expenses that will continue are: administrative salaries, $28,625; interest, $8900; taxes, $12,434; insurance, $5040; salaries of office help, supervisors, and foremen that must be retained, $108,475; and miscellaneous expenses, $15,923.

3 Mr. Daniel Wageman planned to build a summer and weekend cabin for his own use. In conformance with the state law he deposited $100 on a workmen's compensation insurance premium. Upon completion of the cabin, his labor costs and insurance rates per $100 of wages paid were as follows: carpenters, $1200 at $12.27; electricians, $200 at $13.20; plumbers, $500 at $14.25; painters, $300 at $18.20; miscellaneous labor, $600 at $8.90. Find the additional premium or refund due on his policy.

4 A deposit of $300 was made on a workmen's compensation insurance policy. The payroll audit showed the following wage payments and insurance rates per $100 of wages paid: $9085 at $9.28; $6071 at $10.20; $2344 at $13.20; and $5983 at $11.09. Find the additional premium or refund due on the policy.

5 The Merchant Company group health and accident insurance plan provided the following benefits for employees who became incapacitated through nonoccupational sickness or accident: 6 months but less than 2 years of service, 35 percent of wages, maximum of $75 for 8 weeks; 2 but less than 5 years of service, 50 percent of wages, maximum of $120 for 16 weeks; 5 but less than 10 years of service, 65 percent of wages, maximum of $165 for 24 weeks; and 10 or more years of service, 80 percent of wages, maximum $210 for 32 weeks. Find the total benefits received by (a) Ralph Stocker, employed 6 years with average earnings of $250 per week and ill for 15 weeks; (b) Bette Jo Murphy, employed 9 months with average earnings of $125 per week and ill for 10 weeks; (c) Ben Fitzsimmons, employed 19 years with average earnings of $425 per week and ill for 28 weeks.

6 The health and accident insurance plan of the Apley's Manufacturing Corporation provided benefits as follows: 1 but less than 10 years of service, full pay for 4 weeks, half-pay for the next 8 weeks, and one-fourth pay for the next 12 weeks; more than 10 years of service, full pay for 6 weeks, three-fourths pay for the next 12 weeks, and half-pay for the next 18 weeks. Find the benefits received by the following employees: (a) Mr. John Hunter, employed 4 years and earning $272.50 per week, who was incapacitated for 15 weeks; (b) Mrs. Sara Alden, employed 11 years and earning $351.60 per week, who was incapacitated for 23 weeks.

7 Group life insurance provided without charge to all employees of the Raymond Specialty Company was 1 month's salary for each year of service with a maximum of 12 months' salary or $6000, whichever was lower. Find the insurance provided for (a) Jim Hunter, employed 4 years at $12,400 per year, (b) Beth Scott, employed 11 years at $14,000 per year, (c) Helene McGovern, employed 5 years at $11,400 per year, (d) Fred Foultz, employed 9 years at $21,600 per year.

8 The General Manufacturing Corporation group life insurance plan for all employees determined the face of the policies as follows: earnings of $12,500 per year or less, $2000 of insurance; earnings of more than $12,500 per year, $2000 of insurance plus $50 of insurance for each full $100 of

earnings in excess of $12,500 per year. Employee contributions per month per $100 of insurance were computed by age groups as follows: under thirty years, 60 cents; thirty but under forty years, 70 cents; forty but under fifty years, 85 cents; fifty but under sixty years, $1.05; sixty years and over, $1.30. Find the monthly insurance contributions by (a) employee A, age thirty-eight, and earning $12,000 per year, (b) employee B, age sixty-eight, and earning $25,900 per year, (c) employee C, age forty-eight, and earning $25,500 per year.

Appendix 1

Binary, Octal, and Hexadecimal Number Systems

Unit A1.1   Binary, Octal, and Hexadecimal Number Systems in Business

With the increasing use of electronic computers and computer courses in business schools or curricula, it is becoming increasingly important for business students to possess a knowledge of the numeral systems employed by most computer systems. Computers store information in their "memories" and perform their calculations on a charge–no charge basis, or the base 2 (binary) number system which has but two characters. Binary numbers can be long (some computers treat 36 binary digit numbers as a unit of information), and it would be cumbersome for the machine language programmer to communicate with the computer in binary.

The base 8 (octal) and base 16 (hexadecimal) number systems are closely interrelated with the binary system, and enable the human machine language programmer to communicate with the computer in a much less cumbersome manner than with the binary system.

Review of Base 10 (Decimal) Number System

Chapter 1 presented the decimal system which represents a number system with a base of 10 and the 10 admissible characters of 0, 1, 2, 3, 4, 5, 6, 7, 8, and 9. The value of each character is determined by that character (is it a 5 or an 8?) and the position it occupies in relation to the radix (decimal) point. In a base 10 system, the first digit position to the left of the decimal point represents a value of 10^0 or 1, and the value of each of the admissible characters in this position is the product of the particular character times 10^0 or 1. Thus the value of 6 in the first digit position to the left of the decimal point is determined by $6 \times 10^0 = 6$. As we proceed to successive digital positions to the left of the decimal point, the value of each position increases by successive *higher positive* powers of 10. Thus the value of 6 in the second digit position to the left of the decimal point is determined by $6 \times 10^1 = 60$. As we proceed to the right of the decimal point, each successive digital position is determined by successive *negative* powers of 10. Thus the value of 6 in the first digit position to the right of the decimal point is the product of:

$$6 \times 10^{-1} = 0.6 \qquad \left(6 \times 10^{-1} = 6 \times \frac{1}{10} = \frac{6}{10} = 0.6\right)$$

The values of various digit positions in the base 10 (decimal) system shown in Unit 1.1 and matched to the powers of 10 are:

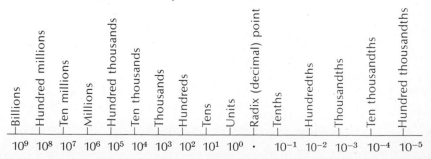

Billions	Hundred millions	Ten millions	Millions	Hundred thousands	Ten thousands	Thousands	Hundreds	Tens	Units	Radix (decimal) point	Tenths	Hundredths	Thousandths	Ten thousandths	Hundred thousandths
10^9	10^8	10^7	10^6	10^5	10^4	10^3	10^2	10^1	10^0	$\cdot$	10^{-1}	10^{-2}	10^{-3}	10^{-4}	10^{-5}

Thus the value of the decimal number 5467.23 is determined as follows:

1 Starting from the decimal point and proceeding to the left:

$$7 \times 10^0(7 \times 1) = 7.$$
$$6 \times 10^1(6 \times 10) = 60.$$
$$4 \times 10^2(4 \times 100) = 400.$$
$$5 \times 10^3(5 \times 1000) = 5000.$$

2 Starting from the decimal point and proceeding to the right:

$$2 \times 10^{-1}\left(2 \times \frac{1}{10}\right) = .2$$

$$3 \times 10^{-2}\left(3 \times \frac{1}{100}\right) = .03$$

3 Sum

$$\overline{5467.23}$$

Base 2 (Binary) Number System

The binary system is a number system having a base of 2 and two admissible characters of 0 and 1. The value of the characters is determined in the same manner as in the base 10 system, except that each digit position now has a value of 2 to the various powers of 2 instead of 10 to the various powers of 10. The values of the various digit positions in the base 2 system are shown in a diagram similar to that illustrating the base 10 system:

256	128	64	32	16	8	4	2	1	Radix or binary point	(0.50) $\frac{1}{2}$	(0.25) $\frac{1}{4}$	(0.125) $\frac{1}{8}$
2^8	2^7	2^6	2^5	2^4	2^3	2^2	2^1	2^0	.	2^{-1}	2^{-2}	2^{-3}

Thus the value of the binary number 11101.101 in terms of base 10 is as follows:

1 Starting from the binary point and proceeding to the left:

$$1 \times 2^0(1 \times 1) = 1.$$
$$0 \times 2^1(0 \times 2) = 0.$$
$$1 \times 2^2(1 \times 4) = 4.$$
$$1 \times 2^3(1 \times 8) = 8.$$
$$1 \times 2^4(1 \times 16) = 16.$$

2 Starting from the binary point and proceeding to the right:

$$1 \times 2^{-1}\left(1 \times \frac{1}{2}\right) = .\frac{1}{2}$$

$$0 \times 2^{-2}\left(0 \times \frac{1}{4}\right) = .0$$

$$1 \times 2^{-3}\left(1 \times \frac{1}{8}\right) = .\frac{1}{8}$$

3 Sum (in terms of a base 10 system)

$$= 29.\frac{5}{8} \text{ or } 29.625$$

Since the characters 0 and 1 in base 2 appear the same as the first two characters in base 10, it is not possible to distinguish the two systems unless some form of identification is used. When working with number systems with different bases, identification is accomplished by placing a subscript at the end of the number; thus:

$$11101.101_2 = 29.625_{10}$$

CONVERSION OF BINARY AND DECIMAL NUMBER SYSTEMS   When converting a *binary number to a decimal number,* proceed generally as above; that is, supply the numerical equivalents of the powers of 2 in the respective digit positions, and then perform the computation in base 10.

Example 1   **Convert 1011101_2 to base 10.**

								Radix point
Binary number	1	0	1	1	1	0	1	.
Powers of 2	64	32	16	8	4	2	1	

Thus $1011101_2 = 64 + 16 + 8 + 4 + 1 = 93_{10}$

When converting a *decimal number to a binary number,* two procedures may be used: (1) successive division by 2, and (2) successive division by the powers of 2.

Example 2   **Convert 849_{10} to base 2.**

Successive division by 2:

1   Divide the decimal number by 2. The remainder then becomes the binary character in the least significant digit position.
2   Divide the integral quotient obtained in (1) again by 2, and the remainder becomes the next significant binary digit.
3   Continue dividing the successive integral quotients by 2 until reduced to less than 2.

Successive division by 2		Integral quotient	Remainder and binary character	
			Radix point	.
$849 \div 2$	$=$	424	$+$	1
$424 \div 2$	$=$	212	$+$	0
$212 \div 2$	$=$	106	$+$	0
$106 \div 2$	$=$	53	$+$	0
$53 \div 2$	$=$	26	$+$	1
$26 \div 2$	$=$	13	$+$	0
$13 \div 2$	$=$	6	$+$	1
$6 \div 2$	$=$	3	$+$	0
$3 \div 2$	$=$	1	$+$	1
$1 \div 2$	$=$	0	$+$	1

Hence $849_{10} = 1101010001_2$.

Successive divisions by powers of 2:

1 Select the highest power of 2 which is less than the base 10 number.
2 Divide the base 10 number by the highest power of 2 selected, noting the integral quotient (it will always be 1 in binary) and the remainder.
3 Divide the remainder by the next highest power of 2, noting the integral quotient and the remainder (in divisions other than the first, the integral quotient will always be 1 or 0 in binary).
4 Continue dividing the remainder until there is no remainder. Unlike the procedure of successive division by 2, the *most significant binary digit is determined first and the least significant last.*

The highest power of 2 less than 849 is 2^9 or 512. Successive lower powers of 2 are 256, 128, 64, 32, 16, 8, 4, 2, and 1.

Successive division of remainder by powers of 2	Remainder	Integral quotient and binary character
$849 \div 512$	337	1
$337 \div 256$	81	1
$81 \div 128$	81	0
$81 \div 64$	17	1
$17 \div 32$	17	0
$17 \div 16$	1	1
$1 \div 8$	1	0
$1 \div 4$	1	0
$1 \div 2$	1	0
$1 \div 1$	0	1
		Radix point .

Hence $849_{10} = 1101010001_2$.

Special Treatment in Converting Decimal Fractions

Some fractional values do not convert accurately to binary because a decimal fraction need not be a finite binary fraction.

Example 3   **Convert $9\frac{1}{2}$ percent, base 10, to base 2 to five binary places.**

1 $9\frac{1}{2}\% = 0.095$

2 Using the successive division of negative powers of 2, we have

$2^{-1} = \frac{1}{2} = 0.50$ $2^{-2} = 0.25$ $2^{-3} = 0.125$ $2^{-4} = 0.0625$

$2^{-5} = 0.03125$

Successive division of remainder by negative powers of 2	Remainder	Binary character
		Radix point .
0.095 ÷ .50	0.095	0
0.095 ÷ .25	0.095	0
0.095 ÷ .125	0.095	0
0.095 ÷ .0625	0.0325	1
0.0325 ÷ .03125	0.00125	1

Although 5 binary places were obtained, the decimal value of $.00011_2$ is:

. 0 0 0 1 1

$0.0625 + 0.03125 = 0.09375$

This discrepancy is solved in the computer through an application identified as *floating-point arithmetic.* Two fields are used in the computer, one for the mantissa, and one for the exponent. Floating-point arithmetic and computer adaptation is explained in connection with the programming portion of computer courses and will not be presented here.

Exercise A1.1

Convert the following binary numbers to base 10:

1 11011_2
2 101101_2
3 1111101.0111_2
4 10101.11_2

Convert the following decimal numbers to base 2:

5 6000_{10}
6 1268_{10}
7 525.25_{10}
8 $6\frac{1}{4}\%_{10}$

Base 8 (Octal) Number System

The octal system is a number system having a base of 8 and the 8 admissible characters of 0, 1, 2, 3, 4, 5, 6, and 7. This system can be converted to the decimal system and the decimal system to the octal system by using the same procedures as described for the binary system. The differences from the decimal and binary systems are (1) each digit position now has a value of 8 to the various powers of 8 in place of 10 to the various powers of 10, and 2 to the various powers of 2, respectively; and (2) there are 8 admissible characters instead of 10 and 2, respectively.

Example 4   **Convert 456_8 to base 10.**

1   A partial chart of powers of 8:

262,144	32,768	4,096	512	64	8	1	.	$\frac{1}{8}$	$\frac{1}{64}$	$\frac{1}{512}$
8^6	8^5	8^4	8^3	8^2	8^1	8^0		8^{-1}	8^{-2}	8^{-3}

2   Computation in base 10:

$$6 \times 8^0 = 6 \times 1 = 6$$
$$5 \times 8^1 = 5 \times 8 = 40$$
$$4 \times 8^2 = 4 \times 64 = \underline{256}$$
$$\text{Sum} = 302$$

3   Hence $456_8 = 302_{10}$

Example 5   **Convert 1268_{10} to base 8 using the procedure of successive division by 8.**

Successive division by 8	Integral quotient	Remainder and octal character
		Radix point .
$1,268 \div 8$	158	4
$158 \div 8$	19	6
$19 \div 8$	2	3
$2 \div 8$	0	2

Hence $1268_{10} = 2364_8$.

Exercise A1.1 (continued)

Convert the following octal numbers to base 10:

9 7541_8
10 1040_8
11 16.50_8
12 $125,413_8$

Convert the following decimal numbers to base 8:

13 6000_{10}
14 936_{10}
15 $.25_{10}$
16 21_{10}

Base 16 (Hexadecimal) Number System

The hexadecimal system is a number system having a base of 16 and 16 admissible characters. Since our popular decimal system has but 10 characters to indicate numbers, six additional characters must be devised. The extra characters have not been standardized, but one computer system at the present time employing the hexadecimal system uses the first six letters of our alphabet: A, B, C, D, E, and F. Thus the 16 admissible characters in this hexadecimal number system would be 0, 1, 2, 3, 4, 5, 6, 7, 8, 9, A, B, C, D, E, and F, where A is equivalent to 10 and F to 15.

   The same procedure described for the binary and octal number systems can be used to convert hexadecimal and decimal to hexadecimal. Each digit position now has a value of 16 to the various powers of 16 and there are 16 admissible characters.

Example 6   **Convert $8E20_{16}$ to base 10.**

   1   A partial chart of powers of 16:

1,050,176	65,536	4,096	256	16	1	.	$\frac{1}{16}$	$\frac{1}{256}$
16^5	16^4	16^3	16^2	16^1	16^0		16^{-1}	16^{-2}

   2   Computation in base 10:

$$\begin{aligned} 0 \times 1 &= & 0 \\ 2 \times 16 &= & 32 \\ E(14) \times 256 &= & 3\,584 \\ 8 \times 4096 &= & 32{,}768 \\ \text{Sum} &= & 36{,}384 \end{aligned}$$

   3   Hence $8E20_{16} = 36{,}384_{10}$

Example 7   **Convert $119{,}609_{10}$ to base 16 using the procedure of successive division by 16.**

Successive division by 16	Integral quotient	Remainder and hexadecimal character
		Radix point .
119,609 ÷ 16	7,475	9
7,475 ÷ 16	467	3
467 ÷ 16	29	3
29 ÷ 16	1	(13)D
1 ÷ 16	0	1

Hence $119{,}609_{10} = 1D339_{16}$.

   The procedure of successive division by the powers of 8 and 16 can also be used to convert decimal numbers to octal and hexadecimal respectively. Since the various powers of 8 and 16 are not usually retained in one's memory, the procedure of successive division by 8 and 16 is generally more convenient when conversion tables are not available.

Exercise A1.1 (continued)

Convert the following hexadecimal numbers to base 10:

17	100000_{16}
18	83_{16}
19	826_{16}
20	$5B341_{16}$

Convert the following decimal numbers to base 16:

21	$10,000_{10}$
22	51_{10}
23	$115,243_{10}$
24	$10,500,000_{10}$

Unit A1.2　　*Interrelationships Between Binary, Octal, and Hexadecimal Number Systems*

The interrelationships between the binary number system and the octal and hexadecimal systems are important in developing workable channels of communication between a human machine language programmer and the computer.

RELATIONSHIP BETWEEN BINARY AND OCTAL　The sum of the decimal values of the first, second, and third digit positions in *binary* is equal to the decimal value of the highest admissible octal character (the character 7). The equivalent decimal value of the first digit position in octal is then the product of:

$$7 \times 8^0 = 7 \times 1 = 7$$

Similarly, the equivalent decimal values of each successive octal digit position—and the sum of the decimal values of each successive set of *three* binary digit positions—is the product of 7 times the successive powers of 8. Thus:

										Radix point
Digit positions	9	8	7	6	5	4	3	2	1	.
Decimal values for binary	256	128	64	32	16	8	4	2	1	
Decimal sum of each set of 3 binary digits		448			56			7		
Decimal values of octal digit positions		$7 \times 8^2 = 448$			$7 \times 8^1 = 56$			$7 \times 8^0 = 7$		

One can therefore *represent* any set of three binary digits in octal by merely noting the sum of the decimal values of each set of 3 binary digits *as if* each such set was in the first, second, and third digit positions. Since we are concerned only with the decimal values of $2^0 = 1, 2^1 = 2$, and $2^2 = 4$, the sum of each triplet of binary digits can be readily ascertained.

Example 1   **Convert 101001111_2 to base 8.**

Radix
point

Binary number	1	0	1	0	0	1	1	1	1	$\cdot$
Powers of 2	256	128	64	32	16	8	4	2	1	

Sum of decimal
values of each
set of 3 binary
digits $\underbrace{\hspace{3cm}}$ $\underbrace{\hspace{3cm}}$ $\underbrace{\hspace{3cm}}$

$$\underline{\underline{320}} \quad + \quad \underline{\underline{8}} \quad + \quad \underline{\underline{7}} \quad \cdot = 335_{10}$$

Binary number $\qquad$ 101 $\qquad\qquad$ 001 $\qquad\qquad$ 111 $\cdot$

Sum of decimal
values *as if* each set
of 3 digits was in the
first, second, and
third digit positions $\qquad$ 5 $\qquad\qquad\qquad$ 1 $\qquad\qquad\quad$ 7 $\quad\cdot = 517_8$

Decimal values of
octal number $\qquad$ 320 $\qquad + \qquad$ 8 $\qquad + \qquad$ 7 $\quad\cdot = 335_{10}$

$\qquad\qquad\qquad$ (5×8^2) $\qquad$ (1×8^1) $\qquad$ (7×8^0)

RELATIONSHIPS BETWEEN BINARY AND HEXADECIMAL   The sum of the decimal values of the first, second, third, and fourth digit positions in binary is equal to the decimal value of the highest admissible character in *hexadecimal* (the character F or 15). The equivalent decimal value of the first digit position in hexadecimal is then the product of:

$$F \times 16^0 = 15 \times 1 = 15$$

The equivalent decimal values of each successive hexadecimal digit position—and the sum of the decimal values of each set of *four* binary digit positions—is the product of 15 times the successive powers of 16. Thus, a binary number can be converted to a hexadecimal number by following the same procedure as was described for conversion to an octal number with the one exception of using sets of four binary digits in place of three. And since we are concerned only with the decimal values of $2^0 = 1, 2^1 = 2, 2^2 = 4$, and $2^3 = 8$, the sum of each quadruplet of binary digits can be easily determined.

Example 2   **Convert 110010001111₂ to base 16.**

Radix
point

Binary number	1	1	0	0	1	0	0	0	1	1	1	1	·
Powers of 2	2,048	1,024	512	256	128	64	32	16	8	4	2	1	

Sum of decimal
  values of each
  set of 4 binary
  digits   3,072   +   128   +   15   = 3,215₁₀

Binary number   1100   1000   1111
Sum of decimal
  values *as if* each
  set of 4 digits was
  in the first, second,
  third, and fourth
  digit positions   12   8   15   = C8F₁₆
Decimal values of
  hexadecimal number   3,072   +   128   +   15   = 3,215₁₀
                        (12×16^2)   (8×16^1)   (15×16^0)

Conversion from Octal and Hexadecimal to Binary

The rules outlined above, when applied in reverse, can be used to convert to binary from octal or hexadecimal.

Example 3   **Convert 517₈ to a binary number.**

Assume that each *octal digit* represents the sum of the decimal values of a set of three binary digits occupying the first, second, and third binary digit positions. Convert such sum into the equivalent binary digits.

Radix point

Octal number   5   1   7   .
                                    ↓   ↓   ↓
Binary number   101   001   111   .
Hence $517_8 = 101001111_2$. (see Example 1.)

Example 4   **Convert C8F₁₆ to a binary number.**

Assume that each *hexadecimal digit* represents the sum of the decimal values of a set of four binary digits occupying the first, second, third, and fourth binary digit positions. Convert such sum into the equivalent binary digits.

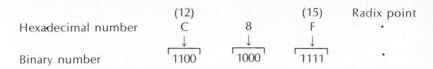

Hence $C8F_{16} = 110010001111_2$. (See Example 2.)

As can be observed from Examples 1 through 4 above, communication with a computer is considerably facilitated when the human machine language programmer can use an octal or hexadecimal number system to represent the long and cumbersome (for a human) binary numbers used by the computer.

Exercise A1.2

Convert the following binary digit numbers to (a) base 8 and (b) base 16:

1 111111111
2 101101101
3 100000001
4 10010011101

Convert the following numbers to base 2:

5 435_8
6 5421_{16}
7 4444_8
8 22222_{16}

Appendix 2

Customary Units; Square Root; Useful Formulas; Roman System

Unit A2.1   *Customary System of Measurements*

Linear Measure

12 inches (in.)	= 1 foot (ft)
3 feet	= 1 yard (yd)
$5\frac{1}{2}$ yards = $16\frac{1}{2}$ feet	= 1 rod
320 rods	= 1 mile
1760 yards	= 1 mile
5280 feet	= 1 mile

Surface Measure

144 square inches (sq in.)	= 1 square foot (sq ft)
9 square feet	= 1 square yard (sq yd)
$30\frac{1}{4}$ square yards = $272\frac{1}{4}$ square feet	= 1 square rod (sq rod)
160 square rods = 43,560 square feet	= 1 acre
640 acres	= 1 square mile (sq mile) or section (Sec)
36 sections (6 miles by 6 miles square)	= 1 township (T)

Cubic Measure

1728 cubic inches (cu in.)	= 1 cubic foot (cu ft)
27 cubic feet	= 1 cubic yard (cu yd)
128 cubic feet (4 by 4 by 8 ft)	= 1 cord (cd) of wood

Liquid Measure

4 gills (gi)	= 1 pint (pt)
2 pints	= 1 quart (qt)
4 quarts	= 1 gallon (gal)
$31\frac{1}{2}$ gallons	= 1 wine barrel (bbl)
231 cubic inches	= 1 gallon; wt. about 8 lb
1 cubic foot	= $7\frac{1}{2}$ gallons = $62\frac{1}{2}$ lb approx.

Dry Measure

2 pints (pt)	= 1 quart (qt)
8 quarts	= 1 peck (pk)
4 pecks	= 1 bushel (bu)
1 bushel	= 2150.42 cu in.
1 cubic foot	= 0.8 bushel approx.

Avoirdupois Weight

16 ounces (oz)	= 1 pound (lb)
100 pounds	= 1 hundredweight (cwt)
20 hundredweight = 2000 pounds	= 1 ton
2240 pounds	= 1 long ton

Measures of Time (see Unit 5.1)

Unit A2.2   *Roots*

The *root* of a given number is one of the *equal factors* of that given number. Restated, it is a number which multiplied by itself two or more times will produce the given number.

As you know (Unit 1.1), the term 6^2 means 6×6, or 6 to the second power, or 6 squared. This second power is obtained by using 6 twice as a factor, and $6 \times 6 = 36$. Thus 36 is the square of 6, or 6 to the second power, or 6^2.

The small 2 to the right of 6 (in 6^2) is called the *exponent*. It indicates the number of times the *base* 6 is to be used as a factor. Thus:

6^3 (6 to the third power or 6 cubed) $= 6 \times 6 \times 6 = 216$
3^4 (or 3 to the fourth power) $= 3 \times 3 \times 3 \times 3 \quad = 81$
2^5 (or 2 to the fifth power) $= 2 \times 2 \times 2 \times 2 \times 2 \ = 32$

The *radical sign* $\sqrt{}$ placed above a number indicates that the root of that number is to be extracted. The index of the root indicates the power (or number of times) of the number to be extracted. Thus:

$\sqrt[2]{}$, ordinarily written simply $\sqrt{}$, indicates that the square root is to be extracted (^{2} is the index of the root).

$\sqrt[3]{}$ indicates that the cube root is to be extracted (^{3} is the index of the root).

$\sqrt[4]{}$ indicates that the fourth root is to be extracted (^{4} is the index of the root).

Square Root

In certain types of measurements, it becomes necessary to find the powers or roots of numbers. Since roots to higher powers than square root are infrequently required in business calculations, this discussion will be confined to a method of extracting square roots.

METHOD OF EXTRACTING THE SQUARE ROOT OF A NUMBER   To understand better the method used to find square root, consider the following:

(a)	(b)	(c)	(d)
$1^2 = \underline{1}$	$10^2 = \underline{1\ 00}$	$100^2 = \underline{1\ 00\ 00}$	$0.1^2 \ = \underline{0.01}$
$3^2 = \underline{9}$	$15^2 = \underline{2\ 25}$	$250^2 = \underline{6\ 25\ 00}$	$0.5^2 \ = \underline{0.25}$
$4^2 = \underline{16}$	$25^2 = \underline{6\ 25}$	$800^2 = \underline{64\ 00\ 00}$	$0.25^2 = \underline{0.06\ 25}$
$8^2 = \underline{64}$	$80^2 = \underline{64\ 00}$	$930^2 = \underline{86\ 49\ 00}$	$2.5^2 \ = \underline{6.\ 25}$
$9^2 = \underline{81}$	$99^2 = \underline{98\ 01}$	$999^2 = \underline{99\ 80\ 01}$	$12.25^2 = \underline{1\ 50.\ 06\ 25}$

It is evident from the preceding that:

1   The square root of a one- or two-digit number is in units, that is, *one* place to the left of the decimal point.
2   The square root of a three- or four-digit number is in tens, that is, *two* places to the left of the decimal point.

3   The square root of a five- or six-digit number is in hundreds, that is, *three* places to the left of the decimal point.
4   The number of decimal places in the square root of numbers expressed in decimals may also be determined. The square root of numbers one or two places to the right of the decimal is in tenths; the square root of numbers three or four places to the right of the decimal is in hundredths; etc.

From the preceding, the reason for the following first step in extracting the square root of a number is apparent.

First step: Point off two digits each to left and right of the decimal point in the number the square root of which is to be found. Thus to find the square root of

$9 = \underline{9}$;	$\sqrt{9}$	will be in one digit
$144 = \underline{1}$ $\underline{44}$;	$\sqrt{144}$	will be in two digits
$1225 = \underline{12}$ $\underline{25}$;	$\sqrt{1225}$	will be in two digits
$50{,}625 = \underline{5}$ $\underline{06}$ $\underline{25}$;	$\sqrt{50{,}625}$	will be in three digits
$4914.1 = \underline{49}$ $\underline{14}$. $\underline{10}$;	$\sqrt{4914.1}$	will be in two digits and one decimal place
$27.5625 = \underline{27}$. $\underline{56}$ $\underline{25}$;	$\sqrt{27.5625}$	will be in one digit and two decimal places

The procedure used to extract square root is illustrated by the following examples:

Example 1   **Find the square root of 625.**

(a)	Point off from decimal	2 $5.$
(b)	Largest square contained in 6 (or 600)	$\sqrt{6\ \ 25.}$
(c)	2 squared $=$	$\underline{4}$
(d)	Subtract; bring down next grouping	$2\ 25$
(e)	2×2, annex $0 = 40 + 5 = 45 \times 5 =$	$\underline{2\ 25}$ $\left\{ \begin{array}{l}\text{40 is trial divisor;}\\ \text{see solution following}\end{array}\right.$
(f)	Remainder 0	0

Since there is no remainder, 25 is the square root of 625, a perfect square.

Proof: $25 \times 25 = 625$

Solution:

(a)   Point off in groups of two digits each way from decimal. Thus $625 = \underline{6}\ \underline{25}$ (the square will be in 2 digits).
(b)   Find the largest square contained in 6, the first grouping. ($2 \times 2 = 4$, the largest perfect square contained in 6.) The number is 2; place it in quotient.
(c)   Square the quotient and subtract from 6 ($6 - 4 = 2$).
(d)   Bring down the next group of two digits (25).
(e)[1]   Double the quotient so far obtained ($2 \times 2 = 4$). To 4 annex one zero:

[1]The actual process at this step is $20 \times 2 = 40$, for there are two groupings in the number 6 25, and the answer will be more than 20^2 (400) and less than 30^2 (900). The procedure of doubling the quotient obtained ($2 \times 2 = 4$) and simply annexing a zero to determine the trial divisor as is illustrated in the fifth step is recommended as easier and less apt to result in error.

40. Use this as a trial divisor. Thus $225 \div 40 = 5$. Add 5 to trial divisor $(40 + 5 = 45)$. Place 5 in quotient and multiply 45 by 5 ($45 \times 5 = 225$).

(f)   Subtract 225. Since there is no remainder, 625 is the perfect square of 25.

If the number 625 were not a perfect square, it would be necessary to annex two zeros at a time, and the process of solution would be continued until the desired degree of accuracy had been attained.

Example 2   **Find the square root of 276,297.4096 to hundredths.**

```
          5  2  5.  6  4
        √27 62 97. 40 96
          25
          ‾‾
          2 62
```

(a)   Point off

(b)   Nearest square (5^2) =

(c)   Subtract; bring down next grouping

(d) $5\underline{0} \times 2 = 100 + 2 = 102 \times 2 =$

(e)   Subtract; bring down next grouping

(f) $52\underline{0} \times 2 = 1040 + 5 = 1045 \times 5 =$

(g)   Subtract; bring down next grouping

(h) $525\underline{0} \times 2 = 10{,}500 + 6 = 10{,}506 \times 6 =$

(i)   Subtract; bring down next grouping

(j) $52{,}56\underline{0} \times 2 = 105{,}120 + 4 = 105{,}124 \times 4 =$

```
          2 04  (100 is trial divisor)
            58 97
            52 25  (1040 is trial divisor)
             6 72 40
             6 30 36  (10,500 is trial divisor)
               42 04 96
               42 04 96  (105,120 is trial divisor)
```

Since there is no remainder, 525.64 is the square root of 276,297.4096.

Proof: $525.64^2 = 276{,}297.4096$

Exercise A2.2   Square Root

Find the square root of the following to nearest hundredths:

1 345	**2** 610	**3** 7.03	**4** 9.80	**5** 1567
6 3046.25	**7** 748.967	**8** 91.7563	**9** 8297.6	**10** 45,678.329

Solve the following problems. *Note:* The square root of the square units of area will be the number of units of linear measure of each side of a square.

11   A square farm contains exactly 360 acres. What is the length of a side in yards? (Suggestion: Express the acreage in square yards before finding the square root.)

12   The floor of a square building contains exactly 31,152.25 sq ft. What is the length of each side of the floor in feet and inches?

13   A two-story square building contains exactly 121,032 sq ft of inside flooring. If the outer walls are 8 in. thick, what is the outside length of each side of the building in yards, feet, and inches?

14   A square field contains exactly 121 acres. What is the length of a side to nearest feet?

15 A square building lot contains exactly 60,616 sq ft. What is the length of a side in feet? (Find answer to nearest tenths.)

16 The floor of a dance pavilion contains exactly 30,925 sq ft. What is the length of each side of the dance floor in feet? (Find answer to nearest hundredths.)

17 A square field contains exactly 372 acres. What is the length of a side to nearest whole feet in rods, yards, and feet? (Suggestion: Express the acreage in square feet before extracting the square root.)

18 A farm in the shape of a square contains exactly 41 acres. What is the length of a side to nearest whole inches in rods, yards, feet, and inches?

19 A square exposition building contains exactly 89,888 sq ft of floor space on its two floors. What is the length of each side of each floor to nearest whole inches in rods, yards, feet, and inches?

TABLE A2.1 TABLE OF SQUARES AND SQUARE ROOTS OF THE NUMBERS 1 THROUGH 99

No.	Sq.	Sq. Root	No.	Sq.	Sq. Root	No.	Sq.	Sq. Root
1	1	1.000	34	1,156	5.831	67	4,489	8.185
2	4	1.414	35	1,225	5.916	68	4,624	8.246
3	9	1.732	36	1,296	6.000	69	4,761	8.306
4	16	2.000	37	1,369	6.082	70	4,900	8.366
5	25	2.236	38	1,444	6.164	71	5,041	8.426
6	36	2.449	39	1,521	6.245	72	5,184	8.485
7	49	2.645	40	1,600	6.324	73	5,329	8.544
8	64	2.828	41	1,681	6.403	74	5,476	8.602
9	81	3.000	42	1,764	6.480	75	5,625	8.660
10	100	3.162	43	1,849	6.557	76	5,776	8.717
11	121	3.316	44	1,936	6.633	77	5,929	8.775
12	144	3.464	45	2,025	6.708	78	6,084	8.831
13	169	3.605	46	2,116	6.782	79	6,241	8.888
14	196	3.741	47	2,209	6.855	80	6,400	8.944
15	225	3.873	48	2,304	6.928	81	6,561	9.000
16	256	4.000	49	2,401	7.000	82	6,724	9.055
17	289	4.123	50	2,500	7.071	83	6,889	9.110
18	324	4.242	51	2,601	7.141	84	7,056	9.165
19	361	4.358	52	2,704	7.211	85	7,225	9.219
20	400	4.472	53	2,809	7.280	86	7,396	9.273
21	441	4.582	54	2,916	7.348	87	7,569	9.327
22	484	4.690	55	3,025	7.416	88	7,744	9.380
23	529	4.795	56	3,136	7.483	89	7,921	9.434
24	576	4.899	57	3,249	7.549	90	8,100	9.486
25	625	5.000	58	3,364	7.615	91	8,281	9.539
26	676	5.099	59	3,481	7.681	92	8,464	9.591
27	729	5.196	60	3,600	7.746	93	8,649	9.643
28	784	5.291	61	3,721	7.810	94	8,836	9.695
29	841	5.385	62	3,844	7.874	95	9,025	9.746
30	900	5.477	63	3,969	7.937	96	9,216	9.798
31	961	5.567	64	4,096	8.000	97	9,409	9.848
32	1,024	5.656	65	4,225	8.062	98	9,604	9.899
33	1,089	5.744	66	4,356	8.124	99	9,801	9.949

Unit A2.3

Useful Formulas for
Work in Measurements

Numbers that represent counting of indivisible units are considered to be exact. Thus a classroom with 35 students and one teacher contains exactly 36 people. But numbers found in a table of measurement that represent divisible units of measurement are considered to be inexact or approximate numbers. If the width of a classroom is 24 ft, such a measurement means that the room is nearer 24 ft than it is to 23 or 25 ft in width. Of course, the width of the room could be expressed more exactly as 24 ft 3 in. which would mean that the width was more than 24 ft 2 in. but less than 24 ft 4 in.

Numbers in the tables of measurement become approximations since measurements without some error probably cannot be made. However, the smaller the unit of measure, the greater should be the degree of accuracy. For example (see Unit 3.5), the established length of the metric unit (meter) is only an extremely close approximation. As another example, $3\frac{1}{7}$ or $\frac{22}{7}$ is a commonly used approximation of π (pi), and π expressed to six digits, or 3.14159, though more accurate, is still an approximate number.

The formulas that follow are among those most useful in the linear measurement of plane surfaces and in the measurement of areas or volume. Many of these formulas may be helpful in personal as well as business or professional activities. Thus you may wish to find lengths, areas, and volumes (such as cubic feet) in your home or yard. Remember, however, not to expect your computations to be more precise than your least accurate unit of measure.

Linear Measure and Area of Plane Figures

Square

Perimeter, or $P = 4b$

$$b = \frac{P}{4}$$

Area, or $A = b^2$

$$b = \sqrt{A}$$

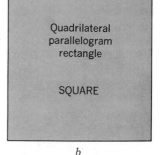

Quadrilateral
parallelogram
rectangle

SQUARE

b

FIGURE A2.1

Rectangle

Perimeter, or $P = 2b + 2h$
$$= 2(b + h)$$

$$b = \frac{P}{2} - h$$

$$h = \frac{P}{2} - b$$

Area, or $A = bh$

$$b = \frac{A}{h}$$

$$h = \frac{A}{b}$$

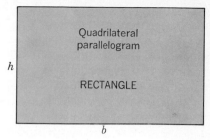

FIGURE A2.2

Rhombus

Perimeter, or $P = 4b$

$$b = \frac{P}{4}$$

Area, or $A = bh$

$$b = \frac{A}{h}$$

$$h = \frac{A}{b}$$

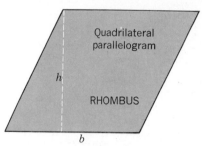

FIGURE A2.3

Rhomboid

Perimeter, or $P = 2b + 2a$
$$= 2(b + a)$$

$$b = \frac{P}{2} - a$$

$$a = \frac{P}{2} \quad b$$

Area, or $A = bh$

$$b = \frac{A}{h}$$

$$a = \frac{A}{b}$$

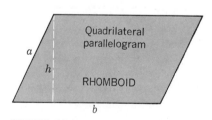

FIGURE A2.4

Trapezoid

Perimeter, or $P = a + b + c + b'$

Area, or $A = h\left(\frac{b + b'}{2}\right)$

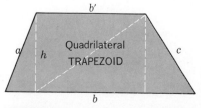

FIGURE A2.5

Triangle

Perimeter, or $P = a + b + c$

$$\text{Area, or } A = \frac{1}{2}bh = \frac{bh}{2}$$

$$b = A \div \frac{h}{2} = \frac{2A}{h}$$

$$h = A \div \frac{b}{2} = \frac{2A}{b}$$

Area may also be determined when the height is unknown if the length of the three sides is known.

If $\quad s = \dfrac{a + b + c}{2}$

then $A = \sqrt{s(s - a)(s - b)(s - c)}$

In a *right-angled* triangle, *the square of the hypotenuse is equal to the sum of the squares of the other two sides.* Thus if c symbolizes the hypotenuse:

$$c^2 = b^2 + h^2$$
$$\text{and } c = \sqrt{b^2 + h^2}$$
$$b = \sqrt{c^2 - h^2}$$
$$h = \sqrt{c^2 - b^2}$$

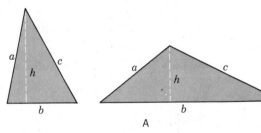

A

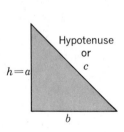 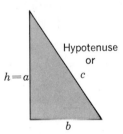

B

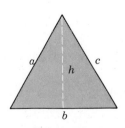 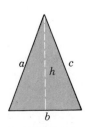

C

FIGURE A2.6

In an *isosceles* triangle, the height may be determined by first forming two equal right-angled triangles by means of a line bisecting the base to the vertex. Then

$$h^2 = c^2 - \left(\frac{b}{2}\right)^2 \qquad \text{or} \qquad h^2 = a^2 - \left(\frac{b}{2}\right)^2$$

$$h = \sqrt{c^2 - \left(\frac{b}{2}\right)^2} \qquad \text{and} \qquad h = \sqrt{a^2 - \left(\frac{b}{2}\right)^2}$$

Note also that in an isosceles triangle there are two equal sides; in an equilateral triangle, all three sides are equal.

Whenever a plane figure can be divided into triangles, squares, rectangles, parallelograms, or any combination of such figures, the area may be found if the needed dimensions of these figures are known or can be determined.

Circle

Circumference, or $C = \pi d$

$$= 2\pi r$$

$$d = \frac{C}{\pi}$$

$$r = \frac{C \div \pi}{2} = \frac{C}{2\pi}$$

Area, or $A = \pi r^2$

$$= \frac{\pi d^2}{4}$$

$$= \frac{Cr}{2} = \frac{\pi dr}{2}$$

$$r^2 = \frac{A}{\pi}$$

$$r = \sqrt{\frac{A}{\pi}}$$

$$d^2 = \frac{4A}{\pi}$$

$$d = \sqrt{\frac{4A}{\pi}}$$

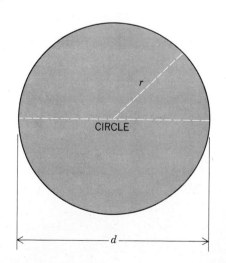

CIRCLE

d = diameter of circle = $2r$

r = radius = $\frac{1}{2}d = \frac{d}{2}$

FIGURE A2.7

Area and Volume of Solids

Cube

Area, or $A = 6b^2$
Volume, or $V = b^3$

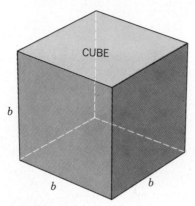

CUBE

b

b

b

FIGURE A2.8

Rectangular Solid

Lateral area $= 2(l + w) \times h$
$= 2h(l + w)$
Area of both bases $= 2lw$
Entire surface area $= 2h(l + w) + 2lw$
Volume, or $V = lwh$
or $=$ area of base $\times$ height

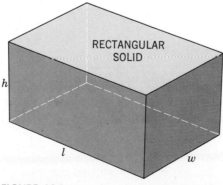

RECTANGULAR
SOLID

h

l

w

FIGURE A2.9

Sphere

Area, or A = circumference $\times$ diameter
$$= \pi d \times d = \pi d^2$$
$$= 4\pi r^2$$

Volume, or $V = \pi d^2 \times \frac{1}{3}r = \pi d^2 \times \frac{1}{6}d = \frac{\pi d^3}{6}$

$$= 4\pi r^2 \times \frac{1}{3}r = \frac{4\pi r^3}{3}$$

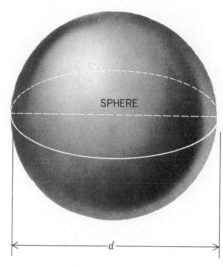

d = diameter of sphere = $2r$

r = radius = $\frac{1}{2}d = \frac{d}{2}$

FIGURE A2.10

Right Circular Cylinder

Lateral area = $\pi dh = 2\pi rh$

Area of both bases = $2\pi r^2$

Total area = $\pi dh + 2\pi r^2$

$$= 2\pi rh + 2\pi r^2$$

Volume, or $V = \pi r^2 h$

RIGHT CIRCULAR CYLINDER

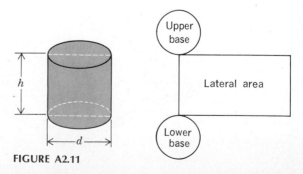

FIGURE A2.11

Regular Pyramid

Lateral area = $\frac{1}{2}$ perimeter of base × slant height
Area of base = as found for any plane polygon
    Total area = sum of lateral area and area of base
Volume, or $V = \frac{1}{3}$ area of base × height

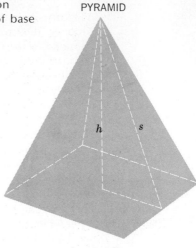

REGULAR
PYRAMID

h = height
s = slant height

FIGURE A2.12

Right Circular Cone

Lateral area = $\frac{1}{2}$ circumference × slant height
           = πr × slant height
Area of base = πr^2
    Total area = sum of lateral area and area of base
Volume, or $V = \frac{1}{3}$ area of base × height

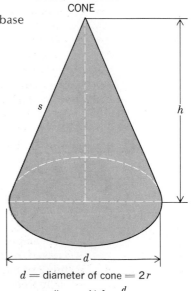

RIGHT CIRCULAR
CONE

d = diameter of cone = $2r$
r = radius = $\frac{1}{2}d = \frac{d}{2}$
s = slant height
h = height

FIGURE A2.13

Optional Exercise A2.3(A)   *Linear Measure*

Solve the following:

1   A factory site in the shape of a rectangle is 250 ft 0 in. long and 231 ft 6 in. wide. If it is to be fenced, (a) how many rods of fencing will be required? If the wire costs $2.25 per linear rod and only whole rods may be purchased, (b) what will be the cost of the wire?

2   It is necessary to put 78 rods 3 yd 2 ft of drain tile in a field at a cost of 80 cents per yard. If 3-ft tile is the shortest length that may be purchased (a) how many feet of drain tile must be bought and (b) what will be the total cost?

3   A field in the shape of a rhomboid has 450 ft 6 in. bases and 231 ft 9 in. sides. How many rods, yards, feet, and inches of fence would be required to enclose the field?

4   A room to be papered is 13 ft 6 in. wide and 14 ft 8 in. long. What minimum number of 18-in. strips of wallpaper will be required? (Disregard the length of the strips.)

5   A 2-ft wide sidewalk is placed 3 ft inside the boundaries of a 70-ft square backyard. Find (a) the exterior perimeter of the walk in feet and (b) the interior perimeter of the walk in feet.

6   The owner of a chicken ranch plans to fence a rectangular chicken yard 32 rods 8 ft 0 in. long and 15 rods 8 ft 6 in. wide. What will be the cost of a wire fence at 33 cents per linear foot?

7   A farmer plans to enclose a field of 160,000 sq yd with a fence. He considers fencing a 400 yd square, or a rectangular area 800 yd long and 200 yd wide. If the cost is 65 cents per linear yard, will the square or the rectangle be the cheaper, and by how much?

8   The edge of a roof in the shape of a rectangle is 33 ft 0 in. long and 21 ft 6 in. wide. Rain gutters 3 in. wide, costing 35 cents per linear foot, are to be placed on the outer edge of the roof. If only one side of the rain gutters may be used for the external face, find (a) the minimum number of feet of gutter required and (b) the total cost of the gutter.

9   A pine baseboard in a room is to be replaced with $\frac{1}{2}$ in.-thick hardwood baseboard finished on one side only (corner joints are angle cut for fit), costing 11 cents per linear foot. The room is of rectangular shape, 22 ft 3 in. long and 14 ft 9 in. wide. A 4-ft opening into the room does not require any baseboard. Find (a) the number of linear feet of baseboard required and (b) the cost.

Solve the following:

10   The triangular sail on a small boat is 6 yd 0 ft 9 in. by 5 yd 1 ft 7 in. by 3 yd 2 ft 5 in. What is the perimeter in feet and inches?

11   On the campus of a certain school is a triangular plot of ground enclosed by a paved roadway. The dimensions of this plot are 47 rods 4 yd 2 ft by 23 rods 2 yd 0 ft by 34 rods 3 yd 1 ft. If the outer edges are to be planted with elm trees on each corner and evenly spaced on each side but not to exceed 23 ft apart, what is the minimum number of trees required?

12   In an airplane race over a triangular course of 200 miles by 273 miles by 325 miles, the winner covered the distance in 3 hr 45 min. What was his average speed in miles per hour? (To nearest tenths.)

13   The winner of a sailboat race covered the first leg of a triangular course in 1 hr 45 min, averaging 9.50 knots; on the next leg he averaged 8.75 knots for 1 hr 30 min; and on the return leg he averaged 10.50 knots for 1 hr 50 min. If a knot is a speed equal to 1 nautical mile per hour and if a nautical mile is equivalent to approximately 1.15 common miles, how long was the course in common miles? (To nearest hundredths.)

14   A pressure tank for a water system has an external radius of 18 in. What is the external circumference in feet? (Let $\pi = 3.1416$.)

15   A water main is made of iron pipe $\frac{1}{2}$ in. thick, having an inside diameter of 12 in. What is the circumference of the exterior in inches? (Let $\pi = 3.1416$.)

16   A silo on a farm has an outside diameter of 14 ft 0 in. The walls are built of concrete 12 in. thick. What are (a) the exterior and (b) interior circumferences in feet and inches (to nearest inches)? (Let $\pi = 3\frac{1}{7}$.)

17   The wheel of an automobile has a tire 6.25-16 or 28.5 in. in diameter. About how many revolutions does this wheel make in traveling 5 miles? (Let $\pi = 3\frac{1}{7}$.)

Optional Exercise A2.3(B)   Area of Plane Figures

Solve the following:

1   At $45 per acre, find (a) the number of acres to nearest thousandths and (b) the total cost of a rectangular field 370 rods long and 150 rods wide.

2   The surface of the face of a brick measures 4 by 8 in. Find the cost of the bricks required to pave a rectangular cellar floor 34 ft 0 in. by 18 ft 8 in., at $45 per M (thousand) brick. (Assume bricks to be laid without joining mortar.)

3   A rectangular field is 796 rods long and has an area of 9,150,020 sq yd. Find the width in feet.

4   A painting hanging in a prominent art gallery has an area of 3960 sq in. If one dimension is 4 ft 6 in., what is the other dimension in feet and inches?

5   A triangular piece of land has a frontage of 150 ft. If the area is 9000 sq ft, what is the depth in feet?

6   If 90 ft is the depth of a triangular piece of land and its area is 13,500 sq ft, what is the length of the frontage in feet?

7   A triangular garden plot has sides of 35, 17, and 22 ft. What is the area to nearest square feet?

8   A house stands 41 ft high. About how long in feet and inches must a ladder be if it is to reach approximately 1 ft above the house and the base of the ladder is 10 ft away from the house? (To nearest inches.)

9   A electric-light pole 38 ft high is to be braced by a wire running from 3 ft below the top to an anchor 22 ft from the base of the pole. Allowing 3 ft for fastening the wire at the top and 2 ft at the bottom, how many feet and inches of wire are necessary? (To nearest inches.)

10   A summer cabin in the mountains is to be 16 by 32 ft, and the height of the ridge to run lengthwise is to be 4 ft above the plate. How long in feet and inches must a rafter be? (To nearest inches.)

Solve the following:

11 A triangular garden plot is 15 ft 7 in. on each side. What is its area to nearest square feet?

12 A rectangular-shaped county is 15 miles 300 rods 4 yd 2 ft wide and 30 miles long. Find the area to nearest tenths of square miles.

13 A ranch in the shape of a rectangle is exactly 2 miles wide and 3 miles 15 rods long. Find the area in acres.

14 A city park in the shape of a triangle extends 330 ft on one side, 264 ft on the second side, and 198 ft on the third side. Find the area in square rods.

15 A three-story factory is built on a lot of the dimensions and shape of a trapezoid, as illustrated by Figure A2.14. Find (a) area of each floor in square feet and (b) total area of the building in square yards.

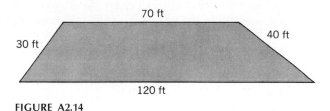

FIGURE A2.14

16 The floor of a circular tower is 90 ft in diameter. What will it cost to pave at 42 cents per sq yd or fraction thereof? (Let $\pi = 3.1416$.)

17 A circular stage is to be covered with hardwood flooring. If the circumference is 235.62 ft, what will be the cost at 28 cents per sq ft or fraction thereof? (Let $\pi = 3.1416$.)

18 The radius of a roller-skating rink is 62 ft 6 in. What is the surface area in square rods to nearest hundredths? (Let $\pi = 3.1416$.)

19 The flat top of a large cylindrical water tank is to be repainted. If two coats are necessary, how many gallons of paint must be purchased if the diameter is 80 ft and it is estimated 1 gal of paint will cover 450 sq ft? (Let $\pi = 3\frac{1}{7}$. Assume that only whole gallons are purchased.)

20 A walk 3 ft wide encloses a circular flower garden 54 ft in diameter. Find the area of the walk to the nearest square yard. (Let $\pi = 3\frac{1}{7}$.)

Optional Exercise A2.3(C)   Area and Volume of Solids

Solve the following:

1 A swimming pool is 60 ft long, 20 ft wide, and 8 ft deep. (a) How many cubic feet of water will it hold? (b) How many gallons?

2 A grain elevator is 125 by 150 by 75 ft high. (a) How many cubic feet of grain will it hold? (b) cubic yards? (c) bushels? (Assume that 1 cu ft = 0.8 bu.)

3 The excavation for the foundation of a building is to be 65 ft long, 27 ft wide, and 9 ft deep. (a) How many cubic feet of ground must be removed? (b) cubic yards? (c) What will it cost at $2.05 per cu yd?

4 Wood was stacked in a pile 16 ft wide, 24 ft high, and 168 ft long. (a) What was the cubic contents in feet? (b) in cubic yards? (c) in cords?

5 A cloud burst deposited $2\frac{3}{4}$ in. of rain on a field of 7 acres. (a) What was the volume of the water in cubic feet and (b) the weight in pounds?

6 A wagon bed is 5 ft wide and 15 ft long. How many inches high must it be to hold 210 bu of wheat? (Assume that 1 cu ft = 0.8 bu.)

7 The concrete foundation walls for a building are to have external measurements of 53 by 22 ft. If the walls are 1 ft 6 in. thick and 7 ft deep, find (a) the number of cubic yards of concrete required and (b) the cost at $4.25 per cu yd.

8 A street 960 ft long and 40 ft wide is to be paved with concrete to a depth of 6 in. (a) How many cubic yards of concrete will be used? (b) What will it cost at $5.50 per cu yd? (Assume a fraction of a cubic yard to cost the same as an entire cubic yard.)

9 A concrete driveway 12 ft wide, 4 in. thick, and 96 ft long is to be built from the street to the garage. (a) How many cubic feet of concrete will be required? (b) cubic yards? (c) What will it cost at $8.25 per cu yd? (Assume a fraction of a cubic yard to cost the same as an entire cubic yard.) (d) What is the cost to nearest cents per square foot of surface area?

10 A room containing 102 cu yd of space is 27 ft long and 12 ft wide. (a) Find the height of the walls in feet and inches and (b) the surface area of the walls in square feet.

11 A rectangular ice-skating rink measures 150 by 200 ft. Water $\frac{1}{4}$ in. deep is used each day to form new ice. The rink is open 365 days per year. 100 cu ft of water costs 18 cents. (a) What is the volume of water in cubic feet used per day? (b) per year? (c) What is the total weight in pounds of water used each year? (d) What is the average cost per day? (e) per year?

Solve the following:

12 The radius of the earth is approximately 4000 miles. (a) To nearest thousands, how many square miles are there on its surface? (b) To nearest hundreds of thousands, how many cubic miles of material are there in the earth? (Let $\pi = 3\frac{1}{7}$.)

13 A spherical steel shell has an outer diameter of 11 ft and an inner diameter of 10 ft. To nearest units, find (a) the number of square feet in the outer surface, (b) the weight of the water in pounds which could be contained within the spherical shell, and (c) the cubic feet of steel necessary to build such a spherical shell. (Let $\pi = 3.1416$.)

14 The surface area of a sphere is 180,956.16 sq in. Find (a) the diameter in inches and (b) the volume in cubic inches. (Let $\pi = 3.1416$.)

15 A service-station owner is installing new equipment. He has replaced an underground cylindrical gas tank with a new one having outside dimensions of 5 ft 10 in. in diameter and 12 ft 6 in. in length. Find the total exterior area to nearest square feet. (Let $\pi = 3\frac{1}{7}$.)

16 A gasoline truck carries a tank with inside measurements of 5 ft in diameter and 14 ft in length. (a) How many cubic feet does it contain? (b) How many gallons of gasoline will it hold? (Let $\pi = 3\frac{1}{7}$.)

17 A silo stands 63 ft high (inside measurement) and 22 ft in diameter

(outside measurement). The walls are 1 ft thick. Find (a) the volume of the interior in cubic feet and (b) the number of bushels of ensilage it will hold. (Let $\pi = 3\frac{1}{7}$ and 1 cu ft = 0.8 bu.)

18   A grain elevator has seven cylindrical storage bins. The inside dimensions of each bin are 25 ft in diameter and 46 ft in height. A level bushel of grain contains 2,150.42 cu in. (a) What is the volume of the elevator in cubic feet? (b) in cubic inches? (c) How many whole level bushels will it hold? (Let $\pi = 3\frac{1}{7}$.)

19   A church spire is in the shape of a regular square pyramid. If each side of the base is 8 ft and the height is 20 ft, (a) to nearest square feet, how much roofing does it require, and (b) how many cubic feet of space are there within the spire? (Do not consider thickness of the roof.)

20   A regular square pyramid has a base of 5 ft on each side, and the slant height is 16 ft. Find (a) the lateral area in square feet and (b) the volume to nearest cubic feet.

21   A monument of solid concrete is in the shape of a right circular cone. The radius of the base is 3 ft 6 in. and the height is 15 ft. Find (a) the lateral area in square feet and (b) the number of cubic feet of concrete in the monument. (Let $\pi = 3\frac{1}{7}$.)

22   A right circular cone is 6 in. in diameter at the base and has a slant height of 11 in. Find (a) the lateral area to nearest square inches and (b) the volume to nearest cubic inches. (Let $\pi = 3\frac{1}{7}$.)

Unit A2.4   The Roman System

The ancient Roman expression of numbers is still in occasional use. Watches, clocks, chapters in books, volume numbers, headings of outlines, cornerstones of buildings, the construction dates of bridges, etc., television and motion-picture productions, and various commemorative events are often designated by the Roman system of notation.

The basis for this system is seven numbers (capital letters) and their values, which are as follows:

I	V	X	L	C	D	M
1	5	10	50	100	500	1000

A line or bar placed above any of these numbers or any combination of them multiplies the value by 1000. Thus:

$$X = 10 \qquad \overline{X} = 10{,}000 \qquad \overline{\overline{X}} = 10{,}000{,}000$$

Repetition of the number repeats the value of the number. Thus:

$$XX = 20 \qquad CCC = 300 \qquad MM = 2000$$

The value of the numbers *following* one of greater value is added to the value of the greater. Thus:

$$VI = 5 + 1 = 6 \qquad CXX = 100 + 10 + 10 = 120$$

$$MCCC = 1000 + 100 + 100 + 100 = 1300$$

The value of a single number *preceding* one of greater value is deducted from the value of the greater. Thus:

$$IV = 5 - 1 = 4 \qquad XC = 100 - 10 = 90$$

$$CM = 1000 - 100 = 900$$

Take special note that the single numbers that may be deducted from the immediately following number of greater value are limited to the following instances: I (1) may be deducted only from V (5) or X (10); X (10) may be deducted only from L (50) or C (100); and C (100) may be deducted only from D (500) or M (1000). The Roman numbers V (5), L (50), D (500), and M (1000) are not used to indicate subtraction.

Thus IX may be used to indicate 9, but IC may not be used to indicate 99; XL may be used to indicate 40, but XD may not be used to indicate 490; VL may not be used to indicate 45, VC may not be used to indicate 95, LD may not be used to indicate 450, etc.

Hence, we have the following order of procedure: First, write the thousands; second, write the hundreds; third, write the tens; and fourth and finally, write the units.

The equivalent of the Arabic numbers 1 to 10 are written in Roman numbers as follows:

1 is I	6 is VI
2 is II	7 is VII
3 is III (never as IIV)	8 is VIII (never as IIX)
4 is IIII or preferably IV	9 is VIIII or preferably IX
5 is V	10 is X

The following procedure is recommended for writing Arabic numbers in Roman numbers:

1 Counting from right to left, separate the Arabic numbers into groups of three digits.
2 Write the Roman number equivalents from left to right and complete each group before beginning the next grouping:
   a Write the thousands (0000).
   b Write the hundreds (000).
   c Write the tens (00).
   d Write the units (0).
3 If a grouping represents the number of thousands, place a line ($\overline{000}$) over the Roman numbers. This multiplies the value of the grouping by 1000.
4 If a grouping represents the number of millions (thousand thousands), place two lines ($\overline{\overline{000}}$) *over* the Roman numbers. This multiplies the value of the grouping by 1 million.

Examples **Write in Roman numbers (a) the Arabic number 486, (b) the Arabic number 29,502, and (c) the Arabic number 205,684,920.**

(a) *Steps* **1** 400 is CD
           2 80 is LXXX
           3 6 is VI

The Roman numbers for 486 are CDLXXXVI

(b) *Steps* **1** 20 is XX
           2 9 is IX
           3 $\overline{\text{XXIX}}$ is 29
           4 $\overline{\text{XXIX}}$ is 29,000
           5 500 is D
           6 2 is II
           7 DII is 502

The Roman numbers for 29,502 are $\overline{\text{XXIX}}$DII

(c) *Steps* **1** 200 is CC
           2 5 is V
           3 $\overline{\overline{\text{CCV}}}$ is 205
           4 $\overline{\overline{\text{CCV}}}$ is 205,000,000
           5 600 is DC
           6 80 is LXXX
           7 4 is IV
           8 DCLXXXIV is 684
           9 $\overline{\text{DCLXXXIV}}$ is 684,000
           10 900 is CM
           11 20 is XX
           12 CMXX is 920

The Roman numbers for 205,684,920 are $\overline{\overline{\text{CCV}}}$DCLXXXIVCMXX

Optional Exercise A2.4 *Roman System of Notation*

Write the following as Arabic numbers:

1	$\overline{\overline{\text{XVI}}}$	**2**	CDXCII
3	$\overline{\text{MCM}}$	**4**	DCLXXXVIII
5	$\overline{\text{MCCXXVI}}$	**6**	MMDCXV
7	$\overline{\text{CCMIX}}$	**8**	CDVI
9	CCXLVII	**10**	MDCLIII

Write the following as Roman numbers:

11	258	**12**	688
13	949	**14**	1890
15	1,000,625	**16**	34
17	1141	**18**	1946
19	1492	**20**	43,500,004

Answers to Odd-Numbered Problems

EXERCISE 1.1

1 (a) 800,000
  (b) 40,030
  (c) 6.4
  (d) 2000.051
  (e) 900,000.7003
  (f) 60,708.0004
3 Five hundred six and twelve hundredths dollars.
5 Forty-eight and three and two-sevenths hundredths.
7 Nine hundred forty-three.
9 Twelve and seven hundred eighty-five thousandths.
11 38.00 5/6
13 3,000,000.2
15 1300.042
17 19.0269
19 2200–2700
21 225–275
23 105–130
25 0.22
27 7.09
29 0.3
31 76.6
33 13,000
35 3,401,000
37 8,678,100
39 400
41 306,760
43 481,510
45 3
47 5721

EXERCISE 1.2

1 9,488,866
3 17,545.0928
5 5955.97
7 19,681.8461
9 433.5239 (check number 2)
11 3678.083 (check number 8)

13 $49,490
15 4031.72 lb
17 $21.097

EXERCISE 1.3

1 66
3 12
5 18
7 39
9 20
11 746
13 68.096
15 171.79
17 2.528339
19 334.8781
21 451.167
23 5114.773
25 .841
27 903.0854
29 1017.916989
31 25,073.89
33 3782.295
35 543,193.48
37 4778.1917
39 446,681.30
41 7817.8678
43 496,460.81
45 530.8714
47 $212.28
49 $53.64
51 9133 ft

EXERCISE 1.4

1 1,885,000
3 524,700,000
5 70,858,800
7 1.43507
9 .363506
11 86
13 .321
15 8524.1

17 60,000 (multiply by 100, divide by 4; or divide by 4, multiply by 100)

19 131,500 (multiply by 1000, divide by 4; or divide by 4, multiply by 1000)

21 110.4138 (check number 0)

23 1521.68 (check number 5)

25 27,030 gal

27 521.64 common miles

29 $1240.80

EXERCISE 1.5

1 5445

3 13.33 1/3

5 94.92 1228/2541

7 .847

9 .8143

11 67,011

13 139.4 (divide by 100, multiply by 4; or multiply by 4, divide by 100)

15 .944 (divide by 100, multiply by 2; or multiply by 2, divide by 100)

17 4764. remainder 15 (check number 3)

19 431. remainder 315 (check number 6)

21 650

23 $43,750

25 274

EXERCISE 1.6

1   2   5   11

3   2   5   7

5   3   5   7

7   None.

9   2

11 4

13 4   6   8   9   10

15 6   9

17 None.

19 4   6   8

21 None.

23 None.

25 2   4   7   8

27 2   4   5   8   10

29 2   3   6   7   9   11

31 2 14/87

33 67 5/7

35 89 2/51

37 129 3/38

39 13 7/9

EXERCISE 1.7

1   966

3   90

5   60,060

7   2394

9   240

11 216

13 2 37/49

15 1539

17 202 1/2

19 70

21 100

EXERCISE 2.1

1   23/44

3   1 4/9

5   2 19/20

7   15 2/21

9   9/20

11 1 5/56

13 4 83/120

15 18 3/10

17 7/24

19 43/72

21 8 1/2

23 43 7/45

25 1 65/88

27 1 229/336

29 2 479/840

31 5 41/48

33 14 117/140

35 194 7/15

37 89 167/252

39 34 5/8

41 53 13/16

43 5 11/12

45 54 5/8

47 (a) 308/693

    (b) 252/693

    (c) 198/693

49 20 15/128

EXERCISE 2.2

1   2/15

3   1 27/28

5   1/14

7   23/240

9   5/12
11 7/24
13 0
15 5
17 23.3
19 $2.28
21 22
23 11
25 19 18/23
27 48 4/9
29 45 7/9
31 24 1/3
33 12 2/9
35 42 1/15
37 3 1/8
39 16 43/45
41 16
43 55 1/6
45 230 2/39
47 13 7/9
49 5/16
51 4 3/8
53 3 79/120
55 12 13/24
57 21 27/32
59 59/210

EXERCISE 2.3

1   1/3
3   1/2
5   4/15
7   5/34
9   91/209
11 2 1/22
13 6
15 21/32
17 3 1/3
19 190 2/3
21 352 2/3
23 163 6/13
25 4 14/15
27 15 1/5
29 42 7/36
31 6537 5/12
33 1680
35 2030 2/5
37 2960
39 1975 10/11
41 2825 10/77

43 4945 11/102
45 29,365 8/63
47 791
49 5312 1/2
51 161 7/48
53 13 1/8
55 502 9/10
57 204
59 $506.60

EXERCISE 2.4

1   72
3   9
5   2/77
7   11/108
9   9/10
11 45/143
13 3 1/45
15 1 4/15
17 28/153
19 2 1/4
21 21/34
23 3 83/147
25 144
27 5/144
29 1 1/2
31 5 1/7
33 4 13/18
35 178/205
37 72
39 1/27
41 21/187
43 5 7/25
45 1 17/40
47 308/549
49 731 3/7
51 14 pieces; remaining length 3/4 in.
53 $42,000
55 8 3/4
57 27
59 $450

EXERCISE 2.5

1   19 3/13
3   29/900
5   1 3/53
7   2340
9   5325

11 1500
13 143.6
15 32 11/12 or 32.9167
17 $4506

EXERCISE 2.6

1 21/25
3 1/150
5 9 89/120
7 4 409/4000
9 1/275
11 3 7/45
13 .3750
15 .6923
17 1.6094
19 1.5040
21 1.2667
23 6.8462
25 $0.\dot{3}$
27 $0.42857\dot{1}$
29 $0.17\dot{3}$
31 $2.99\dot{3}$
33 4/9
35 1/9
37 4/11
39 7/9
41 6 7/15
43 1 13/180
45 19/550
47 6 1/75

EXERCISE 3.1

1 150
3 2700
5 80
7 1.31
9 2600
11 1100
13 80
15 5.76
17 30.24
19 340.00
21 288
23 16.92
25 1601.60
27 1.73
29 40,000
31 $200
33 $0.48

EXERCISE 3.2

1 240
3 31 4/7
5 8 4/27
7 42 2/5
9 50 5/8
11 23 16/27
13 (a) 32
  (b) 36
  (c) 8
15 (a) 925
  (b) 1110
  (c) 9102
17 (a) $25
  (b) $2.50
  (c) $52.50
19 198
21 24 16/25
23 88.2
25 $698.75
27 (a) $156,816
  (b) $93,456
29 $1251.25

EXERCISE 3.3

1 43 1/5
3 1 1/3
5 4 4/5
7 9 1/2
9 14
11 2
13 130
15 8 3/4
17 504
19 37
21 540
23 $107.50

EXERCISE 3.4

1 7/1
3 4/1
5 4/25
7 7/12
9 157/258
11 3/8 = 24/64
13 4/1 = 16/4
15 60/40 = $7\frac{1}{2}$/5
17 75
19 15.20

21	56
23	25 1/2
25	400
27	$3777.78
29	35
31	225.29 miles
33	6 2/3
35	W, $36,000; X, $40,000; Y, $30,000; Z, $10,000

EXERCISE 3.5

1	1875
3	6470
5	.75
7	67,800
9	1,285,000
11	55.93
13	2.48
15	18.59
17	353.15
19	69.16
21	25.4
23	81.65
25	157.48
27	111.43
29	2.36
31	193 cm; 93 kg
33	Dock extends past the liner 2 ft or .6 m.
35	George by 79.9 ml or 2.7 oz.

EXERCISE 3.6

1	12.5 m³	
3	(a)	235.64
	(b)	1968.74
	(c)	.33
5	(a)	343 064 cm²
	(b)	$110.81
7	$62.18	
9	(a)	$16
	(b)	$0.016
	(c)	$30.58
	(d)	$14.52
	(e)	$0.73

11

Ingredients	Customary Units	Metric Units
Eggs	15	15
Sugar	3 1/3 c	830 ml
Melted butter	1 2/3 c	415 ml
Salt	2 1/2 t	12.5 ml
Corn syrup	3 3/4 c	940 ml
Pecan halves	5 c	1250 ml

EXERCISE 4.1

	Fraction	Decimal	Percent
1	—	.125	12.5%
3	36/100	.36	—
5	7/10	—	70%
7	—	1.125	112.5%
9	1/600	.00167	—
11	1 7/8	—	187.5%
13	11/16 less by 1/16		
15	55% less by 3.3%		
17	66 2/3%		
19	12 1/2%		
21	41 2/3%		
23	18 3/4%		
25	28 4/7%		

EXERCISE 4.2

(The percentage model should indicate the following derived answers.)

1	P	98.4
3	B	2500
5	r	6%
7	P	2.1
9	r	9%
11	B	220

EXERCISE 4.3

	Calculation Model	Derived Answers			
		B	P	r	A
1	Amount		40		2040
3	Amount	70.9		21.58	
5	Amount	4			4.48
7	Amount	300	15		
9	Amount		40	5	
11	Amount			5.5	7.9125
		B	P	r	D
13	Difference		264		
15	Difference			22	15,405
17	Difference	150	12		
19	Difference		14.49	21	
21	Difference	425			403.75
23	Difference	1400		8	
		B	P	r	A	A%
25	Amount				840	105
27	Amount	325.4		5.3		105.3
29	Amount	35,000			16,000	128

Calculation Model	Derived Answers				
	B	P	r	A	A%
31 Amount		5.61	6	99.11	
33 Amount	133		1900		2000
35 Amount	18,000	4950	27.5		
37 Amount	400	60			115
39 Amount	1200			1260	105
	B	P	r	D	D%
41 Difference				307.2	96
43 Difference	600		9		91
45 Difference		3150		11,850	79
47 Difference		280	14	1720	
49 Difference		336	24		76
51 Difference	897.5	35.9	4		
53 Difference	5000	950			81
55 Difference	73.75			47.20	64

EXERCISE 4.4

	Calculation Model Used	Answer
1	Percentage Model	460
3	Percentage Model	480
5	Amount Model	.50
7	Amount Model	92
9	Amount Model	6800
11	Amount Model	.20
13	Difference Model	101.4
15	Difference Model	4200
17	Difference Model	.167

EXERCISE 4.5

1   $68,750
3   $29
5   Gain of $200
7   Sales, $227.50; profit margin, $162.50
9   $200
11   $85,500
13   $90,000
15   1136.4 grams

EXERCISE 5.1

1   203 days
3   213 days
5   146 days
7   1155 days
9   954 days
11   1039 days

13   90 days
15   304 days
17   133 days
19   184 days
21   149 days
23   84 days
25   October 8
27   July 19
29   9/15
31   February 2
33   January 11
35   March 30
37   June 15
39   June 3
41   January 20

EXERCISE 5.2

1   $50
3   $285.60
5   $24.75
7   $56
9   $35
11   $200
13   $12.60
15   $285.78
17   $246.58
19   $26.40
21   $5.20
23   $13
25   $80
27   $64.17
29   $210
31   $99
33   $8.28
35   $81.51
37   $126.94
39   $25.90
41   (a) $5112.50
      (b) $5115.00
43   $542.58 principal, $42.58 interest
45   $3512.62

EXERCISE 5.3

1   $1.56
3   $3.12
5   $0.70
7   $1.84
9   $32.60
11   $12.60

13	$2.44
15	$0.72
17	$5.39
19	$17.04
21	$1.40
23	$1.70
25	$0.60
27	$5.69
29	$8.03
31	$34.28
33	$0.40
35	$0.35
37	$10.35
39	$51.25
41	$20.34
43	$16.50
45	$7.82
47	$8.34
49	$2.71
51	$6.30
53	$6.47
55	$9.26
57	$197.10
59	$9.71
61	(a) $58.72
	(b) $2915.52
63	(a) $1584.60
	(b) $47,184.60
65	(a) $21.48
	(b) $665.88
67	(a) $1204.17
	(b) $11,204.17
69	(a) $64.80
	(b) $195.20

EXERCISE 5.4

1	120 days
3	180 days
5	120 days
7	300 days
9	6 1/2%
11	7%
13	10%
15	(a) $625
	(b) $643.75
17	(a) $2189.34
	(b) $2309.51
19	$750.13 (or $750.00)
21	$800

23	(a) $354.54
	(b) $13.29
25	(a) $6208.20
	(b) $34.49
27	$2500

EXERCISE 6.1

1	1.25%
3	6%
5	.75%
7	.0222%
9	20
11	43
13	3635
15	$1783.14
17	$4893.06
19	$2220.59
21	$3498.25
23	$61,881.19
25	$3281.03
27	Blue Lake Savings (effective annual rate, 8.24%).
29	$100,288.45

EXERCISE 6.2

1	$1107.35
3	$1380.33
5	$312.43
7	$271.57
9	Between 4% and 6%.
11	Between 4% and 5%.
13	Between 7 and 7 1/4 years.
15	Between 24 and 25 years.
17	7.94%
19	4.82%
21	5.8 years
23	24.5 years
25	11 years
27	16% $m = 1$
29	7.53%

EXERCISE 6.3

1	$11,331.09
3	$66,753
5	$3756.45
7	$14,869.99
9	$58,153.19

11 $8329.81
13 $3850.88
15 $97,189.48
17 $53,946.93
19 $16,368.40

EXERCISE 6.4

1   $3360.86
3   $4077.10
5   $127,833.56
7   $20,936.51
9   $1974.85
11 $17,615.46
13 $500.08
15 First offer, $3655.42; second offer, $3645.29
17 $2508.03
19 $17,443.61

EXERCISE 6.5

1   $263.33
3   24
5   16%
7   24 regular payments plus 1 smaller payment.
9   5.41%
11 $525.10
13 6%
15 4.86%
17 $100.83
19 29 months
21 $680.69

EXERCISE 6.6

1   Proposal A (16% annual cost rate vs. 20% for proposal B).
3   $1241.17
5   $611.41
7   $579.56

EXERCISE 7.1

1   216
3   16.7%
5   21%
7   $6.50

EXERCISE 7.2

1   $61.25
3   $10.13
5   $17.09
7   Amount to be financed $600; APR 11.25%.
9   Finance charge $258.08; APR 23%.
11 Number of payments 60; APR 10%.
13 Amount of payment $159.59; APR 11%.
15 Finance charge $20,419; amount of payment $95.06.
17 12.33%
19 24.91%
21 (a) $96,016
    (b) $44,225
    (c) 10.25%
    (d) $149,716
23 (a) $222
    (b) $226.83
25 (a) $929.98
    (b) $270.02
    (c) 25.78%

EXERCISE 7.3

1   (a): (1) $7.45,   (2) $179.91
    (b): (1) $7.83,   (2) $179.53
3   (a): (1) $7.67,   (2) $317.26
    (b): (1) $7.96,   (2) $316.97
5   (a): (1) $91.28,   (2) $1555.84
    (b): (1) $102.27, (2) $1544.85
7   $1544.87
9   $2303.37
11 $46,399.27
13 $2311.21
15 $979.11
17 23.54%
19 37.8%
21 7.5%
23 27.8%
25 25%
27 25%

EXERCISE 7.4

1   a
3   a
5   b
7   Should not accept offer.
9   Credit source A.

EXERCISE 8.1

1 (a) $12.20 ∧ 9 = 109.
   (b) $4.20
   (c) $114.00
3 $70.40
5 $883.20
7 $820.46
9 (a) $233.12
   (b) $988.69
   (c) $1221.81
11 $948.37
13 $6.01

EXERCISE 8.2

1 (a) $250.00
   (b) $131.25
   (c) $381.25
3 (a) $126.00
   (b) $12.00
   (c) $138.00
5 (a) $27.08
   (b) $7.13
   (c) $34.21
7 $143.75
9 $163.35

EXERCISE 8.3

1 (a) $216
   (b) $231.12
3 (a) April, $2400; May, $2000; June, $2800
   (b) April, $1800; May, $1500; June, $2100
5 (a) $36.80
   (b) $46.00
   (c) $50.72

EXERCISE 8.4

	(a)	(b)	(c)	(d)
1	$ (320)	$(1000)	$ 700	$(20)
3	$(3900)	$(2000)	$(2000)	$100
5	$ 1005	$ 900	$ 90	$ 15

EXERCISE 8.5

1 $26,812
3 $1120

5 | Name | Net |
   |------|-----|
   | Hunt | $ 249.42 |
   | Scoby | 257.87 |
   | Ryan | 269.04 |
   | Elijah | 238.41 |
   | Anderson | 238.09 |
   | Sodero | 265.10 |
   | Total | $1517.93 |

7 (a) $69.38
   (b) $531.88

EXERCISE 8.6

1 Net proceeds $1698.97.
3 Gross cost $11,684.40.

93.75
6.25

EXERCISE 9.1

1 $200.07
3 $12,926.46
5 $1689.40
7 Company Y is lower by $0.90.
9 56%
11 56.2275%
13 53.6875%
15 (a) $48
    (b) 25%
    (c) $33\frac{1}{3}/20/25$
17 (a) $95.76
    (b) 20%
    (c) 30/25/5/20
19 (a) $5.84
    (b) $17.07
    (c) $449.57
21 (a) $500.50
    (b) $31.91
    (c) $6.20
23 (a) $398.50
    (b) $265.40
25 (a) $21.96
    (b) $485.70
    (c) $7.75

EXERCISE 9.2

1 (a) August 4
   (b) $548.80

3 (a) April 20
   (b) $33.62
   (c) $1086.98
5 $3648.00

	(a)	(b)	(c)	(d)
7	$ 1.76	$ 173.84	$ 175.60	-0-
9	$ 9.28	$ 300.00	$ 309.28	$ 251.47
11	$ 1.71	$ 83.57	$ 85.28	-0-
13	$ 3.75	$ 121.25	$ 125.00	-0-
15	$ 1.85	$ 90.62	$ 92.47	-0-
17	$ 62.50	$1500.00	$1562.50	$1221.50
19	$ 57.45	$ 900.00	$ 957.45	$ 822.55

21 $136.80
23 $173.71
25 (a) Yes
    (b) Interest rate earned by taking cash dis-
         count is 14.7% vs. $10\frac{1}{2}$% interest cost at
         bank.
27 (a) $466.08
    (b) $470.89
    (c) $475.69
    (d) $480.50
29 $15.65

EXERCISE 9.3

1 (a) $6.33
   (b) $697.23
3 (a) $2.56
   (b) $0.43
   (c) $82.23

5	(a)	(b)	(c)
(1)	$ 427.00	$ 1.35	$ 79.74
(2)	$ 223.52	$32.52	$7194.46
(3)	$ 60.59	$ 4.75	$ 944.48

7 (a) $1243.52
   (b) $1243.33

EXERCISE 9.4

	(a)	(b)	(c)
1	$100.00	25%	125%
3	$ 40.00	33.3%	66.7%
5	$ 30.00	$18.00	150%
7	30%	$14.17	$9.92
9	125%	$16.24	$4.06
11	$ 7.00	$ 4.90	70%

	(a)	(b)	(c)
13	$ 25.00	20%	80%
15	$ 31.00	20.97%	120.97%
17	$ 11.55	4.95%	30%
19	10%	$ 6.00	$ 6.60
21	75%	$50.67	$12.67

EXERCISE 9.5

1 1/9
3 2/3
5 3/5
7 9
9 33 1/3%
11 55.55%
13 100%
15 31.58%
17 (No answers requested)

		Number	%	Number	%
19	C				64.10
	M	$ 0.70		$ 0.70	35.90
	S	$ 1.95		$ 1.95	
21	C	$ 2.55		$ 2.55	
	M		66.67		40.04
	S	$ 4.25	166.67	$ 4.25	
23	C	$ 95.00		$ 95.00	54.29
	M		84.21		45.71
	S	$175.00		$175.00	
25	C	$117.49		$117.49	
	M	$ 72.01	61.29	$ 72.01	38.00
	S		161.29		
27	C	$ 27.50		$ 27.50	61.11
	M	$ 17.50	63.64	$ 17.50	38.89
	S				

EXERCISE 9.6

1 $57,323.93
3 ($30.92) (Loss)
5 $14,765.87
7 $66,323.85
9

	Number	%
Sales	$400,000	100
Less cost of goods sold	280,000	70
Gross margin	$120,000	30
Less operating expenses	100,000	25
Operating profit	$ 20,000	5

EXERCISE 10.1

		Amount	%
1	R	—	100
	C	$105	—
	M	70	40
		$175	100
3	R	$312.50	100
	C	—	—
	M	$187.50	60
		$312.50	100
5	R	$920	100
	C	$690	—
	M	—	25
		$920	100

7 $7.33
9 $13.00
11 $1.25
13 23.90%

EXERCISE 10.2

1 52.21%
3 15.45%
5 (a) $4031
  (b) $9744
7 $2376.10

EXERCISE 10.3

1 35%
3 42.99%
5 38.34%
7 6.44%
9 35.92%

EXERCISE 10.4

1 (a) 42%
  (b) 34.09%
3 (a) 27.27%
  (b) 33.33%

5 26.43%
7 $9500
9 (a) 47.62%
  (b) 49.21%

EXERCISE 10.5

1 (a) $80.00
  (b) 15.05%
3 (a) $150.00
  (b) $33\frac{1}{3}$%
5 (a) 14.12%
  (b) 6.55%
7 8.01%

EXERCISE 10.6

1 $8895
3 (a) $27,500
  (b) 14,475
5 5
7 2.38
9 (a) $11,500; 8.78%
  (b) 32.83%
  (c) 34.45%
  (d) 34.67% (.34669927)
  (e) $39,604.65; 30.23%
  (f) 28.93%
  (g) $57,500
  (h) $38,052.33
  (i) 2.28 times
  (j) 2.40 times

EXERCISE 10.7

1 (a) 16.5%
  (b) $55,000
  (c) 6%
  (d) $160,000
  (e) 12%
3 1.58
5 $30,000
7 $13,910
9 $5062.82
11 (a) $17,900
  (b) $10,775.80

EXERCISE 11.1

1 (Check figures only)

Sales	$94,215	111.44%
Net sales	$84,540	100.00%
Less cost of goods sold	45,793	54.38%
Gross margin	$38,567	45.62%
Less expenses	27,890	32.99%
Net income	$10,677	12.63%

EXERCISE 11.2

1 (Check figures only)

	Increase or (decrease)		Percent of total assets	
	$	%	1972	1971
Current assets	14,000	4.5	55.1	53.2
Fixed assets	(8,000)	(2.9)	44.9	46.8
Total assets	6,000	1.0	100.0	100.0
Total liabilities	(24,000)	(6.6)	57.1	61.7
Total stockholders' equity	30,000	13.3	42.9	38.3
Total liabilities and stockholders' equity	6,000	1.0	100.0	100.0

3 7.41 times
5 45.5%
7 (a) 2.2/1 or 2.2
   (b) 2.4/1 or 2.4
9 1.05 times
11 2.32 times

EXERCISE 11.3

1 (a) 153.32
   (b) 153
   (c) 152
3 (a) 56.4
   (b) 58
   (c) 61

5 June 30, $4141.00
   July 31, $4264.67
   Aug 31, $4402.67
   Sept 30, $4439.50
7 June 30, $4140.00
   July 31, $4239.29
   Aug 31, $4291.00
   Sept 30, $4312.56
9 Increase of 10%

EXERCISE 11.4

1 Horizontal graph not drawn
3 (Check figures only)

Advancement	6.0%
Operating	9.6%
Clothing	10.3%
Shelter	13.3%
Food	29.6%
Savings	31.2%

5 Broken-line or curved-line graph not drawn.

EXERCISE 12.1

1 $1.29
3 (a) $289.50
   (b) $17.37
5 3.64
7 (a) 2.803%
   (b) 28.03 mills or $0.02803
   (c) $2.803
   (d) $28.03
9 $593.96
11 $26,726,121.36
13 $24,301.84

EXERCISE 12.2

1

	Annual Depreciation		
Year	Straight line (1/5 or 20%)	Declining balance (30%)	Sum of the years' digits (in 15ths)
First-year depreciation	$ 600	$ 900	$1000
Second-year depreciation	600	630	800
Third-year depreciation	600	441	600
Fourth-year depreciation	600	308.70	400
Fifth-year depreciation	600	216.09	200
Total	$3000	$2495.79	$3000
Unrecovered cost	-0-	$ 504.21	-0-

3 (a) $389.38
  (b) $667.50
5 (a) $1802.78
  (b) $961.48
7 (Single return, first-year additional depreciation limited to $2000)
  (a) $3960
  (b) $1742.22
  (c) $1524.44
  (Joint return)
  (a) $4344
  (b) $1656.89
  (c) $1449.78

9

	Annual Depreciation		
Year	Straight line (1/7 or 14.285%)	Declining balance (2/7 or 28.57%)	Sum of the years' digits (in 28ths)
First-year additional depreciation	$1720.00	$1720.00	$1720.00
First-year ordinary depreciation	857.14	1965.62	1500.00
Total depreciation—first year	$2577.14	$3685.62	$3220.00
Second-year depreciation	857.14	1404.04	1285.71
Third-year depreciation	857.14	1002.90	1071.43
Fourth-year depreciation	857.14	716.38	857.14
Fifth-year depreciation	857.14	511.71	642.86
Sixth-year depreciation	857.14	365.51	428.57
Seventh-year depreciation	857.14	33.84	214.29
Total	$7719.98	$7720.00	$7720.00
Unrecovered cost	$ 880.02	$ 880.00	$ 880.00

EXERCISE 12.3

1 $2571.50
3 (a) $2735.40
  (b) 4.85%
5 (a) 12%
  (b) $876
7 (a) 14.7%
  (b) $9980.16

EXERCISE 12.4

1 $2421
3 $11,195
5 $7250
7 $38,445
9 (a) Cloud: $4080.51
  (b) Mohr: $5099.49
  (c) Redford: $6120

11 (a) $2270.40
   (b) $4128
13 (a) $684,000
   (b) $17,670

EXERCISE 12.5

1 (a) $2280
  (b) $1170
3 Beswick: $1061.19
  Lillard: $1278.81
5 First year: Luckmann: $4150
             Tarnopol: $3950
  Second year: Luckmann: $4924
               Tarnopol: $4976
7 French: $465
  Muscio: $625
  Booher: $375

EXERCISE 12.6

1 (a) $49,400
   (b) $61.75
3 (a) $54,000
   (b) $23.57
5 (a) $66,170
   (b) $44.11
7 (a) $230,640
   (b) $475,000

EXERCISE 12.7

1 (a) $10
   (b) None.
3 (a) $3
   (b) $0.25
5 (a) $2.50
   (b) $0.82
7 (a) $425,000
   (b) $108,000
   (c) $284,000
   (d) $617,000

EXERCISE 12.8

1 (a) $900
   (b) 30%
   (c) 26%
3 (a) $4800
   (b) 53.33%
   (c) 15.33%
5 (a) $12.67
   (b) 15.15% or 15.18%
   (c) 12.67%
7 (a) $43,200
   (b) $10,500
   (c) $53,700
   (d) 24.31%
   (e) 11.19%

EXERCISE 13.1

	(a)	(b)	(c)	(d)
1	3/4	15 3/8	120 1/2	53
3	$ 58.64	$ 8.75	$221.50	$846.81
5	$ 73.35	$136.05	$184.36	$534.41
7	$ 6.00	$ 23.45	$ 17.75	$206.00
9	$141.11	$234.20		

EXERCISE 13.2

	(a)	(b)	(c)
1	$ 3.875	$ 18.75	$ 406.25
3	$19.00	$ 43.50	$ 1943.50
5	$ 5.50	$ 14.30	$ 179.30
7	$ 7.375	$1072.06	$74,822.06

EXERCISE 13.3

	(a)	(b)	(c)	(d)
1	$ 0.03	$3.75	$ 3.78	
3	$ 0.02	$2.18	$ 2.20	
5	$18.25	$3.79	$42.38	$1778.83
7	$ 9.75	$2.52	$29.63	$ 942.85
9	$ 4.00	$0.32	$10.00	$ 89.68

EXERCISE 13.4

	(a)	(b)	(c)	(d)	(e)	(f)
1	$ 4000	102%	$ 41.00	$ 4120.00	$ 30	$ 4151.00
3	$28,000	103.375%	$364.00	$29,309.00	$140	$29,449.00
5	$30,000	95.5%	$568.75	$29,218.75	$150	$29,368.75
7	$20,000	104%	$162.92	$20,962.92	$150	$21,112.92

	(a)	(b)	(c)	(d)	(e)	(f)	(g)
9	$ 4000	102%	$156.00	$0.09	$ 4235.92	$ 30.00	$ 4205.91
11	$ 3000	93%	$ 78.17	$0.06	$ 2868.11	$ 22.50	$ 2845.61
13	$30,000	95.5%	$200.00	$0.58	$28,849.42	$150.00	$28,699.42
15	$13,000	67.25%	$ 94.79	$0.18	$ 8837.11	$ 97.50	$ 8739.61

EXERCISE 13.5

1 $6
3 (a) $5
   (b) $2.83
   (c) $39.17
5 (a) $450
   (b) Loss of $1237.50
   (c) Loss of $787.50
7 (a) $100
   (b) Loss of $218.75
   (c) Loss of $118.75
9 Loss of 26.07%

EXERCISE 13.6

1 6.5%
3 6.3%
5 8.8%
7 8.3%
9 8.7%
11 8.3%
13 6.9%
15 7.2%
17 5%
19 8%

EXERCISE 14.1

		24 years	*35 years*	*55 years*
1	(a)	$ 68.24	$ 80.00	$247.12
	(b)	$167.92	$224.88	$485.76
	(c)	$128.32	$177.52	$395.12
	(d)	$250.48	$306.72	$533.52
	(e)	$199.44	$250.72	$450.48
	(f)	$393.12	$415.28	$566.48
	(g)	$344.24	$353.44	$469.68

3 (a) $6.24
   (b) $124.80
5 (a) $3312
   (b) $6660
   (c) $12,000
7 (a) $96.96
   (b) $85.78
9 (a) $1386
   (b) $3618
   (c) 10 years, 241 days.

EXERCISE 14.2

1 $61
3 $211
5 $101
7 $160
9 $307
11 (a) $261
    (b) $216
13 (a) $145
    (b) $87

EXERCISE 14.3

1 A, $14,000; B, $21,000; C, $35,000
3 $13,000
5 A, $10,357.42; B, $62,142.86; C, $69,047.62;
   D, $55,238.10
7 $8000
9 $5600
11 $796,875

EXERCISE 14.4

1 $040
3 $252.89
5 (a) $2437.50
   (b) $350
   (c) $5880
7 (a) $4133.33
   (b) $6000
   (c) $4750
   (d) $6000

EXERCISE A1.1

1 27
3 125 7/16 or 125.4375
5 1011101110000
7 1000001101.01
9 3937_{10}
11 14 5/8 or 14.625_{10}
13 13560_8
15 $.2_8$
17 $1,050,176_{10}$
19 2086_{10}
21 271_{16}
23 $1C22B_{16}$

EXERCISE A1.2

1 (a) 777_8
   (b) $1FF_{16}$
3 (a) 401_8
   (b) 101_{16}
5 100011101
7 100100100100

EXERCISE A2.2

1   18.57
3   2.65
5   39.59
7   27.37
9   91.09
11 1320 yd.
13 82 yd 1 ft 4 in
15 246.2 ft
17 243 rods 5 yd 1 ft
19 12 rods 4 yd 2 ft 0 in

EXERCISE A2.3(A)

1 (a) 58 4/11 rods (or 59 rods)
   (b) $132.75
3 82 rods 3 yd 2 ft 6 in
5 (a) 256 ft
   (b) 240 ft
7 Square is cheaper by $260.00.
9 (a) 70 ft
   (b) $7.70
11 77 trees
13 56.35 common miles
15 40.8404 in
17 3537 revolutions (approx.)

EXERCISE A2.3(B)

1 (a) 346.875 acres
   (b) 15,609.38
3 6270 ft
5 120 ft
7 149 sq ft
9 46 ft 4 in
11 105 sq ft
13 3900 acres

15 (a) 2280 sq ft
    (b) 760 sq ft
17 $1237.04
19 23 gals

EXERCISE A2.3(C)

1 (a) 9600 cu ft
   (b) 72,000 gals
3 (a) 15,795 cu ft
   (b) 585 cu yd
   (c) $1199.25
5 (a) 69,877.5 cu ft
   (b) 4,367,343.75 lb
7 (a) 56 cu yd
   (b) $238.00
9 (a) 384 cu ft
   (b) 14 2/9 cu yd
   (c) $123.75
   (d) $0.11 per sq ft
11 (a) 625 cu ft per day
    (b) 228,125 cu ft per year
    (c) 14,257,812.5 lb per year
    (d) $1.13 per day
    (e) $410.63 per year
13 (a) 380 sq ft
    (b) 32,725 lb
    (c) 173 cu ft
15 283 sq ft
17 (a) 19,800 cu ft
    (b) 15,840 bu
19 (a) 326 sq ft
    (b) 426 2/3 cu ft
21 (a) 169 sq ft
    (b) 192.5 cu ft

EXERCISE A2.4

1   16
3   1,000,000,900
5   1,000,226
7   100,909
9   247
11 CCLVIII
13 CMXLIX
15 $\overline{\text{M}}$DCXXV
17 MCXLI
19 MCDXCII

Index